Counterparty Credit Risk and Credit Value Adjustment

Second Edition

To Ginnie, George and Christy

Counterparty Credit Risk and Credit Value Adjustment

A Continuing Challenge for Global Financial Markets

Second Edition

Jon Gregory

A John Wiley and Sons, Ltd, Publication

© 2012 John Wiley & Sons Ltd

Registered office
John Wiley & Sons Ltd, The Atrium, Southern Gate, Chichester, West Sussex, PO19 8SQ, United Kingdom

For details of our global editorial offices, for customer services and for information about how to apply for permission to reuse the copyright material in this book please see our website at www.wiley.com.

Reprinted November 2012, June 2013, October 2013

Wiley publishes in a variety of print and electronic formats and by print-on-demand. Some material included with standard print versions of this book may not be included in e-books or in print-on-demand. If this book refers to media such as a CD or DVD that is not included in the version you purchased, you may download this material at http://booksupport.wiley.com. For more information about Wiley products, visit www.wiley.com.

Designations used by companies to distinguish their products are often claimed as trademarks. All brand names and product names used in this book are trade names, service marks, trademarks or registered trademarks of their respective owners. The publisher is not associated with any product or vendor mentioned in this book. This publication is designed to provide accurate and authoritative information in regard to the subject matter covered. It is sold on the understanding that the publisher is not engaged in rendering professional services. If professional advice or other expert assistance is required, the services of a competent professional should be sought.

Library of Congress Cataloging-in-Publication Data
Gregory, Jon, PhD
  Counterparty credit risk and credit value adjustment : a continuing challenge for global financial markets / Jon Gregory. – 2nd ed.
       p. cm.
  Rev. ed. of: Counterparty credit risk. c2010.
  Includes index.
  ISBN 978-1-118-31667-2 (cloth) – ISBN 978-1-118-31665-8 (ebk) – ISBN 978-1-118-31664-1 (ebk)
1.   Derivative securities–Mathematical models. 2.   Risk management.   I. Gregory, Jon, Ph. D. Counterparty credit risk.   II. Title.
  HG6024.A3G74 2012
  332.64'57—dc23
                                                                          2012023249

A catalogue record for this book is available from the British Library.

ISBN 978-1-118-31667-2 (hardback)   ISBN 978-1-118-31665-8 (ebk)
ISBN 978-1-118-31666-5 (ebk)   ISBN 978-1-118-31664-1 (ebk)

Set in 10/12pt Times by Thomson Press
Printed in Great Britain by CPI Group (UK) Ltd, Croydon, CR0 4YY

Contents

Acknowledgements

Less than three years have passed since the first edition of this book was published and yet the subject area has changed and expanded dramatically. I hope his second edition will serve as a timely and thorough update with respect to the subject of counterparty credit risk and all related aspects. Indeed, this is much more than a second edition, most of the subject matter has been re-written and expanded, with several new chapters. To avoid increasing the size of this book significantly, the mathematical appendices are not included but are freely available with the accompanying spreadsheets on my website at www.cvacentral.com. Since many readers do not need to study this material in depth then I hope this is a reasonable separation to make.

I have been fortunate to have been able to obtain feedback on various chapters from various experts within the industry and academia, notably Ronnie Barnes, Karin Bergeron, Liesbeth Bodvin, Alexandre Bon, Christoph Burgard, Andrew Green, Matthew Leeming, Michael Pykhtin, Nicolas Rabeau, Colin Sharpe and David Wigan. I hope it is obvious that any remaining errors are the responsibility of the author.

Thanks go to Aimee Dibbens, Sam Hartley, Lori Laker and Jennie Kitchin at Wiley for helping me through the process. I am very grateful to Rebecca Newenham and Desiree Marie Leedo at Get Ahead VA for much help around administration and proofreading. I would like to also thank my colleagues at Solum Financial Partners in London, notably Vincent Dahinden, Thu-Uyen Nyugen and Rowan Alston.

In the last two and a half years, I have been fortunate to visit Amsterdam, Barcelona, Berlin, Boston, Brussels, Chicago, Dubai, Dusseldorf, Finland, Frankfurt, Geneva, Hong Kong, Iceland, Madrid, Melbourne, Milan, Mumbai, New York, Paris, Rome, Sao Paolo, Singapore, Sydney, Taipei, Toronto, Turkey and Warsaw in relation to counterparty risk assignments. I thank everyone that I have connected with at conferences, training courses and consulting projects for the ideas and questions that kept me thinking about this vast but fascinating subject.

Jon Gregory, August 2012

Spreadsheets

One of the key features of the first edition of this book was the accompanying spreadsheets that were prepared to allow the reader to gain some simple insight into some of the quantitative aspects discussed in the main text. Many of these examples have been used for training courses and have therefore evolved to be quite intuitive and user-friendly (I hope). For this second edition, I have completely updated these spreadsheets to include more sophisticated and additional examples. The spreadsheets can be downloaded freely from my website www.cvacentral.com under the counterparty risk section. New examples will be added over time. Any questions then please contact me via the above website.

Spreadsheet 3.1	Counterparty risk for a forward contract-type exposure.
Spreadsheet 4.1	Simple netting calculation.
Spreadsheet 6.1	Simple monoline example.
Spreadsheet 8.1	EE and PFE for a normal distribution.
Spreadsheet 8.2	EPE calculation.
Spreadsheet 8.3	EPE and effective EPE example.
Spreadsheet 8.4	Simple example of a cross-currency swap profile.
Spreadsheet 8.5	Simple calculation of the exposure of a CDS.
Spreadsheet 8.6	Call and return collateral example with logic relating to independent amounts, thresholds, collateral held, minimum transfer amount and rounding.
Spreadsheet 9.1	Simulation of an interest rate swap exposure with a one-factor Vasicek model.
Spreadsheet 9.2	Illustration of the impact of netting for the examples considered.
Spreadsheet 9.3	Example marginal exposure calculation.
Spreadsheet 9.4	Incremental exposure calculations.
Spreadsheet 9.5	Marginal exposure calculations.

Appendices

The following is a list of Appendices which contain additional mathematical detail. These Appendices can be downloaded freely from my website www.cvacentral.com under the counterparty risk section. Any questions then please contact me via the above website.

Section I: Introduction

This first section covers introductory aspects in relation to counterparty credit risk and CVA and is aimed at providing the background for readers new to the area.

Chapter 1 sets the scene and explains the emergence of counterparty credit risk, especially in relation to the global financial crisis that began in 2007. This discusses the basic problems such as the "too big to fail" phenomenon and the complexities of the activities of banks and the OTC derivative markets. The role of regulation is also introduced.

Some of the important background concepts are covered in **Chapter 2.** This discusses financial risk management in general, outlining the different types of financial risk and their relationship to counterparty risk. The important concept of value-at-risk (VAR) is also defined and explained with the dangers of VAR carefully noted. This chapter discusses OTC (over-the-counter) derivatives markets and their benefits and drawbacks, paying particular attention to credit derivative instruments which allow hedging of counterparty risk but contain significant counterparty risk themselves. The mitigation of counterparty risk, in particular in relation to central clearing, is introduced also.

Chapter 3 is dedicated to defining counterparty risk. This includes outlining the underlying products for which counterparty risk is relevant and discussing the development and nature of exchange traded and OTC derivative markets. The different players in the counterparty risk world are outlined, from large global dealer banks to end-users such as sovereigns and corporates. The components of counterparty risk, such as credit exposure, default probability, credit spreads, recovery rates and replacement costs, are defined. The control and quantification of counterparty risk through credit limits and credit value adjustment (CVA) is discussed. Finally, portfolio effects and hedging are introduced.

1
Introduction

Between 2004 and 2006, US interest rates rose from 1% to over 5%, triggering a slowdown in the US housing market. Many homeowners, who had been barely able to afford their payments when interest rates were low, began to default on their mortgages. Default rates on subprime loans (made to those with a poor or no credit history) hit record levels. US households had also become increasingly in debt, with the ratio of debt to disposable personal income rising. Many other countries (although not all) had ended up in a similar situation. Years of poor underwriting standards and cheap debt were about to catalyse a global financial crisis.

Many of the now toxic US subprime loans were held by US retail banks and mortgage providers such as Fannie Mae and Freddie Mac. However, the market had been allowed to spread due to the fact that the underlying mortgages had been packaged up into complex structures (using financial engineering techniques), such as mortgage-backed securities (MBSs), which had been given good credit ratings from the rating agencies. As a result, the underlying mortgages ended up being held by institutions that did not originate them, such as investment banks and institutional investors outside the US. Financial engineering had created a global exposure to US mortgages.

In mid-2007, a credit crisis began, caused primarily by the systematic mispricing of US mortgages and MBSs. Whilst this caused excessive volatility in the credit markets (which had been quiet for a number of years), it was not believed to be a severe financial crisis (for example, the stock market did not react particular badly). The crisis, however, did not go away.

In July 2007, Bear Stearns informed investors they would get very little of their money back from two hedge funds due to losses in subprime mortgages. In August 2007, BNP Paribas told investors that they would be unable to take money out of two funds because the underlying assets could not be valued due to "a complete evaporation of liquidity in the market". Basically, this meant that the assets could not be sold at any reasonable price. In September 2007, Northern Rock, a British Bank, sought emergency funding from the Bank of England as a "lender of last resort". This prompted the first run on a bank[1] for over a

---

[1] This occurs when a large number of customers withdraw their deposits because they believe the bank is, or might become, insolvent.

century. Northern Rock, in 2008, would be taken into state ownership to save depositors and borrowers.

By the end of 2007, some insurance companies, known as "monolines", were in serious trouble. Monolines provided insurance to banks on mortgage and other related debt. The Triple-A ratings of monolines had meant that banks were not concerned with a potential monoline default, despite the obvious misnomer that a monoline insurance company appeared to represent. Banks' willingness to ignore the counterparty risk had led them to build up large monoline exposures without the requirement for monolines to post collateral, at least as long as they maintained their excellent Triple-A credit ratings. However, monolines were now reporting large losses and making it clear that any downgrading of their credit ratings may trigger collateral calls that they would not be able to make. Such downgrades began in December 2007 and banks were forced to take losses totalling billions of dollars due to the massive counterparty risk they now faced. This was a particularly bad form of counterparty risk, known as wrong-way risk, where the exposure to a counterparty and their default probability were inextricably linked.

By the end of 2007, although not yet known, the US economy was in recession and many other economies would follow. The crisis was now affecting the general public and yet this was only the tip of the iceberg.

In March 2008, Bear Stearns was purchased by JP Morgan Chase for just $2 a share, assisted by a loan of tens of billions of dollars from the Federal Reserve, who were essentially taking $30 billion of losses from the worst Bear Stearns assets to catalyse the sale. This clearly represented a form of bailout, with the US taxpayer essentially funding some of the purchase of Bear Stearns. The sale price of Bear Stearns was shocking, considering that it had been trading at $93 a share only a month previously. Something was clearly going very wrong. In early September 2008, mortgage lenders Fannie Mae and Freddie Mac, who combined accounted for over half the outstanding US mortgages, were placed into conservatorship (a sort of short-term nationalisation) by the US Treasury. Treasury secretary Henry Paulson stated that the combined debt levels posed a "systemic risk" to financial stability.

In September 2008 the unthinkable happened when Lehman Brothers, a global investment bank and the fourth largest investment bank in the US with a century-long tradition, filed for Chapter 11 bankruptcy protection (the largest in history). This occurred after teams of bankers failed during the weekend spent in the Federal Reserve Building to agree any better solution, in particular with Barclays and Bank of America pulling out of buying Lehman. The US government was reluctant to rescue Lehman due to the moral hazard that such bailouts encourage. The bankruptcy of Lehman had not been anticipated, with all major rating agencies (Moody's, Standard & Poor's and Fitch) all giving at least a Single-A rating right up to the point of Lehman's failure and the credit derivative market not pricing an actual default.

Saving Lehman's would have cost the US taxpayer again and exasperated moral hazard problems since a bailout of Lehman's would not punish their excessive risk taking (their exposure to the mortgage market and risky behaviour in understating the need for new funding). However, a Lehman default was not an especially pleasant prospect either. Firstly, there was estimated to be around $400 billion of credit default swap (CDS) insurance written on Lehman Brothers debt. Since the debt was now close to worthless, this would trigger massive payouts on the underlying CDS contracts and yet the opacity of the OTC derivatives market meant that it was not clear who actually owned most of the CDS referencing Lehman.

Another counterparty might now have financial problems due to suffering large losses because of providing CDS protection on Lehman. Secondly, Lehman had around one and a half million derivatives trades with around 8,000 different counterparties that all needed to be unwound, a process that would take years and lead to many legal proceedings. Most counterparties probably never considered that their counterparty risk to Lehman's was a particular issue nor did they realise that the failure of counterparty risk mitigation methods such as collateral and special purpose vehicles (SPVs) would lead to legal problems.

On the same day as Lehman's failed, Bank of America agreed a $50 billion rescue of Merrill Lynch. Soon after the remaining two investment banks, Morgan Stanley and Goldman Sachs, opted to become commercial banks. Whilst this would subject them to more strict regulation, it allowed full access to the Federal Reserve's lending facilities and prevented them suffering the same fate as the bankrupt Lehman Brothers or the sold Bear Stearns or Merrill Lynch.

In case September 2008 was not exciting enough, the US government provided American International Group (AIG) with loans of up to $85 billion in exchange for a four-fifths stake in AIG.[2] Had AIG been allowed to fail through bankruptcy, not only would bondholders have suffered but also their derivative counterparties (the major banks) would have experienced significant losses. Prior to the crisis, the counterparty risk of AIG was typically considered minimal due to their size, excellent credit rating and the fact that (unlike monoline insurers) they did post collateral. The reason for the rescue of AIG and non-rescue of monolines was partly timing – the AIG situation occurred at the same time as the Lehman bankruptcy and immediately after the Fannie Mae and Freddie Mac rescues. However, another important fact was that AIG had an exposure that was not dissimilar to the total exposure of the monoline insurers but concentrated within a single financial entity. AIG was "too big to fail".

Three of the largest US investment banks had now either gone bankrupt (Lehman Brothers) or been sold at fire sale prices to other banks (Bear Stearns and Merrill Lynch). The remaining two had given up their prized investment bank status to allow them to be bailed out. Later in September 2008 Washington Mutual, America's biggest savings and loan company, was sold to JP Morgan for $1.9 billion and their parent company, Washington Mutual Inc., filed for Chapter 11 bankruptcy protection. A CDS contract purchased from any of the aforementioned US banks on any of the other US banks was now clearly seen to have enormous, almost comical amounts of wrong-way counterparty risk.

By now, trillions of dollars had simply vanished from the financial markets and therefore the global economy. Whilst this was related to the mispricing of mortgage risk, it was also significantly driven by the recognition of counterparty risk.

On October 6, the Dow Jones Industrial Average dropped more than 700 points and fell below 10,000 for the first time in four years. The systemic shockwaves arising from the failure of the US banking giants led to the Troubled Asset Relief Program (TARP) of not too much short of $1 trillion to purchase distressed assets and support failing banks. In November 2008, Citigroup, prior to the crisis the largest bank in the world but now reeling following a dramatic plunge in its share price, needed TARP assistance, via a $20 billion cash injection and government backing for around $300 billion of loans.

The contagion had spread far beyond the US. In early 2009, the Royal Bank of Scotland (RBS) reported a loss of £24.1 billion, the biggest in British corporate history. The majority of this loss was borne by the British government, now the majority owner of RBS, having

___
[2] AIG would receive further bailouts.

paid £45 billion[3] to rescue RBS in October 2008. In November 2008 the International Monetary Fund (IMF), together with other European countries, approved a $4.6 billion loan for Iceland after the country's banking system collapsed in October. This was the first IMF loan to a Western European nation since 1976.

From late 2009, fears of a sovereign debt crisis developed in Europe driven by high debt levels and a downgrading of government debt in some European states. In May 2010, Greece received a €110 billion bailout from Eurozone countries and the IMF. Greece was to be bailed out again and support was also given to other Eurozone sovereign entities, notably Portugal, Ireland and Spain. Banks again were heavily exposed to potential failures of European sovereign countries. Again, the counterparty risk of such entities had been considered low but was now extremely high and made worse by the fact that sovereign entities generally did not post collateral.

By now, it was clear that no counterparty (Triple-A entities, global investment banks, retail banks, sovereigns) could ever be regarded as risk-free. Counterparty risk, previously hidden via spurious credit ratings, collateral or legal assumptions, was now present throughout the global financial markets. CVA (credit value adjustment), which defined the price of counterparty risk, had gone from a rarely used technical term to a buzzword constantly associated with financial markets. The pricing of counterparty risk into trades (via a CVA charge) was now becoming the rule and not the exception. Whilst the largest investment banks had built trading desks and complex systems and models around managing CVA, all banks (and some other financial institutions and large derivatives users) were now focused on expanding their capabilities in this respect.

By 2009, new fast-tracked financial regulation was beginning to take shape around the practices of banks. The Basel III global regulatory standard (developed in direct response to the crisis) was introduced to strengthen bank capital bases and introduce new requirements on liquidity and leverage. The US Dodd–Frank Wall Street Reform and Consumer Protection Act 2009 and European Market Infrastructure Regulation (EMIR) were aimed at increasing the stability of the over-the-counter (OTC) derivative markets. Regulatory response to the global financial crisis (as it was now known) revolved very much around counterparty credit risk, with the volatility of CVA, collateral management and wrong-way risk all receiving attention.

The regulatory focus on CVA seemed to encourage active hedging of counterparty risk so as to obtain capital relief. However, the market that would be most important for such hedging, credit derivatives, was having its own problems. Whilst credit derivatives, such as single-name and index credit default swaps, allowed counterparty risk transfer, being OTC instruments, they also introduced their own form of counterparty risk, which was the wrong-way type highlighted by the monoline failures. Indeed, the CDS market was almost seizing up due to this severe wrong-way risk. Counterparty risk was the principle linkage among participants in the CDS market that could cause systemic failures. Regulatory proposals to deal with this problem involved pushing heavily towards the central clearing of certain standard OTC derivatives, notably CDSs. Whilst, prior to the crisis, much of the interest rate swap market was already moving towards central clearing, without regulatory intervention the CDS market was arguably years away.

Whilst central counterparties (CCPs) provided advantages such as transparency that the OTC derivatives market clearly lacked, this also introduced the question of what would

---

[3] Hundreds of billions of pounds were provided in the form of loans and guarantees.

happen if a CCP ever failed. Since CCPs were likely to take over from the likes of Lehman, Citigroup and AIG as the hubs of the complex financial network, such a question was clearly key, and yet not particularly extensively discussed. Furthermore, other potential unintended consequences of increased regulation on counterparty risk could be seen as early as 2010 when, for example, the Bank of England commented that "CVA desks" hedging counterparty risk were causing European sovereign spreads to widen "away from levels solely reflecting the underlying probability of sovereign default".[4] Although the need to ensure investment banks were better capitalised for risk taking was not under debate, arguments developed over the correct level of capitalisation and the potential adverse and unintended consequences of new regulation.

At the same time as a renewed focus on counterparty risk, other changes in derivatives markets were taking place. A fundamental assumption in the pricing of derivative securities had always been that the risk-free rate could be appropriately proxied by LIBOR. However, practitioners realised that the OIS (overnight indexed spread) was actually a better proxy for the risk-free rate. The LIBOR–OIS spread had historically hovered around 10 basis points, showing a close linkage. However, this close relationship had broken down, even spiking to around 350 basis points around the Lehman bankruptcy. This showed that even the simplest types of derivative, which had been priced in the same way for decades, needed to be valued differently, in a more sophisticated manner. Since CVA is an adjustment to the risk-free value of a transaction, this topic was clearly closely related to counterparty risk.

Another, almost inevitable dynamic was that the spreads of banks (i.e., where they could borrow unsecured cash on a longer term than in a typical LIBOR transaction) had increased. Historically, this borrowing cost of a bank was in the region of a few basis points but had now entered the realms of hundreds of basis points in most cases. It was clear that these now substantial funding costs should be quantified alongside CVA. The cost of funding was named FVA (funding value adjustment). Funding costs were also clearly linked to counterparty risk in terms of the calculation and also their similarity to something now known as DVA (debt value adjustment).

DVA for some banks was the only silver lining of the counterparty risk cloud. DVA allowed banks to account for their own default in the value of transactions and therefore acted to counteract counterparty risk-related losses due to an increase in CVA driven by the widening credit spread environment. However, many commentators believed this to be nothing more than an accounting trick as banks reported billions of dollars of profits from DVA simply due to the fact that their own credit spread implied they were more likely to default in the future. Basel III capital rules moved to remove DVA benefits to avoid effects such as "an increase in a bank's capital when its own creditworthiness deteriorates".

The net result of the financial crisis and the impact of regulation led banks to consider the joint impact of risk-free valuation, counterparty risk and funding costs in the valuation of derivatives. Not surprisingly, the increase in funding costs and counterparty risk naturally led banks to tighten up collateral requirements. However, this created a knock-on effect for typical end-users of derivatives that historically had not been able or willing to enter into collateral agreement for liquidity and operational reasons. Some sovereign entities considered posting collateral, not only to avoid the otherwise large CVA and funding costs levied upon them, but also to avoid the issue that banks hedging their counterparty risk may buy CDS protection on them, driving their credit spread wider and potentially causing them

---

[4] This would trigger the consideration of a sovereign exemption with respect to CVA capital charges.

more problems. A sovereign posting their own bonds in collateral would ease the problems but this would not be the ideal answer due to another manifestation of wrong-way risk. Furthermore, corporates other than non-collateral posting entities had issues, for example an airline predicted more volatile earnings "not because of unpredictable passenger numbers, interest rates or jet fuel prices, but because it does not post collateral in its derivatives transactions".[5] End-users of derivatives, although not responsible, were now being hit as badly as the orchestrators of the financial crisis.

Meanwhile, many taxpayers were experiencing poor economic conditions and counting the cost of bailouts via higher taxes and reduced government spending. Businesses and individuals were struggling to borrow money from the heavily capitalised banks. All of this was created by a crisis fuelled to a large extent by counterparty risk.

Because of the above, counterparty risk has become a major subject for global financial markets. It is necessary to consider how to define and quantify counterparty risk. Counterparty risk mitigation methods need to be understood, and their side-effects and any residual risks need to be defined. The question of the role of central counterparties must be examined, alongside the consideration of the risks they will represent. It is important to define how CVA can be quantified and managed, together with other related components such as DVA and FVA. Wrong-way risk must be understood and mitigated or avoided completely. The role and positioning of a CVA desk within a bank or other institution must be defined. The regulation around counterparty risk must be understood, together with the likely impact this will have on banks and the financial markets in which they operate. Finally, the consideration of how all of the above changes are likely to define counterparty risk practices in the future is important.

If any of the above are of interest, then please read on.

---

[5] "Corporates fear CVA charge will make hedging too expensive", *Risk*, October 2011.

2

Background

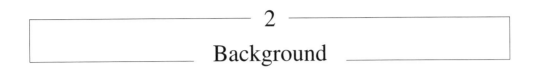

2.1 INTRODUCTION

Financial risk is broken down into a number of different types, one of which is counter-party risk. Counterparty risk is arguably the most complex financial risk to deal with since it is driven by the intersection of different risk types (for example, market and credit) and is highly sensitive to systemic traits, such as the failure of large institutions. Counterparty risk also mainly involves the most complex financial instruments, deriva-tives. Derivatives can be extremely powerful and useful, have aided the growth of global financial markets and have aided economic growth. However, as almost every average person now knows, derivatives can be highly toxic and cause massive losses and financial catastrophes if misused.

In this chapter, we review some of the background to counterparty risk and discuss other forms of financial risk. Counterparty risk should be considered and understood in the context of other financial risks, which we briefly review first. We also discuss the value-at-risk (VAR) concept, which is similar to PFE (potential future exposure), used to assess counterparty risk.

2.2 FINANCIAL RISK

Financial risk management has experienced a revolution over the last two decades. This has been driven by infamous financial disasters due to the collapse of large financial institutions such as Barings (1995), Long-Term Capital Management (1998), Enron (2001), Worldcom (2002), Parmalat (2003) and Lehman Brothers (2008). Such disasters have proved that huge losses can arise from insufficient management of financial risk and cause negative waves throughout the global financial markets. Financial risk is typically sub-divided into a number of different types that will be described below.

2.2.1 Market risk

Market risk arises from the (short-term) movement of market prices. It can be a linear risk, arising from an exposure to the movement of underlying variables such as stock prices, interest rates, foreign exchange rates, commodity prices or credit spreads. Alternatively, it may be a non-linear risk arising from the exposure to market volatility as might arise in a hedged position. Market risk has been the most studied financial risk of the past two decades, with quantitative risk management techniques widely applied in its measurement and management. This was catalysed by some serious market risk-related losses in the 1990s (e.g., Barings) and the subsequent amendments to the Basel I capital accord in 1995 that allowed financial institutions to use proprietary mathematical models to compute their capital requirements for market risk. Indeed, market risk has mainly driven the development of the value-at-risk (described later) approach to risk quantification.

Market risk can be eliminated by entering into an offsetting contract. However, unless this is done with the same counterparty as the original position(s), then counterparty risk will be generated. If the counterparties to offsetting contracts differ, and either counterparty fails, then the position is no longer neutral. Market risk therefore forms a component of counterparty risk.

2.2.2   Credit risk

Credit risk is the risk that a debtor may be unable or unwilling to make a payment or fulfil contractual obligations. This is often known generically as default, although this has slightly different meanings and impact depending on the jurisdiction involved. The default probability must be characterised fully throughout the lifetime of the exposure (e.g., bond maturity) and so too must the recovery value (or equivalently the loss given default). Less severe than default, it may also be relevant to consider deterioration in credit quality, which will lead to a mark-to-market loss (due to the increase in future default probability). In terms of counterparty risk, characterising the term structure of the counterparty's default probability is a key aspect.

2.2.3   Liquidity risk

Liquidity risk is normally characterised in two forms. Asset liquidity risk represents the risk that a transaction cannot be executed at market prices, perhaps due to the size of the position and/or relative illiquidity of the underlying. Funding liquidity risk refers to the inability to fund contractual payments or collateral requirements, potentially forcing an early liquidation of assets and crystallisation of losses. Since such losses may lead to further funding issues, funding liquidity risk can manifest itself via a "death spiral" caused by the negative feedback between losses and cash requirements. Reducing counterparty risk often comes at the potential cost of increasing funding liquidity risk via mechanisms such as collateralisation or central clearing.

2.2.4   Operational risk

Operational risk arises from people, systems, internal and external events. It includes human error (such as trade entry mistakes), failed processes (such as settlement of trades or posting collateral), model risk (inaccurate or badly calibrated models), fraud (such as rogue traders) and legal risk (such as the inability to enforce legal agreements such as those covering netting or collateral terms). Whilst some operational risk losses may be moderate and common (incorrectly booked trades for example), the most significant losses are likely to be a result of highly improbable scenarios or even a "perfect storm" combination of events. Operational risk is therefore extremely hard to quantify, although quantitative techniques are increasingly being applied. Counterparty risk mitigation methods, such as collateralisation, inevitably give rise to operational risks.

2.2.5 Integration of risk types

A particular weakness of financial risk management over the years has been the lack of focus on the integration of different risk types. It has been well known for many years that crises tend to involve a combination of different financial risks. Given the difficulty in quantifying and managing financial risks in isolation, it is not surprising that limited effort is given to combining them. Counterparty risk itself is already a combination of two different risk types, market and credit. Furthermore, the mitigation of counterparty risk can create other types of risk such as liquidity and operational. It is important not to lose sight of counterparty risk as an intersection of many types of financial risk.

2.3 VALUE-AT-RISK

2.3.1 Definition

Quantitative approaches to financial risk management have been widely adopted in recent times, in particular with the popularity of the value-at-risk (VAR) concept. Initially designed as a metric for market risk, VAR has subsequently been used across many financial areas as a means for efficiently summarising risk via a single quantity. A VAR number has a simple and intuitive explanation as the worst loss over a target horizon to a certain specified confidence level. The VAR at the $\alpha\%$ confidence level gives a value that will be exceeded with *no more* than a $(1 - \alpha)\%$ probability. An example of the computation of VAR is shown in Figure 2.1. The VAR at the 99% confidence level is 125 (by convention the "worst loss" is expressed as a positive number) since the probability that this will be exceeded is no more than 1% (it is

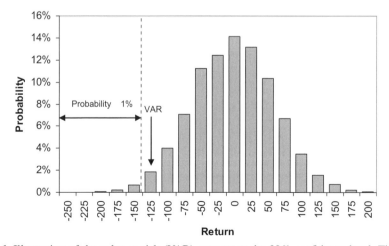

Figure 2.1 Illustration of the value-at-risk (VAR) concept at the 99% confidence level. The VAR is 125, since the chance of a loss (negative return) greater than this amount is no more than 1%.

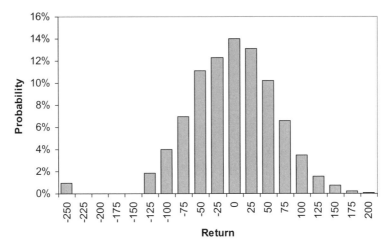

Figure 2.2 Distribution with the same VAR as Figure 2.1.

actually 0.92% due to the discrete[1] nature of the distribution). To find the VAR, one looks for the *minimum* value that will be exceeded with no more than the specified probability.

VAR may be used to set regulatory capital requirements. For example, banks with the relevant approval to use their own internal models may compute their capital requirements for market risk directly via their calculated VAR[2] multiplied by a minimum supervisory factor of three. VAR is also used for internal limit setting and analysis of risks across different risk types.

2.3.2 The dangers of VAR

VAR is a very useful way in which to summarise the risk of an entire distribution in a single number that can easily be understood. It also makes no assumption as to the nature of the distribution itself, such as that it is a normal (Gaussian) distribution.[3] It is, however, open to problems of misinterpretation since VAR says nothing at all about what lies beyond the defined (1% in the above example) threshold. Figure 2.2 shows a slightly different distribution with the same VAR. In this case, the probability of losing 250 is 1% and hence the 99% VAR is again 125 (since there is zero probability of other losses in-between). We can see that changing the loss of 250 does not change the VAR since it is only the *probability* of this loss that is relevant. Hence, VAR does not give an indication of the possible loss outside the confidence level chosen. A certain VAR number does not mean that a loss of 10 times this amount is impossible (as it would be for a normal distribution). Over-reliance upon VAR numbers can be counterproductive as it may lead to false confidence.[4]

---

[1] For a continuous distribution, VAR is simply a quantile (a quantile gives a value on a probability distribution where a given fraction of the probability falls below that level).

[2] The precise relationship is that the capital is defined by the largest of the previous day's VAR and the average of the last 60 days multiplied by the supervisory factor of three or more.

[3] Certain implementations of a VAR model (notably the so-called variance/covariance approach) may make normal distribution assumptions but these are done for reasons of simplification and the VAR idea itself does not require them.

[4] The recent fundamental review of the trading book (see http://www.bis.org/publ/bcbs219.pdf) has recommended replacing VAR with a preferable measure of risk commonly known as expected shortfall.

2.3.3   Models

The use of metrics such as VAR encourages a reliance on quantitative models in order to derive the distribution of returns from which such metrics can be calculated. The use of complicated models facilitates combining many complex market characteristics such as volatility and dependence into one or more simple numbers that can represent risk. Models can compare different trades and quantify which is better, at least according to certain predefined metrics. All of these things can be done in minutes or even seconds to allow institutions to make fast decisions in rapidly moving financial markets.

However, the financial markets have a somewhat love/hate relationship with mathematical models. In good times, models tend to be regarded as invaluable, facilitating the growth in complex derivatives products and dynamic approaches to risk management adopted by many large financial institutions. Only in bad times, and often after significant financial losses, is the realisation that models are only simple approximations to the reality of financial markets fully appreciated. Most recently, following the financial crisis beginning in 2007, mathematical models have been heavily criticised for the incorrect modelling of mortgage-backed securities and other structured credit products that led to significant losses.

The potential for "blowups" in financial markets, especially derivatives, has led to models being either loved or berated depending on the underlying market conditions. Take the most famous model of them all, the Black–Scholes–Merton (BSM) option-pricing formula (Black and Scholes, 1973) as an example. The financial markets took a while to warm to this approach but by around 1977, traders were treating the formula as gospel. On Black Monday (19th October 1987), US stocks collapsed by 23%, wiping out $1 trillion in capital and this was partly due to dynamic-hedging strategies such as CPPI (constant proportion portfolio insurance) made possible by the BSM theory. Nevertheless, in 1995, Myron Scholes and Robert Merton were awarded the Nobel Prize for Economic Sciences.[5] The danger is that models tend to be viewed either as "good" or "bad" depending on the underlying market conditions. Whereas, in reality, models can be good or bad depending on how they are used. An excellent description of the intricate relationship between models and financial markets can be found in MacKenzie (2006).

The changing and inconsistent view of quantitative models within finance also arises from the fact that models are applied to many different problems, some of which are reasonable to model and some of which are not. The rating agencies' willingness to rate highly complex structured credit products with rapidly developed models is an example of the latter category. In this case, the data available was so scarce that statistical modelling, in some cases, should never even have been attempted. VAR provides another good example of the application-of-models dilemma. A 99% VAR over one day[6] is reasonable to model since a one in a hundred daily event is not particularly extreme. Such a measure is also easy to "backtest" as even a year of daily observations gives a reasonable statistical test as to whether the numbers of days the VAR has actually been exceeded is approximately correct.[7] However, when higher confidence levels and/or longer time horizons are involved then risk quantification becomes more complex and difficult to test.

---

[5] Fischer Black had died in 1995.
[6] Most VAR models tend to calculate this measure and then scale to the required 10-day horizon.
[7] Between one and six violations is reasonable at the 95% confidence level, as discussed in more detail in Section 17.4.3.

The modelling of counterparty risk is an inevitable requirement for financial institutions and regulators. This can be extremely useful and measures such as potential future exposure (PFE), the counterparty risk analogue of VAR, are important components of counterparty risk management. However, like VAR, the quantitative modelling of counterparty risk is complex and prone to misinterpretation and misuse. Furthermore, unlike VAR, counterparty risk involves looking years into the future rather than just a few days, which creates further complexity not to be underestimated. Not surprisingly, regulatory requirements over back-testing of counterparty risk models[8] have been introduced to assess performance. In addition, a greater emphasis has been placed on stress testing of counterparty risk, to highlight risks in excess of those defined by models.

2.3.4   Correlation and dependency

Probably the most difficult aspect in understanding and quantifying financial risk is that of dependency between different financial variables. This is well known in VAR methodologies where a large correlation matrix essentially drives the resulting VAR number. Errors in the estimation of the underlying correlations increase the uncertainty of the final VAR number. It is well known that historically estimated correlations may not be a good representation of future behaviour. This is especially true in a more volatile market environment, or crisis, where correlations have a tendency to become very large.[9]

Counterparty risk takes difficulties with correlation to another level, for example compared to traditional VAR models. Firstly, correlations are inherently unstable and can change significantly over time. This is important for counterparty risk assessment, which must be made over many years compared to market risk VAR that is measured over just a single day. Secondly, correlation is not the only way to represent dependency and other statistical measures are possible. Particularly in the case of wrong-way risk (Chapter 15), the treatment of dependencies via measures other than correlation is important.

2.4   THE DERIVATIVES MARKET

2.4.1   Uses of derivatives

Derivatives contracts represent agreements either to make payments or to buy or sell an underlying contract at a time or times in the future. The times may range from a few weeks or months (for example, futures contracts) to many years (for example, long-dated swaps). The value of a derivatives contract will change with the level of one of more underlying assets or indices and possibly decisions made by the parties to the contract. In many cases, the initial value of a derivative traded will be contractually configured to be zero for both parties at inception.

Derivatives are not a particularly new financial innovation; for example, in medieval times, forward contracts were popular in Europe. However, derivatives products and markets have become particularly complex in the last couple of decades. One of the advantages of

---

[8] Under the Basel III regulations.
[9] Either positive or negative.

derivatives is that they can provide very efficient hedging tools, for example, consider the following risks that an institution, such as a corporate, may experience:

- *FX risk*. Due to being paid in various currencies, there is a need to hedge cash inflow in these currencies.
- *IR risk*. They may wish to transform fixed- into floating-rate debt.
- *Commodity*. The need to lock in oil prices when energy costs represent a significant portion of gross margin.

In many ways, derivatives are no different from the underlying cash instruments. They simply allow one to take a very similar position in a synthetic way. For example, an airline wanting to reduce their exposure to a potentially rising oil price can buy oil futures, which are cash-settled and therefore represent a very simple way to go "long oil" (with no storage or transport costs). An institution wanting to reduce their exposure to a certain asset can do so via a derivative contract, which means they do not have to sell the asset directly in the market.

2.4.2 Exchange-traded and OTC derivatives

Within the derivatives markets, many of the simplest products are traded through exchanges. An exchange has the benefit of facilitating liquidity and therefore making trading and unwinding of positions easy. An exchange also mitigates all counterparty risk concerns since the default of a member of the exchange would be absorbed by the exchange (in theory at least, this point is discussed in depth in Chapter 7). Products traded on an exchange must be well standardised to facilitate liquidity and transparent trading. This standardisation typically develops over a lifecycle of many years before a given derivative is suitable for exchange trading.

Compared to exchange-traded derivatives, OTC derivatives tend to be less standard structures and are typically traded *bilaterally*, i.e., between two parties. They are private contracts and not protected by any government insurance programme or customer asset protection programme. Hence, each party takes counterparty risk with respect to the other party. Many players in the OTC derivatives market do not have exceptional credit quality nor are they able to post collateral to reduce counterparty risk. This counterparty risk is therefore an unavoidable consequence of the OTC derivatives market. This also tends to create highly connected counterparties such as in interbank trading.

In 1986, OTC derivatives fell slightly behind exchange-traded instruments with $500 billion notional outstanding.[10] By 1995, OTC derivatives' notional exceeded that of exchange-traded instruments by a ratio of more than 5 to 1, a ratio maintained in 2005.[11] The OTC interest rate market is by far the largest component, having grown since the early 1980s to $284 trillion in notional value. OTC derivatives are significant in other asset classes such as foreign exchange, equities and commodities. Credit derivatives products were first developed to supplement the cash bond market but in many ways are now even more significant than cash bonds. The OTC derivatives market has grown exponentially over the last two decades, offering effective opportunities for risk management and financial innovation, which are key

---

[10] *Source*: ISDA survey 1986 covering only swaps.
[11] *Source*: BIS reports 1995 and 2005.

ingredients for economic growth. OTC derivatives dominate exchange-traded derivatives due to their inherent customisation.

In the last few years, there has been a growing trend to centrally clear derivatives, primarily aimed at reducing counterparty risk. Centrally cleared derivatives retain some OTC features (such as being initiated bilaterally) and therefore represent a halfway house between OTC and exchange trading. A derivative has to be standardised to permit central clearing but it does not need to have all the features that would allow exchange trading, such as sufficient liquidity. Central clearing (Chapter 7) will be a key component in defining the future counterparty risk landscape.

2.4.3   Risks of derivatives

Of course, not all derivatives transactions can be classified as "socially useful". Some involve regulatory arbitrage (i.e., reducing the regulatory capital a bank has to keep without reducing its exposures); some are concerned with changing the tax or accounting treatment of an item; occasionally an OTC derivative is designed by a dealer to appear more attractive than it is to unwary end-users.[12]

The use of derivatives as synthetic versions of cash assets is not particularly worrying. However, a key difference of derivatives instruments is *leverage*. Since most derivatives are executed with only a small (with respect to the notional value of the contract) or no upfront payment made, they allow significant leverage. If an institution has the view that US interest rates will be going down, they may buy US treasury bonds.[13] There is natural limitation to the size of this trade, which is the cash that the institution can raise in order to invest in bonds. However, entering into a receiver interest rate swap in US dollars will provide approximately the same exposure to interest rates but with no initial investment.[14] Hence, the size of the trade, and the effective leverage, must be limited by the institution themselves, their counterparty in the swap transaction or a regulator. Inevitably, it will be significantly bigger than that in the previous case of buying bonds outright.

Derivatives have been repeatedly shown to be capable of creating major market disturbances. They have been given such labels as "financial weapons of mass destruction". The fact is that, as with any invention that offers significant advantages such as commercial aircraft or nuclear power, derivatives can be extremely dangerous. Some take the view that derivatives should be wholly exchange-traded or even, in some cases, outlawed (e.g., see Soros, 2009). On the other hand, many express the opposite sentiment, for example: "*The only thing more dangerous than having too many derivatives floating around the financial system, it seems, is having too few of them.*"[15]

2.4.4   Too big to fail and systemic risk

Systemic risk in financial terms concerns the potential failure of one institution that creates a chain reaction or domino effect on other institutions and consequently threatens the stability

---

[12] Some people would include speculation in this list of non-socially useful applications of OTC derivatives and some large synthetic transactions involving the subprime mortgage market have been widely criticised as having no redeeming qualities. However, speculators are an important source of liquidity in many derivatives markets.

[13] This may not be the most effective way to act on this view but is simply an example.

[14] Aside from initial margin requirements and capital requirements.

[15] "The perils of prudence", *Economist*, 20th June 2009.

of the entire financial markets and even the global economy. Systemic risk may not only be triggered by actual losses; just a heightened perception of risk and resulting "flight to quality" away from more risky assets causes serious disruptions. Derivatives have always been strongly linked to systemic risk, due to the relatively large number of dominant counterparties, the leverage in the market together, unfortunately, with the short-sighted greed of many of the participants within these markets.

A key, but subtle, problem serves as a threat to the stability of derivatives. OTC derivatives have evolved into a market dominated by a relatively small number of financial intermediaries (often referred to as dealers). These financial intermediaries act as common counterparties to large numbers of end-users of derivatives and actively trade with each other to manage their positions. The centralisation of OTC derivatives with a small number of high-quality counterparties was perceived by some as actually adding stability – after all, surely none of these counterparties would ever fail.

It seems to have been a widely held view for many years prior to 2007 that large firms would not fail, since they could hire the best staff and adopt the best risk management practices. Such a view ignores the political, regional and management challenges within a large institution that can lead to opaque representation and communication of risks, especially at a senior level. Recent events have taught the financial markets that this concept is a fundamentally flawed one. A dramatic point in the global financial crisis was the realisation that a number of counterparties were "too big to fail" since their failure would have systemic consequences and knock-on effects that were simply not an option. Institutions such as AIG, Bear Stearns, Dexia and Royal Bank of Scotland were all given some form of a bailout by their central banks in order to avert such events.

The problem of the too big to fail mentality is illustrated by AIG (American International Group Inc.) which had written[16] insurance (credit derivatives) on a notional amount of around half a trillion dollars. AIG did not have to set aside capital or reserves and had limited collateral requirements. Counterparties were presumably happy to transact with AIG on the basis of their strong credit quality and the fact that collateral terms could be contractually tightened in the event of AIG experiencing credit quality deterioration. However, AIG suffered a \$99.3 billion loss in 2008 and failed in September 2008 due to liquidity problems,[17] causing the US Department of Treasury and Federal Reserve Bank of New York to arrange loans as support for a "too big to fail" institution. AIG required over \$100 billion of US taxpayers' money to cover losses due to the excessive risk-taking. Monoline insurers *collectively* had a comparable exposure to AIG but, since this exposure was spread across a number of financial institutions, their failure was more palatable.

A stable derivatives market is not one heavily dominated by a few large institutions but rather a market with smaller institutions that can and will fail, but with less dramatic consequences. A financial system that is "safe to fail" is more readily achievable than one that is "failsafe". Having too big to fail institutions such as large dealers, insurance companies and central counterparties is not ideal.[18] However, policymakers and regulators seem to have accepted that this is an unavoidable consequence of global financial markets and such

---

[16] Through AIG Financial Products (AIGFP), a subsidiary that was able to command the strong reputation of its parent AIG.
[17] The downgrade of AIG's bonds triggered collateral calls that the insurer was unable to make.
[18] It could be argued that even if it was possible to avoid the existence of any too big to fail counterparties, there may be counterparties in particular regions or sectors that would be so interconnected as to produce the same problem (for example, a number of small banks in a country all failing simultaneously).

entities must then be regulated with extreme caution and given special status due to their "SIFI" (systemically important financial institution) status, which is a less crude way of saying too big to fail. A key reaction to the global financial crisis has been to mandate central clearing via central counterparties (CCPs). Yet, by its very nature, a CCP will be a SIFI.

SIFIs create moral hazard problems since they and their counterparties may behave less cautiously due to the implicit or explicit promise that they will always be supported in financial distress by their central bank. A key question for counterparty risk assessment is whether certain counterparties can be regarded to all intents and purposes as "risk-free". It seems in the case of SIFIs that the answer is yes. However, one of the key lessons of the global financial crisis was that it was precisely these types of institutions that can be the most dangerous counterparties. Furthermore, it should not be assumed that a government-sponsored bailout would protect any counterparty in full. No counterparty should ever be regarded as risk-free.

2.4.5 Credit derivatives

The credit derivatives market, whilst relatively young, has grown swiftly due to the need to transfer credit risk efficiently. The core credit derivative instrument, the credit default swap (CDS), is simple and has transformed the trading of credit risk. However, CDSs themselves can prove highly toxic since, whilst they can be used to hedge counterparty risk in other products, there is counterparty risk embedded within the CDS itself. The market has recently become all too aware of the dangers of CDSs and their usage has partly declined in line with this realisation. It is generally agreed that CDS counterparty risk poses a significant threat to global financial markets. Credit derivatives can, on the one hand, be very efficient at transferring credit risk but, if not used correctly, can be counterproductive and highly toxic.

One of the main drivers of the move towards central clearing of standard OTC derivatives is the wrong-way counterparty risk represented by the CDS market. Furthermore, as hedges for counterparty risk, CDSs seem to require the default remoteness that central clearing apparently gives them. However, the ability of central counterparties to deal with the CDS product, which is much more complex, illiquid and risky than other cleared products, is crucial and not yet tested.

2.5 COUNTERPARTY RISK IN CONTEXT

2.5.1 The rise of counterparty risk

Counterparty risk is traditionally thought of as credit risk between OTC derivatives counterparties. Since the global financial crisis, the importance of OTC derivatives in defining crises has made counterparty risk *the* key financial risk. Historically, many financial institutions limited their counterparty risk by trading only with the most sound counterparties. The size and scale of counterparty risk has always been important but has for many years been obscured by the myth of the creditworthiness of the "too big to fail" institutions such as those mentioned in Chapter 1. For many years, institutions ignored counterparty risk with high-quality (e.g., Triple-A) rated institutions, sovereigns, supranational or collateral posting entities. However, the financial crisis showed that these are often the entities that represent the *most* counterparty risk. The need to consider counterparty risk in all counterparty relationships and the decline in credit quality generally has caused a meteoric rise in interest in and around counterparty risk. Regulatory pressure has continued to fuel this interest. Whereas in the past, only a few large dealers invested heavily in assessed counterparty risk, it has rapidly become the problem of all financial institutions, big or small.

2.5.2   Counterparty risk and CVA

Counterparty risk represents a combination of market risk, which defines the exposure, and credit risk, which defines the counterparty credit quality. A counterparty with a large default probability and a small exposure may be considered preferable to one with a larger exposure and smaller underlying default probability – but this is not clear. CVA puts a precise value on counterparty risk and can distinguish numerically between the aforementioned cases. CVA values the counterparty risk that an institution takes and potentially allows it to be traded (hedged).

Many banks essentially accounted for CVA many years prior to the global financial crisis in line with the common practice in taking "reserves" against potential future losses. Such reserves tend to be estimated based on historical data and by their nature did not change much from day to day. A CVA calculated in this way is to be interpreted as a statistical estimate of the expected future losses from counterparty risk. This treats CVA as a banking book item since it is not marked-to-market but rather estimated actuarially. CVA is analogous to a loan loss reserve, which aims to absorb the future potential credit risk losses on a loan book.

Part of the global regulation arising in the aftermath of the global financial crisis (e.g., Basel III) seems to view CVA as necessarily being a marked-to-market trading book component, alongside the OTC derivatives position from which it is derived. Some large dealers had been following this approach for many years, due essentially to not having a banking book (retail banking activities). CVA treated as a mark-to-market represents the cost of hedging counterparty risk in a perfect market. "Trading book CVA" will typically be much larger and certainly much more volatile than "banking book CVA" but, in theory, can be risk-transferred by methods such as hedging and securitisation.

The distinction between banking book and trading book CVA is an important one. On the one hand, trading book CVA is more relevant since it reflects the current market conditions and cost of transferring the risk, rather than some subjective actuarial assessment. On the other hand, the illiquidity of the credit component of counterparty risk and resulting difficulty in hedging may suggest that a more passive banking book approach, with emphasis on fundamental credit analysis, is preferable. Regulators seem not to take this view, but this subject will be discussed further in Chapter 17.

2.5.3   Mitigating counterparty risk

There are many ways to mitigate counterparty risk. These include netting, margining (collateralisation) and hedging. All can reduce counterparty risk substantially but at additional operational cost. Mitigating counterparty risk changes the nature of the underlying market risk component and creates other risks such as liquidity, operational and systemic risk. Indeed, a continuing theme as we discuss this topic in more detail will be that mitigation of counterparty risk generates other forms of financial risk. Hence, it is especially important to look at counterparty risk in the context of other financial risks. The full understanding of counterparty risk therefore involves the appreciation of all aspects of financial risks and the interplay between them, specifically:

- *Market risk*. Taking collateral to minimise counterparty risk creates market risk since exposure exists in the time taken to receive the relevant collateral amount and collateral itself may have price and FX volatility.
- *Operational risk*. The management of counterparty risk relies on practices such as netting and collateralisation that themselves give rise to operational risks, as will be discussed in more detail in Chapter 4.
- *Liquidity risk*. Collateralisation of counterparty risk may lead to liquidity risk if the collateral needs to be sold at some point due to a default. This may also be described as "gap risk". Such aspects are also tackled in Chapters 5 and 8. Rehypothecation (reuse) of collateral (Chapter 3) is also an important consideration here.
- *Systemic risk*. Central counterparties (CCPs) act as intermediaries to centralise counterparty risk between market participants. Whilst offering advantages such as risk reduction and operational efficiencies, they potentially allow dangers such as moral hazard and asymmetric information to develop and flourish. CCPs may ultimately create greater systemic risk in the market due to the possibility that they themselves might fail. This is discussed at length in Chapter 7.

Hence, this is not just a book on counterparty risk; it is a book on market, credit, liquidity, operational and systemic risk. More importantly, it explores the linkages between different risk types and the good and bad points in relation to counterparty risk mitigation.

2.5.4   Counterparty risk and central clearing

There are many solutions to counterparty risk problems, all of which may help to mitigate the risk. Policymakers and regulators seem to believe that a centralised clearing system will reduce counterparty risk, particularly in the credit derivatives market. Whilst central clearing may be beneficial if introduced correctly, it is no panacea. The best mechanism for controlling counterparty risk will be a full understanding of all aspects, including the many possible risk mitigants and hedging possibilities. As market participants and regulators become more knowledgeable, the control of this new dimension of financial risk will become achievable.

2.6   SUMMARY

This chapter has provided some context and background to counterparty risk, examining its importance in financial markets and links to other risk types. A number of basic points, such as the nature of the derivatives market and VAR methods, have been described. The need to mitigate counterparty risk, and the potential dangers in doing so, have also been introduced. The next chapter will define counterparty risk in more detail.

3

Defining Counterparty Credit Risk

An expert is a person who has made all the mistakes that can be made in a very narrow field.
Niels Bohr (1885–1962)

3.1 INTRODUCING COUNTERPARTY CREDIT RISK

. . . probably the single most important variable in determining whether and with what speed financial disturbances become financial shocks, with potential systemic traits

Counterparty Risk Management Policy Group (2005)

Counterparty credit risk (often known just as counterparty risk) is the risk that the entity with whom one has entered into a financial contract (the counterparty to the contract) will fail to fulfil their side of the contractual agreement (e.g., they default). Counterparty risk is typically defined as arising from two broad classes of financial products:

- OTC (over-the-counter) derivatives, some well-known examples being
  - interest rate swaps,
  - FX forwards, and
  - credit default swaps.
- Securities financing transactions, for example
  - repos and reverse repos,
  - securities borrowing and lending.

The former category is the more significant due to the size and diversity of the OTC derivatives market and the fact that a significant amount of risk is not collateralised.

Mitigating counterparty risk creates other financial risks. A complete understanding of counterparty risk requires knowledge of all financial risks, such as market, credit, operational and liquidity. Furthermore, the interaction of different financial risks is critical in defining the nature of counterparty risk. As has been shown in the market events of the last few years, counterparty risk is complex, with systemic traits and the potential to cause, catalyse or magnify serious disturbances in the financial markets. Hence, the need to understand, quantify and manage counterparty risk is crucial. Without this, the future health, development and growth of derivatives products and financial markets in general will be hindered.

3.1.1 Counterparty risk versus lending risk

Traditionally, credit risk can generally be thought of as lending risk. One party owes an amount to another party and may fail to pay some or all of this due to insolvency. This can apply to loans, bonds, mortgages, credit cards and so on. Lending risk is characterised by two key aspects:

- The notional amount at risk at any time during the lending period is usually known with a degree of certainty. Market variables such as interest rates will typically create only moderate uncertainty over the amount owed. For example, in buying a fixed-coupon bond with a par value of $1,000, the notional amount at risk for the life of the bond is close to $1,000. A repayment mortgage will amortise over time (the notional drops due to the repayments) but one can predict with good accuracy the outstanding balance at some future date. A loan or credit card may have a certain maximum usage facility, which may reasonably be assumed fully drawn[1] for the purpose of credit risk.
- Only one party takes lending risk. A bondholder takes considerable credit risk but an issuer of a bond does not face a loss if the buyer of the bond defaults.[2] This point does not follow for other contracts.

With counterparty risk, as with all credit risk, the cause of a loss is the obligor being unable or unwilling to meet contractual obligations. However, two aspects may differentiate contracts with counterparty risk from traditional credit risk:

- The value of the contract in the future is uncertain, in most cases significantly so. The value of a derivative at a potential default date will be the net value of all future cash flows required under that contract. This future value can be positive or negative and is typically highly uncertain (as seen from today).
- Since the value of the contract can be positive or negative, counterparty risk is typically *bilateral*. In other words, in a derivatives transaction, each counterparty has risk to the other.

The primary distinguishing feature of counterparty risk compared with other forms of credit risk is that the value of the underlying contract in the future is uncertain, both in magnitude and in sign!

3.1.2 Settlement and pre-settlement risk

A derivatives portfolio contains a number of settlements equal to multiples of the total number of trades (for example, a swap contract will have a number of settlement dates as cash flows are exchanged periodically). Counterparty risk is mainly associated with

---

[1] On the basis that an individual unable to pay their credit card bill is likely to be close to their limit.
[2] This is not precisely true in the case of bilateral counterparty risk (DVA), discussed in Chapter 13, although we will show that conventions regarding closeout amounts can correct for this.

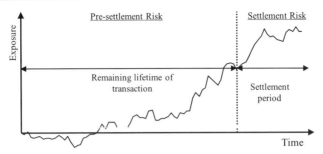

Figure 3.1 Illustration of pre-settlement and settlement risk. Note that the settlement period is normally short (e.g., hours) but can be much longer in some cases.

pre-settlement risk, which is the risk of default of the counterparty prior to expiration (settlement) of the contract. However, we should also consider settlement risk, which is the risk of counterparty default *during* the settlement process.

- *Pre-settlement risk.* This is the risk that a counterparty will default prior to the final settlement of the transaction (at expiration). This is what counterparty risk usually refers to.
- *Settlement risk.* This arises at final settlement if there are timing differences between when each party performs on its obligations under the contract.

The difference between pre-settlement and settlement risk is illustrated in Figure 3.1.

Whilst settlement risk gives rise to much larger exposures, default prior to expiration of the contract is substantially more likely than default at the settlement date. However, settlement risk can be more complex when there is a substantial delivery period (for example, as in a commodity contract where one may be required to settle in cash against receiving a physical commodity over a specified time period).

Whilst all derivatives technically have both settlement and pre-settlement risk, the balance between the two will be different depending on the contract. Spot contracts have mainly settlement risk whilst long-dated swaps have mainly pre-settlement risk. Furthermore, various types of netting (see next chapter) provide mitigation against settlement and pre-settlement risks.

Unlike counterparty risk, settlement risk is characterised by a very large exposure, potentially 100% of the notional of the trade. Settlement risk is a major consideration in FX markets, where the settlement of a contract involves a payment of one currency against receiving

---

Example. Suppose an institution enters into a forward foreign exchange contract to exchange €1m for $1.4m at a specified date in the future. The settlement risk exposes the institution to a substantial loss of $1.4m. which could arise if €1m was paid but the $1.4m was not received. Pre-settlement risk exposes the institution to just the difference in market value between the dollar and euro payments. If the foreign exchange rate moved from 1.4 to 1.45 then this would translate into a loss of **$50,000**. This type of cross-currency settlement risk is sometimes called Herstatt risk (see box below).

> **Bankhaus Herstatt.** The most well-known example of settlement risk is shown by the failure of a small German bank, Bankhaus Herstatt. On 26th June 1974, the firm defaulted but only after the close of the German interbank payments system (3:30pm local time). Some of Bankhaus Herstatt's counterparties had paid Deutschemarks to the bank during the day believing they would receive US dollars later the same day in New York. However, it was only 10:30am in New York when Herstatt's banking business was terminated and consequently all outgoing US dollar payments from Herstatt's account were suspended, leaving counterparties fully exposed.

the other. Most FX now goes through CLS[3] and most securities settle DVP,[4] but there are always exceptions and settlement risk should be recognised in such cases. Cash flows in a cross-currency swap may not go through CLS so this may give rise to settlement risk. Settlement risk may also arise on securities financing transactions if the exchange of securities and cash is not DVP.

Settlement risk typically occurs for only a small amount of time (often just days or even hours). To measure the period of risk to a high degree of accuracy would mean taking into account the contractual payment dates, the time zones involved and the time it takes for the bank to perform its reconciliations across Nostro[5] accounts. Any failed trades should also continue to count against settlement exposure until the trade actually settles.

There are clearly circumstances where banks need to measure settlement risk but it is important to avoid double counting this with pre-settlement or counterparty risk. Institutions typically set separate settlement risk limits and measure exposure against this limit rather than including settlement risk in the assessment of counterparty risk. It may be possible to mitigate settlement risk, for example by insisting on receiving cash before transferring securities.

We also note that one of the recent initiatives to mitigate counterparty risk and some of its side-effects such as liquidity risk, the SCSA, does this at the cost of introducing more settlement risk. This is discussed further in Chapter 14 (Section 14.5.1).

3.1.3 Exchange-traded derivatives

Some derivatives are exchange-traded where the exchange is a central financial centre where parties can trade standardised contracts such as futures and options at a specified price. Exchanges have been used to trade financial products for many years. An exchange promotes market efficiency and enhances liquidity by centralising trading in a single place. The process by which a financial contract becomes exchange-traded can be thought of as a long journey where a reasonable trading volume, standardisation and liquidity must first develop.

Whilst an exchange provides efficient price discovery,[6] it also typically provides a means of mitigating counterparty risk. An exchange will also "clear" trades or have a central

---

[3] The largest multi-currency cash settlement system, see http://www.cls-group.com.
[4] Delivery versus payment where payment is made at the moment of delivery, aiming to minimise settlement risk in securities transactions.
[5] This is a bank account held in a foreign country, denominated in the currency of that country. Nostro accounts are used for settlement of foreign exchange transactions.
[6] This is the process of determining the price of an asset in a marketplace through the interactions of buyers and sellers.

counterparty attached to it that will provide this clearing service. The clearing function guarantees the contract performance and eliminates counterparty risk. Indeed, when trading a typical exchange-traded derivative, the actual counterparty to the contract is the exchange. Derivatives traded on an exchange are therefore normally considered to have no counterparty risk since the only aspect of concern is the solvency of the exchange itself. However, this point requires much further analysis that will be described in Chapter 7.

3.1.4 OTC-traded derivatives

Due to the need for customisation, a much greater notional amount of derivatives are traded OTC (over the counter). OTC derivatives are typically traded bilaterally and each party takes counterparty risk to the other. The market for OTC derivatives has grown dramatically in the last decade and is significantly larger than the exchange-traded market, as illustrated in Figure 3.2. The strong growth of OTC derivatives against exchange-traded derivatives is partly due to exotic contracts and new markets such as credit derivatives (the credit default swap market increased by a factor of 10 between the end of 2003 and the end of 2008). However, the more important factor influencing the popularity of OTC products is the ability to tailor contracts more precisely to client needs, for example, by offering a particular maturity date. Exchange-traded products, by their very nature, do not offer customisation.

The total notional amount of all derivatives outstanding was $601 trillion at 2010 year-end. The curtailed growth towards the end of the history can be clearly attributed to the global financial crisis where firms have reduced balance sheets and reallocated capital and clients have been less interested in derivatives, particularly as structured products. However, the reduction in recent years is also partially due to compression exercises that seek to reduce counterparty risk via removing offsetting and redundant positions (discussed in more detail in the next chapter).

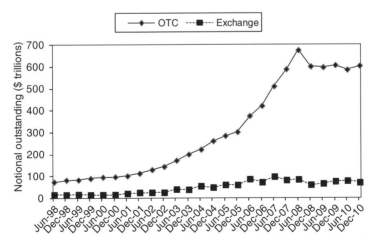

Figure 3.2 Total outstanding notional of OTC- and exchange-traded derivatives transactions. The figures cover interest rate, foreign exchange, equity, commodity and credit derivative contracts. Note that notional amounts outstanding are not directly comparable to those for exchange-traded derivatives, which refer to open interest or net positions whereas the amounts outstanding for OTC markets refer to gross positions, i.e., without netting.
Source: BIS.

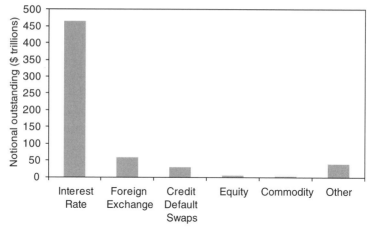

Figure 3.3 Split of OTC gross outstanding notional by product type as of end 2010.
Source: BIS.

The split of OTC derivatives by product type is shown in Figure 3.3. Interest rate products contribute the majority of the outstanding notional, with foreign exchange and credit default swaps seemingly less important. However, this gives a somewhat misleading view of the importance of counterparty risk in other asset classes, especially foreign exchange and credit default swaps. Whilst most foreign exchange products are short-dated, the long-dated nature and exchange of notional in cross-currency swaps means they carry a lot of counterparty risk. Credit default swaps not only have a large volatility component but also constitute significant "wrong-way risk" (discussed in detail in Chapter 15). So, whilst interest rate products make up a significant proportion of the counterparty risk in the market (and indeed are most commonly used in practical examples), one must not underestimate the important (and sometimes more subtle) contributions from other products.[7]

A key aspect of derivatives products is that their exposure is substantially smaller than that of an equivalent loan or bond. Consider an interest rate swap as an example; this contract involves the exchange of floating against fixed coupons and has no principal risk because only cash flows are exchanged. Furthermore, even the coupons are not fully at risk because, at coupon dates, only the difference in fixed and floating coupons or *net* payment will be exchanged. If a counterparty fails to perform then an institution will have no obligation to continue to make coupon payments. Instead, the swap will be unwound based on independent quotations as to its current market value. If the swap has a negative value for an institution then they stand to lose nothing if their counterparty defaults. For this reason, when we compare the actual total market of derivatives against their total notional amount outstanding, we see a massive reduction as illustrated in Table 3.1. For example, the total market value of interest rate contracts is only 3.1% of the total notional outstanding.

---

[7] Indeed, in a survey of banks I carried out in 2009, "Credit value adjustment and the changing environment for pricing and managing counterparty risk", banks were asked which asset classes they felt their counterparty risk came from. Interest rate products were indeed most significant overall (52%), but foreign exchange (18%) and credit derivatives (21%) were significant. This survey can be found at www.cvacentral.com.

Table 3.1 Comparison of the total notional outstanding and the market value of derivatives ($ trillions) for different asset classes as of December 2010

	Gross notional outstanding	Gross market value[*]	Ratio
Interest rate	465.3	14.6	3.1%
Foreign exchange	57.8	2.5	4.3%
Credit default swaps	29.9	1.1	4.5%
Equity	5.6	0.6	11.5%
Commodity	2.9	0.5	18.0%

[*]This is calculated as the sum of the absolute value of gross positive and gross negative market values, corrected for double counting.
Source: BIS

3.1.5 Repos and securities lending

A repurchase agreement or *repo* is a mechanism to reduce the cost of financing although, as the repo market has grown, the application and strategies have also developed. In a repo transaction, one party exchanges securities in return for cash with an agreement to repurchase the securities at a specified future date. The securities essentially act as collateral for a cash loan. The repurchase price is greater than the original sale price with the difference effectively representing the repo rate, which equates to an interest rate on the transaction plus any counterparty risk charge. The collateral tends to be liquid securities (traditionally bonds, although other securities are also used) of stable value. A haircut is applied to mitigate the counterparty risk arising due to the chance that the borrower will fail to pay back the cash *and* the value of the collateral will fall. Repos are of great importance in international money markets and the market has been growing and developing substantially in recent years. A *reverse repo* is simply the same transaction from the other party's point of view.

A repo is essentially a loan with collateral taken against it to mitigate the otherwise substantial credit risk. However, some residual counterparty risk will remain. The seller of securities may default by failing to repurchase them at the maturity date. This means that the buyer may liquidate the securities in order to recover the cash lent. There is a risk that the securities may have lost value due to market movements and not cover this amount. To mitigate this risk, repos are often overcollateralised (via the haircut) as well as being subject to daily mark-to-market margining. Hence, the residual risk is essentially a "gap risk" in that the market moves quickly or "gaps" in a short space of time prior to the default of the seller. Conversely, if the value of the security rises, the borrower in a repo transaction may experience credit risk. The greater the degree of overcollateralisation, the greater this risk will be. The counterparty risk in a repo is subject to many factors such as the term (maturity), liquidity of security and the strength of counterparties involved.

Securities lending transactions involve one party borrowing securities from another and providing collateral of comparable value. This is similar to a repo transaction except that securities are exchanged for collateral rather than cash for collateral. Whilst a repo transaction always involves cash on one side, securities lending does not since the collateral used may be bonds or other securities. In addition to the collateral, securities lending typically involves a mark-to-market margining as for repo.

3.1.6 Mitigating counterparty risk

Counterparty risk can be reduced by various means. Netting and collateral agreements have been common tools to achieve this. These are often bilateral and therefore aim to reduce the risk for *both* parties. In the event of default, netting allows the offset of amounts owed to and by a counterparty. However, the impact of netting is finite and heavily dependent on the type of underlying transactions involved. Collateral can reduce counterparty risk further and, in theory, eliminate it but creates significant operational costs and other risks, such as liquidity and legal. Chapter 4 examines these points in more detail.

Central counterparties, such as exchanges and clearing houses, can allow the centralisation of counterparty risk and mutualisation of losses. This at first seems like a simple solution to the problem raised by significant bilateral risks in the market, which can lead to a systemic crisis whereby the default of one institution creates a "domino effect". However, central counterparties can create moral hazard and asymmetric information problems by eliminating the incentive for market participants to monitor carefully the counterparty risks of one another. In Chapter 7, we will discuss the strengths and weaknesses of central counterparties in detail.

The growth of the credit derivatives market has made hedging of counterparty risk a viable option. Credit derivatives products called contingent credit default swaps (CCDSs) have even been developed specifically for this purpose. Credit derivatives also create the opportunity to diversify counterparty risk by reducing counterparty exposure to the clients of a firm, taking instead exposure to other parties who may be clients only of a competitor. However, hedging can be expensive and creates wrong-way risk (Chapter 15). Chapter 16 discusses hedging in more detail.

We emphasise strongly that *any* mitigation of counterparty risk is a double-edged sword since it will not necessarily reduce overall risks and could potentially allow financial markets to develop too quickly or to reach a dangerous size. A very simple example can explain this. Suppose there are 100 units of risk in a market dominated by 10 dealers. The market cannot develop further since the 10 dealers are unable or unwilling to increase their positions and further market participants are unable, or simply do not see it as being profitable for them, to enter the market. Now, suppose some form of risk mitigation is developed, and allowed by regulators, which reduces the total amount of risk to 25 units. The market is now likely to develop strongly due to existing dealers increasing their exposures and new entrants to the market. Eventually, the market may increase in size and return to the situation of 100 units of risk. The risk mitigation has been extremely efficient since the market size (in terms of the original risk taken) has quadrupled. However, suppose the risk mitigation has some weaknesses and its impact has therefore been overstated, either due to dealers' over-optimistic assessments of their risks and/or regulators allowing too aggressive a reduction in capital. In this case, the overall risk in the market has actually increased due to the risk mitigation. Worst still, market participants and regulatory bodies are blind to these risks.

Understanding the balance between good and bad risk mitigation has not been easy for markets exposed to counterparty risk. We will devote separate chapters to understanding the full impact of collateralisation and netting (Chapter 4), central counterparties (Chapter 7), hedging (Chapter 16) and regulatory aspects (Chapter 17).

3.1.7   Counterparty risk players

The range of institutions that take significant counterparty risk has changed dramatically over recent years (or more to the point, institutions now fully appreciate the extent of counterparty risk they may face). Let us characterise these institutions generally:

- Large derivatives player
  - typically a large bank, often known as a dealer;
  - will have a vast number of OTC derivatives trades on their books;
  - will trade with each other and have many other clients;
  - coverage of all or many different asset classes (interest rate, foreign exchange, equity, commodities, credit derivatives);
  - will post collateral against positions (at least as long as the counterparty will make the same commitment and sometimes even if they do not).
- Medium derivatives player
  - typically a smaller bank or other financial institution such as a hedge fund or pension fund;
  - will have many OTC derivatives trades on their books;
  - will trade with a relatively large number of clients;
  - will cover several asset classes although may not be active in all of them (may, for example, not trade credit derivatives or commodities and will probably not deal with the more exotic derivatives);
  - will probably post collateral against positions with some exceptions.
- Small derivatives player
  - typically a large corporate or sovereign with significant derivatives requirements (for example, for hedging needs or investment) or a small financial institution;
  - will have a few OTC derivatives trades on their books;
  - will trade with potentially only a few different counterparties;
  - may be specialised to a single asset class (for example, some corporates trade only foreign exchange products, a mining company may trade only commodity forwards, a pension fund may only be active in interest rate and inflation products);
  - typically, will be unable to commit to posting collateral or will post illiquid collateral.

Historically, the large derivatives players have had much stronger credit quality than the other participants. However, some small players, such as sovereigns and insurance companies, have had very strong (Triple-A) credit quality and have used this to obtain favourable terms such as one-way collateral agreements. Historically, a large amount of counterparty risk has been ignored simply because large derivatives players (the credit spreads of large, highly rated, financial institutions prior to 2007 amounted to just a few basis points per annum[8]) or Triple-A entities were assumed default free.

However, the above has since 2007 been very clearly seen as a myth and hence the bilateral nature of counterparty risk is ever-present. The impasse between derivatives counterparties caused by the bilateral nature of the risk has caused significant problems with previously liquid-trading activity becoming log-jammed (we discuss the quantification of bilateral

---

[8] Meaning that the market priced their debt as being of very high quality and practically risk-free.

counterparty risk and so-called DVA in Chapter 13). Now, all institutions facing counterparty risk *must* take it seriously and build their abilities in quantification, pricing and hedging aspects. No institution has such poor credit quality that they need not concern themselves with counterparty risk and no institution has such strong credit quality that their potential bankruptcy at some future date can be ignored.

Aside from the parties taking counterparty risk through their trading activities, other major players in the market are third parties. Third parties offer, for example, collateral management, software, trade compression and clearing services. They allow market participants to reduce counterparty risk, the risks associated with counterparty risk (such as legal) and improve overall operational efficiency with respect to these aspects.

3.2   COMPONENTS AND TERMINOLOGY

3.2.1   Credit exposure

Credit exposure (hereafter often simply known as exposure) defines the loss in the event of a counterparty defaulting. Exposure is characterised by the fact that a positive value of a financial instrument corresponds to a claim on a defaulted counterparty, whereas in the event of negative value, an institution is still obliged to honour their contractual payments (at least to the extent that they exceed those of the defaulted counterparty). This means that if an institution is owed money and their counterparty defaults then they will incur a loss, whilst in the reverse situation they cannot gain[9] from the default by being somehow released from their liability.

Exposure is clearly a very time-sensitive measure since a counterparty can default at any time in the future and one must consider the impact of such an event many years from now. Exposure is needed in the analysis of counterparty risk since, for many financial instruments (notably derivatives), the creditor is not at risk for the full principal amount of the trade but only the *replacement cost*. A measure of exposure should encompass the risk arising from actual claims (current claims and those a financial institution is committed to provide), potential claims (possible future claims) as well as contingent liabilities. Essentially, characterising exposure involves answering the following two questions:

- What is the current exposure (the maximum loss if the counterparty defaults today)?
- What is the exposure in the future (what could be the loss if the counterparty defaults at some point in the future)?

The second point above is naturally far more complex to answer than the first, except in some simple cases. We emphasise that all exposure calculations, by convention, will ignore any recovery value in the event of a default. Hence, the exposure is the loss, as defined by the value or replacement cost that would be incurred assuming zero recovery value.

Finally, a very important point:

> Exposure is conditional on counterparty default.

---

[9] Except in some special and non-standard cases that we will consider later.

Exposure is relevant only if the counterparty defaults and hence the quantification of exposure should be "conditioned" upon this event, i.e.,

- What is the exposure in 1 year assuming the counterparty will default in 1 year?
- What is the exposure in 2 years assuming the counterparty will default in 2 years?
- And so on.

Having said this, we will often consider exposure independently of any default event and so assume implicitly no "wrong-way risk". Such an assumption is reasonable for most products subject to counterparty risk, although the reader should keep the idea of conditional exposure in mind if possible. We will then address wrong-way risk, which defines the relationship between exposure and counterparty default, in more detail in Chapter 15.

3.2.2   Default probability, credit migration and credit spreads

When assessing counterparty risk, one must consider the credit quality of a counterparty over the entire lifetime of the relevant transactions. Such time horizons can be extremely long. Ultimately, there are two aspects to consider:

- What is the probability of the counterparty defaulting[10] over a certain time horizon?
- What is the probability of the counterparty suffering a decline in credit quality over a certain time horizon (for example, a ratings downgrade)?

Credit migrations or discrete changes in credit quality, such as due to ratings changes, are crucial since they influence the *term structure* of default probability. They should also be considered since they may cause issues even when a counterparty is not yet in default. Suppose the probability of default of a counterparty between the current time and a future date of (say) 1 year is known. It is also important to consider what the same annual default rate might be in 4 years, in other words the probability of default between 4 and 5 years in the future. There are three important aspects to consider:

- Future default probability[11] as defined above will have a tendency to decrease due to the chance that the default may occur before the start of the period in question. The probability of a counterparty defaulting between 20 and 21 years in the future may be very small. Not because they are very creditworthy (potentially quite the reverse) but rather because they are unlikely to survive for 20 years!
- A counterparty with an expectation of deterioration in credit quality will have an increasing probability of default over time (although at some point the above phenomenon will reverse this).
- A counterparty with an expectation of improvement in credit quality will have a decreasing probability of default over time, which will be accelerated by the first point above.

---

[10] We will for now use the term default to refer to any "credit event" that could impact the counterparty. Such credit events will be described in greater depth in Chapter 10.

[11] Here we refer to default probabilities in a specified period, such as annual.

A trader has to assess the expected loss on a new FX forward trade due to counterparty risk. The potential loss at the maturity of the trade is estimated to be $10m whilst the default probability of the counterparty over the 5-year period is 10%. The trader argues that since the current exposure of the trade is zero, then the average loss over the life of the trade will be half the final value and hence the expected loss will be

$$\$10m \times 50\% \times 10\% = \$0.5m$$

This is not a very accurate calculation. Firstly, the estimate of average exposure is not 50% of the final value because the exposure does not increase linearly. Worse than this, there is an implicit assumption that the default probability is homogeneous through time. If the default probability actually increases through time, the actual expected loss can be considerably higher (see the example in Spreadsheet 3.1 where it is $0.77m). The counterparty may be more likely to default closer to the 5-year point (where the loss is $10m) than today (when the loss is zero).

Spreadsheet 3.1 Counterparty risk for a forward contract-type exposure.

There is a well-known empirical mean-reversion in credit quality as evidenced by historical credit ratings changes. This means that good (above-average) credit quality firms tend to deteriorate and vice versa. Hence, a counterparty of good credit quality will tend to have an increasing default probability over time whilst a poor credit quality counterparty will be more likely to default in the short term and less likely to do so in the longer term. The term structure of default is very important to consider, as the above example (box) demonstrates.

We note finally that default probability may be defined as real-world or risk-neutral. In the former case, we ask ourselves what is the *actual* default probability of the counterparty, which often is estimated via historical data. In the latter case, we calculate the risk-neutral (or market-implied) probability from market credit spreads. The latter case is relevant when hedging counterparty risk and the former otherwise.[12] The difference between real-world and risk-neutral default probabilities is discussed in detail in Chapter 10. When considering counterparty risk via credit spreads, then credit spread volatility is an important consideration in addition to credit migration and default risk.

3.2.3   Recovery and loss given default

Recovery rates typically represent the percentage of the outstanding claim recovered when a counterparty defaults. An associated variable to recovery is *loss given default*, which is linked to recovery rate on a unit amount by the simple relationship *loss given default = 1 − recovery rate*.

---

[12] We note that Basel III regulatory capital rules (discussed in detail in Chapter 17) advocate the risk-neutral approach even though hedging may often be difficult.

Recovery rates can vary substantially which is important because, for example, a recovery of 60% of a claim will result in only half the loss compared to a recovery of 20%. Credit exposure is traditionally measured gross of any recovery (and hence is a worst-case estimate) but recovery rates play a critical role in the quantification of counterparty risk via credit value adjustment (CVA).

In the event of a bankruptcy, the holders of OTC derivatives contracts with the counterparty in default would normally be *pari passu*[13] with the senior bondholders. OTC derivatives, bonds and credit default swaps (CDSs) therefore reference senior unsecured credit risk and therefore may appear to relate to the same recovery value. However, there are two complexities around such aspects. Firstly, whilst CDS contracts are designed as hedges for bonds and loans, they do not necessarily correspond to exactly the same recovery values. This is due to structural features of CDS contracts such as cheapest-to-deliver optionality and delivery squeezes. Whilst recent changes to the CDS market, such as the "big bang protocol", have minimised their impact, these must be understood to fully appreciate hedging of counterparty risk through CDS contracts. Secondly, there is a timing issue. When a bond issuer defaults, the recovery rate can be realised immediately as the bond can be sold in the market. CDS contracts are also settled within days of the defined "credit event" via the CDS auction (Section 10.2.3). However, OTC derivatives (unlike bonds) cannot be freely traded or sold, especially when the counterparty to the derivative is in default. This essentially leads to a different recovery value for derivatives. These recovery aspects, very important in the Lehman Brothers bankruptcy of 2008, are discussed in more detail in Chapter 10.

3.2.4 Mark-to-market and replacement cost

The mark-to-market (MtM) with respect to a particular counterparty defines what could be potentially lost today. However, this is dependent on the ability to net the trades in the event the counterparty defaults. Furthermore, other aspects that will reduce the exposure in the event of default, such as collateral legally held against the contracts and possibly hedges, must be considered. These considerations are discussed in more detail in Chapter 4.

Current MtM does not constitute an *immediate* liability by one party to the other but rather is the present value of all the payments an institution is expecting to receive, less those it is obliged to make. These payments may be scheduled to occur many years in the future and may have values that are strongly dependent on market variables. MtM may therefore be positive or negative, depending on whether a transaction is in an institution's favour or not.

Contractual features of transactions, such as closeout netting and termination features, refer to *replacement costs*. Risk-free MtM is clearly closely related to replacement cost, which defines the entry point into an equivalent transaction(s) with another counterparty. Models tend to assume, for reasons of simplicity, that the two are the same. However, the actual situation is more complicated.

The replacement cost of a transaction, whilst closely coupled to the MtM value of a transaction, will not be the same. To replace a transaction, one must consider costs such as bid–offer spreads, which may be significant for highly illiquid securities. Note that even a standard and liquid contract might be non-standard and illiquid at the default time. In such a

---

[13] This means they have the same seniority and therefore should expect to receive the same recovery value.

case, one must then decide whether to replace with an expensive non-standard derivative or with a more standard one that does not match precisely the original one. Documentation suggests that such cost can essentially be passed on via the replacement cost concept, therefore ignoring transaction costs when quantifying counterparty risk seems reasonable.[14]

Unfortunately, counterparty risk *itself* causes further complication here. Documentation suggests that the creditworthiness of the surviving (or exercising in the case of a contractual termination) party can also be considered in a replacement cost. This means that the future counterparty risk (via CVA and DVA components) actually defines the future replacement cost. This creates a recursive problem since we cannot define counterparty risk without knowing the future counterparty risk and vice versa. Chapter 13 (Section 13.4.2) addresses this topic. For now, we emphasise that basing replacement cost on risk-free valuation is a reasonable approximation to the more complicated, actual situation.

3.2.5 Mitigating counterparty risk

The many ways to mitigate or limit counterparty risk are discussed in more detail in the next chapter. Some are relatively simple contractual risk mitigants, whilst other methods are more complex and costly to implement. No risk mitigant is perfect and there will always be some residual counterparty risk, however small. It is therefore important to consider carefully the benefit of risk mitigants when quantifying counterparty risk. Chapter 8 covers this extensively. In addition to the residual counterparty risk, it is important to keep in mind that risk mitigants do not remove counterparty risk *per se* but instead convert it into other forms of financial risk, some obvious examples being:

- *Netting.* Being legally able to offset positive and negative contract values with the same counterparty, in the event of their default, reduces exposure at the counterparty level. However, this also creates **legal risk** in cases where a netting agreement cannot be legally enforced in a particular jurisdiction.
- *Collateral.* Holding cash or securities against an exposure can clearly reduce that exposure. However, this leads to **operational and liquidity risks** through the necessity to run a complex collateral management function. Indeed, many counterparties cannot agree to collateral terms due to these risks and their inability to handle them effectively.
- *Central counterparties.* Create operational and liquidity risks, for the reasons above, and **systemic risk** since the failure of a central counterparty could amount to a significant systemic disturbance.
- *Hedging.* Hedging clearly has the aim of reducing counterparty risk but may lead to additional **market risks** through the mark-to-market volatility of the hedging instruments.

3.3   CONTROL AND QUANTIFICATION

It is important for an institution to control the counterparty risk that they face. This must recognise the fact that counterparty risk varies substantially depending on aspects such as the transaction and counterparty in question. In addition, it is important to give the correct

---

[14] This is still not perfect since, whilst documentation suggests that by using a replacement cost concept, transactions costs can be claimed from the counterparty, if the counterparty is in default then only a proportion of these costs will be received.

benefit arising from the many risk mitigants (such as netting and collateral) that may be relevant. Control of counterparty risk has been traditionally the purpose of credit limits, used by most banks for well over a decade.

However, *credit limits* only limit counterparty risk and, whilst this is clearly the first line of defence, there is also a need to correctly quantify and ensure an institution is being correctly compensated for the counterparty risk they take. This is achieved via *credit value adjustment* (CVA), which has been used increasingly in recent years as a means of putting a value or price on the counterparty risk faced by an institution.

An institution is faced with counterparty risk from many counterparties and must control the portfolio impact and link this to capital requirements, regulatory or economic. Finally, the hedging of a counterparty must also be considered. Let us examine these components and how they fit together.

3.3.1   Credit limits

Let us consider the first and most basic use of exposure, which is as a means to control the amount of risk to a given counterparty over time. The basic idea of diversification is to avoid putting all your eggs in one basket. Market participants can achieve this by limiting credit exposure to any given counterparty, in line with the default probability of that counterparty. This is the basic principle of credit limits (or credit lines). By trading with a greater number of counterparties, an institution is not so exposed to the failure of any one of them. Diversification is not always practical due to the relationship benefits from trading with certain key clients. In such cases, credit exposures can become excessively large and must be mitigated by other means.

Attribute a credit limit specific to each counterparty as illustrated in Figure 3.4. The idea is to characterise the potential future exposure (PFE) to a counterparty over time and ensure that this does not exceed a certain value (the credit limit). The PFE represents a worst-case scenario and is similar to the well-known VAR measure described in Chapter 2. PFE will be described in more detail in Chapter 4. The credit limit will be set arbitrarily according to the risk appetite of the institution in question. It may be time-dependent, reflecting the fact that exposures at different times in the future may be considered differently.

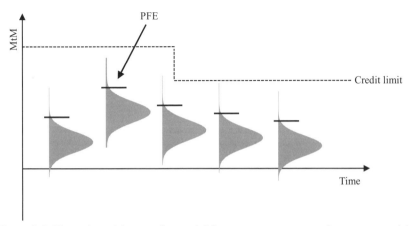

Figure 3.4 Illustration of the use of potential future exposure to control counterparty risk.

Credit limits will often be reduced over time, effectively favouring short-term exposures over long-term ones. This is due to the chance that a counterparty's credit quality may deteriorate over a long horizon. Indeed, empirical and market-implied default probabilities for good quality (investment grade) institutions tend to increase over time (see Chapter 10 for more details). Such an increase in default probability justifies the reduction of a credit limit. The credit limit of a counterparty with poor credit quality (sub-investment grade) arguably should increase over time since, if the counterparty does not default, then its credit quality will be expected to improve eventually.

Any trade that would breach a credit limit at any point in the future is likely to be refused. Credit limits allow a consolidated view of exposure with each counterparty and represent a first step in portfolio counterparty risk management.

When assessing PFE against credit limits, possible future transactions are not considered. However, it is possible for changing market conditions (spot rates and volatilities, for example) to increase PFEs and cause credit limits to be breached. An institution must have not only a policy regarding credit limits, which defines the ability to transact further, but also a rule about the circumstances under which existing positions must be adjusted when a credit limit is breached due to market moves. For example, a credit limit of $10m ("soft limit") might restrict trades that cause an increase in PFE above this value and may allow the PFE to move up to $12m ("hard limit") as a result of changes in market conditions. In the event of a triggering of the higher limit, it may be necessary to reduce the PFE to within the original $10m limit by adjusting positions or using credit derivatives to hedge the exposure.

A credit limit controls exposure in a rather binary way, without any dynamic reference to the relevant variables below:

- default probability of counterparty;
- expected recovery rate of counterparty;
- downgrade probability (worsening credit quality) of counterparty;
- correlation between counterparties (concentrations).

All of the above variables are likely to be built into the defined credit limit in some way. For example, a low default probability or high recovery may lead to a larger limit, whilst a significant chance of downgrade may lead to a decreased credit limit over time (as is the case in Figure 3.4). Finally, a counterparty that is highly correlated to others should have a lower credit limit than an equivalent counterparty, which is less correlated. However, such decisions are made in a qualitative fashion and the nature of credit limits leads to either accepting or rejecting a new transaction with reference to exposure alone and not the actual profitability of the transaction. This is a key motivation for the pricing of counterparty risk via CVA.

3.3.2   Credit value adjustment

Traditional counterparty risk management, as described above, works in a binary fashion. The use of credit limits, for example, gives an institution the ability to decide whether to enter into a new transaction with a given counterparty. If there were a breach of the credit limit then a transaction would be refused (except in special cases). The problem with this is that the risk of a new transaction is the only consideration whereas the return (profit) should surely be a factor also.

By pricing counterparty risk, one can move beyond a binary decision-making process. The question of whether to do a transaction becomes simply whether or not it is profitable once the counterparty risk component has been "priced in". As we will show in Chapter 12, the risky price of a derivative can be expressed as the risk-free price (the price assuming no counterparty risk) less a component to correct for the counterparty risk. The latter component is often called CVA (credit value adjustment). Ensuring that the profitability of a transaction exceeds the CVA is a first hurdle to the proper treatment of counterparty risk. The CVA "charge" should be calculated in a sophisticated way to account for all the aspects that will define the CVA:

- the default probability of the counterparty;
- the default probability of the institution (in the case of bilateral pricing and DVA, this is covered in Chapter 13);
- the transaction in question;
- netting of existing transactions with the same counterparty;
- collateralisation;
- hedging aspects.

CVA moves beyond the binary nature of credit limits and prices counterparty risk directly. A transaction is not refused or accepted directly but an institution needs to make a profit that more than covers the incremental CVA of the transaction, i.e., the increase in CVA taking into account netting effects due to any existing trades with the counterparty. Other aspects, such as collateral, should also be considered. Such pricing aspects are considered in detail in Chapter 12.

CVA is not the be all and end all of counterparty risk though. Broadly speaking, there are three levels to assessing the counterparty risk of a transaction:

- *Trade level*. Incorporating all characteristics of the trade and associated risk factors. This defines the counterparty risk of a trade at a "stand-alone" level.
- *Counterparty level*. Incorporating the impact of risk mitigants such as netting and collateral for each counterparty individually. This defines the incremental impact a trade has with respect to existing transactions.
- *Portfolio level*. Consideration of the risk to all counterparties knowing that only a small fraction may default in a given time period. This defines the impact a trade has on the total counterparty risk faced by an institution.

CVA only addresses the first two components above.

3.3.3   CVA or credit limits?

Both.

CVA focuses on evaluating counterparty risk at the trade level (incorporating all specific features of the trade) and counterparty level (incorporating risk mitigants). In contrast, credit limits essentially act at the portfolio level by limiting exposures to avoid concentrations. When viewed like this, we see that CVA and credit limits act in a complementary fashion as illustrated in Figure 3.5. Indeed, CVA encourages *minimising* the number of counterparties an institution would trade with since this maximises the benefits of netting whilst credit

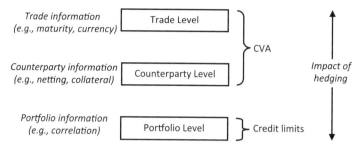

Figure 3.5 High-level illustration of the complementary use of CVA and credit limits to manage counterparty risk.

limits encourage *maximising* this number. Hence, CVA and credit limits are typically used together as complementary ways to quantify and manage counterparty risk.

3.3.4 What does CVA represent?

Since counterparty risk has a price via CVA then an immediate question is what defines this price. The price of a financial instrument can generally be defined in one of two ways:

- The price represents an expected value of future cash flows, incorporating some adjustment for the risk being taken (the risk premium). We will call this the *actuarial price*.
- The price is the cost of an associated hedging strategy. This is the *risk-neutral* (or market-implied) price.

A price defined by hedging arguments may often differ dramatically from one based on expected value + risk premium. Hence, it is natural to ask ourselves into which camp CVA falls. The answer is, unfortunately, both since CVA can be partially but not perfectly hedged. If we have a current exposure of $10m, we may not be able to hedge the resulting loss if the counterparty defaults. Even if we can hedge this current exposure, we might not be able to hedge the future variability of that exposure.

Hence, we must understand the *hedging* implications but also the *portfolio-level* considerations of the residual risks (that cannot be hedged). It is important to emphasise at this point that, whatever the viability of hedging and the extent of an institution's wish to hedge their CVA, Basel III regulatory capital rules advocate a risk-neutral approach to CVA (Chapter 17). CVA quantification, hedging, portfolio aspects and regulatory capital rules are all important considerations for properly dealing with counterparty risk.

3.3.5 Hedging counterparty risk

The growth of the credit derivatives market has facilitated hedging of counterparty credit risk. Suppose an institution has a $10m netted exposure (uncollateralised), which is causing concern and furthermore preventing any further trading activity with the counterparty. Buying $10m notional of CDS protection referenced to this counterparty will hedge this credit exposure. The hedging depends on the ability to trade CDSs on the counterparty in question and comes at a cost. However, hedging enables one to reduce the exposure and hence provides a means to transact further with the counterparty. It can be considered that CDS

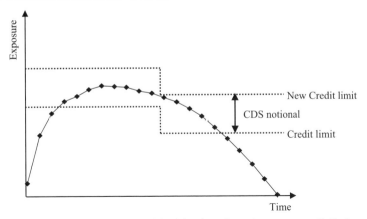

Figure 3.6 Illustration of CDS hedging in order to increase a credit limit.

hedging therefore increases a credit limit by the notional of the CDS protection purchased.[15] This provides a means to use CDS protection to hedge the extent to which a transaction exceeds a credit limit. The combination of hedging some portion of the exposure may be considered the most economically viable solution to trading with some counterparties. This is illustrated in Figure 3.6.

More tailored credit derivative products such as CCDSs have been designed to hedge counterparty risk even more directly. CCDSs are essentially CDSs but with the notional of protection indexed to the exposure on a contractually specified derivative. They allow the synthetic transfer of counterparty risk linked to a specific trade and counterparty to a third party. Suppose institution A trades a contract with party X and has counterparty risk. If A now buys CCDS protection from a party Y referencing both counterparty X and the underlying contract involved, then it has effectively passed the counterparty risk to Y (without X needing to be involved in the arrangement).

Hedging will be addressed in detail in Chapter 16.

3.3.6 Portfolio counterparty risk

Take the above example of counterparties X and Y. Institution A now has risk to only the joint default or "double default" of counterparties X and Y. This means one needs to consider the joint likelihood of these counterparties defaulting. More generally, we should consider the impact of the default probability of all counterparties. For a typical bank, the number of counterparties with whom they have exposure is in the thousands and so this is a difficult but important task.

The concept of assigning capital against financial risks is done in recognition of the fact that unexpected losses are best understood at the portfolio, rather than the transaction, level. Capital requirements may be economic (calculated by the institution in question for accurate quantification of risk) or regulatory (imposed by regulators). Either way, the role of capital is

---

[15] There are some technical factors that should be considered here, which may mean that the hedge is not effective. Chapters 10 and 16 will discuss these aspects in more detail.

to act as a buffer against unexpected losses. Hence, while pricing counterparty risk via CVA involves assessment of expected losses at the counterparty level, the concept of capital allows one to make decisions at the portfolio level (for example, all counterparties an institution trades with) and consider unexpected as well as expected losses.

The computation of capital for a credit portfolio is a rather complex issue since the correlation (or more generally dependency) between the defaults of different counterparties must be quantified. A high positive correlation (strong dependency) means that multiple defaults are possible, which will therefore increase the unexpected loss and associated capital numbers. Assessment of capital for counterparty risk is even more important due to the asymmetric nature of exposure. One must not only understand the correlation between counterparty default events, but also the correlation between the resulting exposures. For example, suppose an institution has a transaction with counterparty A and hedges that transaction with counterparty B. This means the MtM positions with the two counterparties will always offset one another and *cannot* therefore both be positive. Hence, default of both counterparties A and B will create only a single loss in relation to whichever counterparty the institution has exposure to at the default time. Essentially, the negative correlation of the exposures reduces the overall risk. In case the MtM values of transactions with counterparty A and B were positively correlated, joint default would be expected to give rise to a greater loss. Portfolio counterparty risks will be addressed in more detail in Chapter 11.

Finally, it is important to consider regulatory capital. Whilst this should be aligned with economic capital, the necessity for relatively simple regulation tends to restrict this. Furthermore, with the creation of the Basel III capital requirements, the variability of CVA itself must be capitalised, alongside the more traditional measure of the default component of counterparty risk. This is discussed in more detail in Chapter 17.

3.4 SUMMARY

In this chapter, we have defined counterparty risk, introducing the key components of credit exposure, default probability and recovery, and outlining the risk mitigation approaches of netting and collateralisation. We have discussed various ways of quantifying and managing counterparty risk from the traditional approach of credit limits to the more sophisticated approaches of pricing via CVA and the consideration of portfolio and hedging aspects.

The next section of this book, Chapters 4–7, will deal in depth with the mitigation of counterparty risk.

Section II: Mitigation of Counterparty Credit Risk

In this section, we discuss the many diverse ways of mitigating counterparty credit risk. The aim will be to highlight the mechanisms and the overall magnitude of risk reduction. However, just as important will be the assessment of the additional costs and risks that such risk mitigants will create. Counterparty risk can only be reduced and not completely eliminated. Furthermore, counterparty risk is reduced only by transformation into other financial risks, such as market, legal, operational and liquidity. It is important not to lose sight of the materiality of these risks.

The first way of mitigating counterparty risk is to reduce the credit exposure (current and/ or future). The counterparty may default and the aim is to minimise the resulting loss. The most common ways of doing this are netting and collateral.

Closeout netting is a very standard risk mitigation method for counterparty risk. However, in most business relations, netting is not a significant issue. Generally, an institution either buys from or sells to another firm, but rarely does both simultaneously. Therefore, in the event of bankruptcy, few if any contracts offset one another. However, OTC derivatives markets often generate large numbers of bi-directional transactions between counterparties. Netting allows amounts owed *to* a counterparty to be offset with those owed *by* the counterparty to arrive at a net obligation or claim. Closeout permits the simultaneous and immediate termination of the relevant contracts. Netting can reduce counterparty risk substantially and closeout allows trades to be immediately replaced, without the delays caused by lengthy bankruptcy proceedings. Netting is discussed in **Chapter 4** alongside some other simple methods such as terminations and resets which may be used at the trade level for particular trade types. These aspects are all relatively simple and represent minimal additional risk.

A further way to reduce credit exposure is via the use of collateral. Collateral management has been a key way in which to control counterparty risk over the last two decades and has recently been thrust still further into the limelight. Collateral management began in the 1980s, with Bankers Trust and Salomon Brothers taking collateral against credit exposures. There were no legal standards, and most calculations were performed manually on spreadsheets. Collateralisation of derivatives exposures became widespread in the early 1990s, with collateral typically in the form of cash or government securities. Standardisation began in 1994 via the first ISDA documentation. In the 1997/1998 period, collateral management had a greater focus with the default of Russia, the Asian crisis and the failure of the large hedge fund Long-Term Capital Management (LTCM). These events resulted in tighter credit controls and a greater interest in risk mitigation techniques. The use of collateral is more complex than netting and gives rise to significant legal and operational risks. In addition, liquidity risk is important since counterparties need to provide collateral at short notice as market conditions become volatile. A shortage of high-quality collateral at times of market stress can cause additional problems. The operational aspects and risk of collateral are covered in **Chapter 5**.

A second way to mitigate counterparty risk is to trade only with counterparties with excellent credit quality so that their default is highly unlikely (even if the exposure to them is potentially very large).

However, when a default-remote entity is created specifically for this purpose, such as in the case of special purpose vehicles (SPVs), then substantial legal risk can be created. Furthermore, the concept of "too big to fail" counterparties for years created an illusion in financial markets that counterparty risk was not particularly prevalent. Triple-A ratings made the problem worse, especially since Icelandic banks, monoline insurance companies, Fannie Mae and Freddie Mac all had Triple-A status prior to their failure. The failure (or bailout) of these and other high-quality institutions such as Lehman Brothers has changed the counterparty risk landscape for ever. We discuss default-remote entities in **Chapter 6**, which will largely be a historical analysis of their role in the global financial crisis and the lessons to be learned.

Finally in this section, we discuss central counterparties (CCPs). CCPs are essentially another kind of default-remote entity that politicians, regulators and policymakers identified as a key solution to many of the counterparty risk-related problems that were highlighted in the global financial crisis, especially in relation to the bankruptcy of Lehman Brothers. CCPs have essentially been mandated to have a large role in the mitigation of counterparty risk in the coming years and their operation will therefore be critical to the financial stability of financial markets. We will take a closer look at the operational aspects, advantages and disadvantages of CCPs in **Chapter 7**.

IS RISK MITIGATION ALWAYS GOOD?

Before we discuss the many forms of risk mitigation, it is important to put things in context. Most creditors are unable to enforce their rights when a firm is in bankruptcy, whereas OTC derivatives contracts tend to provide additional rights. Netting, closeout and prompt access to collateral without being subject to prolonged legal proceedings in one sense allow OTC derivatives counterparties to jump the bankruptcy queue. The main arguments used as to why derivatives creditors require special protection outside the normal bankruptcy process applied to other creditors are:

- Derivatives markets are critical to the smooth functioning of the financial system, so that their operation deserves special protection.
- Derivatives markets are particularly susceptible to systemic failures due to the volatile nature of the value of derivatives contracts.

Derivatives markets have long been viewed as a major source of systemic risk and require measures to limit the possibility of severe systemic damage to financial markets and economies. Does this mean that the special provisions discussed in this chapter are valid regardless of the costs to other market participants and creditors of a failed institution?

An alternative way to look at the above question is posed by Bliss and Kaufman (2005), who turn the argument on its head somewhat. Netting, closeout and collateralisation have facilitated counterparty risk management to the extent that they have allowed a massive expansion of the OTC derivatives market, with major dealers having massive notional risks (for example, Lehman Brothers had a total notional amount of $800 billion of OTC derivatives at the time of their bankruptcy). Without such risk mitigants, the size, liquidity and concentrations seen in the derivatives dealer network would simply not exist. Increasing the capital required to engage in derivatives dealing by a significant factor (for example, due to the lack of netting) would materially alter the economics of derivatives markets.

Netting is clearly aimed at protecting surviving institutions rather than the counterparty in financial distress. Netting gives preferential benefit to derivatives counterparties at the expense of other creditors (for example, bondholders and shareholders) of an institution. Whilst this can easily be justified to be "fair" in a simple case such as a trade unwind, the strong risk-mitigating benefits of netting have surely been a catalyst for the significant notional amount of OTC derivatives traded. Shareholders and bondholders could argue that this adversely influences their position due to the increase in default probability and reduction of recovery potentially caused by sizeable derivatives exposure. Whilst netting reduces exposure dramatically, it means that resulting exposures may be highly volatile (on a relative basis[1]), making the control of exposure more complex. Some have argued that netting should be reduced as it may, for example, lead to systemic problems (e.g., see Edwards and Morrison, 2005) and reduce incentives to monitor credit quality. However, policymakers seem to follow the opinion of market participants that the benefits of netting outweigh any such disadvantages.

Netting and collateral may increase systemic risk by allowing a concentration of dealers to develop. Closeout is potentially a source of systemic risk by making it more difficult to manage insolvency of a major dealer as its counterparties choose to terminate all transactions. Together these mechanisms may make it more difficult to avoid the failure of a distressed but still financially viable (in the long run) major dealer.

Market participants are likely to overestimate the benefit of risk mitigation. Since counterparty risk acts to reduce profits on transactions, it would not be surprising that the reduction in risk offered by a risk mitigant would be overstated (consciously or unconsciously) in order to maximise the profitability of such transactions. Regulators may overestimate risk reduction in this way, either through a lack of complete understanding of all aspects or pressure from market participants, or both. We are left, therefore, with a dilemma. Are netting, closeout and collateral critical elements in reducing counterparty risk in the derivatives market? Alternatively, is the massive global OTC derivatives market and its associated counterparty risk actually an artefact of these mechanisms being granted to derivatives counterparties?

Counterparty risk mitigation methods are critical, but it is also important not to overstate their benefits and ignore their dangers.

---

[1] Meaning that the net exposure will typically be reduced by a greater amount than the overall volatility. Whilst a netted position will be less volatile, the fact that netting allows an institution to trade a greater notional value means that the overall volatility of their positions is likely to be increased.

Netting, Compression, Resets and Termination Features

One ought never to turn one's back on a threatened danger and try to run away from it. If you do that, you will double the danger. But if you meet it promptly and without flinching, you will reduce the danger by half.

Sir Winston Churchill (1874–1965)

4.1 INTRODUCTION

4.1.1 The origins of counterparty risk

The classic counterparty credit risk problem is illustrated in Figure 4.1, supposing an institution executes a trade with counterparty A and hedges this with counterparty B.[1] For example, the institution could be a bank providing an OTC derivative trade to a customer (A) and hedging it with another bank (B). In this situation, the institution has no volatility of their overall profit and loss (PnL) and, consequently, no market risk. However, they do have counterparty risk to both counterparties A and B since, if either were to default, then this would leave exposure to the other side of the trade.

4.1.2 The ISDA master agreement

The International Swaps and Derivatives Association (ISDA) is a trade organisation for OTC derivatives practitioners. The ISDA Master Agreement is a bilateral framework, which contains terms and conditions to govern transactions between parties. It is designed to eliminate legal uncertainties and to provide mechanisms for mitigating counterparty risk. It specifies the general terms of the agreement between parties with respect to general questions such as netting, collateral, definition of default and other termination events. Multiple transactions can be subsumed under this general Master Agreement to form a single legal contract of indefinite term, covering many or all of the transactions traded. Individual transactions are incorporated by reference in the trade confirmation to the relevant Master Agreement. Trading then tends to occur without the need to update or change any aspect of the relevant ISDA agreement.

---

[1] Note that the hedge may, in fact, be a series of trades.

Figure 4.1 Illustration of the typical situation in which counterparty risk arises.

4.2   NETTING

Consider a holder of a debt security from a bankrupt company. Not only do they expect to make a substantial loss due to the default, but they also must expect it to be some time (often years) before they will receive any recovery value linked to the notional amount of their claim. Whilst this is problematic, it has not been considered a major problem, for example, in the predominantly buy-to-hold, long-only, cash bond market.

Derivatives markets are fast moving, with participants regularly changing their positions and where many instruments offset (hedge) one other. When a counterparty defaults then the market needs a mechanism whereby participants can replace (re-hedge) their position with other counterparties. Furthermore, it is desirable for an institution to be able to offset what it owes to the defaulted counterparty against what they themselves are owed. The following two mechanisms facilitate this:

- *Payment netting*. This gives an institution the ability to net cash flows occurring on the same day. This typically relates to settlement risk.
- *Closeout netting*. This allows the termination of all contracts between the insolvent and a solvent counterparty, together with the offsetting of all transaction values (both in an institution's favour and against it). This typically relates to counterparty risk.

Netting legislation covering derivatives has been adopted in most countries with major financial markets. ISDA has obtained legal opinions supporting the closeout and netting provisions in their Master Agreements in most relevant jurisdictions. (At the time of writing, they currently have such opinion covering 54 jurisdictions.) Thirty-seven countries have legislation that provides explicitly for the enforceability of netting. However, there remain jurisdictions where netting is not allowable.

4.2.1   Payment netting

Payment netting covers the situation where an institution will have to make and receive more than one payment during a given day. The Bankhaus Herstatt example from the 1970s, described in the previous chapter (Section 3.1.2), illustrates the risks of such a situation. Payment netting allows an institution to combine same-day cash flows into a single net payment. This reduces settlement risk and enhances operational efficiency. For example, if a \$305m floating swap payment is to be made and a \$300m fixed payment received (on the same day), then the institution in question would simply make a net payment of \$5m with the \$300m payment having no associated risk.

Payment netting would appear to be a simple process, which gives the maximum reduction of any risk arising from payments made on the same day. However, it does leave operational risk, which has been illustrated in a recent high-profile case during the financial crisis (see box below).

The KfW Bankengruppe transaction, giving rise to the problem outlined below, was a regular currency swap with euros being paid to Lehman and dollars paid back to KfW. On the

The case of KfW Bankengruppe ("Germany's dumbest bank"). As the problems surrounding Lehman Brothers grew ever-more apparent, most of Lehman's counterparties stopped doing business with the company. However, government-owned German bank KfW Bankengruppe made what they described as an "automated transfer" of €300m to Lehman Brothers literally hours before the latter's bankruptcy. This provoked an outcry, with one German newspaper calling KfW "Germany's dumbest bank". Two of the bank's management board members[*] and the head of the risk-control department were suspended in the aftermath of the mistake. Since the bank was government-owned, the transfer would have cost each German person around €4. The bank's total loss, including other deals with Lehman Brothers, was calculated to be nearer €600m.

[*]One has since successfully sued the bank for his subsequent dismissal.

day Lehman Brothers declared bankruptcy, KfW made an automated transfer of €300m despite the obvious fact that the stricken Lehman Brothers would not be making the opposite dollar payment.

4.2.2 The need for closeout netting

It is not uncommon to have many different trades with an individual counterparty. Such trades may be simple or complex and may cover a small or wider range of products across different asset classes. Furthermore, trades may fall into one of the three following categories:

- Trades may constitute hedges (or partial hedges) so that their values should naturally move in opposite directions.
- Trades may constitute unwinds in that, rather than cancelling a transaction, the reverse (or mirror) trade may have been executed. Hence two trades with a counterparty may have equal and opposite values, to reflect the fact that the original trade has been cancelled. Although compression exercises can sometimes reduce such exposures (see later), such trades can otherwise exist for many years.
- Trades may be largely independent, e.g., from different asset classes or on different underlyings.

In light of the above points, it is rather worrying that from a legal point of view the loss on a counterparty defaulting is the *sum* of the exposures. Consider the case of a trade (trade 1) being cancelled via executing the reverse transaction (trade 2). Suppose there are two scenarios in that trade 1 and trade 2 can take the values +10 and −10, respectively, or vice versa. Table 4.1 shows the possible outcomes.

Whilst the total value of the two trades is zero (as it should be since the aim was to cancel the original trade), the total exposure is +10 in both scenarios. This means that if the counterparty defaults, in either scenario there would be a loss due to having to settle the trade with the negative MtM but not being able to claim (either directly or via offsetting) the trade that has a positive MtM. This is a rather perverse situation since any valuation system would show the above position as having zero MtM value and furthermore a market risk system

Table 4.1   Illustration of the exposure of two equal and opposite trades with and without netting

	Scenario 1	*Scenario 2*
Trade 1 value	+10	−10
Trade 2 value	−10	+10
Total value	0	0
Trade 1 exposure	+10	0
Trade 2 exposure	0	+10
Total exposure (without netting)	+10	+10

would show the position as having zero market risk. Yet the counterparty credit exposure of the position is far from zero.

Bankruptcy proceedings are, by their nature, long and unpredictable processes. During such proceedings, likely counterparty risk losses are compounded by the uncertainty regarding the termination of proceedings. A creditor who holds an insolvent firm's debt has a known exposure, and while the eventual recovery is uncertain, it can be estimated and capped. However, this is not the case for derivatives where constant rebalancing is typically required to maintain hedged positions. Once a counterparty is in default, cash flows will cease and an institution will be likely to want or need to execute new replacement contracts.

4.2.3   Closeout netting

Closeout netting comes into force in the event of the default of a counterparty. Its aim is to allow a timely termination and settlement of the net value of all trades with that counterparty. Essentially, this consists of two components:

1. *Closeout.* The right to terminate transactions with the defaulted counterparty and cease any contractual payments.
2. *Netting.* The right to offset amounts[2] due at termination of individual contracts to determining a *net balance*, which is the sum of positive and negative transaction values, to determine a final closeout amount.

Closeout netting permits the immediate termination of all contracts between an institution and a defaulted counterparty and to offset the amount it owes a counterparty against the amount it is owed to arrive at a net payment. If the institution owes money then it makes this payment whilst if it is owed money then it makes a bankruptcy claim for that amount. Closeout netting allows the surviving institution to *immediately* realise gains on transactions against losses on other transactions and effectively jump the bankruptcy queue for all but its net exposure, as illustrated in Figure 4.2. Without the ability to closeout their positions at the time a counterparty becomes

---

[2] The calculations made by the surviving party may be disputed later via litigation. However, the prospect of a valuation dispute and an uncertain recovery value does not affect the ability of the surviving party to immediately terminate and replace the contracts with a different counterparty.

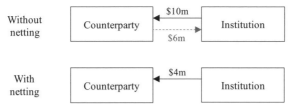

Figure 4.2 Illustration of the benefit of closeout netting. Without netting, the institution must pay $10m to the defaulted counterparty whilst losing some or all of the owed $6m. With netting, the institution is allowed to pay only the net amount of $4m, thereby gaining the $6m owed in entirety.

insolvent, market participants would find themselves locked into contracts that fluctuate in value and are impossible to hedge (due to the uncertainty of future recovery).

Whilst payment netting reduces settlement risk, closeout netting is relevant to counterparty risk since it reduces pre-settlement risk. Netting allows counterparties to reduce the risk to each other via a legal agreement that becomes active if either of them defaults. Netting agreements are crucial in order to recognise the benefit of offsetting trades with the same counterparty.

Netting is a critical way to control the exposure to a counterparty across two or more transactions. Without netting, the loss in the event of default of a counterparty is the sum of the value of the transactions with that counterparty that have *positive MtM value*. This means that derivatives with a negative value have to be settled (cash paid to the defaulted counterparty) whilst those with a positive value will represent a claim in the bankruptcy process. Perfectly offsetting derivatives transactions or "mirror trades" with the same counterparty (as arises due to cancellation of a trade) will *not* have zero value if the counterparty is in default. The argument that the purpose of a trade was to cancel a previous one does not justify the netting of their values.

Example. Consider five difference transactions with a particular counterparty with current MtM given by $+7, -4, +5, +2, -4$. The total exposure is

$$+14 \text{ (without netting)}$$
$$+6 \text{ (with netting)}$$

Spreadsheet 4.1 Simple netting calculation

Note that "set-off" is similar to closeout netting and involves obligations between two parties being offset to create an obligation that represents the difference. Typically, set-off relates to actual obligations whilst closeout netting refers only to a calculated amount. Set-off can be treated differently in different jurisdictions but is sometimes used interchangeably with the term closeout netting.

4.2.4 Netting sets and subadditivity

We will use the concept of a "netting set" which will correspond to a set of trades that can be legally netted together in the event of a default. A netting set may be a single trade and there may be more than one netting set for a given counterparty. Across netting sets, exposure will always be additive, whereas within a netting set MtM values can be added.

A very important point is that within a netting set, quantities such as expected exposure and CVA are non-additive. Whilst this is beneficial, since the overall risk is likely to be substantially reduced, it does make the quantification of exposure (Chapter 9) and CVA (Chapter 12) more complex. This complexity arises from the fact that a transaction cannot be analysed on its own but must be considered with respect to the entire netting set.

4.2.5   The impact of netting

Netting has been critical for the growth of the OTC derivatives market. Without netting, the current size and liquidity of the OTC derivatives market would be unlikely to exist. Netting means that the overall credit exposure in the market grows at a lower rate than the notional growth of the market itself. This has historically allowed dealers to build a large book on a limited capital base. The expansion and greater concentration of derivatives markets has increased the extent of netting steadily over the last decade such that netting currently reduces exposure by close to 90% (Figure 4.3). Note that netted positions are inherently more volatile than their underlying gross positions, which can create systemic risk.

Netting has some subtle effects on the dynamics of derivative markets. Suppose an institution wants to trade out of a position. OTC derivatives are often not liquid and readily tradable. If the institution executes an offsetting position with another market participant, whilst removing the market risk as required, they will have counterparty risk with respect to the original and the new counterparty. Netting means that executing the reverse position with the original counterparty offsets not only the market risk but also the counterparty risk. A counterparty knowing that an institution is heavily incentivised to trade out of the position with them may offer unfavourable terms to extract the maximum financial gain. The institution can either accept these unfavourable terms or trade with another counterparty and accept the resulting counterparty risk.

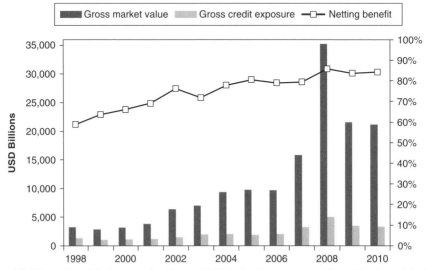

Figure 4.3 Illustration of the impact of netting on OTC derivatives exposure. The netting benefit is defined by dividing the gross credit exposure by the gross market value and subtracting this result from 100%.
Source: ISDA and BIS.

The above point extends to establishing multiple positions with different risk exposures. Suppose an institution wants both interest rate and foreign exchange hedges. Since these trades are imperfectly correlated, by executing the hedges with the same counterparty the overall counterparty risk generated is reduced. This institution may obtain more favourable terms (for example, via a smaller CVA charge).

An additional implication of netting is that it can change the way market participants react to perceptions of increasing risk of a particular counterparty. If credit exposures were driven by gross positions then all those trading with the troubled counterparty would have strong incentives to attempt to terminate existing positions and stop any new trading. Such actions would likely result in even more financial distress for the troubled counterparty. With netting, an institution will be far less worried if there is no current exposure (MtM is negative). Whilst they will be concerned about potential future exposure and may require collateral, netting reduces the concern when a counterparty is in distress, which may in turn reduce systemic risk.

4.2.6   Product coverage

Some institutions trade many financial products (such as loans and repos as well as interest rate, foreign exchange, commodity, equity and credit products). The ability to apply netting to most or all of these products is desirable in order to reduce exposure. However, legal issues regarding the enforceability of netting arise due to trades being booked with various different legal entities across different regions. The legal and other operational risks introduced by netting should not be ignored.

Bilateral netting is generally recognised for OTC derivatives, repo-style transactions and on-balance-sheet loans and deposits. Cross-product netting is typically possible within one of these categories (for example, between interest rate and foreign exchange transactions). However, netting across these product categories (for example, OTC derivatives and repos) is usually not possible.

4.3   TERMINATION FEATURES AND TRADE COMPRESSION

Whilst netting reduces OTC derivative exposure by almost an order of magnitude, there is still a need to find ways of reducing it still further. Typical ISDA netting agreements by their very nature operate bilaterally between just two counterparties. One idea is to take netting further and gain *multilateral* netting benefits via the cooperation of three or more counterparties. The first way in which this can be achieved is via trade compression.

Long-dated derivatives have the problem that, whilst the current exposure might be relatively small and manageable, the exposure years from now could have easily increased to a relatively large, unmanageable level. An obvious way to mitigate this problem is to have a contractual feature in the trade that permits action to reduce a high exposure. This is the role of break clauses and reset agreements.

4.3.1   Reset agreements

A reset agreement avoids a trade becoming strongly in-the-money by means of readjusting product-specific parameters that reset the trade to be more at-the-money. Reset dates may

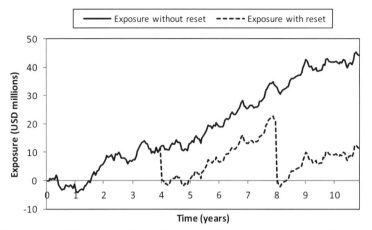

Figure 4.4 Illustration of the impact of reset features on the exposure of a long-dated cross-currency swap. Resets can be seen to occur at 4 and 8 years.

coincide with payment dates or be triggered by the breach of some market value. For example, in a resettable cross-currency swap, the MtM on the swap (which is mainly driven by FX movements on the final exchange of notional) is exchanged at each reset time in cash. In addition, the FX rate is reset to (typically) the prevailing spot rate. The reset means that the notional on one leg of the swap will change. Such a reset is similar to the impact of closing out the transaction and executing a replacement transaction at market rates and consequently reduces the exposure. An example of the impact on exposure is shown in Figure 4.4.

4.3.2   Additional termination events

Additional termination events (ATEs) or so-called break clauses are useful in giving the possibility for an institution to terminate a trade prior to their counterparty's creditworthiness deteriorating to the point of bankruptcy. Under ISDA documentation, break clauses can be defined via "Additional Termination Events". A break clause may occur at one or more pre-specified dates in the future and may be used by one or both counterparties to the transaction. If the break is exercised then the exercising party can terminate the transaction at its current replacement value. This introduces a complexity in terms of the definition of the replacement cost and whether it, for example, incorporates the credit quality of the replacement counterparty[3] and other aspects as discussed in Chapter 3.

A break clause may be considered particularly useful when trading with a relatively good credit quality counterparty on a long-maturity transaction (for example, 10 years or greater). Over such a time horizon, there is ample time for both the MtM of the transaction to become significantly positive and for the credit quality of the counterparty to decline. A *bilateral* break clause will often be relevant since both parties to the transaction may be in the same situation. The break clause will typically only be possible after a certain period (for example, 3 years) and possibly at pre-specified dates (for example, annually) thereafter.

---

[3] This in turn should incorporate the value of any break clause in the replacement contract and so on to infinity.

A break clause goes one step further than a refix and actually specifies the termination of transactions. However, they are not always freely exercisable. Typically, such events can be defined to fall into three categories:

- *Mandatory.* This means that the transaction will definitely terminate at the date of the break clause.
- *Optional.* This means that one (unilateral break clause) or both (bilateral break clause) counterparties have the option to terminate the transaction at the pre-specified date(s).
- *Trigger-based.* This means that a trigger (typically a ratings downgrade[4]) must occur before the break clause(s) may be exercised. There is no ISDA standard ATE and events are therefore a result of negotiations between the parties concerned.

A mandatory break clause is simple to understand and is just a natural continuation of a reset feature (see Figure 4.5). However, as discussed in Chapter 3, there is a complexity in terms of the definition of the replacement cost and whether it, for example, incorporates the credit quality of the replacement counterparty. Optional and trigger-based break clauses lead to more subtle problems in terms of defining their benefits. The problem with optional break clauses is that they need to be exercised early before the counterparty's credit quality declines significantly and/or exposure increases substantially. Exercising them at the "last minute" is unlikely to be useful due to systemic risk problems.[5] However, clients do not generally expect break clauses to be exercised (especially before the aforementioned changes in credit quality and exposure) and banks, for relationship reasons, very rarely do choose to exercise them. Hence, banks have historically avoided exercise for the good of the relationship with the counterparty in question and, in hindsight, many bilateral break clauses

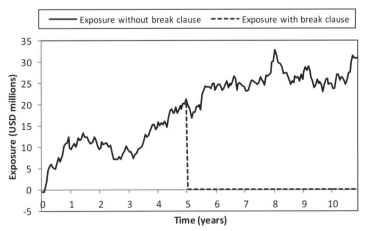

Figure 4.5 Illustration of the impact of a reset feature on the exposure of a long-dated cross-currency swap which occurs at the 5-year point. This example is relevant for a mandatory reset since it assumes termination will definitely occur.

---

[4] They may be based on as little as a 1-notch downgrade in a credit rating or a more substantial downgrade, for example to sub-investment grade status.

[5] By this point, the counterparty is usually in severe financial distress and the exercise of the break clause achieves no more than catalysing a failure. This is especially problematic if many parties have similar types of break clause and exercise at similar times.

have been gimmicks, which have not been utilised when they should have been. This is essentially part of a moral hazard problem, where front-office personnel may use the presence of a break clause to get a trade done but then later argue against the exercise of the break to avoid a negative impact on the client relationship. Banks should have clear and consistent policies over the exercise of option break clauses and the benefit they assign to them from a risk reduction point of view.[6]

Trigger-based break clauses, typically using credit ratings,[7] create further problems. Firstly, unlike default probability, rating transitions probabilities cannot be implied from market data. This means that historical data must be used which is, by its nature, scarce and limited to some broad classification. Secondly, ratings have in many circumstances, especially during the financial crisis, been shown to be extremely slow in reacting to negative credit information.[8] Indeed, under the Basel III rules for capital allocation, no positive benefit for ratings-based triggers is allowed (Section 17.4.5).

The dangers of credit rating triggers. Certain debt contracts may contain an *acceleration* clause that permits the creditor to accelerate future payments (for example, repayment of principal) in the event of a rating agency downgrade, default or other adverse credit event. Acceleration features are clearly aimed at protecting creditors. However, the acceleration of required payments can precipitate financial difficulties and catalyse the insolvency of a firm. As such, these triggers can increase systemic risk.

Consider the case of American International Group Inc. (AIG), which failed in September 2008 due to liquidity problems. The liquidity problems stemmed from the requirement for AIG to post an additional $20 billion[9] of collateral (relating to CDS trades) as a result of its bonds being downgraded. An institution trading with AIG may have thought the requirement for AIG to post collateral due to a downgrade would provide a safety net. However, since the downgrade was linked to the extremely poor performance of AIG's positions and collateral would be required to be posted to many institutions, in retrospect it is unlikely that a feature such as this would do anything more than catalyse a counterparty's demise. Luckily (for them and their counterparties if not the US taxpayer), AIG was bailed out but this story illustrates the limitation of any trigger linked to a credit rating change.

Prior to the financial crisis, break clauses were typically required by banks trading with some non-collateral-posting counterparties. More recently, various counterparties (for example, asset managers and pension funds) have demanded break clauses linked to banks' own credit ratings due to the unprecedented credit quality problems within the banking sector.

---

[6] Furthermore, usage of break clauses is becoming common. Institutions will exercise break clauses (or use their presence as leverage for agreeing other risk mitigating actions).

[7] Alternatives include decline in net asset value of funds, mergers, changes of management or "key person" events.

[8] One obvious extension of this idea is to create triggers based on more continuous quantities such as credit spreads. However, this can lead to death spiral effects.

[9] AIG 2008 Form 10-K.

4.3.3 Walkaway features

A final point of note is that some OTC derivatives have been documented with "walkaway" or "tear-up" features. Such a clause effectively allows an institution to cancel transactions in the event that their counterparty defaults. They would clearly only choose to do this in case they were in debt to the counterparty. Whilst a feature such as this does not reduce credit exposure, it does allow an institution to benefit from ceasing payments and not being obliged to settle amounts owed to a counterparty. These types of agreements, which were common prior to the 1992 ISDA Master Agreement, have been less usual since and are not part of standardised ISDA documentation. However, they have sometimes been used in transactions since 1992. Whilst walkaway features do not mitigate counterparty risk *per se*, they do result in potential gains that offset the risk of potential losses.

Walkaway agreements were seen in the Drexel Burnham Lambert (DBL) bankruptcy of 1990. Interestingly, in this case counterparties of DBL decided not to walk away and chose to settle net amounts owed. This was largely due to relatively small gains compared with the potential legal cost of having to defend the validity of the walkaway agreements or the reputational cost of being seen as taking advantage of the DBL default.

Even without an explicit walkaway agreement, an institution can still attempt to gain in the event of a counterparty default by not closing out contracts that are out-of-the-money to them but ceasing underlying payments. Another interesting case is that between Enron Australia (Enron) and TXU Electricity that traded a number of electricity swaps which were against TXU when Enron went into liquidation in early 2002. Although the swaps were not traded with a walkaway feature, ISDA documentation supported TXU avoiding paying the MtM owed to Enron (A\$3.3 million) by not terminating the transaction (closeout) but ceasing payments to their defaulted counterparty. The Enron liquidator went to court to try to force TXU effectively to settle the swaps but the (New South Wales Supreme) court found in favour of TXU in that they would not have to pay the owed amount until the individual transactions expired (i.e., the obligation to pay was not cancelled but it was postponed).

Some Lehman counterparties chose (like TXU) not to closeout swaps and stop making contractual payments (as the ISDA Master Agreement seems to support). Since the swaps were very out-of-the-money from the counterparties' point of view (and therefore strongly in-the-money for Lehman), there were potential gains to be made from doing this. Again, Lehman administrators challenged this in the courts. US and English courts came to different conclusions with respect to the enforceability of this "walkaway event", with the US court[10] ruling that the action was improper whilst the English court[11] ruled that the withholding of payments was proper.

Any type of walkaway feature is arguably rather unpleasant and should be avoided due to the additional costs for the counterparty in default and the creation of *moral hazard* (since an institution is potentially given the incentive to contribute to their counterparty's default due to the financial gain they can make).

4.3.4 Trade compression and multilateral netting

Standard netting arrangements such as described previously in this chapter are undertaken *bilaterally*, i.e., between two institutions only. Whilst bilateral netting has a significant

---

[10] The Bankruptcy Court for the Southern District of New York.
[11] High Court of England and Wales.

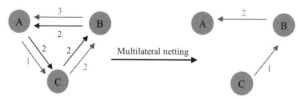

Figure 4.6 Illustration of the potential exposure reduction offered by multilateral netting. The black and grey exposures indicate positions in similar transactions, differing only in notional amount. The exposures in black are removed completely whilst those in grey are reduced by one unit.

impact on reducing overall credit exposure, it is limited to pairs of institutions within the market. Suppose that institution A has an exposure to institution B, whilst B has the same exposure to a third institution C that has another identical exposure to the original institution A. Even using bilateral netting, all three institutions have exposure (A has exposure to B, B to C and C to A). Some sort of trilateral (and by extension multilateral) netting between the three (or more) institutions would allow the exposures to be netted further, as illustrated in Figure 4.6. Even non-matching exposures could be reduced to their lowest level, as also shown.

However, implementation of multilateral netting is not trivial. In addition to the operational costs, it would give rise to questions such as how losses would be allocated between institutions A and B if, for example, institution C were to default. Problems such as this mean that some membership organisation needs to be at the centre of multilateral netting. Typically, such an entity will be an exchange or clearing house that will handle many aspects of the netting process such as valuation, settlement and collateralisation. A disadvantage of multilateral netting is that it tends to mutualise and homogenise counterparty risk, reducing incentives for institutions to scrutinise the credit quality of their counterparties. This will be discussed in much more detail in Chapter 7.

A way to attempt multilateral netting without the complexity of a membership organisation such as an exchange or central counterparty is via trade compression. This has developed since OTC derivatives portfolios grow significantly through time but contain redundancies due to the nature of trading (e.g., with respect to unwinds). This suggests that the trades can be reduced in terms of number and gross notional without changing the overall risk profile. This will reduce operational costs but also minimise counterparty risk. A simple example is given in Table 4.2 for single-name CDS contracts.

Trade compression by its very nature needs the cooperation of multiple participants. Participants submit their relevant trades for compression, which are matched according to the counterparty to the trade and cross-referenced against a trade-reporting warehouse. Participants must also specify tolerances since, whilst the aim of compression is to be totally market risk- and cash-neutral, allowing some very small changes in PnL and risk profile can increase the extent of the compression possible. It is also important not to breach an institution's credit limit to a given counterparty. Based on trade population, redundancies and tolerances, unwinds are determined based on redundancies in the multilateral trade population. Once the proposed terminations and replacement trades are accepted by all participants then the process is finished and all trade terminations and replacements are legally binding. Compression is subject to diminishing marginal returns over time as the maximum multilateral netting is achieved. It also relies to some degree on counterparties being readily interchangeable which implied they need to have comparable credit quality.

Table 4.2 Simple illustration of trade compression for single-name CDS contracts. An institution has three contracts with the same reference credit and maturity but traded with different counterparties. It is beneficial to "compress" the three into a net contract, which represents the total notional of the long and short positions. This may most obviously be with counterparty A as a reduction of the initial trade although this may not be the case in practice. The coupon of the new contract is the weighted average of the three original ones. This can be also set to a standard value which will involve some PnL adjustment (Section 10.2.1).

Reference credit	Notional	Long/short	Maturity	Coupon	Counterparty
ABC Corp.	40	Long	20/12/2015	200	Counterparty A
ABC Corp.	25	Short	20/12/2015	150	Counterparty B
ABC Corp.	10	Short	20/12/2015	325	Counterparty C
ABC Corp.	**5**	**Long**	**20/12/2015**	**200**	**Counterparty A**

Companies such as TriOptima[12] provide compression services covering major OTC derivatives products such as interest rate swaps (in all global currencies), credit default swaps (single-name, indices and tranches) and energy swaps. This has been instrumental in reducing exposures in OTC derivatives markets, especially in rapidly growing areas such as credit derivatives.[13] The CDS market has made changes to promote compression, such as the adoption of standard coupons and maturity dates (see Section 10.2.1). We note that compression services can also be used in conjunction with central clearing.[14]

4.4 CONCLUSION

In this chapter, we have described the primary ways of mitigating counterparty risk via exposure. Closeout netting is a crucial way to control credit exposure by being legally able to offset transactions with positive and negative mark-to-market values in the event a counterparty does default. Reset features allow the periodic resetting of an exposure. Early termination events allow the termination of a transaction to mitigate an exposure combined with a deterioration of the credit quality of a counterparty, possibly linked to some event such as a credit ratings downgrade. Compression reduces gross notional and therefore also the associated net exposure.

In the next chapter, we discuss the use of collateral, which is the other main method for reducing credit exposure.

---

[12] www.trioptima.com

[13] For example, "TriOptima tear-ups cut CDS notional by $9 trillion", http://www.risk.net/risk-magazine/news/1505985/trioptima-tear-upscut-cds-notional-usd9-trillion. "CDS Dealers Compress $30 trillion in Trades in 2008", REUTERS, 12th January 2009.

[14] "TriOptima and LCH.Clearnet terminate SwapClear USD interest rate swaps with notional principal value of $7.1 trillion" http://www.lchclearnet.com/media_centre/press_releases/2011-08-04.asp.

5

Collateral

5.1 INTRODUCTION

Collateralisation (also known as margining) provides a further means to reduce credit exposure beyond the benefit achieved with netting and the other methods described in the previous chapter. Indeed, the use of collateral is essentially a natural extension of break clauses and resets. A break clause can be seen as a single payment of collateral and cancellation of the transaction. A reset feature is essentially the periodic payment of collateral to neutralise an exposure. Standard collateral terms simply take this further to much more frequent collateral posting. Collateral agreements may often be negotiated prior to any trading activity between counterparties or may be agreed or updated prior to an increase in trading volume or change in other conditions.

5.1.1 Rationale for collateral

Suppose that a netted exposure (sum of all the values of transactions with the counterparty) is large and positive. There is clearly a strong risk if the counterparty is to default. A collateral agreement limits this exposure by specifying that collateral must be posted by one counterparty to the other to support such an exposure. The collateral receiver only becomes the economic owner of the collateral if the collateral giver defaults. Like netting agreements, collateral agreements may be two-way which means that either counterparty would be required to post collateral against a negative mark-to-market value (from their point of view). Both counterparties will periodically mark all positions to market and check the net value. Then they will check the terms of the collateral agreement to calculate if they are owed collateral and vice versa. To keep operational costs under control, posting of collateral will not be continuous and will occur in blocks according to predefined rules.

Collateral is an asset supporting a risk in a legally enforceable way

Derivatives collateral is fundamentally different in both type and nature from the use of physical assets as security for debts. Secured creditors have a claim on particular assets but their ability to realise the value of the assets is subject to delays in the bankruptcy process. It is possible for secured creditors to petition the bankruptcy court to release their security but this is a complicated process (e.g., see Baird, 2001). In contrast, collateral posted against derivatives positions is, in most cases, under the control of the counterparty and may be liquidated immediately upon an "event of default". This arises due to the laws governing derivatives contracts and the nature of the collateral (cash or liquid securities).

Exposure, in theory, can be completely neutralised as long as a sufficient amount of collateral is held against it. However, there are legal obstacles to this and issues such as rehypothecation (or relending, discussed in detail later). This was a significant issue in the Lehman Brothers bankruptcy of 2008.

The motivation for collateral management is clearly to reduce counterparty risk but can be summarised in more detail as follows:

- To reduce credit exposure so as to be able to do more business. To maintain exposures within credit lines and not have to cease trading with certain counterparties.
- To enable one to trade with a particular counterparty. For example, ratings restrictions may not allow uncollateralised credit lines to certain counterparties.
- To reduce capital requirements. For example, as discussed in Chapter 17, Basel regulatory capital rules give capital relief for collateralised exposures.
- To give more competitive pricing of counterparty credit risk (see Section 12.5 for an example).

The fundamental idea of collateral management is very simple in that cash or securities are passed from one counterparty to another as security for a credit exposure. However, effective collateral management is much harder than one might initially think, and there are many pitfalls along the way. In particular, it is important to note that, whilst collateral can be used to reduce credit exposure, it gives rise to new risks, such as market, operational and liquidity. All of these risks must be correctly understood, quantified and managed.

5.1.2   Analogy with mortgages

A collateralised position is analogous to a mortgaged house in many ways. As such, it is useful to consider the risks that a mortgage provider faces when making such a loan for their client to purchase a property. The risk that the mortgagor is unable or fails to make future mortgage payments is *default risk*. This risk is mitigated by the house being pledged as collateral for the mortgage, but this will in turn create other risks as outlined below.

- The risk that the value of the property in question falls below the outstanding value of the loan or mortgage. This is often known as the situation of "negative equity" and corresponds to *market risk*. Note that this depends on both the value of the property (collateral) and the value of the mortgage (exposure).

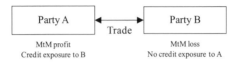

Figure 5.1 Illustration of the basic principle of collateralisation.

- The risk that the mortgage giver is unable, or faces legal obstacles, to take ownership of the property in the event of the failure to make mortgage payments and faces costs in order to evict the owners and sell the property. This corresponds to *operational or legal risk*.
- The risk that the property cannot be sold immediately in the open market and will have a falling value if property values are in decline. To achieve a sale, the property may then have to be sold at a discount to its fair value if there is a shortage of buyers. This is *liquidity risk*.
- The risk that there is a strong dependence between the value of the property and the default of the mortgagee. For example, in an economic downturn, high unemployment and falling property prices make this rather likely. This is a form of *correlation* (or even *wrong-way*) risk.

5.1.3   The basics of collateralisation

The basic idea of collateralisation is very simple and illustrated in Figure 5.1. In a transaction between parties A and B, party A makes a mark-to-market (MtM) profit whilst party B makes a corresponding MtM loss. Party B then posts some form of collateral to party A to mitigate the credit exposure that arises due to the positive MtM. The collateral may be in cash or other securities, the characteristics of which have been agreed before the initiation of the contract.

Note that, since collateral agreements are often bilateral, collateral must be returned or posted in the opposite direction when exposure decreases. Hence, in the case of a positive MtM, an institution will call for collateral and in the case of a negative MtM they will be required to post collateral themselves.

5.1.4   Collateral usage

Collateral posting across the market is quite mixed depending on the type of institution (Table 5.1). The main reasons for doing this are the need to post cash or high-quality

Table 5.1   Collateral posting by type of institution

Institution type	Collateral posting
Dealer Banks	Very High
Other Banks	High
Supranationals, Local authorities, Private Equity Funds	Low
Corporates	Low
Sovereigns	Very Low

Source: Adapted from ISDA Market Review of OTC Derivatives Bilateral Collateralisation Practices 36–38 (2010).

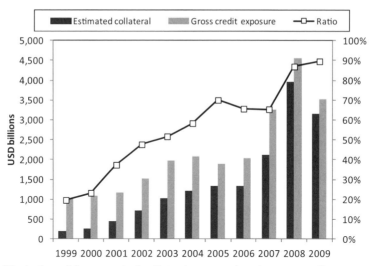

Figure 5.2 Illustration of the amount of collateral compared to the gross credit exposure (i.e., after netting has been accounted for) and the ratio given the extent of collateralisation of OTC derivatives.
Source: ISDA and BIS.

securities and the operational workload associated with posting collateral under stringent collateral agreements. Other aspects may include external restrictions (e.g., negative pledge provisions) and the economic view that uncollateralised trading is cheaper than collateralised trading. This last point may be considered to be related to CVA charges being too low or not even present.

Nevertheless, collateral usage has increased significantly over the last decade, as illustrated in Figure 5.2, which shows the estimated amount of collateral and gross credit exposure. The ratio of these quantities gives an estimate of the fraction of credit exposure that is collateralised. This has grown year on year to a ratio of around 90% in 2009 but is a slightly misleading figure due to the presence of overcollateralisation. Nevertheless, the impact of collateralisation is reported to reduce overall exposure by around four-fifths (Ghosh *et al.*, 2008). Incorporating the fact that credit exposures are first decreased through netting and the remaining net exposures are further mitigated by the pledging of collateral reduces total market exposure by nearly 93% (Bliss and Kaufman, 2005).

5.1.5   The credit support annex

Within an ISDA Master Agreement (see previous chapter), it is possible to append a credit support annex (CSA) which permits the parties to mitigate their credit risk further by agreeing to various collateral posting.[1] As with netting, ISDA has legal opinions throughout a large number of jurisdictions regarding the enforceability of the provisions within a CSA.

---

[1] 92% of collateral agreements in use are ISDA agreements. *Source*: ISDA Margin Survey 2010.

The CSA is therefore at the centre of any collateral agreement as it governs the mechanics of collateral with respect to issues such as:

- Method and timings of the underlying valuations.
- The calculation of the amount of collateral that will be posted.
- The mechanics and timing of collateral transfers.
- Eligible collateral.
- Collateral substitutions.
- Dispute resolution.
- Interest rate payments on collateral.
- Haircuts applied to collateral securities.
- Possible rehypothecation (reuse) of collateral securities.
- Triggers that may change the collateral conditions (for example, ratings downgrades that may lead to enhanced collateral requirements).

In addition, the nature of a CSA is critically defined by a number of key parameters that essentially define the amount of collateral that will be posted. The most important parameters are:

- *Threshold.* Defines the level of MtM above which collateral is posted. When the exposure is above the threshold, the threshold amount is *undercollateralised*. When the exposure is below the threshold then it is not collateralised at all.
- *Independent amount.* This defines an amount of extra collateral that must be posted irrespective of the exposure. Hence, the exposure is *overcollateralised*. An independent amount is similar in concept to an initial margin required by an exchange or central counterparty (Chapter 7). An independent amount is not common in CSAs, although it is used in some specific cases and will be required under new regulations in many cases (e.g., inter-bank trades).
- *Minimum transfer amount.* This defines the minimum amount of collateral that can be called for at a time.

Note that thresholds and independent amounts essentially work in opposite directions. Mathematically, an independent amount is a negative threshold and vice versa.

The process by which two counterparties will agree to collateralise their exposures can be summarised as follows:

- Parties negotiate and sign a collateral support document containing the terms and conditions under which they will operate.
- Trades subject to collateral are regularly marked-to-market, and the overall valuation including netting is agreed (unless this amount is disputed as discussed later).
- The party with negative MtM delivers collateral (subject to minimum transfer amounts and thresholds as discussed later).
- The collateral position is updated to reflect the transfer of cash or securities.
- (Periodic reconciliations should also be performed to reduce the risk of disputes.)

CSAs must explicitly define all the parameters of the collateralisation and account for all possible scenarios. The choice of parameters will often come down to a balance between the

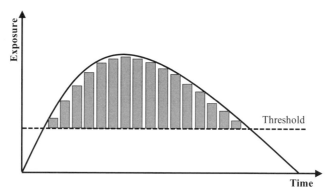

Figure 5.3 Illustration of the impact of collateral on exposure. The collateral amount is depicted by the grey areas.

workload of calling and returning collateral versus the risk mitigation benefit of doing so. We will now analyse the components that make up the collateral process in more detail.

5.1.6   Impact of collateral

The impact of collateral on a typical exposure profile is shown in Figure 5.3. There are essentially two reasons why collateral cannot perfectly mitigate exposure. Firstly, the presence of a threshold[2] means that a certain amount of exposure cannot be collateralised. Secondly, the delay in receiving collateral and parameters such as the minimum transfer amount create a discrete effect, as the movement of exposure cannot be tracked perfectly.[3] This is illustrated by the grey blocks in Figure 5.3.

5.2   COLLATERAL TERMS

5.2.1   Valuation agent

The valuation agent is normally the party calling for delivery or return of collateral and thus must handle all calculations. Large counterparties trading with smaller counterparties may insist on being valuation agents for all purposes. In such a case, the "smaller" counterparty is not obligated to return or post collateral if they do not receive the expected notification, whilst the valuation agent is under obligation to make returns where relevant. Alternatively, both counterparties may be the valuation agent and each will call for collateral when they have an exposure.

The role of the valuation agent in a collateral calculation is as follows:

- To calculate credit exposure under the impact of netting.
- To calculate the market value of collateral previously posted.
- To calculate the uncollateralised exposure.

---

[2] Note that a threshold can be zero, in which case this is not an issue. However, even many interbank CSAs have non-zero thresholds.
[3] The purpose of an independent amount is to mitigate this risk by providing a buffer.

- To calculate the delivery or return amount (the amount of collateral to be posted by either counterparty). This is likely to differ from the uncollateralised exposure due to the discrete nature of collateral agreements, which means that collateral is transferred in blocks. This is covered in more detail in Section 8.5.1.

Third-party valuation agents provide operational efficiencies, and can also help prevent disputes that are common in bilateral collateral relationships.

5.2.2   Types of collateral

Cash is the major form of collateral taken against OTC derivatives exposures (Figure 5.4). The ability to post other forms of collateral is often highly preferable for liquidity reasons, but the credit crisis has shown that even government agency securities (for example, Fannie Mae and Freddie Mac) and Triple-A MBS securities are far from the high-quality assets with minimal price volatility that they were once assumed to be. Non-cash collateral also creates the problems of reuse or rehypothecation (discussed later) and additional volatility arising from the price uncertainty of collateral posted (see Section 9.7.6) and its correlation to the original exposure (Section 15.4.6). On the contrary, in extreme market conditions, cash tends to be in limited supply.

If the credit rating of an underlying security held as collateral declines below that specified in the collateral agreement, then normally it will be necessary to replace this security immediately. When two counterparties do not have the same local currency, one of them will have to take FX risk linked to the collateral posted, even when it is in the form of cash. Securities in various currencies may be specified as admissible collateral but may also attract larger haircuts due to the additional FX risk. FX risk from posted collateral can be hedged in the spot and forward FX markets but it must be done dynamically as the value of collateral changes.

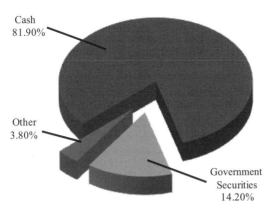

Figure 5.4 Breakdown of the type of collateral used for OTC derivatives. Around three-quarters of cash is posted in USD and EUR currencies with more than 97% being covered by these two currencies plus GBP and JPY. Likewise, over 95% of government securities are posted in these four currencies. The other category contains collateral such as government agency securities, supranational bonds, covered bonds, corporate bonds, letters of credit and equities.

Source: ISDA Margin Survey 2010.

5.2.3 Coverage of collateralisation

As illustrated in Figure 5.5, a large proportion of all OTC derivatives trade under collateral agreements. The percentages are highest for credit derivatives, which is not surprising due to the high volatility of credit spreads[4] whilst the fact that many FX transactions are short-dated explains the relatively low number for this asset class.

Collateral agreements will reference the netted value of some or all trades with a specific counterparty. From a risk mitigation point of view, one should include the maximum number of trades but this should be balanced against the need to effectively value all such trades. Product and regional impacts are often considered when excluding certain trades from collateral agreements. Collateral agreements do require the transfer of the undisputed amount immediately, which means that the majority of products should still be collateralised even when there are disputes regarding a minority. However, the cleaner approach of leaving such products outside a collateral agreement is sometimes favoured.

5.2.4 Disputes and reconciliations

Collateral management is one of the few areas of banking that has not fully embraced technological advances and still relies heavily on manual process and data standards. The use of spreadsheets is still quite common. Clearly, such practices can lead to significant disputes between counterparties.

A dispute over a collateral call is common and can arise due to one or more of a number of factors:

- trade population;
- trade valuation methodology;
- application of netting rules;

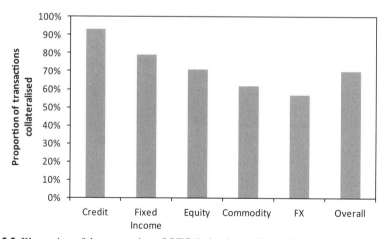

Figure 5.5 Illustration of the proportion of OTC derivatives collateralised shown by product type.
Source: ISDA Margin Survey 2010.

---

[4] In addition, the wrong-way risk embedded in credit derivatives may be driving this aspect although it is not clear whether collateral strongly mitigates this component (Section 15.4.6).

- market data and market close time;
- valuation of previously posted collateral.

If the difference in valuation or disputed amount is within a certain tolerance specified in the collateral agreement, then the counterparties may "split the difference". Otherwise, it will be necessary to find the cause of the discrepancy. Obviously, such a situation is not ideal and will mean that one party will have a partially uncollateralised exposure at least until the origin of the disputed amount can be traced, agreed upon and corrected. The following steps are normally followed in the case of a dispute:

- The disputing party is required to notify its counterparty (or the third-party valuation agent) that it wishes to dispute the exposure or collateral calculation no later than the close of business on the day following the collateral call.
- The disputing party agrees to transfer the undisputed amount and the parties will attempt to resolve the dispute within a certain timeframe (the "resolution time"). The reason for the dispute will be identified (e.g., which transactions have material differences in valuation).
- If the parties fail to resolve the dispute within the resolution time, they will obtain MtM quotations from several market makers for the components of the disputed exposure (or value of existing collateral in case this is the component under dispute).

Rather than being *reactive* and focussing on dispute resolution, it is better to be *proactive* and aim to prevent disputes in the first place. Reconciliations aim to minimise the chance of a dispute by agreeing on valuation figures even though the resulting netted exposure may not lead to any collateral changing hands. They can even be performed using dummy trades before two counterparties transact with one another. It is good practice to perform reconciliations at periodic intervals (for example, weekly or monthly) so as to minimise differences in valuation between counterparties. Such reconciliations can pre-empt later problems that might arise during more sensitive periods. Reconciliations may be rather detailed and will therefore highlight differences that otherwise may be within the dispute tolerance or that by chance offset one another. Hence, problems that may otherwise appear only transiently should be captured in a thorough reconciliation.

The global financial crisis highlighted many problems in the collateral management practices of banks. Regulators have reacted to this in the Basel III proposals (see Chapter 17), which give less credit to collateral as a risk mitigant in some cases. Collateral management is improving, mainly via a simplification of collateral terms (e.g., using cash collateral only). This is also driven by the issues that collateral creates in terms of valuation (Chapter 14).

5.2.5 Margin call frequency

Margin call frequency refers to the periodic timescale with which collateral may be called and returned. A longer margin call frequency may be agreed upon, most probably to reduce operational workload and in order for the relevant valuations to be carried out. Some smaller institutions may struggle with the operational and funding requirements in relation to the daily margin calls required by larger counterparties. Whilst a margin call frequency longer than daily might be practical for asset classes and markets that are not so volatile, daily

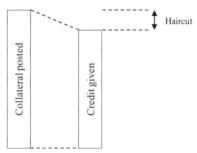

Figure 5.6 Illustration of a haircut applied to collateral.

margining is becoming standard in OTC derivatives markets. Furthermore, intraday margining is common for vanilla products such as repos and for derivatives cleared via central counterparties (Chapter 7).

5.2.6   Haircuts

A haircut is a discount applied to the value of collateral to account for the fact that its value may deteriorate over time. Cash collateral in a major currency will require no haircut but other securities will have pre-specified haircuts depending on their individual characteristics. A haircut of $x\%$ means that for every unit of that security posted as collateral, only $(1 - x)\%$ of credit (or "valuation percentage") will be given, as illustrated in Figure 5.6. The collateral giver must account for the haircut when posting collateral.

Haircuts are primarily used to account for the price volatility of collateral posted. Default relating to a security posted as collateral would clearly reduce the value of that collateral substantially and the haircut is very unlikely to cover such an event. For this reason, only high-quality debt securities are typically allowed to be used as collateral. Haircuts are designed to cover price volatility of assets only and it is therefore crucial that every effort is made to avoid collateral with significant default risk.

Some examples of haircuts together with eligible collateral types are shown in Table 5.2.

Table 5.2   Example haircuts in a collateral agreement

	Party A	Party B	Valuation percentage	Haircut
Cash in eligible currency	X	X	100%	0%
Debt obligations issued by the governments of the US, UK or Germany with a maturity less than 1 year	X	X	98%	2%
Debt obligations issued by the governments of the US, UK or Germany with a maturity between 1 and 10 years	X	X	95%	5%
Debt obligations issued by the governments of the US, UK or Germany with a maturity greater than 10 years	X		90%	10%

The important points to consider before assigning a haircut are:

- time taken to liquidate the collateral;
- volatility of the underlying market variable(s) defining the value of the collateral;
- default risk of the security;
- maturity of the security;
- liquidity of the security;
- any relationship between the default of the counterparty and the value of the collateral (wrong-way risk).

For example, a high-quality long-dated government or corporate bond has significant interest rate volatility due to the long maturity, although default and liquidity risk will probably not be of great concern. Such a security might therefore attract a haircut of around a few percent. Collateral with greater credit risk must be assigned a larger haircut to account for the credit spread volatility and default risk. Volatile collateral such as commodities (e.g., gold) and equities should be assigned higher haircuts as compensation for their price volatility and potential illiquidity. Finally, it is important to consider the potential correlation between the exposure and the valuation of collateral. All these points will be discussed in a more quantitative fashion in Chapter 9.

Example. Consider a security that attracts a haircut of 5% and is being posted to cover a collateral call of $100,000. Only 95% of the value of this security is credited for collateral purposes and so the actual amount of collateral posted must be

$$\text{Market value of collateral} = \$105,263$$
$$\text{Haircut} = \$5,263 \ (5\% \ of \ \$105,263)$$
$$\text{Credit given} = \$100,000 \ (\text{difference between the above})$$

It is the collateral giver's responsibility to account for haircuts when posting collateral so that if a collateral call is made as above then (assuming they do not dispute the amount) the counterparty could post $100,000 in cash but $105,263 in terms of the market value of a security attracting a 5% haircut.

5.2.7   Coupons and interest payments

As long as the giver of collateral is not in default then they remain the owner from an economic point of view. Hence, the receiver of collateral must pass on coupon payments, dividends and any other cash flows. The only exception to this rule is in the case where an immediate margin call would be triggered. In this case, the collateral receiver may typically keep the minimum component of the cash flow in order to remain appropriately collateralised.

Interest will typically be paid on cash collateral at the overnight indexed swap (OIS[5]) rate (for example, EONIA in Europe, Fed Funds in the US). The logic behind this is that since collateral may only be held for short periods (due to the variation of exposure), then only a

---

[5] Discussed in more detail in Section 14.2.2.

short-term interest rate can be paid. However, OIS is not necessarily the most appropriate collateral rate, especially for long-dated exposures where collateral may be held in substantial amounts for a long period. This may lead to a negative carry problem due to an institution funding the collateral posted at a rate significantly above LIBOR but receiving only the OIS rate (less than LIBOR) for the collateral posted. Sometimes, a collateral receiver may possibly agree to post a rate higher than OIS to compensate for this funding mismatch. Another reason for a collateral giver to pay a return in excess of OIS would be to incentivise the posting of cash over other more risky and volatile securities.

5.2.8 Substitution, funding costs and rehypothecation

Sometimes a counterparty may require or want securities posted as collateral returned (for example, to meet delivery commitments).[6] In this case, they can make a substitution request and post an alternative amount of eligible collateral with the relevant haircut applied. The requested collateral does not need to be released until the substitute collateral has been received. If substitution is optional (no consent required), then a substitution request cannot be refused[7] (unless it is not valid). Alternatively, substitution may only be allowed if the holder of the collateral gives consent. Whether or not collateral can be substituted without consent is an important consideration in terms of the funding costs and benefits of collateral (Chapter 14).

For collateral to provide benefit against funding costs, it must be usable (since the economic ownership remains with the collateral giver) via rehypothecation, which means it can be posted as collateral or pledged via repo. To understand the importance of this, consider Figure 5.7. Collateral in securities that cannot be rehypothecated reduces counterparty risk but creates a funding problem. We will refer to this as funding liquidity risk.

Rehypothecation would seem to be obvious because it keeps the flow of collateral moving around the financial system without any blockage. The question arises as to whether rehypothecating a security in this way creates additional risk due to a loss of control of collateral. An institution faces two possible risks in this respect:

- Collateral pledged in a collateral agreement against a negative MtM to another counterparty may be rehypothecated and consequently not be returned (in the event of a default of the counterparty coupled to an increase in the MtM).
- Collateral received from party A and then rehypothecated to party B. This may not be retrieved in the event that party B defaults, creating a liability to party A.

Figure 5.7 Illustration of the importance of rehypothecation of non-cash collateral. An institution trades with counterparty A and typically hedges this transaction with counterparty B, both under CSA agreements. If counterparty B posts collateral then ideally it should be possible to pass this collateral on to counterparty A to minimise funding costs.

---

[6] Note that the collateral returned needs not be exactly the same but must be equivalent (e.g., the same bond issue).
[7] For example, on grounds that the original collateral has been repoed, posted to another counterparty, sold or is otherwise inaccessible.

Prior to the credit crisis in 2007, the pledging, reuse and rehypothecation of collateral was strongly encouraged. This was viewed as being critical to the entire financial system (Segoviano and Singh, 2008). However, the practice of rehypothecation probably became too widespread, especially in the interbank market (presumably since there was little concern of actual bank defaults). The bankruptcy of Lehman Brothers has illustrated the potential problems with rehypothecation. One example is that customers of Lehman Brothers Inc. (US) were being treated more favourably than the UK customers of Lehman Brothers International (Europe) in terms of the return of rehypothecated assets (due to differences in customer protection between the UK and the US[8]).

Singh and Aitken (2009) have reported a significant drop in rehypothecation, which is safer from a systemic risk perspective but leads to an increase in funding liquidity risk. Hedge funds are tending to be unwilling to allow rehypothecation, which will surely lead to an increase in prime broker fees. The problems with rehypothecation are another driving force behind cash collateralisation becoming increasingly the standard and, in many cases, the only option that most institutions are willing to adopt.

When posting and receiving collateral, institutions are becoming increasingly aware of the need to optimise their collateral management as, during the financial crisis, funding efficiencies have emerged as an important driver of collateral usage. Collateral management is no longer a back-office cost centre but can be an important asset optimisation tool delivering the most cost-effective collateral. An institution must consider the "cheapest-to-deliver" cash collateral and account for the impact of haircuts and the ability to rehypothecate non-cash collateral. For example, different currencies of cash will pay different OIS rates and non-cash collateral, if rehypothecated, will earn different rates on repo. Chapter 14 provides a more in-depth study of these aspects.

5.3 DEFINING THE AMOUNT OF COLLATERAL

5.3.1 Types of CSA

Due to the very different nature of OTC derivatives counterparties, many different collateral arrangements exist. Broadly speaking, these can be categorised into the following.

(i) No CSA

There are two reasons why an institution may be unable or unwilling to post collateral. Firstly, it could be because their credit quality is far superior to their counterparty. Secondly (or additionally), it may occur because they cannot commit to the operational and liquidity requirements that arise from committing to a CSA.

One result of the above is that in some trading relationships, CSAs are not used because one or both parties cannot commit to collateral posting. A typical example of this is the relationship between a bank and a corporate where the latter's inability to post collateral means that a CSA is not usually in place (for example, a corporate treasurer may find it almost impossible to manage their liquidity needs if they transacted under a CSA).

---

[8] The liquidator of Lehman Brothers (PWC) stated in October 2008, shortly after the bankruptcy, that certain assets provided to Lehman Brothers International (Europe) had been rehypothecated and may not be returned.

(ii) Two-way CSA

For two similar counterparties, a two-way CSA is more typical. This is common, for example, in the interbank market. A two-way CSA is typically beneficial to both parties. Two-way CSAs may be skewed in some way. For example, one party may have a lower threshold than the other, which may be due to their inferior credit rating.

(iii) One-way CSA

In some situations, a one-way CSA is used which is beneficial to only the collateral receiver. Indeed, a one-way CSA represents additional risk for the collateral giver that puts them in a worse situation than if they were in a no-CSA relationship (Section 9.7.5). One example of this would be a bank trading with a hedge fund and requiring collateral posting (possibly including an independent amount) to mitigate the significantly increased (and opaque) counterparty risk of the hedge fund. Another typical example is a high-quality entity such as a Triple-A sovereign or insurer trading with a bank.

Note that not all one-way CSAs are truly one-way. For example, one party may not post collateral immediately but may be required to do so if, for example, their credit rating deteriorates. Prior to the financial crisis, Triple-A entities such as monoline insurers traded through one-way CSAs but with triggers specifying that they must post collateral if their ratings were to decline. This seemed to put banks in a safe position but quite the reverse was true.

5.3.2   Linkage of collateral parameters to credit quality

It is quite common to attempt to link the precise terms of a collateral agreement to the credit quality of one or both counterparties. The motivation for doing this is to minimise the operational workload whilst a counterparty has strong credit quality but have the ability to tighten up the terms of collateralisation when their credit quality deteriorates. The quantities to which collateral terms can obviously be linked are:

- credit ratings;
- traded credit spread;
- market value of equity;
- net asset value (sometimes used in the case of hedge funds).

The most commonly used of the above have been credit ratings, and examples will be given below. Linking a tightening of collateral terms to a credit rating (for example, a downgrade to sub-investment grade) might seem a rather easy and obvious method of mitigating an increase in counterparty risk. However, this type of agreement can lead to rather unpleasant discontinuities since a downgrade of a counterparty's credit rating can occur rather late and then cause further credit issues due to the requirement to post collateral (similar to the discussions around additional termination events in Section 4.3.2).

5.3.3   Threshold

A threshold is a level of exposure below which collateral will not be called. The threshold therefore represents an amount of uncollateralised exposure. If the exposure is above the threshold, only the *incremental* exposure will be collateralised. In return for taking the risk

Table 5.3 Illustration of linkage of threshold to credit rating

Rating	Threshold
AAA	$100m
AA	$50
A	$25m
Lower	Zero

of a moderate uncollateralised exposure, the operational burden of calling and returning collateral will be reduced. Put another way, many counterparties may only consider collateralisation important when the exposure exceeds a certain level, the threshold. A threshold of zero implies that any exposure is collateralised whilst a threshold of infinity is used to specify that a counterparty will not post collateral under any circumstance. An example of thresholds and their linkage to credit rating is shown in Table 5.3.

A downgrade of the counterparty may trigger an immediate collateral call. As discussed previously, if such an agreement is in place with many counterparties then it may cause cash flow issues at precisely the worst time. This is exactly what happened with AIG and monoline insurers and will be discussed in more detail in Chapter 15.

5.3.4 Independent amount

An independent amount can be thought of (intuitively and mathematically) as a negative threshold. It is typically held as a cushion against "gap risk", the risk that the market value of a transaction(s) may gap substantially in a short space of time. An independent amount can be significant and reduce exposure to practically zero. Independent amounts and gap risk are discussed further in Chapter 7 in the context of central counterparties. Sometimes the posting of an independent amount may be linked to a downgrade in a counterparty's credit rating.

We can think of an independent amount as transforming counterparty risk into "gap risk". A transaction with a risky counterparty might be collateralised with both frequent margin calls and additionally an independent amount. The aim is then that the transaction is always overcollateralised by the independent amount so that even if the counterparty defaults, it is highly unlikely that any loss will be suffered. The residual risk is that, when the counterparty defaults, the value of the transactions will move dramatically or "gap" before it can be unwound. The independent amount is often considered large enough to make such a gap event in the relevant time horizon highly unlikely.

Independent amounts are often specific to a particular trade and are common for counterparties considered to be of relatively poor credit quality (such as hedge funds). However, future regulation seems likely to make them much more common.

5.3.5 Minimum transfer amount and rounding

Collateral cannot be transferred in blocks that are smaller than the minimum transfer amount and hence this must be considered when calculating the amount of collateral that could be called. This will typically mean that an increasing exposure will be slightly under-collateralised due to minimum transfer restrictions. In contrast, a decreasing exposure will typically mean an institution has a small overcollateralisation since they do not need to return collateral continuously.

A minimum transfer amount is the smallest amount of collateral that can be transferred. It is used to avoid the workload associated with a frequent transfer of insignificant amounts of collateral. The size of the minimum transfer amount again represents a balance between risk mitigation versus operational workload. The minimum transfer amount and threshold are additive in the sense that the exposure must exceed the sum of the two before any collateral can be called. We note this additively does not mean that the minimum transfer amount can be incorporated into the threshold – this would be correct in defining the point at which the collateral call can be made but not in terms of the collateral due.[9] Again, minimum transfer amounts may be linked to ratings. When the counterparty has a weaker credit rating then the additional operational workload required to make a larger number of smaller collateral calls is a reasonable price to pay for being able to reduce the exposure.

A collateral call or return amount will always be rounded to a multiple of a certain size to avoid unnecessarily small amounts. The rounding may be always up (or down) or might always be in favour of one counterparty (i.e., up when they call for collateral and down when they return collateral). This is typically a relatively small amount and will have a small effect on the impact of collateralisation. However, the impact of rounding can be considered alongside the other factors above and will cause minor but noticeable impacts on the overall exposure.

5.4   THE RISKS OF COLLATERALISATION

Whilst collateral management is a very useful tool for mitigating counterparty risk, it has significant limitations that must be considered. Essentially, the counterparty risk is converted into other forms of financial risk, such as legal risk (for example, if the terms defined in a CSA cannot be upheld within the relevant jurisdiction). Correlation risk (where collateral is adversely correlated to the underlying exposure), credit risk (where the collateral may default or suffer an adverse credit effect) and FX risk (due to collateral being posted in a different currency) are also important. However, the three most important risks to consider are market, operational and liquidity risk.

5.4.1   Market risk and the margin period of risk

Collateral can never completely eradicate counterparty risk and we must consider the residual risk that remains under the collateral agreement. This is mainly due to contractual parameters such as thresholds and minimum transfer amounts that effectively delay the collateral process, in addition to the normal delay since collateral cannot be received immediately. This can be considered a market risk as it is related to the extent of market movements after the counterparty last posted collateral. Whilst the residual risk may be only a fraction of the uncollateralised risk, it may be more difficult to quantify (Section 9.7) and indeed hedge (see Section 16.6.3, which discusses the impact of collateral on hedging).

---

[9] For example, for a minimum transfer amount (MTA) and threshold (K), the collateral call can be made when the (potentially already collateralised) exposure (E) exceeds MTA + K but the collateralisation required is $E - K$. Using the approximation of adding MTA and K would (conservatively) model the collateralisation required as $E - K - $ MTA.

Whilst there is a contractual period between collateral calls (often daily), one must consider what we shall call the "margin period of risk". This is the *effective* time assumed between a collateral call and receiving the appropriate collateral (or in a worst-case scenario putting the counterparty in default, liquidating existing collateral, closing out and re-hedging the trade). Under Basel II regulations, this should be a *minimum* of 10 days for OTC derivatives and the new Basel III regime defines a more conservative 20-day minimum in certain cases. The experience of most participants in the Lehman Brothers bankruptcy was that this period was approximately 5–10 business days. We will discuss this period in more detail in Section 8.5.2.

5.4.2   Operational risk

The time-consuming and intensely dynamic nature of collateralisation means that operational risk is a very important aspect. The following are examples of specific operational risks:

- missed collateral calls;
- failed deliveries;
- computer error;
- human error;
- fraud.

There is clearly no point in having a collateral management programme that reduces significantly many credit exposures only to find that, in the event of an actual default, losses are not mitigated due to some lack of control or error. The following is a list of points to consider in relation to operational risk:

- Legal agreements must be accurate and enforceable.
- IT systems must be capable of automating the many daily tasks and checks that are required.
- The regular process of calls and returns of collateral is complex and can be extremely time-consuming with a workload that increases in markets that are more volatile.
- Timely accurate valuation of all products is key.
- Information on independent amounts, minimum transfer amounts, rounding, collateral types and currencies must be maintained accurately for each counterparty.
- Failure to deliver collateral is a potentially dangerous signal and must be followed up swiftly.

5.4.3   Liquidity risk

Collateralisation of counterparty risk leads to demanding liquidity requirements. Indeed, this is why some counterparties do not sign CSAs in the first place. One of the most obvious manifestations of this liquidity risk is in the event that collateral has to be liquidated following the default of a counterparty. Firstly, the surviving institution faces transaction costs (bid–offer) and market volatility over the liquidation period. Secondly, there is the risk that by liquidating an amount of a security that is large compared with the volume traded in that security, the price will be driven down and a potentially large loss incurred. If one chooses to liquidate the position more slowly in small blocks then there is exposure to market volatility for a longer period.

When agreeing to collateral that may be posted and when receiving securities as collateral, important considerations are:

- What is the total issue size or market capitalisation posted as collateral?
- Is there a link between the collateral value and the credit quality of the counterparty? Such a link may not be obvious and predicted by looking at correlations between variables.[10]
- How is the relative liquidity of the security in question likely to change if the counterparty concerned is in default?

Because of these liquidity impacts, a concentration limit of 5–10% may be imposed to prevent severe liquidation risk in the event of a counterparty defaulting.

5.4.4 Funding liquidity risk

The above considerations only come into play when a counterparty has actually defaulted. A more significant aspect of liquidity risk arises from the funding needs that arise due to CSAs. We refer to this as funding liquidity risk.

Despite the increased use of collateral, a significant portion of OTC derivatives remain uncollateralised. This arises mainly due to the nature of the counterparties involved, such as corporates and sovereigns, without the liquidity and operational capacity to adhere to daily collateral calls. In such cases, an institution must consider the funding implications that arise. Since most banks aim to run mainly flat (hedged) OTC derivatives books, funding costs arise from the nature of hedging: a non-CSA trade being hedged via a trade done within a CSA arrangement. This relationship was illustrated in Figure 5.7, where the institution will incur a funding cost when the uncollateralised trade moves in their favour and experience a benefit when the reverse happens. In the recent financial crisis where funding has become costly, the need to assess this carefully has become paramount. We dedicate Chapter 14 to discussing such aspects.

The implications of funding liquidity risk arising from CSAs are even more important for non-banking organisations such as institutional investors, corporates and sovereigns that trade under CSAs with banks.[11] The conversion of counterparty risk into funding liquidity risk will be beneficial in normal, liquid markets where funding costs are low. However, in abnormal markets where liquidity is poor, funding costs can become significant and may put extreme pressure on an institution.

The BP Deepwater Horizon oil spill. In 2010, British Petroleum (BP) experienced the largest accidental marine oil spill in the history of the petroleum industry. This caused loss of life, severe environment problems and, of course, severe financial losses for BP themselves. In the immediate aftermath, some banks gave some flexibility to BP in terms of collateral posting. An obvious way to interpret this is that the banks believed that, whilst BP was certainly experiencing significant idiosyncratic credit problems,

---

[10] In the case of the Long-Term Capital Management (LTCM) default, a very large proprietary position on Russian government bonds made these securities far from ideal as collateral. Even a European bank posting cash in Euros gives rise to a potentially problematic linkage.

[11] Note that the posting of collateral here by the institutions mentioned may be subject to downgrade triggers.

it was unlikely to default. Forcing the contractual posting of collateral (which may have been triggered by the resulting credit rating downgrades of the company) may have caused BP liquidity problems that would have made their default more likely.

The above is a good example of the dangers of funding liquidity risk. By not demanding collateral, a bank is essentially converting this risk back into counterparty risk, presumably with the view that long-term counterparty risk is better than short-term liquidity risk. The mitigation of counterparty risk via collateral is clearly useless in such a case.

5.5   SUMMARY

In this chapter we have discussed in detail the use of collateral management in controlling credit exposure, which is a crucial method when trading involving large positions and/or relatively risky counterparties. We have described the mechanics of collateral management and the variables that determine how much collateral would be posted. The significant risks that arise from collateral use have also been considered.

Collateral management should be understood as a way to improve recovery in the event of a counterparty actually defaulting but it is certainly not a replacement for a proper ongoing assessment of credit quality and quantification of credit exposure. Furthermore, the use of collateral mitigates counterparty risk but can aggravate funding liquidity risk and create other financial risks.

In our description of risk mitigation we have now covered all the methods of reducing credit exposure. We now move to assessing how counterparty risk can be reduced via the default probability of a counterparty.

6

Default Remote Entities and the Too Big to Fail Problem

> *We have a new kind of bank. It is called too big to fail. TBTF, and it is a wonderful bank.*
> Stewart B. McKinney (1931–1987)

6.1 INTRODUCTION

In the early days of the derivatives market, there was a tendency to deal only with the most creditworthy counterparties. Weaker credit quality counterparties were either excluded entirely or required to pay substantial premiums in order to trade. For many corporates and sovereigns, this would correspond to trading only with the most financially sound banks and broker dealers. Large dealers within the derivatives market needed strong credit ratings for this reason and set up Triple-A rated bankruptcy-remote subsidiaries – known as DPCs – to handle their derivatives dealing operations.

Obviously, the bankruptcy of Lehman Brothers and bailouts of other large banks have clearly had a very negative impact on the perceived long-term credit quality of banks globally. In addition, the trustworthiness of credit ratings has been severely reduced. For example, Lehman Brothers had a reasonably good "Single-A" rating at the time of its bankruptcy[1] and Icelandic banks had the best quality "Triple-A" ratings just weeks prior to their complete collapse.

6.1.1 Default remoteness and too big to fail

A "default remote entity" is a general concept that can be applied to several different ideas that have been or are important for the management of counterparty risk. The general idea of a default remote entity is that it provides a counterparty of such good credit quality that the default probability and thus the counterparty risk are essentially negligible. In the days when credit ratings were viewed as being informative, this generally applied to Triple-A credit quality. Such entities have proved historically very useful for mitigating counterparty risk as the default of the counterparty is argued to be a highly unlikely event. If this sounds too good to be true and implies a laziness in market practice then that is probably because it is, and it does.

---

[1] Standard & Poor's, one of the major credit rating agencies, have defended this since, claiming the Lehman Brothers bankruptcy was a result of "a loss of confidence . . . that fundamental credit analysis could not have anticipated". See http://www2.standardandpoors.com/spf/pdf/fixedincome/Lehman_Brothers.pdf

Related to a default remote concept is the well-known "too big to fail" one. Such a counterparty may well fail but it is simply too large and correlated to other risks to be allowed to fail. Hence, the same laziness in assessing counterparty risk can be applied. Too big to fail counterparties have been more formally known as systemically important financial institutions (SIFIs). Regulators are aiming to identify SIFIs (for example, via their size and linkage of assets and revenue to financial activities[2]) and break them up or demand that they face higher capital requirements and tougher regulatory scrutiny. Such efforts are aimed at avoiding a repeat of the abrupt collapse of Lehman Brothers and the financial catastrophe that this catalysed. Whilst these will be useful steps, a moral hazard problem will remain since institutions may trade with SIFIs purely on the basis that they believe they have implicit support from governments and central banks.

The idea of default-remoteness or too big to fail has proved to be the Achilles heel of financial markets with respect to counterparty risk. Triple-A ratings have been assigned to counterparties or legal entities based on flawed logic in relation to aspects such as the underlying business model or legal structure. Triple-A ratings may even be correct but just misunderstood. A more subtle problem, as discussed in detail in Chapter 15 in relation to wrong-way risk, is that the absolute credit quality of a counterparty should become less of a focus for very out-of-the-money products. Furthermore, moral hazard causes a behaviour of market participants in relation to the "too big to fail" institutions that further accentuates the illusion that there is little or no underlying counterparty risk. The failure of institutions such as AIG, Fannie Mae, Freddie Mac and monoline insurers has had a massive impact on the way in which counterparty risk is perceived and managed.

We will consider the role of derivatives product companies, monoline insurers and credit derivatives product companies within the financial markets and how ideas of their default-remoteness were so badly founded. Whilst this will be mainly a backward-looking reflection, the discussion will form the basis for some of the arguments in the next chapter examining the concept of central counterparties which themselves are essentially default-remote entities most of which are likely to be SIFIs.

Derivatives markets, like most markets, need some form of insurance or re-insurance in order to transfer risk or a method to mutualise losses. These are roles played respectively by monoline insurers and central counterparties. However, if this insurance or mutualisation fails then it can be catastrophic. We will discuss how this was the case for monoline insurers and ask the question as to why this happened and whether there are lessons to be learned, especially in terms of the rapidly expanded role that central counterparties will have in future OTC derivatives markets.

6.1.2 From OTC to exchange-traded

Exchange-traded derivatives are standardised liquid contracts with little or no counterparty risk since the exchange guarantees the derivative (and is probably too big to fail). The reason for all exchanges offering clearing services is the need to control counterparty risk. OTC derivatives markets, on the other hand, are very different with an institution being exposed to risks unique to each of their counterparties. Furthermore, there is no formal institution to provide guarantees and little formal regulation governing transactions. In the early days of OTC derivatives markets, the bankruptcy of major players caused problems.

---

[2] Obvious SIFIs are large banks but the categorisation could also apply to non-banks if they are considered large enough and have businesses that are likely to be intertwined with a financial downturn.

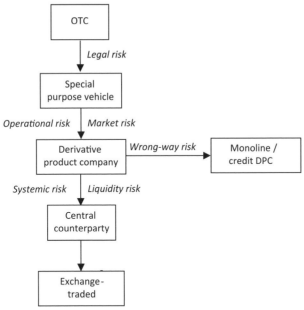

Figure 6.1 Illustration of the progression from OTC derivative to exchange-traded derivative via various approaches to managing counterparty risk together with the financial risks that are introduced.

The gulf between exchange-traded and OTC derivatives in terms of counterparty risk has been closed in several ways. All of these methods essentially replicate some of the benefits of an exchange while preserving the flexibility of OTC derivatives. This can be seen as a progression (although not a chronological one), as illustrated in Figure 6.1. The roles played by the intermediate entities shown are loosely defined as:

- *Special purpose vehicle (SPV)*. An SPV is a wrapper creating a bankruptcy-remote entity and giving a counterparty preferential treatment as a creditor in the event of a default.
- *Derivative product company (DPC)*. A DPC essentially takes this idea further by having additional capital and operational rules to reduce the counterparty risk for those trading with it. Monolines and credit DPCs can be seen as a specific application of this idea to credit derivative products.
- *Central counterparty (CCP)*. A CCP adds a more frequent collateral process and a membership organisation leading to loss mutualisation.

We will examine the structure and operation of these entities in more detail below. We note that the process may mitigate counterparty risk by converting it into different risks. For example, SPVs create legal risk, DPCs create operational and market risk, monolines and credit DPCs create wrong-way risk and central counterparties create systemic[3] and liquidity risks. These aspects will also be explored.

---

[3] CCPs are intended to reduce systemic risk but they can create it also, as described in the next chapter.

6.2   SPECIAL PURPOSE VEHICLES[4]

A special purpose vehicle (SPV), sometimes called a special purpose entity (SPE), is a legal entity (for example, a company or limited partnership) created typically to isolate a firm from financial risk. A company will transfer assets to the SPV for management or use the SPV to finance a large project without putting the entire firm or a counterparty at risk. Jurisdictions may require that an SPV is not owned by the entity on whose behalf it is being set up.

SPVs aim essentially to change bankruptcy rules so that, if a derivative counterparty is insolvent, a client can still receive their full investment prior to any other claims being paid out. SPVs are most commonly used in structured notes where they use this mechanism to guarantee the counterparty risk on the principal of the note to a very high level (Triple-A typically), better than that of the issuer. The creditworthiness of the SPV is assessed by rating agencies who look in detail at the mechanics and legal specifics before granting a rating.

An SPV transforms counterparty risk into legal risk. The obvious legal risk is that of *consolidation*, which is the power of a bankruptcy court to consolidate the SPV with the originator. The basis of consolidation is that the SPV is substantially the same as the originator. This would mean that the assets transferred to the SPV are treated as a part of the assets of the originator. Thus, the isolation of the SPV becomes irrelevant. Consolidation may depend on many aspects such as jurisdictions. US courts have a history of consolidation rulings, whereas UK courts have been less keen to do so, except in cases such as outright fraud.

Unfortunately, legal documentation often evolves through experience and the enforceability of the legal structure of SPVs was not tested for many years. When it was tested in the case of Lehman Brothers, there were problems, although this depended on jurisdiction. Lehman essentially used SPVs to shield investors in complex transactions such as CDOs from Lehman's own counterparty risk (in retrospect a great idea). The key provision in the documents is referred to as the "flip" provision, which essentially meant that if Lehman were bankrupt then the investors would be first in line for their investment. However, the US Bankruptcy Court ruled the flip clauses were unenforceable – putting them at loggerheads with the UK courts, which ruled the flip clauses *were* enforceable.

Just to add to the jurisdiction-specific question of whether a flip clause and therefore an SPV was a sound legal structure, Lehman has settled cases out of court.[5] The only thing that can be stated with certainty is that converting counterparty risk into legal risk is a dangerous process, as the SPV concept has illustrated.

6.3   DERIVATIVE PRODUCT COMPANIES

6.3.1   Standard DPCs

Long before the global financial crisis of 2007 onwards, whilst no major derivatives dealer had failed, the bilaterally cleared dealer-dominated OTC market was perceived as being inherently more vulnerable to counterparty risk than the exchange-traded market. The derivatives product company (or corporation) evolved as a means for OTC derivatives markets to

---

[4] Many of the aspects in this chapter could be described in the past tense. We use the present tense but note that many of the concepts around SPVs, DPCs and monolines are relevant only from a historical point of view.
[5] For example, see "Lehman opts to settle over Dante flip-clause transactions", http://www.risk.net/risk-magazine/news/1899105/lehman-opts-settle-dante-flip-clause-transactions

mitigate counterparty risk (e.g., see Kroszner, 1999). DPCs are generally Triple-A rated entities set up by one or more international banks. A DPC is typically a bankruptcy-remote subsidiary of a major dealer, which, unlike an SPV, is separately capitalised to obtain a Triple-A credit rating.[6] The DPC structure provides external counterparties with a degree of protection against counterparty risk by protecting against the failure of the DPC parent. A DPC therefore provides some of the benefits of the exchange-based system while preserving the flexibility and decentralisation of the OTC market. Examples of some of the first DPCs include Merrill Lynch Derivative Products, Salomon Swapco, Morgan Stanley Derivative Products and Lehman Brothers Financial Products.

The ability of a sponsor to create their own "mini derivatives exchange" via a DPC was partially as a result of improvements in risk management models and the development of credit rating agencies. DPCs maintain a Triple-A rating by a combination of capital, collateral and activity restrictions. Each DPC has its own quantitative risk assessment model to quantify their current credit risk. This is benchmarked against that required for a Triple-A rating. Most DPCs use a dynamic capital allocation to keep within the Triple-A credit risk requirements. The rating of a DPC typically depends on:

- *Minimising market risk.* In terms of market risk, DPCs can attempt to be close to market-neutral via trading offsetting contracts. Ideally, they would be on both sides of every trade as these "mirror trades" lead to an overall matched book. Normally the mirror trade exists with the DPC parent.
- *Support from a parent.* The DPC is supported by a parent with the DPC being bankruptcy-remote (like an SPV) with respect to the parent to achieve a better rating. If the parent were to default then the DPC would either pass to another well-capitalised institution or be terminated with trades settled at mid-market.
- *Credit risk management and operational guidelines (limits, collateral terms, etc.).* Restrictions are also imposed on (external) counterparty credit quality and activities (position limits, collateral, etc.). The management of counterparty risk is achieved by having daily MtM and collateral posting.

Whilst being of very good credit quality, DPCs also give further security by defining an orderly workout process. A DPC defines what events would trigger its own failure (rating downgrade of parent, for example) and how the resulting workout process would work. The resulting "pre-packaged bankruptcy" was therefore supposedly more simple (as well as less likely) than the standard bankruptcy of an OTC derivative counterparty. Broadly speaking, two approaches exist, namely a continuation and termination structure. In either case, a manager is responsible for managing and hedging existing positions (continuation structure) or terminating transactions (termination structure).

6.3.2 The decline of DPCs

There was nothing apparently wrong with the DPC idea, which apparently worked well since its creation in the early 1990s. DPCs were created in the early stages of the OTC derivatives market to facilitate trading of long-dated derivatives by counterparties having less than Triple-A credit quality. However, was such a Triple-A entity of a Double-A or worse bank

---

[6] Most DPCs derived their credit quality structurally via capital but some simply did so more trivially from the sponsor's rating.

really a better counterparty than the bank itself? In the early years, DPCs experienced steady growth in notional volumes, with business peaking in the mid-to-late 1990s. However, the increased use of collateral in the market, and the existence of alternative Triple-A entities, led to a declining demand for DPCs.

The global financial crisis essentially killed the already declining world of DPCs. After their parent's decline, the Bear Sterns DPCs were wound down by JP Morgan with clients compensated for novating trades. The voluntary filing for Chapter 11 by two Lehman Brothers DPCs, a strategic effort to protect the DPCs' assets, seems to link a DPC's fate inextricably with that of their parent. Not surprisingly, the perceived lack of autonomy of DPCs has led to a reaction from rating agencies who have withdrawn ratings.[7]

Whilst DPCs have not been responsible for any catastrophic events, they have become largely irrelevant. As in the case of SPVs, it is clear that the DPC concept is a flawed one and the perceived Triple-A ratings of DPCs had little credibility as the counterparty being faced was really the DPC parent, generally with a worse credit rating. Therefore, DPCs illustrate that a conversion of counterparty risk into other financial risks (in this case not only legal risk as for SPVs but also market and operational risks) simply doesn't work.

6.4   MONOLINES AND CREDIT DPCs

6.4.1   Rationale

As described above, the creation of DPCs was largely driven by the need for high-quality counterparties when trading OTC derivatives. However, this need was taken to another level with the birth and exponential growth of the credit derivatives market from around 1998 onwards.

The first credit derivative product was the single-name credit default swap (CDS). The CDS represents an unusual challenge since its value is driven by credit spread changes whilst its payoff is linked solely to one or more credit events. This so-called wrong-way risk (see Chapter 15 for more detail) meant that the credit quality of the CDS counterparty became even more important than it would be for other OTC derivatives. Beyond single-name credit default swaps, senior tranches of structured finance CDOs had even more wrong-way risk and created an even stronger need for a "default-remote entity". Put simply, the credit derivatives market needed Triple-A protection sellers and, given its rapid growth, it needed them fast.

6.4.2   Monoline insurers

Monoline insurance companies (and similar companies such as AIG[8]) are financial guarantee companies with Triple-A ratings that they utilise to provide *credit wraps* which are *financial guarantees*. Monolines began providing credit wraps for US municipal finance but then entered the single-name CDS and structured finance arena in a big way to achieve diversification and better returns. In order to justify their ratings, monolines have capital requirements driven by the possible losses on the structures they "wrap". For example, a rating

---

[7] For example, see "Fitch withdraws Citi Swapco's ratings", http://www.businesswire.com/news/home/20110610005841/en/Fitch-Withdraws-Citi-Swapcos-Ratings

[8] For the purposes of this analysis we will categorise monoline insurers and AIG as the same type of entity, which, based on their activities in the credit derivatives market, is fair.

agency may consider both a base case and stress scenario and set the monoline capital requirements as a required percentage (100% or more) of the losses in these scenarios. The monoline capital requirements are also dynamically related to the portfolio of assets they wrap, which is similar to the workings of the DPC structure.

The expected (and even stressed) losses for a monoline are expected to be low due to the good-quality assets they wrap (often Triple-A themselves). This means that the amount of capital a monoline holds compared with the total amount of notional insured is small. The implicit leverage of a monoline can therefore be quite high. Due to this high leverage, a monoline has a problem with negative MtM changes on positions since losses will be magnified by the leverage factor. However, being an insurance company, they do not have to consider the mark-to-market of their positions. Nor do monolines have to post collateral (at least in normal times) against a decline in the mark-to-market value of their contracts (due to their historical Triple-A credit rating). This is just as well since posting collateral is essentially the same as marking-to-market in terms of forcing losses to be realised.

Since monolines do not post collateral, they will adhere to the strict operating guidelines summarised below, which in theory justify the Triple-A rating. The basic aim is to require that once the monoline no longer justifies Triple-A credit quality, as measured dynamically via the capital model, it may be required to post collateral to mitigate the increased counter-party risk:

- *Normal state*. The monoline will typically be rated Triple-A partly because of a (ratings-based) capital model which is run daily for the exposures it faces. As long as the required capital does not exceed the actual available equity capital (unexpected loss) then the company can operate within its normal operating guidelines.
- *Restricted state*. This typically is invoked if a capital breach has occurred and will result in restrictions on investments and funding. After a certain period, the Triple-A rating may be withdrawn at the discretion of the rating agency and this in turn may trigger contractual clauses requiring the posting of collateral. In theory, a monoline can return to a normal state and regain their Triple-A rating by raising new capital or restructuring/unwinding existing trades.
- *Run-off*. This corresponds to a hibernation state where the monoline will essentially be static, trades will gradually mature and any default losses will be settled as and when they occur (assuming there is equity capital to cover them). There is no recovery from this state and, whilst it is not the same as a bankruptcy, in practice the result is similar.

Does the above quite complex operating structure of a monoline essentially provide some magical way of reducing counterparty risk? We have already seen that similar questions for SPVs and DPCs imply a negative answer. Why should monolines be any different?

6.4.3   Credit derivative product company

A credit derivative product company (CDPC) is essentially a vehicle inspired by the DPC and monoline concepts described above. CDPCs extend the DPC idea to credit derivative products. A CDPC is a special purpose entity set up to invest in credit derivatives products on a leveraged basis, typically selling protection on corporate, sovereign and asset-backed securities in single-name or portfolio form as CDS contracts. CDPC sponsors include asset managers, hedge funds, insurers and banks. However, whereas a DPC is simply a bankruptcy-remote subsidiary of an institution, a CDPC was an entity set up with the aim of making profit from selling credit derivative protection. Like monolines, CDPCs have the three operating modes described above.

A CDPC will typically offer to provide single-name and, more importantly, tranche protection on credit portfolios. CDPCs may have offsetting positions to some extent, for example, by buying and selling single-name protection. However, in general they break a key rule of a DPC, which is that they have significant market risk due to not having a balanced set of positions. CDPCs therefore have a problem created by the asymmetry of risk for CDS positions, compared, for example, with traditional swaps. They fill a role as a Triple-A counterparty but do so largely on only one side of the market,[9] as sellers of credit protection.

6.4.4 The massive monoline failure

From 2000 onwards, as a result of their massively expanded (and highly profitable) structured credit activities, banks were generating massive amounts of so-called "super senior" exposure, largely from pools of mortgage loans. For reasons which were often regulatory and not economically motivated,[10] banks needed to offload such exposures even though they were considered virtually risk-free. Monoline insurers such as MBIA, FGIC, AMBAC or other insurers like AIG were Triple-A rated and seemed therefore to be ideal counterparties for such transactions. Since they would potentially benefit most from assets offering the most substantial risk premiums, super senior tranches were attractive investments. Banks were comfortable with such a risk transfer, for example the following is from a bank's credit research department published in 2001:

The credit quality of monolines (quote[11] from 2001) "The major monoline bond insurers enjoy impeccably strong credit quality, offering investors excellent credit protection, which combined with the underlying issuer is tantamount to better than triple A risk. In fact, the risk of capital loss for investors is practically zero and the risk of a downgrade slightly greater. Given the state of their risk profiles, the triple A ratings of the monolines are well entrenched. Each of the four major monolines display adequate capital levels, ample claims paying resources against risk positions and limited if any single large exposures."

By not posting collateral, monolines can avoid MtM losses, which might otherwise push them into bankruptcy. They can essentially try and "ride the wave" of short-term volatility and illiquidity that may imply large losses on positions. However, does this enhance their credit quality from the point of view of an institution trading with them? If monolines were required to post collateral then an institution could always retain the option to waive a collateral call if they believed it would enhance the financial stability of the monoline (protection

---

[9] Some CDPCs have taken both long and short positions but this has not been especially common.

[10] For example, banks needed to offload super senior exposures not because economically they did not want the exposure but more because it led to large capital requirements and limited the ability to take profits on structured credit transactions.

[11] See http://www.securitization.net/pdf/nabl_mono_0402.pdf. It should be noted that this report was written a number of years before the financial crisis prior to the monolines undertaking the activities that were to lead to their downfall.

seller) in the long run. However, by doing this they would be taking a firm bet that the monoline's position would (re)gain value in the future. However, for the monoline to gain in the future, the institution (protection buyer) must lose money. The Triple-A rating gained from not posting collateral just does not add up.

We note the posting of collateral means the crystallisation of losses for the monoline. Without the need to post collateral, a monoline can always hope that any MtM losses will be regained at some point in the future. However, in the common scenario that ratings degradation of a portfolio is preceded by MtM losses, then significant losses are likely. This may lead to the monoline being essentially suffocated due to being unable to post collateral or unwind/ restructure trades to reduce the capital accordingly. This creates a "death spiral" where a monoline is unable to regain its Triple-A rating and is eventually forced into some form of termination (for example, see definition in previous section).

The Triple-A ratings granted to monolines are interesting in that they were typically achieved due to the monoline *not* being obliged to post collateral against transactions. Hence, an institution trading with a monoline is critically relying on this Triple-A rating to minimise their counterparty risk. One might reasonably ask the question as to why an institution's credit quality is somehow improved by the fact that they do *not* post collateral (monolines would typically be unable to gain Triple-A ratings if they entered into collateral agreements). Indeed, this point is a first clue to the fundamental flaw in the Triple-A ratings granted to monolines. Nevertheless, there is another more worrying way to look at the need for monolines to not post collateral. It would have been impossible for them to enter the structured finance area in the same way if they had been required to post collateral since mark-to-market volatility would have severely limited their leverage capabilities. Consider the following example:

Example A monoline provides financial guarantees or credit wraps on a total of $10bn notional of structured finance underlyings. Since these underlyings are of very good credit quality, the expected losses are 0.3% ($30 m) and the losses in a stress scenario are 0.9% ($90 m). The monoline has capital of $100 m set against possible losses and achieves a Triple-A rating.

Now suppose the monoline experiences MtM losses on its positions of 2%* or $200 m. Does it still justify a Triple-A rating?

*Assume the average duration of the positions is 8 years. A spread widening of 25 bps across the board would result in such a loss, i.e., it is not a particularly extreme event.

The answer to the above problem is yes . . . and no. Yes, the monoline would still justify a Triple-A rating based on the assessment of its capital against expected or stressed losses, which would not have changed since they are based on statistical estimates (this has been the standard practice of rating agencies). No, since if the monoline were forced to unwind its positions immediately then it would default with no better than a 50% recovery rate (likely to be worse due to the costs and impact of unwinding a large notional of positions). If the monoline were required to post collateral then it would be forced into bankruptcy.

In December 2007 the market was around four months into a "credit crisis" that was to become a global financial crisis and prove longer and more painful than most market participants thought possible. Concerns started to rise over the Triple-A ratings of monolines and that they had insufficient capital to justify their ratings. However, this placed the ratings agencies in a subtle situation since the downgrading of monolines would potentially trigger a chain reaction. Investors would be required to mark down assets due to loss of Triple-A ratings (on these assets) and monolines would potentially be forced to raise more capital due to being required to post collateral against positions with exposed counterparties. Swift ratings action could therefore have triggered an immediate crisis with so much resting on the viability of the monolines' ratings. For example, in November 2007 ACA Financial Guarantee Corporation stated that a loss of its Single-A credit rating would trigger a need to post collateral, which they would not be able to meet. On the other hand, by leaving the monoline rating alone, as long as the crisis did not worsen, then some MtM losses would eventually be recovered (due to spreads tightening again on assets that were of high credit quality) and the ratings would again look firm.

It is difficult when ratings agencies find themselves in this type of situation where the removal of a Triple-A rating (or Single-A in the case of ACA), whilst the correct action, causes default of the monoline (and potential systemic failure of all monolines). Rating agencies appeared to choose a wait-and-see approach to monolines at the start of the credit crisis, seemingly implicitly making a bet that the crisis would be a short one. For example:

- *XL Financial Assurance Ltd.* In December 2007, Standard & Poor's (S&P) reaffirmed the rating of XL Financial Assurance Ltd with negative outlook. In late December, Fitch placed their Triple-A rating under review, saying that $2bn of new capital needed to be raised. By mid-2008, XL Financial Assurance Ltd had been downgraded below investment grade by at least one rating agency. In May, Syncora Guarantee (the monoline formerly known as XL Capital Assurance) suffered a credit event.
- *AMBAC Insurance Corporation.* In early 2008, Moody's and S&P affirmed Ambac's Triple-A rating after it succeeded in raising new capital. In June 2008, Moody's downgraded Ambac's credit rating three notches to Aa3. Since then, their rating continued to decline until they finally filed for Chapter 11 bankruptcy protection in November 2010.
- *MBIA Insurance Corporation.* In February 2008, Moody's affirmed the Triple-A rating of MBIA but in June 2008 they downgraded MBIA's credit rating 5 notches to A2 and by November 2008 it had been further downgraded further to Baa1. In June 2009, the rating had further deteriorated to Ba1 and then in March 2010 it was B3.

The death of monolines as measured by the equity markets was much more sudden, as Figure 6.2 illustrates for MBIA and AMBAC.

Many banks found themselves heavily exposed to monolines due to the massive increase in the value of the protection they had purchased. For example, as of June 2008, UBS was estimated to have $6.4bn at risk to monoline insurers whilst the equivalent figures for Citigroup and Merrill Lynch were $4.8bn and $3bn, respectively (*Financial Times*, 2008).

The situation with AIG was more or less the same, as the joint result of a ratings downgrade and AIG's positions moved against them rapidly, leading to the requirement to post large amounts of collateral. This essentially crystallised massive losses for AIG and led to potentially large losses for their counterparties if they were to fail. The latter did not happen since AIG was bailed out by the US Government to the tune of approximately $182bn. Why AIG was bailed out and the monoline insurers were not could be put down to the size

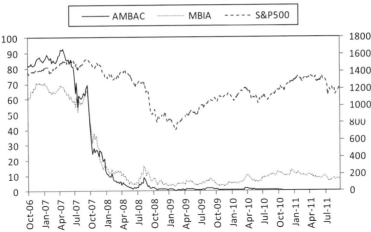

Figure 6.2 Share price (in dollars) of the monoline insurers AMBAC and MBIA (left axis) compared to the S&P500 index (right axis).

of AIG[12] and the timing of their problems (close to the Lehman Brothers bankruptcy and Fannie Mae/Freddie Mac problems).

CDPCs, like monolines, are highly leveraged and typically do not post collateral. They fared somewhat better during the credit crisis but only for timing reasons. Many CDPCs were not fully operational until after the beginning of the credit crisis in July 2007. They therefore missed at least the first "wave" of losses suffered by any party short credit protection (especially super senior[13]). Nevertheless, the fact that the CDPC business model is close to that of monolines has not been ignored. For example, in October 2008, Fitch withdrew ratings on the five CDPCs that it rated.[14]

Was the monolines' and CDPCs' venture into structured finance a case of being in the wrong place at the wrong time and is the difference between a good and bad monoline/ CDPC simply a matter of timing?

There are strong arguments that the monoline insurer business model was fatally flawed all along. An insurance company typically has a long-term view and aims to remain largely immune to any short-term market volatility (and possible losses) and focus mainly on long-term returns. This can stabilise markets by balancing out the herd mentalities that sometimes exist in volatile markets. However, insurance companies must not become too highly exposed to a single risk type. From this point of view, the term "monoline insurer" appears to be a misnomer. Whilst the insurance term "monoline" does not mean that they operate in only a single market, it does imply they do not diversify into other forms of insurance, such as life or property. Knowing how interconnected financial markets can be, a monoline diversified across different asset-backed and corporate securities investments does not sound very diversified at all. From the point of view of the buyer of insurance, i.e., the banks, this would be like purchasing property insurance from a company that insured only the houses in your neighbourhood.

---

[12] Whilst the monolines together had approximately the same amount of exposure as AIG, their failures were at least partially spaced out.
[13] The widening in super senior spreads was on a relative basis much greater than credit spreads in general during late 2007.
[14] See, for example, "Fitch withdraws CDPC ratings", *Business Wire*, 2008.

Another clue as to the inherent problems with monolines is that the motivation for insurance is aversion to large losses (tail losses). However, it must be emphasised that if it is worth having an insurance contract then one must be able to envisage the scenario in which the insurance is needed. Prior to 2007, banks buying insurance from monolines saw the resulting "negative basis trade" as an accounting trick and not insurance they would ever need and neither the ratings agencies nor the monolines themselves thought they would ever face financial distress. This is dangerous since, for example, Thompson (2009) shows that if an insurer has a belief that a claim is highly unlikely to occur, they will invest in more illiquid assets, which earn higher returns. The safer the underlying claim is perceived to be, the more severe the resulting moral hazard problem and consequently the higher the counterparty risk. This result seems to link very directly to monolines looking to insure the illiquid Triple-A tranches of structured finance transactions.

6.4.5 Why the rating agencies got it wrong

The serious problems for monolines and CDPCs showed their business model to be fundamentally flawed as it rapidly became clear that they had insured insane amounts of risk with relatively miniscule amounts of capital to protect against actual defaults. The rating agencies, who assigned the much-coveted Triple-A ratings awarded to these institutions, have also been heavily criticised. The failure of monolines had a knock-on effect as banks suffered billions of dollars of write-downs as a result of the now almost worthless insurance they held.

A key element of bankruptcy-remote entities such as DPCs, monolines and CDPCs is the Triple-A rating since without this coveted measure of creditworthiness they have practically no value. The crucial aspect of these Triple-A ratings from the point of view of investors is that they are largely given after quantification of future losses based on historical data. Let us try to illustrate some potential pitfalls to understand where the ratings went wrong.

First, consider a simple monoline that sells protection on a portfolio security (for example, a CDO tranche which will be discussed in more detail in Chapter 10), which itself has a Triple-A rating. Rating agencies typically use an expected loss-based measure to define such a Triple-A rating.[15] Now, suppose the monoline has just a dollar of capital – a ridiculous notion. However, on an expected loss basis the monoline is Triple-A rated[16] since it can only make a loss when the CDO tranche takes a loss (a Triple-A probability) and even then it has capital (albeit only one dollar!) to set aside against such a loss. This is illustrated in Figure 6.3. Assigning a Triple-A rating to the monoline is meaningless since it just restates the fact that the underlying CDO tranche itself is Triple-A, which does not provide any additional information to a counterparty.

Of course, ratings agencies were not so naïve as to apply such a flawed methodology to assign a Triple-A rating (although they seemed to do little more than use metrics other than expected loss to quantify future losses of the vehicle in question; see, e.g., Tzani and Chen, 2006; Remeza, 2007). However, this example does illustrate a potential pitfall in that a monoline or CDPC-type vehicle might appear to have Triple-A credit quality largely because they sell protection on (or wrap) Triple-A underlyings. A counterparty buying protection from such a vehicle would need significantly more reassurance regarding their

---

[15] S&P have always rated CDOs based on a first dollar of loss or equivalent default probability basis but the same argument will follow in this case.

[16] This follows from the simple mathematical idea that $E[(L - \alpha)^+] \leq E[L]$ as long as α is a positive quantity.

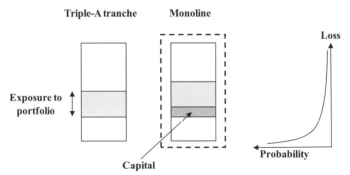

Figure 6.3 Illustration of the illusion by which a monoline (or similar entity such as a CDPC) may always appear to have a Triple-A rating as long as they insure ("wrap") a Triple-A underlying. The monoline provides a guarantee on the Triple-A tranche shown. As long as they have some additional capital (however small), the expected loss of the monoline can be no worse than the Triple-A tranche.

creditworthiness since, if the underlying in question suffers losses, they need there to be a strong likelihood that the vehicle will still be solvent in order to honour their contract.

6.4.6 A (very simple) quantitative analysis of monolines

We can illustrate the problems with a monoline (or CDPC) using a very simple model for the value of protection purchased on a non-collateralised basis. The model assumes a digital payoff for the protection purchased[17] and requires a parameter that represents the correlation between the value of the digital contract and the inverse[18] credit quality of the counterparty. The formula is given in Appendix 6A for reference. We assume the monoline has a default probability (during the life of the contract) of 0.1%. In Figure 6.4 we show, as a function of

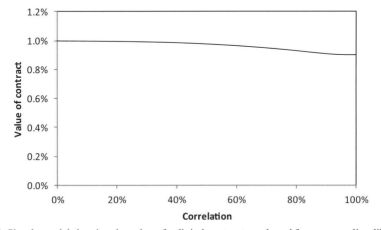

Figure 6.4 Simple model showing the value of a digital contract purchased from a monoline-like counterparty with no collateral posting as a function of correlation. The value of the risk-free digital contract is 1%.

---

[17] This is relevant for a single-name CDS and hence is only an approximation for a portfolio structure as in a CDO tranche.

[18] As the value of the contract increases, the credit quality of the monoline deteriorates.

correlation, the value of such a digital contract with a risk-free value of 1%. We can see that the value is close to this value for all correlations, although it is slightly diminished when the correlation is high. In this case, counterparty risk does not appear to be a major problem.

Spreadsheet 6.1 Simple monoline example

We show a similar example in Figure 6.5 with the only difference being that the risk-free value of the digital contract is just 0.05% (more akin to the event probabilities the monolines were dealing with[19]). Now there is fundamentally different behaviour since, whilst at low levels of correlation the value of the contract is close to 0.05%, at a higher correlation the contract value can be significantly less and eventually worthless.

This simple model illustrates that, for example, buying insurance on a Single-A credit from a Triple-A insurer does not obviously cause a problem but buying insurance on a better than Triple-A credit from that same Triple-A insurer is a crazy notion.

More formally, there are two important points we discuss in more detail in Chapter 15:

- Wrong-way risk increases with correlation (between the monoline's default and the value of the underlying contract).
- Wrong-way risk is dramatically more severe for more out-of-the-money contracts (e.g. more senior tranches).

The original historical activity of monolines, insuring debt such as municipal bonds, does not cause a conflict with the above points but their activities in structured credit did. This is because they specialised in the rather senior (out-of-the-money) tranches. Secondly, their

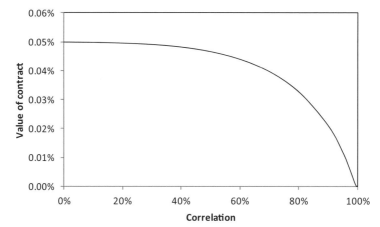

Figure 6.5 Simple model showing the value of a digital contract purchased from a monoline-like counterparty with no collateral posting as a function of correlation. The value of the risk-free digital contract is 0.05%.

---

[19] Or at least they thought they were.

involvement in this market became so large (in terms of notional insured – which was in the tens of billions of US dollars) that the correlation between the value of such assets and their own default probability was by construction extremely high.

The reader may ask from whom banks could have purchased the billions of dollars of insurance for Triple-A and better tranches that they required in order to support their thriving and profitable structured credit businesses. The answer is probably that, due to the inherent counterparty risk, there was simply no way of affecting such a large notional risk transfer. A realisation of this by the banks or their regulators would have significantly curtailed the securitisation of mortgages, averting any "originate to distribute" activity and therefore possibly avoiding the need for a global financial crisis.

6.5   CENTRAL COUNTERPARTIES

6.5.1   Introduction

The lesson so far – after considering SPVs, DPCs, monolines and CDPCs – appears to be that relying on a default-remote entity as one's counterparty is a poor way to mitigate counterparty risk. No matter what their underlying credit quality, never assume your counterparty cannot possibly fail. Assuming they are too big to fail may be more reasonable but this creates moral hazard, which, at least from a regulator's and policymaker's perspective, is highly unpleasant. It might seem strange then that the solution to counterparty risk is another default-remote entity, called a CCP.

The global financial crisis from 2007 onwards triggered grave concerns regarding counterparty risk, catalysed by events such as Lehman Brothers, the failure of monoline insurers (with Triple-A ratings), the bankruptcy of Icelandic banks (more Triple-A ratings) and losses arising from some (yes, you've guessed it, Triple-A) structured products. Counterparty risk in OTC derivatives, especially credit derivatives, was identified as a major risk to the financial system. Whilst there are many ways to control and quantify counterparty risk better, in times of crisis maybe it is natural to look for a panacea. A central counterparty (CCP) offers such a solution since counterparties would simply trade with one another through the CCP, which would effectively act as guarantor to all trades. All OTC derivatives traded through a CCP would then be free of counterparty risk.

In 2010, both Europe (via the European Commission's formal legislative proposal for regulation on OTC derivatives, central counterparties and trade repositories) and the US (via the Dodd–Frank Wall Street Reform and Consumer Protection Act) put forward proposals that would commit all standardised OTC derivatives to be cleared through CCPs by the end of 2012. Part of the reason for this was that, when the financial markets were in meltdown after the collapse of Lehman Brothers in September 2008, CCPs were more or less alone in operating well. As a result, policymakers seemed to focus on CCPs as something close to a panacea for counterparty risk, especially with respect to the more dangerous products such as credit default swaps.

Whilst counterparty risk in OTC derivatives markets has remained primarily a bilateral matter, the growth of the interest rate, foreign exchange, equity derivatives and commodities markets has not been dramatically held back (although firms have certainly needed to advance their methods for risk management). Arguably, it is the dramatic growth of the credit derivatives market in the past decade, together with the global financial crisis, that triggered the significant interest in CCPs.

6.5.2 Exchanges and clearing

Exchange-traded derivatives are rather standardised, transparent products with no counterparty risk. This is because the exchange or a third party normally guarantees the contract, which is the clearing function of the exchange that virtually all exchanges offer through the associated CCP. The disadvantages of exchanges are that products must be highly standardised and liquid. Indeed, the progression of a derivative product from its creation until the day it becomes exchange-traded is a long one.

One can trace the CCP idea all the way back to the 19th century (and even further), when exchanges were used for futures trading. Originally, such exchanges were simply trading forums without any settlement or counterparty risk management functions. Transactions were still done on a bilateral basis and trading through the exchange simply provided certification by the counterparty being a member of the exchange. The development of "clearing rings" followed as a means of standardisation to ease aspects such as closing out positions and enhancing liquidity. After this, methods for mitigating counterparty risk, such as margining, were developed. Finally, by the late 19th century, there was some sort of loss mutualisation via financial contributions to form reserves to absorb member default losses. Virtually all exchange-traded contracts are now, by default, subject to CCP clearing. The CCP function may either be operated by the exchange or provided to the exchange as a service by an independent company.

Exchange-traded derivatives initially dominated OTC derivatives markets due to the benefits in terms of liquidity and counterparty risk management provided by exchanges. However, OTC derivatives growth has been substantial in the past three decades thanks to advances in quantitative finance, risk management and hedging, and the notional size of the OTC derivatives markets has grown significantly to exceed that of exchange-traded derivatives. OTC and exchange-traded derivatives have generally two distinct mechanisms for clearing and settlement: bilateral for OTC derivatives and CCP for exchange-traded structures. Risk management practices, such as collateralisation, are dealt with bilaterally by the counterparties to each OTC contract, whereas for exchange-traded derivatives the risk management functions are typically carried out by the associated CCP.

However, an OTC derivative does not have to become exchange-traded to benefit from central clearing. CCPs have for many years operated as separate entities to control counterparty risk by mutualising it amongst the CCP members. In 2009, almost half the interest-rate swap market was centrally cleared by LCH Clearnet (although almost all other OTC derivatives were still bilaterally traded).

6.5.3 Basics of central clearing

A key concept in central clearing is that of contract novation. Novation means that the exchange essentially steps in-between parties to a transaction (see Figure 6.6) and therefore acts as an insurer of counterparty risk in both directions. In order for a clearing entity to act in this way, strong counterparty risk management techniques such as daily margining and loss mutualisation are required.

In a CCP world the failure of a counterparty, even one as large and interconnected as Lehman, is supposedly less dramatic. This is because the CCP absorbs the "domino effect" by acting as a central shock absorber. In the event of default of one of its members (say C), a CCP will aim to swiftly sever financial relations with that counterparty without suffering any

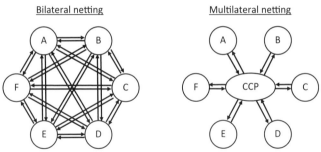

Figure 6.6 Illustration of the exchange and CCP concepts in reducing the complexity of bilateral trading.

losses. From the point of view of surviving members, the CCP guarantees the performance of their trades with C. This will normally be achieved not by closing out and exchanging the fair valuation but rather by replacement of counterparty C with one of the other clearing members for each trade. This is typically achieved via the CCP auctioning the defaulted members' positions amongst the other members.[20]

The CCP concept is obviously is not without its drawbacks. A CCP, by its very nature, represents a membership organisation, which therefore results in the pooling of member resources to some degree. This means that any losses due to the default of a CCP member may be to some extent shared amongst the surviving members. This risk-sharing creates *moral hazard*, which is a well-known problem in, for example, the insurance industry. Moral hazard has negative impacts such as disincentivising good counterparty risk management practice by CCP members (since all the risk is passed to the CCP). Institutions have no incentive to monitor each other's credit quality and act appropriately because a third party is taking all the risk.

CCPs are also vulnerable to *adverse selection* which occurs, for example, if members trading OTC derivatives know more about the risks than the CCP themselves (for example, the wrong-way risk). In such a situation, firms may selectively pass these more risky products to CCPs rather than the less risky ones. Obviously, firms such as large banks specialise in OTC derivatives and may have better information and knowledge on pricing and risk than a CCP.

As illustrated in Figure 6.6, CCPs will change dramatically the topology of the global financial system. An obvious problem here is that a CCP represents the centre of a "hub and spoke" system and consequently its failure would be a major systemic and financially catastrophic event (even in the context of the recent global financial crisis). Nevertheless, do the advantages of using CCPs to mitigate OTC counterparty risk outweigh the disadvantages? It is often stated that CCPs will reduce the interconnections between institutions, especially those that are SIFIs. However, CCPs will rather change the connections – potentially in a favourable way of course.

Likewise, it is also stated that CCPs will reduce systemic risk. This is not clear as CCPs may clearly reduce systemic risk (for example, by lessening the impact of a large counterparty default) but also have the possibility to increase systemic risk in various ways. Overall, in accordance with a concept that has been mentioned many times already, CCPs will not lessen counterparty risk but rather distribute it and convert it into different forms such as liquidity, operational and legal risks. CCPs concentrate these risks in a single place and therefore magnify the systemic risk linked to their own potential failure.

---

[20] A CCP also aids transparency due to seeing the positions of all members.

One thing is for sure, policymakers are ensuring that a large portion of the OTC derivatives market will be moved to centralised clearing over the coming years. This is clearly a highly significant dynamic for all market participants. Hence, we have to understand in detail the function of a CCP and the positives and negatives when trading through them. Only after understanding the precise workings of a CCP and tracing what happens to the counterparty risk they mitigate will it be possible to attempt to understand the likely benefits of the large move to central clearing. We will dedicate Chapter 7 to doing this.

7

Central Counterparties

7.1 CENTRALISED CLEARING

In this chapter, we consider the role of central counterparties (CCPs) to provide a means for centralisation, mutualisation and reduction of counterparty risk. Following the global financial crisis that started in 2007, there has been a significant regulatory interest in expanding the role of CCPs for mitigating counterparty risk. In particular, the interest has been strong for credit derivatives products with their embedded wrong-way risks. Channelling OTC derivatives transactions through CCPs has two main objectives. The first is to reduce counterparty credit risk. The second is to increase transparency so that regulators are more easily able to quantify the positions being taken and carry out stress tests. We will discuss the function of a CCP in detail and aim to highlight the strengths, weaknesses and possible unintended consequences of a large move towards central clearing. Around a quarter of the OTC derivatives market (by notional) is already centrally cleared and this fraction is likely to increase significantly over the coming years. Clearly, a close look at the strengths and weaknesses of central clearing is relevant.

7.1.1 Systemic risk

One of the key concerns over the global OTC derivatives market has always been systemic risk. Systemic risk does not have a firm definition but is essentially financial system instability exacerbated by distress of financial intermediaries. In the context of counterparty risk, systemic risk could arise from the failure of a large financial institution or intermediary and the inevitable knock-on effects, creating financial problems for other market participants. These institutions may then, in turn, fail and continue the "domino effect".

Systemic risk will therefore generally involve some initial spark followed by a proceeding chain reaction, potentially leading to some sort of explosion in financial markets. Thus, in order to control systemic risk, one can either minimise the chance of the initial spark, attempt to ensure that the chain reaction does not occur or simply plan that the explosion is controlled and the resulting damage limited.

Reducing the default risk of large, important market participants reduces the possibility of an initial spark caused by one of them failing. Capital regulation and prudential supervision can contribute to this but there is a balance between reduction of default risk and encouraging financial firms (and the economy) to grow and prosper. DPCs and monolines, discussed previously, are good examples of this balance. Placing very stringent capital and operational limitations on such an entity will make it extremely creditworthy and yet simultaneously make it impossible to generate the returns required to function profitably as a corporation. However, without the correct management and regulation, ultimately, even financial institutions that once seemed like fortresses can collapse.

Given that firms will inevitably fail, having efficient market mechanisms and structures for containing the failure of key firms in place and absorbing a large shock is key. OTC derivatives markets have netting, collateral and other methods to minimise counterparty risk. However, such aspects create more complexity and may catalyse growth to a level that would never have otherwise been possible. Hence, it can be argued that initiatives to stifle a chain reaction may achieve precisely the opposite and create the catalyst (such as many large exposures supported by a complex web of collateral) to cause the explosion.

The ultimate solution to systemic risk may therefore be simply to have the means in place to manage periodic explosions in a controlled manner, which is the role of a CCP. If there is a failure of a key market participant then the CCP will guarantee all the contracts of that counterparty executed through them as "clearing members". This will mitigate concerns faced by institutions and prevent any extreme actions by those institutions that could worsen the crisis. Any unexpected losses[1] caused by the failure of one or more counterparties will be shared amongst all members of the CCP (just as insurance losses are essentially shared by all policyholders) rather than being concentrated within a smaller number of institutions that may be heavily exposed to the failing counterparty. This "loss mutualisation" is a key component as it mitigates systemic risk and prevents a domino effect.

7.1.2   The impact of the crisis

In 2007, a US housing crisis led to a credit crisis, which caused the failures of large financial institutions and a severe economic downturn. Authorities had to make key decisions over failing institutions such as Lehman and AIG with a very opaque view of the situations the firms were in and the potential knock-on impact of any decisions made. The dramatic increase in counterparty risk in the early stages of the global financial crisis and the realisation that no counterparty was immune to potential financial distress brought many calls for a dramatic solution. Regulators were swift to act and CCPs seemed to emerge as a panacea for solving counterparty risk problems.

For example, US policymakers fast-tracked a number of changes to improve the derivatives markets, in particular with respect to CDS contracts. In May 2009, the Obama administration (through the US treasury) proposed a new framework for greater market regulation and oversight of the OTC derivatives market.[2] This framework, broadly speaking, mandated central clearing of all CDS transactions as well as prudent regulation of CDS market participants and increased transparency. At the end of 2008, the SEC approved a series of temporary conditional exceptions that allowed trading index CDSs through CCPs without the delays and hurdles that full regulation would create. The SEC did this in the belief that a

---

[1] Meaning those above a certain level that will be discussed later.
[2] Press Release, US Department of Treasury, *Regulatory Reform OTC Derivatives*, 13th May 2009 (http://ustreas.gov/press/releases/tg129.htm).

CCP can reduce systemic risk, operational risks, market manipulation and fraud and contribute to overall market stability.[3]

By late 2010, both EU (via the European Commission) and US regulation (via the Dodd–Frank Wall Street Reform and Consumer Protection Act) had published formal legislative proposals that all standardised OTC derivatives should be cleared through CCPs. Basel III capital requirements (Chapter 17), first published in 2009, incentives central clearing through relatively low capital requirements for CCP-cleared (as opposed to bilateral) trades. Whilst there will be technical standards and implementation details to be decided, it appears clear that the OTC derivatives market will move significantly more towards central clearing in the coming years.

7.1.3   CCPs in perspective

Most CCPs were originally created by the members of futures exchanges to manage default risk more efficiently and were not designed as the saviour of the global financial system. However, they operated well in the otherwise chaotic financial markets around the Lehman default and this appears to be a key driver for the logic behind regulators and policymakers deciding that the future OTC derivatives market needs to be mainly CCP-based. However, many market participants do not believe that CCPs will definitely make financial markets a better and safer place in the long-term.

The aim of this chapter is to present a critical analysis of CCPs, without attempting the futile task of predicting what their overall impact on future financial markets will be. Some important points to explore are:

- A CCP cannot make counterparty risk disappear. It can only centralise it in a single place and convert it into different forms of risk such as operational and liquidity.
- As with most risk mitigation, for every advantage of a CCP, there are related disadvantages. The benefit of a CCP is not to be a panacea but rather to lead to more advantages than disadvantages.
- CCPs can *reduce* systemic risk (which is well documented) but can also *increase* it.
- There are likely to be unintended consequences of the expanded use of CCPs, which are hard to predict *a priori*.

CCP must have a fine-tuned structure with respect to collateralisation, settlement and risk management and obviously must be extremely unlikely to fail. Furthermore, the very nature of what a CCP does creates potentially dangerous problems such as moral hazard and adverse selection. Finally, the failure of a CCP will clearly be an extremely problematic event, potentially far worse than the failure of any other financial institution.

A large part of the motivation for the regulatory push towards central clearing arises from strong concerns regarding the regulation and practices within the CDS market. However, such concerns must not be overstated due to the unprecedented nature of the crisis. The start of the crisis was largely the result of systematic mispricing of mortgage-related debt and not directly due to the growth of the credit derivatives market. The systemic failure of counterparty risk in CDSs occurred only because of regulated financial guarantors (such as AIG) selling risky protection on assets such as MBS. AIG's excessive risk-taking via CDSs was

---

[3] See http://sec.gov/rules/exorders/2008/34-59164.pdf

part of a broader problem related to seeking returns from mispriced mortgages and mortgage-backed securities.

7.1.4 Function of a CCP

As mentioned already, a CCP is traditionally an entity set up to manage the counterparty risk that exists on an exchange. All derivatives exchanges have adopted some form of CCP. Clearing is what takes place between trade execution and trade settlement (when all legal obligations have been made). When trading a derivative, the counterparties agree to fulfil specific obligations to each other. By interposing itself between two counterparties, which are clearing members, a CCP assumes all such contractual rights and responsibilities. As a result, an institution no longer needs to be concerned about the credit quality of its counterparty, indeed the counterparty to all intents and purposes is the CCP.

The legal process whereby the CCP is positioned between buyer and seller is known as novation. Novation is the replacement of one contract with one or more other contracts. This will not happen immediately and therefore bilateral counterparty risk will exist for a short period.[4] The viability of novation depends on the legal enforceability of the new contracts and the certainty that the original parties are not legally obligated to each other once the novation is complete. Because of novation, the contract between the original parties ceases to exist and they therefore do not have counterparty risk to one another. Because it stands between market buyers and sellers, the CCP bears no net market risk, which remains with the original party to each trade. On the other hand, it does take the counterparty risk, which is centralised in the CCP structure. A CCP will attempt to mitigate most of this risk by demanding financial resources from its members that cover the potential losses in the event they default.

CCPs use collateral to mitigate the counterparty risk they face although this is normally referred to as "margin". In addition to the standard "variation margin" that covers the change in the valuation of the relevant positions as with the collateral in a standard CSA,[5] CCPs will require "initial margin" that overcollateralises[6] the counterparty risk they face. Initial margin exists for the life of the trade and can be increased or reduced depending on market conditions and the remaining risk. Members will also need to commit other financial resources to the CCP such as through what is often known as the "default fund" or "reserve fund". The initial margin and reserve fund contributions required globally for the future move of OTC derivatives to CCPs are significant and comparable with the increases in capital required due to regulatory changes since the crisis. Clearing members may also partially own the CCP.

By taking initial margin and overcollateralising positions, a CCP transforms some counterparty risk into other forms of risk. Most obviously, liquidity risk arises due to the nature of margining but operational and legal risks also exist.

The ideal way for CCP members to contribute financial resources is a "defaulter pays" approach. This would mean that a member would contribute all the necessary funds to pay for their own potential future default. This is impractical though because it would require costly initial margin (and reserve fund contributions) to be set at an impractically high level. For this reason, the purpose of initial margin is to cover most (around 99% or more as

---

[4] Currently a few days but in future likely to be just a few hours as most CCPs aim to clear trades by the end of the relevant business day.
[5] This acts like a two-way CSA with a zero threshold for both counterparties.
[6] Initial margin therefore is analogous to an independent amount.

discussed later) scenarios where a member would default. This leaves a small chance of losses not following the "defaulter pays" approach being borne by the other clearing members. Whilst this is a consequence of the need to reduce systemic risk, it creates problems such as moral hazard, which must be considered carefully.

7.1.5 Multilateral netting

The primary advantage of a CCP is multilateral netting, which can alleviate systemic risk by reducing exposures more than in bilateral markets. Let us compare the different netting schemes in relation to an example set of exposures between three counterparties as shown in Figure 7.1:

- *No netting*. Default of any institution will give rise to losses of 3 and 5 for the remaining institutions. For example, a default of A will cause a loss of 5 for B and 3 for C whilst A will still claim a total amount of 8 owed to them.
- *Bilateral netting*. Default of A will cause a reduced loss of only 2 for B whilst C will suffer no loss at all (since they owe A).
- *Multilateral netting*. No institution is exposed to another since none has any outstanding exposure. Nor does the CCP have risk (in this stylised example) since all positions net.[7]

Whilst multilateral netting is clearly more beneficial when all trades are covered, in reality fragmentation will be a problem. In such cases, one has to assess the benefits of multilaterally netting a subset of trades against losing the bilateral benefits that these trades have. A simple and intuitive quantitative treatment of the benefits of a CCP is given by Duffie and Zhu (2009). Their results are based on considering the netting benefit (based on the measure known as EPE, which is defined in Section 8.2.6) for trading a single class of contracts through a CCP as opposed to bilateral clearing. They show, using a simple model,[8] the required number of dealers trading through the CCP for a single asset class to achieve netting

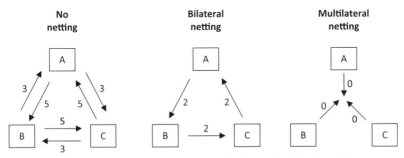

Figure 7.1 Comparison of netting schemes. An arrow indicates the direction of money owed (exposure) so that – under no netting, for example – entity A has an exposure of 3 to entity B whilst B has an exposure of 5 to A.

---

[7] In the example, the matching exposures may be by chance or may arise due to perfectly matching (mirror) trades. In the former case, the CCP will have risk but the point is to illustrate that multilateral netting decreases exposure still further compared with bilateral netting.
[8] Simplifying assumptions of symmetry and equal variance of exposure are used in this case.

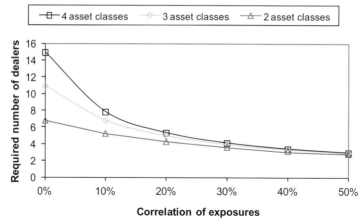

Figure 7.2 Required number of dealers for a single asset class CCP to improve netting efficiency calculated using the formula of Duffie and Zhu (2009).

reduction. The results are plotted in Figure 7.2 as a function of correlation and number of asset classes. For example, for four uncorrelated asset classes, there must be at least 15 dealers to make clearing a single asset class through the CCP valid.[9]

The above example assumes equal distribution of exposure across asset classes. Duffie and Zhu also consider a non-homogeneous case and derive an expression[10] for the fraction of a dealer's exposure that must be concentrated in a particular asset to make a CCP for that asset class viable. This fraction is shown in Figure 7.3. For example, with 10 dealers, using a CCP for a given class of derivatives will be effective only if three-quarters of the dealers' bilaterally netted exposure resides in that class of products.

The Duffie and Zhu results illustrate that achieving overall netting benefits from central clearing (compared to bilateral trading) is not a foregone conclusion. Increased netting

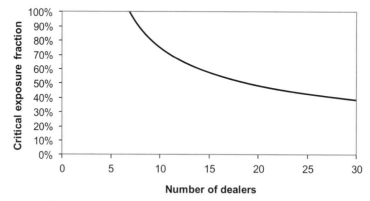

Figure 7.3 Required fraction of exposure attributed to a single asset class ("critical exposure fraction") to make a CCP for that asset class effective. The results as a function of the number of dealers are calculated using the formula of Duffie and Zhu (2009).

---

[9] Interestingly, the impact of correlation between asset classes makes a CCP more effective since bilateral netting is less effective in this case.
[10] This assumes independence between asset classes.

benefits can only be achieved by a relatively small[11] number of CCPs clearing a relatively large volume of transactions. However, it could be argued that the success of central clearing does not depend on the reduction of exposure but rather the control of systemic risk (although the two are partly related).

Given CCPs are unlikely to reduce exposure, the collateral requirements for central clearing are likely to be high. For example, Singh (2010) estimates \$2 trillion globally. However, it is argued (e.g., Milne, 2012) that the overall private cost of collateral is low due to Modigliani–Miller-type arguments (firms holding extra collateral can simply borrow more) and the social cost is lower still.

7.1.6   How many CCPs?

A further result of the Duffie and Zhu study mentioned above is that, not surprisingly, if a CCP is viable then it is inefficient to have more than one CCP in the market. In reality, many competing forces will define the number of CCPs that exist globally. Factors favouring a small number of CCPs are the multilateral netting benefits and other economies of scale. There is likely to be a degree of consolidation of CCPs to reflect these forces. Often a CCP may start with a single goal and therefore be focused in terms of region and asset classes. Growth will naturally involve expanding the geographical base, markets and products covered. The move to central clearing is naturally limited in the early stages due to the lack of benefit until a critical mass of products is cleared.

However, there are a number of factors that will push the total number of CCPs upwards. Jurisdictional fragmentation is the first obvious hurdle to CCP consolidation. Regulators in several major jurisdictions have made it clear that products traded in them or by firms located there must be cleared there. CCPs clearing two or more different types of products are also problematic. The less liquid product takes longer to closeout. This could create a priority where members predominantly trading in the more liquid products (for example, interest rate swaps compared to credit default swaps) would benefit by having an effective first claim on the initial margin and reserve fund of the defaulted member. This is one reason why some CCPs have typically been focused around a single asset class and even product type.

The number of CCPs also depends on the need for competition between CCPs. In one sense, competition may be preferable, as market forces will determine the CCP landscape and costs (via margins) may be competitive. However, too much competition may be counterproductive for the overall risks that CCPs represent. The potential danger of competition for risk assessment was provided by ratings agencies. Up to 2007, a plethora of ever-more-complex products were given good-quality ratings driven by the fact that ratings agencies were essentially paid for giving such ratings and competing with one another. Competition between CCPs can be dangerous and perhaps a preferable solution would be a single monopolistic CCP that concentrates on strong risk management and not on providing attractive costs to potential members. Indeed, this model has existed in Brazil for a number of years.[12]

The balance of forces described above means that it seems likely that some sort of equilibrium may be established with the total number of CCPs globally being in double figures but potentially not too far into double figures. It seems reasonable that the financial markets

---

[11] See also the later comments on interoperability.

[12] In Brazil, only a single clearing house exists (BM&F Bovespa) which clears some OTC derivatives and also acts as a central securities repository.

would be best served via a moderate number of CCPs, which are large enough to offer good product coverage but not so large that they create monopolistic issues, severe systemic risk or geopolitical problems.

7.1.7 Coverage of CCPs

CCPs have historically been closely affiliated with exchanges and have therefore been responsible for the clearing of standard exchange-traded products. Only a few CCPs have offered central clearing services for OTC derivatives (e.g., LCH Clearnet's SwapClear). Central clearing of OTC products presents a number of problems due to a number of aspects, and many products are likely to remain OTC for the foreseeable future. Regarding the types of product tradable through a CCP, the considerations are:

- *Standardisation.* Given the nature of clearing a trade, which involves responsibility over contractual payments and valuation for the purposes of margin calculation, products must be relatively standard. For example, in 2009 there was a standardisation of CDS contracts,[13] which was a prerequisite to any migration to CCPs.
- *Complexity.* Complex derivatives are more problematic for CCPs since their contractual features and valuation will be less straightforward. Note that a complex or exotic derivative may be standardised but still problematic for these reasons.
- *Liquidity.* More illiquid products have less accurate pricing information and typically less historical data for calibrating risk models (for the purposes of initial margin calculation). It is also more costly to replace illiquid trades in the event a CCP member defaults. Note that the liquidity of a trade may well be transient, i.e., it may be liquid at inception but illiquid later. This could be due to either contractual terms or market factors.
- *Wrong-way risk.* Wrong-way risk products are more dangerous for CCPs since there is expected to be a larger exposure in the event of default of the clearing member. This is the main reason why CDS products are more complex to clear than interest rate swap products (even if the additional volatility in the CDS spreads has been accounted for).

The result of the above is that currently only a relatively small number of OTC derivatives products are suitable for central clearing. However, given the size of the interest rate swap market, just clearing this product type will have a very significant impact. CDS indices are also currently cleared and, whilst they are standardised, they are more complex, illiquid and have wrong-way risk. Single-name CDSs will be even more problematic due to their inherent "jump to default" risk. Finally, the OTC derivatives that contributed so significantly to the global financial crisis, namely tranches of bespoke credit portfolios, are extremely difficult to imagine within a CCP environment.

With the above comments in mind, there are two schools of thought with respect to centrally cleared products. The first is that by clearing products that are relatively easy to deal with, such as interest rate swaps and the simpler (index) credit default swaps, a large fraction of OTC derivatives notional can be cleared with the residual remaining forever OTC. An alternative view could be that the products that are difficult to clear are precisely the biggest danger in terms of potential future crises. This would imply that a long-term aim should be to

---

[13] Defined in Section 10.2.1.

clear as many OTC derivatives as possible. However, it is hard to envisage exotic, illiquid or highly structured OTC derivatives being centrally cleared in the near future, or ever.

An example of the opposing views was illustrated with respect to FX products. Market participants have resisted the idea of central clearing for FX products on the basis that the exposures are generally much smaller and settlement risk is more problematic. However, Duffie (2011) argues against this, pointing out that whilst many contracts are short dated, some FX trades have significant credit exposure because FX rates can be volatile, have fat tails and be linked strongly to sovereign risk.

We noted above that a contract could be standardised but still complex. This is a particularly important point to note for credit derivatives products. A single-name CDS is standard and has a payoff that appears quite simple: it is a swap where one party pays a premium in return for receiving a contingent payment if a pre-specified credit event occurs. However, we could also describe this product as being an American-style out-of-the-money barrier option.[14] A CDS index would then be a portfolio of out-of-the-money barrier options. Furthermore, CDS contracts are relatively illiquid (compared to IRS, for example) and become even more so in a crisis. The standardisation of a product does not make it less complex or more liquid.

Pirrong (2009) argues that asymmetric information costs will be higher in centrally cleared markets compared to bilateral ones, especially for exotic products traded by complex, opaque intermediaries. This is argued to be due to the specialisation of dealers with respect to valuing exotic derivatives together and the fact that dealers are more effective at, and have more incentive for, good monitoring and pricing of counterparty risk compared to a CCP. Market participants trading with a CCP may be incentivised to create larger positions than they would otherwise like to, or even be able to, occupy. Put another way, a CCP may therefore suffer from a form of "winner's curse". Such a phenomenon is well known in insurance markets where an insurance company will naturally end up with more risk due to policyholders automatically finding the cheapest premiums[15] given their circumstances.

7.2   LOGISTICS OF CENTRAL CLEARING

7.2.1   Clearing members

From the point of view of trading through a CCP, one can consider three types of participant:

- General clearing member (GCM) – a member of the CCP who is able to clear third parties as well as their own trades.
- Individual clearing member (ICM) – a member of the CCP who clears only their own trades.
- Non-clearing member (NCM) – an institution having no relationship with the CCP but which can trade through a GCM.

These relationships are illustrated in Figure 7.4.

---

[14] Out-of-the-money because the credit event is usually relatively unlikely; barrier because default is similar to the crossing of a barrier; and American-style because default can occur at any time.
[15] For example, an insurance company specialising in insuring drivers with motoring convictions may be able to charge higher premiums but market forces will ensure that they end up with more risky drivers on their books.

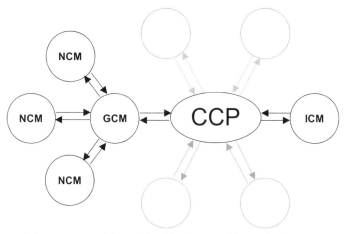

Figure 7.4 Illustration of the relationship between CCPs and clearing members.

A GCM or ICM will typically be a large bank or dealer who has a large number of coun-terparties. An NCM is more obviously characterised by an end-user of OTC derivatives that may channel most or all of its trades through a single counterparty. By this counterparty being a GCM, the end-user can gain benefits from central clearing even though they are not a clearing member. Whilst these are the more obvious roles of members, they are not the only characterisations: for example, a GCM may in fact be another CCP and an NCM may be a smaller bank.

7.2.2   Variation margin

Variation margin is a simple concept, which is an adjustment for the change in valuation of the relevant positions at periodic intervals of at least daily frequency. A CCP may also make intraday margin calls if large price movements threaten to exhaust margin funds in a clearing member's account. Such practices are becoming increasingly common and are supported by technology advances. Valuation is typically straightforward since a prerequisite for clearing is that the underlying trades are standardised. Hence, there is little subjectivity over variation margin amounts.[16] Variation margin will typical be cash in major currencies (or alternatively highly liquid securities). As a counterparty to all trades, CCPs are calculation agents, valuing all positions and collecting or paying respective margins.

7.2.3   Impact of default of a CCP member

In the event of a default, the responsibilities of a CCP are broadly:

- Auctioning the positions of the defaulted member.
- Transferring client positions to surviving clearing members ("porting", see later).
- Allocation of any excess losses to surviving clearing members.

---

[16] Although aspects such as OIS discounting and funding (Chapter 14) have made even the valuation of standard interest rate swaps a complex problem.

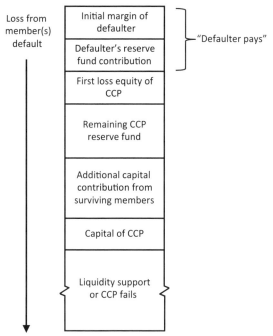

Figure 7.5 Illustration of a typical loss waterfall defining the way in which the default of one or more CCP members is absorbed.

The viability of a CCP depends on its ability to withstand the default of one or more clearing members. As in bilateral markets, the first line of defence for a CCP in such a scenario will be to essentially closeout all positions for the member in question and apply netting of such positions. However, as mentioned previously, we note that CCPs will probably auction positions amongst surviving members rather than terminate them completely.[17] In an ideal world, the termination of positions with a defaulting member would be matched perfectly by the variation margin with respect to that member. In reality, whilst the variation margin should cover any associated losses at a time just prior to the default event, the actual period of time the CCP is exposed to the positions will be longer than this. Hence, there is a need for additional financial resources to absorb further losses. A CPP will have several layers in order to absorb such losses and a typical "loss waterfall" is represented in Figure 7.5.

In most cases, the initial margin is intended to cover the losses from a defaulting member. If this is not sufficient then losses are absorbed from the defaulter's contribution to the reserve fund. Within these amounts, the "defaulter pays" approach, where the defaulting member covers all losses, is being followed.

In extreme scenarios, where the initial margin and reserve fund contributions of the defaulted member(s) have been exhausted, further losses may be taken from the first loss equity of the CCP (for example, current annual profits). After this point, the financial resources contributed by other members via the remaining reserve fund contributions are used. This is the point at which moral hazard appears as other members are paying for the

---

[17] In the case positions were terminated, members would be likely to attempt to execute replacement trades, which then may be subject to central clearing by the CCP. The auction is a quicker and more efficient way to achieve this.

failure of the defaulted member. Indeed, it is possible for a clearing member to lose some of their reserve fund when another member, with whom they have avoided trading, defaults.

Losses wiping out the entire reserve fund of a CCP are clearly required to be exceptionally unlikely.[18] However, if this does happen then the surviving members of the CCP are required to commit some additional "capital" to support the CCP. This contribution is not unlimited and is capped (often in relation to a member's initial reserve fund contribution) as a means to mitigate moral hazard. After the cap is reached then the remaining capital of the CCP would be used to cover losses.

At this point, assuming losses still persist, the CCP will fail unless they receive some external liquidity support (via a bailout from a central bank, for example). We should note that, in order to reach the bottom of the loss waterfall, many layers of financial support must be eroded. Hence, although unquantifiable to any relative precision, this will be an extremely low probability event.[19]

We will now discuss the key elements of the loss waterfall, namely the initial margin and reserve fund in more detail.

7.2.4 Initial margin

Initial margin is, by contrast to variation margin, much more complex and its magnitude is highly subjective. Initial margin is a buffer posted to cover the closing out of positions without loss to the CCP in a worst-case scenario. Initial margin requirements need to be set carefully depending on the trade in question, any existing trades and the required confidence level of the CCP. A final important consideration is the assumed time-period that the CCP would be exposed to the value of a member's positions after their default event (including any grace period). A confidence level of 99% and time-period of around 5 days are typical.

Initial margin depends primarily on the market risk of the centrally cleared trades and only a small component, if any, is linked to the credit quality of the clearing member. Since the posting of cash or high-quality assets imposes higher costs for members, margin requirements must not be too conservative as this may reduce trading volumes through the CCP. On the other hand, they need to be large enough to provide the right level of risk mitigation. A CCP must balance the need to be competitive by incentivising central clearing (low margins) with maximising their own creditworthiness (high margins), i.e., to what extent the default of a member can be absorbed.

The following components are important considerations in deciding on initial margin:

- *Volatility*. The most obvious aspect is the volatility of the trade in question. This is driven by the volatility of the underlying market variable(s) and the maturity of the trade.
- *Tail risk*. Whilst volatility typically measures continuous price variability, some products such as CDSs can suffer from tail risk due to jumps or gaps in the underlying market variables.
- *Dependency*. Since CCP members typically hold a variety of trades with a CCP, it is important to understand the offsetting nature of such trades. If correlation between the price moves of different trades is small then clearly the overall portfolio is less risky and the benefit of this is that less margin needs to be charged. Gemmill (1994) has illustrated

---

[18] Indeed reserve funds are typically calibrated based on the assumed default of the two largest members.
[19] However, never as low as we think.

the diversification offered to a CCP from clearing several markets that are not highly correlated. Indeed, CCP members will be actively looking to receive the benefits of such favourable dependencies in the form of lower initial margins. CCPs tend to offer benefit from same-asset-class trades but less so from cross-asset-class interactions, although this is likely to become more common.

It should be noted that the above calculations, ideally, should all be made under the assumption that the member in question is in default. For example, if a member's default is expected to produce particular volatility in the CDS market then this volatility is the appropriate measure to use when setting initial margin.[20] This is essentially accounting for wrong-way risk, which is discussed in more detail in Chapter 15.

Historically, systems such as SPAN[21] have been used for initial margin, evolving risk factors combinatorially based on movements in either direction based on a certain confidence level (this is similar to some methods now used for stress-testing purposes, for example). The worse-case scenario is normally used to define the initial margin. Whilst such methods work well and are tractable for simple portfolios such as futures and options, they have severe drawbacks. Mostly notably, they do not scale well to a large number of dimensions (as the number of combinations of moves grows exponentially as 2^n where n is the number of dimensions). They also do not clearly attach an underlying probability to the scenario defining the initial margin.

More advanced initial margin calculations follow value-at-risk (see Chapter 2 for a description of VAR) approaches. One lesson from many years of application of VAR methodologies is that "reasonable" losses can be quantified with some success, whereas more severe losses fall outside the abilities of quantitative approaches. Not surprisingly, this can lead to an underestimate of required margin. For example, Figlewski (1984) has shown for equity markets that for a confidence level of 95% such an approach can work reasonably well whereas for a higher confidence level of 99% the empirical margin requirements are much higher than those predicted using normal assumptions.[22] Bates and Craine (1999) showed that following the 1987 crash, the expected losses conditional on a margin call being breached increased by an order of magnitude. Clearly, it is important to attempt to incorporate any "fat tail" effects in the calculation of margins. Beyond the univariate assumptions applied to margin calculations, it is important to consider the multivariate behaviour of different positions (for example, in different currencies) to understand how the total margin would be reduced due to netting effects.

VAR approaches for initial margin will aim to calculate the worst-case loss for a set of trades of any dimensionality and accounting for all cross-dependencies. This will typically rely on a certain window of historical data for the calibration of parameters such as volatility and correlation. Such an approach is scalable to any number of products and risk factors and can allow initial margins to be calculated for large multi-asset portfolios, giving all the relevant netting benefits. Indeed, CCPs are looking in some cases to offer such netting benefits by combining

---

[20] Alternatively, this could be a component of the reserve fund contribution although then the confidence level for initial margin will be implicitly lowered.

[21] Standard Portfolio Analysis of Risk, used historically, for example, by US futures clearing houses and the London Clearing House.

[22] A more complex approach such as extreme value theory (EVT) potentially provides a more sophisticated way to attempt to capture the possibility of extreme price movements. A weakness of EVT is that it requires significant historical data whereas most CCPs prefer to set margin based on a small and recent data sample. EVT may capture potential extreme moves and will therefore lead to higher initial margins.

margins for different product types.[23] However, whilst multidimensional modelling of risk factors can lead to increased benefits from margin offsets, it does increase the model risk. Dependencies of financial variables are notoriously hard to model, especially in certain cases such as involving credit spreads.

Finally, we note that on top of the univariate and multivariate challenges in computing initial margin, there is a procyclicality problem. In benign markets, volatility and correlations will be low and calculated margins therefore smaller. However, this means that, in more volatile times, margins will be insufficient to provide the coverage that the confidence level and time period intended. Since volatility can increase and dependencies change rapidly, it may be necessary to increase margins in periods that are more turbulent. Indeed, the fact that this practice has become *de rigueur* has made the term "initial margin" somewhat confusing since it implies that this margin will be fixed over the lifetime of a transaction where, in reality, market conditions may cause it to increase. The above quantitative difficulties can be resolved by being conservative, especially during periods of low market volatility. Such an approach would mirror the stressed VAR and EPE (Section 17.4.2) requirements for capital under Basel III, where the model must always be calibrated to a dataset including period of stress.

However, initial margin should be at a level to cover all but extreme price movements, but not so high as to damage market liquidity and/or discourage the use of the CCP. High margins have been shown empirically to have a detrimental impact on trading volumes (e.g., see Hartzmark, 1986; Hardouvelis and Kim, 1995).

Whilst it may seem reasonable for a CCP to call for more initial margin during turbulent periods, by doing this the CCP creates systemic risk by, to put it crudely, sucking liquidity out of the market at a critical time. Brady (1988) discusses the crash of 1987 and its impact on some clearing houses arising in an extreme market event with associated liquidity problems. Whilst a moderate increase in margins during more volatile periods may not be unreasonable, a significant hike in margins close to a crisis could have a severely destabilising impact on prices and create unpleasant knock-on effects. Whilst CCPs are generally intended to reduce systemic risk, increasing initial margins is one way in which they may achieve the reverse. The analogy of using stressed market data as a basis for VAR calculations would be that CCP initial margins should upfront contain a contribution relating to a more volatile period to reduce the need to call for additional margin later.

Initial margin will normally be required in cash or in some cases other very liquid securities. Non-cash margins posted with CCPs will typically not be rehypothecated, as this creates the need for more liquid assets and potentially puts a strain on liquidity.

A critical point to emphasise is that CCPs do not vary initial margin significantly based on the credit quality of the clearing member.[24] Therefore, members of a CCP are essentially treated equally. This has an obvious implication that CCP members must be rather similar in credit quality. Even then, there are asymmetric information problems since weaker members will be gaining at the expense of stronger members. Indeed, Pirrong (2000) argues that the delay in adopting central clearing on certain exchanges was related to stronger credit quality members not wishing to subsidise weaker ones.

---

[23] See, for example, "Clearinghouses seek to merge margin accounts for CDS clients", *Dow Jones Newswires*, 7th October 2011.
[24] Some CCPs do base margins partially on credit ratings, for example by requiring more when a member's rating falls below a certain level. However, this is clearly problematic since credit ratings are imprecise and granular measures of credit quality and such triggers requiring more margins are well known to be potentially destabilising and create systemic risk.

7.2.5   Reserve funds, capital calls and loss mutualisation

Whilst keeping the likelihood of exceeding margin over a single day to a high confidence level (such as 99%) is viable, breaches will always be possible. CCPs don't only focus on having margin requirements that cover losses in all but the most extreme cases. They aim to ensure that there is adequate coverage of losses due to the default of a member following a margin-depleting price move. The ability of a CCP to survive such extreme losses, potentially arising from default of several members, is critical.

Another important aspect of CCPs is the reserve fund that has been accumulated over time by initial and ongoing contributions from clearing members and/or built up from other sources such as CCP profits. A determination of the correct reserve fund is significantly more difficult than the already complex initial margin calculation outlined above. By their very nature, losses hitting the reserve fund are infrequent and typically represent a 1% or lower probability **and** the default of at least one clearing member. Calculating the conditional exposures in such scenarios is plagued by problems such as fat tail events, complex dependencies and wrong-way risk. For these reasons, CCPs typically calibrate the size of a reserve fund more qualitatively via stress tests typically framed in terms of the number of defaults a CCP can withstand (two large defaults, for example). However, the true probability of a CCP exhausting their reserve fund is very difficult to quantify with any accuracy as it is linked to events involving default of more than one clearing member together with extreme moves in the positions of such members.

Losses above the defaulting member's reserve fund contribution will begin to hit other clearing members. This loss mutualisation is a key point since it spreads extreme losses from the failure of a single counterparty across all other clearing members. This has the potential to ameliorate any systemic problems arising in bilateral markets due to an institution heavily exposed to a defaulted counterparty. Loss mutualisation (along with margining requirements) completes the process of homogenisation of counterparty risk across all clearing members.

When the reserve fund is exhausted, there will be additional contributions or "capital calls" from remaining clearing members. Such contributions are capped, which reduces moral hazard problems. However, this means that a CCP could become insolvent and without some external injection of capital would fail.

7.2.6   Interoperability

As mentioned above, it seems likely that jurisdictional issues and potential product segregation will create a relatively large number of CCPs. Clearing the same product in multiple CCPs causes fragmentation and limits the benefits of clearing, especially in terms of multilateral netting. Local regulators requiring clearing by CCPs in their own region will also create a need for interoperability. An obvious way to improve such a situation is to link CCPs. Such interoperability would have the advantage of increasing multilateral netting benefits and therefore giving clearing members lower initial margin requirements thanks to the offsetting nature of positions even though they trade those positions through more than one CCP.

Interoperability will firstly require cooperation between CCPs on the initial margin required, taking into account the netting benefits from the linkage of the CCPs. For example, a bank may clear CDS through CCP1 and IRS through CCP2. The CCPs must decide on the total initial margin required for these two sets of trades, knowing that they are not perfectly correlated. Then there is the question of where to hold this margin and how to allocate it in the event the bank were to fail. Even theoretically, such loss sharing is not an obvious calculation (see discussion on marginal exposure in Section 9.6.1). Linking CCPs across different jurisdictions and regulatory regimes will also clearly be difficult and require some harmonisation of regulatory rules and cross-border bankruptcy rules.

Interoperability can mitigate problems due to multiple CCPs and increase the benefits of clearing but would expose CCPs to each other's failure and create a more interconnected CCP landscape similar to the one on the left-hand side of Figure 6.6.

7.2.7   Non-clearing members and end-users

One of the key challenges of moving OTC derivatives to CCPs is persuading "end-users" such as hedge funds, asset managers, insurance companies, corporates and sovereigns to move their positions with dealers. Firstly, end-users often have limited margin (collateral) arrangements with banks and may benefit from not posting margin or posting only limited margin (due to a threshold in the CSA). They may also be able to post illiquid margin (for example, corporate bonds, gold and in extreme circumstances aeroplanes). In order to trade through a CCP, an NCM will either have to commit to frequent posting of liquid margin as required by the CCP or will have to rely on their GCM to provide some sort of "collateral upgrade" service with respect to margin transformation. For example, it is possible that an NCM may post less liquid margin to a GCM and then the NCM will in turn post the required more liquid margin to the CCP. Already the business of collateral conversions has begun in earnest with banks offering the service for their clearing clients via their securities lending and repo desks. Obviously, the GCM would charge for such a service, probably via demanding a significant haircut on the more illiquid margin.

The extreme case of the above is margin lending, where a GCM or other third party essentially funds the NCM for the margin that they need to post. Indeed, Albanese *et al.* (2011) have proposed this as a solution to the significant initial margin funding requirements for central clearing. However, we note that such a liquidity provision creates potentially dangerous problems because the fee for margin lending will increase as the credit quality of the borrower increases. Furthermore, the failure of entities such as conduits and SIV (structured investment vehicles)[25] during the crisis suggests that, in extreme markets, margin-lending mechanisms could simply freeze completely. In Chapter 14 (Section 14.5.2), we discuss in more detail the conversion of counterparty risk to funding liquidity via CSAs, CCPs and margin lending mechanisms.

There are arguments that some end-users should be excused from CCP clearing on the basis that it will be too difficult and expensive to hedge their genuine risk profiles. For example, US regulation provides exemptions for hedgers who are not dealers or "major swap market participants". At the time of writing, it is not completely clear what organisations are covered by such a definition.

Another important consideration is issues that arise over segregation of margin. When customer collateral is commingled in "omnibus" accounts, it is at risk in the event of the

---

[25] Essentially such vehicles made use of short-term funding to make long-term investments. They failed because it was simply impossible to "roll" the short-term funding.

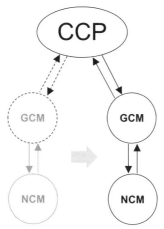

Figure 7.6 Illustration of the "porting" of non-clearing member positions from a defaulting general clearing member to a surviving general clearing member.

clearing member's default. Furthermore, clearing members may be able to utilise margins of non-defaulting customers to offset the obligations of another defaulting customer. This latter effect can be seen as another form of moral hazard where good credit quality clients of a clearing member are in danger of experiencing losses due to the failure of weaker clients. Segregation of margin reduces the risk that a client will lose some or their entire margin in the event of a default (of their clearing member or of another client of their clearing member). There is no free lunch, however, as greater segregation is more costly, both operationally and in terms of the requirement that reserve funds be larger (to cover the losses that would otherwise be taken from surviving institutions margin). There is also the question of the legal enforcement of segregation across jurisdictions.

The final issue is that, in the event of default of their clearing member, clients not only want not to lose their margin, but they also require the ability to "port" their positions to a surviving clearing member (Figure 7.6). This is clearly highly preferable to having all positions closed out or distributed via multiple clearing members through an auction (which would lead to the requirement to post more margin due to the loss of netting benefits). Whilst having all positions moved to a single clearing member is useful, there is the question of whether, in the potentially turbulent markets around a clearing member default, another member will require significant additional margin or simply refuse to accept some or all of the trades.

Note that greater segregation and the ability to port positions creates more moral hazard since a client is less likely to monitor the health of their clearing member.

7.3   ANALYSIS OF THE IMPACT AND BENEFITS OF CCPs

In the description of the mechanics of CCP trading, advantages and disadvantages emerge. We have also described the creation of effects such as moral hazard and adverse selection. These are not insurmountable disadvantages (after all, the insurance market operates despite such problems), but may lead to unintended consequences. We now look at the strengths and weaknesses of CCPs in more detail.

7.3.1 The advantage of centralised clearing

The advantages of trading through a CCP are:

- *Multilateral netting*. Contracts traded between different counterparties but traded through a CCP can be netted. This increases the flexibility to enter new transactions and terminate existing ones and reduces margin costs. Trading out of positions through a CCP is easy and, unlike bilateral markets, can be done with any other counterparty where the multilateral netting benefit is provided by the CCP. Furthermore, reducing the total positions that need to be replaced in the event of a default reduces price impact.
- *Loss mutualisation*. Even when a default creates losses that exceed the financial commitments from the defaulting member, these losses are distributed throughout the CCP members, reducing their impact on any one member. Thus, a counterparty's losses are dispersed partially throughout the market, making their impact less dramatic and reducing the possibility of systemic problems.
- *Legal and operational efficiency*. The margining, netting and settlement functions undertaken by a CCP potentially increase operational efficiency and reduce costs. CCPs may also reduce legal risks in providing a centralisation of rules and mechanisms. A CCP working with regulators on the best procedures is likely to be more efficient than individual market participants taking this collective responsibility.
- *Liquidity*. A CCP will improve market liquidity through the ability of market participants to trade easily and benefit from multilateral netting. Market entry is enhanced through the ability to trade anonymously and the mitigation of counterparty risk. Derivatives traded through a CCP need to be valued on a daily basis due to daily margining and cash flow payments leading to a more transparent valuation of products.
- *Transparency*. A CCP is positioned to understand the positions of all market participants and therefore is privy to potentially sensitive trading information via the overall exposure of a member. Since the CCP does not bear market risk, it has no incentive to use such information. This disperses panic that might otherwise be present in bilateral markets due to a lack of knowledge of the exposure faced by institutions. On the other hand, if a member has a particularly extreme exposure, the CCP is in a position to act on this and limit trading.
- *Default management*. A well-managed central auction is liquid and may result in smaller price disruptions than uncoordinated replacement of positions during a crisis period associated with default of a clearing member.

The distinction between bilateral and CCP-cleared OTC transactions is recognised under Basel III, which gives a relatively low 2% weighting for trade exposures to a CCP.[26]

7.3.2 Have CCPs failed before?

Historically, there are some cases of CCP failures, although they have obviously been rare. Significant examples are:

---

[26] Trade exposure means initial and variation margin. There is also a requirement to capitalise reserve fund exposures, which is much more complicated. The method for doing this is described in Chapter 17 (Section 17.5).

- *French Caisse de Liquidation (1973).* This occurred as a result of a sharp drop in sugar prices and the failure of one large trading firm to post margin.
- *Commodity Clearinghouse in Kuala Lumpur (1983).* This was a result of a crash in palm oil futures and failed margin calls from several brokers who defaulted because of the dramatic price fall.
- *Hong Kong Futures Exchange Clearing Corporation (1987).* As described in detail by Hills *et al.* (1999), this CCP was bailed out as a result of problems with margin calls arising from the global stock market crash.

Indeed, the 1987 stock market crash, not surprisingly, caused quite severe problems for CCPs. Options traders lost large amounts of money but, since trades were reconciled only at the end of the day, many had highly leveraged positions and experienced losses far in excess of their capital. Many traders simply headed straight to the airport – the origin of the expression "airport play". This pushed US CCPs close to default as their members failed or faced severe funding strains. In the wake of the 1987 crash, both the CME and OCC had problems in receiving margin and came close to failure. Without the liquidity that the Federal Reserve injected and support from banks, a large CCP failure was more than a possibility.

Some of the lessons that can be learnt from past CCP failures and near-failures are:

- Operational risk must be controlled as much as possible (for example, after the 1987 crash, electronic reporting of trades was introduced so that the system would not be exposed to these weaknesses again).
- Variation margins should be recalculated frequently and collected promptly (intradaily if possible).
- Initial margin and reserve funds should be resilient to large negative asset shocks or gaps in market variables and to extreme co-dependency (for example, the concept of correlation increasing in a crisis).

7.3.3   The impact of homogenisation

If a major derivatives player defaults, it may not be clear how big the associated counterparty risk losses will be, nor which institutions will bear the brunt of them. This uncertainty is mitigated through a CCP allocating extreme losses across all of its members. The neutrality and ability of a CCP to disperse losses mitigates information asymmetry that can propagate stress events in bilateral markets.

A benefit of clearing is that it improves fungibility of contracts by making counterparties interchangeable and reduces systemic risk by loss mutualisation. However, this reduces the costs that riskier firms face to the detriment of the less risky firms. The former therefore can expand their trading relative to the latter. Heterogeneity of credit quality causes members' interests to diverge and they will be less likely to commit to a CCP. This could be compared to the problems that the euro currency has suffered from 2010 due to the severe credit problems of some of its member countries, especially Greece.

The homogenising of counterparty risk and use of mutualised loss-sharing reduces asymmetric informational problems and allows anonymous trading and settlement (although, as mentioned earlier, this may be costly). In a centrally cleared market using a CCP, all parties are essentially equal and the CCP acts as guarantor for all obligations. An institution has no need to assess the creditworthiness of counterparties they trade with through the CCP and may therefore reduce resources spent on monitoring individual members. They need only have confidence in the creditworthiness of the CCP. An institution with better-than-average risk management (credit quality assessment, collateral management, hedging) may lose out by trading through a CCP.

In a bilateral market, the pricing of counterparty risk will naturally cause institutions with a worsening credit quality to have higher costs and therefore provide an incentive for them to improve this aspect. However, when trading through a CCP, as long as a member is posting the relevant margin, the issue of their declining credit quality may be ignored (up to a point). This may allow poor-quality institutions to build up bigger positions more cheaply than they would normally be able to do in bilateral markets. CCPs may be more popular with counterparties with below-average risk management abilities and firms with weaker credit quality who can only achieve a limited amount of bilateral trading. The products that members may be most keen to clear through a CCP may be the more toxic ones, for example due to wrongway risk, that cannot be readily managed in a bilateral market.

7.3.4   Will a CCP be allowed to fail?

Funnelling market activity through one institution leads to a concentration of risk. A key component for regulators is to ensure that, especially in buoyant markets, CCPs do not become more competitive and therefore increase their likelihood of failing during volatile markets and crashes. However, despite the best efforts of CCPs, their members and regulators, one must still contemplate the possibility that, at some point, a CCP will fail.

The failure of a CCP would necessarily lead to at least a temporary breakdown of the market, as the whole structure through which positions are established, maintained and closed out would be disrupted. It would also have cross-border dimensions due to the global nature of the OTC derivatives market. Given the mandate being given to CCPs to clear many more OTC products, such a failure could be expected to be far worse than even the failure of a large bank. Whilst the *probability* of CCP failure might be smaller than that of an individual institution (thanks to tight regulation and mutualisation of losses), it represents a far more extreme and systemic event.

Relying on banks or other market participants to provide liquidity or capital to a stricken CCP may be naïve, as the market conditions that caused the CCP default may mean that such institutions are also severely financially constrained. This implies that a liquidity injection from a central bank is the only way to avoid a potentially catastrophic CCP failure. Regulators are divided on whether a CCP should essentially be given such liquidity support. The obvious problem is that taxpayers bailing out a CCP is no better than bailing out other financial institutions, such as banks. Furthermore, the view that a CCP is too big to fail will lead to problems with the way CCP members (and possibly the CCP itself) behave (moral hazard again).

There is no obvious answer to the above dilemma. A critical point is that, as noted by Pirrong (2011), an institution such as a CCP could be *solvent* but *illiquid* due to massive liquidity problems in the financial markets. In such a situation, a CCP should have access to liquidity, which probably needs to come from the relevant central bank. However, this liquidity support should ideally not extend to the central bank providing an unlimited backstop for the CCP.

7.3.5   Could OTC derivatives survive without CCPs?

During the financial crisis, taxpayers essentially had to bail out failing financial institutions to quite staggering levels and the only attempt to avoid the inherent unfairness and moral hazard from such bailouts, the Lehman bankruptcy, was an unmitigated disaster. Clearly, aspects within financial markets and OTC derivatives markets in particular need to change. Hence, it is not appropriate to argue that the move towards central clearing is simply wrong.

A reasonable question to ask might rather be whether there is a better way to mitigate systemic risk and other problems in the OTC derivatives market. In order to do this, let us recall the general functions a CCP performs:

- *Pricing and settlement.* A CCP provides the valuation of the relevant OTC derivatives and associated settlement functions.
- *Netting/trade compression.* A CCP can recognise offsetting trades. This is equivalent to netting and trade compression in bilateral markets.
- *Collateral management.* A CCP performs a collateral management function by making margin calls.
- *Reporting.* CCPs can increase transparency and provide information to regulators by maintaining records and providing reporting functionality.
- *Loss mutualisation.* A CCP provides insurance via a loss mutualisation process whereby any excess loss that is caused by the default of a CCP member is absorbed by all other CCP members.
- *Auction process.* In the event of default of a member, a CCP will auction their positions and CCP members are normally required to participate in this auction.

One could argue that of the above six tasks, bilateral markets can perform the first four adequately without CCP intervention via existing pricing/settlement methods, netting/trade compression, CSAs and trade repositories.[27] It might be that CCPs may perform them better and more efficiently but this is not completely clear as it depends on the eventual CCP landscape (for example, the number of CCPs and their product coverage). For example, considering the second point, a CCP provides multilateral netting whereas a bilateral market relies on bilateral netting and trade compression services. Only if the CCP is large enough does it reduce exposure more than other methods in the bilateral market. Furthermore, if CCPs can perform the first four functions better than bilateral markets then there would be no need to mandate clearing of any products as market participants would naturally seek CCP benefits.

The loss mutualisation point is certainly not a feature of bilateral markets. However, as discussed above, the overall benefits of this are not clear since homogeneity leads to additional problems due to moral hazard.

This leaves the final point, the auction process, as the main advantage of a CCP and the one function that is, without doubt, performed significantly better than in bilateral markets (as illustrated during the Lehman bankruptcy, for example). Any criticism of the widespread adoption of central clearing would have to provide an alternative to the CCP auction for dealing with the unwinding and/or replacement of positions resulting from a bankruptcy of a large financial institution. Specifying the protocol and legal structure for an OTC derivatives auction in the event of a major default outside CCPs is not unrealistic. The CDS market achieved something similar via the "big bang protocol" in 2009 (Section 10.2.3), which paved the way for auction settlement for CDS credit events, covering all CDS trades, even legacy ones that pre-dated the big bang protocol.

---

[27] For example, the US Depository Trust & Clearing Corporation (DTCC) maintains CDS data, which it shares with authorities.

7.3.6 Hurdles and challenges for the growth of the CCP market

OTC market products tend to be customised, and relatively illiquid, which limits the ability to clear them through a CCP. A certain amount of standardisation – for example, of contractual term and valuation – is required before a product can be CCP-traded. Standardisation of products to aid central clearing is a major hurdle but a necessary one, so that CCPs can offer broad product coverage. However, a danger here is that the most important products to be traded through CCPs are probably the most risky from the point of view of the stability of the CCP, and vice versa. There has been much recent interest in trading all CDS index products and single-name products through CCPs. Complexity of products may increase adverse selection problems, where dealers may have better knowledge of the inherent risk of a trade than the CCP through which they clear.

Another hurdle is cost. Moving OTC derivatives to a CCP creates costs via increased amounts and liquidity of initial margin, and a reduction in rehypothecation. It will also lead to a loss of netting benefits, although these may be recovered if the CCP market reaches a critical size.

A CCP also centralises legal and operational risks. Like all market participants, CCPs are exposed to operational risks such as systems failure and fraud. A breakdown of any aspect of a CCP's infrastructure would be catastrophic since it would affect a relatively large number of counterparties within the market. Aspects such as segregation and the movement of margin and positions through a CCP, whilst enforceable in the CCP's home jurisdiction, might be subject to legal risk from other jurisdictions.

Finally, there is the danger that the push to central clearing will influence the behaviour of market participants in potentially unintended ways. From this point of view, it is important to remain open-minded about the potential unintended consequences of CCPs and analyse their potential side-effects in as much detail as possible (e.g., see Pirrong, 2011). This does not need to be seen as a negative for central clearing but rather it can give added confidence that most of the potential weaknesses of CCPs are exposed and not hidden.

7.4 CONCLUSIONS

Bilateral OTC markets have been extremely successful and their growth has been greater than that of exchange-traded products over the last 15 years. Whilst it seems obvious that a bilaterally cleared market is more vulnerable to systemic risk, this is not an argument for the naïve introduction of CCPs. CCPs reallocate counterparty risk, but they do not make it disappear. This can be beneficial – for example, a corporate hedging their balance sheet may be wiped out if a major dealer defaults. In a CCP world, this risk is potentially reallocated to market participants who can bear it more reasonably (at a cost, of course).

CCPs reduce systemic risk (e.g., mitigating the impact of clearing member failure) and increase it (e.g., by increasing margins during a period of stress where firms may have to liquidate assets to meet large margin calls which in turn may exacerbate price volatility). Hence, CCPs transform systemic risk but do not definitely reduce it overall.

The question as to whether CCPs really reduce counterparty and/or systemic risk *overall* should be carefully considered. In bilateral markets, dealers compete for business partially based on their ability to manage counterparty risk. A CCP takes away the incentive to properly price and manage the counterparty risk created when entering a trade. Regulation may favour a certain CCP and this will create sub-optimal outcomes and market instability. A

CCP would, of course, have its own risk management capabilities and be subject to prudent supervision and capital requirements in order to make its failure highly unlikely. Yet these are exactly the same measures applied to banking institutions before the 2007 crisis! The lessons from problems experienced by the Triple-A rated monolines during the 2007–2009 period must serve as a warning.

Given the global nature of OTC derivatives markets and the fact that CCPs will operate internationally, there is a need for close cross-border coordination of regulation to avoid regulatory arbitrage and mitigate systemic risk. Operational procedures should be carefully implemented and, in particular, margin should be monitored extremely carefully. CCPs clearing different markets must develop sophisticated modelling techniques to provide an aggregated assessment of the overall risk of open positions. They should perform default simulations to practice for the eventual failure of a member.

CCPs must not be focused only on clearing the products that caused the last crisis, but also those that may cause the next. The next crisis may not involve credit derivatives, indeed it may involve a class of derivatives yet to be invented. Like a financial institution, CCPs cannot be immune to financial distress. CCP access to central bank liquidity has been a controversial issue. However, CCPs could fail due to lack of liquidity. Unlimited liquidity support could lead to a bailout, of which the explicit or even implicit promise creates moral hazard. Furthermore, bailing out a CCP is ultimately no better than bailing out any other financial institution.[28]

---

[28] Indeed, one author has written about central clearing, "It gives the impression that regulators and legislators are reasserting control over the wild beasts of finance. In reality, the proposal may not work or materially reduce the risks it is intended to address". See "Tranquillizer solutions. Part I: A CCP idea", *Wilmott Magazine*, May 2010.

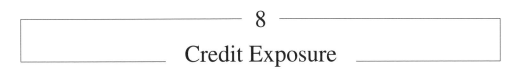

8

Credit Exposure

> *There is no security on this earth, there is only opportunity.*
> General Douglas MacArthur (1880–1964)

This chapter will be concerned with defining credit exposure (often known just as exposure) in more detail and expanding the key characteristics. We then explain the important metrics used for the quantification of credit exposure. Typical exposure profiles for various instruments will be discussed and we will explain the impact of netting and collateral on exposure. Understanding exposure is relevant for the following reasons:

- Trade approval by comparing against credit limits.
- Pricing (and hedging) counterparty risk (CVA).
- Calculating economic and regulatory capital.

8.1 CREDIT EXPOSURE

8.1.1 Definition

A defining feature of counterparty risk arises from the asymmetry of potential losses with respect to the value[1] of the underlying transaction(s). In the event that a counterparty has defaulted, an institution may closeout the relevant contract(s) and cease any future contractual payments. Following this, they may determine the net amount owing between them and their counterparty and take into account any collateral that may have been posted. Note that collateral may be held to reduce exposure but any posted collateral may have the effect of increasing exposure.

Once the above steps have been followed, there is a question of whether the net amount is positive or negative. The main defining characteristic of credit exposure is related to whether the effective value of the contracts (including collateral) is positive (in an institution's favour) or negative (against them), as illustrated in Figure 8.1.

- *Negative value.* In this case, an institution is in debt to its counterparty and is still legally obliged to settle this amount (they cannot walk away from the transaction or transactions except in specific cases – see Section 4.3.3). Hence, from a valuation perspective, the position appears essentially unchanged. An institution does not gain or lose from their counterparty's default in this case.

---

[1] The definitions of value will be more clearly discussed below.

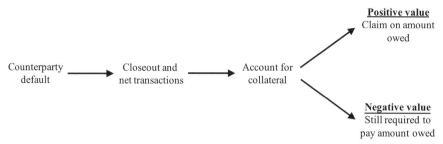

Figure 8.1 Illustration of the impact of a positive or negative value in the event of the default of a counterparty.

- *Positive value.* When a counterparty defaults, they will be unable to undertake future commitments and hence an institution will have a claim on the positive value at the time of the default, typically as an unsecured creditor. They will then expect to recover some fraction of their claim, just as bondholders receive some recovery on the face value of a bond. However, this unknown recovery value is, by convention, not included in the definition of exposure.

The above feature – an institution loses if the value is positive and does not gain if it is negative – is a defining characteristic of counterparty risk. We can define exposure simply as

$$\text{Exposure} = \text{Max}(\text{value}, 0) \tag{8.1}$$

This would mean that defining exposure at a given time is rather easy. One simply values the relevant contracts, aggregates them according to the relevant netting rules and finally applies an adjustment corresponding to any collateral held against the positions. This appears to be a reasonably simple measure of exposure and is usually the one applied in pricing and risk management calculations.

8.1.2 Bilateral exposure

A key feature of counterparty risk is that it is bilateral as both parties to a transaction can default and therefore both can experience losses. For completeness one must consider losses arising from both defaults. From an institution's point of view, their own default will cause a loss to any counterparty they are in debt to. This can be defined in terms of *negative exposure*, which by symmetry is

$$\text{Negative exposure} = \text{Min}(\text{value}, 0) \tag{8.2}$$

A negative exposure leads to a gain, which is relevant since the counterparty is making a loss.[2]

Finally, it is important to note that recovery values are relevant in the case of exposure and negative exposure. In the former case, an institution will be paid only a recovery fraction (Rec_C) of their exposure in the event their counterparty defaults. This is a loss for the

---

Table 8.1   Illustration of payoff in the event of an institution or their counterparty defaulting. Rec_C and Rec_I denote recovery values for the counterparty and institution respectively.

		Impact	*Payoff*
Counterparty defaults	Exposure	Loss	$\text{Rec}_C \times \text{Max}(\text{value}, 0)$
Institution defaults	Negative exposure	Gain	$\text{Rec}_I \times \text{Min}(\text{value}, 0)$

institution. In the latter case, the counterparty will receive only a recovery fraction (Rec_I) of the negative exposure in the event the institution defaults. This is a gain for the institution. The bilateral payoffs defining counterparty risk are illustrated in Table 8.1.

8.1.3   The closeout amount

The amount represented by "value" above represents the valuation of the relevant contracts at the default time of the counterparty (or institution), including the impact of netting and collateral. An institution therefore would presumably aim for the relevant documentation and legal practices to align this amount as closely as possible to the value of the contracts (and collateral) from their point of view. In practice, this is not completely trivial as it is necessary to agree with the counterparty (or the administrators of their default) the relevant valuations. In cases where such an agreement cannot be reached, the valuation must be made by following the relevant procedures in the documentation.

ISDA documentation uses the term "closeout amount" to define what is referred to above as "value". However, the precise definition of closeout is, perhaps not unreasonably, rather vague[3] and can give rise to several issues. In determining a closeout amount, according to ISDA (2009), an institution should "act in good faith and use commercially reasonable procedures in order to produce a commercially reasonable result". Whilst efforts have been made to define closeout language in the most appropriate way and to learn from problems relating to historic bankruptcies, there will clearly always be the chance of a dispute over closeout amounts.

Whilst subjectivities and disagreements over the precise definition of the closeout amount may lead to uncertainties, this should still correspond closely to a standard risk-free value appearing in formula (8.1) corrected for any relevant costs in replacing transactions. This would make the above simple definition of exposure a reasonable proxy, albeit with some (hopefully small) uncertainty due to the difficulty in defining the closeout amount. However, there is also a potentially important and systematic effect. ISDA (2009) specifies that the closeout amount may include information related to the creditworthiness of the surviving party. This implies that an institution can potentially reduce the amount owed to a defaulting counterparty or increase their claims in accordance with their *own* counterparty risk, which would be relevant in a replacement transaction (this component is called DVA and is the subject of Chapter 13). In the event the institution defaults then the counterparty is able to do

---

[3] Historically there have been two methods to govern the calculation of closeout amounts. The first is a "Market Quotation" approach that requires quotes from dealers (a minimum number of quotes may be specified) in the relevant market for replacement transactions that represent the economic equivalent of those being terminated. However, in cases of extreme volatility and even a breakdown of the market (following a major default, for example) it may still be difficult to achieve the quote required to establish such an amount. Another approach is the "Loss" method, where an institution may determine its losses (including costs) because of terminating the relevant transactions and re-establishing the equivalent positions.

the same. The result of this is a recursive problem where the very definition of an institution's counterparty risk depends on their own counterparty risk in the future. We will discuss this problem in more detail when discussing DVA in Chapter 13. Before then, we will base exposure on standard risk-free valuation.

A final point to note about the above problems in determining closeout amounts is the time delay. Until an agreement is reached, an institution cannot be sure of the precise amount owed or the value of their claim as an unsecured creditor. This will create particular problems for managing counterparty risk, as discussed in Chapter 18. In a default involving many contracts (such as the number of OTC derivatives and the Lehman bankruptcy), the sheer operational volumes can make the time taken to agree on such valuations considerable.

8.1.4   Exposure as a short option position

Counterparty risk creates an asymmetric risk profile as shown by equation (8.1). When a counterparty defaults, an institution loses if the value is positive but does not gain if it is negative. The profile can be likened to a short[4] option position. Familiarity with basic options-pricing theory would lead to two obvious conclusions about the quantification of exposure:

- Since exposure is similar to an option payoff, a key aspect will be *volatility* (of the value of the relevant contracts and collateral).
- Options are relatively complex to price (compared with the underlying instruments at least). Hence, to quantify credit exposure even for a simple instrument may be quite complex.

By symmetry, an institution has long optionality from their own default. We note that this is not relevant from a risk management or regulatory point of view but may be relevant for pricing (via DVA, discussed in Chapter 13).

8.1.5   Future exposure

A current valuation of all relevant positions and collateral will lead us to a calculation of current exposure (admittedly with some uncertainty regarding the actual closeout amount). However, it is even more important to characterise what the exposure might be at some point in the future. This concept is illustrated in Figure 8.2, which can be considered to represent any situation from a single trade to multiple netted trades with some collateral arrangement associated with them. Whilst the current (and past) exposure is known with certainty, the future exposure is defined probabilistically by what may happen in the future in terms of market movements and contractual features of transactions, both of which are uncertain. Hence, in understanding future exposure one must define the level of the exposure and also its underlying uncertainty.

Quantifying exposure is extremely complex due to the long periods involved, the many different market variables that may influence the exposure and risk mitigants such as netting and collateral. Doing this will be the subject of the next chapter, whereas this chapter focuses on defining exposure and discussing intuitively the impact of aspects such as netting and collateral.

---

[4] The short option position arises since exposure constitutes a loss.

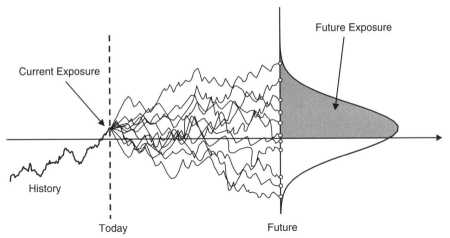

Figure 8.2 Illustration of future exposure with the grey area representing exposure (positive future values). The white area represents negative exposure.

8.1.6   Comparison to value-at-risk

In financial risk management VAR methods have, for almost two decades, been a popular methodology to characterise market risk. Any reader familiar with VAR will recognise from Figure 8.2 that the characterisation of exposure shares similarities with the characterisation of VAR. This is indeed true, although we note that in characterising exposure we are faced with additional complexities, most notably:

- *Time horizon.* Unlike VAR, exposure needs to be defined over multiple time horizons (often far in the future) so as to understand fully the impact of time and specifics of the underlying contracts. There are two important implications of this. The first is that "ageing" of transactions must be considered. This refers to understanding a transaction in terms of all future contractual payments and changes such as cash flows, exercise decisions, cancellations (e.g., callability) and more exotic aspects such as barrier crossings. Such effects may also create path dependency where the exposure at one date depends on an event defined at a previous date. In VAR models, due to the 10-day horizon used,[5] such aspects can be neglected. The second important point here is that, when looking at longer time horizons, the trend (also known as drift) of market variables (in addition to their underlying volatility and co-dependence structure) is relevant (as depicted in Figure 8.2). In VAR the drift can be ignored, again since the period is so short.
- *Risk mitigants.* Exposure is typically reduced by risk mitigants such as netting and collateral and the impact of these mitigants must be considered in order to properly estimate future exposure. In some cases, such as applying the correct netting rules, this requires knowledge of the relevant legal agreements. However, in the case of future collateral amounts, another degree of subjectivity is created since there is no certainty over the type of collateral and precise time that it would be received. Other contractual features of

---

[5] In many cases this is a 1-day horizon, which is simply scaled to 10 days.

transactions, such as termination agreements, may also create subjectivity and all such elements must be modelled, introducing another layer of complexity and uncertainty.

- *Application.* VAR is a risk management approach. Exposure must be defined for both risk management and pricing (i.e., CVA). This creates additional complexity in quantifying exposure and may lead to two completely different sets of calculations, one to define exposure for risk management purposes (Chapter 9) and one for pricing purposes (Chapter 12).

In other words, exposure is much more complex than VAR (which is itself a complex concept). Moreover, exposure is only one component of counterparty risk. However, no-one told you this was going to be easy did they?

8.2   METRICS FOR CREDIT EXPOSURE

In this section, we define the measures commonly used to quantify exposure. The different metrics introduced will be appropriate for different applications. There is no standard nomenclature used and some terms may be used in other contexts elsewhere. We follow the Basel Committee on Banking Supervision (2005) definitions, which are probably the most commonly used although, unfortunately, not the most intuitively named.

We begin by defining exposure metrics for a given time horizon. Note that in discussing exposure below, we are referring to the total number of relevant trades, netted appropriately and including any relevant collateral amounts. We will refer to this as the netting set.

8.2.1   Expected future value

This component represents the forward or expected value of the netting set at some point in the future. As mentioned above, due to the relatively long time horizons involved in measuring counterparty risk, the expected value can be an important component, whereas for market risk VAR assessment (involving only a time horizon of 10 days), it is not. Expected future value (EFV) may vary significantly from current value for a number of reasons:

- *Cash flow differential.* Cash flows in derivatives transactions may be rather asymmetric. For example, early in the lifetime of an interest rate swap, the fixed cash flows will typically exceed the floating ones (assuming the underlying yield curve is upwards sloping as is most common). Another example is a cross-currency swap where the payments may differ by several percent annually due to a differential between the associated interest rates. The result of asymmetric cash flows is that an institution may expect a transaction in the future to have a value significantly above or below the current one. Note that this can also apply to transactions maturing due to final payments.

- *Forward rates.* Forward rates can differ significantly from current spot variables. This difference introduces an implied drift (trend) in the future evolution of the underlying variables in question (assuming one believes this is the correct drift to use, as discussed in more detail in Section 8.6.2). Drifts in market variables will lead to a higher or lower future value for a given netting set even before the impact of volatility. Note that this point (although not always) may be simply another way to state the above point on cash flow differential since in many transactions such as swaps, the cash flow differential is essentially a result of forward rates being different from spot rates.

• *Asymmetric collateral agreements.* If collateral agreements are asymmetric (such as a one-way CSA) then the future value may be expected to be higher or lower reflecting respectively unfavourable or favourable collateral terms. (This is illustrated in the next chapter – Section 9.7.5.)

8.2.2 Potential future exposure

In risk management, it is natural to ask ourselves *what is the worse exposure we could have at a certain time in the future.* PFE will answer this question with reference to a certain confidence level. For example, the PFE at a confidence level of 99% will define an exposure that would be exceeded with a probability of no more than 1% (one minus the confidence level). PFE is therefore exactly the same measure as VAR except for the obvious differences that PFE needs to be defined at more than one future date and represents gains[6] (exposure) rather than losses. PFE is illustrated in Figure 8.3. Note[7] also that, as shown, the centre of the distribution can differ significantly from zero (this represents the future value of the transactions having a significantly positive or negative expected value).

The confidence level is consistent with the probability of losses exceeding the PFE. For example, a 99% confidence level means that the small probability of a loss greater than PFE in Figure 8.3 is 1%.

8.2.3 Expected exposure

In addition to PFE, which is clearly a risk management measure, the pricing of counterparty risk will involve expected exposure (EE), illustrated in Figure 8.4. This is the average of all exposure values. Note that only positive values (the grey area) give rise to exposures and other values have a zero contribution (although they contribute in terms of their *probability*). This means that the expected exposure will be above the expected future value (this is similar to the concept of an option being more valuable than the underlying forward contract).

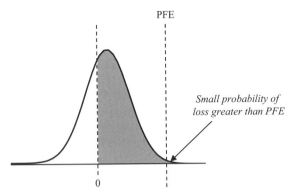

Figure 8.3 Illustration of potential future exposure. The grey area represents positive values which are exposures.

---

[6] Such a gain may not be an actual gain as there will be a corresponding hedge with a different counterparty.

[7] Note that the normal distribution used to depict the distribution of future values does not need to be assumed and also that PFE is often defined at confidence levels other than 99%.

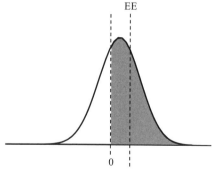

Figure 8.4 Illustration of expected exposure. The grey area represents positive values, which represent exposures.

8.2.4   EE and PFE for a normal distribution

In Appendix 8A we give simple formulas for the EE and PFE for a normal distribution. These formulas are reasonably simple to compute and will be useful for some examples used throughout this book.

Spreadsheet 8.1 EE and PFE for a normal distribution.

Example. Suppose future value is defined by a normal distribution with mean 2.0 and standard deviation 2.0. As given by the formulas in Appendix 8A, the EE and PFE (at the 99% confidence level) are

$$EE = 2.17$$
$$PFE = 6.65$$

If the standard deviation was increased to 4.0, we would obtain

$$EE = 2.79$$
$$PFE = 11.31$$

Note that the EE, like the PFE, is sensitive to standard deviation (volatility).

8.2.5   Maximum PFE

Maximum or peak PFE simply represents the highest PFE value over a given time interval, thus representing the worst-case exposure over the entire interval. This is illustrated in Figure 8.5.

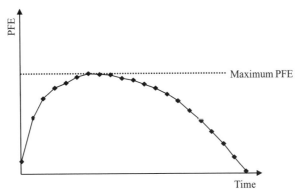

Figure 8.5 Illustration of maximum PFE.

8.2.6 Expected positive exposure

Since EE is already an average over all exposures, it is perhaps natural to continue this averaging over time. Expected positive exposure (EPE) is defined as the average exposure across all time horizons. It can therefore be represented as the weighted average of the expected exposure across time, as illustrated in Figure 8.6.

Spreadsheet 8.2 EPE calculation.

This single EPE number is often called a "loan equivalent", as the average exposure is equivalent to the average amount lent (via an exposure) to the counterparty in question. It is probably obvious that expressing a highly uncertain exposure by a single EPE or loan-equivalent amount can represent a fairly crude approximation, as it averages out both the randomness of market variables and the impact of time. However, we shall see later that EPE has a strong theoretical basis for pricing (Chapter 12) and assessing portfolio counterparty risk (Chapter 11).

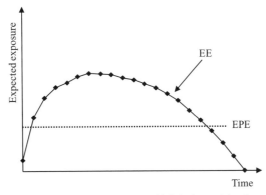

Figure 8.6 Illustration of expected positive exposure, which is the weighted average (the weights being the time intervals) of the EE profile.

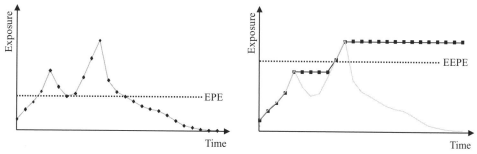

Figure 8.7 Illustration of effective EE and effective EPE.

8.2.7 Negative exposure

Exposure is represented by positive future values. Conversely, we may define negative exposure as being represented by negative future values. This will obviously represent the exposure from a counterparty's point of view. We can therefore define measures such as negative expected exposure (NEE) and expected negative exposure (ENE), which are the precise opposite of EE and EPE. Such measures will be useful for computing DVA (discussed in Chapter 13).

8.2.8 Effective expected positive exposure

Measures such as EE and EPE may underestimate exposure for short-dated transactions and not capture properly "rollover risk". This arises from current short-dated transactions that will be rolled over into new transactions at their maturity. For these reasons, the terms effective EE and effective EPE (EEPE) were introduced by the Basel Committee on Banking Supervision (2005). Effective EE is simply a non-decreasing EE. Effective EPE is the average of the effective EE. These terms are shown in comparison with EE and EPE in Figure 8.7. These measures approximately assume that any maturing transactions will be replaced.[8] The role and definition of EEPE is discussed in more detail in Chapter 10.

Spreadsheet 8.3 EPE and effective EPE example.

We emphasise that some of the exposure metrics defined above, whilst common definitions, are not always used. The definitions above are used by the Basel Committee on Banking Supervision (2005) and will be used consistently throughout this book.

8.3   FACTORS DRIVING CREDIT EXPOSURE

We now give some examples of the significant factors that drive exposure, illustrating some important effects such as maturity, payment frequencies, option exercise, roll-off and default. Our aim here is to describe some key features that must be captured, whilst the next chapter

---

[8] They essentially assume that any reduction in exposure is a result of maturing transactions. This is not necessarily the case.

will give actual examples from real trades. In all the examples below, we will depict PFE defined as a percentage of the notional of the transaction in question.

8.3.1 Loans and bonds

The exposures of debt instruments such as loans and bonds can usually be considered almost deterministic and approximately equal to the notional value. Bonds typically pay a fixed rate and therefore will have some additional uncertainty since, if interest rates decline, the exposure may increase and vice versa. In the case of loans, they are typically floating-rate instruments but the exposure may decline over time due to the possibility of prepayments.

8.3.2 Future uncertainty

The first and most obvious driving factor in exposure is future uncertainty. Forward contracts such as forward rate agreements (FRAs) and FX forwards are usually characterised by having just the exchange of two cash flows or underlyings (often netted into a single payment) at a single date, which is the maturity of the contract. This means that the exposure is a rather simple increasing function reflecting the fact that, as time passes, there is increasing uncertainty about the value of the final exchange. Based on normal distribution assumptions, such a profile will follow a "square root of time" rule, meaning that it will be proportional to some constant times the square root of the time (t):

$$\text{Exposure} \propto \sqrt{t} \qquad (8.3)$$

This is described in more mathematical detail in Appendix 8B. Such a profile is illustrated in Figure 8.8. We can see from the above formula that the maturity of the contract does not influence the exposure (except for the obvious reason that there is zero exposure after this date). For similar reasons, a similar shape is seen for vanilla options with an upfront premium. More exotic options may have more complex profiles.

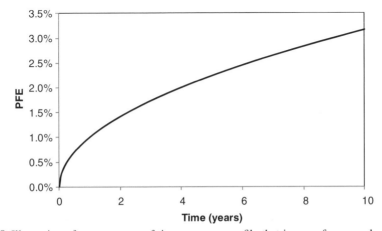

Figure 8.8 Illustration of a square root of time exposure profile that is seen, for example, in forward contracts and vanilla options positions.

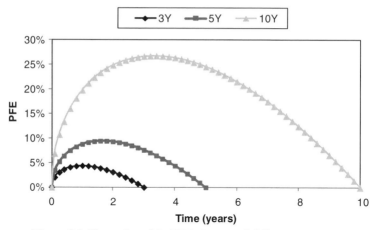

Figure 8.9 Illustration of the PFE of swaps of different maturities.

8.3.3 Periodic cash flows

Many OTC derivatives include the periodic payment of cash flows, which has the impact of reversing the effect of future uncertainty. The most obvious and common example here is a swap which is characterised by a peaked shape as shown in Figure 8.9. The shape arises from the balance between future uncertainties over payments, combined with the roll-off of swap payments over time. This can be represented approximately as

$$\text{Exposure} \propto (T - t)\sqrt{t} \qquad (8.4)$$

where T represents the maturity of the trade in question. This is described in more mathematical detail in Appendix 8C. The above function is initially increasing due to the $\sqrt{t}$ term but then decreases to zero as a result of the $(T - t)$ component, which is an approximate representation of the remaining maturity of the trade at a future time t. It can be shown that the maximum of the above function occurs at $T/3$, i.e., the maximum exposure occurs at one-third of the lifetime.

A swap with a longer maturity has much more risk due to both the increased lifetime and the greater number of payments due to be exchanged. An illustration of the swap cash flows is shown in Figure 8.10.

An exposure profile can be substantially altered due to the more specific nature of the cash flows in a transaction. A basis swap where the payments are made more frequently than they are received will then have more risk than the equivalent equal payment swap. This effect is illustrated in Figures 8.11 and 8.12.

Another impact the cash flows have on exposure is in creating an asymmetry between opposite trades. In the case of an interest rate swap, this occurs because of the different cash flows being exchanged. In a "payer swap", fixed cash flows are paid periodically at a deterministic amount (the "swap rate") whilst floating cash flows are received. The value of future floating cash flows is not known until the fixing date although, at inception, their risk-neutral value will be equal to that of the fixed cash flows. The value of the projected[9] floating cash

---

[9] By projected we mean the risk-neutral expected value of each cash flow.

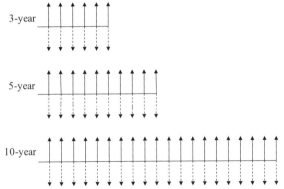

Figure 8.10 Illustration of a cash flows swap transaction of different maturities.

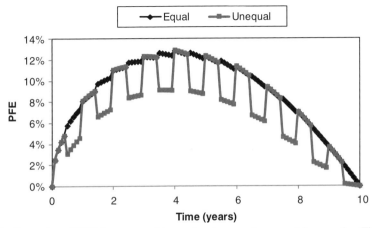

Figure 8.11 Illustration of PFE for swaps with equal and unequal payment frequencies. The latter corresponds to a swap where cash flows are received quarterly but paid only semi-annually.

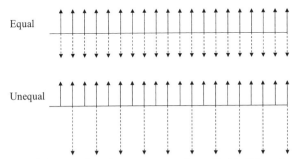

Figure 8.12 Illustration of the cash flows in swap transactions of with different payment frequencies.

flows depends on the shape of the underlying yield curve. In the case of a typical upwards-sloping yield curve, the initial floating cash flows will be expected to be smaller than the fixed rate paid whilst later in the swap the trend is expected to reverse. This is illustrated schematically in Figure 8.13.

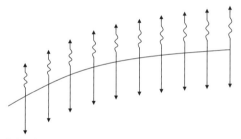

Figure 8.13 Illustration of the floating against fixed cash flows in a swap where the yield curve is upwards sloping. Whilst the risk-neutral expected value of the floating and fixed cash flows is equal, the projected floating cash flows are expected to be smaller at the beginning and larger at the end of the swap.

The net result of this effect is that the exposure of the payer swap is higher due to the expectation to pay net cash flows (the fixed rate against the lower floating rate) in the first periods of the swap and receive net cash flows later in the lifetime (Figure 8.14). Another way to state this is that the forward value of the swap is positive (by an amount defined by the expected net cash flows). The opposite "receiver" swap has a correspondingly lower exposure.

The above effect can be even more dramatic in cross-currency swaps where a high-interest-rate currency is paid against one with lower interest rates (as was the case, for example, with widely traded dollar versus yen swaps for many years before the dramatic US interest rate cuts of 2008/09), as illustrated in Figure 8.15. The overall high interest rates paid are expected to be offset by the gain on the notional exchange at the maturity of the contract,[10] and this expected gain on exchange of notional leads to a significant exposure for the payer of the high interest rate. In the reverse swap, it is increasingly likely that there will be a negative MtM on the swap when paying the

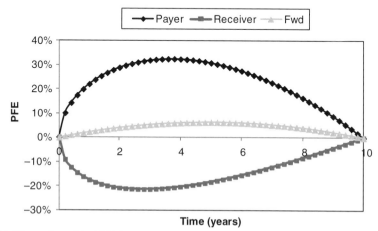

Figure 8.14 Illustration of the PFE for payer and receiver swaps and the associated forward value. The receiver swap is shown for ease of exposition as a negative exposure.

---

[10] From a risk-neutral point of view.

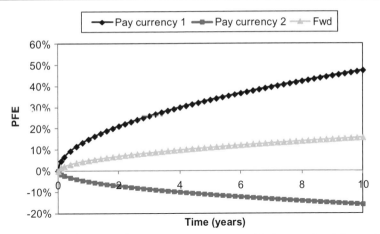

Figure 8.15 Illustration of the PFE for cross-currency swaps with the associated forward value with currency 1 having higher interest rates than currency 2. The latter case is shown for ease of exposition as a negative exposure.

currency with the lower interest rates. This creates a "negative drift", making the exposure much lower.

8.3.4 Combination of profiles

Some products have an exposure that is driven by a combination of two or more underlying risk factors. An obvious example is a cross-currency swap, which is essentially a combination of an interest rate swap and an FX forward trade.[11] This would therefore be represented by a combination of the profiles shown in Figures 8.8 and 8.9, as described in more mathematical detail in Appendix 8D. Figure 8.16 illustrates the combination of two such profiles. Foreign exchange exposures can be considerable due to the high FX volatility driving the risk coupled to the long maturities and final exchanges of notional. The contribution of the interest rate swap is typically smaller, as shown. We note also that the correlation between the two interest rates and the FX rate is an important driver of the exposure (in Figure 8.16 a correlation of 20% is assumed, which increases the cross-currency exposure[12]).

Spreadsheet 8.4 Simple example of a cross-currency swap profile.

In Figure 8.17 we illustrate the exposure for cross-currency swaps of different maturities. The longer-maturity swaps have marginally more risk due to the greater number of interest rate payments on the swap.

---

[11] Due to the exchange of notional at the end of the transaction.

[12] The impact of correlation can be seen in Spreadsheet 8.4. We note that the correlation here is not directly between the two interest rates and the FX rate, as would be required in practice.

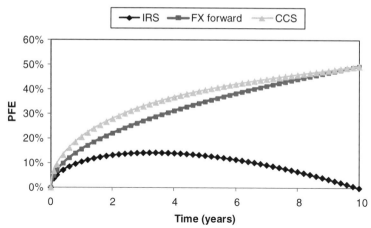

Figure 8.16 Illustration of a cross-currency swap (CCS) profile as a combination of an interest rate swap (IRS) and FX forward.

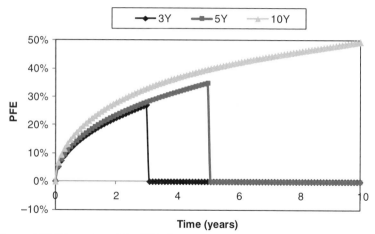

Figure 8.17 Illustration of the PFE of cross-currency swaps of different maturities.

8.3.5 Optionality

The impact of exercise decisions creates some complexities in exposure profiles. In Figure 8.18, we show the exposure for a European-style interest rate swaption that is swap-settled (physical delivery) rather than cash-settled.[13] The underlying swap has different payment frequencies also. We compare it with the equivalent forward swap. Before the exercise point, the swaption must always have a greater exposure than the forward swap[14] but thereafter, this trend will reverse since there will be scenarios where the forward swap has positive value but the swaption would not have been exercised. This effect is illustrated in Figure 8.19, which shows a scenario that would give rise to exposure in the forward swap but not the swaption.

---

[13] The cash-settled swaption has an identical exposure until the exercise date and then zero exposure thereafter. Physically settled swaptions are standard in some interest rate markets.

[14] The option to enter into a contract cannot be worth less than the equivalent obligation to enter into the same contract.

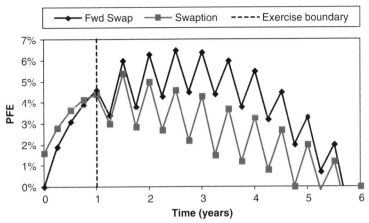

Figure 8.18 PFE for a swap-settled (physically settled) interest rate swaption and the equivalent forward swap. The option maturity is 1 year and the swap maturity 5 years.

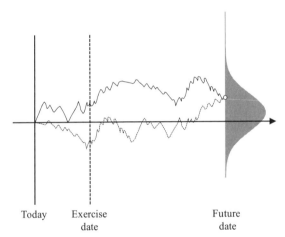

Figure 8.19 Illustration of exercise of a physically settled European swaption showing two potential scenarios of future value for the underlying swap. The solid line corresponds to a scenario where the swaption would be exercised, giving rise to an exposure at the future date. The dotted line shows a scenario that would give rise to an identical exposure but where the swaption would not have been exercised. The exercise boundary (point at which the swaption is exercised) is assumed to be the x-axis.

We can make a final comment about the swaption example, which is that surely in exercising one should incorporate the views on counterparty risk at that time. In other words, CVA should be a component in deciding whether to exercise or not. Yet we have not calculated CVA yet! We will discuss this recursive problem again in Chapter 12 (Section 12.4.3).

8.3.6 Credit derivatives

Credit derivatives represent a big problem for counterparty risk assessment due to wrong-way risk, which will be discussed extensively in Chapter 15. Even without this as a consideration, exposure profiles of credit derivatives are hard to characterise due to the discrete payoffs of the instruments. Consider the exposure profile of a single-name CDS as shown in

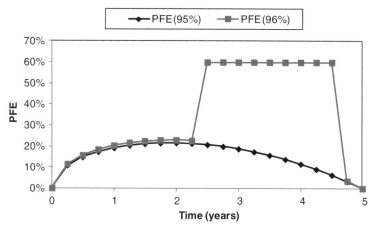

Figure 8.20 PFE for a long protection single-name CDS trade computed at confidence levels of 95% and 96%. A PFE of 60% arises from default with an assumed recovery rate of 40%.

Figure 8.20 (long CDS protection). The exposure increases in the early stages, which corresponds to scenarios in which the CDS premium (credit spread) will have widened. However, the maximum exposure on the CDS corresponds to the reference entity experiencing a credit event, which triggers an immediate payment of the notional less a recovery value (60% in the example, assuming a 40% recovery value). This is a rather unnatural effect[15] (see also Hille *et al.*, 2005), as it means that PFE may or may not represent the actual credit event occurring and is sensitive to the confidence level used. In the example, at 3 years the 95% PFE is defined by a large credit spread widening whilst the 96% PFE is defined by the credit event (and is three times larger). Using a measure such as expected shortfall[16] partially solves this problem.

Spreadsheet 8.5 Simple calculation of the exposure of a CDS.

8.4   UNDERSTANDING THE IMPACT OF NETTING ON EXPOSURE

We now consider in more depth the impact of netting on exposure. Since netting allows the future values of trades to offset one another, then the aggregate effect of all trades must be considered. As we shall see, there are several different aspects to contemplate before understanding the full netting impact on overall exposure with respect to a particular counterparty. In the next section, we will consider the impact of collateral on exposure. In both cases, we will describe the general points to consider before analysing netting and collateral from a more detailed and quantitative view in the next chapter.

---

[15] We comment that the above impact could be argued to be largely a facet of common modelling assumptions, which assume default as a sudden unanticipated jump event with a known recovery value (40%). Using a more realistic modelling of default and an unknown recovery value gives behaviour that is more continuous.

[16] Expected shortfall is a measure used in preference to VAR in some cases since it has more mathematically convenient properties and, unlike VAR, is a "coherent risk measure". In this case, it corresponds to the expected exposure conditional on being above the relevant PFE value.

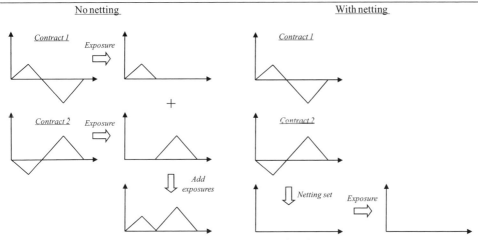

Figure 8.21 Illustration of the impact of netting on exposure.

8.4.1 The impact of netting on future exposure

We illustrate the impact of netting on exposure in Figure 8.21 with exactly opposite transactions. When there is no legal agreement to allow netting then exposures must be considered additive. This means that the positions do not offset one another. With netting allowable (and enforceable), one can add values at the netting set level before calculating the exposure and therefore the profiles shown give a zero exposure at all points in the future.

8.4.2 Netting and the impact of correlation

When considering the netting benefit of two or more trades, the most obvious consideration is the correlation between the future values (and therefore exposures also). A high positive correlation between two trades means that future values are likely to be of the same sign. This means that the netting benefit will be small or even zero. We illustrate this in Table 8.2, where we can see that the two sets of values create very little netting benefit. Netting will only help in cases where the values of the trades have opposite signs, which occurs only in

Table 8.2 Illustration of the impact of netting when there is positive correlation between MtM values. The expected exposure is shown assuming each scenario has equal weight

	Future value		Total exposure		
	Trade 1	Trade 2	No netting	Netting	Netting benefit
Scenario 1	25	15	40	40	0
Scenario 2	15	5	20	20	0
Scenario 3	5	−5	5	0	5
Scenario 4	−5	−15	0	0	0
Scenario 5	−15	−25	0	0	0
EE			13	12	1

Table 8.3 Illustration of the impact of netting when there is negative correlation between future values. The expected exposure is shown assuming each scenario has equal weight

	Future value		Total exposure		
	Trade 1	Trade 2	No netting	Netting	Netting benefit
Scenario 1	25	−15	25	10	15
Scenario 2	15	−5	15	10	5
Scenario 3	5	5	10	10	0
Scenario 4	−5	15	15	10	5
Scenario 5	−15	25	25	10	15
EE			18	10	8

scenario 3. The EE (average of the exposures assuming equally weighted scenarios) is reduced by only a small amount.

Highly correlated exposures[17] (as in Table 8.2) will provide the least netting benefit and, in case of identical distributions (add 10 to each scenario for trade 2 to see this effect), this simply corresponds to increasing the size of a given transaction, in which case there will be no netting benefit at all. Negative correlations are clearly much more helpful as future values are much more likely to have opposite signs and hence the netting benefit will be stronger. We illustrate this in Table 8.3, where we see that netting is beneficial in four out of the five scenarios. The EE is almost half the value without netting.

The extreme case of perfect negative correlation (as in Table 8.3) will provide the maximum netting benefit. In the case of identical distributions (subtract 10 from each scenario for trade 2 to see this effect), this simply corresponds to perfectly offsetting transactions (perhaps due to a cancellation via an unwind) in which case the netting benefit is 100% since there is no overall risk.

A majority of netting may occur across instruments of different asset classes that may be considered to have only a small correlation. One should note that this would still create a positive benefit. Indeed, for a simple example in Appendix 8E we show the reduction corresponding to the case of normal variables with zero mean and equal variance. We derive the following formula for the "netting factor" with respect to exposure under the assumption that future values follow a multivariate normal distribution:

$$\text{Netting factor} = \frac{\sqrt{n + n(n-1)\bar{\rho}}}{n} \qquad (8.5)$$

where n represents the number of exposures and $\bar{\rho}$ is the average correlation. The netting factor represents the ratio of net to gross exposure and will be $+100\%$ if there is no netting benefit $(\bar{\rho} = 100\%)$ and 0% if the netting benefit is maximum $(\bar{\rho} = -(n-1)^{-1})$.[18]

---

[17] Note that the future values in Table 8.2 have a correlation of 100% but the exposures do not.
[18] Note that there is a restriction on the correlation level that ensures the term inside the square root in equation (8.5) does not become negative. This is explained in appendix 8E.

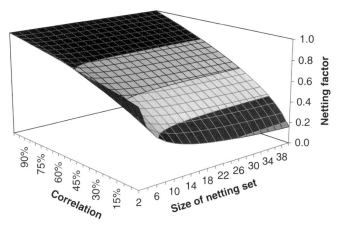

Figure 8.22 Illustration of the netting benefit in a simple example as a function of the size of the netting set (number of trades) and correlation as derived in Appendix 8E. Only positive correlations are shown.

We illustrate the above expression in Figure 8.22, where we can see that the netting benefit improves (lower netting value) for a large number of exposures and low correlation as one would expect, since these conditions maximise the diversification benefit. We note that this is a stylised example but it shows the general impact of correlation and the size of the netting set.

With no correlation, the simple formula tells us that the overall netting factor for n exposures is $1/\sqrt{n}$. This means, for example, that two independent exposures with zero mean and equal volatility have a netted exposure reduced to 71% of the exposure without netting. For five exposures, the netting factor decreases to 45%.

8.4.3   Netting and absolute value

In Table 8.2 the correlation between future values is 100% but the correlation of exposures is only 96%. We can therefore see that the netting benefit depends not only on the correlation of future values but also on the relative offset of the future values (in Table 8.2, trades 1 and 2 have positive and negative expected future values respectively which reduces the netting benefit). Netting not only depends on the *structural* correlation between the future values of trades, but also on the relative offset of those values from zero.

Consider the results shown in Table 8.4. Trade 1 has a strongly negative future value in all scenarios and therefore offsets the positive future value of trade 2 in scenarios 1–3. The EE is reduced from 9 to just 1. This is a result of trade 1 having an overall negative future value and is not solely linked to the structural correlation between the trades (indeed the future values have been constructed to have zero correlation). For example, if the trade 1 future values are increased by +10 then the reduction is only 3 even though the correlation of future values is the same.

An illustration of the impact of negative future value of a netting set is shown in Figure 8.23. Negative future value will create netting benefit irrespective of the structural correlation between trades.

A positive future value can be considered also to have a beneficial impact with respect to netting. Consider the results shown in Table 8.5. Trade 1 has positive future value in all scenarios, which nets with the negative future value of trade 2 in scenarios 4 and 5 even though the correlation of the trade 1 and trade 2 future values is 100%.

Table 8.4 Illustration of the impact of netting when there is an initial negative future value. The expected exposure is shown assuming each scenario has equal weight

	Future value		Total exposure		
	Trade 1	*Trade 2*	*No netting*	*Netting*	*Netting benefit*
Scenario 1	−20	25	25	5	20
Scenario 2	−25	15	15	0	15
Scenario 3	−15	5	5	0	5
Scenario 4	−15	−5	0	0	0
Scenario 5	−25	−15	0	0	0
EE			9	1	

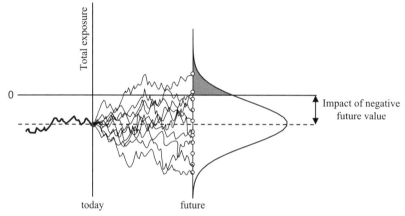

Figure 8.23 Schematic illustration of the impact of a negative future value.

Table 8.5 Illustration of the impact of netting when there is a positive future value. The expected exposure is shown assuming each scenario has equal weight

	Future value		Total exposure		
	Trade 1	*Trade 2*	*No netting*	*Netting*	*Netting benefit*
Scenario 1	45	15	60	60	0
Scenario 2	35	5	40	40	0
Scenario 3	25	−5	25	20	5
Scenario 4	15	−15	15	0	15
Scenario 5	5	−25	5	0	5
EE			29	24	5

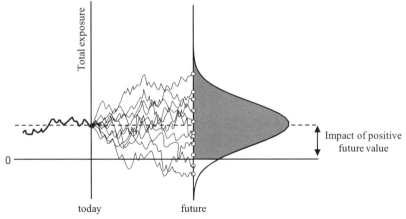

Figure 8.24 Schematic illustration of the impact of a positive future value.

An illustration of the impact of the positive future value of a netting set is shown in Figure 8.24. It is important to emphasise that even highly correlated trades can give rise to netting benefits as the exposure may not be as highly correlated (as in the example in Table 8.2). A practical example of this could be two otherwise identical swaps but with different swap rates.

8.5 CREDIT EXPOSURE AND COLLATERAL

We now describe the key components in understanding the impact of collateral on credit exposure. Collateral typically reduces exposure but there are many (sometimes subtle) points that must be considered in order to assess properly the true extent of any risk reduction. To account properly for the real impact of collateral, parameters such as thresholds and minimum transfer amounts must be properly understood and represented appropriately. Furthermore, the "margin period of risk" must be carefully analysed to determine the true period of risk with respect to collateral transfer.

In addition to reducing it, collateral transforms counterparty risk into other risks, which must be thoroughly appreciated. Most notably, collateral leads to operational risk, legal risk and liquidity risk. Effective collateral management is counterproductive unless these risks are well understood and properly managed. We will highlight these risks in this section, although the reader is also referred to a more comprehensive treatment of the liquidity risks that can arise due to the use of collateral in Chapter 14.

Collateralisation of credit exposure can substantially reduce counterparty risk but to quantify the extent of the risk mitigation is not trivial and requires many, sometimes subjective, assumptions. To the extent that collateral is not a perfect form of risk mitigation, there are three considerations, which are illustrated in Figure 8.25. Firstly, there is a granularity effect because it is not always possible to ask for all of the collateral required due to parameters such as thresholds and minimum transfer amounts (note that this can sometimes lead to a beneficial overcollateralisation as seen in Figure 8.25 where the collateral amount is for a short period greater than the exposure). Note that this must also consider the impact of collateral that an institution must themselves post. Secondly, there is a delay in receiving collateral which involves many aspects such as the operational components of requesting and receiving collateral to the possibility of collateral disputes. Thirdly, we must consider a

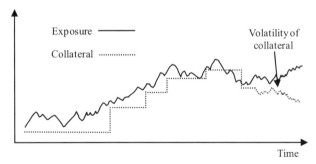

Figure 8.25 Illustration of the impact of collateral on credit exposure showing the delay in receiving collateral and the granularity receiving and posting collateral amounts discontinuously. Also shown is the impact of the volatility of collateral itself (for ease of illustration this is shown in the last period only).

potential variation in the value of the collateral itself (if it is not cash). We also emphasise that the treatment of collateral is path-dependent since the amount of collateral called for at a given time depends on the amount of collateral called (or posted) in the past. This is especially important in the case of two-way collateral agreements.

8.5.1 How much collateral?

The first question to ask is how much collateral may be requested at a given point in time. The parameters in a typical collateral support annex (CSA) do not, by design, aim for a continuous posting of collateral. This is because the operational cost and liquidity requirements of collateral posting are significant and one or both parties may find it beneficial to reduce such requirements within reason. The threshold and minimum transfer amount (discussed in Chapter 5) serve this purpose. The threshold is an amount below which collateral may not be called and the minimum transfer amount is the smallest amount that can be requested at a particular time. Note that in the case of a two-way CSA, both parties are subjected to the impact of thresholds and minimum transfer amounts.

The following steps define the amount of collateral required at a given time:

1. Add or subtract any specified independent amount to the market value of the trades (V).
2. Calculate the required collateral amount, taking into account the threshold using the formula

$$\max(V - \text{threshold}_I, 0) - \max(-V - \text{threshold}_C, 0) - C \qquad (8.6)$$

   where V represents the current mark-to-market value[19] of the relevant trades, threshold_I and threshold_C represent the thresholds for the institution and their counterparty, respectively and C represents the amount of collateral held already. If the above calculation results in a positive value then collateral can be requested, whilst a negative value indicates the requirement to post collateral (subject to the points below).
3. Determine whether the absolute value of the amount calculated above is above the minimum transfer amount. If not, then no call can be made.

---

[19] In comparison to previously, this can be considered to be the mark-to-market value.

4. If the amount is above the minimum transfer amount then round it to the relevant figure as specified in the CSA.

Spreadsheet 8.6 Call and return collateral example with logic relating to independent amounts, thresholds, collateral held, minimum transfer amount and rounding.

Let us consider a collateral calculation assuming a two-way CSA with the threshold, minimum transfer amount and rounding equal to $1,000,000, $100,000 and $25,000, respectively. Initially we show an example in Table 8.6 where there is an exposure resulting in $775,000 of collateral being called for. Whilst the mark-to-market of the underlying trades or "portfolio value" is $1,754,858, the first million dollars of exposure cannot be collateralised due to the threshold. The required collateral is assumed to be rounded up to the final amount of $775,000. Of course, assuming the counterparty agrees with all the calculations they will calculate a value of −$775,000, meaning that they will post this amount.

In Table 8.7 the situation has changed since the collateral has been received and the exposure of the institution has dropped. The result of this is that they are required to post collateral back. Note that, whilst they still have uncollateralised exposure, they are required to do this because of the threshold, i.e., they must return collateral as their net exposure of $848,920[20] has fallen below the threshold.

Table 8.6   Example collateral calculation

	Collateral calculation
Portfolio value	$1,754,858
Collateral held	—
Required collateral (equation (8.6))	$754,858
Above minimum transfer amount?	YES
Rounded amount	$775,000

Table 8.7   Example collateral calculation with existing collateral

	Collateral calculation
Portfolio value	$1,623,920
Collateral held	$775,000
Required collateral (equation (8.6))	−$151,080
Above minimum transfer amount?	YES
Rounded amount	−$150,000

---

[20] This is the portfolio value of $1,623,920 less the collateral held of $775,000.

8.5.2 Margin period of risk

Now we consider how long it will take to receive collateral. This involves estimating the "margin period of risk", which is much more than the contractual time between collateral (margin) calls. Such a period is crucial since it defines the length of time without receiving collateral where any increase in exposure will remain uncollateralised. It is important to model the exposure evolution over the margin period of risk to understand properly the impact of collateral. Where collateral is in a different currency and/or security then the variation in the FX rate and collateral price must also be accounted for as this adds additional risk. An example of having a bond as collateral will be discussed in the next chapter (Section 9.7.6).

In order to assess the margin period of risk, it is important to consider all of the following effects that may slow down the collateral process:

- *Valuation/margin call.* This represents the time taken to compute current exposure and the current market value of collateral, working out if a valid call can be made and finally making that call. This should include the time delay due to the contractual period between margin calls (often daily calls are contractual but sometimes longer periods may apply).
- *Receiving collateral.* The delay between a counterparty receiving a collateral request (fax/email) to the point at which they release collateral. The possibility of a dispute (i.e., the collateral giver does not agree with the amount called for) should be incorporated here.
- *Settlement.* Collateral will not be received immediately as there is a settlement period depending on the type of collateral. Cash collateral may settle on an intraday basis whereas other securities will take longer. For example, government and corporate bonds may be subject to 1-day and 3-day settlement periods, respectively.
- *Grace period.* In the event a valid collateral call is not followed by the receipt of the relevant collateral, there may be a relevant grace period before the counterparty would be deemed to be in default. This is sometimes known as the cure period.
- *Liquidation/closeout and re-hedge.* Finally, it will be necessary to liquidate collateral and closeout and re-hedge positions.

We finally note that all of the above assessments should be considered in a scenario where the relevant counterparty is defaulting. This worst-case scenario is valid since one must base all calculations on the assumption that a counterparty *will* default, as discussed in Chapter 3. An institution is not concerned with the time taken to receive collateral in normal cases and normal market conditions (which may well be small) because collateral performs no function (in terms of mitigating counterparty risk at least[21]) in these situations. Instead, the institution must consider a scenario where their counterparty is in default and market conditions may be far from normal. In such a scenario, the time before being able to take delivery of collateral after a valid call (or alternatively to put the counterparty into default) can be significant.

Under Basel II rules the minimum margin period of risk which must be assumed for OTC derivatives is 10 days (business) assuming collateral may be called for on a daily basis.[22] OTC derivatives and repo transactions are considered separately since they are governed by different documentation. Collateralisation in repo markets is generally tighter and the

---

[21] For example, in such a situation collateral may provide funding benefit as discussed in Chapter 14 in more detail.
[22] If this is not the case then the additional number of contractual days must be added to the time interval used.

Table 8.8 Example timeline for the margin period of risk in a worst-case scenario based on the assumption of a daily margin call. This does not consider the additional delay potentially caused by disputes. The Basel II minimum period (see Chapter 11 for more details) is also shown

	OTC derivatives (CSA[a]*)*	*Repo (GMRA*[b]*)*
Valuation/margin call	2 days	—
Receiving collateral	1 day	1 day
Settlement	2 days	1 day
Grace period	3 days	—
Liquidation/closeout and re-hedge	2 days	1 day
Total	10 days	3 days
Basel II minimum period	10 days	5 days

[a]Credit support annex.

[b]Global master repurchase agreement.

minimum period assumed is therefore lower due partly to the more complex nature of OTC derivatives, which makes valuation more complex. A possible scenario equating to such an assumption is shown in Table 8.8.

The above periods could easily be argued to be different depending on the precise assumptions and legal interpretations. Longer margin periods of risk could be appropriate depending on the collateral agreement and counterparty in question, as well as legal considerations and even the management structure of the institution concerned (institutions may be more lenient with certain counterparties to maintain good relations). In particular, Table 8.8 does not assess potential delays because of disputes or longer grace periods, which may be likely in practice. In particular, under Basel III, a margin period of risk of 20 days must be assumed in certain cases (Section 17.4.8). An institution should decide carefully on the relevant margin period of risk with all of these considerations taken into account.

For the examples in the next chapter, we will use a period of 10 days (or multiples thereof). Clearly, the margin period of risk is a rather crude "catch-all" parameter. By definition, there is little empirical data on this parameter[23] and the correct modelling of collateral calls is complex. For example, in the case of a dispute, the protocol that should be followed is that the undisputed amount is transferred and then the parties involved enter into negotiations to agree on the disputed amount. The latter procedure may take some significant time, as experienced by many institutions during the financial crisis. This process is illustrated in Figure 8.26. In theory, receiving collateral should be divided into two parts, the undisputed and disputed amounts with associated periods. In practice this is probably extraneous.

A simple example of the impact of collateral on exposure is given in Table 8.9 assuming a two-way CSA. In scenarios 1–3 the exposure is reduced significantly, since collateral is held. The exposure is not perfectly collateralised, which may be the case in practice due to factors such as thresholds and minimum transfer amounts. In scenario 4, the value of the portfolio is

---

[23] Although experiences such as the Lehman Brothers bankruptcy, where market participants typically took around 5-10 business days to closeout portfolios, are reasonably consistent with this value.

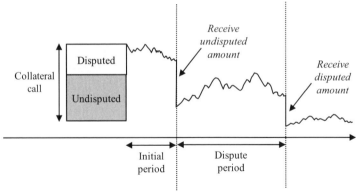

Figure 8.26 Illustration of the impact of a dispute on the margin period of risk period assuming that the institution does eventually receive the full amount, including the disputed component. We note that a fixed margin period of risk is a simple representation of the two periods above.

negative and collateral must therefore be posted but this does not increase the exposure (again in practice due to aspects such as thresholds and minimum transfer amounts). Finally, in scenario 5, the posting of collateral *creates* exposure.[24] In comparison with the benefits shown in the other scenarios, this is not a particularly significant effect, but it is important to note that collateral can increase as well as reduce exposure. These scenarios will be seen in actual cases in Section 9.5 of the next chapter.

8.5.3   Impact of collateral on exposure

Figure 8.27 shows an example of the impact of collateral on exposure. There are two main effects to notice. Firstly, the effect of a threshold is effectively to cap the exposure around the threshold amount. The collateral has little effect at the beginning and end of the profile where the exposure is relatively small. The second effect is the impact of the delay in receiving collateral; the need to post collateral and parameters such as minimum transfer amounts create some risk above the threshold.

Table 8.9   Illustration of the impact of collateral on exposure. The expected exposure is shown assuming each scenario has equal weight

	Future value		*Exposure*		
	Portfolio	*Collateral*	*No collateral*	*With collateral*	*Benefit*
Scenario 1	25	23	25	2	23
Scenario 2	15	12	15	3	12
Scenario 3	5	3	5	2	3
Scenario 4	−5	−2	0	0	0
Scenario 5	−15	−18	0	3	−3

---

[24] In practice, this can happen when previously posted collateral has not yet been returned as required.

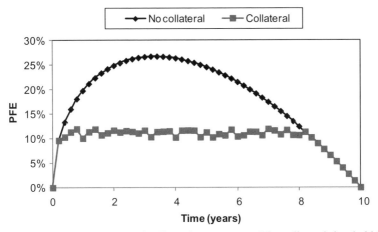

Figure 8.27 Illustration of the impact of collateral on exposure. The collateral threshold is assumed to be 10%.

8.5.4 Repos and overcollateralisation

Repos represent collateralised loans as discussed in Section 3.1.5. An institution borrowing cash and pledging some security as collateral is entering into a repo (repurchase agreement) whilst the other party is entering into a reverse repo. As a reverse repo is effectively a collateralised loan, it carries counterparty risk. The exposure on a reverse repo transaction is Exposure = Max(cash value − bond value, 0). To protect against counterparty risk, the collateral will attract a haircut meaning that the bond value at trade inception will exceed the amount of cash borrowed. In some repo transactions, variation margin (collateral) may be taken which will minimise the impact of changes in the bond price. Since a reverse repo is overcollateralised by the embedded haircut then the counterparty risk should be relatively small. There is a chance that a decline in the bond price (in-between variation margin calls) can create some counterparty risk. Figure 8.28 illustrates the exposure of a reverse repo transaction for different haircut levels assuming that variation margin is also used. The exposure (shown in terms of a bond notional of

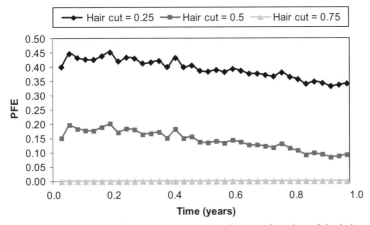

Figure 8.28 Illustration of the risk of a reverse repo transaction as a function of the haircut of maturity 1-year with the underlying collateral being a 5-year bond of notional amount 100. The margin period of risk is assumed to be 5 days.

100) is quite small and almost negligible if the haircut is reasonably large.

The above example assumes a 1-year repo transaction. Whilst this is possible, repos are typically of much shorter term (e.g., overnight or 1 week). This and the over-collateralisation mean that the counterparty risk in reverse repos is typically small in comparison with other cases.

8.6   RISK-NEUTRAL OR REAL-WORLD?

A final consideration in terms of defining credit exposure is whether it should be done with respect to risk-neutral or real-world parameters. In the most simple terms, pricing (CVA) should use the former whilst risk management (PFE) the latter. However, the actual situation is more complicated.

8.6.1   The importance of measure

Scenario generation for risk management purposes and arbitrage pricing theory use different "measures". Arbitrage-based pricing uses the so-called *risk-neutral* measure, which is justified through hedging considerations. Parameters (and therefore probability distributions) such as drifts and volatilities are market-implied and need not correspond to the real distributions (or even comply with common sense). For a risk management application, one does not need to use the risk-neutral measure and should be focused rather on the *real-world measure*, estimated using, for example, historical data. Risk-neutral parameters are typically used in pricing applications (CVA), whilst real-world parameters generally form the basis of risk management models (PFE). This is the general distinction but there are necessary exceptions, which we discuss below.

The types of parameters to be considered are:

- *Drift* – the trend of market variables.
- *Volatility* – the future uncertainty of market variables.
- *Correlation* – the co-movement between market variables.

In addition to the above general definitions, effects like mean-reversion should be considered. Many market variables (for example, commodities and interest rates) tend to mean-revert over time, which pulls long-term rates back to some average level. Mean-reversion has an impact on future spot prices and volatilities. Risk-neutral mean-reversions, whilst often hard to calibrate, tend to be smaller than mean-reversions estimated from historical data.

8.6.2   Drift

A key difference between VAR analysis for market risk (for example) and credit exposure quantification for CVA purposes is the time horizon concerned. In the relatively short market risk horizon (for example, 10-days in VAR approaches), the drift of an underlying asset is of secondary importance vis-à-vis its volatility and is often ignored. However, in the longer time horizons required for assessing credit exposure and CVA, drift will be a key consideration alongside volatility. In other words, the *trend* of an underlying variable can be just as important as its *uncertainty*.

One area where risk-neutral parameters tend to be used even for risk management simulations is the determination of the drifts of underlying risk factors, which are typically calibrated from forward rates. The consideration of drifts is important since the impact of volatility approximately follows the square root of time scaling whereas the drift scales more linearly – so in the end a strong drift will eventually dominate. Futures (or equivalently forward) prices have long been an important mechanism of price discovery in financial markets as they represent the intersection of expected supply and demand at some future point in time. Forward rates can sometimes be very far from spot rates and it is important to understand whether or not this is truly the "view of the market". Some important technical factors are:

- *Commodity prices.* In addition to market participants' view of the direction of commodity prices, storage costs (or lack of storage), inventory and seasonal effects can move commodities futures apart from spot rates. For high inventories the futures price is higher than the spot price (contango). When inventories are low, commodity spot prices can be higher than futures prices (backwardation).
- *Interest rates.* Yield curves may be upwards-sloping or downwards-sloping (and a variety of other shapes) due to the risk appetite for short-, medium- and long-term interest rate risk and the view that rates may increase or decrease.
- *Credit spreads.* Credit curves may be increasing or decreasing either due to demand for credit risk at certain maturities or the view that default probability will be increasing or decreasing over time.
- *Foreign exchange (FX) rates.* Forward FX rates are determined from an arbitrage relationship between the interest rate curves for the relevant currency pair. Expectation of future FX rates may have an influence on the current interest rate curves in the corresponding currencies. For example, FX forward rates are determined by a differential in the underlying interest rates. There has long been doubt regarding the ability of long-term forward rates to predict future spot rates; see, for example, Meese and Rogoff (1983) and a review by Sarno and Taylor (2002).

There has been much empirical testing of the relationship between spot and futures prices across different markets. It is a generally held belief that the futures price is a biased forecast of the future spot price, contrary to the efficient market hypothesis. If we take the view that the forward rate is the best expectation of the future spot rate then this may lead to a strong drift assumption. If this assumption is wrong then it will significantly overstate or understate the risk.

Despite the above problems with drifts, most PFE and CVA calculations will calibrate to forward rates in the market. From the CVA point of view, this is justified by hedging and more discussion is given in Section 16.3.1. For PFE purposes, this is often done more for convenience's sake, since it means that simple instruments are by construction priced properly and circumvents the need to attempt to estimate the "real-world" drift of risk factors.

The key point to take away is that markets are imperfect and so we cannot always expect current futures prices to be the best estimate of spot prices in the future. We should bear this in mind when assessing and pricing counterparty risk, especially for long time horizons. Advocating the estimation of real-world drifts is not the intention here. However, it is

Example. Consider a transaction whose future value has a volatility of 10% and a drift of 5% over 1 year.

The expected exposure based on the usual formula is

$$[5\% \times \Phi(5\%/10\%) + 10\% \times \varphi(5\%/10\%)] = 6.98\%$$

On the other hand, consider the reverse transaction. The expected drift would be -5% and the expected exposure

$$[-5\% \times \Phi(-5\%/10\%) + 10\% \times \varphi(-5\%/10\%)] = 1.98\%$$

Is it correct that the first transaction has a CVA that is approximately three and a half times greater than the second?

important to be aware of the implications of using risk-neutral drifts for PFE quantification and for CVA calculations when hedging is not perfect.

8.6.3 Volatility

To quantify exposure, one might use a historical estimate of volatility. However, to calculate CVA, implied volatilities are more relevant. Again there is the caveat related to the extent to which the volatility component of CVA can (and will) be hedged. We also note that (positive) mean-reversion has the effect of reducing long-term volatilities and thus is an important parameter to estimate.

If one uses a historical estimate of volatility then the implicit assumption is that the past will be a good indication of the future. It is also necessary to decide what history of data to use; a short history will give poor statistics whereas a long history will give weight to "old" meaningless data. In quiet markets, the lack of volatility in historical time series will give low risk numbers which may be misleading (recent changes to Basel capital rules require always using a stress period of data to overcome this – see Section 17.4.2), creating procyclicality. When markets suddenly become more volatile, the historical estimate will only gradually increase to reflect this as the window of data moves.

For most markets, there is likely to be implied volatility information, potentially as a function of strike and the maturity of the option. Implied volatility which will react quickly when the market becomes more uncertain and may be justified via the "market knows best" (or at least the market knows better than historical data). However, risk premiums embedded in market-implied volatilities will lead to a systematic overestimate of the overall risk. It has been argued that implied volatility is a superior estimator of future volatility (e.g., see Jorion, 2007, chapter 9) compared with historical estimation via time series approaches. The stability of the volatility risk premium and the fact that an overestimate of volatility will always lead to a more conservative[25] risk number give greater credence to this idea.

---

[25] Using implied volatility might be expected to produce an upwards bias due to a risk premium, leading to higher (more conservative) risk numbers.

8.6.4   Correlations

Whilst it is at least conservative to assume volatilities are high, the same is not true of other quantities. When estimating correlation for modelling exposure, there may not be an obvious way of knowing whether a high or low (or positive or negative) value is more conservative. Indeed, in a complex portfolio it may even be that the behaviour of the exposure with respect to correlation is not monotonic.[26] Therefore, the use of some market-implied parameters cannot be justified on the basis that the resulting risk numbers will be conservatively high.

Implied correlations are sometimes available in the market. For example, a quanto option has a payoff in a different currency and thus gives information on the implied correlation between the relevant FX rate and the underlying asset. One key aspect of correlation is to determine wrong-way risk. For example, a quanto CDS (a CDS where the premium and default legs are in different currencies) potentially gives information on the correlation between the relevant FX rate and the credit quality of the reference entity in the CDS (Section 15.4.2).[27]

Whilst implied correlation can sometimes be calculated, for most quantities no market prices will be available. This also means that the sensitivity of CVA to correlation parameters cannot generally be hedged and historical data will probably be used. A sensitivity analysis of correlation will be useful to understand the importance of a particular correlation parameter.

8.6.5   Conclusion

In summary, exposure quantification for risk management (PFE) should generally focus on real parameters, with market-implied parameters used when there are good reasons (such as in the example of using drifts and implied volatility above). Exposure quantification for pricing (CVA) should *generally* focus on (risk-neutral) market-implied parameters. An obvious exception here would be the need to use historical correlations since market-implied parameters are typically not observed. The potential difference between real-world and risk-neutral exposure will be discussed in Section 12.2.2, and we discuss the topic of hedging in more detail in Chapter 16.

8.7   SUMMARY

In this chapter we have discussed credit exposure. Some key definitions of potential future exposure, expected exposure and expected positive exposure have been given. The factors impacting future exposures have been explained and we have discussed the impact of netting and collateral. The next chapter will be concerned with the actual quantification of exposure, including all components discussed here such as netting and collateral.

---

[26] Meaning, for example, that the worse correlation may not be +100% or −100% but somewhere in-between.
[27] Assuming we can also observe the premiums of the "vanilla" or single-currency CDS.

Section III: Credit Value Adjustment

In this section, we discuss the pricing of counterparty credit risk via credit value adjustment (CVA). CVA is becoming an increasingly important concept for banks and other financial institutions, driven by accounting standards, regulation and best practice. In its most simple form, CVA quantification is relatively simple, respecting just a combination of exposure and default probability as already discussed in Chapters 9 and 10. Nevertheless, being able to compute CVA in an efficient, accurate and timely fashion represents a number of challenges. **Chapter 12** will cover the basics of CVA and methods for quantifying CVA. Of particular importance is that CVA is increasingly commonly calculated with reference to market parameters (risk-neutral) rather than real-world (e.g., historical) ones. This means that daily, and even intradaily, CVA calculations are increasingly becoming the norm. The pricing of new trades is often done with real-time *incremental CVA* calculations, which are challenging to make accurately. The market standard calculations and methodology for CVA will be described.

Another component of counterparty credit risk is debt value adjustment (DVA), which is the subject of **Chapter 13**. DVA is a mirror image of CVA as it represents the pricing of counterparty risk considering an institution's *own* default. This might sound somewhat counterintuitive but is a common practice, which is supported by accountancy standards. DVA has some theoretically nice properties as it provides a symmetry whereby market participants can agree on counterparty risk pricing. It also, however, has some difficult side-effects, which have sometimes formed a criticism of DVA (for example, an institution reports greater profits when their credit quality deteriorates). Indeed, some of the perceived negative aspects of DVA have led to it being excluded from Basel III capital rules (covered later in Chapter 17). We will go through the basics of DVA with examples and summarise the positive and negative factors behind it.

The calculation of CVA and DVA is done with respect to a "risk-free" value. Pricing financial instruments such as derivatives has always been relatively complex. However, certain aspects of valuation have been considered rather trivial. One of these is the use of LIBOR as a discount rate. In the good old days, a vanilla derivative such as a swap could be valued almost trivially by discounting cash flows on the LIBOR curve. Nowadays, the problem is much more complex and involves "OIS" or "dual-curve" discounting. Since this problem is related to counterparty risk valuation, we discuss valuation issues in **Chapter 14**. This chapter also discusses the implication of funding costs on transactions via FVA, which is an additional component, similar in many aspects to CVA. Like risk-free valuation, funding is a peripheral subject to counterparty risk, but is important to cover especially in understanding the relationship between DVA and funding. It also discusses the impact of collateral (CollVA) on valuation.

The valuation of counterparty credit risk often makes the assumption that exposure (market risk) and default probability (credit risk) are *independent*. This is a convenient assumption that makes much of CVA (and also DVA and FVA) quantification achievable. Unfortunately, this assumption is almost inevitably always incorrect as independence of financial variables is an idealistic assumption, especially during volatile periods and crises. Hence, there is a need to assess wrong-way (and right-way) risk, which arises from the dependence between exposure and default probability. **Chapter 15** is dedicated to this, where we will discuss practical ways in which CVA approaches can incorporate wrong-way risk. Wrong-way risk in different asset classes will be considered and the impact of collateral on mitigating wrong-way risk will be described. Consideration will be given to the impact of wrong-way risk on central counterparties, which is an important topic given the central clearing of credit derivative products.

9

Quantifying Credit Exposure

> *The trouble with our times is that the future is not what it used to be.*
>
> Paul Valery (1871–1945)

9.1 INTRODUCTION

In this chapter, we present an overview of the various methods to quantify exposure. These vary from the simple but crude to the more complex generic approach of Monte Carlo simulation. This latter approach forms the majority of the discussion, as it is the most complex and has rapidly become a standard. We will define, in detail, the methodology for exposure quantification via Monte Carlo simulation, including a discussion of the approaches to modelling risk factors in different asset classes and their co-dependencies.

To illustrate many of the concepts here and in the previous chapter, we will then show a number of real examples, looking in particular at the impact of netting and collateral as well as other relevant effects.

At the heart of the problem of quantifying exposure lies a balance between the following two effects:

- As we look into the future, we become increasingly uncertain about market variables. Hence, risk increases as we move through time.
- Many financial instruments have cash flows that are paid over time, and this tends to reduce the risk profiles as the instruments "amortise" through time.

Nevertheless, the practical calculation of exposure involves choosing a balance between sophistication and operational considerations.

9.2 METHODS FOR QUANTIFYING CREDIT EXPOSURE

9.2.1 Add-ons

The simplest approach to approximate future exposure is to take the current positive exposure and add a component that represents the uncertainty of the PFE in the future. This type of approach is highly simplistic and forms the basis of the Basel I capital rules (discussed in Section 17.3.1), often known as the "current exposure (CEM)" approach. At the trade level, the "add-on" component should account for:

- the time horizon in question;
- the volatility of the underlying asset class.

For example, longer time horizons will require larger add-ons, and volatile asset classes such as FX and commodities should attract larger add-ons. Add-on approaches are fast and allow exposures to be pre-calculated and distributed via simple "grids". Such grids allow a very quick look-up of the PFE impact of a new trade.

However, an add-on approach does not typically account for more subtle effects, including:

- the specifics of the transaction in question (currency, specifics of cash flows);
- if the transaction has a mark-to-market very far from zero (other than the addition of this mark-to-market when it is positive);
- netting;
- collateral.

It is difficult to incorporate such effects except with rather crude rules (for example, Basel I allows 60% of current netting benefit to apply to future exposure). More sophisticated add-on methodologies have been developed (e.g., Rowe, 1995; Rowe and Mulholland, 1999), although the increased complexity of such approaches must be balanced against the power afforded by a more generic method such as Monte Carlo simulation.

9.2.2   Semi-analytical methods

Semi-analytical methods are generally more sophisticated than the simple add-on approaches but still require some approximations. Their advantage lies in avoiding the time-consuming process of Monte Carlo simulation. A semi-analytical method will generally be based on:

- making some simple assumption regarding the risk factor(s) driving the exposure;
- finding the distribution of the exposure as defined by the above risk factor(s);
- calculating a semi-analytical approximation to a risk metric for that exposure distribution.

Some simple and general analytical expressions were described in the last chapter and formulas can be found in the appendices.

More product-specific analytical formulas[1] can be found in, for example, Sorensen and Bollier (1994) who show that the EE of an interest rate swap can be defined in terms of a series of interest rate swaptions. Arvanitis and Gregory (2001) extend this idea to consider a physically settled interest rate swaption (accounting for the exercise decision). Brigo and Masetti (2005b) consider the netting impact and derive formulas for portfolios of interest rate swaps in restricted cases. Obvious drawbacks of such approaches are:

- Semi-analytical calculations depend on simplifying assumptions made with respect to the risk factors involved. Hence, complicated distributional assumptions cannot typically be incorporated.

---

[1] We note that these analytical formulas are generally concerned with calculating risk-neutral exposures using underlyings such as traded swaption prices. Such approaches can also be used for real-world calculations (as is usual for PFE) by simply using alternative data sources.

- Path-dependent aspects, such as exercise decisions, will be hard to capture although Arvanitis and Gregory (2001) give one such example as described above.
- When collateral is present, the analytical expressions must be altered to account for this (although as we shall see later in this chapter, collateral itself can sometimes make exposure easier to approximate).
- Such calculations typically ignore netting effects (Brigo and Masetti is an exception), which are hard to incorporate in their most general fashion.

The last point above is the most significant one. Whilst some useful analytical formulas exist, these are only easy when there are a very small number of risk factors involved, such as is the case for single trades. However, netting implies a problem with potentially many dimensions and requires the use of more flexible simulation methods.

Before writing off faster analytical methods against the flexible, generic but slower approach of Monte Carlo simulation it is worth noting two points. Firstly, many netting sets (especially for non-collateralised counterparties) will actually be quite simple due to the rather narrow requirements of end-users of OTC derivatives. For example, a counterparty may trade only interest rate swaps in a single currency. Secondly, the nature of collateral changes a long-dated exposure into a mainly short-dated one (10-days, for example, as discussed in the last chapter). This suggests that a simpler approach based on value-at-risk methods may be relevant. Indeed, we will discuss the approximation of collateralised exposures at the end of this chapter.

Whilst simple and/or collateralised netting sets may permit analytical calculations that will be much faster than Monte Carlo approaches, they do create difficulties from an operational point of view. A counterparty trading single currency swaps wanting to trade an FX forward may create a netting set that no longer can be handled within the analytical approximation used. Alternatively, a sharp drop in the MtM of trades in a netting set may take the exposure below the CSA threshold and deem the collateral approximation less accurate (see later for details on why a CSA with a threshold is harder to approximate). Hence, whilst Monte Carlo approaches may sometimes be unnecessarily complex, their generality is a significant advantage.

9.2.3 Monte Carlo simulation

Monte Carlo simulation, whilst the most complex and time-consuming method to assess exposure, is completely generic and copes with many of the complexities, such as transaction specifics, path dependency, netting and collateralisation, that simpler approaches may fail or struggle to capture. It is the only method which, in the case of a high-dimensionality netting set, can realistically capture the relatively large number of risk factors and their correlations. Whilst add-on and analytical approaches still exist, Monte Carlo simulation of exposure has been considered state-of-the-art for some time.

9.3   MONTE CARLO METHODOLOGY

9.3.1 Simulation model

The first task is to define the relevant risk factors and decide on the models to be used for their evolution. However, it is important to strike a balance between a realistic model and one which is parsimonious. For example, there are 50–60 or more risk factors defining an interest rate curve, whereas the simplest interest rate models involve only one factor. A model involving two or three factors may represent the right compromise. Such an approach will capture more of the possible curve movements than would a single-factor model, but without producing the unrealistic curve shapes and arbitrageable prices that a model for each individual risk factor might generate.

Another reason for simpler underlying models for risk factors is the need to incorporate co-dependencies (correlations)[2] in order to capture the correct multidimensional behaviour of the netting sets to be simulated. The correct description of the underlying risk factors and correlations leads to a significant number of model parameters. A balance is important when considering the modelling of a given set of risk factors (such as an interest rate curve) and the correlation between this and another set of risk factors (such as an interest rate curve in another currency). There is no point in having sophisticated univariate modelling and naïve multivariate modelling. Due to expertise in different product areas, an institution may have good univariate models for interest rates, FX, inflation, commodities, equities and credit. However, these may be linked via the naïve use of correlations. We will give examples of specific models in Section 9.4.

Whilst the choice of models for the underlying market variables is a key aspect, calibration of these models is just as important since future scenarios will depend on this. Models calibrated using historical data predict future scenarios based on statistical patterns observed in the past and assume that this previous behaviour is a good indicator of the future; such models are sometimes slow to react to changes in market conditions. Models calibrated to market prices tend to be more forward-looking but contain components such as risk premiums and storage costs that introduce bias. Furthermore, they may produce exposures that jump dramatically, for example during a period of high volatility.

Generally, the choice of whether to use historical or market data depends on the application. For risk management purposes, a model must provide a reasonable distribution of the possible risks of the transactions and thus account for a large fraction of the future plausible scenarios. The model will typically be calibrated to historical data. For pricing, the most important aspect is matching current market data and providing stable hedge ratios. Given the two very different applications, PFE and CVA, whilst using the same underlying simulation framework, are often calculated with different parameterisations (or the same or even different models). We do note that there are exceptions to this rule. Typically, even risk management models will be calibrated to current forward rates in the market. Arguably, this is done more for reasons of convenience than because it is the most appropriate choice (this was discussed more in Section 8.6.2). Also, when using pricing models calibrated to market data, there are still parameters that cannot be implied from market prices and must be estimated historically (correlations between risk factors being the obvious example).

Model choice must also involve decisions over effects such as mean-reversion. Failure to include mean-reversion can lead to unrealistically large exposures at long time horizons. However, calibration of these quantities may not be easy (mean-reversions, for example, are not trivial to calibrate from either historical or market data). Other specific features that need to be considered for one or more asset classes are seasonality, jumps, credit migrations and defaults.

---

[2] Correlation is often the specific way in which to represent co-dependency and is very commonly used. We will use correlation from now on but note that there are other ways to model co-dependency, as discussed further in Chapter 15 (Section 15.2.4).

It must be possible and practical to simulate discrete scenarios of the risk factors using the model. Typically, many thousands of scenarios will be required at many points in time and hence there must be an efficient way in which to generate these many scenarios.

It is important to emphasise that the simulation model must be generic to support consistent simulation of the many risk factors that would be required to value a quite complex netting set. This is very different to modelling in the front office, where many models (and individual calibrations thereof) will be used. This leads to unavoidable differences (hopefully small) between current valuation as seen from the counterparty risk system and the relevant front-office systems.

9.3.2   Scenario generation

Having made a choice of risk factors and underlying model, it is necessary to generate scenarios via simulation of these risk factors. Each scenario is a joint realisation of risk factors at various points in time. Scenarios should be *consistent* since it must be possible to see the impact of various risks offsetting one another,[3] at least within a given netting set. Scenario consistency outside netting sets, where risks are additive, is not important as long as a sufficient number of simulations are used.

One will first need to choose a grid for simulation, as illustrated in Figure 9.1. The number of grid points must be reasonably large to capture the main details of the exposure, but not so large as to make the computations unfeasible. A typical value is in the region of 50–200. The final simulation date must obviously be greater than or equal to the longest maturity instrument under consideration. Note that the spacing of the above dates need not be uniform for reasons such as roll-off (discussed below) and identifying settlement risk. In addition, since intervals between simulation points are often greater than the length of the margin period of risk, it may be necessary to include additional "look-back" points for the purposes of simulating the impact of collateral (Figure 9.2). Furthermore, the ability to change grids for different counterparties is beneficial due to different maximum maturity dates, collateral terms and underlying instrument type.

When exposure is calculated at only discrete points, it is possible to miss key areas of risk or "hotspots". Exposure profiles can be highly discontinuous over time due to maturity dates, option exercise, cash flow payments and amortisation. The risk of missing jumps in exposure caused by these aspects is called "roll-off risk". Such jumps may be small in duration but large in magnitude. Daily jumps correspond to settlement risk (Section 3.1.2). The impact of roll-off risk is shown in Figure 9.3.

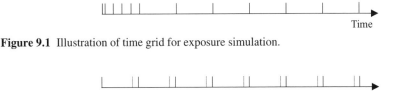

Figure 9.1 Illustration of time grid for exposure simulation.

Time

Figure 9.2 Illustration of time grid for exposure simulation with additional points included for collateral calculations.

---

[3] So a given scenario represents the same state of the world across trades.

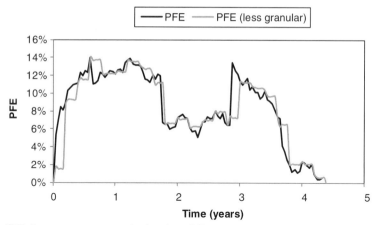

Figure 9.3 PFE for a counterparty calculated at different levels of granularity. In the normal case, the time intervals are spaced by 10 business days, while in the less granular case, the interval is five times greater.

Roll-off risk can be controlled by using non-time-homogeneous time grids (as in Figure 9.1), at least providing a better definition as discrepancies become closer. However, this can mean that the PFE may change significantly from day to day due to exposure jumps gradually becoming engulfed within the more granular short-term grid. A better approach is to incorporate the critical points where exposure changes significantly (for example, due to maturity dates, settlement dates and cash flow payment dates) into the time grid. This must be done separately for each netting set. The ability to use different grids is important; for example, to provide more granularity for certain instrument types or shorter maturities.

Another question to decide is whether the simulation should be done pathwise or via a direct simulation as illustrated in Figure 9.4. As described by Pykhtin and Zhu (2007), a pathwise approach simulates an entire possible trajectory whereas a direct approach simulates each time point independently. Both methods should produce the same underlying distributions and results. However, the pathwise method is more suitable for path-dependent derivatives and those with American or Bermudan features. Therefore, for simulating exposure (although not necessarily for CVA calculations), the best approach is pathwise.

9.3.3 Revaluation

Once the scenarios have been generated, it is necessary to revalue the individual positions at each point in time in the future. For example, to revalue an interest rate swap in a given scenario at a given point in time, one must calculate the corresponding risk factors (interest rates), and then use the standard pricing function for the swap as a function of these interest rates (for example, via a formula for reconstructing the yield curve at this particular point in time).

The revaluation step clearly requires the use of efficient valuation models and algorithms. Suppose the total population of trades and exposure calculation involves:

- 250 counterparties;
- on average, 40 trades with each counterparty;
- 100 simulation steps;
- 10,000 scenarios.

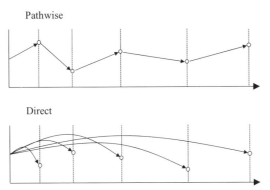

Pathwise

Direct

Figure 9.4 Illustration of the difference between pathwise and direct simulation. Note that the direct simulation may be more time-consuming and problematic with capturing path dependence because it does not use the previous time point as a starting point.

Then the total number of instrument revaluations will be $250 \times 40 \times 100 \times 10,000 = 10,000,000,000$ (10 billion). This has very significant implications for the computation speed of pricing models as this step usually represents the bottleneck of a PFE or CVA calculation.

Pricing functions for vanilla instruments must be highly optimised with any common functionality (such as calculating fixings) stripped out to optimise the calculation as much as possible. Whilst such pricing functions are usually relatively fast, the sheer volume of vanilla products makes this optimisation important.

Exotic products may present more of a problem since, whilst there may be fewer of them, pricing often involves lattice-based or Monte Carlo methods that may be too slow. There are three ways to get around this problem:

- *Approximations.* Sometimes crude ad hoc approximations may be deemed of sufficient accuracy; for example, approximating a Bermudan swaption as a European swaption (which admits a closed-form formula).
- *Grids.* Grids giving the MtM of a trade can be used as long as the dimensionality of the problem is not too large. Such grids may be populated by front-office systems and therefore be in line with trading desk valuation models. The PFE calculation will look up (and possibly interpolate) the relevant values on the grid rather than performing costly pricing.
- *American Monte Carlo methods.* This is a generic approach to utilising future Monte Carlo simulations to provide good approximations of the exposure[4] at a given point in time. Examples of this and related approaches can be found in Longstaff and Schwartz (2001), Glasserman and Yu (2002) and Cesari *et al.* (2009). This may be the best solution for CVA quantification but may not be as relevant for PFE and risk management (see Section 9.4.1).

Alternatively, methods such as described by Gordy and Juneja (2008) can be utilised to have a more efficient calculation of EE values. Such an approach makes use of the

---

[4] It can be used for both expected exposure (for CVA purposes) and potential future exposure (for risk management purposes). However, the accuracy in the latter case is typically worse. Furthermore, being a generic approach, this will not match front-office valuations exactly.

fact that, in exposure calculation, the *distribution* of instrument values is the key element to be estimated.

Whilst there are many ways to improve the efficiency of the revaluation step, it is likely that this will have to be backed up by some quite significant hardware with thousands of CPUs. Given that a large institution may have to calculate the exposure of millions of trades in thousands of paths for hundreds of time steps, this is not surprising.

9.3.4 Aggregation

Once the revaluation step has been done, there will be a large amount of data in three dimensions corresponding to the trade (k), simulation (s) and time step (t). We represent the future value as a function of each of these components: $V(k, s, t)$. This information must now be aggregated to the netting set level. This requires knowledge of the relevant netting conditions for the counterparty in question. Let us assume that trades $k = 1, K$ all belong to a single netting set (*NS*). The future value for this netting set is characterised by the matrix

$$V_{NS}(s, t) = \sum_{k=1}^{K} V(k, s, t). \tag{9.1}$$

Now, $V_{NS}(s, t)$ defines the net future value of the netting set at simulation s and time step t. This is a major component required for subsequent analysis and will typically need to be stored. It may not be necessary to store all of the individual trade information, $V(k, s, t)$, although this might be needed for calculating certain quantities (for example, see the discussion on marginal exposure in Section 9.6.3).

9.3.5 Post-processing

The previous step provides future values in all scenarios and time steps, aggregated to the appropriate level (e.g., netting set). The purpose of post-processing is to go through these values and apply the logic corresponding to a certain risk mitigant, the most obvious being collateral. Post-processing for a collateralised exposure means analysing each simulation path and applying the relevant logic to determine, at each point, how much collateral would be posted. Typically, this can be done independently of (but after) the previous steps under the assumption that the collateral parameters do not depend on any of the underlying market variables but only on the total exposure in one or more netting sets.

Post-processing can also apply to features such as additional termination events (break clauses), discussed in Section 4.3.2. We note that these must be typically accounted for at the trade level. We will discuss post-processing in Section 9.7.

9.3.6 Extraction

Finally, once all the above steps have been completed, one can extract any metrics desired (for example, for risk management, pricing or regulatory purposes). Whilst scenarios can be collapsed into metrics such as EE and CVA, in order to account for future trades all of the $V_{NS}(s, t)$ values must be kept (for example, to facilitate the calculation of incremental exposure, which is discussed later in Section 9.6.2).

9.4   MODELS FOR CREDIT EXPOSURE

In this section, we provide details on models used for exposure simulation considering some basic points on the modelling in different asset classes (see also Appendix 9A for more mathematical detail). We consider the calibration issues, the balance between complex and simple models, and give some specific examples for various asset classes. We will provide only an overview and the reader is directed to Cesari *et al.* (2009) for a more mathematical treatment of the modelling of credit exposure.

A key point to bear in mind is that, sometimes, simple and parsimonious approaches with fewer parameters can justifiably be favoured over ones that are more complex. Modelling many risk factors to define a curve evolution is unnecessary and may lead to excessive complexity and unrealistic future scenarios. This is especially true given the complex co-dependencies that may need to be modelled and the fact that problems such as wrong-way risk (Chapter 15) are still to be addressed. Whilst the total number of risk factors needing to be modelled is likely to be in the hundreds (depending on asset class coverage), it is important to keep this number to a minimum.

Whilst more advanced models for exposure are important, the possibility of false accuracy must also be considered. If there are other components of CVA with a large degree of uncertainty then a more sophisticated modelling of exposure may be futile. An obvious example of such a component would be the assessment of the credit spread of a counterparty, which can be rather subjective and prone to inaccuracy.

9.4.1   Risk-neutral vs real-world

In the last chapter (Section 8.6), the difference between risk-neutral and real-world approaches was discussed. In general, for risk management of counterparty risk, measures such as PFE are computed under the real-world measure whilst pricing (CVA) is risk-neutral. There are fundamental differences between PFE and CVA approaches, as illustrated in Table 9.1. PFE methods for risk management tend to use historical data, are conservative and tie in with passive approaches such as credit limits. On the other hand, CVA pricing approaches are based on market data and need to be accurate to reflect correct pricing and hedging mechanisms. Exposure simulation must typically be able to support both approaches concurrently

A more subtle problem with the separation between real-world and risk-neutral approaches is illustrated in Figure 9.5. Revaluation of trades at future dates should always be done using risk-neutral valuation as this is what happens in reality. Risk management

Table 9.1   Illustration of the different requirements for PFE and CVA approaches

	PFE	*CVA*
Approach	Real-world	Risk-neutral
Calibration	Historical data	Market data
Precision	Conservative	Accurate
Mitigation	Limit	Hedging

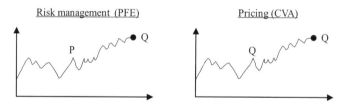

Figure 9.5 Illustration of the different requirements from scenario models for risk management and pricing of counterparty risk. For risk management, simulations tend to be done under the real-world (P) measure whilst revaluations must be risk-neutral (Q-measure). For pricing purposes, both scenarios and revaluations are typically risk-neutral.

of counterparty risk therefore needs to use real-world (denoted by P for P-measure) simulations and risk-neutral (Q-measure) pricing. This inconsistency can cause difficulties, for example, in using American Monte Carlo methods as discussed in Section 9.3.3. On the other hand, pricing (CVA) is all under the Q-measure and is therefore self-consistent and less problematic.

This problem with PFE is one reason why some practitioners may suggest that risk-neutral simulations should also be used for risk management purposes. However, this is not necessarily a better solution, as risk-neutral parameters can often be biased compared with real-world ones (see discussion in Section 8.6). Using risk-neutral parameters for risk management may cause excess volatility, which makes approaches such as credit limit control unnecessarily complex. It also invalidates standard procedures such as backtesting that are done in the real world.

Finally, we should re-emphasise that pricing, whilst always done risk-neutrally, depends critically on the ability to hedge, which for CVA is far from trivial (as will be discussed in Chapter 16). There is therefore the argument that the right-hand side of Figure 9.5 contains significant dependence on real-world parameters.

9.4.2 Interest rates

The simplest interest rate model that has historically been used for estimating exposure is the one-factor Hull and White (or extended Vasicek) model (Hull and White, 1990). In this model, the short rate follows a Brownian motion with mean-reversion. Mean-reversion dictates that when the rate is above some "mean" level, it is pulled back towards that level with a certain force. The mean-reversion level can be time-dependent, allowing this model to be fitted to the initial yield curve.

**Spreadsheet 9.1 Simulation of an interest rate swap exposure
with a one-factor Vasicek model.**

In practice, multi-factor models tend to be used for simulation of yield curve movements. Historically, a substantial portion of the observed movements in yield curves can be explained in terms of three principal factors (e.g., see Rebonato, 1998). These factors

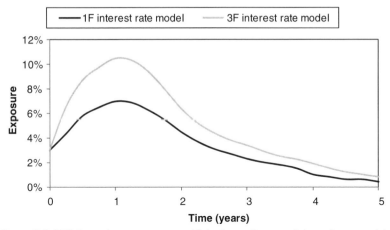

Figure 9.6 PFE for an interest rate cap with both one-factor and three-factor models.

correspond to parallel shifts, twists and butterfly movements. Such approaches have been described as more realistic models for interest rate risk modelling by Jamshidian and Zhu (1997) and Reimers and Zerbs (1999). To illustrate the need for multi-factor models, we show the PFE of an interest rate cap in Figure 9.6 with both one-factor and three-factor approaches calibrated against the same historical data. A one-factor model generally only captures parallel moves in the yield curve with some limited steepening and flattening movements. The more sophisticated three-factor approach, on the other hand, produces more complex changes in the shape of the yield curve. This leads to a significantly greater PFE for the interest rate cap, which has a strong sensitivity to changes in yield curve shape. For CVA purposes, the need for multi-factor models is similar but more driven by the need to have the flexibility to match market prices.

Two fundamental types of model tend to be chosen for multi-factor interest rate modelling, namely short-rate or LIBOR market models (LMM; e.g., Brace *et al.*, 1997). Short-rate models have the advantage that they are typically numerically simpler in terms of calibration and simulation and are usually easier to combine with models for other asset classes. However, moving to non-Gaussian short-rate models (to avoid the possibility of negative interest rates) reduces tractability. LMM models tend to be more complex numerically, requiring state-dependent drift terms so that simulation is slower, but are more flexible in terms of calibration to other instruments such as caplets and swaptions. For the latter reasons, LMM models tend to be more suitable for CVA approaches.

As discussed in Chapter 14, the importance of funding may mean that the funding curve should be modelled as another interest rate process. This may also be related as a basis to the CDS spread.

9.4.3 FX and inflation

A traditional model for FX rates is to assume a standard geometric Brownian motion, which ensures that the FX rates are always positive. The drift is typically calibrated to the forward rates (although in the case of PFE we note the potential problem with doing this in Section 8.6.2).

For PFE purposes, historical volatility may be used and it may be relevant to add some mean-reversion to avoid FX rates becoming unrealistically large or small, especially for long time horizons. This long-term mean may be set at the current spot level or set to a different level due to the view of a risk manager, historical analysis, forward rates or simply to be conservative. Whilst it is conservative to ignore mean-reversion, in such a model, long-term FX rates can arguably reach unrealistic levels.

CVA approaches will typically calibrate spot FX volatility to the prices of FX options (although this can be problematic for long-dated options). However, it will not match options on currency cross-rate options. More sophisticated FX approaches are much more costly, especially in the context of the other asset classes.

In some circumstances, it may be relevant to include jumps in FX rates that could occur due to a shock to the economy of a given currency or even a devaluation, perhaps linked to a sovereign default. Jump-diffusion processes have often been used to characterize emerging markets or pegged currencies. The shorter the time horizon, the greater the importance of capturing such jumps (e.g., see Das and Sundaram, 1999). We will address these points in detail in Section 15.4.2.

Inflation products can be modelled in a similar way to FX since the underlying real and nominal rates can be treated as local and foreign currencies. The standard yield curve essentially determines the local currency whilst inflation-linked bonds can be used to calibrate the foreign currency. Volatility may be calibrated to inflation-linked options.

9.4.4 Commodities

Commodities tend to be highly mean-reverting around a level, which represents the marginal cost of production (e.g., see Geman and Nguyen, 2005; Pindyck, 2001). Furthermore, many commodities exhibit seasonality in prices due to harvesting cycles and changing consumption throughout the year. For commodities, the use of risk-neutral drift is particularly dangerous due to strong backwardation and contango present for some underlyings (see Section 8.6.2). However, non-storable commodities (for example, electricity) do not have an arbitrage relationship between spot and forward prices and therefore the forward rates might be argued to contain relevant information about future expected prices.

9.4.5 Credit spreads

Credit products have significant wrong-way risk and so a naïve modelling of their exposure without reference to counterparty default is dangerous, a problem we return to in detail in Chapter 15. Credit spreads, like the above asset classes, require a model that prevents negative values although such models are less tractable. They also, more than any other asset class, are extremely volatile and might be expected to have jumps caused by a sudden and discrete change in credit quality (such as an earnings announcement or ratings downgrade or upgrade).

9.4.6 Equities

The standard model for equities is a geometric Brownian motion, which assumes that the equity returns are normally distributed. The underlying volatility could also be either market-implied or determined from historical analysis. For practical purposes, it may not be advisable to attempt to simulate every single underlying stock. Not only is this highly time-consuming, but it also leads to a large correlation matrix that may not be of the appropriate form.[5] Rather, one may choose to simulate all major indices and then estimate the change in the individual stock price by using the beta[6] of that stock.

9.4.7 Correlations

A typical exposure simulation will model hundreds, perhaps even thousands, of risk factors. This then requires a large correlation matrix to specify the multidimensional dependency. Even for a single trade, this dependency can be important: a cross-currency swap has risk to the FX rate and the two interest rates and hence at a minimum three risk factors and the three correlations between them must be accounted for. However, individual correlations will have very different importance in defining future exposure. For two interest rate swaps in different currencies, the correlation between the interest rates may be a very important parameter. However, the correlation between, for example, the price of oil and an FX rate may be unimportant or completely irrelevant. It will be informative to make a distinction between *intra* and *inter* asset class correlations.

The nature of a lot of business for institutions is asset class-specific by counterparty. For example, interest rate products may be traded with one counterparty and commodities with another. Intra asset class dependencies will be important components. For example, to specify the future exposure of two interest rate trades in different currencies, the correlation between the interest rates is important. Indeed, it may be a more important factor than the impact of subtle yield curve movements, which justifies the use of a relatively parsimonious (low-factor) interest rate model. Such correlations can be straightforwardly estimated from time series and may also be observed via the traded prices of products such as spread options, baskets and quantos.

In some cases, the population of trades with a given counterparty will cover two or more asset classes or contain cross asset class trades such as cross-currency swaps. The inter asset class correlation between the risk factors must then be considered carefully. Inter asset class correlations are harder to estimate from historical time series as the correlations are more likely to be unstable due to the complex interactions between asset classes. Furthermore, they are less likely to be able to be implied from the prices of market instruments. Inter asset class correlations, especially for the non-collateral-posting counterparties, can often be less important due to single asset class transactions. Having said that, even a relatively simple end-user of derivatives, such as an airline, could need to trade across commodities, FX and interest rate products, creating a future exposure dependent on many inter and intra asset class correlation parameters.

The hundreds of risk factors required in a typical exposure simulation engine give rise to tens of thousands of correlations,[7] many of which will represent zero or very little impact on future exposure. However, some will be very important and it is necessary to understand such effects and perform sensitivity analysis to not rely solely on naïve correlation estimation from time-series data.

---

[5] Such aspects can be solved; in particular, there are methods to regularise correlations, to obtain the closest possible valid (positive semi-definite) correlation matrix. However, this is time-consuming and may be viewed as being too complex with simpler methods preferred, especially if equity constitutes only a moderate portion of the overall exposure.
[6] As defined by the Capital Asset Pricing Model (CAPM), the beta represents the covariance of the stock and index returns divided by the variance of the index returns.
[7] The number is $N(N-1)/2$, where N is the number of risk factors.

9.4.8 Stochastic volatility

Another component that may be important to consider including is that of stochastic volatility, which is one way to incorporate non-normal assumptions in the underlying distributions of risk factors. Stochastic volatility models add sophistication as they can be used to match model dynamics to the volatility smile (or skew). This can be an important effect, especially for legacy trades that may be off-market and therefore not primarily driven by at-the-money volatilities. Furthermore, in Chapter 15 we will argue that stochastic volatility models may be required as a prerequisite for proper modelling of wrong-way risk in some cases (e.g., Section 15.4.1).

Another component of stochastic volatility modelling is the need to model the *future implied volatility* of volatility-sensitive products. Constructing such an approach is a significant challenge and there is limited market information to calibrate forward volatilities. Even state-of-the-art CVA approaches tend to be reasonably basic in their representation of volatility.

9.5 NETTING EXAMPLES

9.5.1 Examples

We now consider the netting benefit achieved in several examples.[8] The trades considered are as follows:

- Base case. Payer interest rate swap, GBP, 5-year maturity, "Payer IRS GBP 5Y".
- Trade 1. Payer interest rate swap, GBP, 6-year maturity, "Payer IRS GBP 6Y".
- Trade 2. Payer interest rate swap, EUR, 5-year maturity, "Payer IRS EUR 5Y".
- Trade 3. Receiver interest rate swap, EUR, 5-year maturity, "Receiver IRS EUR 5Y".
- Trade 4. Cross-currency swap paying GBP, receiving USD, "CCS GBPUSD 5Y".

All trades have a notional of 100m in the relevant currency except the CCS, which has a smaller notional of 25m.[9] Unless otherwise stated, the exposures have been simulated at time intervals of 10 calendar days with a total of 10,000 simulations. We show the trade-level EE and PFE profiles (both positive and negative) in Figure 9.7.

The reader may notice that the interest rate swaps have a worst-case exposure (95% PFE), which is bigger than the negative worst-case exposure (5% PFE) whilst the EE is generally less than the NEE. It will be useful to characterise this difference, which will be discussed further in Chapter 12 when we consider risk-neutral exposure. Firstly, we explain the reason for the EE being smaller than the NEE, which can be understood from the drift assumptions. Since this calculation was done at a time when interest rates had been declining, the historical calibration creates a negative drift on interest rates. This then tends to push the future value of a payer swap to be negative, since a falling interest rate environment will lead to a negative theta[10] on such a transaction. The

---

[8] I am grateful to Algorithmics for providing the simulation data for these examples.
[9] This is to prevent the inherently more risky cross-currency swap dominating the results.
[10] A payer swap in an upwards-sloping yield curve environment will have a swap rate higher than short-term interest rates. This means that initial fixed payments on the swap are greater than the floating payments received. If interest rates are not assumed to be increasing then this creates the negative theta (time decay) effect where the payer swap is expected to have a negative future value.

reverse will occur for a receiver swap (which is represented by the NEE). The reason for the 95% PFE being greater is due to the skew in the underlying interest rate distribution. Interest rates can potentially increase to very high levels with small probabilities but cannot go negative. Hence a payer swap has a greater worst-case exposure (95% PFE driven by rates increasing substantially) than the equivalent negative exposure, which represents a receiver swap (5% PFE driven by rates reducing). This effect is strong enough to reverse the negative theta trend that leads to the EE being smaller than the NEE.

Base case. Payer IRS GBP 5Y

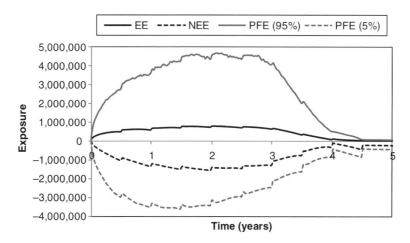

Trade 1. Payer IRS GBP 6Y

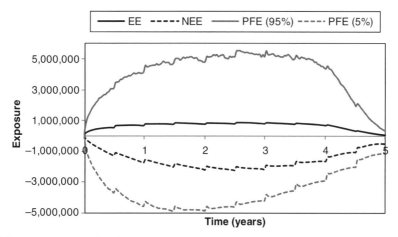

Figure 9.7 EE and PFE profiles for the trades used in the examples. The exposure from the counterparty's point of view is represented by the NEE and 5% PFE. Note that the receiver swap (not shown) is simply the reverse of the equivalent payer. All currencies in base units.

Trade 2/3. Payer IRS EUR 5Y (receiver is opposite)

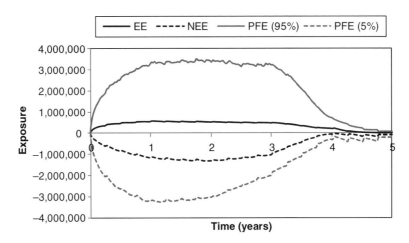

Trade 4. CCS GBPUSD 5Y

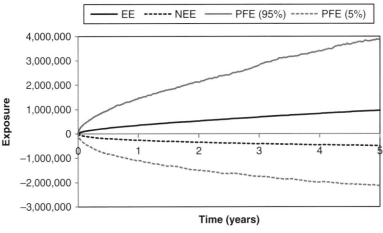

Figure 9.7 (Continued)

9.5.2 Exposure profiles

We now consider exposure profiles that would arise in several different cases. In all examples, we start with the base case "Payer IRS GBP 5Y" trade and consider the impact of netting this with the other four trades listed above. We will see different impacts depending on the relationship between the trades in question.

**Spreadsheet 9.2 Illustration of the impact of netting for
the examples considered.**

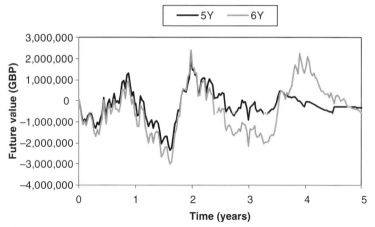

Figure 9.8 Example scenario of the future values of the 5-year and 6-year interest rate swaps.

Case 1: Payer IRS GBP 6Y

This trade will be rather highly correlated to the base case since they differ only in maturity date. An example scenario showing their future values is given in Figure 9.8. The high structural correlation means that the values are highly dependent, similar to Table 8.2 in the previous chapter. We note that the relationship between the two swaps depends subtly on the precise evolution in the shape of the yield curve that will be quite model-sensitive. The decorrelation is stronger towards the end of the profile as the relative difference in remaining maturity increases. Indeed, we can see a small amount of netting benefit around the 4.5-year point. However, even this small impact does not occur in most paths and the netting effect is therefore minimal overall. We show the EE values in Figure 9.9, which are almost additive with the average netting factor[11] being only 98.6%.

Case 2: Payer IRS EUR 5Y

We now look at the impact of swaps in different currencies. Both swaps pay the fixed rate and have the same maturity. Furthermore, the correlation between moves in the different interest rates is positive. However, the imperfect correlation between the currencies is expected to create a reasonable netting benefit. This is illustrated in Figure 9.10, where the average netting factor is 82.9%.

Case 3: Receiver IRS EUR 5Y

We now consider the impact of opposite swaps, albeit in different currencies. Here, we have effectively reversed the correlation between interest rates to become structurally negative, which should imply an even stronger netting benefit. Not surprisingly, the total netted EE is much smaller than either of the individual trade EEs. See Figure 9.11. The average netting factor is 43.7%.

---

[11] As in Section 8.4.1, the netting factor is the ratio of net to gross exposure. We define the average netting factor as the average ratio of the EE with netting to the EE without netting.

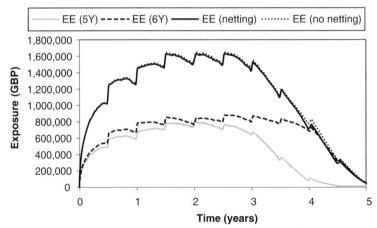

Figure 9.9 EE profiles for the 5-year pay fixed interest rate swap and a 6-year pay fixed interest rate swap. Also shown is the total EE with and without netting. The EE components are almost additive due to the very high correlation.

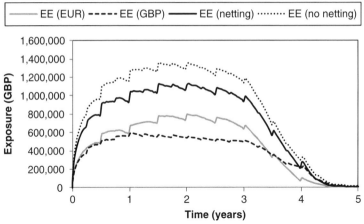

Figure 9.10 EE profiles for the 5-year pay fixed GBP interest rate swap and the 5-year pay fixed EUR interest rate swap. Also shown is the total EE with and without netting.

Case 4: CCS GBPUSD 5Y

Finally, we consider the combination of the base case 5-year IRS with a cross-currency swap (CCS) of the same maturity. Since the CCS is dominated by the FX component, as described in the last chapter, there is a small[12] correlation between the trades and again this should create a reasonable netting benefit. The EE profiles are shown in Figure 9.12 and the netting factor is 66.7%. This is quite close to the simple approximation of $1/\sqrt{2} = 70.7\%$ as discussed in Section 8.4.2.

---

[12] The interest rate-FX correlation is small.

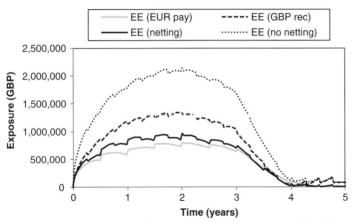

Figure 9.11 EE profiles for the 5-year pay fixed GBP interest rate swap and the 5-year receive fixed EUR interest rate swap. Also shown is the total EE with and without netting. There is a strong netting benefit due to the negative correlation between the swaps.

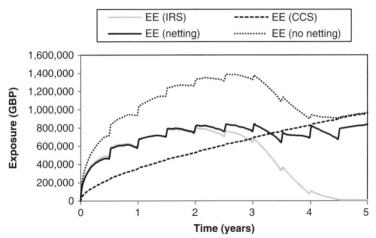

Figure 9.12 EE profiles for the 5-year pay fixed GBP interest rate swap and the 5-year pay GBP receive EUR cross-currency swap. Also shown is the total EE with and without netting.

9.6 ALLOCATING EXPOSURE

It is clear from the above examples that netting benefits can be substantial. It is not clear though how to allocate these benefits to the individual trades. If the EE (or PFE) of the trades is considered on a stand-alone basis then this will overstate the actual risk. However, there is no single way to distribute the netted exposure amongst the trades.

9.6.1 Simple two-trade, single-period example

Suppose we have two exposures defined by normal distributions with different mean and standard deviation as illustrated in Figure 9.13. The distributions are rather different, the first

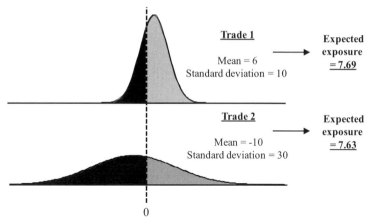

Figure 9.13 Distribution defining the exposures for the simple example.

having a positive mean and a smaller standard deviation and the second a negative mean but a larger standard deviation. The result of this is that the EEs are similar at 7.69 and 7.63[13] for trade 1 and trade 2, respectively. Assuming zero correlation, the total expected exposure of both trades would be 10.72.[14]

Now the question is how to allocate the exposure of 10.72 between the two trades. The most obvious way to do this is to ask simply in which order they arose. If trade 1 was first then by definition it would contribute an EE of 7.69 at that time. By a simple subtraction, trade 2 would then have to represent only 3.03. If the order were reversed then the numbers would be almost the opposite. We will refer to this as *incremental exposure* since it depends on the incremental effect, which in turn depends on the ordering. Incremental allocation is usually most relevant because the nature of trading is sequential, potentially with trades being done years apart.

However, incremental allocation seems unfair because in the above example the first trade always gets charged more and the second trade is given all the netting benefit. This may seem unfair, but life is unfair and, since we cannot (usually) predict future trading activity, incremental allocation is seemingly the only reasonable approach to use. It is also consistent with a charging approach where the charge must be defined at the time of initiation and must not subsequently change.[15]

Suppose that instead we did not wish to look at exposures sequentially but rather wanted to find a fair breakdown of exposure, irrespective of the order in which they were originated. This could be relevant if two trades are initiated at the same time (e.g., two trades with the same counterparty on the same day) or for analysing exposure to find the largest contributions at the current time. We could simply *pro rata* the values in line with the stand-alone EEs. Whilst this may seem reasonable, it is not theoretically rigorous. A more robust way to do this is via *marginal exposure*.

---

[13] These EE numbers can be computed using the formula in Appendix 9B. This effect is similar to an in-the-money option having a similar value to an out-of-the-money option with a greater underlying volatility.

[14] Since the distributions are independent, we can calculate the combined mean and variance as $6 - 10 = -4$ and $10^2 + 30^2 = 1000$, respectively and then use the formula in Appendix 9B.

[15] This is leading to a transfer pricing concept for CVA at trade inception without the need to charge more (or less) in the future.

Table 9.2   Summary of different EE decompositions for the trades in Figure 9.13 assuming independence between exposures

	Incremental (1 first)	Incremental (2 first)	Pro rata	Marginal
Trade 1	7.69	3.09	5.38	3.95
Trade 2	3.03	7.63	5.34	6.77
Total	10.72	10.72	10.72	10.72

Marginal risk contributions are well-studied concepts due to the need to allocate risk measures back to individual constituents. For example, they have been described by Arvanitis and Gregory (2001) for credit portfolios and a discussion on marginal VAR can be found in Jorion (2007). In most situations, a marginal contribution can readily be calculated as the derivative of the risk measure with respect to its weight. Hence, we need numerically to calculate the derivative of the total EE with respect to each constitution exposure in order to know the marginal EEs. This will be described more intuitively below. The marginal EEs will, under most circumstances, sum to the total EE as required. More mathematical details are given in Appendix 9B.

We calculate the marginal EEs under the assumption of independence between the two exposure distributions and summarise the overall results[16] in Table 9.2, comparing also to incremental exposure and the crude pro rata approach. We can see that the marginal EE of exposure 2 is actually quite significantly higher than that of exposure 1, even though the standard EE is lower. The exposure with a smaller expected value and a larger volatility is more risky than the exposure with the opposite characteristics.

Spreadsheet 9.3 Example marginal exposure calculation.

In summary, incremental exposure is relevant when exposure is built up sequentially, which is usually the case in practice. It is potentially unfair in that the incremental exposure depends on the timing as well as individual characteristics. Marginal allocation is fair but changes each time a new exposure is added, which is not appropriate for charging to the originator of the risk (credit limits or CVA). In order to illustrate this, consider adding a third exposure based on a normal distribution with mean 7 and standard deviation 7 (again with a similar stand-alone EE of 7.58). The numbers change as in Table 9.3. Whilst the marginal EEs seem fairer, the impact of the third exposure is to change the magnitude of the first two (indeed, the first is increased while the second is reduced). By construction, the incremental exposures do not change.

We will now give some real examples of incremental and marginal exposure and discuss how they are both useful in practice. We then give some additional calculation details.

[16] In the case of normal distributions, the analytical expression makes the calculation of marginal EE quite easy without the need for simulation, as shown in Spreadsheet 9.3.

Table 9.3   As Table 9.2 with a third trade added

	Incremental (1 first)	*Incremental (2 first)*	*Pro rata*	*Marginal*
Trade 1	7.69	3.09	4.86	4.45
Trade 2	3.03	7.63	4.82	5.67
Trade 3	3.76	3.76	4.79	4.36
Total	14.48	14.48	14.48	14.48

9.6.2   Incremental exposure

We look at the examples shown in Section 9.5.2 showing the netting effect via the incremental exposure. The incremental exposure is defined easily via

$$\text{EE}_i^{\text{incremental}}(u) = \text{EE}_{NS+i}(u) - \text{EE}_{NS}(u). \tag{9.2}$$

In other words, it is the exposure of the netting set with the new trade added ($NS + i$) minus that of the netting set alone (NS). A similar formula can be used for PFE. We now show in Figure 9.14 the incremental exposure when the base case trade (i) is added to the four other example trades. In other words the "netting set" is originally assumed to contain one of the four trades and we consider the impact of adding the 5-year GBP payer swap to this. The stand-alone EE is always the same whereas the incremental EE depends on the existing trade.

Spreadsheet 9.4 Incremental exposure calculations.

Payer IRS GBP 6Y

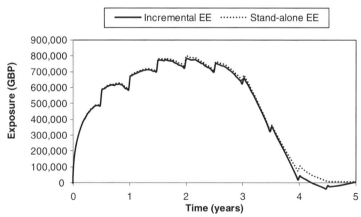

Figure 9.14 Incremental exposure of adding the base case trade (Payer IRS GBP 6Y) to each of the four different other example trades.

Payer IRS EUR 5Y

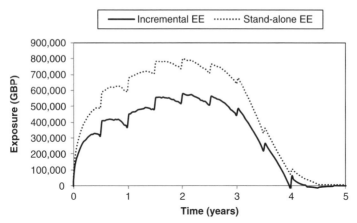

Receiver IRS EUR 5Y

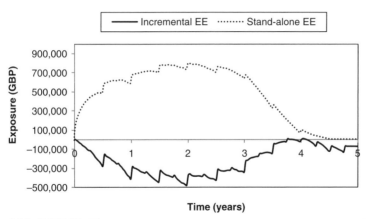

CCS GBPUSD 5Y

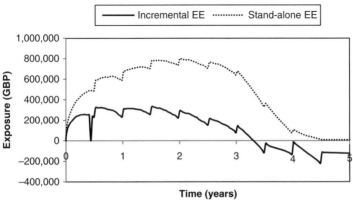

Figure 9.14 (Continued)

We can explain the results as follows. The 6-year swap has virtually no impact, with the incremental being very close to the stand-alone. The different currency EUR swap produces a reasonable reduction due to the imperfect (but still positive) correlation between the two interest rate curves in question. The incremental EE is negative in the third example. Since there is a positive correlation between the interest rates in question, the receiver EUR swap has a negative correlation with the payer GBP, creating a strong netting benefit and a negative incremental effect. Finally, in the cross-currency swap, firstly, there is a cancellation of the cash flows between paying floating GBP and the equivalent receive leg in the GBP interest rate swap. Secondly, there is a favourably low correlation between the USD/GBP FX rate and the GBP interest rate (of approximately 30%). The result of this is that the netting benefit is strong and increases through time. The incremental EE is therefore reduced significantly and even becomes negative towards the end of the lifetime.

We have shown above that incremental exposure can vary dramatically depending on the existing netting set and even be negative. It is clearly very important to be able to characterise the effect properly to understand the true magnitude of the risk being added. We also note that different institutions will see different exposures for the same trade with a given counterparty as they will have different existing netting sets. Indeed, a counterparty should find it easier to trade with an institution with more favourable existing trades. The extreme case of this is that it should be easiest to execute a reverse trade (unwind) with the same counterparty with which the existing trade is done.[17]

9.6.3 Marginal exposure

In risk management, it is common and natural to ask the question of from where the underlying risk arises. Risk managers find it useful to be able to "drill down" from a number representing counterparty exposure and understand which trades are contributing most to the overall risk. This can be important information when considering whether to unwind transactions or enter into more business. Marginal exposure is useful in this context since, just because trade level (stand-alone) expected exposures are similar, it does not mean that the contributions to the total netted exposure are also similar.

Let us first repeat the simple exercise in Section 9.6.1 for a range of correlation values as shown in Figure 9.15 (these calculations can be seen in the aforementioned Spreadsheet 9.3). The total EE is smallest at −100% correlation and increases with the correlation as the overall netting benefit is reduced. The breakdown of total EE into marginal components depends very much on the correlation. At zero correlation, as we have already seen, trade 2 has a larger contribution to the overall EE. At negative correlation, the more "risky" trade 2 has a positive marginal EE that is partly cancelled out by trade 1 having a negative marginal EE. At high correlations, the marginal EEs are both positive and of almost equal magnitude (since there is little or no netting benefit).

The point being emphasised here is that for trades with low or negative correlation, marginal EEs are particularly important to understand. The marginal EE of a trade depends on the relationship of that trade to others in the netting set. A trade which is risk-reducing (negative marginal EE) in one netting set might not have the same characteristic in a different netting set.

There are two obvious reasons why marginal exposure might be a meaningful measure. Firstly, the situation where two or more trades happen simultaneously (or within a short

---

[17] This may not necessarily be true as it depends also on the other trades in the netting set.

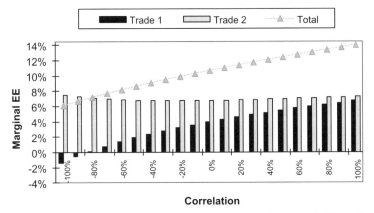

Figure 9.15 Marginal EEs for the simple two-trade example shown in Figure 9.13 as a function of the correlation between the normal distributions.

time interval) and incremental allocation would therefore be inappropriate (and unfair). The second is when it is important to allocate the exposure back to constituents in order to make some decision, such as which trades to terminate.

Let us look at the first use of marginal exposure, for trades happening at the same time. We now look at a general example of marginal EE calculation using the interest rate swap (base case example) and cross-currency swap (case 4 from Section 9.5.1). Figure 9.16 shows the expected exposure allocated incrementally (in both ways) and marginally. We note that the top line is the same in all cases as this represents the overall exposure. We can see that the second trade allocated incrementally has a relatively small exposure, to the detriment of the first trade. The marginal allocation is fairer and would be appropriate if the trades occurred at the same time.[18]

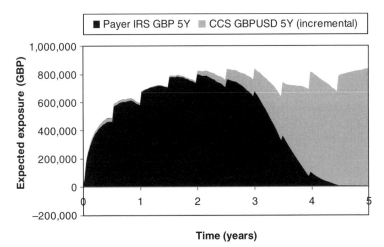

Figure 9.16 Illustration of the breakdown of the expected exposure of the interest rate and cross-currency swaps via incremental (CCS first), incremental (IRS first) and marginal.

---

[18] There is still some problem of allocation here since, for trades occurring at the same time, we wish to allocate marginally whilst the total impact of the trades should be allocated incrementally with respect to existing trades in the netting set. An obvious way to get around this problem is to scale the marginal contributions of the trades so that they match the total incremental effect.

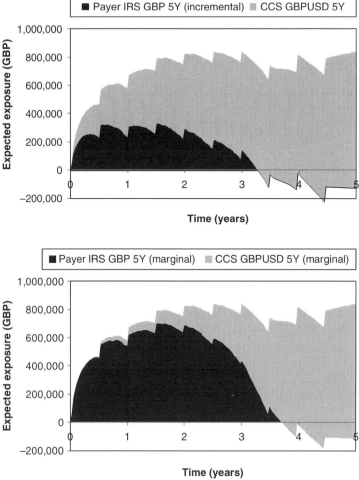

Figure 9.16 (Continued)

We will return to this example and show the respective CVA numbers in Chapter 12 (Section 12.4.1).

The second use of marginal exposure is to drill down within a counterparty exposure and understand which trades are driving the risk at different points in time. Let us look at the total expected exposure of the four aforementioned trades (Section 9.5.2) excluding the receiver (trade 3, since this will simply cancel out the impact of the previous payer swap). The marginal allocation of expected exposure is shown in Figure 9.17 and compared to the stand-alone contributions (which are overall larger) in Figure 9.18.[19]

Suppose it is important to reduce the overall exposure of the trades in the above example. For example, this may be in order to comply with the credit limit[20] or because the CVA to a counterparty is deemed excessive (and cannot be readily hedged). All other things being equal,

---

[19] These have been shown previously in Figure 9.14.
[20] In such a case PFE, rather than EE, would be the appropriate metric to consider. We have checked that, whilst the marginal PFE numbers are systemically higher than the EEs shown, there is no change in the qualitative behaviour.

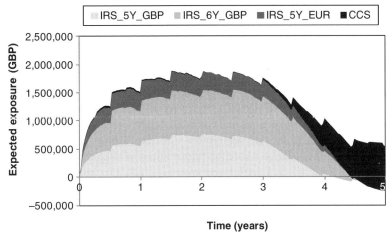

Figure 9.17 Illustration of the marginal expected exposure of the three interest rate and one cross-currency swaps.

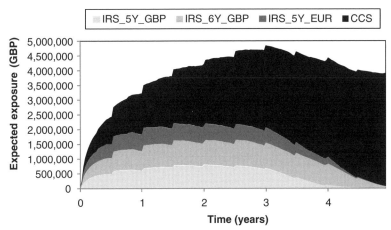

Figure 9.18 Illustration of the stand-alone expected exposure of the three interest rate and one cross-currency swaps to be compared with the marginal exposures shown in Figure 9.17.

Spreadsheet 9.5 Marginal exposure calculations.

---

the trade with the higher marginal EE (or PFE) is the most relevant to look at. There are two points of interest here. Firstly, the marginal allocation is not homogeneous with time and so, depending on the horizon of interest, the highest contributor will be different. Secondly, it is not always easy to predict, *a priori*, which trade will be the major contributor. From the stand-alone contributions of the trades, it would be expected that the cross-currency swap would have a significant marginal component. However, the marginal contribution of the cross-currency swap is rather small and practically zero for the first 4-years. Even towards the end of the 5-year profile, the large risk coming from the exchange of notional is significantly offset by the three IRSs.[21]

9.6.4 Calculation of incremental and marginal exposure

We consider the most efficient way in which to compute incremental and marginal exposure. A netting agreement allows two parties to net a set of positions (explicitly covered by the netting agreement) in the event of default of one of them. This is a critical way to control exposure but can typically be only quantified effectively in a Monte Carlo framework. Netting benefits arise in scenarios where the future values of two trades are of opposite signs. Hence, to calculate the impact of netting one must aggregate (Section 9.3.4) at the individual transaction level, as illustrated by equation (9.3).

In order to calculate the incremental exposure we simply need to add the simulated values for a new trade i to those for the rest of the netting set. Working from equation (9.1), we can write

$$V_{NS+i}(s,t) = \sum_{k=1}^{K} V(k,s,t) + V(i,s,t) = V_{NS}(s,t) + V(i,s,t), \qquad (9.3)$$

giving the future value of the netting set, including the new trade in each simulation (s) and at each time point (t). From this, it is easy to calculate the new EE, which can be compared with the existing EE as required by equation (9.2). What is helpful here is that we need only know the future value of the netting set, not the constituent trades. From a systems point of view this reduces the storage requirements from a cube of dimension $K \times S \times T$ (which could be extremely costly) to a matrix of dimension $S \times T$.

Typically, systems handle the computation of incremental exposure by calculating and storing the netting set information $V_{NS}(s,t)$ (often in an overnight batch) and then generating the simulations for a new trade, $V(i,s,t)$ "on-the-fly" as and when required. The "re-aggregation" in (9.3) and recalculation of measures such as EE is then a simple and quick calculation.

The calculation of marginal EE is more difficult than incremental EE. As mentioned above, the marginal exposure can be defined by a derivative, which in turn can be calculated as a small change in the underlying exposure (see Appendix 9B for more detail). This does not require any additional simulation but just a rescaling of the future values of one trade by an amount $1 + \varepsilon$ followed by a recalculation of the EE for the netting set.[22] The marginal EE of the trade in question is then given by the change in the EE divided by ε. The sum of the marginal EEs will sum to the total EE.[23]

However, as described by Rosen and Pykhtin (2009), there is an alternative way to compute marginal EE, which is more intuitive and easier to calculate via a *conditional expectation*. This can be written as

$$EE_i^{\text{marginal}}(t) = \sum_{s=1}^{S} V(i,s,t)I(V_{NS}(s,t) > 0)/S, \qquad (9.4)$$

---

[21] This is mainly because, under the drift assumptions discussed above, the three IRSs are expected to have negative net payments at the end of their lifetime that cancel with any positive payment (exposure) in the CCS.
[22] ε is a small number such as 0.001.
[23] At least in the current case where no collateral is assumed, see Rosen and Pykhtin (2009) for more detail.

where $I(.)$ is the indicator function that takes the value unity if the statement is true and zero otherwise. The intuition behind the above formula is that the future values of the trade in question are added only if the netting set has positive value at the equivalent point. A trade that has a favourable interaction with the overall netting set may then have a negative marginal EE since its future value will be more likely to be negative when the netting set has a positive value.

Whilst marginal EE is easy to calculate as defined above, it does require full storage of all the future values at the trade level. From a systems point of view, marginal EE could be calculated during the overnight batch with little additional effort whereupon the trade-level future values can be discarded. However, for analysing the change in marginal EE under the influence of a new trade(s) then, unlike incremental EE, all trade-level values must be retained.

9.7   EXPOSURE AND COLLATERAL

Uncollateralised credit exposure should be considered over the full time-horizon of the transaction or transactions in question. Long-term distributional assumptions, such as mean-reversion and drift, are important and the specifics of the transactions, such as cash flow dates and exercise times, must be considered. Collateral changes the above picture by transforming a risk that should be considered usually over many years into one that need only be considered over a much shorter period (the margin period of risk). This is illustrated in Figure 9.19, which shows some future point where a position is well collateralised (e.g., no threshold in the CSA) and hence the main concern is the relatively small amount of risk over the margin period of risk (for example, the cash flows shown in Figure 9.19 are not as important due to the length of the margin period of risk). Hence, some of the intricacies of modelling potential future exposure can hopefully be ignored as long as the counterparty is well collateralised. The problem now becomes a short-term market risk issue and therefore shares many commonalities with market risk VAR methodologies.

Whilst the above may seem plausible, we will see that the overall impact of collateral is not always straightforward and may not reduce the risk as much as might be hoped.

9.7.1   Collateral assumptions

We will now give some basic details and results on the modelling of collateral. As discussed above, collateral can be accounted for after the simulation of exposure, under the

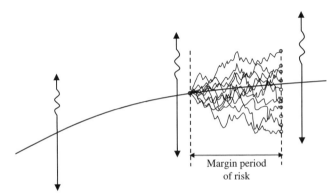

Margin period
of risk

Figure 9.19 Schematic illustration of the impact of collateralisation on potential future exposure.

Table 9.4 Base case parameters used for the collateral examples (two-way CSA)

	Party A (institution)	Party B (counterparty)
Independent amount	—	—
Threshold	—	—
Minimum transfer amount	100,000	100,000
Rounding	20,000	20,000

assumption that the collateral agreement depends only on the net future value and not other market variables.[24] We have described in the previous chapter (Section 8.5.1) the specifics of the calculation of the amount of collateral that may be called, considering the impact of parameters such as thresholds and minimum transfer amounts. We have also discussed the choice of margin period of risk, with 10 or 20 business days being a reasonably standard choice.

In the collateral simulations that will be shown below, the following assumptions apply:

- The collateral amounts to be called by either party will be calculated as described in the previous chapter (Section 8.5.1).
- Collateral called for will take 30 calendar days[25] to arrive (this is close to the assumption of 20 business days under Basel III). Collateral posting to the counterparty will be immediate. There are no other assumptions on collateral disputes other than those captured by the 30-day margin period of risk assumption.
- Collateral posted is not retrievable in the event of a counterparty default. This assumes that it is not held in a segregated account (or in the case of non-cash collateral is rehypothecated).
- All collateral will be in cash (non-cash collateral will be discussed later) in a liquid currency such that any mismatch can easily be hedged in the FX market.

The base case parameters used are shown in Table 9.4.

All of the examples below will be based on the four trades used above and described in Section 9.5.2.

Spreadsheet 9.6 Quantifying the impact of collateral on exposure.

9.7.2 Base case example

We start by assessing the risk of a fully collateralised position, by which we mean that the collateralisation is not subject to any threshold amount. To understand the impact of collateral, first consider a single simulation path as illustrated in Figure 9.20. We can see that the impact of collateral on exposure is not perhaps as strong as one might first have thought.

---

[24] There are situations where this assumption may not be entirely appropriate; for example, collateral parameters may be defined in different currencies from the deals to which they apply. In practice, this means some FX translations may be required when the collateral parameters are applied within the simulation. However, in the majority of situations the assumptions made will be valid and will greatly simplify the analysis of collateralised exposures.

[25] This is because the simulations used are discretised in calendar and not business days with a step size of 10 days.

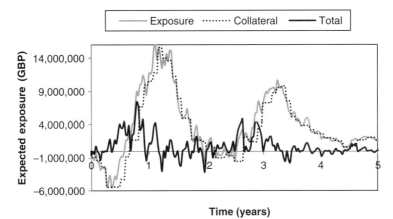

Figure 9.20 Illustration of an individual simulation path and the impact of collateral on that path with the assumptions described.

Firstly, whilst the collateral amount approximately tracks the exposure, this is imperfect due to the margin period of risk and the minimum transfer amounts, which create a potential further delay. Secondly, collateral can also increase exposure, such as during the first period when the future value is negative. This leads to a posting of collateral, which is not retrievable,[26] when the future value increases and the counterparty defaults.

The overall impact of collateral on EE is shown in Figure 9.21. Whilst there is a benefit, a significant exposure remains with prominent spikes due to the exchange of cash flows,[27] which creates a peak in the exposure for a length of time corresponding to the margin period of risk. The overall reduction in exposure (measured via the EPE) is 2.25 times, which is surprisingly low since a 5-year uncollateralised exposure has been collateralised with no threshold with only a 30-day (61 times shorter than the maturity!) risk horizon.

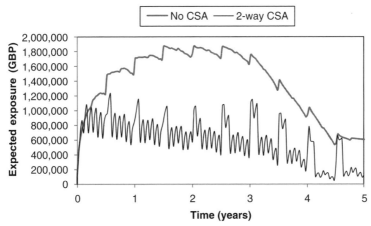

Figure 9.21 Illustration of EE calculated with and without collateral assumptions.

---

[26] This is the assumption of non-segregated or rehypothecated collateral mentioned above.
[27] In this example, all four swaps pay cash flows on the same dates.

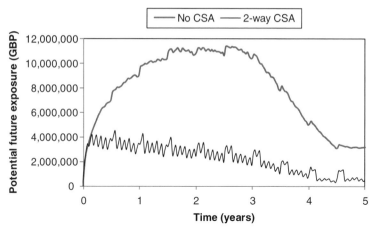

Figure 9.22 Illustration of PFE calculated with and without collateral assumptions.

In Figure 9.22, we show the equivalent PFE (95% confidence level) under the same assumptions showing that the relative impact of collateral is superior. This is because not all simulations contribute equally to the PFE and those with the most contribution (when the exposure is high) are precisely the ones where the most collateral is taken (the average improvement in PFE is 3.52 times compared to 2.25 for EE).

9.7.3 Impact of margin period of risk

The first aspect to consider for a collateralised exposure is the uncertainty of the exposure over the margin period of risk. In Appendix 9C we give simple formulas for the PFE and EE based on normal distribution assumptions. For example, the EE in our case is given by

$$\text{EE}(u) \approx 0.4 \times \sigma_E \times \sqrt{\Delta t}(T - u), \tag{9.5}$$

where σ_E represents the (annual) volatility for the underlying positions, Δt the margin period of risk in years and T is the final maturity. The factor $(T - u)$ is an amortisation component, which assumes linear decay.[28] The volatility of the positions can be estimated from a variance/covariance-type analysis, which is well known from market risk VAR calculations.

In Figure 9.23 we show the impact of a shorter 10-day margin period of risk (calendar days) on the EE and illustrate the above approximation,[29] which fits quite well apart from the spikes caused by cash flows. We can see that a shorter margin period of risk significantly improves the EE, with an average (i.e., EPE) reduction of 5.23 (compared with 2.25) times.

We note that analytical formulas, such as the one above, can be useful for characterising the impact of collateral. For example, Gibson (2005) derives a simple semi-analytical formula for a collateralised exposure incorporating collateral thresholds, which is shown to agree well with a full simulation approach. However, to capture all effects such as cash flows,

---

[28] This is a rather crude approximation in this case as it is a reasonable assumption for interest rate swaps but not for the cross-currency swap due to the exchange of notional.

[29] The approximation is only illustrated for the 10-day margin period of risk but gives similarly good agreement for the 30-day one.

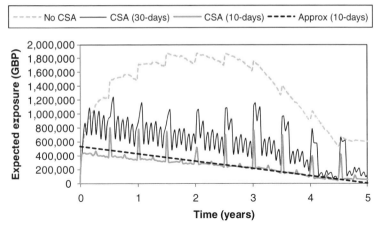

Figure 9.23 Illustration EE calculated with different margin period of risk assumptions (in calendar days) and compared with the simple approximation described.

as Figure 9.23 shows, full simulation is required. Approximations to collateralised exposure, available under Basel II and III, will be discussed again in Chapter 17 (Section 17.3.6).

9.7.4   Impact of threshold and independent amount

We consider the impact of threshold (for both parties) in Figure 9.24. As expected, it makes the reduction in exposure worse (the EPE is improved by only a factor of 1.15 with a 10m threshold compared to 2.25 in the zero-threshold case). One important use of thresholds is to minimise the operational costs associated with exchanging collateral at the expense of increasing future exposure.[30] The balance between risk reduction and operational workload is important in collateral management. A low threshold will significantly reduce the exposure

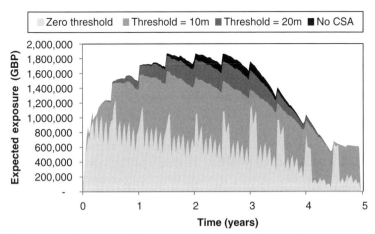

Figure 9.24 Illustration EE calculated with different threshold assumptions.

---

[30] We note that this might come from an institution or their counterparty's point of view since if the CSA is likely to give rise to operational effort then the counterparty may be unable to commit to collateral posting.

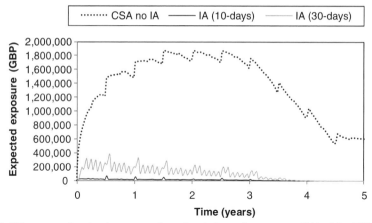

Figure 9.25 EE computed under the assumption of an independent amount (IA) of 2m EUR calculated with different margin period of risk assumptions (in calendar days) and compared to the base case (CSA but no IA and with a 30-day margin period of risk).

with a high workload for the collateral management unit. On the other hand, decreasing the number of collateral calls can only be achieved by accepting a larger exposure.

Whilst the reduction and comments above are reasonable for credit limits purposes (and indeed the PFE is improved by a slightly more significant amount as for the zero-threshold case discussed above and shown in Figure 9.22), they are not so relevant or useful for mitigating CVA, as discussed in more detail in Chapter 12. A key theme with CSAs so far has been that, whilst they can reduce exposure, they certainly cannot eradicate it. From the perspective of, for example, central counterparties, there is a need to mitigate exposure more strongly. This can only be achieved by using an independent amount.

Let us return to the case of zero thresholds and assume an additional independent amount (IA) of 2m EUR posted by the counterparty to the institution. In Figure 9.25 we show the impact on EE compared with the base case (CSA but no IA) for 10-day and 30-day margin periods of risk. The shorter period has the impact of practically eradicating exposure (the EPE is 123 times smaller than the CSA with no IA). However, the increase to 30 days creates almost an order of magnitude more EE (now only 13.6 times better). Whilst an IA can be useful, to quantify the benefit achieved is a very subtle problem.

One way of looking at an IA is that it converts counterparty risk into gap risk. The gap risk is defined in this case by the chance of the exposure "gapping" through the 2m IA in the space of 10 (or 30) days. It is now more relevant to look at the problem in terms of gap risk and this is much harder to do with reasonable accuracy. The reason for this is that the scenarios where the IA is breached are relatively extreme and therefore the impact of changes in assumptions is more dramatic. Firstly, as seen, there is much more sensitivity to the margin period of risk (in Figure 9.23 the impact of reducing this from 30 to 10 days is 2.33 whilst in Figure 9.25 it is a 9.1 times reduction in EPE). Secondly, when assessing gap risk one should be more concerned about distributional assumptions such as fat tails, jumps and extreme co-dependency. None of these is considered in the modelling of the exposure, but in the non-IA cases this is less of a concern.

Note that IAs (which are rather called initial margins) are essentially the first line of defence through which central counterparties mitigate their risk. The difficulty in setting the

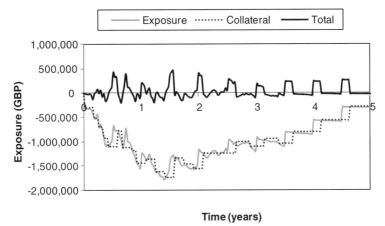

Figure 9.26 Illustration of an individual simulation path and the impact of collateral on that path for a single-name CDS protection position (short protection) calculated with and without a two-way collateral agreement (as defined in Table 9.4).

correct initial margin should be clear since this depends so subtly on the assessment of the gap risk that remains.

9.7.5 Are two-way CSAs always beneficial?

Two-way collateral agreements may in some specific cases increase exposure. Take the example of single-name CDS protection. As discussed in the last chapter (Section 8.3.6), such products create a very skewed exposure distribution. When selling CDS protection, exposure is moderate compared with the negative exposure due to the possibility of an extreme credit spread widening or a credit event. The overall result of this is that in a short CDS protection position collateral is much more likely to be posted than received, as illustrated for one simulation in Figure 9.26. The net result is to increase the overall EE, as shown in Figure 9.27.

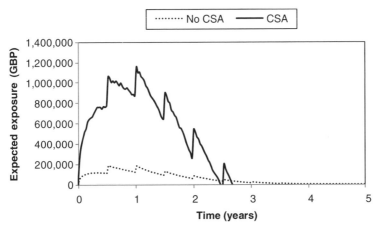

Figure 9.27 EE for a single-name CDS protection position (short protection) calculated with and without a two-way collateral agreement (as defined in Table 9.4).

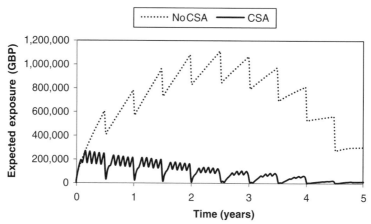

Figure 9.28 EE for a single-name CDS protection position (long protection) calculated with and without a two-way collateral agreement (as defined in Table 9.4).

The increased risk from posting collateral has dominated the reduced risk from receiving it. For a long protection single-name CDS position (Figure 9.28) the situation is reversed and the CSA is seen to be beneficial.

There are other cases where the skew of the exposure distribution is important to consider when looking at the benefit of collateral. Examples would be long option positions, strongly off-market netting sets and wrong-way risk exposures (covered in more detail in Chapter 15).

9.7.6 Non-cash collateral

Non-cash collateral will have a price volatility that should be considered since a decline in collateral value will potentially lead to an uncollateralised exposure. For this reason, haircuts are assigned. The levels of haircuts are usually estimated according to market price volatility and foreign exchange volatility (in the case of securities denominated in foreign currency). Furthermore, typical haircuts take into account the type of security, its credit rating and the duration of its maturity. An obvious way in which to derive a haircut would be to require that it covers a potential worst-case drop in the value of the underlying collateral during a given time period as illustrated in Figure 9.29. The time would depend on the liquidity of the underlying collateral.

Under normal distribution assumptions, such a formula is easy to derive:

$$\text{Haircut} = \Phi^{-1}(\alpha) \times \sigma_C \times \sqrt{\Delta t}, \tag{9.6}$$

where $\Phi^{-1}(\alpha)$ defines the number of standard deviations the haircut needs to cover, involving the cumulative inverse normal distribution function[31] and the confidence level α (e.g., 99%). Also required is the volatility of the collateral, σ_C, and the time (similar to the margin period of risk) denoted Δt. In order to test this assumption, we look at the standard haircuts defined under Basel II in Table 9.5. Assuming a 99% confidence level and a margin period of risk of 10 days (Basel II specifies a minimum of 5 days, as discussed in Chapter 17), the 2% haircut on a 5-year Triple-A government bond would need to assume an underlying volatility

---

[31] NORMSINV(.) in Excel[TM], for example.

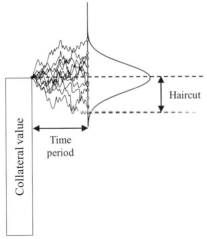

Figure 9.29 Illustration of the methodology for estimating a haircut.

Table 9.5   Illustration of Basel II haircuts

		Up to 1 year	*1–5 years*	*Above 5 years*
Sovereign debt	AAA/AA	0.5%	2%	4%
	A/BBB	1%	3%	6%
	BB	15%		
Corporates and financials	AAA/AA	1%	4%	8%
	A/BBB	2%	6%	12%
	BB	15%		
Other assets	Cash	0%		
	Equity	15–25%		
	Gold	15%		
	FX	8%		

Source: Adapted from BCBS (2006)

of 4.3%.[32] Given an approximate duration of 4.5 years, this would translate into an assumed interest rate volatility of around 1%, which is reasonable.[33]

Haircuts applied in this way should not only compensate for collateral volatility but also reduce exposure overall since they will create an overcollateralisation in 99% of cases and only 1% of the time will they be insufficient. Whilst this is generally true, it ignores the possibility of a relationship between the collateral and the exposure.

---

[32] $2\%/\Phi^{-1}(99\%)/\sqrt{10/250}$ assuming 250 business days in a year.
[33] This should not be taken to imply that these precise assumptions were used to derive the results in Table 9.5.

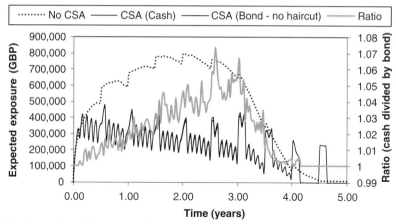

Figure 9.30 Illustration of the impact of cash and non-cash collateral (without a haircut) on the exposure of a swap. It is very hard to see the difference between the cash and non-cash cases, so the ratio of the two is also shown.

Consider a payer interest rate swap collateralised by a Triple-A bond. Since the bond has little or no default risk and given the relevant haircut, surely the position is not a risky one? However, imagine the impact of interest rates going up: the value of the swap increases, whilst the bond price goes down. This negative correlation between collateral and exposure is non-desirable. In the case of a receiver interest rate swap, the situation is reversed and we have a beneficial positive correlation.

A simple way to represent the impact of the correlation between exposure and collateral is via

$$\sigma_{CE} = \sqrt{\sigma_E^2 + \sigma_C^2 - 2\rho_{E,C}\sigma_E\sigma_C}, \tag{9.7}$$

where σ_E, σ_C and σ_{CE} represent the standard deviation of the exposure, collateral and combined positions, respectively and $\rho_{E,C}$ is the correlation between the exposure and collateral. This is a standard formula for combining standard deviations, with the minus sign being structural since the collateral acts in the opposite direction to the exposure. We can see from equation (9.7) that a negative correlation is clearly not desirable (as in the payer swap and bond).

We have simulated the impact of this effect by taking the base case trade (Payer IRS GBP 5Y) and assuming collateral is posted in a fixed-rate UK treasury bond denominated in GBP bond (also 5Y maturity). The results are shown in Figure 9.30. The effect is small and imperceptible for the EE but the ratio (EE with cash collateral divided by EE with bond collateral) is clearly above 1. Indeed, we can see that a haircut of 2% (as implied from Table 9.5) would not be adequate as the ratio is above 1.02 at many points in the profile.[34]

The above effect is rather small, which is due to the relevant amount of swap and bond. The standard deviation of the bond will be much smaller since it will have a much smaller notional amount. For example, the swap has a notional of 100m EUR but the amount of collateral will rarely get close to 10m EUR. However, this does illustrate that a simple methodology for setting haircuts is not appropriate when there is a significant correlation between exposure and collateral. This would have a much stronger impact for more volatile collateral.

---

[34] The crises from the correlation between the exposure and value of the collateral.

In such cases, the correlation of the collateral and the underlying exposure is clearly very important as wrong-way risk will mean that even a haircut estimated at a high confidence level may be worse than cash collateral.

9.8   SUMMARY

In this chapter we have described the quantification of credit exposure by various methods, ranging from simple approximations to a more general simulation approach. We have outlined the method for simulating exposure for different asset classes. Examples have been given to show the impact of netting on exposure and we have discussed the allocation of exposure either incrementally or marginally. We have also discussed the quantification of exposure in the presence of collateral, showing that the presence of a collateral agreement changes the nature of future exposure quite significantly but does not always reduce the risk as much as may be imagined.

So far, this book has been concerned mainly with credit exposure. Whilst this is a critical component of counterparty risk, it is not the only component. Assessing the potential magnitude of a credit exposure is a useful step but is meaningless without an associated quantification of the probability that a counterparty will default. In Chapter 10, we will turn our attention to credit risk and default probability to define counterparty risk more fully as credit exposure coupled to the likelihood of an actual default event.

10

Default Probability, Credit Spreads and Credit Derivatives

> *Creditors have better memories than debtors.*
>
> Benjamin Franklin (1706–1790)

So far, this book has been largely concerned with credit exposure, the market risk component of counterparty risk. Now we focus on the credit risk component arising from the probability of counterparty default and the loss incurred as a result. We will also discuss recovery rates, which define the amount of a claim that is received from a defaulted counterparty.

Default probability plays a critical role in counterparty risk assessment and valuation (CVA). There are different ways to define default probability which we will explain, noting the important difference between using real-world (e.g., historical data) and risk-neutral probabilities (market data). In the latter case, we consider mapping methods that may be used for estimating the credit spread of a counterparty where this cannot be estimated directly. We also consider the term structure of default probability (how default probability changes over time) and show that this is an important consideration. The empirical relationship between real-world and risk-neutral default probabilities (a very important point for defining CVA) is discussed.

Finally, we will examine single-name and portfolio credit derivative products, which are important for hedging purposes (Chapter 16) and the consideration of wrong-way risk (Chapter 15).

10.1 DEFAULT PROBABILITY AND RECOVERY RATES

An example of historical default rates for investment- and speculative-grade assets is shown in Figure 10.1, illustrating that default rates tend to vary substantially through the economic cycle.

10.1.1 Defining default probability

In Appendix 10A we define default probability in more mathematical detail. We refer to the cumulative default probability, $F(t)$, which gives the probability of default any time from now (assuming the counterparty is not currently in default) until time t. This is illustrated in Figure 10.2. The function must clearly start from zero and tend towards 100% (every counterparty defaults eventually!). A *marginal* default probability, which is then the probability

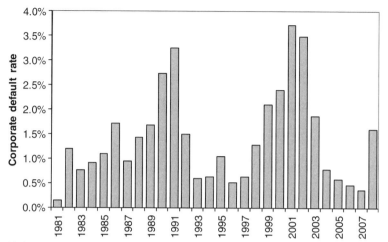

Figure 10.1 Corporate annual default rates (average of investment and speculative grade rates).
Source: Standard & Poor's (2008).

of a default between two specified future dates, is given by

$$q(t_1, t_2) = F(t_2) - F(t_1) \quad (t_1 \leq t_2). \tag{10.1}$$

We can see that $F(.)$ must be monotonically increasing to avoid marginal default probabilities being negative.

10.1.2 Real and risk-neutral default probabilities

It is well known in finance that there is a difference between a real-world parameter (for example, the historical volatility of an asset) and a risk-neutral one (for example, the implied volatility derived from an option price). Real-world (also known as physical) parameters aim to reflect the true value of some financial underlying whilst risk-neutral parameters reflect parameters derived from market prices. The distinction between real and risk-neutral parameters is important.

For our current purpose, real default probabilities will be the assessment of future default probability for the purposes of risk management or other analysis. Risk-neutral default

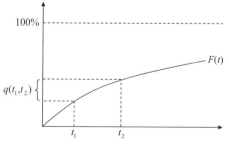

Figure 10.2 Illustration of cumulative default probability function, $F(t)$, and marginal default probability, $q(t_1, t_2)$.

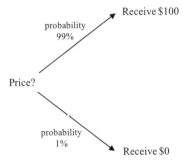

Figure 10.3 Illustration of the difference between real and risk-neutral default probabilities.

probabilities are not estimates of the actual probabilities of default but rather reflect the market price of default risk.

There is reason to expect that real and risk-neutral default probabilities will be very different. This can be understood from a simple example illustrated in Figure 10.3, which is a bet in which there are two possible outcomes: a gain of $100 with 99% probability or a zero gain with 1% probability. This example is equivalent to a zero-recovery, zero-coupon bond in a zero-interest-rate environment. A quick calculation would suggest that the price of the bond is $99 (99% × $100 + 1% × $0). However, no rational investor would enter into such a bet for $99 as the expected payoff is no greater and there is the risk of losing the entire stake.

Rational investors are risk-averse and would never accept risk without the expectation of making a positive return. Suppose an investor was willing to pay only $97 for the "bond" in the example above. They are (quite rationally) expecting a $2 reduction as compensation for the uncertainty of the return. We could call this a *default risk premium*, i.e., the premium that investors need in order to accept default risk. This would require probabilities in Figure 10.3 of 97% and 3%. Furthermore, suppose the investor is worried about the liquidity of the bond above as they may need or want to sell it at some point in the future. For this reason, they may only pay $94 for the bond. The further $3 could be described as a *liquidity premium*. The probabilities would now have to be 94% and 6%. These are not the real default probabilities, but rather constructed risk-neutral probabilities to make the numbers balance assuming that investors have no aversion to risk and will therefore take on the fair bet that Figure 10.3 will then represent. If $94 were the market price of the bond then the risk-neutral default probability would be 6%. We emphasise that this is an artificial probability derived from the market price and has nothing to do with the actual likelihood of the bond defaulting (which is 1%), as illustrated in Figure 10.4.

It is important to understand that a difference in real-world and risk-neutral default probabilities is not conflicting and simply represents a difference in what they represent. Indeed, in line with the above, Altman (1989) tracks the performance of portfolios of corporate bonds for a given rating and finds that the returns outperform a risk-free benchmark (which is a portfolio of Treasury bonds). The reason for the outperformance is that the return on the corporate bonds is more than adequate to cover the default losses experienced. This shows clearly that bond investors are being compensated for components above expected default losses and that the size of these components is significant. Risk-neutral default probabilities are materially higher than real-world ones.

There is no conflict between risk-neutral and real default probabilities. Real-world default probabilities are the actual assessment of the probability of a counterparty defaulting, which is therefore relevant for any quantitative assessment of return or risk management approach.

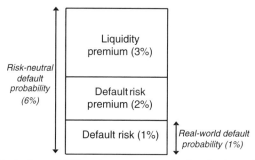

Figure 10.4 Example illustration of different components of a bond price and the difference between real and risk-neutral default probabilities.

Risk-neutral default probabilities reflect the market price and are therefore relevant for hedging purposes. Let us discuss the methods for estimating both and then return to the question of defining this difference, which will be discussed in Section 10.1.6.

We note that the above discussion applies to risk-neutral default probabilities from bond prices, but similar behaviour should be expected with respect to CDS-implied default probabilities. This is discussed in more detail below (Section 10.1.6).

10.1.3   Estimating real default probabilities – historical data

The most obvious assessment of real default probability comes from examining historical data and using past default experience to predict future default likelihood. For example, in Table 10.1 we show a transition matrix based on many years of data as published in Tennant *et al.* (2008). This matrix gives the historical probability of moving from a given rating (on the left-hand column) to another rating (in the top row) during a period of 1 year. It also defines the default probabilities in the far right column. For example, the probability of an A rating being downgraded to BBB after 1 year is 5.14% and the chance of it defaulting is 0.03%.

Not only does Table 10.1 give information on the probability of default, it also provides greater structure for defining how defaults occur. For example, we see that a Triple-A credit has only a 0.01% chance of defaulting in a year but a 7.7% chance of deteriorating to a

Table 10.1   1-year transition matrix for Moody's ratings

	AAA	AA	A	BBB	BB	B	CCC	Default
AAA	91.61%	7.70%	0.66%	0.00%	0.02%	0.00%	0.00%	0.01%
AA	1.13%	91.29%	7.21%	0.27%	0.06%	0.02%	0.00%	0.02%
A	0.07%	2.84%	91.30%	5.14%	0.51%	0.09%	0.02%	0.03%
BBB	0.05%	0.20%	5.15%	88.83%	4.54%	0.81%	0.24%	0.18%
BB	0.01%	0.06%	0.42%	6.25%	82.95%	8.48%	0.63%	1.20%
B	0.01%	0.05%	0.18%	0.39%	6.21%	81.93%	6.23%	5.00%
CCC	0.00%	0.03%	0.03%	0.19%	0.73%	11.22%	68.57%	19.23%

Source: From Tennant *et al.* (2008)

Table 10.2 Cumulative default probabilities implied from the 1-year transition matrix shown in Table 10.1

	AAA	AA	A	BBB	BB	B	CCC
1	0.01%	0.02%	0.03%	0.18%	1.20%	5.00%	19.23%
2	0.02%	0.04%	0.08%	0.48%	2.75%	10.37%	32.99%
3	0.03%	0.07%	0.16%	0.90%	4.60%	15.72%	43.03%
4	0.05%	0.10%	0.27%	1.43%	6.68%	20.85%	50.54%
5	0.07%	0.15%	0.42%	2.06%	8.92%	25.65%	56.27%
6	0.09%	0.20%	0.60%	2.78%	11.26%	30.09%	60.77%
7	0.11%	0.27%	0.82%	3.58%	13.65%	34.15%	64.36%
8	0.14%	0.35%	1.09%	4.45%	16.05%	37.85%	67.30%
9	0.18%	0.45%	1.39%	5.39%	18.43%	41.22%	69.75%
10	0.22%	0.57%	1.73%	6.38%	20.76%	44.28%	71.83%

Double-A credit. A Triple-C has a large 19.23% chance of default but a 12.2% chance[1] of improving in credit rating over a year.

By making several assumptions, we can derive the cumulative default probabilities, $F(.)$, for each credit rating from Table 10.1. The main assumption[2] required in order to do this is that the matrix is constant through time. This is clearly a naïve assumption as default and transition probabilities would be expected to change through the economic cycle, but it is reasonable for estimating default probabilities over long periods. Under such assumptions, we can simply multiply this matrix by itself $n - 1$ times to derive an n-year matrix. The resulting cumulative default probabilities are shown in Table 10.2 and plotted in Figure 10.5.

Spreadsheet 10.1 Analysis of historical default probabilities.

Looking at the above results, apart from the obvious conclusion that firms with good credit ratings default less often than those with worse ratings, we can also notice the following.

- *Investment-grade credits.* These tend to have default probabilities that increase over time. For example, the 5-year Single-A (A) default probability is 0.42% but the 10-year probability is 1.73%, which is more than four times bigger.
- *Non-investment-grade credits.* These credits tend to show the reverse effect, with default probabilities that increase much less strongly over time. For example, the 2-year Triple-C default probability is less than double the 1-year one (32.99% compared with 19.23%[3]).

---

[1] The sum of the first six numbers in the bottom row of Table 10.1, which represent the total probability of an upgrade.
[2] Other assumptions are that in the data, only a maximum of one credit rating move was experienced in a given year and that credit ratings have no "memory" – e.g., a given rating that has been upgraded or downgraded recently is not different from the same rating not subject to such a move.
[3] A key point to consider is that poor credit quality firms have default probabilities concentrated in the short term, not necessarily because their credit quality is expected to improve over time but instead because default in a future period can only be achieved by surviving to the start of this period. However, all other things being equal, we would expect the 2-year default probability to be 19.23% + 19.23% × (1 − 19.23%) = 34.76%. The actual 2-year default probability is less than this, illustrating that there is still a reduction in default probability and there is another component to be considered.

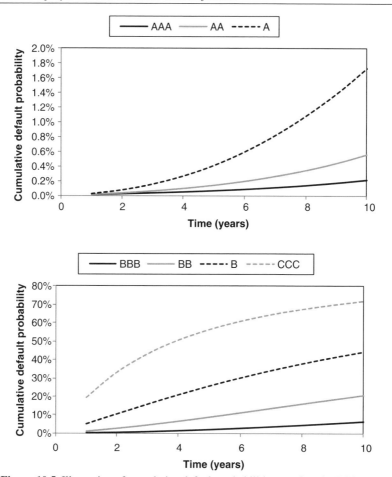

Figure 10.5 Illustration of cumulative default probabilities, as given in Table 10.2.

The above results can be explained by the mean-reversion of credit ratings, where above-average counterparties tend to deteriorate and vice versa. Hence (conditioning on no prior default), a good credit quality counterparty is much more likely to be downgraded than upgraded whilst the reverse is true for a counterparty with a low rating. Such trends can easily be seen when looking at transition matrices as shown in Table 10.1. For example, the probabilities of being upgraded and downgraded from A are respectively 2.91% and 5.76%, whilst the equivalent numbers for CCC are 12.2% and zero.

In computing CVA, not only will the cumulative default probability be important but also so will the way in which this is distributed marginally. We illustrate this in Figure 10.6, which shows annual default probabilities for A- and CCC-rated credits. The former increases significantly through time and the latter reduces. If an A-rated credit defaults then it is likely to be towards the end of the 10-year horizon considered, whilst a CCC-rated credit is likely to default much earlier.

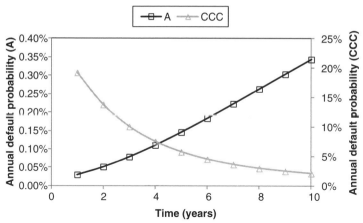

Figure 10.6 Annual historical default probabilities for Moody's A-rated firms computed using the data in Table 10.2. For example, the point at 3 years represents the default probability in the interval 2 years to 3 years, which is $0.16\% - 0.08\% = 0.08\%$.

10.1.4 Estimating real default probabilities – equity-based approaches

Equity-based approaches aim to estimate default probability from stock market information. In the classic Merton (1974) framework, the value of a firm (asset value) is considered stochastic and default is modelled as the point where the firm is unable to pay its outstanding liabilities when they mature. The original Merton model assumes that a firm has issued only a zero-coupon bond and will not therefore default prior to the maturity of this debt. Through option-pricing arguments, Merton then provides a link between corporate debt and equity via pricing formulas based on the value of the firm and its volatility (analogously to options being valued from spot prices and volatility). The problem of modelling default is transformed into that of assessing the future distribution of firm value and the barrier where default would occur. Such quantities can be estimated non-trivially from equity data and capital structure information. A key contribution of the Merton approach is that low-frequency binary events can be modelled via a continuous process and calibrated using high-frequency equity data.

KMV^{TM} (now Moody's KMV) developed the Merton-style approach (e.g., see Kealhofer and Kurbat, 2002; Kealhofer, 2003) with the aim of predicting default via the assessment of 1-year default probability defined as EDF^{TM} (expected default frequency). The KMV approach relaxed many of the stylised Merton assumptions. Their approach can be summarised broadly in three stages:

- estimation of the market value and volatility of a firm's assets;
- calculation of the distance to default, which is a standardised measure of default risk;
- scaling of the distance to default to the actual probability of default using a historical default database.

The distance to default (DD) measure is a standardised distance a firm is away from default. A key element of the KMV approach is to recognise the model risk inherent in this approach and rather to estimate the default probability empirically from many years of default history (and the calculated DD variables). For a firm with a DD of 4.0 (say), the question KMV attempt to answer is how often firms with the same DD have defaulted historically. The answer is likely to be considerably higher than the theoretical result of 0.003%.[4] This mapping of DD to actual default probability could be thought of as an empirical correction for model error. Note that, although the KMV approach relies on historical data, the EDF measure will still be dynamic due to constantly changing equity data.

A more recent and related, although simpler, approach is CreditGrades^{TM}. The aims of CreditGrades are rather similar to those of KMV, except that the modelling framework (see Finger *et al.*, 2002) is rather simpler and more transparent; in particular, there is no use of empirical data in order to map to an eventual default probability. In CreditGrades, default probability is defined by a simple formula with just a few model parameters.

Equity-based models for default probabilities have a place due to their ability to define default probability dynamically. This can be an advantage in a situation where historical default probabilities are considered too static a measure whilst probabilities defined directly from the credit market (discussed next) may be considered highly volatile and conservative due to the embedded default risk and liquidity premiums.

10.1.5   Estimating risk-neutral default probabilities

Risk-neutral default probabilities are those derived from credit spreads observed in the market. There is no single definition of a credit spread and it may be defined in slightly different ways and with respect to different rates. Common ways to define a credit spread are:

- from the premiums of single-name CDSs;
- from the traded spreads of asset swaps;[5]
- from bond prices, typically compared with some benchmark such as a treasury or LIBOR curve;
- using some proxy or mapping method.

All of the above are (broadly speaking) defining the same quantity, but small differences do exist in practice. The basis between CDS and bond spreads will be discussed in Section 10.2.4 and the definition of credit spreads with respect to LIBOR (and other) rates will be covered in more detail in Chapter 14. For now, we will focus on deriving risk-neutral default probabilities from the defined credit spread, which reflects the market price of credit risk.

Suppose a counterparty has a certain constant probability of default each year of (say) 10%. This must be the conditional default probability (i.e., the default probability assuming default has not yet occurred) as otherwise, after more than 10 years, the total default probability would be greater than 100%. This is illustrated in Figure 10.7. The probability of defaulting in the second year is equal to the probability of surviving the first year and defaulting the next, which would be 90% × 10% = 9%. The probability of defaulting at any time in the first two years is then 10% + 9% = 19%. By similar arguments, the probability of defaulting in the third year must be 90% × 90% × 10% = 8.1%, and so on.

---

[4] This arises since $\Phi^{-1}(-4.0) = 0.003\%$.
[5] An asset swap is essentially a synthetic bond, typically with a floating coupon.

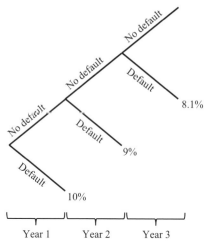

Figure 10.7 Illustration of the default process through time assuming a conditional default probability of 10% per year.

A more formal mathematical description of the above (see Appendix 10B) is that default is driven by a Poisson process and the default probability for a future period u is given by

$$F(u) = 1 - \exp(-hu), \tag{10.2}$$

where h defines the hazard rate of default, which is the conditional default probability in an infinitesimally small period. By choosing a hazard rate of 10.54%,[6] we can reproduce the results corresponding to the 10% annual default probability; for example, $1 - \exp(-10.54\% \times 2) = 19\%$ is the default probability in the first two years.

In Appendix 10B we show that an approximate[7] relationship between the hazard rate and credit spread is

$$h \approx \frac{\text{spread}}{(1 - \text{recovery})}, \tag{10.3}$$

where the assumed recovery rate is a percentage. Combining the above two equations gives the following approximate expression for risk-neutral default probability up to a given time u:

$$F(u) = 1 - \exp\left[-\frac{\text{spread}}{(1 - \text{recovery})} u\right]. \tag{10.4}$$

The reason that risk-neutral default probability depends on recovery can be explained as follows. Suppose a bond will default with a probability of 2% but the recovery value would be 50%. The expected loss is 1%, which is the same as if the bond had a 1% probability of default but the recovery value was zero. In the market we see only a single parameter (the credit spread) and must imply two values from it. Common practice is then to fix the recovery rate and derive the default probability. A higher recovery must

---

[6] This can be found from inverting equation (10.2) at the 1-year point as $-\log(1 - 10\%)$, where log represents the natural logarithm.
[7] This assumes that the credit spread term structure is flat (credit spreads for all maturities are equal) and that CDS premiums are paid continuously, as discussed in Appendix 10B.

be balanced (good for the bondholder) by a larger assumed default probability (bad for the bondholder).

The above formula is a good approximation generally, although to compute the implied default probabilities accurately we must solve numerically for the correct hazard rate, assuming a certain underlying functional form. The reader is referred to Appendix 10B and O'Kane (2008) for a more detailed discussion. Such an approach is also required to take into account the term structure of credit spreads and incorporate other aspects such as the convention of using upfront premiums (Section 10.2.1) in the CDS market.

Spreadsheet 10.2 Calculating market-implied default probabilities.

In terms of marginal default probability between dates t_{i-1} and t_i, an obvious approximation would be to take the difference between the relevant cumulative default probabilities in equation (10.4), leading to

$$q(t_{i-1}, t_i) \approx \exp\left[-\frac{\text{spread}_{t_{i-1}}}{(1 - \text{recovery})} t_{i-1}\right] - \exp\left[-\frac{\text{spread}_{t_i}}{(1 - \text{recovery})} t_i\right]. \qquad (10.5)$$

This approach is used to define CVA under Basel III (Chapter 17). It is only an approximation because it does not account for the shape of the credit curve prior to the time t_{i-1} (and the more sloped the curve is, the worse the approximation). We compared the simple formula with the more accurate calculation[8] in an example shown in Table 10.3.

We note that the annual default probabilities increase over time since the credit curve is increasing (upwards-sloping), which is a similar effect to that seen in Figure 10.5 for historical default probabilities (e.g., for an A rating). Indeed, the shape of a credit curve plays an

---

Table 10.3 Comparison of simple and accurate calculations for an example credit curve

Tenor	Spread	Hazard rate	$F(u)$	Annual default probability (equation (10.5))	Annual default probability (exact)
1Y	300 bps	5.00%	4.88%	4.88%	4.82%
2Y	350 bps	5.83%	11.01%	6.13%	6.14%
3Y	400 bps	6.67%	18.13%	7.12%	7.28%
4Y	450 bps	7.50%	25.92%	7.79%	8.22%
5Y	500 bps	8.33%	34.08%	8.16%	8.93%

---

[8] The more accurate calculation assumes constant continuously compounded interest rates of 5% and piecewise constant hazard rates.

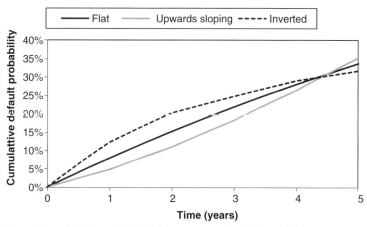

Figure 10.8 Cumulative default probabilities for flat, upwards-sloping and inverted curves as described in the text. In all cases, the 5-year spread is 500 bps and the recovery value is assumed to be 40%.

important part in determining the distribution of risk-neutral default probability, as we shall see in an example.

Suppose we take three different credit curves: the upwards-sloping one from Table 10.3, a flat curve at 500 bps and an inverted curve with, respectively, spreads of 800 bps, 700 bps, 600 bps, 550 bps and 500 bps. The cumulative default probability curves are shown in Figure 10.8. Note that all have a 5-year credit spread of 500 bps and assumed recovery rates of 40%. The only thing that differs is the shape of the curve. Whilst all curves agree reasonably well on the 5-year cumulative default probability of approximately 33%, the precise shape of the curve up to that point gives very different results. This is seen in Figure 10.9, which shows annual default probabilities for each case. For an upwards-sloping curve, default is less likely in the early years and more likely in the later years, whilst the reverse is seen for an inverted curve. In order to calculate risk-neutral default probabilities properly, in addition to defining the level of the credit curve it is also important to know the precise curve shape.

10.1.6 Comparison between real and risk-neutral default probabilities

The difference between real and risk-neutral default probabilities outlined in Section 10.1.2 has been characterised in a number of empirical studies. For example, Giesecke *et al.* (2010) use a dataset of bond yields that spans a period of almost 150 years from 1866 to 2008 and find that average credit spreads (averaging across all available bond data) have been about twice as large as realised losses due to default. Studies that are more specific include Fons (1987), the aforementioned work by Altman (1989) and Hull *et al.* (2005a). For example, Fons finds that 1-year risk-neutral default probabilities exceed actual realised default rates by approximately 5% (corresponding therefore to the numbers shown in Figure 10.4). The difference between real and risk-neutral default probabilities from Hull *et al.* (2005a) is shown in Table 10.4 as a function of credit rating. We see that the difference is large, especially for better quality credits.

There has been much work on understanding the components of credit spreads and their relation to actual default rates and recoveries. See, for example, Collin-Dufresne *et al.*

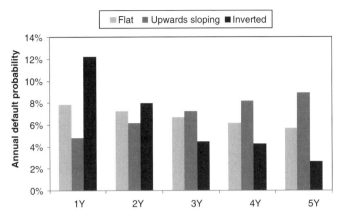

Figure 10.9 Annual default probabilities for flat, upwards-sloping and inverted curves as described in the text. In all cases, the 5-year spread is 500 bps and the recovery value is assumed to be 40%.

(2001) and Downing *et al.* (2005). These studies find that the difference between credit spreads and actual default losses is due to:

- the relative illiquidity of corporate bonds requiring a liquidity risk premium;
- the limited upside on holding a bond portfolio, or negative skew in bond returns;[9]
- the non-diversifiable risk of corporate bonds requiring a systemic risk premium.

We do not require here to understand in detail the relationship between credit spreads and historical default losses, but it is important to appreciate the impact on quantifying and managing counterparty risk. If one does not seek to hedge the default component of counterparty risk, then it is more relevant to consider the real world default probabilities estimated empirically via (for example) historical data.[10] If, on the other hand, one intends to hedge against

Table 10.4 Comparison between real and risk-neutral default probabilities in basis points

	Real default intensity	*Risk-neutral default intensity*	*Ratio*
Aaa	4	67	16.8
Aa	6	78	13.0
A	13	128	9.8
Baa	47	238	5.1
Ba	240	507	2.1
B	749	902	1.2
Caa	1690	2130	1.3

Source: Hull *et al.* (2005)

---

[9] This refers to the fact that the positive return from holding a bond is relatively modest whilst the loss on default can be relatively large.
[10] Although we note that Basel III regulation is not consistent with the use of real-world default probabilities irrespective of whether the intention is to hedge or not.

counterparty defaults then it is important to consider market credit spreads and associated risk-neutral default probabilities. Clearly, hedging counterparty risk appears to be much more costly than not hedging (Table 10.4). We will return to this discussion in Chapter 16.

Most of the empirical evidence compares risk-neutral default probabilities from bond spreads with historical default probabilities. Longstaff *et al.* (2005) argue that the CDS market, being more liquid, will not give rise to the liquidity premium represented in Figure 10.4. This would imply that the corresponding ratio between CDS-implied risk-neutral and historical default probabilities would be lower. However, this assumption is not supported by a consistently negative CDS–bond basis (Section 10.2.4). Hence, it seems reasonable that the relationship discussed above is broadly the same when using risk-neutral default probabilities from the CDS market.

10.1.7 Recovery rates

In order to estimate risk-neutral default probabilities, we must know the associated recovery rate. Recovery rates refer to the amount that would be recovered in the event of a counterparty defaulting. Common recovery rates are assumed to be a percentage of the notional amount (the exposure). This is in line with the legal right of all creditors to receive a proportion of what they are owed. Recovery rates are sometimes expressed via loss given default (LGD), which is simply one minus the recovery rate (in percentage terms). For example, a low recovery rate of 20% implies a high loss given default of 80%.

Ideally, recovery rates would be derived from market prices. A recovery swap is an agreement between two parties to swap a realised recovery rate (when and if the relevant credit event occurs) with a fixed recovery rate that is specified at the start of the contract. The reference price reflects the fixed recovery such that the recovery swap has zero value initially. Since the swap is issued at a price of zero, if the reference entity does not default in the term of the swap, then the swap expires with no cash flows having taken place. If a default does occur, the fixed recovery payer in the swap will compensate the other party, if the actual recovery is less than the fixed recovery, and vice versa. Since recovery swaps do not trade (except occasionally for distressed credits), we must normally look to historical analysis of recovery rates.

Recovery values, like default probabilities, tend to show a significant variation over time, as illustrated in Figure 10.10. We can see further variation according to variables such as

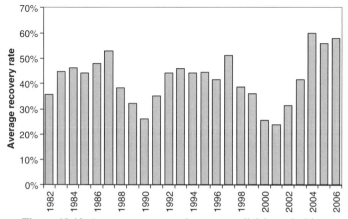

Figure 10.10 Average recovery values across all debt seniorities.
Source: Moody's Investors Service (2007).

Table 10.5   Recovery rates by sector

Industry	Recovery rate average
Public utilities	70.5%
Chemicals, petroleum, rubber and plastic products	62.7%
Machinery, instruments and related products	48.7%
Services (business and personal)	46.2%
Food and kindred products	45.3%
Wholesale and retail trade	44.0%
Diversified manufacturing	42.3%
Casino, hotel and recreation	40.2%
Building material, metals and fabricated products	38.8%
Transportation and transportation equipment	38.4%
Communication, broadcasting, movie production, printing and publishing	37.1%
Financial institutions	35.7%
Construction and real-estate	35.3%
General merchandise stores	33.2%
Mining and petroleum drilling	33.0%
Textile and apparel products	31.7%
Wood, paper and leather products	29.8%
Lodging, hospitals and nursing facilities	26.5%
TOTAL	**41.0%**

Source: Altman and Kishore (1996)

sector (Table 10.5). Recoveries also tend to be negatively correlated with default rates (e.g., see Hamilton *et al.*, 2001). This negative correlation means that a high default rate will give rise to lower recovery values. Hence, the random nature of default probability and recovery over time coupled to the negative correlation creates strong variability in default losses.

Recovery rates also depend on the seniority of the claim (Table 10.6). Normally, OTC derivatives would rank *pari passu* with senior unsecured debt, which in turn is the reference in most CDS contracts. When the recovery claim for counterparty risk is different then this must be quantified.

A final point on recovery is related to the timing. CDSs are settled quickly following a default and bondholders can settle their bonds in the same process (the CDS auction discussed in Section 10.2.3). However, OTC derivatives cannot be settled in a timely manner. This is partly due to their bespoke nature and partly due to netting (and collateral), which means that many trades are essentially aggregated into a single claim and cannot be traded individually. The net claim (less any collateral) is then often quite difficult to define for the portfolio of trades. This creates two different recovery values:

- *Settled recovery.* This is the recovery that could be achieved following the credit event; for example, by selling a defaulted bond.

Table 10.6 Recovery rates by original debt seniority

Debt seniority	Recovery rate average	
	Investment grade	Sub-investment grade
Senior secured	54.8%	56.4%
Senior unsecured	48.2%	48.7%
Senior subordinated	32.7%	39.9%
Subordinated	31.9%	31.7%
Discount and zero-coupon	24.1%	24.4%
Total	41.0%	

Source: Altman and Kishore (1996)

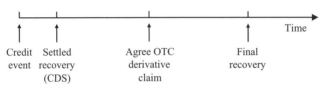

Figure 10.11 Schematic illustration of recovery settlement after a credit event. The settled recovery rate is achieved very close to the credit event time (for example, by participating in the CDS auction). The final recovery occurs when the company has been completely wound up. The actual recovery for a derivative claim may be realised sometime between the settled and final recoveries.

- *Actual recovery*. This is the actual recovery paid on the debt following a bankruptcy or similar process.

In theory, settled and actual recoveries should be very similar but in reality, since bankruptcy processes can take many years, they may differ materially. This is illustrated in Figure 10.11. It should be possible to agree on the claim with the bankruptcy administrators prior to the actual recovery, although this process may take many months. This would allow an institution to sell the claim and monetize the recovery value as early as possible. In the case of the Lehman Brothers bankruptcy, the settled recovery was around 9% whereas some actual recoveries traded to date have been substantially higher (in the region of 30–40%).

10.2   CREDIT DEFAULT SWAPS

The credit derivatives market has grown quickly in recent years, fuelled by the need to transfer credit risk efficiently and develop ever-more sophisticated products for investors. A credit derivative is an agreement designed to shift credit risk between parties and its value is derived from the credit performance of a corporation, sovereign entity or security. Credit derivatives can be traded on a single-name basis (referencing a single component such as a corporate) or a portfolio basis (referencing many components such as 125 corporate names).

Credit derivatives instruments are important since they represent opportunities for trading, hedging and diversification of counterparty risk. However, credit derivatives as a product class give rise to a significant amount of counterparty risk. Indeed, the continued development of the credit derivative market is contingent on control of this counterparty risk. This is a key role of CCPs, as discussed in Chapter 7.

10.2.1 Basics of CDSs

Many credit derivatives take the form of a CDS, which transfers the default risk of one or more corporations or sovereign entities from one party to another. In a single-name CDS, the protection buyer pays an upfront and/or periodic fee (the premium) to the protection seller for a certain notional amount of debt for a specified reference entity. If the reference entity specified undergoes a credit event then the protection seller must compensate the protection buyer for the associated loss by means of a pre-specified settlement procedure (the protection buyer must also typically pay an accrued premium at this point as compensation, due to the fact that premiums are paid in arrears). The premium is paid until either the maturity date or the credit event time, whichever comes first. The reference entity is not a party to the contract, and it is not necessary for the buyer or seller to obtain the reference entity's consent to enter into a CDS. The mechanics of a single-name CDS contract are shown in Figure 10.12 (index contracts are discussed later in Section 10.4.1).

CDS contracts trade with both fixed premiums and upfront payments. This reduces annuity risk in the hedge and unwinding of CDS contracts. Although it is not compulsory, the standard is that a CDS, on investment-grade reference entities, typically has a fixed premium of 100 basis points whilst high-yield reference entities trade at 500 basis points.[11] The scheduled termination dates of CDSs are March 20th, June 20th, September 20th or December 20th.

CDS documentation refers to a reference obligation and reference entity. The reference entity may be a corporate, a sovereign or any other form of legal entity which has incurred debt.[12] The reference obligation defines the seniority of the debt that can be delivered. Commonly, all obligations of the same or better seniority can be delivered (in the case of no reference obligation being specified then the seniority is senior unsecured).

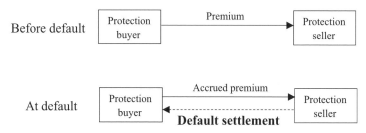

Figure 10.12 Illustration of a typical CDS contract on a single reference entity.

---

[11] Fixed premiums of 25, 100, 500 and 1000 (and 300 and 750) basis points may also trade. Historically, CDSs traded without any upfront payment, leading to many different running premiums traded at any one time.
[12] Occasionally, CDSs trade on names with little or no outstanding debt, often in the case of sovereign entities.

10.2.2 Credit events

Generally, the term "default" is used (as in default probability, for example) instead of the more accurate generic term "credit event". There are various credit events, which can all potentially lead to losses for creditors. Some credit events are well-defined, such as Chapter 11 bankruptcy in the US, whereas some other technical credit events, for example involving a breach of some contractual terms, are less so.

The three most important credit events are:

- *Bankruptcy*. This will be triggered by a variety of events associated with bankruptcy or insolvency proceedings, such as winding up, administration and receivership, under English and New York law or analogous events under other insolvency laws.
- *Failure to pay*. This event covers the failure to make a payment of principal or interest. A minimum threshold amount must be exceeded before this event is triggered (default value $1m). Failure to make a collateral posting even after the relevant grace period falls into this category, as discussed in Chapter 5.
- *Restructuring*. This covers the restructuring of debt causing a material adverse change in creditworthiness.

A significant risk when hedging with CDS contracts is that there is an economic loss but the credit event in the contract is not triggered.[13] Obvious examples of this may be restructuring-type credit events such as a debt-to-equity swap, a distressed exchange or another form of restructuring. The voluntary haircuts taken by most holders of Greek debt in 2012 were not enough to trigger a credit event. Whilst the exercise by Greece of the "Collective Action Clause" forcing all bondholders to participate did eventually trigger a restructuring credit event, this illustrates that default losses and the triggering of a credit event are in danger of being misaligned. CDSs may well appear to be good hedges for counterparty risk but may completely or partially fail when the credit event actually occurs.

10.2.3 CDS settlement

The fundamental aim of a CDS is to compensate the protection buyer for the loss of par value on a defaulted security such as a bond. However, debt securities will typically not be worth zero when there has been a credit event, but will rather trade at some recovery value. Hence, the protection buyer needs to be paid par minus this recovery value. There are fundamentally two ways in which this payoff has been achieved in CDSs:

- *Physical settlement*. In this case, the protection buyer will deliver to the protection seller defaulted securities of the reference entity with a par value equal to the notional amount of the CDS contract. In return, the protection seller must make a payment of par in cash. For example, an investor buying a bond and holding CDS protection for the same notional may deliver the defaulted bond against receiving par. This mechanism is clearly attractive since no other parties need to be involved and there can be limited dispute over payments.

---

[13] In 2008, the conservatorship of Fannie Mae/Freddie Mac gave the reverse case by triggering the bankruptcy clause without a bankruptcy filing. However, the bonds traded very close to par due to a delivery squeeze and the explicit guarantee by the US government. In this case, sellers of CDS protection faced costs due to settlement even though there was no economic loss.

- *Cash settlement.* Here, the protection seller will compensate the protection buyer in cash for the value of par minus recovery value. An obvious problem with this is that the recovery value must be determined through some market consensus of where the debt of the defaulted entity is trading (dealer poll or more recently an auction process described below).

In a CDS contract settled via physical delivery, since the credit event is not specific to a given security, there is no single bond that needs to be delivered. The protection buyer therefore has some choice over the security that can be delivered and will naturally choose the cheapest available in the market (the "cheapest-to-deliver option"). Obvious choices for cheapest-to-deliver bonds may include those with low coupons (including convertible bonds) and illiquid bonds. Restructuring credit events are particularly significant in this respect, as bonds are more likely to be trading at different levels. The market has evolved to different restructuring options in CDS contracts to try to minimise cheapest-to-deliver risk. The current standards in the US and Europe are modified restructuring (MR) and modified modified restructuring (MMR), respectively. These both include restructuring as a credit event in a CDS contract but limit the securities that can be delivered following such a credit event.

A large proportion of protection buyers do not hold the original risk in the form of bonds. This "naked" CDS position may arise due to pure speculation or may be linked to counterparty risk hedging. There have been efforts and calls to ban naked CDSs and only allow the buying of CDS protection when the buyer holds the underlying debt security (as is the case in insurance contracts where the owner of insurance needs to own the insured risk at the claim time). Aside from the fact that this will make the CDS market inefficient, this can restrict CDS protection being held against credit exposure to hedge counterparty risk. Since future credit exposure is uncertain, it is not clear what an appropriate amount of CDS protection to hold as a hedge would be.[14] An institution may understandably want to buy more CDS protection than their current exposure to mitigate a potential increase in exposure in the future.

Another problem in the CDS market is a *delivery squeeze* that can be created if the amount of notional required to be delivered (total outstanding CDS protection on the reference entity) is large compared with the amount of outstanding debt. In a delivery squeeze, bond prices will increase to reflect a lack of supply and this in turn will suppress the value of the CDS (since the payoff is par less recovery). This is another important consideration in the hedging of counterparty risk since it can create a significant discrepancy between the recovery value of the security itself and the recovery as defined by the CDS contract.

The problems of cheapest-to-deliver options and delivery squeezes have been limited by the adoption of an auction protocol in settling credit events. In 2009, there were a number of changes to CDS documentation and trading practices, aimed at reducing some of the risks described above and improving standardisation. One was the incorporation of auction settlement provisions as the standard settlement method for credit derivatives transactions. The so-called "Big Bang Protocol" allowed this auction to also be included for legacy CDS trades (as long as both counterparties signed up to the Big Bang Protocol). Most major credit events on liquid reference credits should now be settled in this fashion, via a pre-planned auction of defaulted bonds to determine a fair price for cash settlement of all CDSs referencing the credit in question. Whilst this eliminates most basis risks, the problems of settled and final recovery in the hedging of counterparty risk (Figure 10.11) remains.

---

[14] For example, even if the exposure to a counterparty was currently zero, an institution may reasonably want to buy CDS protection to hedge a potential increase in the counterparty credit spread (see Section 16.4.1).

Table 10.7   Recovery rates for CDS auctions for some credit events in 2008. The impact of a delivery squeeze can be seen in that Fannie Mae and Freddie Mac subordinated debt traded at higher levels than the senior debt

Reference entity	Seniority	Recovery rate
Fannie Mae	Senior	91.5%
	Subordinated	99.9%
Freddie Mac	Senior	94.0%
	Subordinated	98.0%
Washington Mutual		57.0%
Lehman		8.6%
Kaupthing Bank	Senior	6.6%
	Subordinated	2.4%
Landsbanki	Senior	1.3%
	Subordinated	0.1%
Glitnir	Senior	3.0%
	Subordinated	0.1%
Average		38.5%

In Table 10.7 we show recovery values settled following credit events for some CDS auctions in 2008. We see a wide range of recoveries from Fannie Mae and Freddie Mac that were close to 100%, thanks largely to the guarantee from the US government, making this a more technical credit event than Lehman Brothers and Icelandic banks that recovered very little.

10.2.4   The CDS–bond basis

It is possible to show theoretically (Duffie, 1999) that, under certain assumptions, a (short) CDS protection position is equivalent to a position in an underlying fixed-rate bond and a payer interest rate swap.[15] This combination of a bond and interest rate swap corresponds to what is known as an asset swap. This implies that spreads, as calculated from the CDS and bond markets, should be similar. However, a variety of technical and fundamental factors means that this relationship will be imperfect. The difference between CDS and bond spreads is known as the CDS–bond basis. A positive (negative) basis is characterised by CDS spreads being higher (lower) than the equivalent bond spreads.[16]

Factors that drive the CDS–bond basis are:

- *Counterparty risk.* CDSs have significant wrong-way counterparty risk (Chapter 15), which tends to make the basis negative.
- *Funding.* The theoretical link between bonds and CDSs supposes that LIBOR funding is possible. Funding at levels in excess of LIBOR will tend to make the basis positive, as CDSs do not require funding. Contributing further to this effect is that shorting cash bonds tends to

---

[15] Specifically, the interest rate swap is not standard, as it must terminate if the underlying credit event in the CDS occurs.
[16] We note that the definition of bond spread is subjective, as it must be defined by some "risk-free" benchmark. In Chapter 14 (Section 14.2.2), this aspect is discussed in more detail.

be difficult, as the bond needs to be sourced in a fairly illiquid and short-dated repo market in which bonds additionally might trade on special, making it expensive to borrow the bond.

• *Credit event definition.* CDS credit events should, in theory, perfectly coincide with the concept of credit-related losses for bondholders. However, credit events are vulnerable to divergence from bond documentation, despite improvements by ISDA in standardising and harmonising CDS legal documentation. Technical credit events may cause CDS protection to pay out on an event that is not considered a default by bondholders. Alternatively, a credit event may not be triggered even though bondholders take credit losses (see comment on Greek debt in Section 10.2.3). The former effect would tend to push the basis into positive territory whilst the latter would make it negative.

• *Cheapest-to-deliver option.* The delivery option (Section 10.2.3) in a CDS contract may have some additional values in certain circumstances, such as restructuring credit events. This would tend to make the basis *positive.*

• *Delivery squeeze.* A delivery squeeze (Section 10.2.3) involves a shortage of CDS deliverable debt and would tend to make the basis *negative.*

• *Bonds trading above or below par.* Fixed-rate bonds can trade significantly above or below par because of changes in interest rates. CDS protection is essentially indexed to the par value of a bond and bonds trading above (below) par will tend to make the basis negative (positive). The use of fixed coupon CDS (Section 10.2.1) reduces this effect.

• *Accrued interest.* In the event of default, a bond typically does not pay accrued interest for any coupons owed, whereas a CDS does require protection buyers to pay the accrued premium up to the credit event. This will cause the basis to be negative.

• *Other technical factors.* Historically, other technical factors, such as synthetic CDO issuance, have had an impact on the basis.

Generally, prior to the global financial crisis, the basis tended to be positive due to effects such as funding and the cheapest-to-deliver option. More recently, the basis has been negative due partially to CDS counterparty risk concerns.

10.2.5   Contingent credit default swaps

In a standard single-name CDS, the protection buyer has protection on a fixed contractual notional amount. Such a contract is reasonably well tailored towards credit exposures arising from instruments such as loans and bonds. For example, $10m of CDS protection would give protection against holding bonds with par value of $10m.[17] However, a key aspect of counterparty risk is that the loss as determined by the credit exposure at the credit event time is usually unknown.

A CCDS is an instrument that is the same as a standard single-name[18] CDS but with one key difference, in that the notional amount of protection is referenced to another transaction(s). This underlying transaction can be potentially any product across any asset class. Hence, a CCDS can provide perfect protection against the counterparty risk on a derivative since the protection amount can be linked directly to the exposure of that derivative. Whilst CDSs are generally products which have many applications, CCDSs are products that are

---

[17] This is only approximately true due to the triggering of a credit event not being aligned with the bond loss as mentioned above, and due to the potentially different recovery values (Section 10.1.7).

[18] We refer here to single-name CCDSs. Index CCDSs will be discussed in Section 15.4.5.

tailor-made to hedge counterparty risk. As such, CCDSs potentially allow for the possibility of a complete disentangling of counterparty risk from all other financial risks.

A CCDS represents a contract tailor-made to transfer counterparty risk from one institution to another. However, except in limited cases, CCDSs have not proved particularly popular. Some reasons for this are:

- *Complexity of documentation.* A CCDS must contain a "termsheet within a termsheet" since it must reference the transaction for which the counterparty risk is to be transferred. Confidentiality may also be a problem here since a CCDS counterparty would have information on all trades with the counterparty whose risk is being hedged.
- *No recognition of netting/collateral.* A CCDS typically references a single trade and not a netting set, which would be more relevant. A CCDS referring an entire netting set would be complex and would not cover subsequent trades within that netting set. Additionally, a CCDS does not account for the potential collateralisation of a credit exposure.
- *Double default.* A CCDS is not effective unless the CCDS provider has a very high credit quality and/or is uncorrelated with the original counterparty. These aspects are very hard to achieve, the latter especially so for counterparties of good credit quality. This is discussed in more detail in Section 16.2.2.
- *Lack of sellers of protection.* As with the single-name CDS market, there is a lack of sellers of single-name CCDS protection.

There have been attempts to ignite the CCDS market. For example, Novarum group[19] set up a dedicated vehicle to sell fully collateralised CCDS protection in 2009. However, this initiative has not seen great success, probably mainly due to the double default aspect mentioned above. For example, for an OTC derivative dealer to hedge a large component of their CVA with such an entity they would have to be very certain of this entity's ability to withstand a high default rate environment in order to feel that the hedges were effective. Regulators would need to have the same confidence to allow capital relief and provide a strong credit rating to the protection seller.

10.3   CURVE MAPPING

In Section 10.1.5, we discussed the quantification of risk-neutral default probabilities from the credit spread of a counterparty. Such a credit spread may be derived in a variety of ways from the market prices of bonds, asset swaps and single-name CDSs. However, a key aspect in quantifying CVA is to obtain credit spreads for non-observable names, i.e., those counterparties for which there is no defined credit spread trading in the market.

Whilst using subjective mapping methods to determine a credit spread may seem rather non-scientific, it is generally a necessary process for banks to value illiquid assets, such as bonds and loans, held on their trading books. Furthermore, Basel III capital rules impose similar requirements for capital allocation against CVA, stating (BCBS, 2011): "Whenever such a CDS spread is not available, the bank must use a proxy spread that is appropriate based on the rating, industry and region of the counterparty." Banks and authors (e.g., Gregory, 2010) have argued against this requirement on the basis that banks do not attempt to mark-to-market much of their illiquid credit risk (including CVA).

---

[19] See http://www.novarumgroup.com

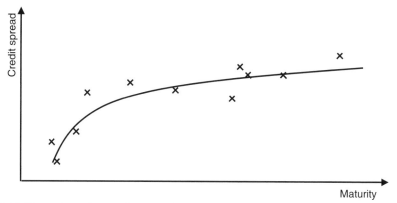

Figure 10.13 Illustration of a mapping procedure. The crosses represent observable spreads as a function of maturity.

10.3.1 Basics of mapping

The fundamental aim of credit curve mapping is to use some relevant points to achieve a general curve based on observable market data, as illustrated in Figure 10.13. This illustrates a case where a number of points can be used at various different maturities (as in the case of the secondary bond market). A best fit to these spreads (perhaps with some underlying weighting scheme also used to bias towards the more liquid quotes) gives the entire curve. The classification may be rather broad (e.g., a Single-A curve), in which case there will be a large number of data points to fit but less distinguishing between different counterparties. In contrast, a more granular classification (e.g., rating, sector and geography – for example, a Single-A US utility company) distinguishes better between different counterparties but provides less data for each curve calibration.

We note that this representation is troublesome from a hedging perspective as all points represent hedging instruments. There is also the problem that a recalibration (either periodic or, for example, due to removal of an illiquid data point) will cause a curve shift and a resulting move in CVA with an associated (unhedgeable) PnL impact.

10.3.2 Indices and classification

Whilst bond spreads provide some mapping information, a key component of a mapping methodology is the link to the hedging of CVA (Chapter 16). Credit indices therefore represent a better choice for mapping credit curves. An example classification of European counterparties according to credit indices[20] is given in Figure 10.14. Reading from the bottom, the first choice would obviously be to map to a single-name CDS or a relevant proxy such as a parent company. If such information were not available then the counterparty would be mapped to the relevant index depending on whether it is a corporation, financial or sovereign entity. Corporations may be further sub-divided according to credit quality.

Note that further, more detailed classifications can be made that are not shown in Figure 10.14. For example, iTraxx SovX is sub-divided into Western Europe (WE) and Central & Eastern European, Middle Eastern and African (CEEMEA). Corporates may also be sub-

---

[20] See http://www.markit.com/en/products/data/indices/credit-and-loan-indices/itraxx/itraxx.page

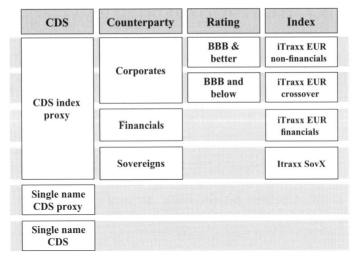

CDS	Counterparty	Rating	Index
CDS index proxy	Corporates	BBB & better	iTraxx EUR non-financials
		BBB and below	iTraxx EUR crossover
	Financials		iTraxx EUR financials
	Sovereigns		Itraxx SovX
Single name CDS proxy			
Single name CDS			

Figure 10.14 Illustration of a classification of counterparties according to European credit indices.

divided into sectoral indices (in addition to financials and non-financials), such as TMT, industrials, energy, consumers and autos. Whilst these sub-divisions give a more granular representation, they have to be balanced against the available liquidity in the CDS market.

10.3.3 Curve shape

A final consideration that is relevant is the case where a single-maturity credit spread (typically 5 years) can be defined (either directly or via some mapping) but the rest of the curve cannot. The obvious solution in such a case is to use the most appropriate index to define the curve shape, as illustrated in Figure 10.15. So, for example, if the 5-year point defined is 130% times the equivalent index maturity, then all points are mapped to 130% of the index curve.

The topic of mapping will be discussed again in Chapter 16 in relation to beta hedging.

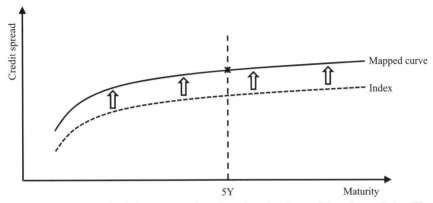

Figure 10.15 Illustration of defining a curve shape based on the shape of the relevant index. The cross shows the 5-year point that is assumed to be known for the curve in question.

10.4 PORTFOLIO CREDIT DERIVATIVES

In this final section, we give a brief overview of portfolio credit derivatives products such as index tranches and collateralised debt obligations (CDOs). A basic understanding of these structures is useful for the discussions on wrong-way counterparty risk in Chapter 15. A more in-depth coverage of portfolio credit derivatives and their uses (and abuses) is given in Tavakoli (2008).

10.4.1 CDS index products

Up until 2004, the majority of credit default swaps were written on single names, but thereafter a major impetus to growth and market liquidity of the credit derivative market has been credit default swaps on indices. A credit index can usually be thought of as an equally weighted combination of single-name CDSs and hence the fair premium on the index will be close to the average CDS premium within that index.[21] The two most common credit indices are:

- *DJ iTraxx Europe*. This contains 125 European corporate investment-grade reference entities, which are equally weighted.
- *DJ CDX NA IG*. This contains 125 North American (NA) corporate investment-grade reference entities, which are equally weighted.

Other indices exist for different underlying reference entities and regions but they are less liquid. Indices can be traded in either CDS (unfunded) or CLN[22] (funded) form. Buying CDS protection on \$125m of the DJ CDX NA IG index is almost[23] equivalent to buying \$1m of CDS protection on each of the underlying reference entities within the index.

An important feature of credit indices is that they "roll" every 6 months. A roll will involve:

- *Adjustment of maturity*. Typical traded maturities are 5, 7 and 10 years. Fixed maturity dates[24] will be used such that the initial maturities are 5.25, 7.25 and 10.25 years. After 6 months, the maturities will have become 4.75, 6.75 and 9.75 and these will be re-set to their original values.
- *Adjustment of portfolio*. Names will be removed from a credit index according to predefined criteria in relation to credit events, ratings downgrades and increases in individual CDS premiums beyond a certain threshold. The overall aim is to replace defaulted names and maintain a homogenous credit quality. Names removed from the index will be replaced with other names meeting the required criteria.

---

[21] This is not quite true for two reasons. First, a theoretical adjustment must be made to the average CDS premium to account for the heterogeneity of the constituents. Second, the index will typically trade at a basis to the average CDS premiums (bid–offer costs will prevent arbitrage of this difference).

[22] Credit linked note, which is a CDS funded to create a synthetic bond.

[23] Aside from the theoretical adjustment due to a premium mismatch and the fact that the index protection may involve an upfront payment.

[24] International Monetary Market (IMM) dates are used.

- *Premium.* In the 6-month period before a roll, the index premium is fixed at a given level of either 100 or 500 bps and trades on the index will involve an upfront payment from one party to the other to compensate for the difference between the fair premium and traded premium. This greatly facilitates unwinding positions and monetising MtM gains (or losses), and is similar to the use of a fixed premium for US CDS contracts discussed in Section 10.2.1. At the roll, the index premium may be reset (to either 100 or 500 bps) depending on its fair theoretical level based on the individual CDS levels at that time.

We note that rolls only influence new trades and not existing ones (which still reference the old index and other terms).

10.4.2   Index tranches

Following on from the standardisation of credit indices was the development of index tranches. Whilst a credit index references all losses on the underlying names, a tranche will only reference a certain portion of those losses. So, for example, an [$X\%$, $Y\%$] tranche will reference losses between $X\%$ and $Y\%$ on the underlying index. The "subordination" of the tranche is $X\%$ whilst $Y\%$ is referred to as the "detachment point". The size of the tranche is $(Y - X)\%$. The standard index tranches for the DJ iTraxx Europe and DJ CDX NA indices are illustrated in Figure 10.16. The index tranche that takes the first loss, [0–3%], is referred to as the equity tranche, with the very high-up tranches referred to as senior or super senior and the intermediate tranches referred to as mezzanine.

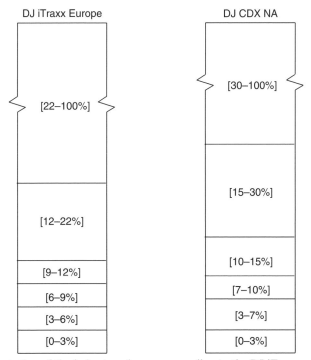

Figure 10.16 Illustration of the index tranches corresponding to the DJ iTraxx and DJ CDX North American credit indices. All tranches are shown to scale except the [22–100%] and [30–100%].

Irrespective of trading convention, the important aspect of an index tranche is that it covers only a certain range of the losses on the portfolio. Index tranches vary substantially in the risk they constitute: equity tranches carry a large amount of risk and pay attractive returns whilst tranches that are more senior have far less risk but pay only moderate returns. At the far end, super senior tranches might be considered to have no risk whatsoever (in terms of experiencing losses) but this is a point we will analyse in more depth in Chapter 8. Tranching creates a leverage effect since the more junior tranches carry more risk than the index whilst the most senior tranches[25] have less risk.

10.4.3 Super senior risk

As we shall see in Chapter 15, the more senior a tranche, the more counterparty risk it creates. Not surprisingly then, super senior tranches have created a big headache for the credit market in terms of their counterparty risk. Let us start by asking ourselves how many defaults would cause a loss of either super senior tranche of DJ iTraxx and DJ CDX. We can represent the number of defaults a given tranche can withstand by

$$\text{Number of defaults} = n \frac{X}{(1 - \text{recovery})}, \tag{10.6}$$

where X represents the attachment point of the tranche (%), n is the number of names in the index and the recovery is the (weighted[26]) average recovery rate for the defaults that occur.

Example. How many defaults can the super senior tranches of DJ iTraxx and DJ CDX withstand at assumed average recoveries of 40% and 20%?
From the previous formula, we have for DJ iTraxx

$$125 \times 22\%/(1 - 40\%) = 45.8 \text{ defaults } (40\% \text{ recovery})$$

$$125 \times 22\%/(1 - 20\%) = 34.4 \text{ defaults } (20\% \text{ recovery})$$

And for DJ CDX

$$125 \times 30\%/(1 - 40\%) = 62.5 \text{ defaults } (40\% \text{ recovery})$$

$$125 \times 30\%/(1 - 20\%) = 46.9 \text{ defaults } (20\% \text{ recovery})$$

Super senior tranches clearly have very little default risk. Let us consider a super senior tranche of the longest maturity (10-years). From Table 10.2, the Moody's cumulative default probability for the worst investment-grade rating of Triple-B for this

---

[25] Due to its size, usually only the super senior may have a leverage of less than one and all other tranches may be more highly leveraged than the index.
[26] Since the default that actually hits the tranche may have only a fractional impact, as in the previous example.

period is 6.38%. The even assuming the lower 20% recovery, default rates of 4.3 and 5.9 times the historical average would be required to wipe out the subordination on the iTraxx and CDX super senior tranches respectively.[27] This default remoteness has led to terms such as "super Triple-A" or "Quadruple A" being used to describe the risk on super senior tranches. From the counterparty risk perspective, the important question is: from whom can an institution buy super Triple-A protection?

10.4.4   Collateralised debt obligations

There are many different types of collateralised debt obligations. They contain different asset classes and have different structural features. However, the approximate classification of risk defined in the last section (equity, mezzanine, senior) will always follow. For example, any CDO structure will have an associated super senior tranche that will be considered extremely unlikely ever to take credit losses.

CDOs can be broadly divided into two categories:

- *Synthetic CDOs.* Alternatively called collateralised synthetic obligations (CSOs), these are very similar to index tranches except that the underlying portfolio, attachment and detachment points, maturity and other specifics will be bespoke or tailor-made for a given transaction(s). Most commonly, a tranche will be traded in isolation from the rest of the capital structure. Banks have traditionally had large "correlation desks" that trade many different tranches of synthetic CDOs on various different portfolios.
- *Structured finance securities.* This very large class of securitisation structures covers cash CDOs, collateralised loan obligations (CLOs), mortgage-backed securities (MBSs) and CDOs of ABSs. The main difference between these structures and synthetic CDOs is that the structure and tranche losses occur by means of a much more complex mechanism. This means that tranches of these deals cannot be traded in isolation and all tranches must be sold more or less simultaneously[28] as a so-called "full capital structure" transaction.

From the point of view of counterparty risk, the key aspect is that issuers of CDOs need to place (buy protection) on all tranches across the capital structure. In a full capital structure or structured finance-type structure, this is clear from the need to place all of the risk. In a synthetic CDO, it is less obvious but arises because a book cannot be risk-managed effectively unless it has a reasonable balance between equity, mezzanine and senior tranches. Therefore, issuers of CDOs are super senior protection buyers, not necessarily because they think super senior tranches have value but rather because:

- They need to buy protection or place the super senior risk in order to have efficiently distributed the risk. Failure to do this may mean holding onto a very large super senior piece and potentially not being able to recognise P&L on a transaction.

---

[27] For example, for iTraxx $34.4/(125 \times 6.38\%) = 4.3$. Where the factor of 34.4 is calculated in the above example.

[28] Unless some can be "recycled" and put in the next structure, a practice that has become widely regarded as far from ideal from an investor's perspective.

OR

- Buying super senior protection is required as a hedge for other tranche positions. Without going into too much detail, we note that structured product traders may buy a product such as an option or tranche, not because they think it is undervalued, but rather because it allows them to hedge. In options terminology they may pay for the "gamma" (the convexity of the price with respect to market movements). In this case, a CDO correlation trader may buy protection on a super senior tranche, not because he thinks it will have a payoff (losses hitting the tranche), but rather because it provides positive gamma.

We will return to these aspects when we show how CDOs fail in Chapter 15.

10.5 SUMMARY

This chapter has been concerned with an overview of default probability, credit spreads and credit derivatives. We have described default probability, estimation methods and the differences between real and risk-neutral default probabilities. The impact of recovery rates has also been discussed. Detail necessary to calculate risk-neutral default probabilities from credit spreads, which will be required in CVA calculations later, has been given. We have described the important credit derivatives instruments that will be essential for discussing wrong-way risk (Chapter 15) and hedging (Chapter 16). Finally, we have discussed curve-mapping procedures that are an important component of CVA quantification.

In Chapter 11, we consider the nature of portfolio counterparty risk, where we focus on the joint default probabilities of many counterparties at the same time.

11

Portfolio Counterparty Credit Risk

The policy of being too cautious is the greatest risk of all.

Jawaharlal Nehru (1889–1964)

11.1 INTRODUCTION

In the last chapter, we considered the default probability of a single counterparty. The next component to consider is portfolio-level aspects, requiring consideration of the risk posed by two or more counterparties. We will first do this for two counterparties and discuss "double default risk", which is an important consideration in assessing the hedging benefits that may be derived from credit derivatives. The concept of economic capital applied to credit portfolios has been much studied over the past two decades. We will consider how the uncertainty of exposure influences economic capital. This will be discussed in more detail in Chapter 17 with the Basel II requirements for counterparty risk.

11.2 DOUBLE DEFAULT

11.2.1 Joint default events

Suppose an institution has an exposure to counterparty A and insures that exposure through counterparty X (as in the case of a CCDS discussed in Section 10.2.5). The institution now has a (reduced) risk, as it is only exposure in the case of counterparties A and X **both** defaulting. Let us consider four possible outcomes, as illustrated in Figure 11.1. We need to consider the following relationships between entities A and X:

- *Mutually exclusive*. Mutually exclusive events cannot occur at the same time. For default events to be mutually exclusive there would have to be negative correlation between them. This is unlikely to be the case for defaults, except in rare circumstances where two competitors may be considered unlikely to default together since the failure of one would give the other an increased market share.[1]
- *Independent*. Independent events happen with no underlying linkage so that occurrence of one event makes it neither more nor less probable that the other event occurs. When throwing two coins, the outcomes are independent. Independent events can happen

---

[1] Even then, there is likely to be some systemic scenario (such as a downturn in the sector) that could lead both counterparties to default.

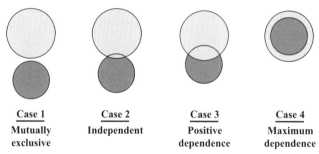

Figure 11.1 Illustration of the relationship between the defaults of two entities. The area of each circle represents the default probability (a larger circle is a more risky name). The overlap between the circles signifies joint default.

together (circles overlapping), although this will be unlikely if their underlying probabilities are small.

• *Positive dependence.* Positive dependence means that if one event happens then another is more likely to occur. This is the key area for portfolio defaults since one default may increase the probability of other defaults. Positive dependence means that the probability of two defaults is increased compared with the independent case.

• *Maximum dependence.* The maximum dependence between two default variables corresponds to the highest possible joint probability. Note that the circles cannot overlap perfectly (since the individual default probabilities differ). Hence, the maximum joint default probability is the minimum of the two individual default probabilities.

> **Example.** Suppose an institution has exposure to a counterparty (A) with a default probability of 2% but then buys protection on that exposure (through a CCDS, for example) with another counterparty (X) with a smaller default probability of 1%.
>
> The institution now has risk to the "double default" (default of both counterparties A and X). What is this probability?
>
> *Answer.* At this point, we can do no more than attempt to put boundaries on the problem. Assuming that the default events of A and X cannot be mutually exclusive, the best case corresponds to independence when the joint default probability will be 0.02% (1% × 2%) – case 2 in Figure 11.1. The worst case of maximum correlation would correspond to a joint default probability of 1% (the minimum of the two default probabilities) – case 4 in Figure 11.1. The joint default probability will therefore be between 0.02% and 1%, and the relative benefit of the CCDS could be anything from double (2% reduced to 1%) to 100 times (2% reduced to 0.02%).

11.2.2 Merton-style approach

The modelling of joint default events is conceptually difficult due to the binary[2] nature of default and the lack of data regarding default events (especially joint default events). What is

---

[2] Meaning simply that default can either occur or not, so there are just two (rather than a continuum of) states to consider. The nature of default, as in this two-state process, means that the application of classical statistical concepts such as correlation is not straightforward.

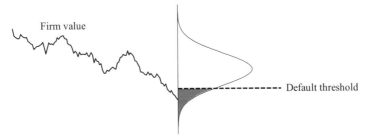

Figure 11.2 Illustration of the Merton approach to default modelling. If the underlying firm value falls below a certain default threshold then default will occur.

required is an intuitive way to generate dependence between defaults with some underlying economic structure. This has been classically achieved using a Merton-inspired approach. The Merton model was described briefly in Chapter 10 for a single default process and is now extended for multiple defaults. In the Merton model, we simply write default as being the point at which a process for the asset value falls below a certain "default threshold", as illustrated in Figure 11.2. The change in the firm value is typically assumed to follow a normal distribution.

The assumption that the change in firm value is driven by a normal distribution is key. However, since the default probability of the firm is already known (by other methods as described in Chapter 10), the precise distributional specification of the normal distribution (drift and volatility) is unimportant. One must simply set the default barrier in order to retrieve the correct default probability. This involves an inversion, often written as $k = \Phi^{-1}(p)$, where $\Phi^{-1}(.)$ is the inverse of a cumulative normal distribution function, p is the default probability of the name over the time horizon of interest and k is the default threshold.

11.2.3   Impact of correlation

The above modelling framework[3] might first appear to be nothing more than a mapping exercise. However, the power of the approach lies in its elegance and intuition when introducing another default event. Now the joint default probability can be defined by a two-dimensional or bivariate Gaussian distribution function. Hence, in the "double default" model of interest, the joint default probability of two names A and X, p_{AX}, is given by

$$p_{AX} = \Phi_2(k_A, k_X; \rho_{AX}),\qquad(11.1)$$

where Φ_2 is a cumulative bivariate distribution function, ρ_{AX} is the correlation between A and B, often referred to as the "asset correlation", and k_A and k_X are the default barriers as defined above. An illustration of this is given in Figure 11.3. It can be seen that positive correlation has the impact of increasing the joint default probability.

> **Spreadsheet 11.1 Calculation of joint default probabilities with a bivariate normal distribution function.**

---

[3] Although there is a clear link between this simple approach and the Merton model, we have ignored the full path of the asset value process and linked default to just a single variable. A more rigorous approach, however, does not differ significantly and is much more complex to implement (see Hull *et al.*, 2004).

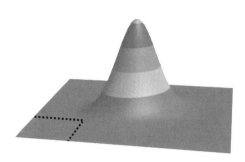

Figure 11.3 Illustration of the two-name correlation approach which is driven by a bivariate Gaussian distribution with positive dependence (correlation = 30%). The area shown by the dotted lines corresponds to joint default.

We now have the means to calculate joint default probabilities as a function of correlation using equation (11.1). This is shown in Figure 11.4 for the earlier example of names with default probabilities of 1% and 2%. We can see that with negative correlation, the joint default probability is extremely small, tending towards zero at maximum negative correlation (mutually exclusive). With zero correlation (independence), the joint default probability is 0.02% (1% × 2%) whilst at maximum correlation it increases to 1%. Not surprisingly, the magnitude of the correlation is clearly crucial in determining the impact of counterparty risk for two or more names.

In order to fully illustrate the last point, we must now consider the effectiveness of a single-name CDS (or CCDS) hedge. We look at the reduction in default risk corresponding to the unhedged default probability (original counterparty only) and the hedged case of joint default probability (both counterparties). This gives an idea of the benefit of hedging and the impact of the residual "double default risk". Consider the following ratio:

$$\text{Hedge effectiveness} = \frac{\text{default probability (no hedge)}}{\text{joint default probability (with hedge)}} = \frac{p_A}{p_{AX}} \geq 1. \tag{11.2}$$

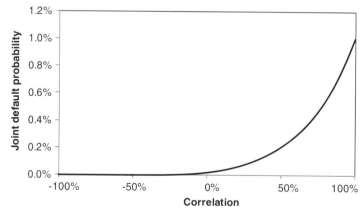

Figure 11.4 Joint default probability as a function of asset correlation for two counterparties with individual default probabilities of 2% and 1%.

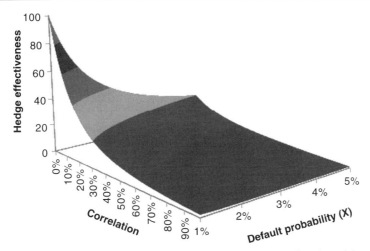

Figure 11.5 Illustration of effectiveness of a single-name CDS hedge as a function of the default probability of the counterparty and the correlation between the default of the counterparty and the original counterparty. The hedge effectiveness is defined as the original counterparty default probability (2%) divided by the joint default probability.

The larger the above ratio, the more effective the hedge. This ratio is shown in Figure 11.5 for the example where the original counterparty default probability is 2%. We can see that, not surprisingly, for the CDS hedge to be effective the counterparty must have a low default probability (with respect to the original counterparty) and/or there should be a low correlation between this counterparty and the original counterparty. As the correlation and the hedge counterparty default probability increase then the ratio tends to unity, illustrating no benefit at all.

Whilst this effect may seem obvious, what is particularly striking is the impact of correlation on the effectiveness of the hedge. Whilst in this particular example 0% correlation gives a maximum effectiveness of 100, with a correlation of above 30% this falls to below 20 times and at 50% it falls to below 10. This is the first evidence of extreme wrong-way risk in CDSs, which can render them almost useless in certain situations due to the double default problem. This will be discussed further in Chapter 15.

11.3   CREDIT PORTFOLIO LOSSES

The concept of portfolio losses is fundamental to any quantification of credit risk. In order to properly account for counterparty risk at the portfolio level, there must be some statistical estimate of the possibility of significant losses in the event that many counterparties were to default in a given period of time (such as 1 year).

The quantification of counterparty risk at the portfolio level requires knowledge of the following factors:

- counterparty default probabilities;
- correlations between counterparty default events;
- randomness of future counterparty exposures;
- correlation between future counterparty exposures.

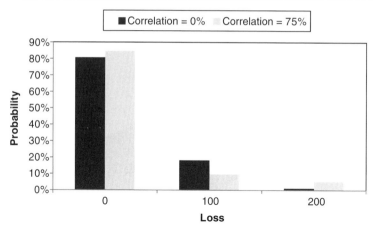

Figure 11.6 Illustration of the loss distribution in the simple two-counterparty case for different correlation assumptions assuming individual default probabilities of 10%.

Whilst the first two components above are standard inputs for most credit portfolio models, the last two are specific to counterparty risk and create significant complications when treating OTC derivatives within a typical credit portfolio framework. Whilst the randomness and correlations of exposures can be assessed accurately with detailed knowledge of the relevant transactions with each counterparty, it may also be important to be able to treat these components in a simple fashion to avoid complex calculations.

11.3.1   Simple two-name example

We start with a simple example, considering losses arising from default events of two counterparties A and B[4] with a direct exposure of 100 to each and default probabilities of 10%. In Figure 11.6 we show the loss probabilities for the case of no correlation and a high correlation value of 75% obtained using equation (11.1). We can see that the impact of correlation is to increase the likelihood of extreme losses (in this case 200 due to both names defaulting). This is a key result driven by the correlation of defaults.

Take a very simple example of a random exposure of either 200 or 0 occurring with equal probabilities. This gives a simple proxy of a typical bilateral derivatives position. We further assume the same exposure to two different counterparties but with a perfect negative correlation between exposures (as would be the case when the trades with the counterparties are hedging one another). The assumptions are illustrated in Table 11.1. We note that a loss of +400 is not possible since, even in the event both counterparties default, there cannot be an exposure to both at the same time.

What is the error when we approximate this simple case with the expected positive exposure (EPE)[5] of 100? Figure 11.7 shows the loss probabilities for the simple random exposure example compared with the fixed exposure case. We use the same previous correlation parameter of 75%. Although the expected exposure with respect to each counterparty is

---

[4] We use A and B to refer to two counterparties whose exposure is side by side rather than the previous notation of A for the original counterparty and X for the secondary CDS counterparty.

[5] Note that in this single-period case, the EPE and EE are equivalent. For reasons that will become clear, we will use EPE for all discussions.

Table 11.1 Illustration of the scenarios in the simple two-counterparty example. The probability of each scenario occurring is assumed to be 50%

	Perfect negative correlation		Perfect positive correlation	
	Scenario 1	Scenario 2	Scenario 1	Scenario 2
Counterparty 1	200	0	200	0
Counterparty 2	0	200	200	0

unchanged, the chance of a large loss (200) is greater in the random exposure case. Random exposures increase the possibility of extreme losses.

It is not only the correlation of defaults that is important in determining portfolio losses, but also the correlation of exposures. In the previous example, the exposures were assumed perfectly negatively correlated. Now we compare this to the case when they are perfectly positively correlated. In this case, a joint default will potentially create a large loss of 400. In Figure 11.8 we show that the impact of positive correlation between exposures increases the possibility of extreme losses still further.

11.3.2 Loss distributions and unexpected loss

Loss distributions are useful for understanding the nature of portfolio losses. Figure 11.9 illustrates the general approach for a typical fat-tailed distribution of credit losses. The expected loss of the portfolio (which is the CVA[6]) is reasonably small compared with the

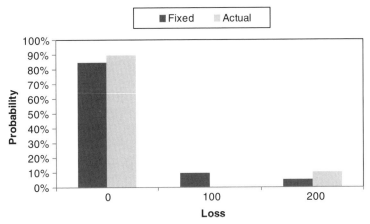

Figure 11.7 Illustration of the loss distribution in the simple two-counterparty case assuming individual default probabilities of 10%. The fixed exposure case corresponds to deterministic exposures of 100 for each counterparty whilst the random exposure case considers perfectly negatively correlated random exposures with an expected exposure of 100 as in Table 11.1.

---

[6] CVA has not yet been defined but for the purpose of this chapter can be thought of as the expected loss of the portfolio. One important distinction here is that this is the CVA calculated with real-world parameters and not the risk-neutral CVA discussed in Chapter 12.

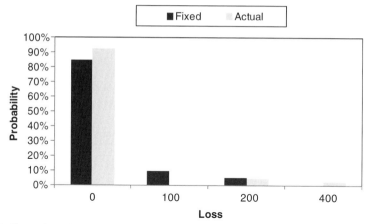

Figure 11.8 Illustration of the loss distribution in the simple two-counterparty case assuming individual default probabilities of 10%. The fixed exposure case corresponds to deterministic exposures of 100 for each counterparty whilst the random exposure case considers perfectly positively correlated random exposures with an expected exposure of 100 as in Table 11.1.

unexpected loss, which is usually measured via some high percentile (e.g., 99.9%). Whilst the CVA covers the expected loss, the unexpected loss represents the loss severity above that expected in a "normal" scenario.

One important property of expected loss is that is does not depend on the correlation in the portfolio as unexpected loss does (Figure 11.10). The linearity of the expected loss means that the total CVA at the portfolio level is simply the sum of the counterparty-level CVA contributions. However, the unexpected loss does not have this quality and depends on the

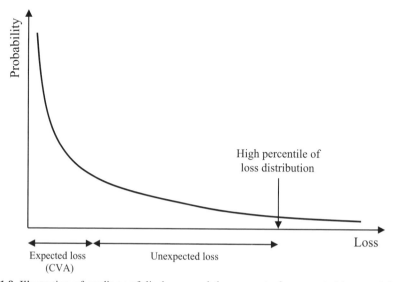

Figure 11.9 Illustration of credit portfolio losses and the concept of unexpected loss as defined by a high percentile of the distribution. The unexpected loss represents the uncertainty above the expected loss to a given confidence level.

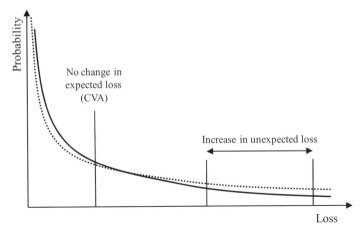

Figure 11.10 Illustration of the impact of correlation on credit portfolio losses. The dotted line represents a higher correlation of defaults and therefore corresponds to a higher worst-case loss and a higher economic capital value.

nature of the portfolio, where aspects such as default correlations are very important. Clearly, it is important to characterise both expected and unexpected losses. Expected losses relate to the CVA that should be allocated to each counterparty and charged appropriately (this is the subject of the next chapter). However, an institution will still be exposed to unexpected losses, which could cause significant problems if they are not anticipated and mitigated against. Unexpected loss relates to measures such as economic and regulatory capital, the purpose of which is to absorb losses in scenarios that are far worse than average. This may be used as an additional performance indicator.

Unexpected loss may be significant and depend on many aspects such as the number of counterparties, their default probability and correlation. The key driver of credit portfolio losses is correlation (or more generally dependence). However, positive correlation between default events makes large losses more likely and therefore increases the uncertainty of actual losses compared with expected losses. This will cause the unexpected loss, and consequently any associated capital number, to increase. In addition, the characteristics of the exposure to each counterparty will be important (as illustrated in Figures 11.7 and 11.8).

Note that if it were possible to perfectly hedge counterparty risk then unexpected loss would be unimportant, but since hedging is far from perfect then it remains a key concept. Hedging is dealt with in more detail in Chapter 16.

11.3.3   Example

We will now seek to look at the impact of certain factors on the required regulatory or economic capital to cover the counterparty risk of a given portfolio. We do not go into detail on credit portfolio models; more detail is given in Appendix 11A and, for example, Gupton *et al.* (1997), Bluhm *et al.* (2003), Duffie and Singleton (2003) or, in relation to counterparty risk, De Prisco and Rosen (2005).

In order to compute the distribution of losses, one must define a model for the behaviour of exposures and default events. We will follow the two-name case introduced in Section 11.2.3, in which case the default events will be driven by a multivariate normal distribution.

We will also make the following assumptions:

- The recovery rates are fixed known percentages. This topic was discussed in Chapter 10.
- The individual default probabilities are known. Again, the methods for doing this were described in Chapter 10.
- The exposure distributions are known for each counterparty, the calculation of these has been discussed previously in Chapter 9. The correct modelling of exposures will account for both the randomness of future exposures and the correlation between future exposures with respect to different counterparties.
- The exposures are independent of the default events.

The first three assumptions are common and will be assumed throughout the analysis of this chapter. The final point corresponds to the assumption of no wrong-way risk, which we will relax later.

Most credit portfolio models focus on fixed exposures, which are characteristic of the classic debt instruments such as bonds and loans. Little attention has been given to random exposures that arise in counterparty risk, although they have been described by Arvanitis and Gregory (2001), and several papers (e.g., Pykhtin, 2003) have tackled the related problem of stochastic recovery rates.[7]

Spreadsheet 11.2 Calculation of unexpected losses and "alpha" factor for a credit portfolio with random exposures.

We consider a portfolio with 100 counterparties and an average default probability of 1.5%. The correlations are assumed to be 20% for all counterparty pairs. We assume that the future values with each counterparty follow a normal distribution with a mean of zero and standard deviation of ten. This gives an expected exposure (EPE) of 3.99,[8] as illustrated in Figure 11.11. Recovery values are assumed zero since they typically only manifest themselves as multiplicative factors. We calculate the distribution of losses in the following two cases:

- *Random exposure*. The exposure is uncertain and characterised as shown in Figure 11.11. The values for different counterparties are independent.
- *Fixed exposure*. The exposure with each counterparty is assumed fixed and equal to 3.99.

The time horizon is arbitrary since it only relates to the choice of default probability, but we note that a 1-year time horizon is normally used in such cases.

By using the expected exposure we ensure that we get the same *expected* loss on the portfolio in each case (fixed and random). However, what is interesting is the behaviour of the unexpected loss. In all results below we have used 500,000 Monte Carlo simulations for the

---

[7] The difference between random exposure and random recovery is simply that the recovery rate is bounded by zero and one, whereas the exposure is unbounded.

[8] This is computed using the formula derived in Appendix 8A. Since we are using a single time horizon, EPE is the same as expected exposure (EE).

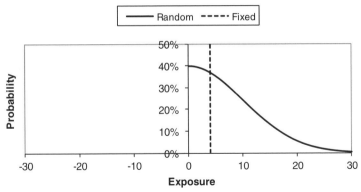

Figure 11.11 Illustration of random and fixed exposures used for the example.

calculations. This is relatively large in order to achieve a reasonably high resolution of the low-probability events.

Figure 11.12 shows the loss exceedance probabilities (probability that the loss will exceed a given level expressed as a percentage). We can clearly see that the impact of random exposure is to change the shape of the distribution of losses substantially and, in particular, to increase the possibility of larger losses. Indeed, the 99% unexpected loss[9] of the random exposure cases is 55.6, larger than that in the fixed exposure case of 43.9.

The additional uncertainty introduced by random exposures creates a corresponding uncertainty in the portfolio loss. For fixed exposures, a given number of defaults results in a fixed loss. However, with random exposures, the loss for a given number of defaults is uncertain, depending on the exposures with respect to each defaulted counterparty. It is this additional uncertainty of exposure that increases the unexpected loss.

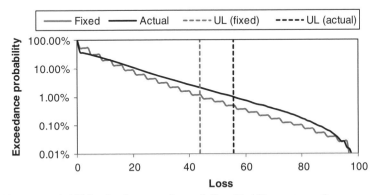

Figure 11.12 Loss probabilities for the example portfolio with 100 counterparties, an average default probability of 1.5% and a correlation of 20%. The random exposure case assumes normally distributed future values with zero mean and a standard deviation of ten. The fixed exposure case assumes deterministic exposures of 3.99 for each counterparty, which is the EPE.

---

[9] Economic capital is defined here as the 99% VAR number. As mentioned previously, it is sometimes defined as this value minus the expected loss, although given the latter quantity is quite small compared with the former this will not change the results substantially.

11.3.4   The alpha factor

Practitioners have long used the concept of a "loan equivalent" in order to represent a random exposure in a simple way. Regulatory aspects are a key driver for this and will be discussed at length in Chapter 17. A loan equivalent represents the fixed exposure that would have to be used in order to mimic a random exposure. However, a loan equivalent must be defined with reference to a given characteristic of the loss distribution of the portfolio in question. It is important to emphasise that a loan equivalent will be an arbitrary correction or "fudge factor" that will depend on the nature of the underlying portfolio.

The basis of using loan equivalents is to separate the calculation of regulatory (or economic) capital into two stages, as illustrated below:

$$\text{Derivatives position(s)} \quad \rightarrow \quad \text{loan equivalent} \quad \rightarrow \quad \text{capital.} \tag{11.3}$$

The above separation means that, from the point of view of capital calculations, derivatives positions can be treated in the same way as more simple positions such as loans. The main issue is then determination of the suitable loan equivalent amount.

The basis for calculating loan equivalents for random exposure derivatives portfolios is that, as shown by Wilde (2001), under the following conditions:

- infinitely large portfolios (number of counterparties) of small exposures (i.e., infinite diversification);
- no correlation of exposures;
- no wrong-way or right-way risk.

Then EPE is the true (accurate) loan equivalent measure. Whilst this is only relevant as a theoretical result, it implies that EPE is a good starting point for a loan equivalent. One can then define a factor that will correct for the granularity of the portfolio in question. This factor has been named alpha (α). The loan equivalent used will be $\alpha \times \text{EPE}$ and can be calculated from the following expression:

$$\alpha = \frac{\text{UL(actual)}}{\text{UL(fixed)}}, \tag{11.4}$$

where UL(actual) is the actual unexpected loss (incorporating random exposures) and UL(fixed) is the unexpected loss using a fixed exposure for each counterparty equal to the EPE value. Doing this for the previous example (Figure 11.12), we have $\alpha = 55.6/43.9 = 1.27$ and therefore the EPE must be increased to $1.27 \times 3.99 = 5.05$, which gives the results shown in Figure 11.13. Note that, whilst the distributions do not agree perfectly, the relevant point corresponding to the 99 percentile does. This means that the 99% values are the same with both calculations but any other measure is likely to differ. Other than the point used for the calculation of alpha, the distributions may differ substantially.[10] Furthermore, changes in both the portfolio and market variables will cause the true alpha measure to also change.

One might ask what could be the point of alpha given that its estimation requires the knowledge of the correct result. The purpose of an alpha correction will be to allow calculations with fixed exposures to mimic the impact of random derivatives exposures. Suppose an institution runs a daily calculation of credit losses. In order to include derivatives positions in

---

[10] Since they are plotted on a log-scale, the distributions shown in Figure 11.13 look rather similar, but there are material differences.

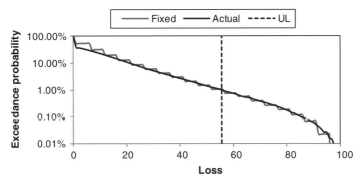

Figure 11.13 Loss probabilities for the example portfolio with fixed exposures adjusted by the relevant alpha factor of 1.266 computed at a 99% confidence level. The dotted line shows the 99% unexpected loss, which is the same for each distribution.

this calculation, they calculate some appropriate value of alpha using a simulation-based analysis of their total portfolio (or even some heuristic estimate). The daily calculations will then use $\alpha \times$ EPE as the fixed exposure for all derivatives counterparties. The value of alpha may be recalculated periodically, which is reasonable since the overall nature of the portfolio will evolve gradually and not change over a short timeframe. Alpha is also useful for defining regulatory capital (as discussed in Chapter 17). In this case, an institution may use a sophisticated approach to evaluating alpha for their own portfolio or they may revert to the regulator's (probably more conservative) estimate.

The alpha factor defined as above will be greater than one,[11] and reflect the extent to which the portfolio deviates from the stylised theoretical case. The advantage of defining a loan equivalent via $\alpha \times$ EPE is that the role of alpha is intuitive, as it will correct for the granularity of the portfolio in question. Since alpha can be benchmarked against certain portfolio characteristics (as we shall do below), it may be reasonable to use a loan equivalent value as a simple proxy of the contribution of a random exposure to the overall portfolio loss.[12]

We will see that the following characteristics are important in determining the magnitude of alpha:

- the granularity of the portfolio;
- the correlation between the exposures of different counterparties;
- the correlation between exposures and defaults (wrong-way risk).

In the following, we present a sensitivity analysis on the value of alpha using the example portfolio introduced in Section 11.3.3. Similar results were originally reported by Canabarro *et al.* (2003). We show alpha as a function of various portfolio characteristics in Table 11.2.

We can see that the following aspects will all cause a decrease in the value of alpha:[13]

- larger portfolio;
- larger average default probabilities;

---

[11] Except in special cases such as right-way risk, which will be discussed in Section 10.5.3.

[12] The actual measure used is actually known as EEPE not EPE, which will be discussed in detail in Chapter 17.

[13] We can also note that, as shown by Canabarro *et al.* (2003), the dispersion of exposures in a portfolio also causes the alpha value to increase. This is not surprising since it is a similar impact to decreasing the size of the portfolio.

Table 11.2   Illustration of change in alpha values computed for different portfolio characteristics. The base case is shown in bold

Portfolio size	Alpha	Default probability	Alpha	Correlation	Alpha	Confidence level	Alpha
50	1.45	0.5%	1.45	0%	1.80	90%	1.27
75	1.39	1.0%	1.35	10%	1.39	95%	1.26
100	**1.25**	**1.5%**	**1.25**	**20%**	**1.25**	**99%**	**1.25**
200	1.09	2.0%	1.16	30%	1.12	99.9%	1.22
400	1.04	2.5%	1.15	40%	1.05	99.97%	1.21

- larger correlations;
- higher confidence levels.

All of the above aspects can be understood by a single point. Suppose the unexpected loss is defined by a relatively large number of counterparty defaults. This could be due to a relatively large portfolio, higher average default probability, higher correlation or a higher confidence level. The law of averages now dictates that the total loss will be closer to the sum of EPEs. Hence, the EPE will be a better approximation to the loan equivalent and the alpha value will be closer to unity.

11.3.5   Alpha and wrong-way risk

The sensitivity analysis shown in Table 11.2 illustrates that the value of alpha is dependent on a number of variables but generally varies from just above unity for a large portfolio to around 1.4 to 1.5 for a smaller portfolio. These results are consistent with previous studies (e.g., Canabarro *et al.*, 2003; Wilde, 2005) and seem to constitute a reasonable range. As we shall discuss more in Chapter 17, the regulatory value of alpha (for regulatory capital purposes) is set at 1.4. However, there are some important aspects that can lead to far higher alpha values, such as:

- asymmetric and fat-tailed exposures;
- correlation of exposures;
- wrong-way risk.

Wrong-way risk has been studied previously by Wilde (2005) and Canabarro *et al.* (2003), who reported only modest increases in the value of alpha (for example, in Canabarro *et al.* the alpha increased from 1.09 to 1.21 when considering a market credit correlation of around 45%). In contrast to these previous studies that consider reasonably large diversified portfolios, we will now look at the impact of wrong-way risk in a more extreme situation.

We consider a CDS portfolio based on the 1-year exposures for the CDS position used in Section 9.7.5 assuming that the institution is long protection. This represents a highly skewed distribution of future value where the expected exposure is 122,201 but with exposures more than an order of magnitude larger than this. We show the loss distributions in Figure 11.14,

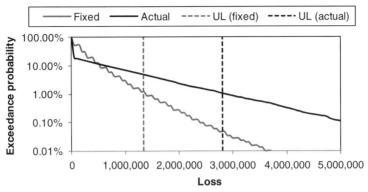

Figure 11.14 Loss probabilities for the example long single-name CDS protection portfolio with 100 counterparties, an average default probability of 1.5% and a correlation of 20%. The fixed exposure case assumes deterministic exposures according to the EE.

which are significantly different with an associated alpha value of 2.09. If we furthermore consider the exposures to be correlated,[14] then the alpha increases to 2.71 and including wrong-way risk it takes alpha to a factor of over 5.0.[15]

Whilst a well-diversified portfolio may have an alpha within the regulatory level, a highly concentrated portfolio or one with significant wrong-way risk could be far more risky than such a multiplier might suggest. Whilst the true value of alpha is hard to determine, the depth and complexity of some counterparty risks has recently provided a lesson that it may in some cases be rather higher than has generally been believed.

Alpha is clearly a very useful measure for reasonably large multi-asset OTC derivatives portfolios and this is justified by estimated values not far above unity. However, the extreme cases of asymmetric exposure and wrong-way risk that may be characterised by specific instruments such as credit derivatives are more subtle. The use of alpha in such cases may give rise to a false sense of security as the true alpha may be significantly greater than one, difficult to estimate and may change significantly over time. Even a large portfolio with a relatively small concentration of wrong-way risk exposures could have a significantly higher alpha. Dealing with instruments such as credit derivatives in a more sophisticated framework and not relying on loan equivalent measures may be important.

11.4 SUMMARY

In this chapter we have described the basics of modelling credit portfolio risk and therefore addressed the issue of defining the default of two or more counterparties. Initially, the two-name case has been described and the efficiency of a CDS product in hedging counterparty risk has been assessed. Following this, the multiple-name case has been considered, including the impact of random (derivatives) exposures on the distribution of losses. The

---

[14] The correlation of exposures is assumed to be 50%.
[15] In this case, we assume a correlation of 20% between the exposure and the default probability. The methodology for doing this is described in more detail in Chapter 15.

quantitative foundations for the use of "loan equivalents" based on EPE have been described. We show that, whilst in most cases EPE provides a good approximation of the risk at the portfolio level, there are cases such as credit derivatives where this is clearly not the case. In Chapter 17 we will discuss portfolio aspects in relation to the regulatory treatment of counterparty risk. We will also describe in more detail how the concept of loan equivalents and the alpha factor has been incorporated into regulatory capital rules within Basel II.

12

Credit Value Adjustment

Do not worry about your difficulties in Mathematics. I can assure you mine are still greater.
Albert Einstein (1879–1955)

The last section focused separately on credit exposure and default probability. Now we proceed to combine these two components in order to address the pricing of counterparty credit risk via CVA.[1] We will see that under certain commonly made assumptions it is relatively simple to combine default probabilities and exposures to arrive at the CVA.

Accurate pricing of counterparty risk involves attaching a value to the risk of all outstanding positions with a given counterparty. This is important in the reporting of accurate earnings information and incentivising trading desks and businesses to trade appropriately. If counterparty risk pricing is combined with a systematic charging of new transactions, then it will also be hedged generated funds that will absorb potential losses in the event that a counterparty defaults. Counterparty risk charges are increasingly commonly associated with hedging costs.

For the purpose of this chapter, we will make three key assumptions that will greatly simplify the initial exposition and calculation of CVA. These aspects will then be dealt with in more detail in the remaining three chapters in this section. The key assumptions are:

- *The institution themselves cannot default.* The first assumption corresponds to ignoring the DVA (debt value adjustment) component, which is discussed in the next chapter.
- *Risk-free valuation is straightforward.* We have to assume that the risk-free valuation can be performed. However, this is far from simple due to the lack of a clear discount rate (in the past Libor was considered acceptable) and the increased importance of funding. These aspects are discussed in Chapter 14.
- *The credit exposure and default probability[2] are independent.* This involves neglecting wrong-way risk, which will be discussed in Chapter 15.

This above separation of concepts should make it easier to explain all the key features around CVA.

Reference papers on the subject of CVA include Sorensen and Bollier (1994), Jarrow and Turnbull (1992, 1995, 1997), Duffie and Huang (1996) and Brigo and Masetti (2005a).

---

[1] Also sometimes referred to as counterparty value adjustment.
[2] And, also, the recovery value.

12.1 DEFINITION OF CVA

12.1.1 Why pricing CVA is not easy

Pricing the credit risk for an instrument with one-way payments, such as a bond, is relatively straightforward – one simply needs to account for default when discounting the cash flows and add any default payment. However, many derivatives instruments have fixed, floating or contingent cash flows or payments that are made in both directions. This bilateral nature characterises credit exposure and makes the quantification of counterparty risk dramatically more difficult. Whilst this will become clear in the more technical pricing calculations, a simple explanation is provided in Figure 12.1, which compares a bond to a similar swap transaction. In the bond case a given cash flow is fully at risk (its value may be lost entirely) in the event of a default, whereas in the swap case only part of the cash flow will be at risk due to partial cancellation with opposing cash flows. The risk on the swap is clearly smaller due to this effect.[3] However, the fraction of the swap cash flows that are indeed at risk are hard to determine as this depends on many factors such as yield curve shape, forward rates and volatilities.

12.1.2 CVA formula

We first define the formula for calculating CVA and will discuss after this the motivation and precise use of CVA within an institution. When valuing a financial transaction such as an OTC derivative or repo, counterparty risk must be included. However, it is possible to separate the components according to

$$\text{Risky value} = \text{risk-free value} - \text{CVA.} \tag{12.1}$$

The above separation is theoretically rigorous, with the full derivation given in Appendix 12A. This separation is clearly extremely useful because the problem of valuing a transaction and computing its counterparty risk can be completely separated. The first implication of this is that it is possible to deal with all CVA components centrally

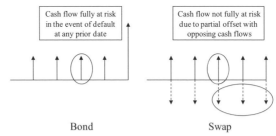

Bond   Swap

Figure 12.1 Illustration of the complexity when pricing the credit (counterparty) risk on a derivative instrument such as a swap, compared with an instrument such as a bond. In the bond the cash flow circled is fully at risk (less recovery) in the event of default of the issuer but in the swap the equivalent cash flow is not fully at risk due to the ability to partially offset it with current and future cash flows in the opposite direction (the three dotted cash flows shown circled).

---

[3] It is also smaller due to the lack of a principal payment but this is a different point.

and "transfer price" this away from the originating trader or business. This is critical since it allows separation of responsibilities within a financial institution: one desk is responsible for risk-free valuation and one for the counterparty risk component. Transactions and their associated counterparty risk may then be priced and risk-managed separately. Therefore, for example, a swap trader in a bank need not understand how to price and hedge CVAs[4] as this will be handled by the bank's "CVA desk" who will charge the appropriate CVA for the trade in question. This is discussed in more detail in Chapter 18.

If this sounds too good to be true, there is a hidden complexity in the seemingly simple equation (12.1) which is that it is not linear. Due to risk mitigants such as netting and collateral, CVA is not additive with respect to individual transactions. This means that the risky value of a given transaction cannot be calculated individually, as it is defined with respect to other transactions within the *same* netting set. We will therefore have to consider the allocation of CVA just as we considered allocation of exposure in Chapter 8.

Nevertheless, under the above assumptions, a standard equation for CVA (see Appendix 12B for more detail) is

$$\text{CVA} \approx (1 - \text{Rec}) \sum_{i=1}^{m} \text{DF}(t_i)\text{EE}(t_i)\text{PD}(t_{i-1}, t_i). \tag{12.2}$$

The CVA depends on the following components:

- *Loss given default (1 – Rec)*. In the event of counterparty default, some percentage amount of the claim would be recovered; this is the percentage amount of the exposure expected to be lost if the counterparty defaults. Note that LGD = 1 – Rec.
- *Discount factor (DF)*. This is the relevant risk-free discount factor. Discounting is relevant since any future losses must be discounted back to the current time.
- *Expected exposure (EE)*. The term is the expected exposure (EE) for the relevant dates in the future given by t_i for $i = 0, n$. Calculating EE was the subject of Chapter 9, although we will discuss the need to use risk-neutral exposures below.
- *Default probability (PD)*. The expression requires the marginal default probability in the interval between date t_{i-1} and t_i. Default probability estimation was covered in Chapter 10.

It should not be a surprise that CVA involves default probability (how likely is the counterparty to default), EE (what is expected to be lost in default) and recovery (what will be recovered). It should also not be a surprise that the formula has a time dimension, since EE and PD have been shown in Chapters 9 and 10 to be rather time inhomogeneous. The formula therefore must integrate over time to take into account the precise distribution of EE and PD (and not just their average values). An illustration of the CVA formula is given in Figure 12.2.

Hence, CVA simply depends on combining components from potentially different sources. For example, an exposure team within a financial institution may compute EE, which is a market risk. The credit department and/or credit derivatives trading desk may provide loss

---

[4] Indeed, the trader need know nothing whatsoever about CVA although, since CVA is a charge to their PnL, it is likely they will want at least a basic understanding of what CVA is and how it is calculated.

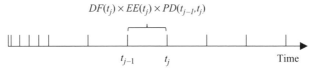

$$DF(t_j) \times EE(t_j) \times PD(t_{j-1}, t_j)$$

Figure 12.2 Illustration of CVA formula. The component shown is the CVA contribution for a given interval. The formula simply sums up across all intervals and multiplies by the loss given default.

given default and default probability information. Crucially, none of the areas needs to be aware of what the other is doing, as all the components are assumed independent.

A further important advantage of computing CVA via equation (12.2) is that default enters the expression via default *probability* only. This means that, whilst one may require a simulation framework in order to compute CVA, it is not necessary to simulate default events, only the exposure (EE). This saves significantly on computation time by avoiding the need to simulate relatively rare default events.

Spreadsheet 12.1 Simple CVA calculation.

We illustrate the above CVA formula with a simple example of a forward contract-type exposure[5] using the simple expression from Chapter 8 (Section 8.3.3) and a default probability defined by equation (10.5). We assume a constant credit spread of 500 bps, a recovery value of 40% and a constant continuously compounded interest rate of 5%.[6] We assume an interval of 0.25 years between the dates in equation (12.2), which involves evaluation at a total of 20 points. With these assumptions, the expected exposure and marginal default probability are as shown in Figure 12.3. The CVA is calculated to be 0.262%, which is expressed in terms of percentage of notional value (since the EE was expressed in percentage terms).

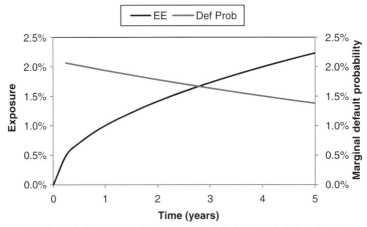

Figure 12.3 Illustration of the expected exposure and default probability for the example CVA calculation.

---

[5] The expected exposure is given by $EE(t) = \sqrt{t} \times 1\%$ as a percentage of notional.
[6] This means the discount factors are given by $DF(t) = \exp(-5\% \times t)$.

In terms of the accuracy of the integration, the exact result is 0.254%. One can improve the efficiency by choosing more than 20 points. However, it is also best to approximate the exposure and discount by the average of those at the beginning and end of the period, i.e., $\text{EE}(t_j) \rightarrow \big(\text{EE}(t_{j-1}) + \text{EE}(t_j)\big)/2$ and $\text{DF}(t_j) \rightarrow \big(\text{DF}(t_{j-1}) + \text{DF}(t_j)\big)/2$. This gives a more accurate result of 0.253% with the 20 points used above.

We emphasise that, under the assumption of no wrong-way risk, equation (12.2) provides a very efficient way to compute CVA from components that may already be calculated by a financial institution (exposures, default probabilities, discount factors and loss given default). Historically, for many institutions this route has been a very important way to price counterparty risk in a realistic and practical way.

12.1.3   CVA as a spread

Suppose that instead of computing the CVA as a stand-alone value, one wanted it to be expressed as a spread (per annum charge). In Appendix 12C we derive an approximate formula for CVA that will be at least of intuitive interest and will also help in expressing CVA as a running spread. The formula assumes that the EE is constant over time and equal to its average value (EPE). This yields the following approximation based on EPE:

$$\text{CVA} = \text{credit spread} \times \text{EPE}, \tag{12.3}$$

where the CVA is expressed in the same units as the credit spread, which should be for the maturity of the instrument in question, and EPE is as defined in Chapter 8.[7] For the example above, the EPE is 1.54% and therefore the CVA approximation is $1.54\% \times 500 = 7.71$ bps.

A simple calculation would involve dividing the CVA by the risky annuity[8] value for the maturity in question. For the previous calculation, a risky annuity of 3.65 would be obtained using the simple formula described in Appendix 10B (the accurate result for an interval of 0.25 years is 3.59). From the result above, we would therefore obtain the CVA as a spread, being $0.253\%/3.65 \times 10{,}000 = 6.92$ bps (per annum).

The approximate calculation works reasonably well in this case. The simple formula is an overestimate because, whilst the EE profile is certainly not constant as assumed, the marginal default probabilities are reasonably constant. This approximate formula tends to be more accurate for swap-like profiles where the symmetry of the profile helps but is less accurate for monotonically increasing profiles such as the one used in the example above.

The approximate formula in equation (12.2) is often not used for actual calculations but can be useful for intuitive understanding of the drivers of CVA. As counterparty risk became a common component of derivatives transactions from the late 1990s onwards, the above method of representing CVA would be rather common. For example, a bank might tell a corporate client that they would have to pay an extra X bps on a swap to cover the "credit charge" or CVA. The simple formula allows the charge to be broken down into the credit component (the credit spread of the counterparty in question) and the market risk component (the exposure, or EPE, in question).

---

[7] This is the simple average of the EE values in our example, although for non-equal time intervals it would be the weighted average. Discounting is not included in the EPE based on the assumptions used in deriving the approximate formula.
[8] The risky annuity represents the value of receiving a unit amount in each period as long as the counterparty does not default.

12.2   CVA AND EXPOSURE

In Chapter 9, we have discussed in detail how to quantify exposure, which covers the EE term in equation (12.2). Institutions may commonly take EE values from a risk management system, even though that system may have been set up for monitoring credit lines and not computing CVA. However, there is one caveat. For quantifying exposure for risk management, as discussed in Section 9.4.1, one should use the real probability measure whereas for pricing purposes the risk-neutral measure should be used. The use of the risk-neutral versus real probability measure is an important point and hence will be discussed in more detail in Chapter 16. We now discuss some aspects of exposure, not covered in Chapter 9, which relate to the potential need to calculate risk-neutral exposure for CVA purposes.

12.2.1   Exposure and discounting

In the above, we consider a separate discount factor in order to discount future losses to today, and arrive at a price (the CVA). It is reasonable to do this as long as the exposure is calculated in the correct fashion. A problem could arise, for example, in an interest rate product where, when rates are high a larger discount factor should be used, and vice versa. This convexity effect would mean that we would overestimate the CVA of a payer swap and vice versa for a receiver swap.[9] To solve this problem technically means quantifying the underlying exposure using the "T-forward measure" (Jamshidian, 1997). By doing this, discount factors depend on expected future interest rate values, not on their distribution. Hence, moving the discount factor out of the expectation term (for exposure) is theoretically correct.

Working with separate discount factors may sometimes be convenient. For example, the approximation in equation (12.2) works only if discounting is done separately,[10] as described in the derivation in Appendix 12B. However, often expected exposure for CVA purposes will be discounted during the simulation process.

12.2.2   Risk-neutral exposure

For CVA, it may be relevant to calculate a risk-neutral exposure rather than the real-world exposures characterised in Chapter 8. This requires calibration to market, rather than historical, data. For example, interest rate volatilities and mean-reversion parameters would be derived from the prices of interest rate swaptions, caps and floors rather than estimation via historical time series. In addition, the drift of the underlying variables (such as interest rates and FX rates) will need to be calibrated to forward rates, rather than coming from some historical or other real-world analysis.[11] Hence, in terms of risk-neutral exposure, there are two effects to consider which arise from the impact of different volatility and drift assumptions.

We first consider the drift impact on exposure. Taking the base case interest rate swap from Chapter 9 (Payer IRS GBP 5Y[12]), we compute the expected exposure using the risk-neutral drift (i.e., that implied from the shape of the interest rate curve observed in the market) to compute with the original case (Figure 9.6), which uses a historical drift. The results

---

[9] Since a payer swap has the largest exposure when rates are high and these paths would be discounted according to a lower rate.
[10] In other words, the EPE in equation (12.2) does not contain any discounting effects.
[11] As noted in Section 9.4.1, risk-neutral drift may often be used anyway for calculating exposure for risk management purposes.
[12] Payer interest rate swap in GBP with a 5-year maturity and 100m notional.

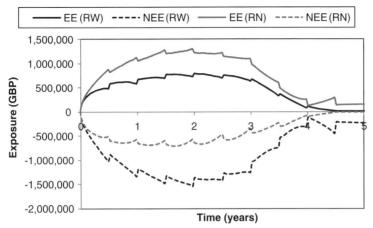

Figure 12.4 Illustration of the EE and PFE of a 5-year interest rate swap paying fixed GBP (notional 100m) and receiving floating GBP computed with both real-world (RW) and risk-neutral (RN) simulations.

are shown in Figure 12.4. Note that, in order to isolate the drift impact, historical volatility is used in both cases.

Recall from Chapter 9 (Section 9.5.1) that in this example the real-world EE is smaller than the NEE due to a negative interest rate "drift" calibrated from historical data. Since the interest rate curve is upwards-sloping (long-term interest rates are higher than short-term rates), the risk-neutral drift is positive, leading to the EE being higher than the NEE (this effect was explained in Section 8.3.3). Hence, the difference between using risk-neutral and real-world drift is to "twist" the exposure distribution, so that the risk-neutral EE is greater and the NEE is smaller, compared with the real-world values.

Now we illustrate the role of volatility. In Figure 12.5, we show the expected exposure of the cross-currency swap described in Chapter 8 under both real-world (historical volatility and drift as discussed in Chapter 8) and risk-neutral (market-implied volatility and drift

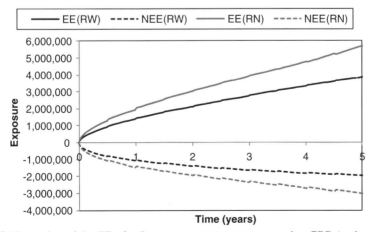

Figure 12.5 Illustration of the EE of a 5-year cross-currency swap paying GBP (notional 25m) and receiving USD computed with both real-world (RW) and risk-neutral (RN) simulations.

implied from forward rates) assumptions. Here the main impact is simply that risk-neutral volatilities tend to be higher than real-world ones and hence both the PFE and EE are bigger.

It is important to consider that the higher risk-neutral exposure in this case may be an indication that the market is pricing in a higher level of volatility than is estimated from a real-world (e.g., historical) analysis. In this case, the risk-neutral exposure may be argued to be a superior measure to the real-world one since it represents the future view and not the view of the past. On the other hand, the risk-neutral exposure may simply be systematically higher due to the well-known presence of risk premiums in market parameters.

12.2.3 CVA semi-analytical methods

In the case of some specific product types, it is possible to derive analytical formulas for the CVA. Whilst such formulas are of limited use since they do not account for netting or collateral, they are valuable for quick calculations and an intuitive understanding of CVA.

The first simple example is the CVA of a position that can only have a positive value, such as a long option position with an upfront premium. In this situation, it is possible to show (Appendix 12C) that the CVA is simply

$$\mathrm{CVA} \approx \mathrm{LGD} \times F(T) \times V, \tag{12.4}$$

where T is the maturity of the transaction in question and V is its (risk-free) valuation. The term $F(T)$ represents the probability that the counterparty will default during the lifetime of the transaction in question. It is intuitive that one simply multiplies the standard risk-free price by this default probability and corrects for the recovery value.

Moving on to contracts that can have both positive and negative value, the calculation of the CVA of an interest rate swap is considered by Sorensen and Bollier (1994). These authors show that the CVA in this case can be expressed as a function of (reverse) swaptions with different exercise dates (Appendix 12D). The intuition is that the counterparty might default at any time in the future and, hence, effectively cancel the non-recovered value of the swap, economically equivalent to exercising the reverse swaption.

The swap exposure and swaption analogy is illustrated in Figure 12.6. The expected exposure of the swap will be defined by the interaction between two factors: the swaption payoff and the underlying swap duration (these are the two components in the simple approach given in equation (8.4)). These quantities respectively increase and decrease monotonically over time. The overall swaption value therefore peaks at an intermediate point.

Spreadsheet 12.2 Semi-analytical calculation of the CVA for a swap.

The Sorensen and Bollier formula gives us a very useful insight on CVA calculations, specifically that a CVA calculation will be at least as complex as pricing the underlying product itself. To price the swap CVA, one needs to know about swaption volatility (across time and strike), components far beyond those needed to price the swap itself. The value of the swap does not depend significantly on volatility and yet the CVA for the swap does.

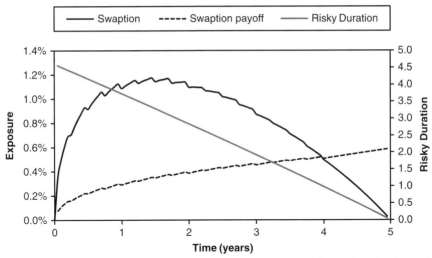

Figure 12.6 Illustration of swap EE as defined by swaption values which are given by the product of the swaption payoff and the risky duration value (shown on the secondary y-axis).

This approach naturally captures effects such as the asymmetry between payer and receiver swap (Figure 12.7) and unequal payment frequencies such as in basis swap (Figure 12.8). In the former case, the receiver (payer) swaptions corresponding to the payer (receiver) swap are in-(out-)of-the-money. In the latter case, the strike of the swaptions moves significantly out-of-the-money when an institution receives a quarterly cash flow whilst not needing (yet) to make a semi-annual one.

The above analogy can be extended to other products where any transaction can be represented as a series of European options. This approach would be the method of choice for evaluating the CVA of a single trade. In some circumstances it can also be extended beyond the single trade level to, for example, a portfolio of single currency swaps as discussed by Brigo and Masetti (2005b). The ability to do this may often be useful, as clients may trade a rather narrow range of underlying products, the exposure of which may be modelled

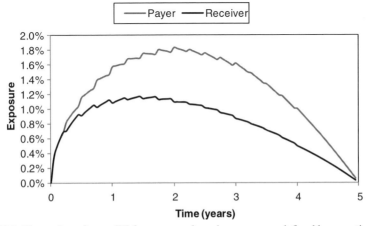

Figure 12.7 Illustration of swap EE for payer and receiver swaps as defined by swaption values.

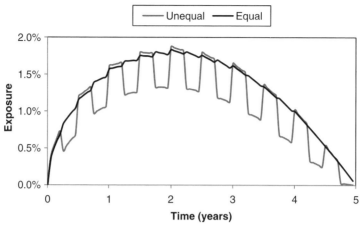

Figure 12.8 Illustration of swap EE for unequal (pay semi-annually, receive quarterly) swaps as defined by swaption values.

analytically. However, multidimensional netting sets will typically need to be treated in a more generic Monte Carlo-style approach.

12.3   IMPACT OF DEFAULT PROBABILITY AND RECOVERY

We now consider the impact of default probability and recovery on CVA. There are several aspects to consider, such as the level of credit spreads, the overall shape of the credit curve, the impact of recovery rates and the basis risk arising from recovery rate assumptions. In all the examples below, we will consider the CVA of the same 5-year GBP payer interest rate swap, described in Section 12.2.2. The expected exposures are the same as those used previously in Chapter 9.[13] The base case assumptions will be a flat credit curve of 500 bps and a recovery rate of 40%. The base case CVA is then calculated to be £91,389.

12.3.1   Credit spread impact

Let us first review the impact of increasing the credit spread of the counterparty in Table 12.1. The increase in credit spread clearly increases the CVA, but this effect is not linear since default probabilities are bounded by 100%. Another way to understand this is that the "jump to default" risk[14] of this swap is zero, since it has a current value of zero and so an immediate default of the counterparty will not cause any loss. As the credit quality of the counterparty deteriorates, the CVA will obviously increase but at some point, when the counterparty is very close to default, the CVA will decrease again. This point will be discussed again in Chapter 16, as it is an important consideration for hedging.

Next, we look at the impact of changes in *shape* of the credit curve. In Chapter 10 (e.g., Figure 10.8), we considered upwards-sloping, flat and inverted credit curves all of which assumed a terminal 5-year credit spread of 500 bps. We discussed how, whilst they gave cumulative default probabilities that were approximately the same, the marginal default

---

[13] We note that these are not risk-neutral but allow a direct comparison with previous results.
[14] This term is generally used to mean a sudden and immediate default of the counterparty with no other factors changing.

Table 12.1   CVA of the base case IRS as a function of the credit spread of the counterparty

Spread (bps)	CVA (GBP)
100	20,915
250	49,929
500	92,593
750	129,004
1000	160,033
10,000	289,190
25,000	224,440
50,000	180,455
Default	0

Table 12.2   CVA of the base case IRS for different shapes of credit curve. The 5-year credit spread is 500 bps in all cases

	CVA (GBP)
Upwards-sloping	84,752
Flat	92,593
Downwards-sloping	94,358

probabilities differed substantially. For a flat curve, default probability is approximately equally spaced whilst for an upwards (downwards)-sloping curve, defaults are back (front) loaded. We show the impact of curve shape on the CVA in Table 12.2. Even though the spread at the maturity of the swap (5Y) is the same in all cases, there are quite different results for the different curve shapes. Indeed, going from an upwards- to a downwards-sloping curve increases the CVA by 11%. We note that for EE profiles that are monotonic, such as forward contracts and cross-currency swaps, this impact is typically stronger (for example, for the case represented in Figure 12.3 the corresponding increase is 40%[15]). This illustrates why we emphasised the shape of the credit curve as being an important part of the mapping process (Section 10.1.5).

12.3.2   Recovery impact

Table 12.3 shows the impact of changing settled and actual recoveries. Recall (Figure 10.11) that the settled recovery is the recovery at the time of default (for example, settled in the CDS auction) whilst the actual recovery is the amount that will actually be received for the

---

[15] This is because for such profiles, the maximum exposure occurs at the end of the contract and for a sufficiently upwards-sloping curve, this is also where the maximum default probability occurs. The combination of these two aspects gives a high CVA.

Table 12.3 CVA of the base case IRS for different recovery assumptions. Simultaneous changes in the settled and final recovery ("both") and a 10% settled recovery and 40% final recovery are shown

Recovery	CVA (GBP)
20% both	96,136
40% both	92,595
60% both	86,003
10%/40%	64,904

claim (i.e., used in equation (12.2)). Changing both recovery rate assumptions has a reasonably small impact on the CVA since there is a cancellation effect: increasing recovery increases the implied default probability but reduces the resulting loss. Indeed, the simple approximation in equation (12.3) has no recovery input. The net impact is only a second-order effect, which is negative with increasing recovery, because the implied default probability increase is sub-linear in recovery, but the loss amount is linear. Different assumptions for settled and actual recovery rates will obviously change the CVA more significantly. For example, assuming a 10% recovery for calculating implied default probabilities and a higher 40% actual recovery (similar to Lehman Brother values as discussed in Section 10.1.7) gives a much lower CVA.

12.4   PRICING NEW TRADES USING CVA

Being able to price the stand-alone CVA on a given transaction is useful, but the need to account for risk mitigation such as netting and collateral is critical for any practical use of CVA.

12.4.1   Netting and incremental CVA

When there is a netting agreement then the impact is likely to reduce the CVA and cannot increase it (this arises from the properties of netting described in Section 8.4). We therefore know that for a set of netted trades (NS):

$$\text{CVA}_{NS} \leq \sum_{i=1}^{n} \text{CVA}_i^{\text{stand-alone}}, \tag{12.5}$$

where CVA_{NS} is the total CVA of all trades under the netting agreement and $\text{CVA}_i^{\text{stand-alone}}$ is the stand-alone CVA for trade i. The above reduction can be substantial and the question then becomes how to allocate the netting benefits to each individual transaction. The most obvious way to do this is to use the concept of *incremental CVA*, analogous to incremental EE discussed in Section 9.6.2.[16] Here the CVA of a transaction i is calculated based on the

---

[16] The reader may wish to refer back to the discussion around incremental exposure in Chapter 9, as many of the points made there will apply to incremental CVA also.

incremental effect this trade has on the netting set:

$$\text{CVA}_i^{\text{incremental}} = \text{CVA}_{NS+i} - \text{CVA}_{NS}. \tag{12.6}$$

The above formula ensures that the CVA of a given trade is given by its contribution to the overall CVA at the time it is executed. Hence, it makes the most sense when the CVA needs to be charged to individual traders and business. The CVA depends on the order in which trades are executed but does not change due to subsequent trades. A CVA desk (Chapter 18) charging this amount will directly offset the impact on their PnL from the change in CVA from the new trade.

As shown in Appendix 12E, we can derive the following formula for incremental CVA:

$$\text{CVA}_i^{\text{incremental}} = (1 - \text{Rec}) \sum_{j=1}^{m} \text{DF}(t_j) \text{EE}_i^{\text{incremental}} (t_{j-1}, t_j) \text{PD}(t_{j-1}, t_j). \tag{12.7}$$

This is the same as equation (12.2) but with the incremental EE replacing the previous stand-alone EE. This should not be surprising since CVA is a linear combination of EE, and netting changes only the exposure and has no impact on recovery values, discount factors or default probabilities. The quantification of incremental EE was covered in detail in Chapter 9.[17] Incremental EE can be negative, due to beneficial netting effects, which will lead to a CVA being negative and, in such a case, it would be possible to transact at a loss due to the overall gain from CVA.

It is worth emphasising, in the relationship defined above, that, due to the properties of EE and netting, the incremental CVA in the presence of netting will never be higher than the stand-alone CVA without netting (except in bilateral CVA cases discussed in the next chapter – see also Duffie and Huang, 1996). The practical result of this is that an institution with existing trades under a netting agreement will be likely to offer conditions that are more favourable to a counterparty with respect to a new trade. Cooper and Mello (1991) first quantified such an impact, showing specifically that a bank that already has a trade with a counterparty can offer a more competitive rate on a forward contract.

The treatment of netting makes the treatment of CVA a complex and often multi-dimensional problem. Whilst some attempts have been made at handling netting analytically (e.g., Brigo and Masetti, 2005b as noted in Section 12.2.3), CVA calculations incorporating netting typically require a general Monte Carlo simulation for exposure (EE) quantification. However, note that under equation (12.7), one does not have to simulate default events as mentioned before.

We will now look at an example of incremental CVA following the previous results for incremental exposure in Section 9.5. As before, we consider a 5-year GBP payer interest rate swap (Payer IRS GBP 5Y) and in Table 12.4 consider the CVA under the assumption of four different existing trades with the counterparty.[18]

We can make the following observations:

- The incremental CVA is never higher than the stand-alone CVA (which assumes no netting benefit due to existing trades). This is not surprising since in Chapter 9 we saw that netting could not increase exposure.

---

[17] Although we note again that the use of risk-neutral exposure may be considered relevant for CVA purposes.

[18] These trades are described in Section 9.5.1.

Table 12.4   Incremental CVA calculations for a 5-year GBP swap paying fixed (Payer IRS GBP 5Y) with respect to four different existing transactions and compared to the stand-alone value. The credit curve is assumed flat at 500 bps with a 40% recovery rate and continuously compounded interest rates of 5% are used

Existing trade	Incremental CVA (GBP)
None (stand-alone calculation)	92,593
Payer IRS GBP 6Y	90,076
Payer IRS EUR 5Y	63,832
Receiver IRS EUR 5Y	−42,446
CCS GBPUSD 5Y	−35,801

- The incremental CVA is only slightly reduced for a very similar existing trade (6-year GBP swap). This follows from the high positive correlation between the two trades.
- The incremental CVA is reduced moderately in the case of a similar swap in a different currency. This is since the trades are still positively correlated.
- The incremental CVA is negative in the last two cases due to the structurally negative correlation (this impact is discussed in detail in Section 9.5.2). A trader may therefore expect a positive P&L in this situation due to reducing the overall risk to the counterparty in question and may therefore execute a trade with otherwise unfavourable terms. We discuss the mechanics of this in Section 18.3.4.

12.4.2   Marginal CVA

Following the discussion in Section 9.6.3, we can define *marginal CVA* in a similar way by simply including the marginal EE in the above formula. Marginal CVA may be useful to break down a CVA for any number of netted trades into trade-level contributions that sum to the total CVA. Whilst it might not be used for pricing new transactions (due to the problem that marginal CVA changes when new trades are executed, implying PnL adjustment to trading books), it may be required for pricing trades transacted at the same time[19] (perhaps due to being part of the same deal) with a given counterparty. Alternatively, marginal CVA is the appropriate way to calculate the trade-level CVA contributions at a given time. This may be useful where a CVA desk is concerned about their exposure to the default of a particular counterparty.

We compute the marginal CVA corresponding to the marginal EE (Figure 9.16) of the interest rate swap (Payer IRS GBP 5Y) and the cross-currency swap (CCS GBPUSD 5Y). We do this for two different credit curves, one flat at 500 bps and one having the form [300 bps, 350 bps, 400 bps, 450 bps, 500 bps] for maturities [1Y, 2Y, 3Y, 4Y, 5Y]. The results are shown in Table 12.5.

---

[19] This could also cover a policy where CVA adjustments are only calculated periodically and several trades have occurred with a given counterparty within that period.

Table 12.5 Illustration of the breakdown of the CVA of the interest rate and cross-currency swap via incremental (CCS first), incremental (IRS first) and marginal. The credit curve is assumed flat or upwards-sloping, recovery rates are 40% and continuously compounded interest rates are 5%

	Flat credit curve			*Upwards-sloping credit curve*		
	Incremental (IRS first)	*Incremental (CCS first)*	*Marginal*	*Incremental (IRS first)*	*Incremental (CCS first)*	*Marginal*
IRS	92,593	27,133	71,178	84,752	18,995	59,580
CCS	34,098	99,558	55,513	48,902	114,660	74,075
Total	**126,691**	**126,691**	**126,691**	**133,655**	**133,655**	**133,655**

We see the effect that the first trade is charged for the majority of the CVA, as seen before, whilst the marginal CVA charges are more balanced. Notice also that, whilst the overall CVA is not changed by much, the breakdown of CVA changes significantly for a differently shaped credit curve. For example, the marginal contribution of the CCS is significantly lower with a flat curve and significantly higher with an upwards-sloping curve. This is because most of the contribution from the CCS to marginal EE comes in the last year of the lifetime (Figure 9.16), which is where the upwards-sloping curve has the highest default probability.

There are some important practical points to understand when incorporating CVA into trades. We start by looking at various CVA decompositions for the four trades in Table 12.6. It can be seen that incremental CVA depends very much on the ordering of the trades. For example, the incremental CVA of the CCS can be almost 20 times smaller if it is the last and not the first trade to be executed. Clearly, the amount of CVA charged can be very dependent on the timing of the trade. This may be problematic and could possibly lead to "gaming" behaviour by traders. However, whilst the marginal contributions are fair, it is hard to imagine how to get around the problems of charging traders and businesses based on marginal contributions that change as new trades are executed with the counterparty.

Table 12.6 Illustration of the breakdown of the CVA for four trades via incremental (the ordering of trades given in brackets) and marginal contributions. The credit curve is assumed flat at 500 bps, recovery rates are 40% and continuously compounded interest rates are 5%

	Stand-alone	*Incremental (1-2-3-4)*	*Incremental (4-1-2-3)*	*Marginal*
Payer IRS GBP 5Y	92,593	92,593	27,133	84,011
Payer IRS GBP 6Y	124,816	122,299	95,520	107,995
Payer IRS EUR 5Y	76,006	37,191	35,694	45,286
CCS GBPUSD 5Y	99,558	5,822	99,558	20,613
Total	**392,973**	**257,905**	**257,905**	**257,905**

12.4.3 CVA as a spread

Another point to consider when pricing CVA into trades is how to convert an upfront CVA to a running spread CVA. This would facilitate charging a CVA to a client via, for example, adjusting the rate paid on a swap. One simple way to do such a transformation would be to divide the CVA by the risky duration for the maturity in question.[20] For example, for the 5Y GBP IRS above (notional 100m), for the stand-alone CVA, we would obtain:

$$\frac{92,593}{3.59 \times 100,000,000} \times 10,000 = 2.58 \text{ bps.} \tag{12.8}$$

However, when adding a spread to a contract such as a swap, the problem is non-linear since the spread itself will have an impact on the CVA. The correct value should be calculated recursively (since the spread will be risky also) until the risky MtM of the contract is zero. Hence, we need to solve an equation $V(C^*) = \text{CVA}(C^*)$, where $V(.)$ is the value of the contract for the adjusted rate C^*. This would ensure that the initial value perfectly offsets the CVA and hence C^* is a minimum hurdle for the trade to be profitable. In this case, for the accurate calculation, the relevant spread is 2.34 bps. Obviously, calculating this spread quickly can be an important component. Vrins and Gregory (2011) consider this effect (including the impact of netting and DVA) and show that it is significant in many cases. There are also accurate approximations for computing the correct spread without the need for a recursive solution.[21]

Another point to emphasise is that the benefit of netting seen in the incremental CVA of a new trade depends also on the relative size of the new transaction. As the transaction size increases, the netting benefit is lost and the CVA will approach the stand-alone value. This is illustrated in Figure 12.9, which shows the incremental CVA of the 5-year IRS EUR payer

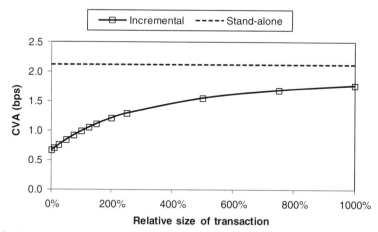

Figure 12.9 Incremental CVA (as a spread in basis points per annum) for a 5-year EUR swap paying fixed (Payer IRS EUR 5Y) with respect to the other three trades in Table 12.6.

---

[20] An even simpler way is to use the approximation from equation (12.3) although, as described above, this can be quite inaccurate in some cases.

[21] Indeed, Vrins and Gregory (2011) show that it is trivial to bound the true spread, which in the example given leads to a range of 2.19–2.67 bps. They also give a reasonably close approximation, which leads to an accurate estimate of 2.36 bps. None of these results requires any additional CVA calculations, as would be required in a full recursive solution.

examined as a function of the relative size of this new transaction. We assume that the existing trades are the other three shown in Table 12.6. The stand-alone and standard incremental CVA values are 76,006 and 35,694,[22] which can be converted approximately into running spreads as in equation (12.8), giving 1.77 bps and 0.99 bps respectively. For a smaller transaction, the CVA decreases to a lower limit of 0.67 bps whereas for a large transaction size it approaches the stand-alone value. Clearly, a CVA quote in basis points is only valid for a particular transaction size.

12.4.4 Numerical issues

Calculating CVA on exotic derivatives can be highly challenging, which is not surprising due to the previous intuition that calculating the CVA on a product is at least as complex (and often more complex) as pricing the product itself. Valuation of exotic products can be rather slow, requiring Monte Carlo or lattice-based modelling. Since each EE value required for calculating CVA requires a rather large number of simulations, this will probably be beyond realistic computational resources. Many pricing functions[23] used by traders may be inadequate to calculate EE.

The CVA calculation as represented by equation (12.2) is costly due to the large number of calculations of the future value of the underlying trade(s). For example, in the above calculations (as described in Chapter 10), there are 10,000 simulations and 183 time points (representing a point every 10 calendar days for 5 years). This means that all the above CVA estimates are based on 1.83m pricing calls. This is likely to be the bottleneck of the CVA calculation, and the first and most obvious method for improving the efficiency of the CVA calculation will be to speed up the underlying pricing functionality. There are many methods that may achieve this, such as (see also discussion below on exotics):

- Stripping out common functionality (such as cash flow generation and fixings), which does not depend on the underlying market variables at a given point in time.
- Numerical optimisation of pricing functions.
- Use of approximations or grids.
- Parallelisation.

Another aspect to consider when computing CVA is whether to use pathwise or direct simulation, as discussed in Chapter 9 (Section 9.3.2). Whilst, for exposure, evaluation of pathwise simulations would seem to be best, it is not clearly the case for CVA. A parallel can be drawn here to pricing synthetic CDOs, which is a similar problem as it involves integration over defaults. Here, practitioners have favoured approaches that simulate defaults directly via the well-known Gaussian copula default time model attributed to Li (2000) rather than, for example, the pathwise default simulation approach of Hull *et al.* (2004). In other words, whilst the evaluation of exposure does not favour a direct simulation approach, the evaluation of the default component in CVA *does*.

We consider the above idea by comparing the evaluation of the CVA of the 5Y GBP IRS above with a similar calculation based on a direct simulation approach. In the former case,

[22] This can be seen from the 4-1-2-3 scenario where this trade is considered after the other three.
[23] Exotic products in this context could imply any product that does not admit a very simple pricing formula (such as a swap or simple option).

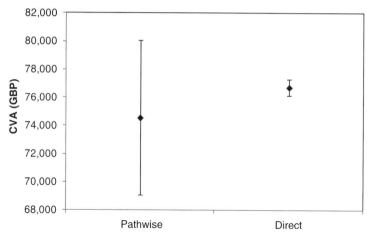

Figure 12.10 Estimate of the CVA for the Payer IRS EUR 5Y calculated with pathwise and direct jump to simulation approaches. In each case, the same numbers of evaluations of the swap are used.

we have 10,000 paths for the exposure at a total of 183 time steps. In the latter approach, there is no time grid and, instead, default times are drawn randomly in the interval [0, 5Y]. The approach of Li (2000) allows this to be done in a way that is consistent with the underlying cumulative default probability. The exposure is then calculated at each of these points directly. A total of 1.83m default times are generated, so that the number of swap evaluations is the same as in the pathwise case.

The comparison of the CVA estimates is given in Figure 12.10, with error bars representing one standard deviation of uncertainty. We can see that the direct simulation approach is much more accurate for CVA than the pathwise approach for the same number of underlying pricing calls. The reason that the pathwise method is less accurate can be understood as follows. Suppose we generate 10,000 paths that overestimate the interest rate at one year in the future (in other words, due to Monte Carlo noise the average interest rate in the simulation is slightly too high). Then we will tend to overestimate the exposure of the payer swap at this point. However, this is likely to overestimate the exposure at, for example, 18 months, since the interest rate paths six months later are more likely to be positively biased. In the direct simulation approach, this is not a problem since all the default times are drawn independently.

The improvement above is quite dramatic, with the standard deviation 9.7 times smaller in the direct approach. Since Monte Carlo error is approximately proportional to the square root of the number of simulations, this actually represents a speed improvement of $9.7 \times 9.7 = 94$ times. In other words, we can do 94 times fewer simulations to achieve the same accuracy. Whilst the above may sound appealing, we must consider the overall improvement. Amdahl's law (Amdahl, 1967) gives a simple formula for the overall speedup from improving one component of a calculation. This formula is $((1 - P) + P/S)^{-1}$, where P is the percentage of the calculation that can be improved and S is the relative speed improvement. For example, if 90% $(P = 0.9)$ of the time is spent on pricing function calls and these can be speeded up by 94 times, then the overall improvement is 9.1 times. This is shown in Figure 12.11, illustrating the improvement depending on the proportion of time spent on the valuation. Clearly, P needs to be close to unity for the overall speedup to be good. Furthermore, going from a pathwise to a direct simulation may be more time-consuming, as illustrated in Figure 9.4. Figure 12.11 also illustrates the impact of the non-valuation stage taking

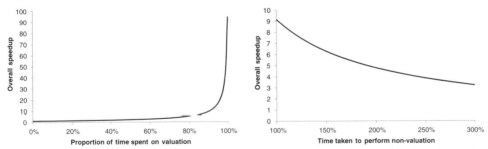

Figure 12.11 Illustration of the overall improvement according to the speedup of 94 times in moving from pathwise to direct simulation for CVA computation. The left-hand graph shows the overall speedup as a function of the proportion of time spent on the valuation stage. The right-hand graph assumes 90% of the time spent on the revaluation and looks at the overall speedup as a function of the increased time to perform the non-valuation components.

longer, which results in a worse speedup. Overall, we can see that a direct simulation approach for CVA may be faster but this will depend on the precise time spent on different components in the Monte Carlo model.

12.4.5 Path dependency, break clauses and exotics

Whilst the above idea may allow some speedup in CVA calculations, it will introduce complexities with path-dependent products. Path dependency in CVA calculations presents a problem since, in order to assess a future exposure at a certain date, one must have information about the entire path from now until that date. This aspect was discussed in Section 8.3.5. Whilst CVA calculations are naturally, and most easily, based on risk-free values, ideally, one should exercise an option based on the risky value (i.e., including CVA). However, this creates a recursive problem where the CVA calculation depends on the exercise decision, which itself depends on the CVA.

Arvantis and Gregory (2001) solve the path-dependent CVA problem for an interest rate swaption with deterministic credit spreads and their results are reported in Table 12.7. We

Table 12.7 Illustration of CVA values for physically settled interest rate swaptions assuming exercise based on the risk-free and risky values. The left-hand column shows the swaption and swap maturity respectively, for example 1Y/5Y indicates a 1-year swaption to exercise into a 5-year swap

	CDS curve = 200 bps flat		CDS curve = 500 bps flat	
	Risk-free exercise	*Risky exercise*	*Risk-free exercise*	*Risky exercise*
1Y/5Y	0.117%	0.116%	0.252%	0.245%
2Y/5Y	0.128%	0.127%	0.268%	0.264%
1Y/10Y	0.334%	0.327%	0.690%	0.654%
2Y/10Y	0.355%	0.349%	0.700%	0.679%

Source: Taken from Arvanitis and Gregory (2001)

can see that exercising based on the optimal risky value lowers the CVA slightly. This is because it avoids exercising in situations where the risk-free value of the swap is positive but the CVA is greater than this value. We also see the effect is stronger for a larger credit spread.

As shown in equation (12.2), the calculation of CVA will be approximated with reference to EE calculated at discrete points in time. Whilst this may be acceptable for certain kinds of path dependencies (for example, Bermudan swaptions), exotic derivatives prices are often based on a continuous sampling of quantities (for example, barrier options). Such cases will also require approximations such as those introduced by Lomibao and Zhu (2005), who use a mathematical technique known as a Brownian bridge to calculate probabilities of path-dependent events that are intermediate to actual exposure simulation points.

Regarding exotic products and those with American-style features, as discussed in Section 9.3.3, there are typically three approaches followed. The first is to use approximations, which may sometimes be upper bounds on the true CVA. Given this, the other uncertainties in quantifying CVA and associated hedging issues, using approximations for exotic products, may not be of great concern. A second, more sophisticated and accurate approach involves using pre-calculated grids to provide the future value of instruments as a function of the underlying variables. This approach works well as long as the dimensionality is not high. Third, American Monte approaches can be used to approximate exposures, handling any exotic feature as well as path dependencies. This is described in detail by Cesari *et al.* (2009).

12.5 CVA WITH COLLATERAL

Finally, we will consider the impact of collateral on CVA, which follows from the assessment of the impact of collateral in Section 9.7. As with netting before, the influence of collateral on the standard CVA formula given in equation (12.2) is straightforward. Collateral only changes the EE (it does not change the default probability of the counterparty or recovery value) and hence the same formula may be used with the EE based on assumptions of collateralisation. The base case scenario will consider the four trades used above and described in Section 9.5. The base case exposure, with and without collateral, can be seen in Figure 9.19. This assumes a zero-threshold, two-way CSA with a minimum transfer amount of 100,000 and a rounding of 20,000. For the CVA calculation, a flat credit curve of 500 bps and recovery value of 40% is assumed. The base case CVA without any collateral considered is 257,905 as can be seen, for example, from Table 12.6.

12.5.1 Impact of margin period of risk

We first consider the impact of the margin period of risk on the zero-threshold CVA calculation, as considered previously in Figure 9.21. The CVA increases, from being very small at a margin period of risk of zero[24] towards the uncollateralised value as shown in Figure 12.12. At a margin period of risk of 30 calendar days, the CVA is almost half the uncollateralised CVA. This is in line with the more conservative assumption of a minimum of 20 business days required in certain circumstances under the Basel III capital rules (see Chapter 17 for more detail).

---

[24] Note that at a margin period of risk of zero there is still a small CVA due to the minimum transfer amount and rounding.

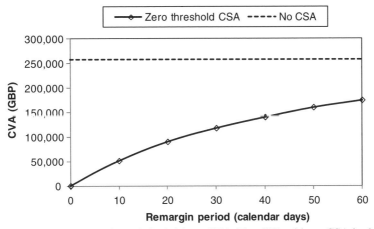

Figure 12.12 Impact of the margin period of risk on CVA. The CVA with no CSA is shown by the dotted line.

12.5.2 Threshold CSAs and independent amounts

Figure 12.13 shows the impact of a threshold on various different CSAs. In the case of a one-way CSA, in favour of the counterparty (and therefore against the institution), the overall CVA is increased compared to the uncollateralised CVA (dotted line). A one-way CSA in favour of the institution (for) reduces the CVA significantly. In both one-way CSA cases, the impact of an increasing threshold is to make the CVA converge to the uncollateralised result. In the case of a two-way CSA the behaviour is not completely monotonic with respect to an increasing threshold such that a (two-way) threshold of $1m appears slightly more beneficial than a zero-threshold CSA. It is interesting to explain this effect in a bit more detail.

This non-monotonic behaviour in the two-way CSA case is related to the discussion in Section 9.5.1 on EE being *less* than NEE whilst 95% PFE is *greater* than 5% PFE. Recall that we are dealing with a set of four trades, three of which have a positive sensitivity to

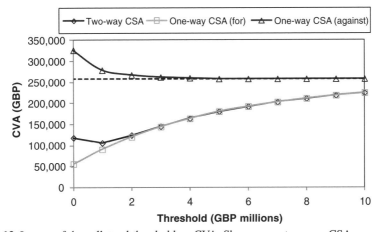

Figure 12.13 Impact of the collateral threshold on CVA. Shown are a two-way CSA, a one-way CSA in the institution's favour (for) and vice versa (against). The dotted line is the uncollateralised CVA.

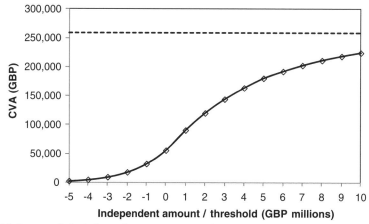

Figure 12.14 Impact of the independent amount (negative values) and threshold (positive values) on CVA. A one-way CSA in the institution's favour is assumed. The dotted line is the uncollateralised CVA.

overall interest rates. In the zero-threshold case, there are many scenarios where the institution must post a relatively small amount of collateral due to a negative drift (relating to the NEE being greater than the EE). This tends to weaken the benefit of the collateralisation. On the other hand, with a small threshold, many of these scenarios do not result in collateral posting and the ability to mitigate the paths around the 95% PFE, where interest rates are high, outweighs the need to post collateral for the paths around the (smaller) 5% PFE.

Figure 12.14 shows the impact of independent amount and threshold on the CVA. Note that an independent amount can be considered as a negative threshold. We can see an increase from zero, where the independent amount is large, to the uncollateralised CVA (dotted line) where the threshold is large.

In Figure 12.15 we look more carefully at the impact of the independent amount on the CVA. We also show error bars arising from an assumed uncertainty in the margin period of

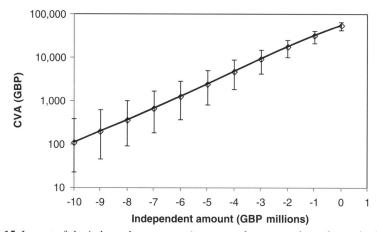

Figure 12.15 Impact of the independent amount (represented as a negative value as in the previous figure) on CVA with a logarithmic y-axis. Also shown are error bars corresponding to changing the assumed margin period of risk by ± 10 calendar days.

risk of ± 10 days (i.e., 20 days or 40 days). Whilst an increase in the independent amount reduces the CVA substantially, the uncertainty over the CVA is relatively greater. With an independent amount, we may believe that the CVA is small but the uncertainty of the estimate is large.

12.6 SUMMARY

This chapter has been concerned with the pricing of counterparty risk via CVA. The computation of CVA has been detailed from the commonly made simplification of no wrong-way risk, which assumes that the credit exposure, default of the counterparty and recovery rate are not related. We have shown the relevant formulas for computing CVA in their simplest possible forms (all the details can be found in the appendices to this chapter, found on cvacentral.com). The concepts of incremental and marginal CVA have been introduced and illustrated in order to provide a means to price new or existing trades. We have discussed the specifics of calculating CVA, including collateral and netting, and covered some more complex aspects such as numerical implementation, exotic products and path dependency.

In the next chapter, we continue to discuss pricing counterparty risk, incorporating the default probability of an institution into the analysis (DVA). Over the last few years, this has been an important and controversial aspect of pricing counterparty risk. We will also consider some other important effects related to DVA.

13

Debt Value Adjustment

> *I don't want to tell you how much insurance I carry with Prudential. All I can say is: When I go, they go!*
>
> Jack Benny (1894–1974)

In the last chapter, we considered the pricing of counterparty risk via credit value adjustment (CVA). One of the assumptions made in deriving the CVA formula was that the institution themselves was risk-free and could not default. This may have seemed like a fairly innocuous and straightforward assumption. Indeed, it is consistent with the "going concern" accountancy concept, which requires financial statements to be based on the assumption that a business will remain in existence for an indefinite period.

However, institutions are allowed by international accountancy standards to consider their own default in the valuation of liabilities. Since credit exposure has a liability component (the negative exposure as defined in Section 8.2.7), this can be included in the pricing of counterparty risk, creating what is often known as the debt value adjustment (DVA) component. DVA is a double-edged sword. On the one hand, it will resolve some theoretical problems with CVA and create a world where risky counterparties can more easily trade with one another. On the other hand, the nature of DVA and its implications and potential unintended consequences may trouble some people.

DVA is controversial. Whilst some practitioners argue in favour of its use, others have criticised it for various reasons, which we will elaborate upon in this chapter. We will look first at the use of DVA in counterparty risk and then step back and consider the broader implications of the use of DVA.

13.1 DVA AND COUNTERPARTY RISK

13.1.1 The need for DVA

CVA has traditionally been a charge for counterparty risk that is incorporated in a transaction in favour of the stronger credit quality counterparty. Historically, banks trading with corporate counterparties have charged CVAs linked to the credit quality of the corporate and the exposure in question. A corporate would not have been able to credibly question such a charge since the probability that a bank would default was considered remote (and indeed the credit spreads of banks have traditionally been very tight and the credit ratings very strong). The suggestion that a large bank such as Lehman Brothers would default was, until 2008, an almost laughable concept.

Now let us fast-forward to the credit crisis beginning in 2007. Gradually, the idea of "default-free" counterparties became not credible and credit spreads of the "strong" financial institutions widened dramatically. Consider the following situation.

A corporate client has traded with a top-tier bank for a number of years. The credit ratings and credit spreads of each institution are as follows:

	Credit rating	Credit spread
Bank	Aa1/AA+	10–15 bps
Corporate	A3/A–	200–300 bps

The bank will always charge a CVA to the corporate on trades and will be transparent about the calculation; for example, explaining the quantities used to come up with the CVA and also giving benefit due to netting (and possibly collateral) agreements that are in place. The corporate is quite used to the CVA charges and has never been concerned that the bank could ever default. Now, as a result of the global financial crisis, the bank's own credit spread has widened to a level that is comparable to that of the corporate (the credit rating is unchanged but that offers little reassurance). The corporate believes that it should not be paying such a significant CVA charge. This would imply that the bank would have to reduce their CVA charge significantly.

Question: How can the bank reduce the price of counterparty risk when the credit market is becoming more risky? What would be the economics behind such a reduction?

An even simpler version of the above dilemma occurs in the interbank market. Surely two banks would trade at mid-market with no adjustment for credit quality. A trade at mid-market where neither bank makes a profit is reasonable since the banks may be hedging profitable client trades. However, both banks incur counterparty risk when trading with each other, which should incur a cost, making the net value of the trade negative from both points of view. This is one reason for having a collateral arrangement, such as through a CSA with a low threshold, which will minimise the counterparty risk faced by both banks. However, as shown in Section 12.5.1, even a zero-threshold CSA does not eradicate counterparty risk entirely. Hence, in a world where all parties use CVA, how can two counterparties of similar credit quality ever agree to trade, even under a collateral arrangement?

DVA, which arises from considering bilateral CVA, solves both of the above two issues, at the *possible* risk of causing greater issues.

13.1.2 Bilateral CVA

Bilateral CVA arises from accounting practices and formally began in 2006, when the FAS 157[1] determined that banks should record a DVA entry. FAS 157 states "Because non-performance risk includes the reporting entity's credit risk, the reporting entity should

---

[1] The Statements of Financial Accounting Standard, No 157.

consider the effect of its credit risk (credit standing) on the fair value . . . ". Although the use of bilateral CVA (BCVA) goes back many years, it has become increasingly relevant and popular since the financial crisis began in 2007. BCVA means that an institution would consider a CVA calculated under the assumption that they, as well as their counterparty, may default. In Appendix 13A, we derive the formula for BCVA under these conditions. The definition of BCVA follows directly from that of unilateral CVA, with the assumption that the institution concerned can also default. Hence, we relax this, and only this,[2] assumption. We will also initially assume that the default of the institution and their counterparty are independent and that simultaneous default cannot occur. These assumptions will be relaxed later. Under these conditions, the BCVA is:

$$
\mathrm{BCVA} = (1 - \mathrm{Rec}_C) \sum_{j=1}^{n} \underbrace{\mathrm{EE}(t_j)}_{\substack{\text{Discounted} \\ \text{expected} \\ \text{exposure}}} \underbrace{\left[1 - \mathrm{PD}_I(0, t_{j-1})\right]}_{\substack{\text{Probability institution} \\ \text{hasn't yet defaulted}}} \underbrace{\mathrm{PD}_C(t_{j-1}, t_j)}_{\substack{\text{Probability} \\ \text{counterparty defaults} \\ \text{(in this interval)}}}
$$

$$
+ (1 - \mathrm{Rec}_I) \sum_{j=1}^{n} \underbrace{\mathrm{NEE}(t_j)}_{\substack{\text{Discounted} \\ \text{expected negative} \\ \text{exposure}}} \underbrace{\left[1 - \mathrm{PD}_C(0, t_{j-1})\right]}_{\substack{\text{Probability counterparty} \\ \text{hasn't yet defaulted}}} \underbrace{\mathrm{PD}_I(t_{j-1}, t_j)}_{\substack{\text{Probability} \\ \text{institution defaults} \\ \text{(in this interval)}}}
$$

$$(13.1)$$

with I representing the institution themselves and C their counterparty. The first term in the BCVA formula is close to the usual CVA term, as given in equation (12.2), but contains an additional multiplicative factor based on the institution's own survival probability. This is not surprising, since an institution can argue that they should not consider losses due to their counterparty defaulting in scenarios where they themselves have defaulted first. Indeed, the termination of the derivative will occur at the "first to default" of the institution and their counterparty. Failure to account properly for this would therefore create a double counting effect, where both counterparties assume their own default is the first event to occur. However, we will show that proper consideration of the closeout in the event of default implies that this should be ignored (Section 13.4.2).

Spreadsheet 13.1 Simple BCVA calculation.

The second BCVA term is a mirror image of the first term and represents a negative contribution (since the NEE will be negative), known as DVA. It corresponds to the fact that in cases where the institution defaults (before their counterparty), they will make a "gain" if the value is negative (a "negative exposure"). A gain in this context might seem unusual but it is, strictly speaking, correct since the institution, in the event of their own default, pays the

---

[2] For example, the assumptions of no wrong-way risk and that risk-free valuation is straightforward as introduced at the start of the last chapter still apply.

counterparty only a fraction (recovery) of what they owe. The negative expected exposure, defined in Section 8.2.7, is the opposite of the EE. This is also the EE from the counterparty's point of view.

It is important to note that, in terms of the standard valuation of cash flows, there is nothing wrong with equation (13.1). Furthermore, there is a very important and attractive implication of the BCVA formula. This is that if two counterparties agree on the approach and parameters for calculation of BCVA then they will agree on a price by the symmetry of equation (13.1). If an institution calculates the BCVA from their point of view to be $+X$ (a loss), then their counterparty should calculate it to be $-X$ (a gain). The counterparty could then pay the institution an amount of X as compensation for counterparty risk.

To easily understand the impact of DVA, let us return to the simple formula for CVA given in equation (12.3). Modifying this to an approximation for the BCVA formula gives

$$BCVA = \text{credit spread}_C \times EPE + \text{credit spread}_I \times ENE. \qquad (13.2)$$

This means that an institution subtracts from the CVA a component equal to their own credit spread times the expected negative exposure (ENE), which is the opposite of the EPE as defined in Section 8.2.7. The ENE is the counterparty's EPE. Finally, if we consider that $EPE = -ENE$,[3] then we obtain simply $BCVA = EPE \times (\text{credit spread}_C - \text{credit spread}_I)$. Thus, an institution can intuitively charge a counterparty for the *difference* in their credit spreads (and if this difference is negative then they should pay the counterparty). Weaker counterparties pay stronger counterparties in order to trade with them based on the differential in credit quality.

13.1.3 Examples of BCVA

We now show an example of BCVA computation based on the CVA calculations in the last chapter. Considering the same four trades which had an overall CVA of 257,905 GBP (e.g., see Table 12.6), we compute the BCVA. The EE, which has been shown before and NEE, which has not, are shown in Figure 13.1.

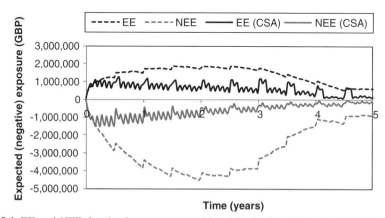

Figure 13.1 EE and NEE for the four swaps considered in the last chapter (e.g., see Table 12.6). Shown are the cases without collateral and with a (zero-threshold, two-way) CSA.

---

[3] This is sometimes a reasonable approximation in practice but we will discuss the impact of asymmetry below.

In this case, the NEE is significantly greater in absolute terms than the EE, as discussed previously in Section 9.5.1. In order to understand the overall impact of bilateral pricing, three distinct CVA measures are considered as outlined below:

- *Unilateral CVA*. This is the standard unilateral CVA formula given by equation (12.2).
- *CVA*. This is the CVA taking into account the survival probability of the institution, i.e., this is the first term in equation (13.1).
- *BCVA*. The bilateral CVA given by equation (13.1). This will be less than the adjusted CVA and may be negative due to the second term in the formula.

Referring to the above equation, we make the following statements about BCVA compared with unilateral CVA:

- CVA will always be less than or equal to the unilateral CVA since it includes multiplication by survival probabilities that must be no greater than unity.
- In turn, BCVA will always be less than the CVA since the institution is pricing a "gain" from their future default.
- In general, BCVA is expected to be positive if the counterparty is more risky than the institution (their credit spread is greater) and negative otherwise.
- BCVA also depends on symmetry of future value (magnitude of EPE compared with ENE). Some trades/netting can have highly asymmetric future values, as we shall see below.

Let us assume as before that the counterparty's CDS curve is flat at 500 bps and the recovery rate is 40%. As before, we assume a constant continuously compounded interest rate of 5%. We assume that the institution has a flat CDS curve of 250 bps (i.e., they are half as risky as implied by the market).

The results showing the three different CVA measures described above are shown in Table 13.1. The CVA is smaller than the unilateral CVA due to adjusting for the probability that the institution may default first. The reduction is modest and can be understood as follows. The 5-year default probability of the institution is approximately 19%.[4] Assuming the institution has a 50% chance of defaulting first, we halve this probability to 9.5%. Finally, we subtract 9.5% from the unilateral CVA value to arrive at a CVA of £233,400, which is reasonably close to the actual value of £237,077.

Table 13.1   Unilateral and bilateral CVA values for the portfolio of four swap trades under the assumption of independence of defaults and no wrong-way risk

	CVA (GBP)
Unilateral CVA	257,905
CVA	237,077
DVA	−245,868
BCVA	−8,791

[4] As discussed in Section 10.1.5, this can be calculated as $1 - \exp(-hu) = 1 - \exp(-4.167\% \times 5) = 18.8\%$, where $h = 250/10,000/(1 - 40\%) = 4.167\%$ is the hazard rate.

Regarding the BCVA, the DVA component is slightly bigger than the CVA one, creating a net BCVA of –£8,791, which represents a benefit for the institution. This seems strange at first, because the institution is only half as risky as their counterparty. However, due to asymmetry of the exposure distribution (Figure 13.1), the NEE is much bigger than the EE. Hence, whilst the institution faces probabilities in the CVA component that are approximately double those in the DVA, the EE in the CVA component is approximately half the NEE component in the DVA. The NEE component is slightly dominant, creating an overall negative effect. Another way to see this is via the simple formula in equation (13.2). The EPE and ENE are £1,371,285 and –£2,806,231, respectively. This gives an approximate CVA per annum of

$$CVA(\text{per annum}) \approx 5\% \times 1,371,285 + 2.5\% \times -2,806,231 = 68,564 - 70,156$$
$$= -£1,592.$$

This example illustrates an important effect, which is that BCVA does not just depend on credit quality. Recall that if the counterparty agrees on the modelling and parameters, then they will, by symmetry, calculate a BCVA of +£8,791. The institution, even though they are half as risky, has to pay the counterparty £8,791 to trade with them since the counterparty faces around double the exposure.

13.1.4 Impact of collateral

We now compute the BCVA in the collateralised case assuming a zero-threshold, two-way CSA. The equivalent results are shown in Table 13.2. The situation is much more balanced, since the impact of the CSA is to create similar amounts of residual exposure for both the institution and the counterparty. The impact of this is that the BCVA is approximately half the CVA (59,737 vs 109,931), in line with the institution's CDS spread being half that of the counterparty (250 bps vs 500 bps).

The above results rely on the assumption of a margin period of risk for the institution as well as the counterparty. This requires an institution to consider a benefit, not only from their own default, but also from their ability to stop posting collateral 10 days[5] prior to their default. Finally, note that by signing a two-way CSA, the institution would realise a loss of £60,023.[6] Their counterparty would realise the same amount as a gain.

Table 13.2 Unilateral and bilateral CVA values for the portfolio of four swap trades under a zero-threshold, two-way CSA and assuming also independence of defaults and no wrong-way risk

	CVA (GBP)
Unilateral CVA	118,311
CVA	109,805
DVA	–58,574
BCVA	51,232

[5] Or whatever the margin period of risk assumption is.
[6] This comes from taking the BCVA in Table 13.2 from the equivalent value in Table 13.1.

13.1.5 Properties of DVA

The reader might be concerned with the concept that an institution is attaching value to their own default. Indeed, there may be some implications of using DVA that may or may not seem reasonable. These are:

- *A risky derivative can be worth more than a risk-free derivative.* The BCVA can be negative (if the second term is larger in magnitude than the first) unlike CVA, which is always positive. A negative BCVA implies that the risky value of a derivative (or netting set of derivatives) is *greater* than the risk-free value.
- *Pricing counterparty risk is a zero-sum game.* If all counterparties in the market agree on the approach and parameters for calculation of BCVA then the total amount of counterparty risk in the market (as represented by the sum of all BCVAs) will be zero. This follows from the symmetry of equation (13.1).
- *Favourable risk mitigants can increase BCVA.* The impact of CVA caused by netting will not always be advantageous; in particular, if the second term in equation (13.1) dominates. Without netting, an institution can cherry-pick contracts, requiring those with a positive value to be settled and leaving those with a negative value as liabilities in the bankruptcy process. This is also true for two-way collateral agreements, as illustrated in Tables 13.1 and 13.2.

However, a very favourable feature of BCVA, which is related to all of the above points, is that parties can agree on pricing. Indeed, the clearing price for counterparty credit risk in the market currently appears to include DVA. With unilateral CVA, theoretically two counterparties will never agree to the terms of a new trade since they will both seek to add a counterparty risk charge. Using bilateral CVA is compelling, largely since it has a symmetry that allows a price agreement. However, this does not mean that BCVA is the right approach to use. To fully understand the strengths and weaknesses of BCVA, we will need to consider its history and the ways in which an institution can attempt to monetise it.

13.2 THE DVA CONTROVERSY

13.2.1 Liability measurement and accounting standards

The issue of DVA in counterparty risk is a small component of a broader issue which is the general incorporation of credit risk in liability measurement. The question is: should an institution measure its liabilities including the possibility of their own financial failure? This has been a very significant question for banks in the last few years since their "own credit risk" (via credit spreads) has seen unprecedented volatility.

Accountancy standards have generally evolved to a point where "own credit risk" can be incorporated in the valuation of liabilities. For example, relevant for the US, the FASB[7] issued in 2006 SFAS 157, relating to fair value measurements, which became effective in 2007. This permits an institution's own credit quality to be included in the valuation of their liabilities, stating "The most relevant measure of a liability always reflects the credit standing of the entity obliged to pay". Amendments to IAS 39 by the International Accounting Standards Board (IASB) in 2005, relevant for the European Union, also concluded that the fair value of a liability should include the credit risk associated with that liability. This position

---

[7] Financial Accounting Standards Board of the United States.

Table 13.3   Illustration of the impact of including own credit on a financial statement

	Method 1		Method 2	
	Before	*After*	*Before*	*After*
Assets	1000	950	1000	950
Liabilities	(800)	(800)	(800)	(760)
Equity	(200)	(150)	(200)	(190)

is reinforced with the introduction of IFRS 13, which unites international and US accounting treatments, at the beginning of 2013.

Why do accounting rules view an institution's own credit risk as being an important component of fair value measurement? In a nutshell, the answer to this is that the fair value of an institution's bonds is considered to be the price other entities are willing to pay for them (which would certainly contain a component for the institution's credit risk). Another reason is that the failure to account for own credit risk could lead to an accounting mismatch, as explained below.

In Table 13.3, we consider two simple accounting approaches. Method 1 values an institution's liabilities at their face value, which is a fixed amount whilst Method 2 values them using the current market valuation. An institution typically has assets and liabilities that are affected by similar market forces (e.g., they hold bonds and have issued their own debt). Suppose that a change in interest rates reduces the value of the assets by 5% (1000 to 950). Under Method 1 in Table 13.3 this creates a distorted view seen as an apparent loss of 50 from the equity of the company. Method 2 appears better because the liabilities also lose $(800 - 760 = 40)$,[8] which balances much of the apparent equity loss leading to an adjustment of only 10.

However, suppose that the change in value of the assets above is caused by a change in credit spreads. Method 2 now corresponds to incorporating "own credit" to create a loss on the liabilities. This may be favoured for similar reasons to those described above. However, the loss on assets is because other issuers (of the bonds held by the institution) are apparently more likely to default. In Method 2, this is cancelled by gains due to the fact that the institution itself is more likely to default. This may not sound quite as persuasive as the interest rate example. However, it is not completely trivial to disentangle the impact of interest rates and credit spreads (i.e., if the yield of an institution's debt increases by, say, 1% it is not easy to determine how much of this is due to interest rate effects and how much to credit effects). Hence, using Method 2 (which uses DVA to value liabilities) in all cases may seem most reasonable and easiest.

However, the inclusion of own credit creates a well-known counterintuitive effect. Consider that the credit spread of the institution widens whilst all other variables (including other credit spreads) are held fixed (Table 13.4). Now the institution reports a profit of 40 due to an increase in the value of their equity, which is driven by their own declining credit quality (as measured by their credit spread trading in the market).

---

[8] We assume they lose the same 5% of value.

Table 13.4   Illustration of the impact of including own credit on a financial statement when an institutions credit spread widens

	With own credit	
	Before	*After*
Assets	1000	1000
Liabilities	(800)	(760)
Equity	(200)	(240)

An institution booking profits from their own declining credit quality, either due to the debt held on their books or with respect to derivatives via a bilateral counterparty risk adjustment, is a subject that has been fiercely debated. It first became widely discussed in 2008, when the widening of banks' credit spreads led to some very large accounting profits which were seemingly treated with caution and even disdain by some observers. In 2009, this story became even more obscure as the reverse effect meant that banks' own credit risk actually began to negatively impact their financial results.[9]

More recently, in 2011 banks have made similar large accounting gains as their credit spreads widened in the midst of the euro crisis and other market turbulence. Articles reporting this have made statements such as "The profits of British banks could be inflated by as much as £4bn due to a bizarre accounting rule that allows them to book a gain on the fall in the value of their debt"[10] and describing DVA as "a counter-intuitive but powerful accounting effect that means banks book a paper profit when their own credit quality declines".[11] Perhaps the most striking illustration of the effect was with UBS, where a "Sfr1.8 billion DVA gain nearly cancelled out the Sfr1.9 billion it lost in an alleged rogue trading incident".[12] There is much scepticism over the use of DVA, but this has come at a time when banks are highly unpopular institutions. Others[13] have defended the use of DVA saying, for example, "they are part of the mark-to-market framework for derivatives, and the profit and loss is as realisable as in any derivatives position".

The criticism of DVA stems mainly from the fact that it is not easily realisable,[14] just as an individual cannot realise gains on their own life insurance policy. Whilst an institution may buy and sell assets on a daily basis, liabilities sometimes cannot be transferred without permission. Hence, it could be argued that the accounting treatment of liabilities should not *necessarily* mirror that of assets. Other criticisms include the idea that the gains coming from DVA are distorted because other components are ignored. For example, Kenyon (2010) makes the point that if DVA is used then the value of goodwill (which is zero at default) should also depend on an institution's credit quality. Losses in goodwill would oppose gains on DVA when an institution's credit spread widened. In addition, funding costs (Chapter 14)

[9] For example, "Banks' own credit risk hampers financial results", 5th August 2009, www.risknews.net
[10] "Banks' profits boosted by DVA rule", *Daily Telegraph*, 31st October 2011.
[11] "Papering over the great Wall St Massacre", efinancialnews, 26th October 2011.
[12] "Cutting edge introduction: the DVA debate", Laurie Carver, *Risk*, 2nd November 2011.
[13] From an anonymous employee at a US bank quoted in the article in the previous footnote.
[14] For example, "It's not the kind of stuff you'd point to in earnings and say, 'now that's sustainable income'. You would want to exclude it from earnings in evaluating how well a company performed". Jack Ciesielski, www.accountingobserver.com

are another component whose valuation, whilst similar to DVA, are not marked to market as DVA benefits are.

In order for the reader to understand the relative merits of DVA in counterparty risk valuation, we therefore need to consider how it can be realised.

13.3   HOW TO MONETISE DVA

Let us return from the world of accountancy standards to the world of counterparty risk. There is clearly a debate over how reasonable the use of DVA is. This debate really hinges around to what extent an institution can ever *realise* a DVA benefit in a reasonable economic way. These arguments are discussed by Gregory (2009a) and are expanded upon below. Note that, in the case of a CSA, the monetisation of DVA must be done over the margin period of risk, i.e., in the days prior to an institution's default. The monetisation of this benefit during the last days before bankruptcy may appear even more difficult.

13.3.1   File for bankruptcy

An institution can obviously realise the BCVA component by going bankrupt but, like an individual trying to monetise their own life insurance, this is not relevant. In fact, this becomes a circular argument; consider a firm with a DVA benefit so substantial that it can prevent their bankruptcy. Yet it is not possible to reverse a bankruptcy.

13.3.2   Unwinds and novations

Returning to the somewhat macabre example of an individual trying to monetise their life insurance, suppose that one instead were to stand at the top of a tall building and call one's life insurance company, offering to settle the contract at, say, half the value. If the life insurer believed this apparent suicide attempt was genuine, they may indeed be willing to settle.[15]

The above example is not as naïve as it may at first sound, as it essentially corresponds to an unwind. Unwinds are quite common ways in OTC derivatives markets to terminate trades early and may allow an institution to realise DVA benefits. Suppose an institution does a trade with a counterparty where the CVA and DVA are exactly balanced at 100 each. However, now assume that the institution's credit quality deteriorates such that their DVA is 300 whilst the CVA is still 100. They ask their counterparty to unwind the transaction, paying them the 200 of DVA benefit. The counterparty has an economic motivation to do this since, by symmetry, they should have 300 of CVA and 100 of DVA. Unwinding can therefore allow the institution to make a gain of 200. A novation (the substitution of one party in a contract with another party) would work in a similar way. Suppose a counterparty has a trade with 300 CVA and 100 DVA but this can be novated to another (better credit quality) counterparty such that both counterparty CVA and DVA are 100. They should be willing to pay 200 for this novation.

There is evidence in OTC derivatives markets of institutions being able to monetise DVA via unwinds and novations. However, there is a problem making this monetisation imperfect. The counterparty, knowing the institution is making a gain via DVA, may wish to profit

---

[15] We note that there are obvious problems here. For example, some life insurance policies may be invalidated by suicide. In addition, paying a suicidal individual five million dollars may alleviate their depression somewhat.

themselves. They will therefore not be willing to unwind at 200 but at a lower value, 100 being the obvious value (split the difference). In such a case only half of the DVA has been monetised.

In practice, the amount of DVA that can be realised in an unwind is more complex than the parties simply agreeing to meet in the middle as it depends on their respective credit quality. For example, monolines have realised substantial DVA benefits from unwinding trades with banks. Such unwinds have represented large CVA-related losses for banks and associated DVA gains for monolines. The monoline insurer XL Capital made billions of dollars of DVA[16] benefits unwinding transactions with banks in 2008. More recently, MBIA monetised a multi-billion dollar derivatives DVA in an unwind of transactions with Morgan Stanley.[17]

Whilst these billions of dollars gained by monolines in unwinding transactions with banks seem to be a clear illustration of monetising DVA, there is a caveat. In May 2009, a credit event was deemed to have occurred in respect of Syncora Guarantee Inc. (formerly known as XL Capital mentioned above). The reason for banks so readily unwinding trades, and paying large DVA benefits in the process, was that they had little choice given the fact that XL Capital was a certainty for bankruptcy. In the case of MBIA, their CDS at the time of the Morgan Stanley settlement was trading at 25 percentage points upfront, representing a highly distressed market price of default risk. With the monolines default, it was more a question of when and not if.

Let us return briefly to the life insurance example. Here, viatical settlements represent the unwind of a life insurance policy prior to maturity. Generally, this occurs when life expectancy has significantly worsened, typically due to terminal illness, and hence the policy has increased in value substantially. In such a case, the unwind (viatical settlement) offers the policyholder a means to monetise the policy early, for example to pay for treatment whilst the insurer can benefit from paying out less than the current policy value.

The parallel between viatical settlement and monolines unwinding transactions is that, in both cases, the impact of ill health (respectively physical and financial) puts them in a strong negotiating position and allows them to unwind and realise close to the full value in the contract. However, a healthy individual trying to obtain a settlement on their life insurance policy or a financially healthy institution attempting to settle a trade, does not permit such an easy monetisation. Monolines do not represent the best example of realising DVA via unwinds since this was achieved only due to the severe deterioration in credit quality of monolines and the fact that they were essentially no longer financially viable.

In summary, unwinds certainly allow some monetisation of DVA. However, this may be easiest to achieve when an institution is in very poor financial health and unlikely to survive. This is not so useful as, rather than realising their DVA by defaulting, they are doing so by getting very close to defaulting (i.e., similar to the analogy with life insurance and terminal illness). If an institution has reasonable credit quality then the negotiation over an unwind or novation will be less easy and they may have to accept that only a proportion (say 50%) of the DVA is monetisable. This links with the practice that a CVA desk may only give a portion (e.g., 50%) of DVA benefit in pricing new trades (Section 18.3.5).

---

[16] Due to different accountancy standards for insurance companies, the monoline does not see this gain as a DVA benefit.

[17] "MBIA and Morgan Stanley settle bond fight", *Wall Street Journal*, 14th December 2011. Although MBIA paid Morgan Stanley $1.1 billion, the actual amount owed (as defined by Morgan Stanley's exposure) was several billion dollars. The difference can be seen as a DVA benefit gained by MBIA in the unwind.

13.3.3 Closeout

Perversely, another way to realise DVA might be to closeout trades in the event of the default of the counterparty. Here, as discussed in Section 8.1.3, an institution may be able to incorporate various factors into the closeout amount. For example, under ISDA (2009) protocol, the determination of a closeout amount "may take into account the creditworthiness of the Determining Party", in other words an institution may use their own DVA in determining the amount to be settled.

As an example, consider that an institution owes a counterparty $1,000 and that counterparty then defaults. But assume that the institution has an associated DVA benefit of $100. The institution may claim that they need only to pay $900 and attempt to realise the full DVA. On the other hand, if an institution is owed $1,000 themselves with $100 of DVA then they can claim $1,100 and receive the recovery rate times the DVA. In the bankruptcy of Lehman Brothers, these practices have been common although courts have not always favoured some of the large DVA (and other) claims.

Suppose an Icelandic bank had entered a trade with Lehman Brothers in 2007. At the time of the Lehman bankruptcy, the replacement cost for the Icelandic bank would be enormous, due to their highly distressed credit spreads. Should the Icelandic bank's claim to this replacement cost (mainly their own substantial DVA) from the Lehman estate be legally upheld? If not, then monetisation of DVA in this way appears delicate and, at the very least, subject to complex legal risks.

13.3.4 Hedging

Not surprisingly, a key way to monetise DVA is via hedging. By contrast, in order to hedge CVA, an institution needs to *short the credit* of their *counterparty*. This can be accomplished by shorting bonds or buying CDS protection. It is possible that neither of these may be achievable in practice, but they are theoretically reasonable ways to hedge CVA. The CVA is monetised (negatively) via paying the carry in the repo transaction or the premiums in the CDS protection position. However, in order to hedge DVA, an institution would need to go *long* with their *own* credit. This can be achieved by buying back their own bonds (or more indirectly via a stock buyback) but cannot be achieved by selling CDS protection on themselves (which is not possible[18]).

Let us first consider an institution buying back their own debt in order to hedge DVA. Institutions normally buy back their bonds (or stock) when they have had a strong performance and are therefore cash rich. An institution with an increasing DVA is normally in the reverse situation, as they must have an increasing credit spread. Furthermore, buying back debt is also a funding management tool and therefore (as discussed in the next chapter) cannot be considered simultaneously to be a way to monetise DVA.

Moving on to other hedging methods, an institution cannot sell CDS protection on themselves but can sell protection on other institutions that are similar. This has been a common and relatively successful way for banks to hedge DVA in the last few years. Obviously, the hedging here cannot be perfect because no other credit spread will have 100% correlation

---

[18] Either because it is illegal or because of the extreme wrong-way risk it will create (Section 15.5.1), meaning that no party should be willing to enter such a trade except at a very low premium.

with that of the institution. For example, some dealers sold protection on Lehman Brothers prior to their default as an attempted "hedge" against their DVA. Furthermore, if the hedging is a good one, then the large correlation that must exist may cause problems. In practice, this is best understood by considering the impact of dealers selling CDS protection on each other. From the dealer's perspective, it may be beneficial but, from the point of view of the counterparties buying CDS protection, it may not be. Buying CDS protection from a dealer on another dealer is not a sensible trade from a counterparty risk perspective. Indeed, it potentially has a lot of wrong-way risk that even collateral may not mitigate particularly well. This will be discussed later in Section 15.5.1.

Finally, index hedges may be used as effectively a short protection position on "own credit", an obvious choice being the Markit iTraxx Senior Financials index although the basis risk can be significant. Index hedging of DVA may not be completely apparent as the index hedge can be combined with long protection on CVA against counterparties' credit spreads with the overall position being a basis hedge (see Section 16.4.3). Again there is the problem here that a highly correlated index will represent wrong-way risk, whilst a low correlation hedge will be ineffective. Essentially, any DVA hedge will only be able to monetise the systematic portion of an institution's credit spread. The idiosyncratic part is non-hedgeable. Furthermore, when an institution's spread is large, the idiosyncratic proportion may be larger (for example, Table 10.4 shows this). Monetisation of DVA therefore becomes more problematic closer to default. These hedges also create systemic risk, especially given the size that is required when banks all sell such protection to hedge their DVA.

13.3.5 Funding

Finally, arguments around the monetisation of DVA claim that it is a funding benefit. The argument here is that, whilst EPE represents a long-term receivable, ENE represents a long-term payable providing some funding benefit and therefore justifying the use of bilateral CVA. We will discuss this in more detail in the next chapter, but for now we simply emphasise that this can lead to double counting unless the funding benefits are adjusted accordingly (which somewhat defeats the object of the exercise).

13.4 FURTHER DVA CONSIDERATIONS

13.4.1 Impact of default correlation

We consider next the impact of dependence between the default events of the institution and their counterparty. The most common way to correlate defaults is via the Gaussian copula approach attributed to Li (2000) and mentioned in the last chapter. A simple way to do this in the current case is given by Gregory (2009a). We show the impact of correlation in Figure 13.2. The impact is very strong, with the benefit of the overall negative BCVA lost at only a small correlation value (around 14%). Thereafter, the BCVA increases towards the unilateral value as the correlation between the default times increases to 100%. This is due to a fairly well-known feature of the Gaussian copula approach where at 100% correlation the default times are *co-monotonic* and where the most risky name is certain to default first and therefore the DVA benefit is lost.

The above approach is not the only way to introduce dependency between default events. However, the main point to emphasise is that, when using BCVA, the dependence between

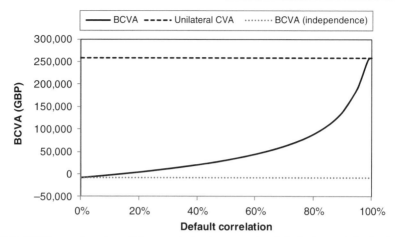

Figure 13.2 BCVA as a function of the correlation between the default times of the institution and their counterparty.

the default of the institution and their counterparty is very significant. However, the effect shown above is potentially an illusion as we discuss in the next section.

13.4.2   DVA and closeout

When defining exposure we noted that, despite the need to define precisely what the termination value of a transaction actually would be, there is no obvious best solution. If one works with risk-free valuation then it is the simplest from a theoretical point of view but introduces jumps in the value of derivatives at various termination points as explained below. Incorporation of components such as CVA and DVA in exposure and termination value introduces a smooth valuation but creates a recursive problem.

In defining exposure (Section 8.1.2) and then deriving the formulas for CVA and DVA, a standard assumption is that, in the event of default, the closeout value of transactions (whether positive or negative) will be based on risk-free valuation. This approximation makes quantification more straightforward but the actual case is more complex and subtle, as discussed in Section 13.3.3. The more natural proxy for a closeout amount is the cost of replacing the transaction with another party. As mentioned above, documentation (e.g., ISDA) allows for the actual transaction replacement cost to be the closeout amount, provided enough market makers were asked for bids on the transaction and the majority of them look reasonably fair.[19] DVA (or equivalently the counterparty's CVA) would definitely be included in this method.

Below we analyse the potential impact of CVA and DVA on the closeout amount. This is much less straightforward since it leads to a recursive problem: to calculate CVA and DVA, we need to define the closeout amount, which defines the EE and NEE. However, it seems that EE and NEE should themselves incorporate the CVA and DVA at the relevant time in the future. We cannot calculate CVA/DVA without first knowing EE/NEE and we cannot calculate EE/NEE without first knowing CVA/DVA!

---

[19] Market quotation in 1992 ISDA. Also included among broader options in the closeout definition of 2002 ISDA.

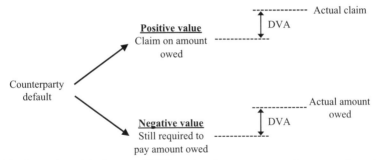

Figure 13.3 Illustration of the impact of DVA on the closeout amount when a counterparty defaults.

In Section 8.1.2 we defined exposure as $\text{Max}(\text{value}, 0)$ and negative exposure as $\text{Min}(\text{value}, 0)$, where "value" was risk-free. This assumes risk-free closeout. However, consider the situation when a counterparty defaults. The CVA disappears but the DVA component remains. Suppose the value is negative, say –$900, with a DVA component making it –$800. A risk-free closeout would require the institution to pay $900 and make an immediate loss of $100. If the DVA can be included in a closeout calculation then the institution pays only $800 and has no jump in their PnL (that would otherwise occur) (Brigo and Morini, 2010).

However, if instead the institution has a positive valuation of $1,000, of which $900 is risk-free value and $100 is DVA,[20] then a risk-free closeout amount is based on $900, leading to a certain loss of $100. A "substitution closeout" allows a claim of $1,000, which matches perfectly. We can see that including DVA in the closeout amount, as supported by standard documentation, seems to make more sense. The new situation is represented in Figure 13.3. Here, a positive value leads to a claim on the amount owed, which includes the cost of DVA that would be incurred on a replacement transaction. Note that only a recovery fraction of this DVA will be received. A negative value requires a settlement of the amount to the counterparty, which is offset by the DVA.

However, an institution also needs to consider the symmetric case which occurs when they themselves default. In this situation, the counterparty can increase their own valuation in exactly the same way. To the institution, this *increase* in valuation from *DVA* appears as a *reduction* in valuation by *CVA*. The four cases are shown in Table 13.5.

In order to account for a substitution closeout, an institution should quantify the additional gain arising when their counterparty defaults. This comes from two components, the first is an additional gain of $R_C \times \text{Max}(\text{value} - \text{DVA}, 0)$ instead of $R_C \times \text{Max}(\text{value}, 0)$ in the event of a positive future value. The second is a gain of $\text{Min}(\text{value} - \text{DVA}, 0)$ instead of $\text{Min}(\text{value}, 0)$ in the event of a negative future value. The equivalent additional losses stemming from CVA in the event of the institution's own default must also be accounted for. The calculation must be done iteratively to deal with the recursive problem described above. More details on the computation are given in Gregory and German (2012).

The results of the BCVA calculation with a substitution closeout are shown in Figure 13.4 compared with the standard risk-free closeout assumptions assumed in all

---

[20] It may appear that there should be no DVA here but it can arise, for example, due to an exposure that is currently positive but has significant possibility of being negative in the future.

Table 13.5   Comparison of payoffs using risk-free and substitution closeout (in the latter case therefore including DVA). When the counterparty defaults, the institution increases the valuation by their own DVA (which is negative by convention, hence minus DVA corresponds to an increase). When the institution themselves defaults, the counterparty can reduce the valuation by their DVA (which from the institution's point of view is their CVA)

		Counterparty defaults	*Institution defaults*
Risk-free closeout	(Positive) Exposure	$R_C \times Max\,(\text{value},0)$	$Max\,(\text{value},0)$
	Negative Exposure	$Min\,(\text{value},0)$	$R_I \times Min\,(\text{value},0)$
Substitution closeout	(Positive) Exposure	$R_C \times Max\,(\text{value} - \text{DVA},0)$	$Max\,(\text{value} - \text{CVA},0)$
	Negative Exposure	$Min\,(\text{value} - \text{DVA},0)$	$R_I \times Min\,(\text{value} - \text{CVA},0)$

previous calculations. We use the same example as discussed previously and shown in Figure 13.2. We see that the default correlation now has a much smaller impact on the BCVA. This is because the institution can benefit from their own DVA even in the event that the counterparty defaults first (and vice versa). For example, consider the large difference at a high correlation value. Here, the more risky counterparty is significantly more likely to default first and the institution's DVA benefit is likely to be large at this time since their own spread is expected to have widened. Under risk-free closeout this DVA benefit is lost, causing the overall BCVA to be large and positive. Under substitution closeout the DVA benefit can be realised even if the counterparty does default first.

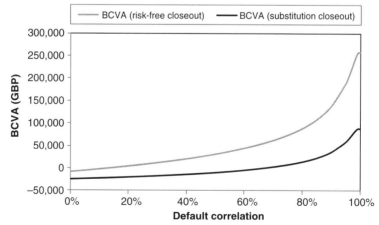

Figure 13.4 BCVA computed with standard risk-free closeout, compared with substitution closeout assumptions, as a function of default correlation.

13.5 SUMMARY

In this chapter, we have discussed DVA, which is a controversial component of counter-party credit risk arising from an institution's ability to value the potential benefits they make from defaulting. We have given the theoretical background to DVA and shown how it can be computed in a very similar manner to CVA. The strengths and weaknesses of accounting for DVA on a balance sheet have been considered. Most importantly, we have described the ways in which an institution can attempt to monetise their DVA. These are far from perfect, although it could be argued that many attempts at monetising intrinsic value in financial markets, especially with respect to derivatives, are not perfect. Finally, we have described some of the complications arising from DVA use, such as the sensitivity to default correlation between the institution and their counterparty. We have shown that the correct evaluation of CVA and DVA with substitution closeout is complex but is reasonably well approximated by the bilateral formula (equation 13.1) but without inclusion of survival probabilities of the institution and counterparty.

DVA is likely to remain a hotly debated subject for some time. Those against DVA will argue that it is unnatural to book benefits from an increased likelihood of defaulting (just as life insurance doesn't make you rich), and may point to potentially unpleasant consequences (such as an institution profiting as their credit quality worsens). Proponents of DVA will argue that it is a natural consequence of pricing counterparty credit risk, that it complements CVA and that it can be monetised, albeit with underlying uncertainty as with any financial benefit. Theoretical results and empirical evidence are unlikely to bridge the gap completely between critics and advocates of DVA. However, the hedging of DVA will be discussed in more detail in Chapter 16.

The important question will be to what extent accounting practice and other regulation continues to support the use of DVA. Whilst there is no indication of changing accounting rules, capital requirements are moving to ignore DVA,[21] which is a significant development. This will be discussed in more detail in Chapter 17.

In the next chapter we will consider funding, which is a subject distinct from, but linked to, counterparty credit risk. The relationship between DVA and funding benefits will be examined. We will look at the impact of funding on derivatives transactions and examine the subtle interplay between funding, DVA and collateral. This will lead to a consideration of the optimal trading with respect to CVA, DVA, funding costs and capital requirements.

---

[21] For example, "Application of own credit risk adjustments to derivatives", Basel Committee on Banking Supervision, http://www.bis.org/press/p111221.htm

14

Funding and Valuation

The value of a man should be seen in what he gives and not in what he is able to receive.
Albert Einstein (1879–1955)

14.1 BACKGROUND

Pricing financial instruments such as derivatives has always been relatively complex. However, certain aspects of valuation have been considered rather trivial. One of these is the use of LIBOR to discount future cash flows. In the event that these cash flows are not risk-free, CVA (or an analogous quantity) must be accounted for. The computation of CVA has been the major subject up to now in this book.

However, the traditional LIBOR discounting of risk-free cash flows, so standard for many years, requires two further assumptions for it to be valid. The first of these is that LIBOR is (or at least is a very good proxy for) the risk-free interest rate. The second is that there are no material funding considerations that need to be considered, i.e., an institution can easily borrow and lend funds at LIBOR. In the last few years both of these key assumptions have been shown to be completely incorrect. Related to these problems is the concept that the credit quality of large financial institutions is homogeneous. This is also far from true and the impact of transacting with counterparty A or counterparty B can be materially different in a number of ways.

Prior to the global financial crisis, pricing of vanilla interest rate products was understood and most attention was on exotics. Credit and liquidity were ignored, since their effects were viewed as negligible. The old-style framework for pricing financial instruments is now undergoing a revolution in order to address the shortcomings highlighted by the crisis and properly and completely incorporate credit risk, collateral and funding into a valuation framework. Generally, there are two questions to be answered:

- What is the correct way to perform "risk-free" valuation?
- How should the funding cost of an institution be accounted for in valuation?

Neither of these issues is specifically a counterparty credit risk and CVA problem. However, the quantification of CVA is inextricably linked to valuation and funding issues, especially in relation to DVA which was discussed in the last chapter.

The relevant discounting rate for transactions is now typically the so-called overnight indexed swap (OIS) rate. This greatly complicates matters for a number of reasons. Pricing a single interest rate swap (IRS) used to use the same rate (LIBOR) for both projecting the future cash flows and discounting them. Now, it is necessary to account for the difference between projected rates (LIBOR) that include credit risk and the rates for discounting which should be risk-free (OIS). This is often known as "dual curve"[1] pricing or "OIS discounting". Pricing and risk-management of a single currency IRS is now an exotic problem involving multiple curves and basis risks.

It is important to note that, even without the intervention of the global financial crisis, OIS discounting should always have been the more correct way to approach valuation. However, prior to the crisis, the difference between this and traditional LIBOR discounting was not particularly material. Figure 14.1 illustrates the clear breakdown between overnight rates and LIBOR rates for US dollars. For example, the difference between US 3-month LIBOR and Fed Funds (OIS) was only a few basis points prior to the crisis but spiked to hundreds of basis points in the aftermath of the Lehman default (September 2008) and has remained significant ever since.

OIS discounting stems from the way in which transactions, such as derivatives, are collateralised via, for example, CSAs (Chapter 5). This is not simply solved by deciding on the correct "risk-free" rate (OIS) and using the relevant additional curves in the valuation methodology. There are also problems from the currency and type of collateral that might be posted or received by an institution. Collateral arrangements are historically quite flexible, allowing the posting of cash in different currencies, high-quality debt (such as corporate or sovereign bonds) and sometimes other assets such as equities or gold. This creates a valuation problem linked to the ability to optimise the collateral that an institution posts, noting

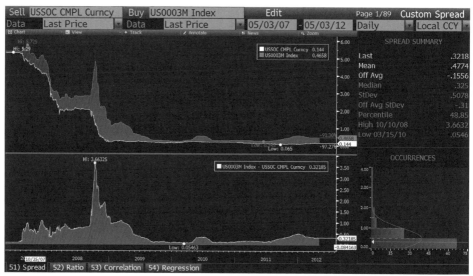

Figure 14.1 Illustration of the historical relationship in US dollars between OIS (Fed Funds) and 3-month LIBOR. The top graph shows the respective levels while the bottom line shows the difference between the two.

Source: Bloomberg (www.bloomberg.com), reproduced with permission.

---

[1] Noting that dual curve pricing is relevant for a single interest rate transaction and different currencies and cross-currency products will require many curves incorporating the various tenor basis and cross-currency basis effects. Optionality from collateral agreements will, in theory, introduce even more curves into the pricing problem.

that their counterparty holds, analogously, a similar option for the collateral that they might post. This is often referred to as the "cheapest-to-deliver collateral" and, unfortunately, has an impact on valuation.

In addition to defining the appropriate "risk-free" valuation method, there is a need to incorporate funding costs when valuing transactions and assess their relationship to DVA, as mentioned in the last chapter. This is typically the case for uncollateralised transactions although, since no collateralisation is perfect, it will also be a component for collateralised ones. This is something that was never considered in the past because unsecured funding for institutions, such as banks, was trivial and could be achieved at more or less risk-free rates. For example, the bond spreads or CDS premium referencing banks, especially large dealers, were only a few basis points prior to 2007 but since then have been more in the region of hundreds of basis points. Now transactions, especially uncollateralised ones, should be treated including the institution's own funding as a component of their valuation. The concept of FVA (funding value adjustment, also known as liquidity value adjustment or LVA) aims to do this. FVA is similar in many ways to CVA and many of the components to calculate the two are shared.

This chapter will aim to explain, in detail, the OIS discounting and FVA concepts and their relationship to CVA. We note that the paradigm shift is probably permanent and it is unlikely that we will ever return to the old days when these components could realistically be ignored. This is similar to the "discovery" of stochastic volatility as a result of the 1987 stock market crash, which has persisted ever since. However, it is likely that some of the problems will be eradicated or mitigated by structural changes in market practice, such as by shifting collateral arrangements to a "standard CSA" as discussed later.

14.2   OIS DISCOUNTING

14.2.1   The impact of CSAs

Collateral arrangements involve parties posting cash or securities to mitigate counterparty risk, usually governed under the terms of an ISDA Credit Support Annex. The typical frequency of posting is daily and the holder of collateral pays a (typically overnight) interest rate such as EONIA or Fed Funds. The use of collateral has increased steadily as the OTC derivatives market has developed. The 2010 ISDA margin survey reports that 70% of net exposure arising from OTC derivatives transactions is collateralised. A CSA converts some (but not all, as seen in Section 9.7) of the underlying counterparty risk into funding liquidity risk, as we shall describe in more detail below.

When a counterparty does sign a CSA then the type of collateral is important. As Table 14.1 illustrates, the type of collateral must have certain characteristics to provide benefits against both counterparty risk and funding. Firstly, in order to maximise the benefits of counterparty risk mitigation, there should, ideally, be no adverse correlation between the collateral and the credit quality of the counterparty which represents wrong-way risk. A sovereign entity posting their own bonds, especially if they are short-dated, provides an example of this.[2] Note that adverse correlations can also be present with cash collateral: an example

---

[2] We note that there are benefits in taking collateral in this form. Firstly, more collateral can be called for as the credit quality of the sovereign deteriorates. Secondly, even a sudden jump to default event provides the recovery value of the debt as collateral. After this, the bank would have access to a second recovery value as an unsecured creditor.

Table 14.1   Impact of collateral type on counterparty risk and funding

		Is collateral in cash or can it be rehypothecated?	
		YES	*NO*
Is collateral subject to	*YES*	Funding benefit	Limited or no benefit
adverse correlation?	*NO*	CVA and funding benefit	CVA benefit

would be receiving euros from European sovereigns or European banks. A second important consideration is that, for collateral to provide benefit against funding costs, it must be usable (since the economic ownership remains with the collateral giver). In the case of cash collateral, this is trivially the case but for non-cash collateral, rehypothecation must be allowed so that the collateral can be reused or pledged via repo.

14.2.2   OIS and LIBOR rates

Traditionally, there have been two measures of a risk-free interest rate. LIBOR rates represent unsecured lending between banks and were generally thought to be largely free of credit risk[3] due to the extremely small default probabilities of banks. Triple-A treasury bond yields represent another alternative, again being free of credit risk due to the extremely high quality rating of the sovereign issuer. LIBOR rates were generally thought to be preferable to treasury bonds due to better liquidity, the lack of problems with technical factors (such as repo specialness and tax issues) and the close links between LIBOR rates and funding costs. Hence, pre-2008 the market standard discount (or funding) curve was the 3- or 6-month LIBOR curve.[4]

The LIBOR rate is the interest charged (determined daily) for banks to borrow from other banks, usually for terms of 3 months, without the need for collateral. The LIBOR provides institutions with the means to quickly access capital at relatively low rates on an unsecured basis. However, LIBOR is risky in the sense that the lending bank loans cash to the borrowing bank with the global financial crisis illustrating this credit risk very clearly. One way in which this can be seen is via basis swap spreads, which represent the exchange of rates in the same currency. For example, the EURIBOR 3-month versus EURIBOR 6-month basis swap spread went from less than 1 bp to over 40 bps in October 2008 after the Lehman bankruptcy. This represents the additional unsecured credit risk in the 6-month tenor versus the 3-month tenor. When banks were perceived as risk-free then such differences did not exist but as soon as this myth dissolved, basis swap spreads blew up dramatically.

A better proxy for a risk-free interest rate would be the OIS, which represents an overnight rate. In Europe, the relevant OIS rate is EONIA, which is a weighted average of overnight unsecured lending rates in the European interbank market. In the US, the relevant rate is

---

[3] For example, a typical quote from a paper discussing derivative pricing prior to the crisis states, "LIBOR is not a risk-free rate, but it is close to it as the participating banks have very strong credit ratings".

[4] Depending on the currency, the most liquid point may have been either maturity. However, the differences between LIBOR at different tenors was extremely small.

Fed Funds. The daily tenor of transactions such as EONIA means they should carry a minimal amount of credit risk. Furthermore, since the aim of collateral is to remove counterparty risk in a transaction, the collateral rate naturally appears as the obvious discounting rate. OIS can be observed across a term structure via products such as OIS–LIBOR swaps. During the global financial crisis, the spreads between Euribor and EONIA OIS swaps diverged for the first time ever. The difference or "spread" between the LIBOR and OIS rates is an important measure of risk and liquidity. A higher spread is typically interpreted as indication of a decreased willingness to lend by major banks.

OIS is also the rate typically specified in a CSA since, with daily margining, collateral is only guaranteed to be held for one day (although in practice it can be held for much longer, which is an important consideration). Hence, there are two reasons why OIS seems to be the correct rate for valuation. Firstly, it is the rate with the least credit risk embedded and it also represents the underlying rate for collateralised derivatives.

Whilst the above considerations, not surprisingly, have led to a shift towards OIS discounting, we note that this is not a unique choice. OIS is simply an obvious benchmark of overnight lending and so is typically used as a convenient "fair" return on cash collateral deposited overnight. However, for a long-duration collateralised position, OIS is far from fair. Collateral posted against, for example, a large negative exposure in a cross-currency swap[5] may persist for months or even years (indeed this is one reason for reset features on such products, as discussed in Section 4.3.1). Collateral agreements may reference other rates such as LIBOR, which clearly complicates the analysis. Despite these problems, the best framework would seem to be one where all collateral arrangements specify daily collateral posting, with OIS as the rate of return paid on collateral, and all valuations are therefore linked to OIS discounting. Even then, the problem of allowing collateral in multiple currencies exists since this in turn references OIS in all of these currencies. Restricting collateral to the currency of the trade in question has obvious problems for multi-currency products (e.g., cross-currency swaps) and netting sets and creates settlement risk (Section 14.5.1).

14.2.3 CSA optionality

CSAs typically allow a range of assets to be posted, and these may include (see Chapter 5):

- cash in different currencies;
- government or corporate bonds;
- other assets such as MBS (mortgage-backed securities), equities and commodities.

This creates a collateral value adjustment (CollVA). Obviously, the nature of the underlying collateral agreement is relevant. Asymmetric terms (such as in a one-way CSA), thresholds and rating triggers can all be important.[6] Also material are any rehypothecation restrictions over the collateral received.

Not surprisingly, cash currency returns are tied to the OIS in the corresponding currency (EONIA, SONIA, Fed Funds). This means that the choice of which currency to post collateral in materially affects the return received. An institution should optimally post the collateral in the highest yielding currency and maximise their "cheapest-to-deliver option".

---

[5] Simply paying the lower interest rate in a cross-currency swap produces this long-term funding cost.
[6] Note that even in a two-way CSA, quantities such as thresholds may differ.

Comparison should be made in some base currency (typically the main funding currency) by comparing yields earned in other currencies after exchanging them back into the base currency at the relevant forward FX rates. This takes into account the cross-currency basis spread which, for example, was extremely large in October 2008. All other aspects being equal, the highest yielding collateral represents the best choice. The counterparty should be expected to follow the same optimal strategy in terms of collateral posting.

Moving on from cash collateral, more complications arise. Other collateral types will attract haircuts such that their market value exceeds the cash equivalent. However, in order to earn interest on this non-cash collateral, it must be rehypothecated in a transaction such as a repo where another haircut will be required. The repo rate must be multiplied by the factor $\frac{1-H_{\text{repo}}}{1-H_{\text{CSA}}}$, where H represents the percentage haircuts in the repo market and CSA, respectively. This rate can be compared with the cash rates discussed above[7] (although other factors may be more important, such as the balance sheet opportunity of posting non-cash collateral).

The extent of the optimisation possible depends on whether a collateral arrangement allows substitution of collateral. If substitution is allowed then there is greater value to the net collateral posted as an institution may, at any time, replace the collateral with a more optimal choice (for example, if the OIS in one currency widens with respect to another). Collateral agreements not allowing substitution (or requiring consent[8]) have less optionality but an institution can still optimise by posting the highest yielding collateral as negative exposure increases (or exposure reduces).

Assessing the value of collateral posting is very difficult, as it must account for all of the factors outlined above throughout the lifetime of the transactions in question. It is a path-dependent problem as it depends on the future evolution of exposure and the amount of collateral required (Section 9.7) in addition to the assessment of the cost or benefit derived from the actual collateral posted or received. Collateral management, which used to be mainly a back-office function, has moved on to become a front-office proactive process. Banks and large institutions have become fairly optimal in managing current collateral. However, it is a great challenge to price and monetise the future value of collateral optionality and "lock in" the value of CollVA that is effectively embedded in a CSA. Furthermore, CollVA clearly represents a zero-sum game and in many situations, the bilateral nature of CSAs limits any significant overall benefit. It seems likely that CSAs will be simplified to minimise or remove CollVA as far as is practical.

14.2.4 Central counterparties

Collateral posting through CSAs is becoming more widespread and streamlined (e.g., more cash usage) but another force will create even more funding requirements for counterparty risk. The financial crisis that developed from 2007 suggested that better ways of controlling counterparty risk needed to be found. Policymakers identified the widespread adoption of central clearing of OTC derivatives as one means of achieving this. Legislation such as the Dodd–Frank Wall Street Reform (passed by the US Congress in 2010) and the new European Market Infrastructure Regulation (EMIR) mandate that certain OTC derivatives transactions be centrally cleared through CCPs.

---

[7] In theory, if this presented an opportunity then the counterparty could repo the collateral and post cash. However, not all parties may have the same access to the repo market.
[8] Since the counterparty's optimal strategy would be not to give consent.

Central counterparties create collateral requirements similar to symmetric CSAs but require more liquid collateral and initial margin. The initial margin therefore represents an additional consideration on top of those described above. It is important to note that CCPs have the ability to increase initial margin requirements, for example in response to a period of higher market volatility, as discussed in Chapter 7.

Not surprisingly, CCPs have been switching to OIS discounting for valuations. In order to mitigate some of the problems with substitutions and cheapest-to-deliver collateral, the collateral requirements are much simpler than in a standard CSA. One approach (for example, used by LCH.Clearnet) is to require collateral to be posted in the currency of the underlying transaction. Cross-currency products are currently not cleared, partly due to the obvious problems this would create. This currency-mixing problem is also one of the reasons why cross-product netting on margins is not recognised. Even then, some practical issues exist, such as if there is no liquid reference for OIS in a currency.

It is also important to note that even non-CCP trades may have large funding requirements. For example, according to the Dodd–Frank act, even for non-cleared OTC derivatives a "swap dealer" must collect initial and variation margin at levels that are likely to be comparable with those of centrally cleared trades.

14.2.5 Methodology

OIS discounting is generally considered the correct way to value derivatives under the following assumptions (e.g., see Piterbarg, 2010):

- The transaction is covered by a symmetric (two-way) CSA with zero threshold, minimum transfer amount and rounding.
- Collateral is in cash only with the relevant OIS rate paid on collateral posted.
- Collateral is settled continuously.[9]

Whilst these assumptions are somewhat stylised in reality (especially continuous settlement of collateral), they are a reasonable basis for the large number of transactions that occur in the interbank market or through CCPs. Additional components such as CVA, DVA, FVA and CollVA can then be added on to this base case as required.

Traditional interest rate curve building typically follows the following steps:

- Select a set of liquid IR securities (cash deposits, futures and swaps).
- Make decisions on overlapping, interpolation etc.
- Fit a single curve via a "bootstrap" procedure, which solves sequentially to fit market prices, or a more complex algorithm.

OIS discounting complicates this process. LIBOR–OIS swaps are generally more liquid than OIS swaps and so OIS and basis curves[10] have to be built simultaneously from these market prices together with standard LIBOR-based swaps. In this calibration, discounting is assumed based on OIS whilst cash flows are projected in the relevant rate (OIS or LIBOR).

---

[9] It also needs to be assumed that the underlying exposure changes continuously and that, in the event of default transactions can be closed out instantaneously.
[10] This defines the basis between LIBOR and OIS.

This "dual curve" problem means that standard simpler bootstrap methods are not applicable. More details on these issues can be found in, for example, Morini and Prampolini (2010), Kenyon (2010) and Mercurio (2010).

Whilst OIS discounting is emerging as a standard, it has not yet been fully implemented across all banks and other financial institutions. This would mean that even perfectly collateralised trades would need to have some funding adjustment (for example, taken as reserves) due to the LIBOR–OIS spreads.

14.3 FUNDING VALUE ADJUSTMENT

14.3.1 The need for FVA

Despite the increased use of collateral, a significant portion of OTC derivatives remain uncollateralised. This arises mainly due to the nature of the counterparties involved, such as corporates and sovereigns, without the liquidity and operational capacity to adhere to daily collateral calls. In such cases, an institution must consider the full impact of counterparty risk and funding of the transactions in question.

A counterparty not adhering to the posting of collateral (non-CSA counterparty) will create a funding requirement for an institution trading with them. This relates to the need for the institution to offset or hedge with other transactions under CSAs (this is explained in more detail below). For unilateral exposures, such as loans, this is a cost for the institution making the loan. For a one-way CSA, this is a cost for the collateral posting institution. For bilateral exposures (such as swaps) under two-way CSAs this can be both a cost and a benefit as the transaction(s) may have both positive and negative value. Transactions with large CVA (and DVA) components may have very significant funding components also. FVA, also known as LVA, is the metric used to quantify this. FVA accounts for funding costs and benefits above the relevant index not already accounted for through (OIS) valuation or other components such as DVA.

In addition, the hedging above is more complex with the relevant ratio not being one-to-one. The OIS curve might be at LIBOR – 30 bps with uncollateralised funding around LIBOR + 200 bps. To properly determine the relevant hedge ratio for uncollateralised to collateralised trades requires a full quantification of the funding components. To properly hedge the difference requires LIBOR–OIS basis swaps for which the underlying market is still quite illiquid (although developing).

14.3.2 The source of funding costs

Since most banks aim to run mainly flat (hedged) books (e.g., for OTC derivatives), funding costs arise from the nature of hedging: a non-CSA trade being hedged via a trade (or trades) done under a CSA arrangement (or on an exchange) which is illustrated in Figure 14.2. This should be interpreted as comparing the uncollateralised trade with a trade done under a perfect (according to the terms at the start of Section 14.2.5) collateral arrangement (where OIS funding is therefore valid). The hedge trade may not actually exist but is relevant for comparison since it represents the case of zero funding costs.

The above analogy implies that funding costs will be driven by the exposure on the uncollateralised trade (since this is the amount posted in collateral due to the negative exposure on the collateralised trade). In the case of a negative exposure, there will be a funding benefit

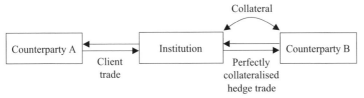

Figure 14.2 Illustration of the way in which funding becomes important. A bank trades with counterparty A with no collateral arrangement but typically hedges with a collateralised (CSA) trade(s). Note that the hedge is for reference purposes and need not be the real hedge.

(since an institution will receive collateral from the CSA hedge, which they will not be required to post in the non-CSA trade). A simpler way to think of this funding cost (benefit) is that an institution would receive (pay) the exposure in cash if a transaction was terminated and hence the funding requirement is in order to maintain the transaction. Another way to think of funding cost is that they relate to cash paid or received in transactions (e.g., via upfront premiums or differentials in swap cashflows. The key point is that, however it is defined, exposure drives a funding cost, just as it drives CVA. By symmetry, negative exposure drives a funding benefit analogous (or perhaps identical) to DVA.

Given the definition of (negative) exposure as a funding cost (benefit), it is important to consider the impact of such funding in the pricing of a transaction such as derivatives. We first illustrate this in a simple example and then give a more quantitative treatment. Consider Figure 14.3, which shows the cash flows and associated funding considerations for a payer interest rate swap assuming an upwards-sloping yield curve (this is similar to the discussion on exposure in Section 8.3.3). In the early stages of the swap, the fixed cash flows being paid are expected (risk-neutrally) to be greater than the floating ones received. This creates a positive exposure which needs to be funded. The exposure increases cumulatively for the

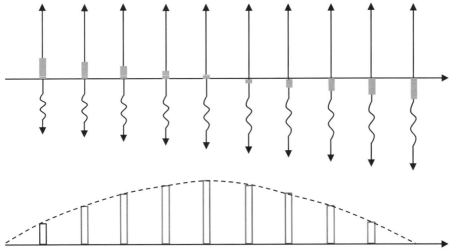

Figure 14.3 (Top) Illustration of the funding needs on a payer interest rate swap which arise due to the future cash flow differential. The grey bars show the net projected funding cost (based on risk-neutral valuation). (Bottom) The cumulative effect over time of the cash flow differential and resulting funding profile.

first five[11] payment dates and then reduces as the projected floating payments start to exceed the fixed ones. This creates an overall funding cost based on the expected future value of the swap. The corresponding receiver swap would have precisely the opposite profile, creating a symmetric funding benefit.

The above example suggests a rather simple treatment of the funding cost (or benefit), which is to discount cash flows at the relevant funding rate. We will refer to this approach as the "discount curve method". This is much simpler than CVA and DVA quantification for reasons discussed in Section 12.1.1 and also in the following section. The discount curve method is a simple way to incorporate funding and also equivalent to discounting cash flows at the institution's funding spread (rather than OIS) in order to account for FVA. Hence, it potentially allows funding to be valued within a transaction without even the need to resort to a specific FVA term.

The discount curve method is clearly a simple way to take funding into account but there are two obvious drawbacks with this approach. Firstly, it implicitly assumes a symmetry between funding costs and funding benefits. Secondly, it does not allow the treatment of situations such as thresholds, or one-way CSAs. These aspects will be considered in more detail below.

14.3.3 DVA formula

Although it is quantifying something quite different, FVA is related to CVA and DVA and will have a rather similar formula. In a sense, FVA will complete the full picture of all possible outcomes. CVA accounts for the situation in which a counterparty defaults but an institution survives which can be written[12] as $PD_C(1 - PD_I)$, as seen from equation (13.2) in the last chapter. DVA accounts for the reverse situation where the institution defaults but their counterparty does not, given probabilistically by $PD_I(1 - PD_C)$. Taking these probabilities away from unity and ignoring simultaneous defaults[13] gives $(1 - PD_C)(1 - PD_I)$, which is the event where neither party defaults. This is the scenario in which funding costs (and benefits) must be considered. Hence, FVA covers the final missing scenario from the CVA/DVA framework, as illustrated in Figure 14.4.

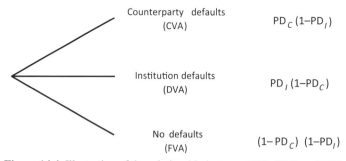

Counterparty defaults
(CVA) $PD_C(1–PD_I)$

Institution defaults
(DVA) $PD_I(1–PD_C)$

No defaults
(FVA) $(1– PD_C)(1–PD_I)$

Figure 14.4 Illustration of the relationship between CVA, DVA and FVA.

---

[11] Note that the reduction in this case occurs exactly halfway through the profile. This is for illustration purposes only and the true profile depends on the precise shape of the yield curve.
[12] This assumes the default of the institution and counterparty are independent, as noted previously. This is for ease of exposition only. It was also noted in the last chapter (section 13.4.2) that the survival probabilities in these components should probably be ignored to best approximate the impact of "substitution closeout". This does not invalidate the intuition here.
[13] We can simply assume a small time interval such that this probability is negligible.

The FVA formula is shown below and should be compared with the BCVA formulas given in equation (13.1) of the previous chapter. There are two terms which represent a funding cost and funding benefit, respectively. The funding benefit and DVA can be shown to be identical except for a basis difference that will be discussed below. More mathematical detail is given in Appendix 14A.

$$\text{FVA} = \sum_{j=1}^{n} \underbrace{\text{EE}(t_j)}_{\substack{\text{Discounted} \\ \text{expected} \\ \text{exposure}}} \underbrace{\left[1 - \text{PD}_C(0, t_{j-1})\right]\left[1 - \text{PD}_I(0, t_{j-1})\right]}_{\substack{\text{Probability neither institution nor} \\ \text{counterparty has yet defaulted}}} \underbrace{\text{FS}(t_{j-1}, t_j)}_{\substack{\text{Funding spread} \\ \text{(for borrowing)}}} \underbrace{(t_{j-1} - t_j)}_{\text{Interval}}$$

$$+ \sum_{j=1}^{n} \underbrace{\text{NEE}(t_j)}_{\substack{\text{Discounted} \\ \text{expected negative} \\ \text{exposure}}} \left[1 - \text{PD}_C(0, t_{j-1})\right]\left[1 - \text{PD}_I(0, t_{j-1})\right] \underbrace{\text{FS}(t_{j-1}, t_j)}_{\substack{\text{Funding spread} \\ \text{(for lending)}}} (t_{j-1} - t_j) \qquad (14.1)$$

We will refer to the first term in the above formula as FCA (funding cost adjustment) and the second as FBA (funding benefit adjustment). There are therefore two major distinctions between the FVA formula and the similar BCVA one (equation 12.2):

- The FVA references an institution's own spread in both terms, since they relate to borrowing and lending rates. In the BCVA formula, the counterparty's spread is referenced in the first term (CVA) and the institution's spread in the second (DVA).
- The spread in question is the funding spread, which is not the same as the CDS spread commonly used to calculate BCVA. See Section 10.2.4 for more discussion on this difference. Based on the earlier discussion that OIS is the most relevant risk-free rate, this spread reflects the funding cost in excess of the relevant OIS.

Similarly to equation (13.2) and assuming a flat funding spread curve, we can also have the following simple approximation for FVA, expressed as a spread:

$$\text{FVA} \approx \text{funding spread}_B \times \text{EPE} + \text{funding spread}_L \times \text{ENE}. \qquad (14.2)$$

If the funding spread is symmetric, i.e., the spreads for borrowing and lending are the same, then the equation depends only on the expected future value (EFV) (see Section 8.2.1) since $\text{EE} + \text{NEE} = \text{EFV}$.[14] This gives a simple approximation of $\text{FVA} \approx \text{funding spread} \times$ average EFV and the FVA is simply the time-averaged expected future value (either positive or negative) multiplied by the funding spread. This is then equivalent to the so-called "discount curve method", discussed in the previous section, where the funding cost or benefit is the institution's funding spread multiplied by the expected future value (see also Figure 14.3). If the latter value is positive overall then there is a cost, whilst a gain results from it being negative.

We can see that the discount curve approach therefore depends critically on the funding rate being the same for both positive and negative cash flows.[15] The quantification of funding

---

[14] See footnote 16.

[15] Furthermore, we note that the discount curve method is relevant only for fully uncollateralised transactions (leading to the use of the basic EPE and ENE) and cannot allow a treatment of partially collateralised cases (such as thresholds and one-way CSAs). Such cases will be discussed in Section 14.3.7.

then only involves the expected future value (EFV), which is insensitive to volatility, rather than the expected exposure (and expected negative exposure), which depend on volatility.[16] However, if the funding spreads for borrowing and lending are considered unequal then the FVA will be sensitive to volatility via the EE and NEE. The assumptions around the funding rates will be discussed in more detail in the next section.

14.3.4   Defining the funding rate

The heart of FVA is the relevant funding rate of an institution and we must therefore consider the appropriate funding rate to use. The different funding rates to consider are shown in Figure 14.5, which also shows the impact of the CDS–bond basis. Derivatives, due to their dynamic nature and the funding approach of banks, are not *term funded*.[17] The funding is generally short-term, although still significantly more expensive than OIS which essentially represents risk-free funding. Furthermore, regulation is pushing banks to rely less on short-term funding. Overall, this means that for an institution to define their appropriate funding curve represents a very subtle and difficult problem. Note also the distinction between bond spreads (that define term funding costs) and CDS spreads (that define CVA and DVA).

On the one hand, an institution may consider a symmetry between lending and borrowing rates (this is the traditional way in which the treasury function in a bank has functioned). However, some institutions may consider that funding rates may be *asymmetric*, i.e., the rate at which an institution is able to borrow unsecured funds is not equal to the rate it is able to achieve when lending. If an institution considers that their funding can be managed by issuing and buying back bonds then the symmetric assumption may be reasonable (with some bid-offer assumption potentially relevant). However, an alternative assumption could be that excess cash (funding benefit) can only provide a risk-free return (OIS) without taking on

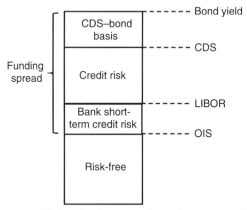

Figure 14.5 Illustration of the differing funding rates depending on type of instrument and maturity together with the CDS–bond basis (note that a negative basis is illustrated based on the convention in Section 10.2.4, although this does not have to be the case in practice). The unsecured funding spread is defined with respect to the OIS rate.

---

[16] Mathematically this occurs because it is essentially possible under funding cost symmetry to combine the expected exposure and negative expected exposure terms via $max(V,0) + min(V,0) = V$.

[17] Meaning, for example, that a 5-year swap is not funded via a 5-year bond issue.

additional credit risk. This would cause the funding benefit term to disappear and lead only to a funding cost.[18]

14.3.5 Examples

We will now illustrate funding costs and benefits (assuming equal funding spreads), taking three examples previously discussed in terms of their exposure and CVA in Section 12.2.2. The examples are the payer interest rate swap (Payer IRS GBP 5Y), using both real-world and risk-neutral parameters, and the cross-currency swap (CCS GBP USD 5Y) with risk-neutral parameters only. The funding spread of the institution is assumed to be 250 bps and the CDS spread and recovery of the institution and their counterparty are assumed to be 250 bps and 40%, respectively (these are relevant for calculating the survival probabilities in equation (14.1)). This assumes zero basis between the funding spread and CDS spread. The results are shown in Table 14.2.

Spreadsheet 14.1 Example FVA calculation.

We consider, first, the interest rate swap. As noted before (Section 12.2.2), this has a negative EFV (EE < NEE) using real-world parameters but a positive EFV (EE > NEE) using risk-neutral parameters. For this reason, the real-world FVA is negative (by convention an overall benefit) whilst the risk-neutral one is positive. It is important to note at this point that funding should not necessarily be considered under the risk-neutral measure since funding costs are generally unhedgeable. Indeed, a treasury valuing the funding for a certain stream of cash flows may use various projections, not based purely on risk-neutral assumptions (as suggested by Figure 14.3). This distinct difference is important to note, although from now

---

Table 14.2 FVA calculations for the three examples using equation (14.1) and the approximation in equation (14.2). The funding spread is assumed to be symmetric at 250 bps and the CDS spreads and associated recoveries of the institution and their counterparty are assumed to be 250 bps and 40%, respectively. The notional amount of the interest rate swaps is 100m whilst the cross-currency swap is 25m

	IRS (RW)	IRS (RN)	CCS (RN)
FCA	46,244	74,489	283,445
FBA	−86,450	−40,528	−174,330
Overall FVA	−40,206	33,960	109,115
Spread (bps)	**−1.10**	**0.93**	**2.99**
EPE	0.47%	0.77%	3.36%
ENE	−0.90%	−0.41%	−2.03%
Approx. spread (bps)	**−1.06**	**0.90**	**3.33**

---

[18] As shown by Burgard and Kjaer (2012), being able to use the transaction (e.g., an OTC derivative) as collateral could also make the funding cost term disappear. However, this is clearly problematic.

on we assume, like CVA, that FVA will be calculated using risk-neutral parameters. Hence, we see that an institution may reduce the fixed rate by around 0.93 bps, when paying fixed in this IRS, to account for the FVA. Due to the symmetry of equation (14.1), the opposite swap will have an equal and opposite FVA (again, assuming symmetry of funding spreads).

The above observations tend to be borne out by market practice. Institutions tend to charge clients for paying fixed and higher quality institutions (with lower funding rates) are able to offer a better rate. A client paying fixed (uncollateralised) may benefit from trading with an institution with higher cost of funding through effectively lending them money as the institution may see the receiver swap as having a funding benefit overall.

Another important point when assessing funding costs, especially since institutions such as banks do not *term fund*, is the change in future funding costs. If an institution believed that their funding costs would drop substantially in the future then they might consider their funding costs lower. This is clearly a dangerous practice but since funding costs do not have to be marked-to-market (like CVA), it is not completely impossible. There is no way for an institution to uniquely derive their future funding costs, or hedge them. For this to be possible, they would have to be able to trade *forward* on their own funding spread.

14.3.6   FVA and DVA

In the discussion on monetising DVA (Section 13.3.5), it was mentioned that treating it as a funding benefit was one argument used to justify using DVA. Figure 14.6 depicts a parallel between DVA and the funding benefit (FBA). The only material difference is the CDS–bond basis shown in Figure 14.5, since DVA is calculated with the CDS spread whilst the funding benefit is calculated with the relevant funding spread. Aside from this basis difference, the DVA and FBA components are theoretically identical.

This illustrates that treating DVA naïvely as a funding benefit is dangerous as it implies a double counting. The precise theoretical analysis of this problem is complex (e.g., see Burgard and Kjaer, 2012), and depends on the precise assumptions made. However, the double counting of FBA and DVA is a practical interpretation of theoretical studies, as noted by previous authors (e.g., Tang and Williams, 2010). Whilst Figure 14.6 suggests a symmetry that may permit both DVA and FBA, they do not appear together in theoretical calculations. In Burgard and Kjaer (2012), the reason for this is the asymmetry assumptions regarding unsecured borrowing and lending. For example, unsecured lending may be assumed to yield only the risk-free rate,[19] whilst borrowing will require the unsecured term funding rate. An alternative explanation of double counting is that an institution cannot sell CDS protection on themselves.

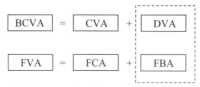

Figure 14.6 Illustration of the link between funding and DVA. Funding benefits are denoted by FBA (funding benefit adjustment) and costs by FCA (funding cost adjustment).

---

[19] Of course, unsecured lending can yield more than the risk-free (or OIS) rate but this then involves taking additional credit risk.

If an institution believes that they can monetise their own default,[20] then it is possible to consider all four terms in Figure 14.6. However, if this is viewed as problematic (see Section 13.3.4), then to avoid double counting of a funding benefit there are two obvious potential frameworks for treating counterparty risk and funding consistently. These are:

- *Symmetric funding and CVA (CVA + FCA + FBA).* This would ignore DVA benefit on the basis that monetisation of DVA (as purely a self-default component) is problematic (Section 13.2.2).
- *Asymmetric funding and BCVA (CVA + DVA + FCA).* This includes DVA as a funding benefit and considers a funding cost only.

Theoretically, neither of the above choices is right or wrong since they can both be derived depending on the assumptions regarding the funding instruments an institution has at their disposal.[21]

Accounting regulations treat both CVA and DVA in a mark-to-market framework (Section 13.1.2), whilst funding costs are considered differently under accrual accounting. This suggests that the asymmetric funding and BCVA approach is relevant and this is indeed the treatment that tends to be favoured by banks as it allows them to capture some of the beneficial features of DVA, such as symmetry of prices (Section 13.1.2). However, such an approach may seem unnatural since funding benefits are accounted for in PnL without the offsetting costs (FCA). In a widening spread environment, an institution may be viewed as offsetting their CVA losses via funding benefits without the associated funding costs (which remain under accrual accounting).

For those arguing that FBA is being arbitrarily renamed DVA in the above, the symmetric funding and CVA framework may seem more natural. In such an approach, a "funding desk" (the treasury department of a bank, for example) considers both funding costs and benefits. Two perfectly hedged trades with the same collateral terms (but potentially different counterparties) have a net zero funding cost as their benefits and costs cancel perfectly.[22] In this approach, a "CVA desk" must consider CVA but ignore DVA. This approach is also in line with the Basel III rules for capital requirement,[23] which do not allow DVA (see Section 17.4.9), but is inconsistent with accounting practices.

There are other important differences between DVA and FBA. DVA and funding benefits at the counterparty level may not be the same if netting is imperfect (e.g., multiple netting agreements). Here, funding benefits can offset across netting sets whereas DVA benefits cannot. This is an important test for any theoretical framework around BCVA and funding.

Let us now look at an example of funding costs together with CVA and DVA. We consider the four trade portfolios, previously characterised in terms of exposure (Section 9.5.1), CVA (Section 12.4) and DVA (Section 13.1.3). We assume, as before, that the CDS spread of the institution and their counterparty are 250 bps and 500 bps, respectively. The funding spread of the institution is assumed symmetric at 300 bps, creating a negative basis of 50 bps. Recovery rates are set at 40%. The BCVA and FVA terms for this portfolio are given in Table 14.3.

---

[20] Which cannot be done via buying back their own bonds since this is the obvious strategy for monetising FBA.

[21] For example, in Burgard and Kjaer (2012), the first choice arises when a zero-coupon bond is a sole funding instrument whilst the second is a consequence of assuming a single bond with recovery is freely tradable.

[22] Aside from the time delay in receiving collateral, discussed in Section 14.3.7.

[23] Note that these rules apply to capital only and hence an institution cannot be required under Basel III to ignore DVA from their accounting PnL.

Table 14.3   BCVA and FVA components for the four-trade portfolio (all figures in GBP)

BCVA		FVA	
CVA	237,077	FCA	118,268
DVA	−245,868	FBA	−294,200
BCVA (total)	−8,791	FVA (total)	−175,932

In this case, both BCVA and FVA give rise to benefits because in this portfolio the NEE dominates the EE. In the case of BCVA the benefit is rather small since the counterparty spread (driving CVA) is double that of the institution (driving DVA). However, in the case of FVA, the large NEE leads to a significant funding benefit.

14.3.7   The impact of collateral

The ability to take collateral should reduce FVA, as illustrated in Figure 14.7, which considers a trade and its associated perfectly collateralised hedge (i.e., OIS discounted) executed with a different counterparty. When the trade moves in the institution's favour they will receive collateral that can be posted on the hedge and vice versa.

In practice, a perfect cancellation of collateral in the above example will not occur for the following reasons:[24]

- *Collateral terms.* Non-zero thresholds, minimum transfer amounts and rounding will mean that collateral balances do not match.
- *Time delay.* An institution may have to release collateral before receiving the equivalent amount corresponding to the hedge trade. Whilst this delay[25] should be small (no more than a few business days), it does leave residual funding liquidity risk even in the ideal situation.

For the above reasons, FVA should also be quantified in a collateralised trade. The most significant effect here is that of a threshold. A positive exposure creates a funding cost only up to the threshold amount, after which collateral would be taken and the exposure above

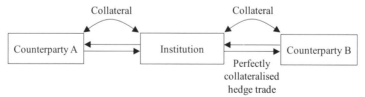

Figure 14.7 Illustration of funding in the presence of collateral agreements. An institution does a collateralised trade which is hedged with a different counterparty under a perfect CSA. The collateral posted between the trade and hedge will partially cancel.

---

[24] Note that another factor here is that different currency, non-cash collateral or securities cannot be posted in the hedge trade. This represents optionality in the CSA (Section 14.2.3) previously described as CollVA rather than an FVA component.
[25] Note that this time delay is not the same as the margin period of risk (Section 8.5.2), which is conditional on counterparty default and is therefore longer.

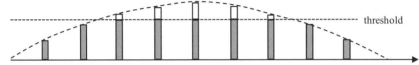

Figure 14.8 Illustration of the funding cost for a partially collateralised trade. In such a case, the exposure must be funded up to the threshold (and a funding benefit is achieved up to the opposite threshold). Due to the uncertainty of the exposure, this must be accounted for via the EE and NEE terms and the discount curve method is not applicable.

the threshold would be essentially capped, reducing the FCA term. This is illustrated in Figure 14.8. Correspondingly, the negative exposure defining the funding benefit would also be capped (at a potentially different threshold), reducing the FBA term. Whilst these calculations may appear complex, they are precisely the same as needed for quantifying exposure in the presence of collateral (Section 9.7). Hence, the discount curve method cannot be applied but a CVA framework can readily be used to calculate FVA in such cases.

Note that funding costs theoretically occur in the zero-threshold, two-way CSA case since OIS discounting alone requires continuous collateral posting (Section 14.2.5), whereas in reality there will be some delay (for example, see the effect in Figure 9.21 and the related discussion).[26] However, market practice is generally to ignore such impacts,[27] similarly to ignoring CVA for well-collateralised counterparties.

The overall funding cost of a non-collateralised trade hedged via a partially collateralised trade will be correctly represented via the sum of the relevant FVAs. For example, suppose an uncollateralised receiver swap has an overall funding benefit. By symmetry, the payer hedge will have an equal and opposite funding cost. However, this cost will be smaller due to the ability to receive collateral above the threshold. Hence, the combination of the two trades has an overall funding benefit. This can be seen as the benefit from receiving collateral above the threshold on the hedge but not posting collateral on the uncollateralised trade minus the cost from posting on the hedge and not receiving.

It may also be relevant to make use of incremental and marginal exposure calculations (Section 9.6) in order to allocate funding at trade level in cases such as threshold collateral arrangements, where trade-level funding costs cannot be calculated.

14.4   OPTIMISATION OF CVA, DVA AND FUNDING COSTS

Collateral agreements reduce CVA, although the residual risk is hard to quantify. Furthermore DVA and FVA complicate the understanding of the overall benefit of a CSA. Therefore, an interesting question is to ask now is how an institution might optimise BCVA and FVA in their trading activities. This will require a look at the impact of collateral agreements on the BCVA and FVA components. We will then consider the impact of central clearing. Finally, we will discuss the overall optimisation of BCVA, FVA and regulatory capital.

14.4.1   The spectrum of trading with BCVA and FVA

Let us consider, in more depth, the impact of collateral on transactions such as derivatives. Generally, there are three broad situations to consider:

---

[26] And also due to aspects such as non-zero minimum transfer amounts.
[27] There could be a further argument that the symmetry of exposure and negative exposure will lead to a cancellation of FCA and FBA. However, this is not necessarily the case (due to drifts and asymmetric distributions), as can be seen in Figure 13.1.

- *Uncollateralised trades.* The advantage of uncollateralised trades is that the main issue is CVA (and the associated regulatory capital charges), which an institution can attempt to quantify and manage. This makes it most straightforward to identify the cost of trading at inception and incorporate this into prices. However, CVA hedging is far from trivial as, under Basel III, capital relief is not achieved on market risk hedges (Section 17.4.5) and only a limited relief[28] is given for credit index hedging (a single-name CDS market, which would allow close to 100% capital relief, does not exist for most counterparties). Furthermore, the difficult topic of DVA must be also considered.
- *CSA trades.* A CSA has the effect of reducing CVA but the extent of this reduction is difficult to quantify and is often only moderate (Section 12.5.1). Furthermore, CSAs create problems with funding liquidity risk, which is more opaque and harder to quantify than counterparty risk. Costs are then harder to define at inception, but may have a positive effect in that such opaque risks are, by their nature, less well capitalised and regulatory capital is therefore lower. The cost (benefit) of posting (receiving) collateral is the difference between the funding rate of that collateral and the return paid under the CSA (normally the overnight indexed swap rate). Another important aspect to look at is the "cheapest-to-deliver" collateral via a CollVA adjustment. Multi-currency CSAs give optionality over collateral posting and, with the differences between the major rates being significant, choosing the best collateral is important.[29]
- *Centrally cleared trades.* In addition to the considerations mentioned above for CSA trades, CCP trades must be assessed based on reduced capital against significant initial margin requirements. CCPs also have different collateral practices, for example requiring variation margin to be posted in cash of the currency of the underlying transaction (with the relevant overnight indexed swap rate used to discount the trade). This implies a change in MtM for a book of OTC trades migrated to a CCP because the potential cheapest-to-deliver collateral terms from the CSA in question are essentially given up. For clearing members acting as intermediaries for non-clearing members and essentially providing margin lending (collateral facility), the long-term cost of this must be considered.

Let us take a closer look at the significant differences to be considered between the main ways in which collateral may be taken, namely overcollateralised (e.g., CCP[30]), collateralised (potentially with some threshold) and no collateral in Figure 14.9. CVA will be most significant when there is no CSA and least significant under central clearing (assuming a very low default probability of the CCP). DVA, being the opposite of CVA, shows the reverse trend (most beneficial with no CSA and least beneficial under central clearing due to the initial margin required). Funding is least problematic with no CSA and becomes increasingly intensive under a CSA[31] (collateralisation) and central clearing (overcollateralisation). Finally, capital charges will be highest for uncollateralised trades whilst benefit

---

[28] As explained in Section 17.4.5, a 50% relief is obtained for index hedges although this can be greater if a high enough correlation is observed between this and the mapped single-name spread.

[29] Since a rational counterparty will always deliver the cheapest collateral then the implicit assumption that one's counterparty will act in the same way is made. This also applies to the substitution of collateral, where this is possible.

[30] We note that bilaterally cleared trades may also be overcollateralised and indeed this may be more common in future.

[31] We assume that CSA trades are more funding-intensive since a completely uncollateralised hedged set of transactions would require no funding whereas a fully collateralised book would require funding even if perfectly hedged (due to the mismatch between receiving and posting collateral). Whilst perfectly collateralised transactions should be valued with OIS discounting and no additional funding considerations, such perfect transactions do not exist in practice due to the delay in receipt of collateral and other aspects such as non-zero thresholds.

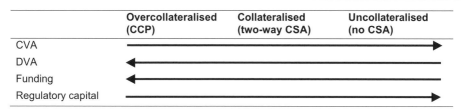

	Overcollateralised (CCP)	Collateralised (two-way CSA)	Uncollateralised (no CSA)
CVA	————————————————————————→		
DVA	←————————————————————————		
Funding	←————————————————————————		
Regulatory capital	————————————————————————→		

Figure 14.9 Illustration of the impact of various factors on different OTC derivative trading arrangements. The arrows denote the relative increasing cost (or benefit reduction) of each factor. For example, CVA is largest in the "no CSA" case and smallest under central clearing.

can be achieved for CSA trades and the requirements are probably smallest for centrally cleared trades.

Uncollateralised trades have the best funding and DVA situation but are the most expensive in terms of CVA and regulatory capital charges.[32] Centrally cleared transactions have the smallest CVA and regulatory capital charges, but costly funding and no benefit from DVA. CSA trades are intermediate in all senses. It is therefore not clear what is the most beneficial trading arrangement. The question to ask is how the combined BCVA and FVA change over the above spectrum and, in general, in which way the most favourable combination of counterparty and funding valuation is achieved. To do this, we first need to look at the impact of central clearing on the BCVA and FVA quantities. We will do this under the assumption of fixed credit quality for the counterparty. This is somewhat stylised, since CCP default probabilities may be considered lower than other typical counterparties, and so we will also show the case assuming CCPs are risk-free.

14.4.2 The impact of CSAs

We begin by considering the impact of collateral on the BCVA and FVA for the four-trade portfolio (see Section 9.5.1). The four terms are shown in Figure 14.10 as a function of the threshold, assuming a two-way CSA. As expected the impact of a decreasing threshold (for

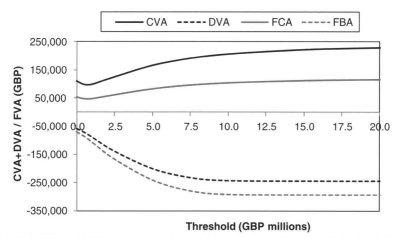

Figure 14.10 BCVA and FVA terms for the four-trade portfolio as a function of the threshold in a two-way CSA.

---

[32] Although we note that capital charges for some CCPs may not necessarily be smaller than for non-CCP trades. This will be discussed in Chapter 17.

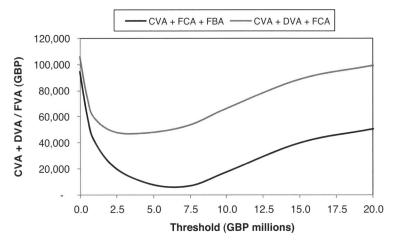

Figure 14.11 Total counterparty risk and funding costs for the four-trade portfolio as a function of the threshold in a two-way CSA for different choices.

both parties) is to reduce all terms (except some small increase close to zero already discussed in Section 12.5.2). Note also that the DVA is greater than the funding benefit mainly due to the basis (funding spread over CDS spread) of 50 bps assumed. At the maximum threshold shown, the values are close to the non-CSA results shown in Table 14.2.

Now we consider the total impact of BCVA and FVA under the two choices described in Section 14.3.6, as shown in Figure 14.11. The cases of symmetric funding and CVA (CVA + FCA + FBA) and asymmetric funding and BCVA (CVA + DVA + FCA) show similar behaviour, mainly differing due to the basis assumption of 50 bps. In both these cases, a moderate positive threshold represents the optimal choice for the institution as it minimises the combined counterparty risk and funding components. An interesting conclusion here is that, rather than focusing solely on CVA minimisation (zero threshold) or funding benefit maximisation (infinitive threshold), the best strategy appears to be a reasonable mitigation of CVA without the creation of excessive funding costs.

14.4.3 Central clearing

The impact of collateral when a transaction is centrally cleared is not as beneficial, due to the need to post initial margin. However, since CCPs are supposed to be of excellent credit quality (or too big to fail), central clearing may be viewed by many as providing the maximum reduction of CVA. Indeed, it is unlikely that the CVA to a central counterparty will even be quantified.[33]

We need to consider the impact of central clearing on the above results. The most important aspect of clearing will be the requirement to post independent amounts (initial margins). As noted previously, we can look at an independent amount as a negative threshold (assuming at this point the CSA is one way, i.e., only the institution posts initial margin). Doing this for the above analysis gives the BCVA and FVA components in Figure 14.12. When the institution posts an independent amount, the DVA and funding benefit disappear quickly as there is little chance of them ever being in debt (negative exposure). On the other hand, the CVA and funding costs increase rapidly at this point.

---

[33] As mentioned earlier, under Basel III, CVA VAR (Section 17.4.5) does not need to include central counterparties.

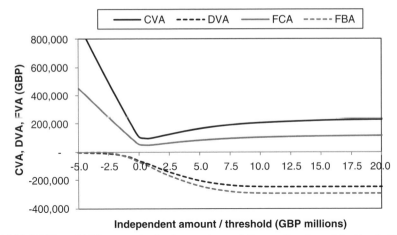

Figure 14.12 BCVA and FVA terms for the four-trade portfolio as a function of the threshold in a two-way CSA.

Looking at the combined BCVA and FVA impact (Figure 14.13) shows that the impact of an independent amount is to cause a significant increase in overall costs. This is even the case if we ignore the CVA component for independent amounts (negative values), this assumption being equivalent to assuming that such trades are with risk-free CCPs. As noted before, the optimum situation for the portfolio in question is a CSA with a small positive threshold. Large positive thresholds are not favoured (due to CVA and funding costs), nor are large negative thresholds or independent amounts as required by central clearing (due to large funding costs even assuming CCPs do not give rise to any CVA). We can note that the local minimum shown for a small negative threshold corresponds to a relatively ideal situation of central clearing with low funding costs, but the assumption that the CCP is risk-free. This is not achievable without the CCP having support from the taxpayer.

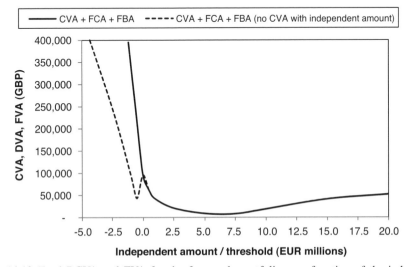

Figure 14.13 Total BCVA and FVA for the four-trade portfolio as a function of the independent amount (negative values) and threshold in a two-way CSA (positive values).

14.4.4 Optimisation and impact of regulatory capital

The above analysis shows a balance of BCVA and FVA which suggests that collateralisation, via two-way CSA with a relatively low threshold, is the most efficient way in which to transact. This, however, ignores the impact of regulatory capital. To include this quantitatively is difficult since it would be necessary to consider standard capital charges for both default risk and CVA (under Basel II and III, respectively), capital charges for CCP trades and liquidity and leverage ratio charges. This will be discussed further in Chapter 17.

It is clear that there is much optimisation possible in the trading of OTC derivatives contracts with respect to counterparty risk, funding and regulatory capital. This can be seen from the activities of banks, such as a closer integration between collateral teams and trading desks. The precise optimisation is clearly a huge challenge due to the complexity in defining costs associated with counterparty risk and funding, together with the cost of holding the required regulatory capital. We will address this in more detail in Chapter 18, in relation to the role of a CVA desk. However, a very simple and compelling conclusion from the above analysis is that CVA cannot be completely eradicated without the creation of significant, and perhaps prohibitive, costs.

14.5 FUTURE TRENDS

14.5.1 Standard CSA

Whilst we have quantified, above, the joint impact of BCVA and FVA in collateralised situations, many of the complexities of CSAs are simply too complex to quantify rigorously. A tremendous amount of optionality exists in a CSA since there are so many possibilities about the type of collateral that can be delivered (and substituted) across currency, asset class and maturity. Knowing the cheapest-to-deliver collateral in the future depends on many aspects, such as the future exposure, basis swap spreads and haircuts. An accurate valuation, via CollVA, of the optionality that an institution has in a CSA (and that their counterparty has) is clearly not achievable. However, an alternative solution is to remove, structurally, most of the optionality to simplify some of the valuation problems linked to funding and CSAs.

The ISDA Standard Credit Support Annex (SCSA) aims to achieve such standardisation and greatly reduce embedded optionality in CSAs, whilst improving collateralisation and promoting the adoption of OIS discounting. At the same time, the mechanics of a SCSA are focussed on being closely aligned to central clearing collateral practices. Additionally, the SCSA aims at creating a homogeneous valuation framework, minimising valuation disputes and making trading and novation more straightforward. The SCSA is still being developed and the reader is referred to the ISDA website (www.isda.org) for the latest status.

In a typical CSA, a single amount is calculated each period for a portfolio, which may cover many currencies. Cash collateral may therefore be posted in different currencies and typically in other securities also. In addition, thresholds and minimum transfer amounts are commonly not zero. A SCSA greatly simplifies the process, requiring:

- Cash collateral only (with respect to variation margin, any independent amounts may be allowed in other securities).
- Only currencies with the most liquid OIS curves (USD, EUR, GBP, CHF and JPY) will be eligible.
- Zero thresholds and minimum transfer amounts (probably).
- One collateral requirement per currency (cross-currency products are put into the USD bucket).

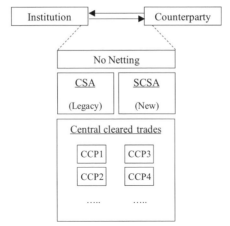

Figure 14.14 Illustration of the different collateral arrangements that may exist.

The SCSA will require parties to calculate, individually, one collateral requirement per currency per day with delivery of cash in the relevant currency. This gives rise to settlement (Herstatt) risk (see Section 4.2.1). With agreement, it will be possible to convert each currency amount into a single amount, with an accompanying interest adjustment overlay (to correct for interest rate differences between the currencies, also known as the "implied swap adjustment mechanism" or "ISA method"). A "safe settlement" platform is being developed to minimise residual Herstatt risk.

A SCSA simplifies bilateral collateralisation as much as possible, removing most of the optionality discussed in Section 14.2.3. Assuming zero thresholds and no independent amount, aligns the practical terms of the CSA closely with the theoretical ideal discussed in Section 14.2.5.[34] It therefore allows such trades to be reasonably discounted at the relevant OIS rate. Cross-currency trades would be discounted in USD (Fed Funds) rates using the relevant FX basis curves. Due to the daily margining (and likely lack of independent amount), BCVA is still an issue as shown previously (Section 9.7.2) and, correspondingly, some FVA component will exist. Note that the BCVA component depends on the margin period of risk, which must be calculated under the assumption of the counterparty (or institution) defaulting whereas the equivalent period for FVA may be much shorter as it arises in non-default scenarios.

Figure 14.14 illustrates the different collateral arrangements that may exist between an institution and their counterparty.[35] Note that trades can be moved from CSAs to SCSAs but not vice versa. Similarly, uncleared trades may be moved to a given central counterparty (CCP) but probably not vice versa.

14.5.2 The conversion of CVA into funding liquidity risk

It is important to emphasise the high-level issue around aspects discussed in this chapter, which is that increasing collateralisation may reduce CVA, but it increases funding liquidity risk. Figure 14.15 illustrates the increasing strength of collateral use starting from the rather flexible CSA. The SCSA is a stronger form of collateralisation since much of the optionality is removed and collateral is cash with thresholds being zero. Central clearing takes this a

---

[34] Problems that still exist are the delay in receiving collateral, jumps in exposure and closeout periods.
[35] As noted in Chapter 5, a CSA is not the only collateral arrangement used but is by far the most common.

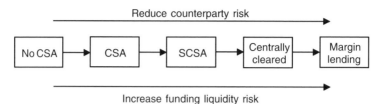

Figure 14.15 Illustration of the increasing impact of collateral on counterparty risk and funding liquidity risk.

stage further by requiring independent amounts (initial margins). The limit of this (as discussed in Section 7.2.7) is margin lending, where collateral posted is funded via a third party.

What is important to appreciate is that, whilst the conversion of counterparty risk to funding liquidity risk is an inevitable result of the completely realistic need to take collateral, it may be pushed too far. This may certainly be the case in the extreme with margin lending as, due to risk aversion and possible asymmetric information, a margin lender must charge more. Furthermore, margin lenders will increase charges in volatile markets and will likely fail or withdraw their services in crises (as illustrated by the complete seizure of the short-term funding market in 2008). CCPs will also increase funding requirements (via initial margin) in volatile markets but will hopefully not fail (especially during a crisis). However, as discussed in Chapter 7, the assessment of the risk of a CCP is extremely complex.

A key decision for market participants and regulators alike is the concentration of various trading on the spectrum represented by Figure 14.15 and the risks that this presents. Whilst pushing to the right minimises counterparty risk, it also increases more opaque and complex funding liquidity risks. In contrast to assessing FVA and complex processes such as central clearing and margin lending, the quantification and management of CVA in the No CSA case on the left hand side of Figure 14.15 is relatively easy!

14.6   SUMMARY

In this chapter, we have described the issues relating to funding, which are rather distinct but, in many ways, entwined with the problems of counterparty credit risk and BCVA. We have characterised the problem of "risk-free" derivatives valuation and the use of so-called "OIS discounting" as a more appropriate standard valuation (before CVA has been accounted for). The problem of FVA quantification and its link to DVA has also been addressed, together with the related issues of "cheapest-to-deliver collateral" and other optionality stemming from standard collateral agreements (CollVA).

The topics addressed in this chapter are broad and growing rapidly. The purpose has been to describe the important issues from a counterparty risk perspective. The interested reader is referred to the many publications on the topic for more general information on OIS discounting and funding.

In the next chapter, we will relax a final and important consideration, until now, which is the independence of exposure and default probability. This is the important and complex topic of wrong-way risk.

15
Wrong-Way Risk

I never had a slice of bread, particularly large and wide, that did not fall upon the floor, and always on the buttered side.

Newspaper in Norwalk, Ohio, 1841

15.1   INTRODUCTION

The last three chapters have been concerned with valuation of counterparty risk and funding via CVA, DVA and FVA under a key simplifying assumption of no wrong-way risk. Wrong-way risk is the phrase generally used to indicate an unfavourable dependence between exposure and counterparty credit quality – i.e., the exposure is high when the counterparty is more likely to default and vice versa. Whilst it may often be a reasonable assumption to ignore wrong-way risk, its manifestation can be rather subtle and potentially dramatic. In contrast, "right-way" risk can also exist in cases where the dependence between exposure and credit quality is a favourable one. Right-way situations will reduce counterparty risk and CVA.

In this chapter, we will identify causes of wrong-way risk and discuss the associated implications on exposure estimation and quantification of counterparty risk. We will give examples of quantitative approaches used and give specific examples such as forward contracts, options and swaps. We will later discuss wrong-way risk in the credit derivative market and analyse what went so dramatically wrong with CDOs in the global financial crisis. The impact of collateral on wrong-way risk will be analysed and the central clearing implications will be discussed.

15.2   OVERVIEW OF WRONG-WAY RISK

15.2.1   Simple example

Imagine tossing two coins and being asked to assess the probability of getting two heads – that is an easy question to answer.[1] Now suppose that you are told that the coins are linked in some way: the first coin to land can magically have some impact on which way up the other coin lands. Clearly, the question is now much more complex.

In Chapter 12, we saw that CVA could be generally represented as credit spread multiplied by exposure. Indeed, an approximate formula for CVA was simply CVA = credit

---

[1] It is, of course, 25% from one-half times one-half.

spread × EPE. However, the multiplication of the default probability (credit spread) and exposure (EPE) terms relies on a key assumption, which is that the different quantities are *independent*. If they are dependent then the analysis is far more complicated and the relatively simple formulas are no longer appropriate. Essentially this corresponds to the integration of credit risk (default probability) and market risk (exposure), which is a very complex task. We could have other dependence such as between loss given default (and equivalently recovery rate) and either exposure or default probability, which will also give rise to other forms of wrong-way risk.

A simple analogy to wrong-way risk is dropping (the default) a piece of buttered bread. Many people believe that in such a case, the bread is most likely to land on the wrong, buttered side (exposure). This is due to "Murphy's Law", which states that "anything that can go wrong, will go wrong". This particular aspect of Murphy's Law has even been empirically tested[2] and, of course, the probability of bread landing butter side down is only 50%.[3] People have a tendency to overweight the times when the bread lands the wrong way against the times they were more fortunate. Since it is in human nature to believe in wrong-way risk, it is rather surprising that it has been significantly underestimated in the derivatives market! The market events of 2007 onwards have illustrated clearly that wrong-way risk can be extremely serious. In financial markets, the bread always falls on the buttered side (or has butter on both sides).

15.2.2 Classic example and empirical evidence

Wrong-way risk is often a natural and unavoidable consequence of financial markets. One of the simplest examples is mortgage providers who, in an economic regression, face both falling property prices and higher default rates by homeowners. In derivatives, examples of trades that obviously contain wrong-way risk across different asset classes, which will be studied in more detail later, are:

- *Put option*. Buying a put option on a stock (or stock index) where the underlying in question has fortunes that are highly correlated to those of the counterparty is an obvious case of wrong-way risk (for example, buying a put on one bank's stock from another bank). The put option will only be valuable if the stock goes down, in which case the counterparty's credit quality will be likely to be deteriorating. As we shall see later, an out-of-the-money put option will have more wrong-way risk than an in-the-money one. Correspondingly, equity call options should be right-way products.
- *FX forward or cross-currency products*. Any FX contract must be considered in terms of a possible linkage between the relevant FX rate and the default probability of the counterparty. In particular, a potential weakening of the currency received by the counterparty vis-à-vis the paid currency should be a wrong-way risk concern. This would obviously be the case in trading with a sovereign and paying their local currency. Another way to look at a cross-currency swap is that it represents a loan collateralised by the opposite currency in the swap. If this currency weakens dramatically, the value of the collateral is strongly diminished. This linkage could be either way: first, a weakening of the currency could

---

[2] On the English BBC TV science programme Q.E.D. in 1993.
[3] Matthews (1995) has shown that a butter-down landing is indeed more likely, but for reasons of gravitational torque and the height of tables rather than Murphy's Law.

indicate a slow economy and hence a less profitable time for the counterparty. Alternatively, the default of a sovereign or large corporate counterparty may itself precipitate a weakening of its local currency.

- *Interest rate products.* Although this is probably an area with limited wrong-way risk, it is important to consider a relationship between the relevant interest rates and the counterparty default probability. Such a relationship could be considered in either direction: high interest rates may trigger defaults whereas low interest rates may be indicative of a recession where defaults are more likely.
- *Commodity swaps.* In an oil swap, one party pays cash flows based on a fixed oil price and receives cash flows based on an average spot price of oil over a period. The exposure of payer swap will be high when the price of oil has increased. Suppose the counterparty is an oil company: high oil prices should represent a scenario in which they are performing well. Hence, the contract *should* represent "right-way risk". The right-way risk arises due to hedging (as opposed to speculation). However, it may not always be as clear-cut as this, as we shall see later.
- *Credit default swaps.* When buying protection in a CDS contract, an exposure will be the result of the reference entity's credit spread widening. However, one would prefer that the counterparty's credit spread is not widening also! In the case of a strong relationship between the credit quality of the reference entity and counterparty then clearly there is extreme wrong-way risk. On the other hand, with such a strong relationship then selling CDS protection should be a right-way trade with little or no counterparty risk. In portfolio credit derivatives, this effect becomes more subtle and potentially dramatic and helps to explain the failure of CDOs.

All of the above cases will be considered in more detail later in this chapter.

General empirical evidence supports the presence of wrong-way risk. For example, Duffee (1998) shows a clustering of corporate defaults in the US during periods of falling interest rates. Regarding the FX example, results from Levy and Levin (1999) look at residual currency values upon default of the sovereign and find average values ranging from 17% (Triple-A) to 62% (Triple-C). This implies the amount by which the FX rate involved could jump at the default time of the counterparty.

Losses due to wrong-way risk have also been clearly illustrated. For example, many dealers suffered heavy losses because of wrong-way risk during the Asian crisis of 1997/1998. This was due to a strong link between the default of sovereigns and of corporates and a strong weakening of their local currencies. A decade later, the credit crisis starting in 2007 caused heavy wrong-way risk losses for banks buying insurance from so-called monolines, as discussed later.

15.2.3   Right-way risk and hedging

Right-way risk indicates a beneficial relationship between exposure and default probability that actually *reduces* counterparty risk. Hedges should naturally create right-way risk because the aim of the hedge is to reduce risk, which should in turn mean less uncertainty over counterparty credit quality.

Wrong-way risk *should* be rather rare in an ideal world. Suppose a mining company wishes to hedge (lock in) the price of gold at some date in the future. This can be achieved via a forward contract on gold. When such a contract is in an institution's favour (and against the mining company), the price of gold will be high. Mining companies are not expected to default when gold is expensive. Assuming most counterparties are hedging and not speculating then they should generate right-way rather than wrong-way risk.

It could be assumed that wrong-way risk will generally be offset by right-way risk. However, we will show later that these assumptions can sometimes be shown to be quite naïve. In the real world, speculation, failed hedges and systemic effects mean that wrong-way risk can occur frequently. Institutions that have exposures to certain market events (such as hedge funds and monolines) will almost surely create wrong-way risk for those trading with them.

15.2.4 Wrong-way risk challenges

Quantifying wrong-way risk will involve somehow modelling the relationship between default probability and exposure. At a high level, there are two potential pitfalls in doing this, which are:

- *Lack (or irrelevance) of historical data*. Unfortunately, wrong-way risk may be subtle and not revealed via any historical time series analysis.
- *Misspecification of relationship*. The way in which the dependency between credit spreads (default probability) and exposure is specified may be inappropriate. For example, rather than being the result of a correlation, it may be the result of a *causality* – a cause-and-effect type relationship between two events.

Suppose an institution makes a statistical study of the correlation between the credit quality of their counterparty and a variable driving the exposure (e.g., an interest rate or FX rate) and finds this correlation is close to zero. There seems to be little evidence of wrong-way risk in this transaction. However, both of the above problems may exist.

Concerning historical data, wrong-way risk by its very nature is extreme and often rather specific. Hence, historical data may not show the relationship. For example, in 2010, the European sovereign crisis began and was accompanied by deterioration in the credit quality of many European sovereigns and a weakening of the euro currency. There is a clear relationship here with sovereign credit spreads widening and their underlying currency weakening. However, historical data did not bear out this relationship, largely since neither the sovereigns concerned nor the currency had ever previously been subject to any adverse credit effects.

Concerning possible misspecification, correlation is only one measure of dependency. It measures only the linear relationship between variables. Suppose one believes that a small move in a market rate will have little or no impact on the credit quality of a counterparty but a much larger move will. This is a second-order relationship that will not be captured by correlation. There may be a causal relationship: for example, the counterparty's credit quality deteriorating significantly moves market variables significantly even though the credit spread of that counterparty previously showed no relationship to the market variable during normal times. It is important to emphasise here, whilst two independent random variables will have zero correlation, the reverse is **not** true. If the correlation between two random variables is measured as zero then this does not prove that they are independent.[4]

---

[4] A classic example of this is as follows. Suppose a variable X follows a normal distribution. Now choose $Y = X^2$. X and Y have zero correlation but are far from independent.

15.2.5 Wrong-way risk and CVA

The presence of wrong-way risk will (unsurprisingly) increase CVA. However, the magnitude of this increase will be hard to quantify, as we shall show in some examples. Wrong-way risk also prevents one from using the (relatively) simple formulas used for CVA in Chapter 12. Whilst independence may exist in everyday life, it almost certainly does not in the interconnected and systemic financial markets. All of the aforementioned formulas are therefore wrong.

All is not lost though. We can still use the same CVA expression as long as we calculate the exposure *conditional* upon default of the counterparty. Returning to equation (12.2), we simply rewrite the expression as

$$\text{CVA} \approx (1\text{-Rec}) \sum_{j=1}^{m} \text{DF}(t_j)\text{EE}(t_j|t_j = \tau_C)\text{PD}(t_{j-1}, t_j), \tag{15.1}$$

where $\text{EE}(t_j|t_j = \tau_C)$ represents the expected exposure at time t_j conditional on this being the counterparty default time (τ_C). This replaces the previous exposure, which was unconditional. As long as we use the conditional exposure[5] in this fashion, everything is correct.

Obviously, calculating the conditional exposure is not at all easy because it depends on the counterparty and future time in question. Two equivalent portfolios of trades with different counterparties will have the same *unconditional* exposure but different *conditional* exposures. Broadly speaking, there are two ways to go about computing conditional exposure:

- Consider the exposure and default of the counterparty together and quantify the economic relationship between them. This method is the "correct" approach but the economic relationship may be extremely hard to define and there may be computation issues in calculating quantities such as CVA in this manner.
- Incorporate wrong-way risk via simple conservative assumptions, "rules of thumb" or simple generic models. This is a much simpler approach that involves minimal effort in the way of systems re-engineering or additional computational requirements.

15.2.6 Simple example

So exposure should always be computed conditionally on the counterparty default. In Appendix 15A we derive a simple formula for the conditional expected exposure for a forward contract-type exposure (an extension of the previous unconditional case given in Appendix 8B). The correlation is introduced by assuming the exposure follows a normal distribution and that the default time is generated from a normal distribution using the so-called Gaussian copula approach (Section 12.4.3). Under these assumptions, the conditional expected exposure can be calculated directly. This gives the EE at a time s under the assumption that the counterparty will have defaulted at time s. The relationship between exposure and counterparty default is expressed using a single correlation parameter. This correlation parameter is rather abstract, with no straightforward economic intuition, but it does facilitate a simple way of quantifying and understanding wrong-way risk.

---

[5] We note that there are other ways to represent this effect. For example, we could instead look at the conditional default probability, as will be done in Section 15.3.2.

Spreadsheet 15.1 Wrong-way risk calculations of expected exposure.

Let us now consider the impact of wrong-way risk on the example forward contract using the following base case parameters:

$\mu = 0\%$ drift of the value of the forward contract
$\sigma = 10\%$ volatility of the value of the forward contract
$h = 2\%$ hazard rate[6] (default probability) of the counterparty
$\rho = \pm 50\%$ correlation between the value of the forward contract and the default time of the counterparty

Figure 15.1 shows the impact of wrong-way (and right-way) risk on the EE. We can see that with 50% correlation, wrong-way risk approximately doubles the EE whilst with −50% correlation the impact of right-way risk reduces it by at least half. This is exactly the type of behaviour expected: positive correlation between the default probability and exposure increases the conditional expected exposure (default probability is high when exposure is high), which is wrong-way risk. Negative correlation causes right-way risk. Note that since the drift is zero, the negative expected exposure would follow exactly the same trend.

Let us look into this simple model in a bit more detail. Consider now the impact of counterparty default probability on the EE with wrong-way risk. Figure 15.2 shows the EE using three different hazard rates, indicating that the exposure decreases as the credit quality of the counterparty also decreases. This result might seem at first counterintuitive but it makes sense when one considers that for a better credit quality counterparty, default is a less

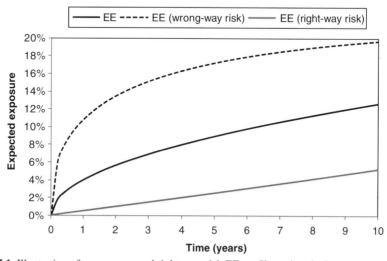

Figure 15.1 Illustration of wrong-way and right-way risk EE profiles using the base-case scenario with correlations of 50% and −50%, respectively.

---

[6] See Section 10.1.5 for the definition of hazard rate.

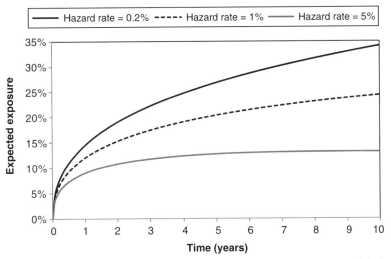

Figure 15.2 Illustration of EE under the assumption of wrong-way risk as a function of the hazard rate. The correlation is assumed to be 50%.

probable event and therefore represents a bigger surprise when it comes. We note an important general conclusion:

Wrong-way risk *increases* as the credit quality of the counterparty *increases.*

Finally, we change the drift of the forward contract to be $\mu = -2\%$ and use a larger hazard rate of $h = 6\%$. The EE profile with and without wrong-way risk is shown in Figure 15.3.

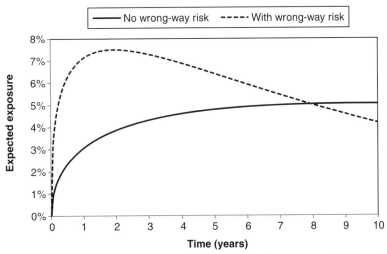

Figure 15.3 Illustration of EE with and without the assumption of wrong-way risk for a drift of $\mu = -2\%$ and hazard rate of $h = 6\%$.

Negative drift will reduce the overall exposure, as we can see. However, there is another effect, which is that the wrong-way risk EE is actually smaller than the standard EE after 8 years. This is because counterparty default in later years is not such a surprise as in earlier years (with a hazard rate of 6% the 8-year default probability is 38%, whilst the 2-year default probability is only 11.3%[7]). Hence, default in early years represents "bad news" whilst in later years default is almost expected! This suggests that wrong-way risk has a term structure effect, with conditional exposure in the shorter term showing a more dramatic effect than in the long-term.

15.3   PORTFOLIO WRONG-WAY RISK

Broadly speaking wrong-way risk can be divided into two categories, namely general and specific. This distinction has been made by the Basel committee in regulatory capital rules (see Chapter 17). General wrong-way risk can be thought of as the general relationship between exposure and default probability due to macroeconomic factors, which is most relevant at the portfolio level. Specific wrong-way risk may be analysed more at the transaction level and often represents more of a structural relationship between the counterparty default probability and the underlying exposure. We will discuss them along similar lines but use the terms portfolio and trade-level wrong-way risk, which do not necessarily coincide with the terms general and specific.

15.3.1   Correlation approach

The simple approach described in Section 15.2.6 above can readily be extended to the general case. To do this it is necessary to map the exposure distribution at each point in time onto a chosen (e.g., normal) distribution. The most obvious way to do this is to sort the exposures in descending order (although other more complex approaches can be used, as discussed below) and then map via a quantile mapping procedure. The approach is described in more detail in Appendix 15A. This approach is then the simplest version of the approaches proposed by Garcia-Cespedes *et al.* (2010) and Sokol (2010) and is illustrated in Figure 15.4. Due to the mapping of the exposures onto a normal distribution, in the positive correlation case an early default time will lead to a higher exposure, as is the case with wrong-way risk. A negative correlation will have the reverse effect and generate right-way risk. Note that there is no need to recalculate the exposures as the original exposures are used directly. The conditional exposures and corresponding CVA are then calculated easily via Monte Carlo simulation. Other distributional assumptions can also be used.

We start with the unilateral case (DVA and wrong-way risk will be discussed later in this section). As before, we assume the counterparty CDS curve is flat at 500 bps and the recovery rate is 40%. The same four-trade portfolio will be used as in previous examples (see Section 9.5.1). This corresponds to the unilateral CVA result reported previously in Table 13.1. We will first look at the expected exposure conditional on the counterparty's default, which is shown in Figure 15.5 for both positive and negative correlation values as well as zero correlation (the independent case shown previously in, for example, Figure 13.1). We see the expected impact that positive (negative) correlation leads to a higher (lower)

---

[7] Recall the simple relationship for the cumulative default probability at time s, being $1 - \exp(-hs)$ where h is the hazard rate.

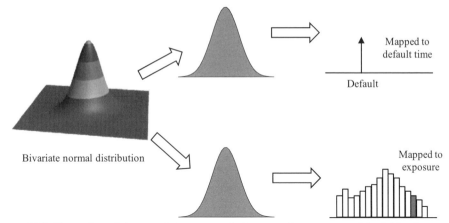

Figure 15.4 Illustration of the correlation approach for general wrong-way risk. A bivariate normal distribution with a certain correlation value drives both default times and exposures. If the correlation is positive then an early default time will be more likely to lead to a high exposure, as illustrated.

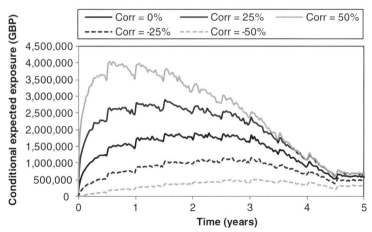

Figure 15.5 Conditional expected exposure calculated with various levels of correlation for the four-trade portfolio.

conditional exposure reflecting wrong-way (right-way) risk. As noted before, this effect is stronger for shorter maturities since an early default is more unexpected.

Figure 15.6 shows the (unilateral) CVA as a function of correlation. Negative correlation reduces the CVA due to right-way risk and wrong-way risk, created by positive correlation, increases it. The effect is quite dramatic, with the CVA approximately doubled at 50% correlation.

15.3.2   Parametric approach

Hull and White (2011) have proposed a different approach to the above. Rather than holding the default probability fixed and calculating the conditional expected exposure, they do the reverse (which is equally as valid). The conditional default probability is then defined by

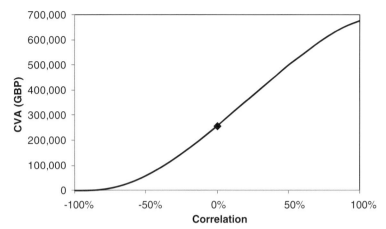

Figure 15.6 Unilateral CVA as a function of the correlation between counterparty default time and exposure. The point marked shows the independence CVA of 257,905 reported previously in Table 13.1.

linking the hazard rate to the underlying future value of the portfolio. One functional form proposed is $h(t) = \ln[1 + \exp(a(t) + bV(t))]$, where $h(t)$ and $V(t)$ represent the hazard rate and the future value and $a(t)$ and b are parameters.[8] An example of this functional form is given in Figure 15.7, which corresponds approximately to a counterparty CDS spread of 500 bps and recovery rate of 40% (a perfect fit will be used below). To give this some context, the unconditional hazard rate is in this case 8.33%, whilst the value at $V(t) = 0$ is 7.89%. Calculating the hazard rate at the EPE of this portfolio, which corresponds to $V(t) = 1,371,285$, gives 10.25% (i.e., an increase of around 30%). Note that a negative b value will give the opposite behaviour and create a right-way risk effect.

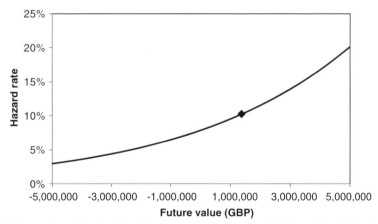

Figure 15.7 Illustration of the functional form proposed by Hull and White (2011) in their wrong-way risk approach. The $a(t)$ function is set constant at -2.5 whilst the b parameter is 2×10^{-7}. The point marked corresponds to the EPE.

---

[8] Hull and White also note that the hazard could be related to other variables (such as interest rates). They also propose an additional noise term and a different functional form but note that these aspects do not generally have a significant impact on the results.

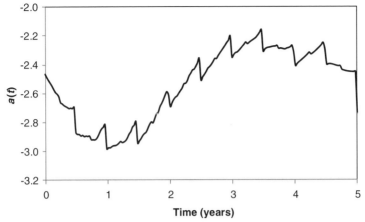

Figure 15.8 Illustration of the $a(t)$ function for the four-trade portfolio in the parametric wrong-way risk approach calibrated assuming the b parameter is 2×10^{-7} and the counterparty CDS and recovery rate are 500 bps and 40%, respectively.

The function $a(t)$ is most naturally used to fit the term structure of default probability, leaving the single parameter b to define the relationship between exposure and default probability. This can be done numerically as shown by Hull and White (2011) and the calibration required for the four-trade portfolio is shown in Figure 15.8.

Finally, we show the CVA as a function of the b parameter in Figure 15.9. As anticipated, a positive b gives a wrong-way risk effect and a higher CVA whilst a negative value gives the reverse right-way risk effect. The overall profile is similar (although more dramatic) than that given in the correlation model above. In the correlation model, the maximum CVA is 677,261 whilst in Figure 15.9 it can be seen to be significantly exceeding this value. Whether or not this is economically reasonable, it illustrates that 100% correlation should not be taken to imply a limiting case.

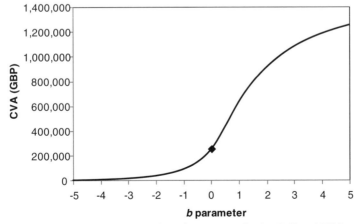

Figure 15.9 Unilateral CVA as a function of the b parameter in the Hull and White approach. The marked point denotes the independence CVA of 257,905 reported previously in Table 13.1.

15.3.3 Calibration issues

The correlation and parametric approaches described are relatively simple ways to incorporate general wrong-way risk without a large computational burden and/or having to rerun the underlying exposure simulations. However, the main challenge of such approaches will be calibration of the relevant parameters.

Firstly, regarding the correlation approach, Garcia-Cespedes *et al.* (2010) suggest using multifactor models and a principal component approach to calibrate the correlation based on historical data. Discussion and correlation estimates are given by Fleck and Schmidt (2005) and Rosen and Saunders (2010).

For the parametric approach, Hull and White suggest using an intuitive calibration based on a what-if scenario. For example, if the exposure of the portfolio increases to $10 million what would the spread of the counterparty increase to? Such a question will give a single point that can be used to calibrate the b parameter. Alternatively, the parametric relationship can be calibrated directly to historical data. This will involve calculating the portfolio value for dates in the past and looking at the relationship between this and the counterparty's CDS spread (hazard rate). If the portfolio has historically had a high value, which has corresponded to a larger-than-average counterparty CDS spread, then this will indicate some wrong-way risk. This approach obviously requires that the current portfolio of trades with the counterparty is similar in nature to that used in the historical calibration.

It is clear that the calibration of market and credit correlation is a very complex task. There is a significant risk of misspecification, for example, the correlation approach gives a maximum CVA of 677,261 (Figure 15.6) whereas the parametric approach can produce much larger values (Figure 15.9). Furthermore, there is likely to be a substantial error in calibration to historical data. Finally, the historical relationship may be completely meaningless with respect to the future relationship. Indeed, many of the events of the global financial crisis, especially those involving large dependencies, were not in any way borne out in historical data prior to the crisis and/or analyses based only on correlation measures.

15.3.4 DVA and wrong-way risk

We should finally mention the impact of wrong-way risk on bilateral CVA (BCVA). For the purposes of calculating BCVA, the conditional negative expected exposure conditional on the institution's own default is also required. This calculation follows in a similar way to the expected exposure. The symmetry of CVA and DVA implies that if one is affected by wrong-way risk then the other should show the effect of right-way risk. There are two obvious cases where the above logic does not work, i.e., one party having wrong-way risk implies that the other party benefits from right-way risk. The first is that the nature of the parties is different, and therefore they are exposed to different risk factors (e.g., a bank and a sovereign). In the interbank market, wrong-way risk and right-way risk are likely to always be side-by-side. However, a bank providing a hedge to an end user may have right-way risk in their trade but the end user will not obviously have wrong-way risk. A second possibility is if the trade payoff is highly asymmetric, so that only one party can have a significant exposure. This is the case in CDS contracts, which are discussed later.

We return to the correlation approach in Section 15.3.1, and look at the DVA impact. We assume as before that the institution's own CDS spread is 250 bps and their recovery value is 40%. The correlation between the exposure and default times is the same for both the counterparty's and the institution's own default (although these correlations could easily be

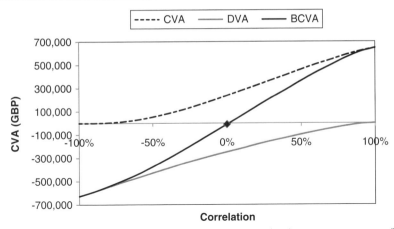

Figure 15.10 Bilateral CVA (BCVA) as a function of the correlation between counterparty/institution default time and exposure. The point marked shows the independence BCVA of −8,791 GBP reported previously in Table 13.1.

different, as mentioned above). We also assume independence between the default times (again, it would be straightforward to relax this assumption as was discussed in Section 13.4.1). The results are shown in Figure 15.10. It can be seen that wrong-way risk (positive correlation) has the impact of reducing the DVA whilst right-way risk (negative correlation) reduces the CVA. The overall impact is therefore very strong. For example, at zero correlation (no wrong- or right-way risk), the BCVA is −8,791 GBP but at just 10% correlation it has increased to 65,523 GBP, i.e., changed sign and almost an order of magnitude larger!

15.4 TRADE-LEVEL WRONG-WAY RISK

We now deal with trade-level wrong-way risk, looking at the different features by asset class. We will illustrate the wide range of wrong-way risk models and the different aspects that are important to consider.

15.4.1 Interest rates

The relationship between changes in interest rates and default rates have been shown empirically to be generally negative.[9] This means that low interest rates are likely to be accompanied by higher default rates. This is most obviously explained by central bank monetary policy being to keep interest rates low when the economy is in recession and the default rate high. Such an effect clearly leads to wrong- and right-way risk in interest rate products, which we will analyse through an interest rate swap.

An obvious way to proceed in light of the empirical evidence is to correlate interest rates and credit spreads (hazard rates) in the quantification of the CVA on an interest rate product. Such approaches have commonly been used in credit derivative pricing (e.g., see O'Kane, 2008). The case above corresponds to a negative correlation. We assume a Hull and White

---

[9] See, for example, Longstaff and Schwartz (1995), Duffee (1998) and Collin-Dufresne *et al.* (2001).

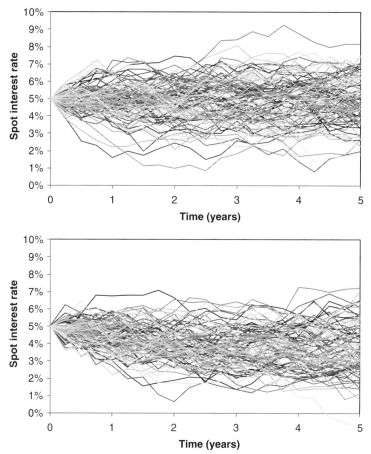

Figure 15.11 Interest rate simulations conditional on counterparty default (at some point in the 5-year period) for the correlated interest rate and hazard rate (credit spread) approach. Cases of zero (top) and −90% (bottom) correlation are used.

(1990) interest rate model[10] with a flat interest rate term structure of 5%. This will give a symmetric exposure profile that will make the wrong- and right-way risk effects easier to identify. We assume a lognormal hazard rate approach so that credit spreads cannot become negative.[11] As before, the counterparty CDS spread and recovery rate are 500 bps and 40%, respectively.

We first show interest rate simulations conditionally on a counterparty default event in Figure 15.11. In the case of zero correlation, these are unaffected by counterparty default and the paths are distributed symmetrically around the starting point of 5%.[12] In the case of negative correlation, the paths are biased downwards towards low interest rates. This happens because low interest rates occur often together with high hazard rates, which leads to a greater chance of default.

---

[10] The mean reversion parameter and volatility are set at 0.1 and 1%, respectively.
[11] The volatility used is 50%.
[12] One of the reasons for using a normal interest rate model was to illustrate this.

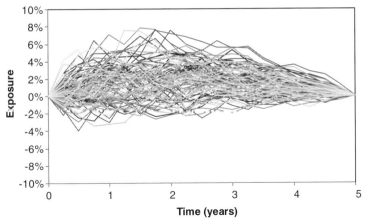

Figure 15.12 Future values for a receiver interest rate swap conditional on counterparty default for the correlated interest rate and hazard rate (credit spread) approach. A correlation of −90% is used. This seemingly large value is chosen to illustrate most clearly the effect.

In Figure 15.12, we show the future values for a 5-year receiver interest rate swap with negative correlation between interest rates and hazard rates. We see a strong wrong-way risk effect: the swap has an exposure when interest rates are low, which is likely to correspond to a higher hazard rate where counterparty default is more likely. Conditionally on default, its exposure is therefore likely to be positive. The payer swap would, by symmetry, show the reverse behaviour. In a positive correlation environment, the payer swap would be the wrong-way product and the receiver would have right-way risk.

In Figure 15.13 we show the expected exposure (EE) and negative expected exposure (NEE) for the receiver swap in the presence of wrong-way risk. For the purpose of

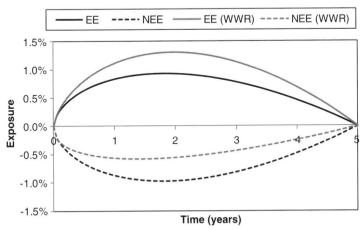

Figure 15.13 Expected exposure (EE) and negative expected exposure (NEE) for a receiver interest rate swap conditional on counterparty default for the correlated interest rate and hazard rate (credit spread) approach. The base case corresponds to an assumed correlation of zero whilst the wrong-way risk (WWR) approach to a correlation of −50%. Note that the EE is computed conditional on the default of the counterparty (500 bps CDS spread assumed) whilst the NEE is conditional on default of the institution (250 bps).

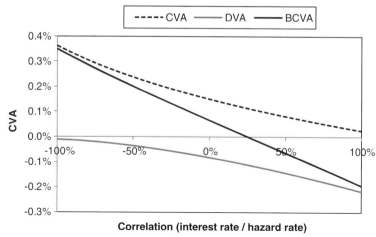

Figure 15.14 Bilateral CVA components for a receiver interest rate swap as a function of the correlation between interest rates and hazard rates. The counterparty and institution CDS spreads are assumed to be 500 and 250 bps, respectively and the recovery rates are 40%.

calculating the NEE, the institution's CDS spread is assumed to be 250 bps as previously, with a 40% recovery rate. A correlation of −50% is assumed in both cases (i.e., both the counterparty's and institution's own hazard rates are correlated to interest rates by −50%), although we note that a different choice may be relevant in practice. Wrong-way risk increases the EE and right-way risk reduces the NEE. Note that the right-way risk effect is stronger: this is because default of the institution is less likely and so has a larger impact on the exposure conditional on the default event.

Finally, we show the bilateral CVA (BCVA) contributions as a percentage of the notional value in Figure 15.14. Due to the institution's default probability being approximately half that of the counterparty, the DVA is expected to be approximately half the CVA. However, also important is the fact that the right-way risk is stronger than the wrong-way risk, as discussed above. This can be seen from the fact that the maximum DVA is more than half the maximum CVA.[13] We see that the overall BCVA is very sensitive to the correlation, for example being three times bigger at −50% correlation than in the standard case (no wrong- or right-way risk).

The above example represents the most obvious way to incorporate wrong-way (and right-way) risk. It is computationally more demanding than the standard BCVA approach since defaults must be simulated explicitly via some hazard rate process. However, there are relatively efficient methods for doing this. The correlations required could be calibrated from the market price of interest rate and credit hybrid products or from a historical time series of interest rates and credit spreads.

Nevertheless, there are uncertainties and possible problems with the above approach. The distributional choices for the interest rate and hazard rates are obviously important. In particular, there is a lack of market information and historical data to calibrate hazard rate processes. Clearly, the estimate of the correlation between interest rates and hazard rates is uncertain. Indeed, since this correlation arises from a recession leading to both higher default rates and causing central banks to lower interest rates, there may also be some inherent time

---

[13] The maximum CVA is 0.36% at −100% correlation and the maximum DVA −0.22% at +100% correlation.

delay. However, the biggest concern should be over the fundamental choice of specifying a dependency between interest rates and hazard rates. In doing so, we assume that a payer swap is a wrong-way (right-way) risk product for negative (positive) correlation whilst a receiver swap will be precisely the reverse (as can be observed from the DVA in Figure 15.6). This is more than a matter of specifying the correct correlation. Empirical evidence is that default rates are high when interest rates are low, as mentioned at the beginning of this section. However, counterparties may also be more likely to default in high-interest rate environments when borrowing costs are high. This could make both payer and receiver swaps wrong-way risk products. A model correlating interest rate *volatility*[14] with default probability would produce this different behaviour.

15.4.2   Foreign exchange example

Ehlers and Schönbucher (2006) have considered the impact of a default on FX rates and illustrated cases where a correlation approach (such as used in the interest rate case above) between the exchange rate and the hazard rate is not able to explain empirical data. The data implies a significant additional jump in the FX rate at default. A simple approach proposed by Levy and Levin (1999) to model FX exposures with wrong-way risk is to assume that the relevant FX rate jumps at the counterparty default time, as illustrated in Figure 15.15. This is a simple approach since the conditional FX rate at default is simply the unconditional value multiplied by some jump factor.[15] The jump factor is often called a residual value (RV) factor of the currency and the assumption is that the currency devalues by an amount $(1 - RV)$ at the counterparty default time and the relevant FX rate jumps accordingly.

The RV approach is most relevant for exposures to sovereigns where their local currency will clearly devalue by a significant amount in the event they default. Indeed, Levy and Levin (1999) provide estimates of residual currency values by rating upon sovereign default, based on 92 historical default events, which are reproduced in Table 15.1. The RV is larger for better-rated sovereigns, presumably because their default requires a more severe financial shock and the conditional FX rate therefore should move by a greater amount. Such an approach can also be applied to other counterparties, as described by Finger (2000). For

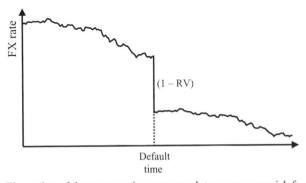

Figure 15.15 Illustration of the currency jump approach to wrong-way risk for FX products.

---

[14] This is analogous to the Merton (1974) idea that shows a relationship between credit spreads and equity *volatility*.
[15] The conditional expected FX rate, $E[FX(s)|s = \tau]$, at the counterparty default time is equal to its unconditional value $E[FX(s)]$ multiplied by a "residual value factor" (RV).

Table 15.1   Residual currency values (RV) upon sovereign default as a function of the sovereign rating prior to default

Rating	Residual value
AAA	17%
AA	17%
A	22%
BBB	27%
BB	41%
B	62%
CCC	62%

Source: From Levy and Levin (1999)

example, a default of a large corporate should be expected to have quite a significant impact on their local currency (albeit smaller than that due to sovereign default).

The conditional expected exposure implied by the devaluation approach is shown in Figure 15.16 (the calculations are described in Appendix 15B). The impact is fairly time homogeneous, which may be criticised based on the previous observation that wrong-way risk may have a different impact for different future horizons.[16] For example, we may think that an immediate default of a sovereign may produce a large currency jump (small RV in the short term) whereas a later default may be less sudden and therefore lead to a smaller effect (larger RV in the medium to longer term).

The above approach may seem rather imprecise and ad hoc, and may not be favoured over an approach similar to the correlation one adopted for interest rates described above. Whilst the devaluation approach is simple and practical, concern may exist over the inability to

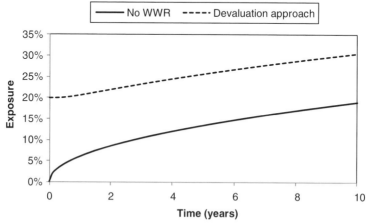

Figure 15.16 Illustration of the conditional expected exposure for the devaluation wrong-way risk approach for an FX forward assuming a residual value factor RV = 80%. The FX volatility is assumed to be 15%.

---

[16] Although the market data shown below approximately supports this homogeneous assumption.

characterise the RV factor (and any associated term structure) for a given counterparty. Compared with the ability to estimate FX and credit spread correlation from historical data, this may seem like a bit of a "finger in the air" approach.

In recent years, however, the devaluation approach has been supported by observations in the CDS market. Most CDSs are quoted in US dollars but sometimes simultaneous quotes can be seen in other currencies. For example, Table 15.2 shows the CDS quotes on Italy in both US dollars and euros. These CDS contracts trigger on the same credit event definitions and thus the only difference between them is the currency received on default. There is a large "quanto" effect, with euro-denominated CDS cheaper by around 30% for all maturities. This shows an implied RV of 69% in the event of the default of Italy using 5-year quotes (91/131). This calculation would require adjustment for forward FX and cross-currency basis spreads. Not only is the RV time homogeneous, supporting the approach above, but it is also apparent several months before the euro sovereign crisis developed strongly in mid-2011 and Italian credit spreads widened significantly from the levels shown in Table 15.2.

Similar effects during the European sovereign crisis were seen later in 2011. For example, implied RVs of the euro were 91%, 83%, 80% and 75% for Greece, Italy, Spain and Germany, respectively.[17] This is again consistent with a higher credit quality sovereign creating a stronger impact. The CDS market therefore allows wrong-way risk effect in currencies to be observed and potentially also hedged.

Table 15.2 CDS quotes (mid-market) on Italy in both US dollars and euros from April 2011

Maturity	USD	EUR
1Y	50	35
2Y	73	57
3Y	96	63
4Y	118	78
5Y	131	91
7Y	137	97
10Y	146	103

15.4.3 Risky option position

In Appendix 15C, we derive a simple formula for the value of a risky European stock option based on the classic Black and Scholes (1973) formula. The expression given allows the computation of the risky option premium with the impact of wrong-way (and right-way) risk. We will use the following parameters in the examples below:

$A = 100$ current asset price
$K = 105.1$ strike price of option
$r = 5\%$ risk-free interest rate

---

[17] For example, see "Quanto swaps signal 9 percent Euro drop on Greek default", Bloomberg, June 2010.

$\sigma = 25\%$ stock volatility

$T = 1$ option maturity

$h = 5\%$ hazard rate of the default of the counterparty

ρ correlation between the stock price and the default time of the counterparty

The first five terms above are standard in the Black–Scholes formula. The magnitude of the counterparty risk impact will depend on the hazard rate, h, and the correlation parameter, ρ. Increasing ρ in absolute terms will increase the wrong-way risk impact whilst changing the sign of ρ will generate right-way risk. The sign of ρ that gives rise to wrong-way or right-way risk will depend on the underlying contract considered.

Spreadsheet 15.2 Black–Scholes formula with counterparty risk.

Since the strike of the option is "at-the-money forward",[18] then the standard (risk-free) value of both call and put options is 9.95. In Appendix 15B, we showed a simple expression for the CVA of an option. We will ignore recovery value (which is just a systematic effect), as a result of which the premium of a risky option (no wrong-way risk) can be obtained by simply multiplying the risk-free premium and the survival probability of the counterparty over the life of the option. This means that the risky value of the call or put in the current example is 9.46[19] – we will refer to this as the "risky Black–Scholes price".

We first show the impact of correlation on the premiums of European calls and puts in Figure 15.17. We can see that the call option value increases with correlation, (compared with the risky Black–Scholes value) is a consequence of right-way risk. Due to

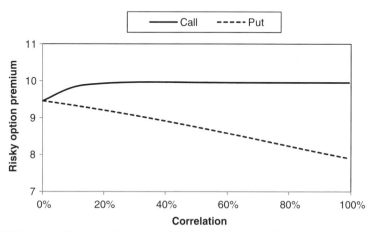

Figure 15.17 Premiums for risky European call and put options as a function of correlation using the base-case parameters described in the text.

---

[18] The strike of the option is determined by the forward value $F = A(t)e^{rT} = 100 \times e^{5\% \times 1} = 105.1$.

[19] The 1-year survival probability given the hazard rate of 5% is $\exp(-5\% \times 1) = 0.951$.

the correlation between the stock price and the counterparty default time, a default becomes increasingly unlikely when the option payoff is positive. For the put option, there is wrong-way risk since a falling stock price leads to the option having a positive payoff but also increases the probability that the counterparty will default. This is intuitive behaviour: buying a put option from a counterparty whose credit quality is positively related to the underlying variable would be dangerous. On the other hand, the equivalent call option (which is in-the-money when the market is on the up) should be less of a concern. We can finally note that the impact of right-way risk is far less dramatic than that of wrong-way risk.

Note that put–call parity, which normally gives a theoretical linkage between European call and put premiums, does not work in this case. Put–call parity involves comparing a long call and a short put position (or vice versa). Since only the long position will have counterparty risk, it does not apply to risky options as a counterparty default will effectively break the underlying static hedge that leads to put–call parity.

We now investigate the relationship between counterparty risk on options and the strike of the option. In Figure 15.18, we show the ratio of the risky to risk-free put option as a function of strike. This ratio will be less than or equal to 100% due to counterparty risk, and the lower the ratio, the greater the wrong-way risk impact. We see that put options of lower strikes show a more significant behaviour. Indeed, for the most out-of-the-money put ($K = 75$) at high correlation the ratio shown approaches 0%, which means that the extent of the counterparty risk is to make the put option almost worthless. Again, this effect is intuitive: a very out-of-the-money put option will only have value when the underlying has dropped significantly, at which point a correlated counterparty's credit quality should be expected to have deteriorated significantly.

An important conclusion is that, where there is wrong-way (or right-way) risk, its magnitude will increase for a contract that has more out-of-the-money characteristics. This example is a somewhat academic exercise as options may trade on exchanges and are not commonly traded out-of-the-money to the extent suggested by Figure 15.18. However, we will show later that CDS positions have a very similar behaviour.

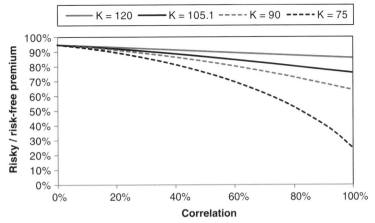

Figure 15.18 Risky option premium divided by the risk-free premium (Black–Scholes price) for put options of different strikes.

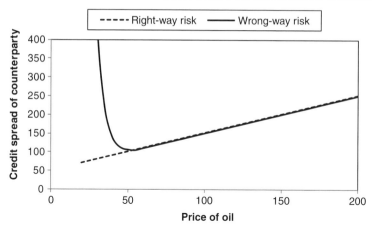

Figure 15.19 Schematic illustration of the value of an oil swap versus the credit spread of an airline counterparty.

15.4.4 Commodities

Wrong-way risk in commodities can be modelled in a similar way to interest rate products. Brigo *et al.* (2008) consider modelling of commodity derivatives CVA in more detail. However, there is another important concept that arises here in certain situations. Consider an institution entering into an oil receiver swap with an airline. Such a contract allows the airline to hedge their exposure to rising oil prices, which is important since aviation fuel represents a very significant cost for the airline industry. From an institution's point of view, such a swap has exposure when the price of oil is low, but at this point, the credit quality of the airline should be sound due to their reduced fuel costs. When the price of oil is high, then the airline may be in a weaker financial situation but this will be the situation of negative exposure. This *should* give rise to right-way risk. However, as illustrated schematically in Figure 15.19, the real situation may be more complex. There is potentially a different linkage here, which is that a low price of oil might mean a severe recession in which case the airline may have financial troubles. This effect was seen in the global financial crisis. What was originally perceived as right-way risk in the sense of a small fall in the price of oil created wrong-way risk in relation to a more substantial price drop. This is seen on the left-hand side of Figure 15.19.

Note that the above effect should be considered in other asset classes. For example, a slow economy driving low interest rates has the potential to produce a similar effect.

15.4.5 Contingent CDS

One observation from the above approaches to wrong-way risk is that they are generally rather complex modelling problems, with the lack of empirical data and problems with representing dependency creating huge challenges. The only approach that has some clarity is the FX approach in Section 15.4.2 where the simple, economically motivated approach can be calibrated directly to hedging instruments available in the market. This suggests that the main way forward with wrong-way risk is to develop hedging instruments.

In Section 10.2.5 we described the contingent credit default swap (CCDS), which is a credit derivative instrument particularly designed for the hedging of counterparty risk. Like a credit default swap, a CCDS pays out following a credit event on a reference entity. However, unlike a CDS, which has a fixed notional amount, the CCDS protection buyer has protection indexed to another referenced transaction. Whilst single-name CCDS contracts have existed for a number of years (and the ISDA published standard documentation in 2007), the market has not developed any liquidity due to a shortage of protection sellers.

More recently, CCDS has been redeveloped referencing indices such as CDX, iTraxx and SovX on underlying transactions such as interest rate swaps and cross-currency basis swaps denominated in USD, GBP, EUR and CAD. This may help different banks to hedge differing positions, such as being exposed to high or low interest rates with respect to CVA. However, a key need that has partially driven the emergence of an index-based product is to encourage a wider universe of investors to enter the market, for example to express a view on the correlation between credit spreads and interest rates. The prices of CCDS products will imply wrong-way risk effects just as the example in Table 15.2, and may be a hedging tool against wrong-way risk problems such as cross-gamma (described later in Section 16.5.3) which are otherwise unhedgeable.

Apart from developing liquidity, a key to the success of index CCDS is capital relief under Basel III. Since Basel III considers only credit spread volatility of CVA, hedges linked to market risk components, as CCDSs are, are partly problematic. This is discussed in more detail in Section 17.4.5.

15.4.6   Wrong-way risk and collateral

Collateral is typically assessed in terms of its ability to mitigate exposure. Since wrong-way risk essentially causes exposure to increase significantly around the counterparty default time, it could be an important aspect to consider. However, this is very hard to characterise because it is very timing dependent. If the exposure increases gradually up to the default time then collateral can be received, whereas a jump in exposure deems collateral useless.

To understand the difficulty in characterising the impact of collateral, consider first the approach taken for general wrong-way risk in Section 15.3.1. Recalculating the CVA under the assumptions of a zero-threshold, two-way CSA (the exposure in this case has been shown in Section 9.7.2, whilst the CVA has been reported in Table 13.2) gives the results shown in Figure 15.20. Interestingly, the collateralised CVA is rather insensitive to wrong-way risk, with the slope of the line being quite shallow. This is because the greater the wrong-way risk, the more collateral that tends to be taken. The relative benefit of collateral is greatest when there is the most wrong-way risk (at +100% correlation) and has a negative impact when there is extreme right-way risk (less than −40% correlation) due to the need to post collateral.

In the above example, collateral seems to mitigate most of the impact of wrong-way risk as more collateral can be taken in wrong-way risk scenarios. However, let us instead consider the impact of collateral in the FX example from Section 15.4.2. The effect here is obvious, but nevertheless is shown in Figure 15.21. Clearly, the jump effect cannot be collateralised and the exposure cannot be below the assumed devaluation of 20%. In this case, the ability of collateral to reduce wrong-way risk is very limited. If the weakening currency is gradual then the exposure can be well collateralised prior to the default. However, if devaluation of a

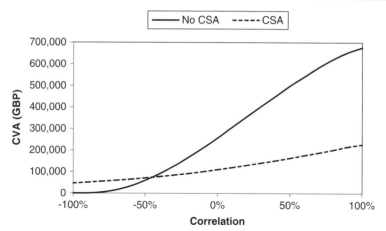

Figure 15.20 Combined impact of collateral (via a two-way CSA) and wrong-way risk on the CVA of the portfolio of four swaps considered previously in Figure 15.6.

currency is linked very closely to a sovereign default, it may be likely to result in a jump in the FX rate that cannot be collateralised in a timely manner.

Not surprisingly, approaches such as the devaluation approach for FX tend to quantify collateral as being useless whereas more continuous approaches such as the correlation approach described above for interest rates (and both approaches described for general wrong-way risk also) suggest that collateral is an effective mitigant against wrong-way risk. The truth is probably somewhere in-between, but the quantification is a challenge. A recent paper by Pykhtin and Sokol (2012) considers that the quantification of the benefit of collateral in a wrong-way risk situation must account for jumps and a period of higher volatility during the margin period of risk. They also note that wrong-way risk should be higher for the default of more systemic parties such as banks. Overall, their approach shows that wrong-way risk has a negative impact on the benefit of collateralisation. Interestingly, counterparties that actively use

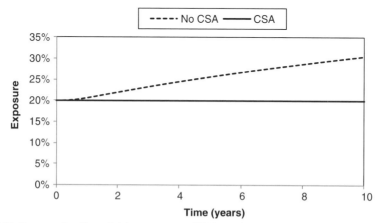

Figure 15.21 Impact of collateral (via a two-way CSA) on the conditional expected exposure of the FX forward shown previously in Figure 15.16.

collateral (e.g., banks) tend to be highly systemic and will be subject to these extreme wrong-way risk problems whilst counterparties that are non-systemic (e.g., corporates) often do not post collateral anyway!

We note also that wrong-way risk can be present on collateral itself. This was shown in Chapter 9 (Section 9.7.6) for a fixed-rate bond collateralising a swap. It is also relevant for cash collateral, for example receiving euro cash from a European sovereign.

15.5 WRONG-WAY RISK AND CREDIT DERIVATIVES

Credit derivatives need particular attention as they effectively represent an entire asset class of wrong-way risk. Furthermore, the problems with monoline insurers described in Section 6.4.4 illustrate the inherent problems with wrong-way risk and credit derivatives. We will analyse the monoline failure in more detail below and explain how wrong-way risk caused such problems. This is not just a historical note: central counterparties intend to clear a significant portion of the credit derivatives market and will therefore have to deal with this wrong-way risk.

15.5.1 Single-name credit derivatives

The wrong-way risk in credit derivatives is a direct consequence of the nature of the products themselves and can lead to serious counterparty risk issues. A protection buyer in a CDS contract has a payoff with respect to a reference entity's default but is at risk in case the counterparty in the contract suffers a similar fate. As mentioned in Section 8.3.6, the CDS product has a highly asymmetric payoff profile due to being essentially an insurance contract. In addition to this, there is also a correlation effect. Buying CDS protection represents a very definite form of wrong-way risk that is made worse as the correlation between the credit quality of the reference entity and the counterparty increases.

In Appendix 15D, we discuss the pricing for a CDS with counterparty risk using a Gaussian copula framework as discussed previously. This requires valuing the two legs of a CDS contingent on the counterparty surviving (since once the counterparty has defaulted an institution would neither make premium payments nor receive default payments) and adding the usual term depending on the future value of the CDS contract at the default time. The pricing of CDS counterparty risk is not trivial, as discussed in Appendix 15D. However, an elegant solution is provided by Mashal and Naldi (2005), who show that there are upper and lower bounds for the value of protection that can be computed more easily. We will take this approach here and use a simple Monte Carlo simulation to value a CDS with counterparty risk. The upper and lower bounds are generally quite close together and we shall therefore report the average. More details can be found in Appendix 15D and in Gregory (2011).

We will ignore the impact of any collateral in the following analysis. This will be conservative since the use of collateral may be considered to reduce CDS counterparty risk. However, due to the highly contagious and systemic nature of CDS risks, the impact of collateral may be hard to assess and indeed may be quite limited (for example, see Section 9.7.5), especially in cases of high correlation. We note also that many protection sellers in the CDS market such as monolines and CDPCs (discussed later) have not traditionally entered into collateral arrangements anyway.

We are interested in the risky value of buying or selling CDS protection as a function of correlation between the reference entity and counterparty (the counterparty is selling

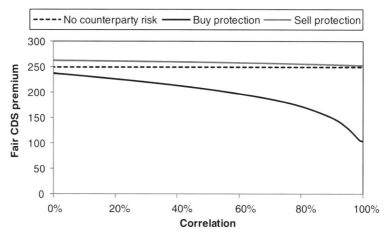

Figure 15.22 Fair CDS premium when buying protection subject to counterparty risk compared with the standard (risk-free) premium. The counterparty CDS spread is assumed to be 500 bps.

protection). We assume that the reference entity CDS spread (without counterparty risk) is 250 bps whereas the counterparty CDS spread is 500 bps. Both recoveries are assumed to be 40%. We assume that the correlation driving joint defaults can only be positive. It is unlikely that negative correlation would ever be seen except in specific cases (for example, the default of a competitor improves the financial health of a counterparty).

We show the fair premium – i.e., reduced (increased) to account for CVA – that an institution should pay (receive) in order to buy (sell) protection in Figure 15.22. When buying protection we can observe the very strong impact of correlation: one should be willing only to pay around 200 bps at 60% correlation to buy protection compared with paying 250 bps with a "risk-free" counterparty. The CVA in this case is 50 bps (running) or one-fifth of the risk-free CDS premium. At extremely high correlations, the impact is even more severe and the CVA is huge. At a maximum correlation of 100%, the CDS premium is just above 100 bps, which relates entirely to the recovery value.[20] When selling protection the impact of CVA is much smaller and reduces with increasing correlation due to right-way risk.[21]

Due to the relatively small CVA impact on selling protection, we can see that the bilateral implications of counterparty risk on CDS contracts are relatively small. For these reasons, we will not consider the impact of DVA although bilateral calculations have been reported by Turnbull (2005).

15.5.2 Credit derivative indices and tranches

Structured credit has given rise to even more complex counterparty risk in the form of tranches. There exist many kinds of CDO structure, which are all broadly characterised by

---

[20] The premium based only on recovery value (i.e., there is no chance of receiving any default payment) is $250 \times 40\% = 100$ bps.

[21] For zero or low correlation values, the protection seller may possibly suffer losses due to the counterparty defaulting when the CDS has a positive MtM (requiring a somewhat unlikely tightening of the reference entity credit spread). However, for high correlation values, the MtM of the CDS is very likely to be negative at the counterparty default time and (since this amount must still be paid) there is virtually no counterparty risk.

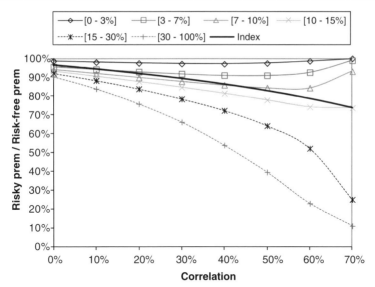

Figure 15.23 Impact of counterparty risk across the capital structure for different tranches. Fair risky tranche premium divided by the risk-free premium for all tranches in the capital structure and compared with the index ([0–100%] tranche). Recovery rates are assumed 10%.

their exposure to a certain range of losses on a portfolio. The counterparty risk problem now becomes more complex, since one needs to assess where the counterparty might default compared with all the reference names underlying the portfolio. The pricing of these instruments and further references are given in Appendix 15D. More details on this can also be found in Turnbull (2005), Pugachevsky (2005) and Gregory (2009b).

We choose tranches according to the standard CDX[22] North American portfolio that are defined by the attachment and detachment points [0%, 3%, 7%, 10%, 15%, 30%, 100%]. Since we are interested only in understanding the qualitative impact of counterparty risk for different tranches, we choose the market standard Gaussian copula model with a fixed correlation parameter of 50%.[23] Due to constraints on the correlation matrix, this means we consider the correlation between the counterparty default and the other names in the portfolio in the range [0, 70%].[24]

We show the impact of counterparty risk across the entire capital structure in Figure 15.23, assuming recovery rates of 10%.[25] In order to compare all tranches on the same scale, we plot the ratio of fair risky premium to risk-free premium: this value will have a maximum at unity and decrease towards the recovery (of the counterparty) as counterparty risk becomes more significant. Indeed, from a counterparty risk perspective, we can view tranching as segregating the counterparty risk: the more senior a tranche, the more risk it contains on a relative basis.

---

[22] www.markit.com

[23] This does not produce prices close to the market, but the standard approach of "base correlation" used to reproduce market prices does not have an obvious associated way in which to price correctly counterparty risk. We have checked that the qualitative conclusions of these results hold at different correlation levels.

[24] The upper limit for this correlation, due to constraints of positive semi-definitiveness on the correlation matrix, is approximately $\sqrt{50\%} = 70.7\%$.

[25] This is consistent with the low recoveries experienced with some defaulting monoline insurers.

In the analysis of options and wrong-way risk (Figure 15.17), we concluded that wrong-way risk increases for more out-of-the-money contracts. We now have an analogous conclusion for tranches that wrong-way risk *increases* for tranches that are more senior. The most senior tranche in the capital structure, the super senior [30–100%] represents the most severe problem. Assuming 40% recovery, there needs to be 62.5% (over half the portfolio) defaults[26] before this tranche takes any loss, and so the chance that the counterparty is still around to honour these payments is expected to be much smaller than for other tranches.

Many of the problems in 2008 and 2009 suffered by monolines were caused by high leverage, coupled with the unprecedented increase in value of super senior protection. The credit spreads of monolines widened from 5–10 bps to several hundred basis points. Banks that had bought super senior insurance from monolines had to realise substantial losses due to the increased counterparty risk. Many transactions were unwound, with banks taking substantial losses due effectively to their positive CVA component. In retrospect, it is not surprising that tranches such as the [30–100%] shown above created severe counterparty risk problems due to their massive wrong-way risk.

15.5.3 The failure of CDOs

Gregory (2008b) presents a theoretical analysis of the protection purchased by monoline insurers and shows that its value is limited by a number of technical factors. Given the sheer size of these tranches, it is counterparty risk that explains much of the failure of CDOs and synthetic securitisation that led to the global financial crisis. Below we make a simple presentation on why CDOs can be efficient and create value, but how they are ultimately due to counterparty risk problems.

CDOs come in many forms, such as cash or synthetic, and cover various different assets from corporate to ABS. However, their basic principle is to take the risk on a given credit portfolio and redistribute it via tranches. A typical CDO is represented in Table 15.3. A number of different classes of securities are issued to cover the full portfolio notional. The riskiness of these securities changes from the bottom unrated equity tranche to the top so-called super senior tranche. Although this latter tranche has no rating, it is above the Triple-A rated class A notes and therefore is at least Triple-A or even better (from where the terms super Triple-A and Quadruple-A arose).

Table 15.3   Illustration of the securities issued from a typical CDO

Class	Amount	Tranching	Rating	Funding
Super senior	850	[15–100%]	NR	Unfunded
Class A	50	[10–15%]	Aaa/AAA	Funded
Class B	30	[7–10%]	Aa2/AA	Funded
Class C	30	[4–7%]	Baa2/BBB	Funded
Equity	40	[0–4%]	NR	Funded

---

[26] $30\% \times 125/(1 - 40\%)$. Although it should be noted that a lower recovery rate assumption is probably more relevant in such an extreme situation.

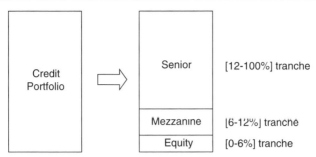

Figure 15.24 Simple CDO structure used for the example.

We can illustrate the key points with a very simple example of a CDO structure illustrated in Figure 15.24. A portfolio is divided into three tranches – equity, mezzanine and senior – and has a 5-year fixed (bullet) maturity. The underlying credit portfolio is assumed to be 100 bonds with Triple-B ratings. From Table 10.2 we can see that the 5-year BBB default probability is 2.06%. Assuming a loss given default of 60%, this will give an expected loss of $2.06\% \times 60\% = 1.24\%$. Finally, we know that a BBB portfolio has to compensate for a loss of more than this due to risk and liquidity premiums. The multiplier from the aforementioned study by Hull *et al.* (2005) from Table 10.4 is 5.1,[27] which suggests that the overall compensation the investors would receive is in fact $1.24\% \times 5.1 = 6.29\%$. We assume the underlying portfolio will provide exactly this amount.[28]

The approximate goal of a CDO is to sell the tranches for less than the return received on the underlying portfolio. In this simple example, this corresponds to paying investors an overall return of less than 6.29% for the equity, mezzanine and senior pieces. In order to sell tranches, they first have to be rated. Assuming an asset correlation (Section 11.2.3) of 20%[29] for all names in the portfolio, the tranches would have ratings of CCC, BBB and AAA for the equity, mezzanine and senior respectively (this process is described in more detail in Appendix 15E). Assuming investors will demand the same return for these investments corresponding to the multiplier in Table 10.4, the economics of the structure are shown in Table 15.4.

The CDO works because most of the risk is sold in the equity tranche, which attracts a relatively low multiplier. It is *relatively* expensive to sell the AAA tranche as the multiplier assumes that for every unit of actual default risk passed on, 16.8 units of return must be paid. However, given the small amount of actual risk that is assessed as being in this tranche, this does not affect the economics of the structure particularly. In Table 15.4, we also show the calculated spreads of the different tranches and the portfolio. Another way to see the value created is via the so-called excess spread, which is the spread paid in versus that paid out. Taking into account the size of each tranche, this is given by $137 - (14 \times 88\%) - (137 \times 6\%) - (1230 \times 6\%) = 43$ bps. This positive excess spread[30] suggests that the overall structure creates a profit. Even if the CDO investors demand a higher relative return for each

---

[27] We note that this uses Moody's ratings (Baa) whilst the default probability data in Chapter 10 is from Standard & Poor's. The results are not changed significantly by using Moody's data throughout.

[28] It should be strongly emphasised that all the above numbers are based on empirical analysis over many years of data but the general conclusions are not changed.

[29] This is conservative with respect to the correlations used by rating agencies for corporate names.

[30] The excess spread is not a perfect guide to the profit since it changes over the lifetime of the CDO as defaults occur. However, it is a reasonable guide to the economics of the structure.

Table 15.4   Illustration of the securities issued from a typical CDO

	5-year default probability	Expected default loss	Multiplier	Size	Cost	Spread
BBB portfolio	2.06%	1.23%	5.1	100%	**6.29%**	137
AAA tranche	0.07%	0.04%	16.8	88%	0.58%	14
BBB tranche	2.06%	1.23%	5.1	6%	0.38%	137
CCC tranche	56.27%	33.76%	1.3	6%	2.63%	1230
				Total	**3.59%**	

rating (this was certainly true in the early days of the CDO market), there is enough value in the structure to pay this return.

The above explains how CDOs can work. Their failure could be ascribed to the rating agency models used to rate the tranches as being incorrect. However, there is no evidence from corporate default rates that the correlation assumptions used by rating agencies are too low. Secondly, a higher correlation does not completely ruin the economics of the structure (for example, a 30% correlation in the above example reduces the excess spread from 43 to 27 bps but changing the tranching can substantially improve this[31]).

The true failure of CDOs lies more in counterparty risk. The above does not take into account the counterparty risk in issuing the tranches of the CDO. Whilst the equity and mezzanine tranches can probably be issued on a fully funded basis,[32] the (super) senior tranche will typically be completely unfunded[33] (see Table 15.3). This unfunded tranche then creates the significant counterparty risk that can be seen in Figure 15.23. The relative size of this tranche,[34] the high seniority and the inability of protection sellers (such as monolines to post collateral) makes the risk transfer highly inefficient, as shown by Gregory (2008b). The only way to achieve this risk transfer is by counterparties who are not highly leveraged and exposed to senior credit risk (as monolines were). This in turn makes the economics of the transaction less beneficial (since the price paid on the senior tranche will be higher) and severely limits the total amount of such transactions that can be done.

15.5.4   Central clearing and wrong-way risk

CCPs convert counterparty risk into gap risk and tail risk. A key aim of a CCP is that losses to the default of a clearing member are contained within resources committed by that

---

[31] The tranches described have not been optimised in any way. For example, by calculating the minimum amount of subordination to achieve a given rating.

[32] The transaction will be a synthetic bond with the investor paying upfront the full notional of the transaction, which is therefore fully collateralised with no counterparty risk.

[33] This will therefore be executed as a credit default swap referencing the underlying tranche. It is therefore subject to counterparty risk.

[34] For example, a typical portfolio size may be around $1 billion, which would make the notional of the senior tranche in this example $880m.

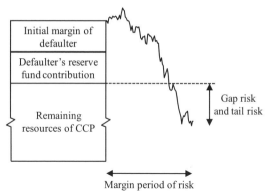

Figure 15.25 Illustration of the tail risk faced by a CCP in the event of the default of one or more members. The effective margin period of risk is as discussed previously (e.g., Section 5.5.1) and is usually considered by CCPs to be around five business days (Section 7.2.4).

clearing member (the so-called "defaulter pays" approach described in Section 7.1.4). A CCP faces tail and gap risk as illustrated in Figure 15.25 since the initial margin and reserve fund contributions (Sections 7.2.4 and 7.2.5, respectively) of the defaulting member(s) may be insufficient to cover their losses. This leads to moral hazard (since other CCP members will suffer losses) and potentially even financial insolvency of the CCP.

CCPs tend to disassociate credit quality and exposure. Institutions must have a certain *credit* quality to be clearing members but members will then be charged initial margins and reserve fund contributions driven primarily[35] by the *market* risk of their portfolio (that drives the exposure faced by the CCP). In doing this, CCPs are in danger of implicitly ignoring wrong-way risk. The drop in value represented in Figure 15.25 can be a result of extreme volatility, downward pressure and gap (jump) events. The impact of wrong-way risk is to make all of these aspects more severe when coupled with the default of the counterparty.

For significant wrong-way risk transactions such as CDSs, CCPs have a problem of quantifying the wrong-way risk component in defining initial margins and reserve funds. As with the quantification of wrong-way risk in general, this is far from an easy task. Furthermore, wrong-way risk increases with increasing credit quality, as shown in Figure 15.2 and Table 15.1 (similar arguments are made by Pykhtin and Sokol (2012) in that a large dealer represents more wrong-way risk than a weaker credit quality counterparty). These aspects suggest perversely that CCPs should require greater initial margin and reserve fund contributions from **better** credit quality members.[36]

15.6   SUMMARY

In this chapter we have discussed wrong-way counterparty risk, which is a phenomenon caused by the dependence between exposure and default probability. Wrong-way risk is a subtle, but potentially devastating, effect that can increase counterparty risk and CVA

---

[35] As noted in Section 7.2.4, some CCPs do base margins partially on credit ratings but this tends to be a secondary impact.
[36] Of course, better credit quality members are less likely to default but the impact in the event that they do is likely to be more severe.

substantially. Portfolio and trade-level wrong-way risk have been described. We have examined some classic examples arising in different asset classes (interest rates, FX, equity and commodities) and associated quantitative approaches. Counterparty risk in credit derivatives has been analysed and the failure of CDOs has been linked to this. Finally, we have considered the impact of wrong-way risk on collateral and argued that it represents a very serious concern for central counterparties.

In the next and final section of this book, we will turn our attention to methods for managing counterparty credit risk including hedging, capital and the operation of a CVA desk.

Section IV: Managing Counterparty Credit Risk

The final section of this book describes the management of counterparty credit risk, which is a critical aspect due to the volatility of financial markets and regulatory changes. We begin by discussing hedging counterparty risk in **Chapter 16**. CVA essentially represents a complex hybrid derivative payoff that is ultimately very difficult to manage with good precision, even compared, for example, with the hedging of exotic derivatives positions. We look at the theoretical hedging for CVA across both market risk and credit risk. The impact of DVA and collateral is also considered, and the impact of wrong-way risk in the form of cross-gamma is described. We describe the practical hedging strategies that are possible, especially in light of the illiquidity of credit hedges for most counterparties. We will also discuss that, due to effects such as mapping credit spreads, CVA hedging of accounting PnL is not always aligned with the true reduction of economic risk.

CVA may be further complicated by the need for banks to reduce capital requirements for counterparty risk. Not surprisingly such capital requirements have been increased significantly in light of the global financial crisis. However, these are made up from a combination of different capital charges. Pre-crisis, CVA default losses were capitalised via the Basel I and II frameworks, which considered default risk analogously to illiquid credit risk such as loans. A key part of the post-crisis Basel III framework is the belief that most counterparty risk capital should be derived as a result of the mark-to-market volatility of CVA. This has led to a new capital charge in the form of "CVA VAR". It is also important to consider the impact of capital requirements where transactions are collateralised and centrally cleared to understand the benefit that will be achieved. **Chapter 17** describes the regulation of counterparty risk, mainly in terms of capital requirements. Since this is a rapidly changing area, updates to this chapter will be posted on www.cvacentral.com.

Finally, in **Chapter 18** we consider the role of the CVA desk, which is the central unit in a bank with the job of quantifying and managing counterparty risk. A CVA desk needs to price CVA in new trades, apply the relevant hedging and optimise the regulatory capital requirements. The CVA desk also has critical interaction with other functions, such as other trading desks, collateral management and the treasury (funding) in a bank. The existence of a CVA desk has become the norm and they have become extremely high profile in many banks.

Even non-banking financial institutions and end-users of OTC derivatives are seeing the need to have some CVA management function.

Counterparty risk is a complex subject with many challenges and its future will be shaped by an interaction between market practice, risk mitigation and regulatory requirements. Many questions remain unanswered, such as the impact of Basel III and central clearing on OTC derivatives markets. In **Chapter 19** we will try to give some idea of the future of counterparty risk and the changing landscape for CVA.

16

Hedging Counterparty Risk

Take calculated risks. That is quite different from being rash.

George S. Patton (1885–1945)

This chapter deals with the hedging of counterparty risk, which has become a key activity over recent years. There are certainly many ways to mitigate counterparty risk. However, without the ability to hedge, an institution may find themselves severely limited in the type and amount of transactions they take and the counterparties they trade with, due to internal or regulatory capital restrictions (Chapter 17). Furthermore, an institution's total CVA (and DVA) may exhibit severe volatility and potentially lead to large losses. However, as we shall see, hedging CVA poses many challenges due to the different market variables involved and the potential linkage between them. Ultimately, the hedging will be far from perfect, the most pragmatic solution being to identify the key components of CVA that can, and should, be hedged as well as those that cannot, or should not.

Trade-level CVAs are relatively small due, primarily, to the relatively low default probability of the counterparty and the exposure-reducing effects such as netting and collateral. A typical CVA will be a fraction of a percentage point of the notional of a trade. However, were the counterparty to default, the actual losses might well be much higher. For example, the four-trade example in Table 13.1 has a CVA of 237,077. However, considering a potential counterparty default at 2 years, then the actual expected exposure is 1.77m and the 95% PFE is 10.86m (this can be seen in Figures 9.21 and 9.22, respectively). Hence, the CVA covers only a small fraction of the potential losses.

There are two possible explanations to the above observation:

1. The CVA is "reserve" against counterparty risk and will certainly not represent the actual losses experienced at the trade level. However, since there are many other trades with many different counterparties, the diversification impact means that the overall CVA is sufficient in a portfolio context.
2. The CVA represents the cost of hedging counterparty risk, irrespective of whether or not the counterparty defaults.

In this chapter, we deal with the second case above and discuss CVA hedging. In Chapter 18, we ask the question of how an institution should manage their CVA effectively, which may represent a combination of the above two points.

16.1 BACKGROUND TO CVA HEDGING

16.1.1 Aim of CVA hedging

A key aspect of CVA, as discussed in Chapter 12, is the ability to separate the risk-free and risky value of a derivative (or set of netted derivatives). This extends to hedging where the risk-free value[1] and CVA can be hedged separately. A simple example of the aim of CVA hedging is given in Table 16.1, which shows the impact of a market move on the risky and risk-free value, which is also illustrated in Figure 16.1. In this example, the market move causes the risk-free value to *increase* but the risky value to *decrease* (due to an increasing CVA). Without hedging the CVA, there would be a net loss on the risky position.

The above approach implies that different trading desks can be responsible for hedging the risk-free and CVA components. For many reasons, such as the required specialism in many different areas (interest rates, FX, commodities) and the impact of netting and collateral agreements on CVA, this split is a natural one. We will discuss this further in Chapter 18.

16.1.2 CVA as an exotic option

The famous Black–Scholes (1973) approach to option pricing created a link between the price of an option and a dynamic hedging strategy. The option price can be proved equal to the expected return under the so-called risk-neutral measure. This is justified theoretically since the option can be replicated via a self-financing strategy. Anyone disagreeing on the price of the option can be proved wrong[2] via being arbitraged! This idea has been critical to the development of exotic options and structured products. To price any complex payoff, one specifies a model, calibrates it to the market (the hedging instruments) and then calculates the risk-neutral price. The underlying justification that there is a practical strategy for replicating the calculated model price is often not considered in enough depth.

In Section 12.2.3, we described the Sorensen–Bollier approach to representing the CVA of a swap via a series of swaptions. This approach can be extended, i.e., a CVA can be represented as a series of options on the underlying product(s). However, in quantifying the value of these options there are many complexities. The quantity of each option is driven by the default probability of the counterparty effectively creating a *hybrid* product. Off-market

Table 16.1 Numerical illustration of hedging of risky value via the CVA and risk-free MtM

	Before	*After*	*Hedge (after)*
Risk-free value	+10	+11	−1
CVA	+2	+4	+2
Risky value	+8	+7	
Gain/loss		−1	+1

---

[1] Noting, as discussed in Chapter 14, that risk-free valuation is much more complex than was historically believed to be the case.
[2] Assuming of course the model's assumptions, in particular that of the volatility, hold true.

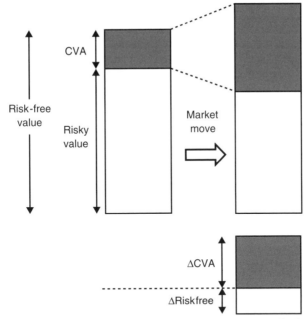

Figure 16.1 Illustration of the ideal hedging of a risky derivatives position via the risk-free and CVA components. The market move causes an increase in the risk-free value that creates a loss on the corresponding hedging instrument. The CVA, however, increases and therefore the associated hedge produces a gain. Overall, the risky value decreases, which is hedged via an overall gain on the CVA versus a loss on the risk-free hedge.

(legacy) trades will lead to in- or out-of-the-moneyness. Out-of-the-money options are more difficult to price as they are more sensitive to the extremes of the underlying distributions. There is no guarantee that the underlying option even exists, for example, it may be too out-of-the-money or the maturity may be too long. Finally, CVA typically needs to be calculated on a netting set of trades, which implies the underlying option may be multidimensional.

With these associated problems, quantifying CVA clearly represents a hybrid exotic option pricing problem. However, since exotic options are priced and hedged, surely CVA can also be. Whilst this point is not incorrect *per se*, some important considerations should be kept in mind:

- *Variables*. The CVA for even a simple product will represent several underlying variables (for example, interest rates, FX rates and credit spreads). Hence, hedging CVA involves several underlying risk factors. Hedges may also be sensitive to term structure, meaning that to hedge one underlying variable effectively may involve positions in hedging instruments with different maturity dates.
- *Cross-dependency*. The dependency or relationship between different variables (for example, interest rates and credit spreads) may be impossible to hedge and lead to difficult cross-gamma effects (Section 16.5.2).
- *Inability to hedge some variables*. There may be some variables that have an impact on CVA but cannot be hedged, either because there is no market instrument with the required sensitivity or because, pragmatically, the hedging costs are prohibitory. Credit parameters,

in particular, are rather expensive to hedge and correlations are often completely unhedgeable.

None of the above points is specific to CVA and all arise in various exotic products. Having said that, from an exotic product perspective, CVA represents a *complex hybrid multi-asset exotic option*. In addition, there is a further point when hedging CVA that should be considered:

- *Lack of arbitrage*. When pricing exotic products, arbitrage is a key aspect. Mispricing of an exotic product can lead to arbitrage as other market participants can dynamically hedge in order to lock in a profit arising from the mispricing. However, if an institution A misprices the CVA[3] to another institution B then an arbitrageur is unlikely to profit since they would need to trade a contract with institution A, referencing the credit quality of institution B. Whilst products like CCDSs (discussed later) make this potentially possible, their usage is still at a very low level.

16.1.3 Risk-neutral or real-world?

As discussed in Section 8.6, the choice of risk-neutral over real-world parameters is a subtle but important one. Risk-neutral parameters tend always to be used for pricing, even though the underlying hedging is not always applied. In such situations, it is important to consider the implications carefully and be cautious with the naïve use of implicit risk-neutral drift parameters, especially drifts. Other parameters such as correlations are not tradable and tend to be estimated historically. The inability to hedge such variables will create unavoidable PnL volatility.

16.1.4 Traditional hedging of fixed exposures

Traditional debt securities, such as bonds and loans, can be hedged using credit default swaps (CDSs). Holding a bond with a $100m face value and buying the same notional of CDS protection referencing the bond issuer is quite an effective hedge for the credit risk of the bond. A potential default of the issuer is hedged against since the CDS payoff will compensate for the bond face value, less recovery, if there is a credit event as illustrated in Table 16.2. Furthermore, the position is hedged against credit migration and credit spread risk, since a fall in the bond price triggered by a deterioration of the issuer's credit quality will be compensated by a MtM gain on the CDS position.

Despite the relatively simple nature of the above example (after all, this is more or less what the CDS product was designed for), there are a number of reasons why the above hedge will not be perfect (this is related to the discussion on the CDS–bond basis in Section 10.2.4):

- *Non-par bonds*. CDS protection will settle based on a fixed notional value whereas bonds can trade above or below par for interest rate (or equity in the case of convertible bonds) reasons.[4] If the CDS notional is equal to the par value of the bond then the hedge will

---

[3] The quantification of CVA is so subjective and no standards exist. Therefore, an actual mispricing of CVA is hard to define.
[4] The bond trading away from par for credit reasons is not relevant since the MtM impact of this will be mirrored by the MtM of the CDS protection.

Table 16.2   Illustration of hedging the default risk in a bond with a CDS showing the payoff at default or the maturity of the bond

	Default	*No default*
Bond	Recovery	Par
CDS	Par – recovery	—
Total	**Par**	**Par**

make a loss[5] (gain) if the bond is trading above (below) par prior to default. Essentially this is a facet of uncertain exposure that is more pronounced in contracts such as derivatives.

- *Annuity risk*. Similar to the effect above, a mismatch between the maturity and the premium of the CDS contract leads to annuity risk (Section 10.2.1).
- *Trigger risk*. There is a risk that the CDS contract may not trigger whilst there will be a credit-related loss on the bond (Section 10.2.2).
- *Seniority*. The CDS must be *pari passu* (Section 10.1.7) and reference the same seniority of debt (typically senior unsecured) so that recovery values are aligned. Derivatives exposures normally rank *pari passu* with senior debt.
- *Cheapest-to-deliver option*. If a CDS contract can be settled physically via the protection buyer delivering bonds then they have the option to find the cheapest bond that may be contractually delivered. A cheaper bond will lead to a lower recovery on the hedge than on the derivative contract and result in a gain for the institution hedging counterparty risk.
- *Delivery squeeze*. Under physical settlement of a CDS, a delivery squeeze is caused by a lack of deliverable obligations in the market and causes inflated bond prices due to strong demand. CDS protection buyers, for the purposes of hedging CVA, will have to buy bonds in order to settle the CDS. This higher bond price will be likely to lead to a loss for the institution hedging counterparty risk.

As discussed previously (Section 10.2.3), the last two problems above, arising from physical settlement of CDSs, have been minimised by adopting an auction method of cash settlement as the primary means of settling CDS contracts. Whilst this removes the problems related to the cheapest-to-deliver option and delivery squeeze, we must now consider any possible differences between the auction recovery rate and the actual recovery rate eventually received on the exposure. Whilst a CDS contract can (and must) be settled in a timely manner, an institution has to wait before receiving the recovery amount on a derivative(s) or otherwise monetising this claim (see Section 10.1.7). Bankruptcy proceedings involve long negotiations and legal proceedings that can last many years. The larger the counterparty, the more complex the bankruptcy period and consequently the longer an institution will have to wait to recover anything on their claim.

---

[5] This assumes implicitly that the bond is marked-to-market and/or its interest rate risk is hedged.

16.2   COMPONENTS OF CVA HEDGING

16.2.1   Single-name CDS

As discussed above, static hedging of a bond or similar security by buying CDS protection is a reasonable hedging strategy, albeit with many small potential risks (and technical risks such as delivery squeezes). Most fixed-rate bonds are unlikely to trade more than 5–10% away from their par value[6] and hence a static hedge will, if implemented carefully, allow a major proportion of the credit risk to be eliminated.

The static hedging of derivatives exposures is much more complex due to the highly uncertain potential future exposure. As an example, we illustrate the hedging of the PFE of a swap-type exposure in Figure 16.2. The hedge notional(s) are chosen to ensure that the PFE is (over) hedged at all points in time. We consider a single CDS hedge and a term structure hedge involving five CDS instruments of different maturities. The latter hedge allows a better replication of the PFE profile.

Since the static hedge is based on 95% PFE, we would expect it to be costly since it will be an over-hedge in at least 95 cases out of 100. Assuming an upwards-sloping credit curve,[7] the total CVA, expressed as a running spread, for the exposure profile in Figure 16.2 is 1.5 bps. The initial cost of the hedge using only 5-year CDS protection is 10.3 bps.[8] The term structure hedge (CDS Hedge 2) provides a better match to the overall exposure profile and has an initial cost of 8.1 bps.[9] We could, of course, choose a lower confidence level, which would make the hedge cheaper at the expense of increasing the probability that, in default, the exposure would be unhedged.

This style of static hedge, whilst extremely simple, is inefficient and costly. It can only be considered for extreme situations such as very profitable trading with a particular

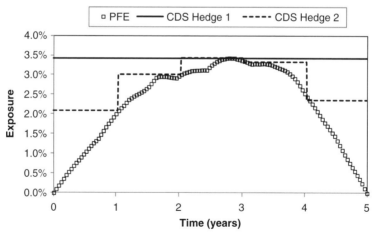

Figure 16.2 Example of static hedging of exposure via the PFE at the 95th quantile. CDS Hedge 1 corresponds to a single-maturity instrument (5 years) whilst CDS Hedge 2 assumes a hedge involving 1-, 2-, 3-, 4- and 5-year CDS protection.

---

[6] For non-credit reasons since this any price changes for credit spread reasons will be hedged by the MtM value of the CDS protection.

[7] 1Y = 100 bps, 2Y = 150 bps, 3Y = 200 bps, 4Y = 250 bps, 5Y = 300 bps.

[8] $300 \times 3.42\%$.

[9] $(100 \times -0.92\%) + (150 \times -0.42\%) + (200 \times 0.11\%) + (250 \times 0.97\%) + (300 \times 2.35\%)$.

counterparty or the urgent need to reduce an exposure to within a confidence level or, equivalently, below a certain credit limit. Furthermore, it assumes the existence of a single-name CDS market.

16.2.2 Contingent CDS

Single-name CCDSs have been described previously in Section 10.2.5. The settlement of a CCDS will work in exactly the same way as that of a standard CDS, except that the notional amount of protection will be determined by the value of the derivative contract referenced by the CCDS at the default time. For example, if the derivative has an exposure of $10m at the counterparty default date, then the CCDS protection buyer may exercise based on a notional amount of $10m. If a CCDS is physically settled then bonds with face value $10m must be purchased to deliver against the contract. If the recovery rate is 40% then the CCDS contract will have a payoff of $6m. The remaining $4m should be recovered from the counterparty. CCDSs will retain the problem of mismatch between CDS auction recovery versus actual final recovery (discussed above). There has been discussion in the market of introducing swap-settled CCDSs where the actual derivative would be assigned to the CCDS counterparty, although legal obstacles of reassignment may prohibit this.

Two obvious risks arise from a CCDS, as illustrated in Figure 16.3. A CCDS contract has to reference another transaction, and hence, in order to perfectly hedge the exposure, all the details of the transaction must be specified (maturity date, reference rates, underlyings, payment frequency, daycount conventions, etc.). If the exact transaction or netting set is not specified, for reasons of practicality or otherwise, then the exposure in question will not be precisely tracked and give rise to residual exposure. A further consideration of CCDSs is that there is still risk due to the joint default of the original counterparty and the CCDS counterparty.

Whilst this might seem a small issue, if the correlation between these counterparties is significant then the problem may be serious, as discussed in more detail in Section 11.2. The "double default" aspect implies two important considerations when trading CCDSs (and indeed CDSs):

1. The CCDS counterparty should be of an equivalent or better credit quality than the original counterparty *and/or*
2. The default correlation between the CCDS counterparty and the original counterparty should be reasonably low.

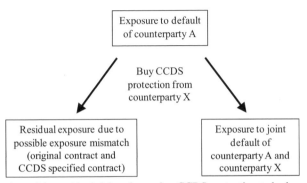

Figure 16.3 Illustration of the residual risks when using CCDS protection to hedge a specific exposure.

Basel III is bringing a renewed interest in CCDSs as they provide some level of capital relief, as discussed in Chapter 17. There is also interest in index CCDSs for hedging wrong-way risk, as discussed in Section 15.4.5.

16.2.3 CVA Greeks

In the next sections we discuss dynamic hedging of CVA, analysing the different Greeks and examining the practical issues with hedging each relevant component. Let us consider the simple unilateral CVA formula given previously in Chapter 12 (hedging of bilateral CVA will be covered later):

$$CVA = spread \times EPE. \tag{16.1}$$

The obvious sensitivities of this formula are

$$\partial CVA = \frac{\partial CVA}{\partial spread} \Delta spread + \frac{\partial CVA}{\partial EPE} \Delta EPE + \frac{\partial^2 CVA}{\partial EPE\, \partial spread} \Delta EPE \Delta spread.,$$

The first two terms above, $\partial CVA/\partial spread$ and $\partial CVA/\partial EPE$, represent the CVA sensitivity with respect to credit spreads and exposure, respectively whilst the final one represents a cross-dependency (cross-gamma).

The credit spread sensitivity covers default probability and recovery rate. The most obvious hedge for the default probability is a single-name CDS with the counterparty as reference entity. Most of the recovery risk will be hedged via such a CDS but there can be some second-order risk and basis risk, which we will analyse later.

The exposure (EPE) sensitivity covers all variables that have an impact on exposure.[10] This can be grouped broadly into three categories:

- *Spot/forward rates.* The sensitivity to spot and forward rates, such as interest rates and FX.
- *Volatility.* The sensitivity to implied volatility, such as FX options or swaptions.
- *Correlation.* The sensitivity to correlation between different exposure variables (such as two different interest rates).

The number of sensitivities that the above categories can constitute is unmanageably large, even in some rather simple cases, let alone for large portfolios of trades. For example, even a single cross-currency swap gives rise to interest rate risk (in two currencies), interest rate volatility risk (two currencies), FX risk, FX volatility risk and correlation risk or cross gamma (between both interest rates and between interest rates and the FX rate).

It is also important to re-emphasise that equation (16.1) is only an approximation to the CVA (as discussed in Section 12.1.3). This means that all hedges should be considered across the term structure. Ideally, hedges themselves should be counterparty risk-free (such as those executed on an exchange) to avoid the problem that the hedges themselves create more CVA. This is the case in the double default problem mentioned in Section 16.2.2.

The final sensitivity given above, $\partial^2 CVA/\partial EPE\, \partial spread$, is a cross-dependency term often known as cross-gamma. This will be relevant when there is a relationship between

---

[10] Note that there will be cross-dependency terms here also representing the cross gamma between different exposure terms (e.g., interest rates and FX).

credit spread and exposure, as in the case of wrong-way (and right-way) risk. This is discussed in Section 16.5.2.

There are clearly a potentially enormous number of CVA Greeks to consider. A CVA book will experience sensitivity to every single parameter which is a sensitivity for the underlying trades in every currency, asset class and product type. Furthermore, a CVA book will have sensitivity specific to CVAs that are not present in the risk-free valuation of the underlying transactions, such as in the case of credit risk, correlations and some additional volatilities. It is therefore crucial to understand which terms are most important, which less so and which can be ignored.

16.3   EXPOSURE HEDGES

The next sections will examine the above CVA components in more detail and from a practical perspective. The following assumptions will be used unless otherwise stated:

Trade:	5-year payer interest rate swap
Interest rates:	Increasing term structure corresponding to 1- to 5-year interest rates of 4.0%, 4.25%, 4.5%, 4.75% and 5.0%, respectively
Volatility:	The interest rate volatility is assumed to be 25%[11]
Credit quality:	We assume the counterparty has an initial CDS premium of 500 bps and recovery rate of 40%
Notional:	100m (most of the results are given as percentages so this is not relevant)

For all quantitative examples, we will tend to assume a complete liquidity of hedging instruments but also comment on the practicality of the strategies due to the availability of the hedging instruments in today's market.

We first consider the hedging of the CVA component arising from the exposure that can be divided into the impact of spot/forward rates and volatilities. Correlation (which is typically not hedgeable) is discussed later.

16.3.1   Spot/forward rates

The hedging of underlying CVA spot rates for CVA usually mirrors hedges corresponding to the risk-free instrument. In Figure 16.4 we show both the risk-free and CVA interest rate sensitivities for the interest rate swap in question.

We can understand the graph as follows. The 5-year payer swap has a positive sensitivity to interest rates since, as rates increase, the value of the floating payments received will increase. Most of the sensitivity is concentrated on the 5-year point. When interest rates increase, the CVA will increase due to the increased exposure but, since CVA represents a cost, this corresponds to a negative sensitivity. The CVA sensitivity on the previous tenors is slightly positive. A combination of the risk-free and CVA sensitivities gives the risky sensitivity, which involves reducing the 5-year hedge and increasing the (small) hedges on the shorter maturities (since counterparty risk shortens the expected lifetime or duration of the swap).

Another way to understand Figure 16.4 is that the swap trader hedges as if the trade were risk-free and the institution had 100% of a swap. However, the institution has less than 100%

---
[11] This is a lognormal volatility of the swap rate.

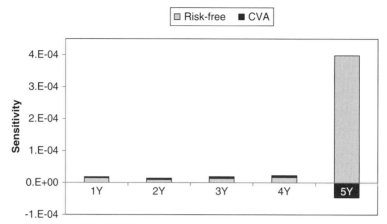

Figure 16.4 Sensitivity of the risk-free swap value and the CVA of the swap to a 1 bp move in the underlying interest rates assuming the counterparty CDS premium is 500 bps.

of a swap since the counterparty is risky and hence the CVA hedge cancels out some of the original hedge. Indeed, some institutions without active CVA desks often hedge only a proportion[12] of the interest rate sensitivity in order to incorporate the CVA sensitivity directly.

This poses the question as to why the interest rate risk should be split and hedged by two separate desks, the swap trader hedging the interest rate risk in the usual manner (as if the swap were risk-free) and another CVA trader hedging the CVA component. It might seem perverse for one trader to execute one hedge position on 5-year rates and another essentially to "unwind" some of this position.[13] Figure 16.5 shows the same sensitivities, assuming the counterparty CDS premium has doubled to 1,000 bps. Whilst the risk-free hedges are

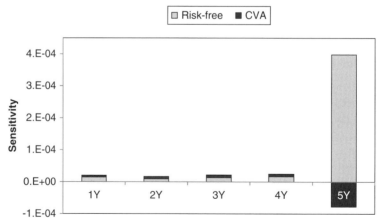

Figure 16.5 Sensitivity of the risk-free swap value and the CVA of the swap to a 1 bp move in the underlying interest rates assuming the counterparty CDS premium is 1,000 bps.

---

[12] This proportion is approximately equal to the survival probability of the counterparty.

[13] An interesting limiting case is when a counterparty is close to default. Here, the risk-free and CVA sensitivities should be almost equal and opposite, leading to an overall net position with close to zero interest rate risk as required. The original trading desk and CVA desk can offset their respective risks by trading directly with each other.

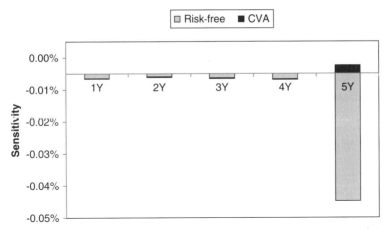

Figure 16.6 Sensitivity of the opposite (receiver) risk-free swap value and the CVA of the swap to a 1 bp move in the underlying interest rates assuming the counterparty CDS premium is 500 bps.

unaffected, the CVA hedges have changed substantially. In Figure 16.6 we show the sensitivities for the opposite receiver swap which are of the opposite sign, but approximately half those of the corresponding payer swap. Whilst the risk-free sensitivities are exactly equal and opposite due to the linearity of the product, the CVA components do not behave in this way. With an upwards-sloping interest rate term structure, the receiver swap will have a smaller sensitivity to interest rates since it has a lower expected exposure. These examples illustrate some of the complexity of CVA hedging, meaning that whilst risk-free and CVA hedges could be combined, the complexity of hedging CVA requires that it be handled by a specialist CVA desk (Chapter 18).

16.3.2 Drift and hedging

Let us return briefly to the discussion on using risk-neutral or real parameters and consider the hedging of the payer and receiver interest rate swaps according to the sensitivities shown in Figure 16.4 and Figure 16.6, respectively. We therefore consider hedges based on all five annual maturities up to 5 years. By using the interest rate term structure given by the market, we are implicitly assuming that interest rates will increase over time. Let us assume that this is not the case, reflected by a flattening of the interest rate term structure. In Table 16.3 we

Table 16.3 Illustration of hedging of CVA corresponding to a flattening of the interest rate term structure (1-year and 2-year rates move up by 5 bps, 4-year and 5-year rates down by 5 bps, 3-year unchanged)

	Payer swap	*Receiver swap*
Initial CVA	0.325%	0.166%
Final CVA	0.306%	0.177%
CVA PnL	0.019%	−0.011%
Hedge PnL	−0.020%	0.010%

show that the hedges perform well with the decrease in the CVA for the payer swap, balanced by a loss on the hedge and vice versa for the receiver swap. The smaller hedge (Figure 16.6) required for the receiver swap is in line with the smaller change in CVA for the interest rate move.

If the interest rate component of the CVA is not being hedged then the use of risk-neutral parameters is dangerous. The implicit assumption that future spot interest rates will follow the current forward rates equates to making a bet that the interest rates will increase and, hence, the payer swap has a larger CVA than the receiver. If this is not the case, as seen by a gradual flattening of the interest rate curve, then the CVA will create a positive PnL on the payer swap and a negative PnL on the receiver swap.

Spot and forward rate sensitivities in interest rate and FX, and also in other areas such as inflation and commodities markets, are generally relatively easy to manage and banks tend to hedge out these components of their CVA (to the extent they are considered material).

16.3.3 Volatility

Managing volatility risk is an important aspect of hedging CVA. Recall that, whilst the underlying derivative may have little or no sensitivity to volatility, the associated CVA could have substantial volatility risk. An institution could have only interest rate swap products to avoid any volatility risk and yet generate volatility risk through the CVA of the swaps! We show in Figure 16.7 the CVA for the payer and receiver interest rate swaps used in the previous examples. The reader may find it helpful to recall that the CVA of an interest rate swap can be represented as a series of swaptions on the reverse swap (Section 12.2.3).

Both the payer and receiver swaps have a monotonically increasing relationship to volatility, as one would expect given exposure represents an option on the underlying (Section 8.1.4). For zero volatility, the payer swap has some CVA due to the swaptions being in-the-money for the upwards-sloping interest rate term structure. At zero volatility, the receiver swap has zero CVA since the swaptions are out-of-the-money.

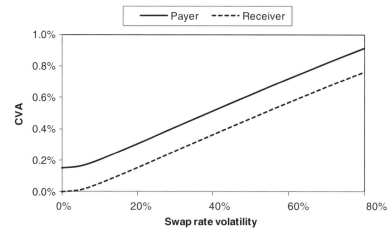

Figure 16.7 CVA as a function of swap rate volatility for the payer interest rate swap and equivalent receiver swap. This assumes a flat volatility term structure.

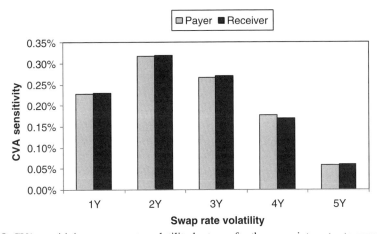

Figure 16.8 CVA sensitivity to swap rate volatility by tenor for the payer interest rate swap and equivalent receiver swap.

The sensitivity of CVA to interest rate volatility can be hedged via swaptions. However, we should also consider the term structure impact of volatility, which is illustrated in Figure 16.8.

In order to understand the pattern in Figure 16.8, we must consider that the short-term swaptions[14] defining the CVA will have little value, due to the short maturity, whilst long-term swaptions will have little value, due to the short duration of the underlying swap. The swaptions that have the most value are those at intermediate maturities. Indeed, this effect gives rise to the classic exposure profile of a swap product.

We see that the volatility sensitivity is approximately the same for payer and receiver swaps, even though the CVA is substantially more for the payer. The payer swaptions are in-the-money by the same amount as the receiver swaptions are out-of-the-money. Since a Vega (volatility) profile is approximately symmetric with the maximum at-the-money, the sensitivities are almost identical. This is no particular use at this stage as all positions are implicitly short Vega on the CVA component. However, it will become interesting when we consider DVA later.

Note that it is possible to use either payer or receiver swaptions to hedge volatility but it is important to consider the sensitivity of swaptions to spot rates. Figure 16.9 shows the spot sensitivity of CVA, as previously shown in Figure 16.4, but assuming that the volatility will be hedged using a 2-year maturity swaption.[15] We can see that hedging volatility with the opposite receiver swaption will reduce the overall spot sensitivity, whereas using a payer swaption to hedge volatility will increase the overall sensitivity and potentially increase hedging costs. From the Sorenson–Bollier analogy, it is not surprising that the more natural hedging instrument is the (opposite) receiver swaption.

---

[14] These swaptions follow the Sorensen and Bollier analogy (Appendix 12D) and are not considered actual hedging instruments.

[15] We assume a 2-year swaption to enter into a 3-year swap, although the swap maturity has only a small impact on the results.

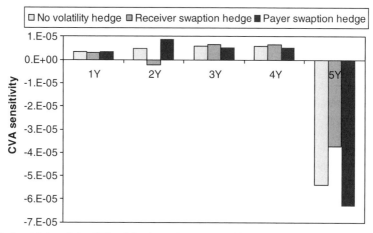

Figure 16.9 Sensitivity of the CVA of the (payer) swap to a 1 bp move in the underlying interest rates, as previously shown in Figure 9.13, but assuming that there is additionally a single volatility hedge corresponding to either a receiver or payer swaption of 2-year maturity.

16.4   CREDIT HEDGES

We will now discuss the hedging of the credit component of CVA. Initially, the focus will be on single-name hedging assuming liquidity of CDS, referencing the counterparty. After this we discuss hedging with indices, which is more practical given the lack of depth in the single-name CDS market.

16.4.1   Credit delta

Unlike a bullet structure, the credit spread hedging of the 5-year swap cannot be closely replicated with a 5-year CDS instrument. We first consider the sensitivity to the CDS spread, as shown in Figure 16.10. There is a significant impact across the CDS tenor. An increase in the 1-year CDS premium, for example, causes the 1-year default probability to increase and the 1-year to 2-year default probability to decrease. This means that the overall CVA will decrease since the EE is smaller in the first year compared with the second year – there is, therefore, a negative sensitivity at 1 year. An increase in the 3-year CDS will move default probability to the 2- to 3-year region from the 3- to 4-year region, where the EE is higher, and therefore creates a positive sensitivity. The impact of changes to the shape of the CDS curve (flat curve versus upwards-sloping curve) has little impact on the CDS risk. This emphasises that the term structure impact arises almost entirely from the EE profile of the swap.

16.4.2   Gamma and jump-to-default risk

Consider the delta hedging of CVA assuming a starting CDS premium of 500 bps. We assume hedging with a 5-year CDS contract only, as this is likely to be the most liquid tenor available. The credit delta hedge at the current CDS premium of 500 bps is calculated to be 1.64%, meaning that one would need to buy 1.64% of the swap notional of CDS protection on the counterparty. However, as noted before (Table 12.1), there is convexity in the CVA profile. The performance of this hedge against moves in the counterparty's CDS premium is shown in

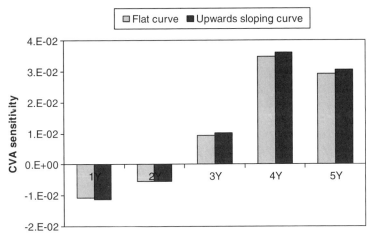

Figure 16.10 Sensitivity of the interest rate swap CVA to changes in CDS premiums of various maturities (represented in terms of CDS notional). The 5-year CDS premium is assumed 500 bps, with both a flat curve and upwards-sloping curve (300, 350, 400, 450 and 500) considered.

Figure 16.11. The concavity of the CVA profile is slightly greater than the convexity of the CDS profile, producing an overall small positive gamma. This means that the position is reasonable to manage since it requires buying CDS protection when credit spreads tighten and vice versa.[16] Positive gamma means that unhedged moves in the CDS premium will create a gain on the hedge in the absence of transaction costs. Note that the effect depends on the maturity of the CDS contract used in the hedge, since the overall gamma decreases with the increasing maturity. For a CDS maturity of, say, 7 years the overall gamma is negative, creating the need to buy more CDS protection as spreads widen. This is not a desirable situation, although the effect is not nearly as significant as when there is wrong-way risk (see later).

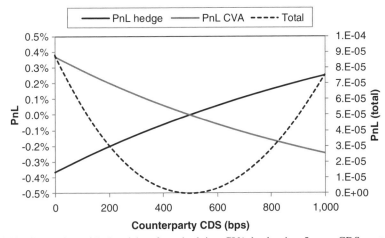

Figure 16.11 Illustration of PnL arising from hedging CVA by buying 5-year CDS protection as a function of the counterparty CDS premium. The counterparty CDS premium is assumed 500 bps.

---

[16] However, whilst this is true in theory, it is seldom the case in practice due to effects such as bid-offer costs and wrong-way risk.

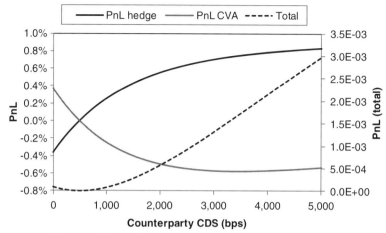

Figure 16.12 As Figure 16.11 but shown over a wider range.

Whilst the hedging of the CVA for reasonable changes in credit spreads seems practical, we must also consider the potential impact of large increases in the spread of the counterparty due to severe credit deterioration and/or a rather sudden credit event. We show the same gamma effect over a much wider range of counterparty credit quality in Figure 6.12.[17] This shows the CVA PnL changing direction at large spreads (around 3,500 bps), due to the fact that a jump to default would cause the CVA to drop to zero. In such a case, there would be a profit of around 1%.[18]

The above example illustrates a key point that the hedging of credit delta and default risk, whilst related, can require very different hedges. An instrument with no current exposure has *no* jump-to-default risk since an immediate default is of no concern. In order to hedge both credit spread and jump-to-default risk one would require positions in at least two different CDS contracts. Whilst it is theoretically possible to hedge both the credit spread sensitivity and jump-to-default component, the liquidity in the single-name CDS market probably prohibits this. Assuming it is possible to buy CDS protection on the counterparty, the pragmatic approach will be to hedge the credit spread sensitivity, unless the name becomes highly distressed, in which case the jump-to-default risk should be the key focus.[19]

16.4.3 Credit hedging with indices

Buying single-name CDS protection on some counterparties (or hedging their credit risk directly in other ways) is impractical. A CDS market may not exist, may be highly illiquid or an institution may simply not consider it worthwhile to trade CDS against certain counterparties. A possible solution is then to hedge via a credit index. This is related to the use of credit indices for mapping credit spreads in the first instance (see Section 10.3.1).

---

[17] We note that the CDS will typically trade with an upfront premium, especially when the name is severely distressed and the numbers shown are the running equivalents.
[18] $1.64\% \times (1 - 40\%) = 0.98\%$ is the payoff of the CDS. Note that at the right-hand side of Figure 16.11 the gain has reached only around 0.6%.
[19] Although we can note that, due to the gamma effect, hedging credit spread risk may be an over-hedge of jump-to-default risk.

Whilst hedging individual exposures is often impractical, a key advantage of using credit indices is the ability to hedge total CVA numbers across all counterparties. In a widening spread environment, an institution would have an increasing total CVA, creating substantial losses, unless hedged. For example, many institutions suffered such problems when credit spreads widened dramatically in 2007. Macro hedging of global credit spreads is possible by buying protection on the relevant credit indices. Such hedges may not be updated extremely frequently due to an inherent approximation due to the basis. The use of credit indices will also simplify (perhaps incorrectly) the hedging of bilateral CVA and the monetisation of DVA. This will be discussed in more detail below.

Whilst hedging with indices is undoubtedly useful and hedging against general credit quality changes as defined by the overall level of credit spreads, it is not perfect. In particular, it does not allow any control over gamma and jump-to-default risk for a given counterparty.[20] Such an approach will hedge systemic credit quality changes but not idiosyncratic ones. A counterparty's CDS premium widening significantly for idiosyncratic reasons would be expected to give rise to an unhedged increase in CVA. Credit spreads tend to become more idiosyncratic closer to default (see, for example, Table 10.4) suggesting that credit hedging (via indices) becomes more difficult in the very situations where it is important.

16.4.4   Recovery rate sensitivity

We have previously discussed the impact of changes in recovery rate assumptions on CVA (Section 12.3.2). In most situations the sensitivity of CVA to recovery rate will be small, assuming the CVA credit component is dynamically hedged with the CDS (as discussed later). This is useful since there is no obvious market instrument that allows recovery rate hedging (see discussion on recovery swaps in Section 10.1.7). A decrease in recovery not only causes an increase in CVA, but also an equivalent increase in the value of the CDS protection used as a hedge. This is consistent with the approximate CVA formula (equation (16.1)) having no recovery rate term.

Counterparties with low CDS premiums will have little recovery sensitivity. A counterparty close to default will also have little or no recovery sensitivity since the loss on the derivative and gain on the CDS contract are expected to net (but there is basis risk here due to settled and final recovery, as discussed in Section 10.1.7). A distressed counterparty, but not imminently likely to default, represents the largest recovery risk, especially if the PFE profile is time inhomogeneous. This is because a change in recovery rate, in turn, changes the implied default probability over time.

16.5   CROSS-DEPENDENCY

We now consider cross-dependency between exposure and credit as characterised by the third term in equation (16.1). This is often known as cross-gamma and can significantly complicate the hedging process and cause large losses even for seemingly well-hedged positions.

16.5.1   Re-hedging costs

Let us first consider the case where exposure and credit are independent (no wrong- or right-way risk). Figure 16.13 shows how the sensitivity of CVA changes as interest rates move up

---

[20] If the counterparty concerned is within the index used for hedging there may be some implicit hedging of these components.

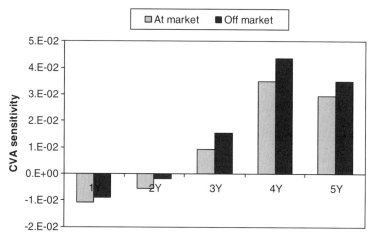

Figure 16.13 Sensitivity of the interest rate swap CVA to changes in CDS premiums of various maturities for an at-market and off-market swap (interest rates moved up by 50 bps). The CDS premiums are assumed flat at 500 bps.

by 50 bps. In this payer swap (receiving the floating rate) example, the swap becomes more in-the-money and there is a reasonable change in sensitivities. A move in interest rates means that the credit hedge will have to be adjusted significantly, even if CDS premiums have not moved. Similar effects can be seen across other variables, for example, a move in volatility causes a similar change in credit hedges. Correspondingly, a move in credit spreads changes interest rate sensitivities.

16.5.2   Cross-gamma

Cross-gamma is the term used to describe a dependency between two underlying variables. If there is correlation between variables then the cross-gamma term(s) will be non-zero. The most important manifestation of cross-gamma is that related to wrong-way risk. An unanticipated relationship between credit quality and exposure will cause hedging problems, even if the credit and exposure terms are correctly hedged in isolation.

Table 16.4 shows a hedging analysis for the receiver interest rate swap, assuming perfectly negatively correlated parallel moves in interest rates and the counterparty CDS spread, and assuming the individual components are hedged for a move of 1 bp. In addition, importantly, it is assumed that there is no wrong-way risk, i.e., interest rates and CDS spreads are treated as independent for the CVA (and delta) calculation. Whilst there are gamma components for individual moves, the largest contribution comes from the cross-gamma component, arising from a joint movement of rates and credit – around 6% of the increase in CVA is unhedged, in this case.[21] Since a negative

---

[21] Note that convexity in the underlying hedging instruments (e.g. interest rate futures and single name CDS) is ignored. This would reduce the gamma effects seen in individual moves but not influence the cross gamma result, which is net of individual gamma components.

Table 16.4   Illustration of the impact of moves in interest rates and CDS spreads on the CVA hedges of a receiver interest rate swap. The interest rate and CDS sensitivity are assumed delta hedged for a 1 bp move and convexity in the hedging instruments is ignored. The unhedged proportion for both moves has the component for the individual moves removed (i.e., it only represents the cross-gamma)

	CVA	Change	Unhedged
Base case	207,711		
CDS spread up 100 bps	241,498	−33,788	1,140
Interest rates down 10 bps	228,317	−20,606	−880
Joint move (negative correlation)	**265,662**	**−57,951**	**−3,557**

correlation between interest rates and credit spreads represents wrong-way risk for this swap (Section 15.4.1), the unhedged component of −3,711 can be seen as a manifestation of wrong-way risk losses. For a joint upwards move of interest rates and credit, there would be an overall gain on the cross-gamma component. This is consistent with positive correlation, reducing the CVA on a receiver swap (Figure 15.14) due to right-way risk.

A hedging simulation for the receiver swap (Figure 16.14) shows the overall impact of the cross-gamma. In the zero-correlation case, the PnL is approximately flat whereas negative (positive) correlation causes an overall loss (gain) due to wrong-way (right-way) risk. This shows the importance of properly accounting for wrong-way risk effects in modelling such that large cross-gamma terms do not present a problem.

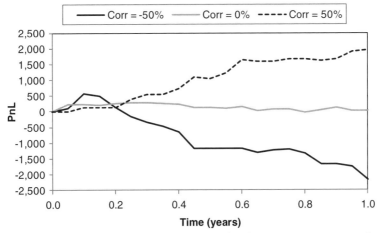

Figure 16.14 Illustration of the hedging of the 5-year receiver interest rate swap over a 1-year period. We assume both the interest rate and CDS spread are delta hedged in a standard CVA model (with no wrong-way risk) and show the resulting PnL in the cases of positive, zero and negative correlation between interest rates and hazard rates.

16.5.3 Hedging wrong-way risk

Wrong-way risk is often not hedgeable, except in specific cases (see also discussion on index CCDS in Section 16.5.5). One such example is the FX devaluation effect discussed in Section 15.4.2. Here, the FX jump can be calibrated from CDSs in different currencies. This leads to a hedging strategy involving buying CDS protection in the base currency and selling protection in the currency that will weaken. For example, suppose an institution has a cross-currency swap with a sovereign paying their local currency and receiving US dollars. They should buy USD CDS protection and sell equivalent protection in the local currency CDS. This is intuitive because it involves buying CDS protection against the receive cash flows whilst selling the pay leg. Any change in the FX rate at the default time will be hedged. However, note that this is a "default-neutral" hedge and deltas would need to be considered separately.

Where wrong-way risk dependencies cannot be directly hedged, the correct specification and calibration of models should keep cross-gamma effects such as the one above to a minimum. In an environment where CVA is being hedged, this is critical, as wrong-way risk (via cross-gamma) may be realised whether or not the counterparty ever defaults.

16.5.4 Unintended consequences of CVA hedging

The above example of wrong-way risk may seem relatively innocuous but if the same effect occurs across many trades it can be severe. One problem of CVA hedging is the linkage between different parameters across many trades. For example, a falling interest rate environment will increase a dealer's exposure,[22] requiring more credit hedging, and increases in CDS spreads will lead to a need to re-hedge interest rate exposure. Such re-hedging is required, even if interest rates and CDS spreads are independent, but, if they are correlated, then the impact is made worse (cross-gamma). Finally, the linkage of both interest rates and CDS spreads to volatility adds a third dimension to the problem. The position then held by all dealers has the potential to cause a huge issue in a volatile market through hedge-inducing feedback effects. Panic-driven re-hedging tends to be accompanied by deteriorating liquidity, which exacerbates the problem still further. In normal markets, rates, credit and volatility may operate more or less independently of one another but, in volatile markets, this structural connection has the potential to make them interlocked for non-economic reasons.

In May 2010, sovereign CDS spreads rose as the first wave of the European sovereign crisis began. This seemed to have caused significant hedging requirements for banks via their CVA desks. In turn, this hedging created some unintended consequences. For example, the Bank of England second quarter bulletin[23] in 2010 stated:

> " . . . given the relative illiquidity of sovereign CDS markets a sharp increase in demand from active investors can bid up the cost of sovereign CDS protection. CVA desks have come to account for a large proportion of trading in the sovereign CDS market and so their hedging activity has reportedly been a factor pushing prices away from levels solely reflecting the underlying probability of sovereign default."

---

[22] For example, due to trading receiver swaps with non-CSA clients and hedging with CSA trades.
[23] http://www.bankofengland.co.uk/publications/quarterlybulletin/index.htm

The implication of this is that the hedging of CVA was one factor in pushing credit spreads to excessively wide levels. This can arise from a feedback loop where a strong need to hedge increases premiums, which in turn increases hedging requirements. Losses will arise from the inevitable imperfect hedging (due to transaction costs and the inability to hedge continuously).

However, this effect was also due to cross-gamma issues as well. In 2010, sovereign CDS spreads, the 10/30[24] euro swap curve and long-dated interest rate volatility all became inextricably linked. Sovereign CDS spreads widened substantially, the 10/30 swap curve flattened significantly and there was an associated increase in long-dated volatility. The magnitude of this problem was illustrated by the realised correlations between the main iTraxx CDS index of credit spreads and the 10/30 euro swap curve, which jumped to around -90%[25] from a historical range not far from zero. A similar result could be seen when measuring the correlation between CDS spreads and long-dated EUR interest rate volatility. The very act of CVA hedging therefore seems potentially to increase CDS spreads, drive rates down further and increase volatility, reinforcing the need to hedge further. This would further drive cross-gamma losses, such as illustrated in the top half of Table 16.4. The fact that the hedging needs of CVA desks are one way makes the problem worse. CVA desks are then forced to re-hedge at the worst levels, crossing bid and offer prices during times of rapid moves and market illiquidity. This causes CVA desks to consider not hedging at all in such a "crowded trade" environment.

16.5.5 Index CCDSs

Products may also be designed specifically to provide wrong-way risk hedges, especially when there are structural hedging problems, such as described in the last section. One example of this is an index contingent credit default swap (index CCDS) which banks, with ISDA, sought to create standard terms for, in light of the wrong-way risk-induced cross-gamma issues they experienced between interest rates and CDS spreads. Index CCDSs work in a similar way to the single-name equivalent discussed in Section 16.2.2, but reference an index such as iTraxx, SovX or CDX instead of a single reference entity. Underlying reference trades can be interest rate swaps but also other products such as foreign exchange and commodities.

Index CCDSs do not readily permit a perfect match of the exposure due to the underlying trades being standardised. However, an institution can use a specific index CCDS to hedge a cross-gamma effect with a single trade covering the market risk exposure and counterparty spread risk simultaneously. This gives a new dimension to the hedging of counterparty risk and provides the possibility to hedge unpleasant correlations, such as those between interest rates and CDS spreads. The indexing of CCDSs to standard and liquidity indices rather than single names should improve liquidity. The index CCDS market may therefore be more successful than the single-name CCDS market.

---

[24] Meaning the long end of the euro interest rate curve from 10 to 30 years.
[25] See Sasura, M., "CVA hedging in rates, gaining in significance", Global Rates Strategy, Barclays Capital, 20th May 2010.

16.6   THE IMPACT OF DVA AND COLLATERAL

16.6.1   Hedging bilateral counterparty risk

As discussed in Chapter 14, bilateral counterparty risk (BCVA) means that an institution manages CVA under the assumption that they, as well as their counterparty, may default with the "own default" component, commonly known as DVA. This aspect will always reduce the price of counterparty risk as defined by BCVA, since an institution will always "gain" when they default due to being not obliged ("able" would be a better word) to make contractual payments. In Chapter 13, it was suggested that monetisation of DVA was potentially problematic. Now we can look more deeply into this aspect with the hedging implications of DVA.

The first implication of using BCVA is that all calculations are conditioned on an institution's own survival, which reduces the CVA in the first component of equation (13.1). In Section 13.1.2, we argued that this was reasonable since an institution need not consider losses due to their counterparty defaulting in scenarios where they themselves default first. Failure to account properly for this "first to default" component would, therefore, create a double counting effect.[26] However, even this aspect is not completely clear when we analyse BCVA on hedging grounds. The obvious hedge for unilateral CVA is to buy CDS protection referencing the counterparty. When BCVA is considered then a more natural hedge would be the same contract that *terminates* in the event of an institution's own default. Of course, such a contract does not exist. However, this is a small issue compared to the second DVA component, which presents much more of a hedging challenge.

It may be useful to recall the intuitive approximate formula for bilateral CVA given in equation (13.2):

$$\mathrm{BCVA} = \mathrm{spread}_C \times \mathrm{EPE} + \mathrm{spread}_I \times \mathrm{ENE}, \tag{16.2}$$

where spread_C and spread_I are the counterparty's and institution's own CDS spreads respectively, EPE the expected positive exposure and ENE the expected negative exposure (EPE from the counterparty's point of view). An institution will, therefore, obtain corresponding sensitivities for the second term in equation (16.2) due to their DVA component. The question is, to what extent these sensitivities offset those generated by the CVA. In all the examples below we will assume that the institution is around half as risky as its counterparty, with a CDS premium of 250 bps compared with 500 bps (credit curves assumed flat and recovery rates set to 40%).

We first show, in Figure 16.15, the sensitivity to interest rates (shown earlier in Figure 16.4) for both unilateral (as discussed previously) and bilateral CVA. The bilateral CVA sensitivity can be seen to have increased. This can be understood since an increase in 5-year interest rates will increase the EPE and, correspondingly, decrease the ENE. Due to their opposite signs, in equation (16.2) these effects both contribute a negative CVA sensitivity.[27]

We now consider how the sensitivity of CVA to swap rate volatility is impacted by the bilateral component. In the classic swaption analogy, an institution is short a series of receiver swaptions (relating to their counterparty's default). DVA implies they are also long a series of the same swaptions (relating to their own default). These swaptions will not match perfectly, due to the difference in credit quality and strike, but one should expect some

---

[26] Although as described in Section 13.4.2 the consideration of a substitution closeout suggests that this component should probably be ignored.
[27] Recall the CVA is a negative term in the context of the value of the derivative. Increasing EPE and decreasing ENE both have negative impacts and increase the negative sensitivity compared with the unilateral case.

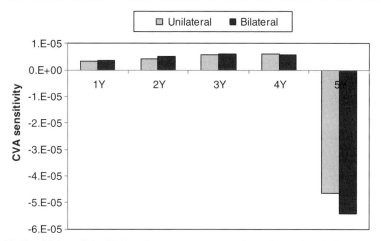

Figure 16.15 Sensitivity of the CVA to interest rate moves for unilateral and bilateral CVA for the payer interest rate swap shown previously in Figure 16.10.

cancellation of the volatility risk. To put it differently, the terms in equation (16.2) will move in opposite directions with increasing volatility (note ENE is negative) and so, overall, the second term will dampen the increase of the first. The balance of the sensitivity to volatility will be determined by:

- The relative riskiness of the institution and their counterparty as defined by their CDS spreads.
- EPE versus the ENE (this is related to the strike of the long and short swaptions).

Under the swaption analogy, one set of swaptions will be in-the-money whilst the other will be out-of-the-money by the same proportion. Since both sets of swaptions will have comparable sensitivity to volatility (the Vega is roughly symmetric), we expect the former component, the relative riskiness, to be the key one. This is indeed the case, as seen in Figure 16.16,

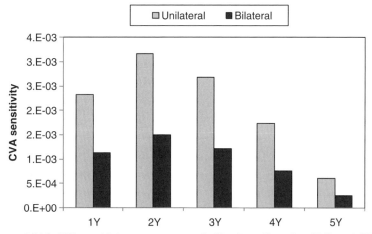

Figure 16.16 CVA sensitivity to swap rate volatility for unilateral and bilateral CVA.

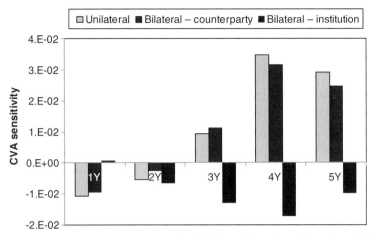

Figure 16.17 Sensitivity of the CVA to changes in CDS premiums for unilateral and bilateral cases. The case "Bilateral – counterparty" shows the impact of a move in the counterparty's CDS premium whilst "Bilateral – institution" refers to a move in the CDS premium of the institution.

which shows the bilateral sensitivity reduced by around 50% in correspondence with the relative riskiness of the institution vis-à-vis their counterparty. The use of DVA reduces the volatility hedge required, which in turn reduces the cost of the hedging in accordance with a smaller BCVA.

Finally, we look at the CDS sensitivities corresponding to bilateral CVA, which are shown in Figure 16.17. The sensitivity to the counterparty CDS premium is reduced slightly under BCVA because the institution may default first (in which case they do not need to have protection on their counterparty). The key impact is the sensitivity that the institution has to their own CDS premium, which is in the opposite direction. This, as discussed in Chapter 13, corresponds to selling self-CDS protection. This is a crucial component in the analysis and can be thought of as being required in order to partially fund the protection bought on the counterparty and therefore justify the lower BCVA. If an institution is unable to monetise the component of BCVA, then using BCVA cannot be properly justified from a hedging point of view.

16.6.2 DVA and index hedging

Whilst hedging DVA is difficult, perversely the general inability to hedge CVA via single-name CDSs (due to a lack of liquidity in the market) helps. In such cases both CVA and DVA can be hedged with equivalent amounts of the relevant index according to the "beta" with respect to the index in question.[28] If the same index is used for hedging both the counterparty and institution CDS spread, then these components can be further aggregated to produce a net hedge. This is illustrated in Figure 16.18.

Clearly, the index mapping procedure will likely dampen the overall CDS sensitivity, as the long protection required to hedge the counterparty spread will be partially cancelled by the short CDS protection hedging the institution's own spread. Note that the net position may

---

[28] In other words, adjusting for the covariance between the credit quality of the counterparty and institution and that of the underlying credit index.

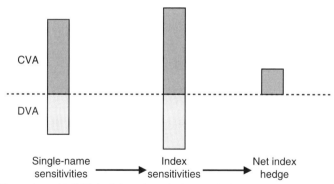

Figure 16.18 Illustration of BCVA hedging via an index. Both the CVA (counterparty CDS) and DVA (institution CDS) components are mapped empirically into an index hedge. If they are mapped to the same index then these hedges can be aggregated further to a net index hedge.

turn out to be short index protection, which can generally be seen as the institution monetising a negative bilateral CVA. There are two obvious problems with this strategy. The first is that the index is not sufficiently correlated with the single-name CDS (or either counterparty or institution) to justify this as a hedging strategy. Positive correlation is not enough here: a simple example suggests that the correlation needs to be in excess of +50% to provide any benefit.[29] One advantage of the index hedges for CVA is the likely scale: they may cover many hundreds or even thousands of counterparties and therefore hedges need only work on an overall basis, with unfavourable behaviour, with respect to a single hedge (e.g., negative correlation) being averaged out by the rest of the portfolio. The DVA hedges do not share this benefit and a lack of correlation between the institution's own CDS spread and the underlying index will cause excess DVA volatility on all positions simultaneously.

The second problem with the above strategy is specific to DVA and concerns the fact that if the index is highly correlated to the institution's own CDS spread, then the hedges will be efficient, but create a large wrong-way risk for the buyer of protection (see Figure 15.22). Indeed, it creates *specific* wrong-way risk, which is often viewed as being a result of badly structured transactions (for example, see Basel III discussion in Section 17.4.1) that should be avoided. In such cases, buyers of protection should expect to do so more cheaply, thereby making the hedge less effective. Indeed, the institution is stuck in a difficult situation here: a low correlation gives an ineffective DVA hedge, whilst a high correlation creates excessive wrong-way risk and should lead to problems selling protection.[30]

The idea of hedging with a credit index seems to fit naturally within the bilateral CVA concept and avoids the problem that an institution cannot sell CDS protection on themselves. However, such an approach may be partially delusional, since it works only when correlations are high. Index hedges are efficient for the systematic component of CDS premiums, but not the idiosyncratic risks of either the counterparty or institution. If the counterparty defaults then the resulting losses may be completely unhedged and yet there may have been

---

[29] Assuming the index and single-name CDS to have the same standard deviation, σ, there would be a combined standard deviation of $\sqrt{\sigma_{\text{index}}^2 + \sigma_{\text{sn}}^2 - 2\rho\sigma_{\text{index}}\sigma_{\text{sn}}} = \sqrt{2(1-\rho)}\sigma$. This quantity is larger than the original standard unless the correlation parameter ρ is greater than 50% and in order to reduce the combined standard deviation to half the original value then the correlation must be 87.5%. More detail is given in Appendix 16A.

[30] More homogeneous markets, such as are created under central clearing, may aid this. However, this implies that CCPs may have to deal with large amounts of wrong-way risk, which may be problematic (Section 15.5.4).

zero (or even negative) BCVA initially. An institution relying on bilateral CVA pricing, together with some systemic credit hedging via indices, may have few problems where their own and their counterparty's spread are mainly systemic with respect to the underlying index. However, when there are idiosyncratic credit quality effects, any potential underestimation of counterparty risk created by bilateral assumption will become apparent via the inefficiency of the underlying hedges.

16.6.3 Impact of collateral on hedging

We now show the impact of collateral on sensitivities and the hedging of CVA. Since collateral reduces exposure, we should expect a reduction in the hedging requirements. We will consider a case of a strong collateral agreement with zero threshold, independent amount, minimum transfer amount and rounding. We assume a 10-day margin period of risk (Section 8.5.2) as a reasonable assessment for daily margining. Clearly, weaker collateralisation will lead to intermediate results (with respect to the uncollateralised case) to those shown below.

The sensitivity, with respect to interest rates (Figure 16.19), is almost zero, reflecting the fact that the drift becomes unimportant with collateral due to the relevant time horizon being so short. CDSs (Figure 16.20) are also reduced substantially, although it should be noted that the overall hedges are all positive across tenors and the sum is still relatively large, reflecting a significant jump-to-default risk. Finally, volatility (Figure 16.21) shows material sensitivity, reflecting the importance these factors have on the risk of a collateralised counterparty. This can be partially understood by the fact that, in contrast to drift-type effects that are linear with respect to time, such as interest rates and CDS spreads, volatility scales approximately as the square root of time.

The summary is that collateral can reduce hedging parameters substantially. The likely key residual components are volatility and jump-to-default risk. It must also be noted that hedges are very sensitive to the terms of the collateral agreement (thresholds, etc.) and the assumed margin period of risk.

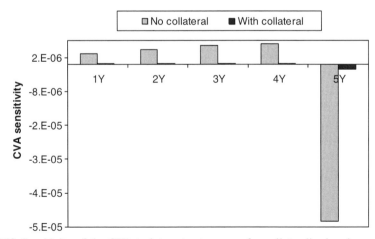

Figure 16.19 Sensitivity of the CVA to interest rate moves for collateralised and uncollateralised positions.

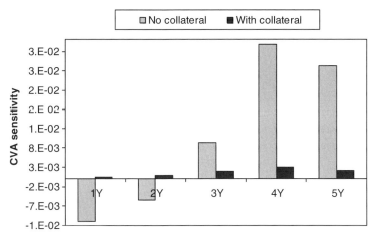

Figure 16.20 Sensitivity of the CVA to changes in CDS premiums for collateralised and uncollateralised positions.

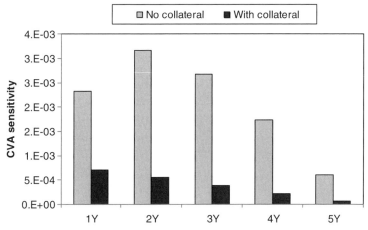

Figure 16.21 Sensitivity of the CVA to swap rate volatility for collateralised and uncollateralised positions.

16.6.4 Aggregation of sensitivities

It is worth discussing the aggregation of sensitivities across an entire CVA portfolio. Exposure-related sensitivities can be aggregated across all counterparties. Key sensitivities, such as interest rate and FX risk, will therefore offset partially across positions and their associated hedges. Such offsets are typically imperfect, due firstly to the fact that, even with equivalent counterparties, CVA sensitivities on opposite trades do not perfectly match (see the example of this for interest rates in Figure 16.4 and Figure 16.6). A second, and probably more important, effect though is the differing nature of trades and their hedges, such as the credit quality of the counterparties, CSA vs. non-CSA trades and so on. For example, a dealer typically providing receiver interest rate swaps for non-CSA clients and hedging them with CSA counterparties (e.g., in the interbank market) will have a large negative sensitivity to interest rates overall. The nature of client business defines such large CVA sensitivities for banks.

Whilst other market variables will offset sensitivity to CVA, volatility is in the same direction for all trades (for example, see Figure 16.8 and aside from the DVA benefit shown in Figure 16.16). Hence, the overall volatility risk will be significant and should be hedged by buying options across term structures for the different underlying asset classes. Foreign exchange volatility is likely to be a particularly important hedge, due to the long-dated nature of many FX exposures, and interest rate volatility risk is likely to be significant due to the sheer notional amount of exposure. Failure to hedge volatility risk correctly could lead to sudden MtM losses, caused by an increase in CVA values resulting from a spike in volatility in one or more asset classes. Volatility risk is reduced by using bilateral CVA (see Figure 16.16) due to a negative sensitivity linked to the institution's own default. This would mean that an institution would have to buy volatility when their credit quality is good but sell volatility when their credit quality worsens.[31] This is another strange quirk arising from the BCVA approach.

Credit risk, unlike the exposure components, cannot be aggregated across counterparties when components, such as jump to default, are considered. Index hedges can obviously be aggregated at the portfolio level as illustrated in Figure 16.18. Single-name CDS protection should, in theory at least, be traded against each counterparty individually to have control over jump-to-default risk. In practice, only the counterparties with significant risk and liquid CDS markets will be hedged in this way. Again, using bilateral CVA will reduce the net overall amount of CDS protection required. Indeed, an institution whose CDS premium is wide compared with the average of their counterparty's may be an overall seller of CDS protection in order to hedge a negative BCVA. Such an approach is perverse since a sudden improvement of the institution's credit quality (CDS premium tightens compared with the rest of the market) will create a large unhedged CVA loss. Trading single-name protection, an institution can be hedged against the idiosyncratic change in the CDS premium of a counterparty. However, since selling self-protection is not possible then the hedging of the equivalent portion of an institution's own spread is not possible.

16.7 SUMMARY

This chapter has been concerned with a thorough analysis of the hedging aspects of CVA. We have shown that a complete hedging of credit risk and exposure components is complex due to the large number of variables, relative illiquidity of the CDS market, and aspects such as cross-gamma and jump-to-default risk. Sensitivities to spot rates, volatility, correlation, cross-dependency and default have all been described. We have also shown the impact of collateral on hedging and discussed the hedging implications of using bilateral counterparty risk. For an institution to manage their counterparty risk effectively requires a prudent choice of which key variables upon which to focus.

The unintended consequences of CVA hedging have been illustrated. Hedging CVA is a new area and traders may be prone to over-reaction. Markets prone to blowups, due to their structural nature and associated re-hedging effects, cannot be avoided altogether. Many markets experience granular flows due to re-hedging caused when specific thresholds are

---

[31] Very perversely, a highly distressed institution will need to be extremely short volatility to hedge the potential increase in BCVA – due to a decrease in the second term of equation (16.2) – if volatility declines.

breached. Sudden thinning of liquidity, volatility increases and gaps cannot be avoided completely. The market may have to bear CVA hedging problems or improve the liquidity, or variety, of credit derivative products for effective risk transfer. However, the sheer complexity of CVA hedging and its cross-asset nature suggest that the question of whether or not to hedge CVA is one that must be considered carefully.

In the next chapters, we explore in more detail the management of counterparty risk, looking at the regulatory aspects in Chapter 17 before discussing the operation of a CVA desk in Chapter 18.

17
Regulation and Capital Requirements[1]

17.1 INTRODUCTION

Since the global financial crisis, regulation has been heavily in the spotlight, as rules need to be improved, and new ones introduced, to prevent a repeat of the almost Armageddon scenario where financial institutions collapsed and had to be bailed out by governments and (effectively) the taxpayer. It is not, therefore, surprising that new regulation has been put together very quickly with the Dodd–Frank act, for example, being signed into law in July 2010, and totalling almost one thousand pages of rules governing financial institutions. In addition, Basel III guidelines for regulatory capital have been developed quickly (compared with, for example, the previous Basel II framework).

A key form of regulation is determining the minimum amount of capital that a given bank must hold. Capital acts as a buffer to absorb losses during turbulent periods and, therefore, contributes significantly to defining creditworthiness. Ultimately, regulatory capital requirements partially determine the leverage under which a bank can operate. The danger of overly optimistic capital requirements has been highlighted during the recent period, with losses not just exceeding, but dwarfing, the capital set aside against them. Banks continually strive for ever-greater profits to be shared by employees (via bonuses) and shareholders (via dividend payments and capital gains). Banks will therefore naturally wish to hold the minimum amount of capital possible in order to maximise the amount of business they can do and the risk they are able to take. There is clearly a balance in defining the capital requirements for a bank; it must be high enough to contribute to a very low possibility of failure and, yet, not so severe as to unfairly penalise the bank (at least in comparison with competitors that operate under a different regulatory regime). Defining capital requirements is clearly a difficult task, as financial markets have a habit of creating surprises that cannot be predicted by models and historical experience.

The definition of sound regulatory capital buffers is also plagued by the complexity of the underlying approach. A simple approach will be transparent and easier to implement but will not be able to capture any more than the key aspects of the risks arising from a complex web of positions often taken by a bank. As such, this may give rise to possible

---

[1] Since regulation is a rapidly and continually evolving subject area, updates to this chapter will be posted on www.cvacentral.com.

"arbitrages" of capital requirements arising from the ability to reduce capital, without a corresponding reduction in the associated risk. Indeed, the growth of the credit derivatives markets was largely driven by regulatory capital arbitrage. A more sophisticated model-based approach may more closely align capital and actual financial risk, but will be less transparent and harder to implement. Added to this is the fact that large dealers may have the resource and expertise to implement complex regulatory capital approaches, whilst smaller banks may prefer to implement a simpler approach, even if this is by its very nature more conservative in ultimate capital requirements. Hence, it is usually necessary, concurrently with advanced methods, to implement alternative simple methodologies. Note that a bank typically cannot "cherry pick" between approaches – once they have approval to adopt a more sophisticated methodology they cannot switch back to a simpler one without permission from the regulator.

Capital requirements, not surprisingly, are also split into various different, very distinct areas such as market, credit, liquidity and operational risk. This leads to potential double counting effects and failure to appreciate offsetting risks. Even in a seemingly individual risk type such as counterparty credit risk, capital requirements are defined by more than one set of rules, with the overall capital being additive.

It has become clear that the capitalisation of counterparty risk was inadequate prior to the global financial crisis. This chapter covers the overall regulation and capital requirements covering all aspects of counterparty credit risk. This quite naturally splits into the regulation present prior to the global financial crisis (mainly Basel II, which includes some aspects of Basel I) and that being introduced in the wake of the crisis (mainly Basel III). The implementation requirements of Basel III supplement, extend and add to those of Basel II rather than replace them. Whilst we will not discuss capital requirements for other areas, it is interesting to note that a large part of the new capital required under Basel III is due to counterparty credit risk alone.

Regulation may also incentivise or require changes to market structure, such as through the introduction of central clearing via CCPs (Chapter 7). Such entities must then be capitalised, as must the exposure of market participants to them. This requires the introduction of a completely new set of rules. A final problem is that regulation is not always consistent globally. Whilst Basel III, for example, constitutes a global set of capital rules, the precise implementation is decided by local regulators (for example, under the Dodd–Frank act or CRD IV) and may differ by region.

Note that in this chapter, the term exposure at default (EAD) will be used. This is similar to the previously used terms of expected exposure (EE) and expected positive exposure (EPE) and essentially refers to the future exposure incurred should the counterparty to the transactions default. EAD for regulatory purposes is defined by a variety of methods which may be necessarily less precise and conservative compared with actual quantities such as EPE.

17.2 BASEL II

17.2.1 Background

Most large banks operate in multiple countries. To minimise the effect that conflicting regulatory practices in different jurisdictions may have on international banks, the Basel Committee on Banking Supervision (BCBS) was established by the central bank governors of the Group of Ten (G10) countries in 1974. The Basel Committee does not possess any formal authority, and its conclusions do not have legal force. Instead, it formulates broad supervisory standards and issues recommendations that reflect its view on the current best practice. The supervisory authorities in the relevant countries follow the BCBS guidelines when they develop their national regulation rules.

In 1988, the BCBS introduced a capital measurement framework known as the Basel Capital Accord (nowadays often referred to as Basel I). This framework was adopted not only in the G10 countries, but also in other countries with internationally active banks. However, the Basel I Accord lacked risk sensitivities, and banks learned how to game the system: reduce the minimum capital requirements without actually reducing the risk taken. To reduce this practice, known as regulatory arbitrage, work on the more risk-sensitive Revised Capital Adequacy Framework, commonly known as Basel II, started in 1999. The Basel II framework, now covering the G20 group of countries, is described in the Basel Committee's document entitled "International Convergence of Capital Measurement and Capital Standards" (BCBS, 2006). It consists of three "pillars":

- *Pillar 1, minimum capital requirements.* Banks compute regulatory capital charges according to a set of specified rules.
- *Pillar 2, supervisory review.* Supervisors evaluate the activities and risk profiles of banks to determine whether they should hold higher levels of capital than the minimum requirements in Pillar 1.
- *Pillar 3, market discipline.* Public disclosures that banks must make, that would provide greater insight into the adequacy of banks' capitalisation (including disclosure about methods used to determine capital levels required), are specified.

We will discuss minimum capital requirements, according to Pillar 1 of Basel II, as they apply to counterparty risk for banks. For a comprehensive review of Basel II in general, the reader is referred to Ong (2006) and Engelmann and Rauhmeier (2006).

17.2.2   General approach to credit risk

We first discuss the general approach taken to capitalise the default risk on typical credit risk instruments, such as loans. Two approaches are available under Basel II:

- *Standardised approach.* Banks assess the risk of their exposures using external ratings. All non-retail exposures are assigned to risk buckets. BCBS (2006) provides tables that specify a capital charge for each risk bucket. This approach has its basis under Basel I but is more granular.
- *Internal ratings-based (IRB) approach.* Banks rely on their own internal estimates of some (foundation IRB) or all (advanced IRB) risk components. These components are probability of default, loss given default (or recovery rate), exposure at default and effective maturity.

Whilst market risk capital requirements have, since 1995, been fully model-based, Basel II has stopped short of allowing this for credit risk. Such a limitation can be put down to the increased complexity of modelling credit risk, together with the limited data and longer time horizons involved. The advanced IRB approach still uses a relatively simple formula to define economic capital, although the origins of this formula have a firm theoretical basis.

The advanced IRB approach of Basel II broadly follows the credit portfolio model described in Section 11.3. The theory rests on the large homogeneous pool (LHP) approximation described in Appendix 17A. This is used to define a conditional (on a confidence level) expected loss under the LHP assumptions of Vasicek (1997) and granularity adjustment formula of Gordy (2004) with a confidence level set at 99.9%. Under the advanced IRB approach, regulatory capital (RC) for a given instrument is defined by the following formula:

$$RC = EAD \times LGD \times [PD_{99.9\%} - PD] \times MA(PD, M) \qquad (17.1)$$

with the following definitions:

EAD   the exposure at default (e.g., the notional of a bond or loan)[2]

LGD   the expected loss given default in relation to the EAD (estimated conditionally on an economic downturn)

PD   the obligor's probability of default (subject to a floor of 0.03%), with $PD_{99.9\%}$ representing an unexpected probability of default[3] at the confidence level of 99.9%. This incorporates an asset correlation parameter (see Section 11.2.3) which may penalise more correlated or systemic exposures

MA   a maturity adjustment factor

The above formula is intuitive: the capital should depend on the size of the position concerned (EAD) and on the probability of default, loss given default, effective maturity and correlation within the portfolio concerned.

17.2.3   Asset correlation and maturity adjustment factor

The asset correlation in the above formula is not constant and, instead, assumed to depend on the default probability itself, uniquely determined by the PD as shown in Figure 17.1 (the formula is given in Appendix 17B). This can be interpreted as asset correlation being believed to decrease as the size of the obligor decreases (smaller obligors tend to have larger default probabilities) or it could be thought of as a correction to the model to produce a more linear function with respect to default probability, which would dampen the effect of procyclicality.[4] Basel III has increased the asset correlation assumed for large financial institutions (see Section 17.4.1).

The maturity adjustment (MA) factor above attempts to capture credit migration risk, the risk that whilst the obligor may not have defaulted at the horizon (1 year), its credit quality may be weaker. The Basel maturity adjustment is not derived from any model – it is a parametric function with its parameters chosen to match the output of a single-factor version of the KMV Portfolio Manager model (KMV Corporation, 1993) as closely as possible. The formula is given in Appendix 17B. Figure 17.2 shows the dependence of the Basel maturity adjustment factor upon the remaining maturity for several values of PD. While the Basel parametric maturity adjustment is certainly a huge simplification over a real credit migration

---

[2] Large exposures are therefore not penalised directly in such a formula since EAD is multiplicative.

[3] This is given by the function $\Phi\big((\Phi^{-1}(PD) + \sqrt{\rho}\Phi^{-1}(0.999))/\sqrt{1-\rho}\big)$, where the functions $\Phi(.)$ and $\Phi^{-1}(.)$ are the standard normal cumulative distribution function and its inverse. This arises from the LHP approximation and granularity adjustment mentioned.

[4] For a comprehensive discussion on procyclicality in regulatory capital and possible ways to reduce it, see Gordy and Howells (2006).

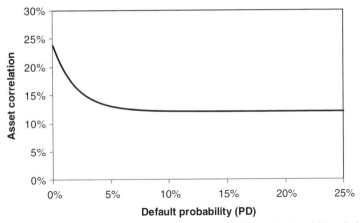

Figure 17.1 Asset correlation as a function of PD according to the Basel II capital rules.

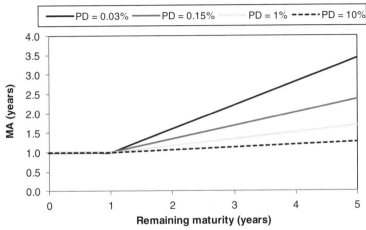

Figure 17.2 Maturity adjustment (MA) as a function of remaining maturity for several values of PD.

model, it does retain two major properties of credit migration risk that we would intuitively expect. First, for any given PD, the maturity adjustment factor increases with remaining maturity. We certainly would expect this behaviour because, with longer remaining maturity, there is more time for the obligor to be downgraded. Secondly, the maturity adjustment factor is higher for obligors with lower PD. This behaviour is also very intuitive because higher-rated obligors have more "space" for downgrade than lower-rated obligors do, as illustrated by the mean-reversion characteristics (Section 10.1.3) of credit migrations.

17.3   EXPOSURE UNDER BASEL II

A main emphasis of the Basel II framework is on instruments with relatively fixed exposures, such as loans. Chapter 11 discusses the computation of economic capital, illustrating the additional complexity posed by derivatives, due to effects such as random exposures, correlation of exposures and wrong-way risk. However, we have discussed that there also exist reasonable theoretical foundations for replacing derivatives exposures by their loan-equivalent values and an additional "alpha" multiplier (Section 11.3.4).

The Basel II framework very much follows the loan-equivalent style for derivatives with minimum capital requirements for counterparty risk in OTC derivatives and securities financing transactions (SFTs), calculated by applying Basel II rules for corporate, sovereign and bank exposures (BCBS, 2006). In applying these rules to counterparty risk in OTC derivatives and SFTs, there are different methods of varying complexity for calculating EAD:

- the current exposure method (CEM);
- the standardised method (SM);
- the internal model method (IMM).

The first two approaches above are normally referred to as the non-IMM methods. These methods are designed to provide a simple and workable supervisory algorithm for those banks that are not able to model credit exposure internally. In addition, there are separate approaches to handle repo transactions. All of these approaches will be described below.

EAD is calculated at the netting set level. From the Basel perspective, a netting set is a group of transactions with a single counterparty subject to a legally enforceable bilateral netting agreement that satisfies certain legal and operational criteria, described in Annex 4 of BCBS (2006). Netting, other than on a bilateral basis, is not recognised for calculating regulatory capital. Each transaction that is not subject to a legally enforceable bilateral netting agreement is interpreted as its own netting set. The interpretation of a netting set according to Basel II is therefore consistent with the earlier definition (Section 8.2).

17.3.1 Current exposure method

Under the current exposure method approach (originating from Basel I), the EAD is computed according to

$$EAD = CE + \text{add-on}, \tag{17.2}$$

where CE is the current exposure and add-on is the estimated amount of the potential future exposure over the remaining life of the contract. The add-on is calculated, for each single transaction, as the product of the transaction notional and the add-on factor, which is determined based on the remaining maturity and the type of underlying instrument (e.g., interest rates, foreign exchange, etc.) according to Table 17.1. For example, a 6-year interest rate swap with a current MtM of 1% would have an add-on of 1.5% and therefore an EAD of 2.5%.

Table 17.1 Add-on factors of the current exposure method (CEM) by the remaining maturity and type of underlying instrument

Remaining maturity	Interest rates	FX and gold	Equities	Precious metals (except gold)	Other commodities
<1 year	0.0%	1.0%	6.0%	7.0%	10.0%
1–5 years	0.5%	5.0%	8.0%	7.0%	12.0%
>5 years	1.5%	7.5%	10.0%	8.0%	15.0%

Under the CEM, it is possible to fully net transactions, covered by a legally enforceable bilateral netting agreement, for the purposes of calculating the CE. This is trivial since it relates to current exposure and means that the CE for a netting set is defined by the *net* portfolio value. The benefit of netting of future exposures via the add-on component is not obvious, since the impact of netting can change significantly over time as the MtM values of individual transactions change. Consider two transactions that net perfectly today since they have equal and opposite MtM values. Only if they are mirror trades (perfect hedges) will the netting be perfect in the future. If the trades happened to net by chance, then some, or all, of this netting benefit will be lost over time. The treatment of netting is described in Appendix 17C. Essentially, only 60% of the current netting benefit is given as credit for netting of future exposures. This accounts for the fact that some netting benefit will be structural (such as mirror trades or hedges) but some will occur only transiently and by chance. This treatment seems conservative as it assumes that the current netting benefit will decay over time, whereas the reverse can also occur.

Finally, for a collateralised counterparty, unlike under Basel I, the current exposure for transactions within a netting set can be reduced by the current market value of the collateral, subject to a (sizeable) haircut.[5] This is defined more thoroughly in Appendix 17C. Essentially, the benefit of collateral on current exposure is recognised via the reduction of CE, but the ability to call for collateral against future exposure is not (no reduction of add-on).

17.3.2   Standardised method

The standardised method (SM) in Basel II was designed for those banks that do not qualify to model counterparty exposure internally, but would like to adopt a more risk-sensitive approach than the CEM – for example, to account more properly for netting. Under the SM, one computes the EAD for derivative transactions within a netting set, as a combination of "hedging sets", which are positions that depend on the same risk factor. Within each hedging set, offsets are fully recognised but netting between hedging sets is not accounted for. As with the CEM, collateral is only accounted for with respect to the current MtM component and future collateral is not specifically considered. More details are given in Appendix 17D. The SM is not particularly common, as banks tend to use the simpler CEM approach described above or the more sophisticated IMM described below.

17.3.3   Treatment of repo-style transactions

For repo-style transactions, the EAD is calculated as the difference between the market value of the securities and the collateral received, and given by

$$EAD = \max[0, MtM(1 + h_S) - C(1 - h_C)], \qquad (17.3)$$

where h_S is the haircut on the security and h_C is the haircut on the collateral. The haircuts must be applied to both the exposure and collateral received in order to account for the risk arising from an appreciation in value of the underlying exposure, and simultaneous decline in value, of collateral received as a result of future market movements. Banks may be permitted

---

[5] This is referred to as "Volatility adjusted collateral", see www.bis.org/publ/bcbs116.pdf.

to calculate haircuts themselves using internal models. In such cases, the relevant confidence level should be 99% and the minimum time horizon 5 days.

To better account for netting, as an alternative method to the use of haircuts as above, banks may take a VAR-based approach to reflect the price volatility of the exposure and collateral received (see discussion and example results in Section 8.5.4). Under the VAR-based approach, the EAD or exposure can be calculated, for each netting set, as

$$EAD = \max(0, MtM - C + VAR),$$

where MtM and C again represent the current market value of trades in the netting set and the current market value of all collateral positions held against the netting set, respectively, and VAR represents a value-at-risk type assessment of the collateralised position over some time horizon. The advantage of the VAR model is to improve the rule-based aggregation under standard haircuts by taking into account correlation effects between positions in the portfolio. The VAR-based approach is available to banks that have already received approval for the use of internal models under the Market Risk Framework – see BCBS (2006, Part 2, Section VI). Other banks can apply separately for supervisory recognition to use their internal VAR models for the haircut calculation on repo-style transactions.

The quantitative and qualitative criteria for recognition of internal market risk models on repo-style transactions, and other similar transactions are, in principle, the same as under the Market Risk Framework. For repo-style transactions, the minimum holding period is five business days (rather than the ten that is standard). The minimum holding period should be adjusted upwards for market instruments, where such a holding period would be inappropriate given the liquidity of underlying security.

17.3.4   Internal model method

Insitutions with competence in market risk modelling are now viewed as suitably qualified to model exposures for derivatives using internal models. Under the IMM, banks are allowed to compute the distribution of exposure at future time points using their own models (with methods similar to those described in Chapter 9). Assuming that this distribution is available, the IMM prescribes a way of calculating EAD and the effective maturity (required for the maturity adjustment factor, MA in equation (17.1)) from the expected exposure profile.

The internal model method (IMM) is the most risk-sensitive approach for EAD calculation available under the Basel II framework. It is intended to provide incentives for banks to improve their measurement and management of counterparty credit risk by adopting practices that are more sophisticated. Even with the volatile environment over the last few years, there is still benefit from using more sophisticated IMM models, which are still less conservative than the CEM approach. Under the IMM, both EAD and effective maturity are computed from the output of a bank's internal models of future exposure. These models must be approved by the bank's supervisors for them to become eligible for the IMM. More details on the effective maturity calculation are given in Appendix 17E.

Not only does the IMM allow a realistic treatment of the important mitigants of netting and collateral, it permits full netting across asset classes and, if relevant, cross-product netting between OTC derivatives and SFT (i.e., repo-style) transactions. In order to achieve cross-product netting, several legal and operational requirements must be met. In particular, there has to be a strong legal opinion that, in the event of default, the relevant courts and authorities (within all relevant jurisdictions) would recognise this form of netting. There is also an operational difficulty of integrating different legal agreements between OTC [ISDA] and SFTs [GMSLA[6]] due to systems capabilities and data problems. Some banks therefore do not consider cross-product netting because of poor data quality and/or operational difficulties. However, we note that netting is given only limited recognition under other approaches and cross-product netting has no recognition at all. Whilst a number of banks achieved IMM approval for EAD prior to 2007, it is only recently, with capital becoming more expensive, that most banks, including smaller ones, aim to use the IMM method to achieve the most realistic treatment of capital.

17.3.5   Exposure at default and alpha

As we have seen in Chapter 11, EPE is the true loan-equivalent exposure for an infinitely fine-grained portfolio. The multiplier alpha (α), first suggested by Picoult (2002), is the correction that accounts for the finite number of counterparties, correlations between exposures and general wrong-way risk.[7] The intuition behind the α multiplier is the same as discussed in Chapter 11, i.e., it corrects for the finite size and concentration of the portfolio in question. In other words, for the purposes of calculating capital, EPE should be multiplied by α in order to reproduce the same result as in the true random exposure case. Since an α of one is valid only for infinite diversification, α is interpreted as a multiplier above unity, which depends on the nature of the portfolio in question. It is clearly an approximation to the true portfolio behaviour but permits a very simple capital model, certainly compared with the complexity that would be required by a more sophisticated portfolio model.

The use of this loan-equivalent approach greatly reduces the complexity of Basel II, since it permits a separate modelling of market and credit risk factors. To be clear, the IMM allows the EAD in equation (17.1) to be defined via a model-based computation, the exposure at the individual counterparty (netting set) level. Under the IMM, α is fixed at a level of 1.4. While this number may be appropriate for banks with small derivative portfolios, it may be conservative when applied to large OTC derivatives dealers (assuming there is no severe wrong-way risk). Alpha has been discussed in detail in Chapter 11, and we summarise some published estimates in Table 17.2.

Banks using the IMM have an option to compute their own estimate of α, subject to the supervisory approval. However, this estimate is subject to a floor of 1.2. In light of the results shown in Table 17.2, this floor seems to be conservative, but could be argued to cover model risk and avoid over-reliance on model-based approaches implying idealistic αs close to unity. We should emphasise that all of the above comments on the behaviour of α assume a reasonably large portfolio with no significant wrong-way risk. The empirical work around α pre-dates the global financial crisis and does not benefit from the hindsight of the potential influence of large concentrated positions in instruments such as credit derivatives (Section 11.3.5 showed the potential large increase in α in this type of situation). Not surprisingly, getting the relevant regulatory approval to model α to values below 1.4 is not straightforward. Indeed, if regulators do not deem a bank's IMM framework to be good enough, then they may increase the prescribed value to above 1.4.

Under the IMM, EAD is calculated at the netting set level. Therefore, in contrast to non-internal methods, full cross-product netting and proper collateral modelling is allowable.

---

[6] Global Master Securities Lending Agreement.
[7] According to Picoult (2002), alpha "expresses the difference between calculating economic capital with full simulation and with a simulation assuming the exposure profile of each counterparty can be represented by a fixed exposure profile".

Table 17.2   Regulatory results and published estimates of α. The study of Wilde (2005) includes wrong-way risk whilst the ISDA survey involved four banks estimating based on their own portfolios and internal models

	Alpha
Infinitely large ideal portfolio	1.0
Canabarro *et al.* (2003)	1.09
Wilde (2005)	1.21
ISDA Survey (2003)	1.07–1.10
Regulatory prescribed value	1.4
Supervisory floor (if using own estimation)	1.2
Possible values for concentrated portfolios	2.5 or more

Given the potential benefits of netting and collateral, this is clearly highly advantageous. The definition of EAD under the IMM is based on the "loan-equivalent" EPE measure. However, there is one final modification to account for potential non-conservative ageing effects. This involves using what is known as effective EE, which is the EE but constrained to be non-decreasing for maturities below 1 year. The average effective EE is then the effective EPE (EEPE), which is, by definition, the same or higher than the EPE. This is illustrated in Figure 17.3.

In essence, the non-decreasing constraint captures[8] the roll-off impact of risk that would otherwise be missed for transactions that are close to maturity but, in practice, are likely to be replaced. This is particularly true for portfolios such as, for example, short-dated FX positions. EEPE will typically be slightly greater than EPE as shown (unless EE is monotonically increasing, in which case they will be identical). It could be argued that EEPE may

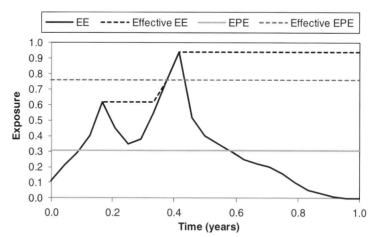

Figure 17.3 Illustration of the difference between EPE and effective EPE. Effective EE is the same as EE but is constrained to be non-decreasing. EPE is the average of the EE over time whilst effective EPE is the average of effective EE over time. A time horizon of only 1 year is shown, since EEPE for longer periods is not used in regulatory formulas.

---

[8] It could be also seen as assuming some worst case default time within the 1-year interval considered.

sometimes be unnecessarily conservative. For example, a profile with a spike in exposure for a very short period (due, for example, to large cash flows) will create an EEPE that is much higher than the EPE.

Finally, the exposure at default is defined by

$$\text{EAD} = \alpha \times \text{EEPE}.$$

17.3.6 Collateral under the IMM

Under the IMM, internal models can be used to calculate collateralised EE, subject to the supervisory approval. The modelling of collateralised exposures from this point of view has been discussed in Chapter 9. Whilst the modelling of collateral should not represent a huge challenge on top of the quantification of exposure, there are complexities to doing this. An obvious issue could be the challenge of including the relevant points for the collateral calculation (Section 9.3.2 and Figure 9.2) at the appropriate margin period of risk (e.g., 10 business days or more).

An alternative[9] to full collateral modelling is to use what has become known as the *shortcut method*. There has been a revision[10] to the shortcut method under Basel III and, for ease of explanation, this is included in the discussion below. The revised shortcut method allows the effective EPE for a collateralised counterparty to be defined by the following quantities:

1a. The current exposure net of any collateral held (but not including any collateral not yet received due to disputes, etc.).
1b. The largest net exposure, including all collateral held or posted under the margin agreement that would not trigger a collateral call. This will include thresholds, minimum transfer amounts[11] and any other components that would cause a delay before collateral could be requested. This is, basically, the largest exposure that could theoretically occur before any collateral call would be triggered.
2. An add-on that reflects the potential increase in exposure over the margin period of risk. This add-on is defined as the expected exposure over some margin period of risk, which (as with other cases) must be at least 5 business days for repo-style transactions and 10 business days for other netting sets.

The capital is defined by the *higher* of 1a and 1b *plus* 2. This can be understood as the worst-case exposure that could occur before collateral would be called for (either the theoretical value 1b or the actual value 1a in case this is larger due, for example, to a collateral dispute) plus the expected exposure generated over the margin period of risk. Finally, the above can be replaced by the effective EPE *without* a collateral agreement in case this amount is higher (which, due to the conservativeness of the approach, can be the case). When accounting for this non-collateralised EEPE, any collateral that has been posted to the counterparty independently of the margining process (e.g., independent amount) must be added.[12]

---

[9] In the case where collateral has been posted across more than one netting set but not all netting sets have exposures computed under IMM (for example, a netting set may use the shortcut method for some trades), there is no rule on how to split the collateral between netting sets. Obviously double counting is not allowable.
[10] This revision arose to correct for cases where collateral has not yet been received (for example, due to disputes) but the supervisory formula allowed it to be included to reduce the exposure. It also prevented independent amounts from being used to reduce exposures.
[11] Which are typically additive with respect to thresholds.
[12] The prevention of independent amounts from being used to offset the uncollateralised exposure calculation, which was a practice that occurred under Basel II, was another change made in Basel III.

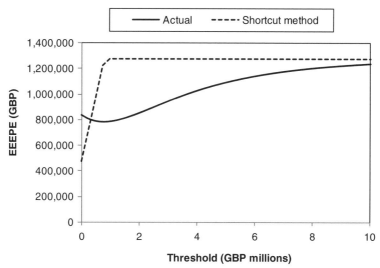

Figure 17.4 EEPE at the 1-year horizon for a four-trade portfolio showing the actual result compared with the shortcut method.

Note that the shortcut method does not make a distinction between unilateral and bilateral collateral agreements – all are treated as unilateral agreements in a bank's favour. Thus, a bank's risk of losing part of the posted collateral (discussed, for example, in Section 9.7.5) is ignored. BCBS (2006) clearly states that the shortcut method is *conservative*, which is probably true, despite the previous comment, because it makes the assumption that all future exposures will be above the threshold or that there will be no benefit from collateral. Figure 17.4 shows an example of the EEPE (at 1 year as required) as a function of the collateral threshold for the shortcut method, compared with the actual result for the four-trade portfolio described in Section 9.5.1.

In this example, the shortcut method underestimates the zero-threshold EEPE as it assumes a simple approximation based on a unilateral CSA only.[13] However, for non-zero thresholds, the shortcut method can significantly overstate the true EEPE. This is not surprising, as it makes no allowance for the fact that the exposure could be below the threshold. For large thresholds, the shortcut method converges to the true solution since this corresponds to taking the uncollateralised result. Hence, we can see that the shortcut method is generally quite conservative, except for the particular cases of a very small or large threshold. This conservativeness means that more banks are aiming to treat collateralised exposures via full simulation (under the IMM) rather than relying on the shortcut method.

17.3.7 Double default

Suppose the credit risk of an exposure is hedged with a product, such as a credit default swap, or otherwise guaranteed by a third party. There should potentially be some capital relief due to this risk reduction, since there is now only risk in the case both parties (original counterparty and party providing the guarantee) default. From Basel II onwards there are two possible ways in which to account for hedged or guaranteed exposures:

---

[13] In the actual case, quite a lot of the risk arises from having to post collateral, as was previously discussed in Section 12.5.2.

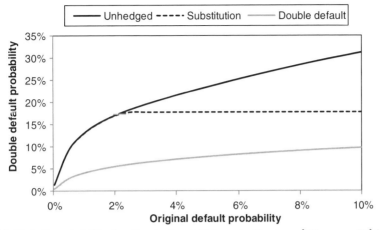

Figure 17.5 Default probability function in Basel II formula (the term $[PD_{99.9\%} - PD]$ in equation (17.1)) for unhedged and hedged exposures. In the latter case, both substitution assumptions and the double default formula are shown. All details are given in Appendix 17E. The obligor default probability is assumed to be 0.1%.

- *Substitution.* The default probability of the "guarantor" (provider of protection or guarantee) may be substituted for the default probability of the original "obligor" (original counterparty). Assuming the guarantor has a better credit quality then this will cause some reduction in risk.
- *Double default.* The "double default effect" is recognised via a formula to account for the fact that risk only arises from joint default. A key consideration in this formula is the correlation between the original counterparty and the guarantor. The reader should bear in mind that the double default treatment has likely been developed with mainly semi-fixed exposures, such as loans and bonds, in mind rather than the more complex case of derivatives products. However, we will discuss the combination of double default and random exposure.

The double default formula[14] (BCBS, 2005) is based on the treatment of the two-default case as described in Section 11.2, where the joint default probability is expressed in terms of a bivariate normal distribution function. Appendix 17E describes the double default formula for computing capital for hedged or guaranteed exposures. The main reduction in capital arises from the decrease in the default probability within the capital formula (there are less significant changes in effective maturity and loss given default). Figure 17.5 contrasts the difference between an unhedged exposure, the substitution and double default approaches. The substitution approach is beneficial only if the conditional default probability of the guarantor is lower than that of the obligor. The double default formula is always beneficial, in recognition of the fact that the probability that both obligor and guarantor will default is usually significantly less than that of the obligor defaulting alone. The Basel Committee has also proposed a simple parametric formula. This approximation, described in Appendix 17E, works well for small obligor default probabilities but is less accurate for high probabilities.

---

[14] This option is only available when using the IRB approach under Basel II.

Indeed, it is possible for the adjustment factor to give a capital requirement higher than that for an unhedged exposure.

The double default formula can most simply be implemented by directly reducing the EEPE of the calculated EEPE for a given counterparty in the same way as a fixed exposure. In this case, the equivalent exposure of the hedge must be included as a separate counterparty with a probability of default defined by the double default formula. Alternatively, the double default hedge could be modelled within the EEPE calculation (similar to the impact of an independent amount under a collateral agreement) with a separate component, again modelled to account for the hedge. The value of α can also include this component so, for example, hedged exposures would not influence the estimate of α. This could mean that a portfolio with well-hedged wrong-way risk exposures could give a low estimate of α due to recognition of the wrong-way risk reduction.

17.4   BASEL III

17.4.1   Basel III, counterparty credit risk and CVA

In December 2009, the BCBS published a document entitled "Strengthening the resilience of the banking sector". This document[15] essentially described changes to regulation and capital requirements in response to the, then relatively new, financial crisis. The crisis highlighted many shortcomings of the Basel II regulatory regime, such as insufficient capital levels, excessive leverage, procyclicality and systemic risk. In response to this, a large number of changes were proposed in order to improve upon previous regulation, which make up Basel III (and in the case of revisions to the market risk framework – Basel 2.5).

A large portion of the Basel III changes relate to counterparty credit risk and CVA (over half of the 80-page document mentioned above is concerned with these aspects). After a consultation period, the final Basel III requirements have been published[16] in "Basel III: A global regulatory framework for more resilient banks and banking systems". In this section, we will explain the aspects of Basel III that concern counterparty credit risk (which are substantial) and are affective from 1st January 2013[17]. Note that these changes also depend on aspects such as CRD IV which at the time of writing are not finalised. A brief summary of the changes (note that some affect overall credit risk also) is given below:

- *Stressed EPE.* Expected positive exposure (EPE) must be calculated with parameter calibration based on stressed data. This has arisen due to the procyclical issues of using historical data where non-volatile markets lead to smaller risk numbers, which in turn reduce capital requirements. This use of stressed data is also intended to capture general wrong-way risk more accurately.
- *Backtesting.* Validation of EPE models must involve backtesting up to a time period of at least one year.
- *Stress testing.* An increased focus on the stress testing of counterparty risk exposures.

---

[15] http://www.bis.org/publ/bcbs164.htm
[16] http://www.bis.org/publ/bcbs189.pdf
[17] However, at the time of going to print, this date appears unfeasible. For example, in early August 2012, the Financial Services Authority (FSA) made the following statement about CRD IV (the legal implementation of Basel III within the European Union): *"It does not appear feasible that the legislation can enter into force in line with the implementation date."* See http://www.fsa.gov.uk/library/communication/statements/2012/crd-iv.shtml

- *Specific wrong-way risk*. There must be procedures for identifying and dealing with specific wrong-way risk. Experiences with, for example, monoline insurers have shown the potentially devastating impact of ignoring such aspects.
- *Increased margin period of risk*. In certain situations, the minimum period for the margin period of risk, as introduced in Section 8.5.2, must be increased from 10 days to 20 days. This has arisen due to the realisation that collateral management practices during the crisis were sometimes extremely suboptimal and issues such as collateral disputes severely influenced the timely receipt of collateral.
- *Asset correlation multiplier*. A multiplier of 1.25 will be applied to regulated financial firms (with assets of at least \$100 billion) and to all exposures to unregulated financial firms. This has arisen due to the observed interconnectedness of such institutions during the crisis.
- *Central counterparties*. A relatively small capital charge of 2% (of the EAD) was introduced to cover exposures[18] to qualifying central counterparties (CCPs). Whilst this is higher than the zero capital charge under Basel II, the aim of this is to encourage the use of CCPs.
- *CVA capital charge*. A capital charge will be introduced for CVA volatility (CVA VAR[19]), in addition to the current charges against counterparty credit risk. This is the most important change and has arisen because a large proportion of the counterparty credit risk-related losses in the crisis were seen as being mark-to-market based (CVA) rather than due to actual defaults, which were the focus of the Basel II regulations.

In addition, there are other small changes, such as an update to the "shortcut method" described in the last section, the preclusion of rating-based collateral clauses and the adjustment of exposure for CVA and DVA. All of these aspects will be discussed further below.

The overall impact of the changes will be a larger capital charge for counterparty credit risk. This will come about from an increased exposure (stressed EPE, increased margin period of risk, wrong-way risk) and the new capital charge for CVA volatility. This, in turn, will incentivise CVA hedging and the use of CCPs in order to benefit from the capital relief given for hedges and the lower capital charges for centrally cleared exposures. Under Basel III, a bank will gain significantly from using the IMM approach rather than the simpler and more conservative methodologies.

17.4.2   Stressed EPE

The requirements over stressed EPE parallel the rules introduced for market risk under Basel 2.5. The danger in calibrating risk models with historical data is that benign and quiet periods tend to precede major crises. This means that risk measures are particularly low at the worst possible time. Indeed, the higher leverage levels that such low-risk measures ultimately allow may increase the likelihood and severity of any crisis. This problem is typically known as procyclicality.

In order to correct for the above problem, it is necessary under Basel III to use stressed inputs (e.g., volatility and correlation) when computing EPE. These stressed inputs must use three years of historical data that include a one-year period of stress (typically defined as

---

[18] Here there is a distinction between exposure via initial and variation margin and that arising from the default fund contribution. This is discussed in detail below.
[19] Value at risk as introduced in Chapter 2.

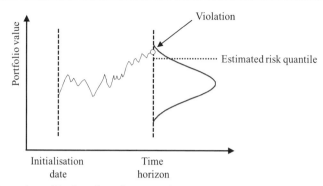

Figure 17.6 Illustration of backtesting via comparing a realised path, at some time horizon, to the estimated risk measure (assumed to be a quantile).

increasing CDS spreads) or, alternatively, market-implied data from this period. This stressed period must be used *in addition* to the "normal" period of at least three years of historical data, which itself should cover a full range of economic conditions. The exposure at default must be on the set of parameters that result in the highest EEPE at the portfolio (not by counterparty) level, i.e., the maximum[20] of the normal and stressed exposure calculations. It is not clear how often this comparison needs to be made, which is to be defined by the regulator. Daily comparisons could be computationally intensive and lead to unnecessary volatility in the EEPE.

The use of the stressed period should resolve procyclicality problems by ensuring that EPE does not become artificially low during quiet periods in financial markets. In addition, it is viewed that the use of stressed EPE should improve the coverage of general wrong-way risk, as the dependencies that contribute to this may be more apparent in stressed periods. Otherwise the treatment of general wrong-way risk as EEPE multiplied by the α factor is unchanged, except for some points related to the robust calculation of α.[21]

17.4.3 Backtesting

The required backtesting of EPE models follows the requirements over (market risk) VAR approaches. A backtesting procedure that could apply to quantile measures such as VAR or PFE is illustrated in Figure 17.6. VAR is typically defined as a 99% confidence level over a 1-day time horizon.[22] Assuming that independence of daily forecasts would imply a simple binomial distribution for exceedances or violations, the expected number of violations over an annual period (250 business days) would be 2.5 and, to a 95% confidence level, violations above six or below one are rejected.[23] The backtesting of VAR models is therefore relatively straightforward. An obvious problem is that the severity of a violation is not considered.

Backtesting of EPE is more challenging than that of market risk VAR for a variety of reasons:

- Multiple time horizons must be considered, which require more data to be stored and processed. The need to look at longer time horizons implies that a much larger historical

---

[20] Note that this is in contrast to the sum which is applied for VAR and CVA VAR.
[21] In particular, it seems banks cannot attain IMM approval without modelling wrong-way risk in some way.
[22] This can then be scaled to the required 10-day interval.
[23] This can be shown via the relevant binomial probabilities or more robustly using the two-tailed approach of Kupiec (1995).

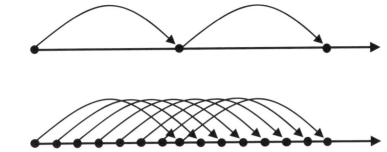

Figure 17.7 Use of non-overlapping (top) and overlapping (bottom) windows for backtesting.

dataset is used and creates problems with effects such as ageing. It is also necessary to keep track of the quarterly recalibration of EPE models.[24]

• Backtesting must be done for different portfolios of trades, as EPE is defined at the counterparty (or netting set) level. However, such portfolios cannot be assumed independent. For example, if one portfolio contains the hedges of another, then they will never be expected to have a high exposure at the same time.

• Measures such as EPE are based on expectations and not a quantile (which defines VAR). Non-quantile-based quantities are harder to backtest.

There are a number of considerations that are necessary to comply with the above. An obvious first is the use of overlapping windows (see Figure 17.7). However, it is then important to deal with the dependence of data (e.g., exceeding an exposure in one period leads to a greater likelihood of exceedance in an overlapping period). This leads to difficulties as most simple statistical tests are based on the assumption of independent observations. For more discussion, see "Sound practices for backtesting counterparty credit risk models".[25]

Backtesting must first be done at the risk factor level. The aim of this is to test the distributional assumptions for each risk factor individually and avoid the potential for these to be diluted or masked at the portfolio level. Secondly, backtesting must be done at the netting set or portfolio level. Assuming the risk-factor backtesting shows acceptable results then the portfolio-level backtesting is relevant for testing the ability to capture important codependencies between different risk factors.

Backtesting must involve multiple time horizons, up to at least one year, and multiple initialisation points. Furthermore, different quantiles must be used to effectively test across the whole exposure distribution. To simplify the workload, given the millions of trades that may exist within a typical large OTC derivatives book, it is possible to backtest "representative portfolios". Such representative portfolios must be chosen based on their sensitivity to the significant risk factors and correlations to which a bank is exposed. This could be done via regression methods or principal components analysis, or may be rather more ad hoc (e.g., based on the largest counterparties, exposures or overall capital contributions). Once representative portfolios have been chosen, a typical backtesting exercise may use, for example, tenors defined at (1W, 2W, 1M, 3M, 6M, 1Y, 2Y) and test 1%, 5%, 25%, 75%, 95%

---

[24] For example, a 3-month and 6-month distribution generated today will be inconsistent with the 3-month distribution generated 3 months from now since a recalibration of the model will be performed.

[25] http://www.bis.org/publ/bcbs185.pdf

and 99% quantiles with weekly initialisation points. The data and systems implications of doing this are considerable. In addition, representative portfolios should presumably be reviewed on a periodic basis. Whilst a typical portfolio will not change materially over the short term, any large market move or significant trading in a particular asset class may create sensitivities in a bank's portfolio that need to be included in the representative portfolios.

17.4.4 CVA capital charge

The objective of the CVA capital charge is to improve upon the Basel II requirements, which effectively capitalise only potential losses due to default (and credit migration). The BCBS, in their December 2009 document, made it clear that this was a key issue and stated that, in the crisis, only one-third of counterparty risk-related losses were due to defaults, with the remaining two-thirds being mark-to-market based.[26] It is not clear what the precise empirical evidence for the value of two-thirds is, and it likely depends on aspects such as banks unwinding trades with monoline insurers (see Section 13.3.2). The highly distressed nature of monolines at the time could be used to argue that these were, in fact, more akin to default losses. Nevertheless, it seems hard to argue against the fact that CVA volatility represents a substantial risk and, as such, must be capitalised.[27] Essentially, Basel III requires that, as a trading book component, a VAR must be calculated to assess the unexpected losses due to CVA. CVA VAR covers OTC derivatives, but not centrally cleared transactions. Securities financing transactions may be covered, this point being still under discussion, and may rest with whether or not the relevant local regulator believes them to be material. In addition, market participants have lobbied for exceptions for other counterparties, such as sovereigns and "non-financials" (taken to mean institutions such as corporates). Any such exemptions may come at the discretion of the local regulator rather than coming under the Basel III definitions.

Developing a methodology for CVA VAR represents a significant challenge. Both VAR and CVA itself are, typically, calculated via Monte Carlo simulations. A calculation of an EE profile can potentially require the consideration of thousands of paths that extend out many years in the future and cover all trades within the netting set. There is clearly a need to avoid a methodology requiring a Monte Carlo within a Monte Carlo calculation and, therefore, simplifications are required. The first proposal (December 2009) suggested a bond-equivalent approach as a reasonable simplification, but this received a critical response (e.g., see Rebonato et al., 2010) and the methodology was subsequently refined in the final Basel III proposals published in June 2011.

From the point of view of CVA VAR, rather than allowing a bank to define CVA in accordance with their own accounting practices, the BCBS defines CVA as follows:

$$\text{CVA} = \text{LGD}_{\text{mkt}} \sum_{i=1}^{T} \max\left(0; \exp\left(-\frac{s_{i-1}t_{i-1}}{\text{LGD}_{\text{mkt}}}\right) - \exp\left(-\frac{s_i t_i}{\text{LGD}_{\text{mkt}}}\right)\right)\left(\frac{\text{EE}_{i-1}D_{i-1} + \text{EE}_i D_i}{2}\right).$$

(17.4)

This is equivalent to the CVA formula in equation (12.2). The term $\text{LGD}_{\text{mkt}} = (1 - \text{Rec})$ defines loss given default, which is simply one minus the recovery rate. The use of a market (mkt) LGD refers to this being based on market expectations and not historical estimates that

---

[26] This implies that the uncertainty of default is twice as important as default itself.

[27] Assuming, of course, that CVA should be marked-to-market in the first place. This aspect is discussed at the end of Section 17.4.7.

might be used for other capital charges. The motivation for this is to ensure that the LGD for pricing CVA is identical[28] to that used for implying default probabilities (the denominator in the exponential functions in equation (7.4)). This partial cancellation of LGD_{mkt} is discussed in Section 12.3.2. The first term inside the summation is an approximation for the future default probability[29] previously defined in equation (10.5) as $q(t_{i-1}, t_i)$. This is defined from the relevant CDS spreads at the beginning and end of the interval, s_{i-1} and s_i, and is floored at zero since it is a probability. The accuracy of this approximation was previously shown in an example in Table 10.3. The second term is the expected exposure and discount factor previously written in equation (12.2) as $DF(t_j)EE(t_j)$. The division by two is simply a more accurate integration, which is relevant if the number of time intervals used (T) is relatively small (Section 12.1.2 discusses the accuracy of the integration in the CVA formula). Formulas for delta and gamma of the CVA are also provided for banks that calculate VAR using these approximations.

It is worth emphasising that the CDS spread defined by s_i in the Basel III CVA definition is clearly defined as a market-implied parameter. Indeed, the BCBS (2011) state: *"Whenever the CDS spread of the counterparty is available, this must be used. Whenever such a CDS spread is not available, the bank must use a proxy spread that is appropriate based on the rating, industry and region of the counterparty"*. This is important because it implies that, even if a bank relied on historical default probabilities for calculating CVA, then the CVA VAR would need to use market-implied (risk-neutral) probabilities. The difference between historical and risk-neutral default probabilities has been emphasised in Section 10.1.6.

Another point to note is that the EE in equation (17.4) is the one calculated by an approved capital model and not defined by accounting purposes when calculating CVA. This is likely to lead to efforts to align this exposure calculation with the (risk-neutral) one used by the CVA desk when pricing and hedging.[30]

17.4.5   CVA VAR – advanced approach

With the above definition of CVA, the so-called advanced approach requires a bank to use their VAR engine to calculate CVA VAR directly. This approach can only be used by banks with IMM approval to use internal VAR models for market risk purposes **and** similar approval for specific risk for bonds. An approved specific risk model gives the ability to simulate the credit spreads that are required in order to calculate CVA as in equation (17.4). Such approaches tend to simulate spreads for generic or proxy curves, generally defined via ratings and potentially also regions and sectors. Hence, this is approximately aligned with the mapping procedures already required to estimate credit spreads for CVA valuation purposes (see Section 10.3.1). The Basel Committee accept that, due to the illiquidity of the CDS and bond markets, proxying CDS spreads will be the norm. The methodology for simulating such CDS spreads is part of the specific risk model approval.

Generally, the calculation is analogous to market risk VAR, using a 99% confidence level and 10-day horizon. Presumably, a similar multiplier of three will be used.[31] In addition, the

---

[28] Except if there is a difference in seniority, in which case different LGDs can be used.
[29] Presumably an accurate calculation as described in Chapter 10 would be acceptable.
[30] However, the use of historial data to calculate exposure in most IMM approved models, together with requirements over the use of stressed data make this alignment very difficult.
[31] The initial version of the CVA VAR proposals included a multiplier of five, which was subsequently dropped. The multiplier of three appears in the capital requirements for market risk (Section 2.3.1), although this can be increased by the supervisor, for example due to poor backtesting performance.

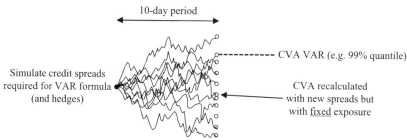

Figure 17.8 Illustration of advanced CVA VAR methodology. Since CVA is by convention a positive number, the VAR is defined by an increasing CVA.

aforementioned changes that require an additional calculation with the simulation of stressed market data (similar to the EPE requirements discussed in Section 17.4.2) also apply. The stressed market data corresponds to both the calculation of exposure with the CVA formula and the simulation of credit spread, and the final number is the sum of the normal and stressed calculations.[32] However, despite the correspondence to the current market risk VAR methodology, the CVA VAR calculation must be run separately.

The critical simplifying assumption (see Figure 17.8) is that the exposure is unchanged (avoiding a costly recalculation probably involving Monte Carlo simulation) and only the impact of credit spread changes is considered. The expected exposure profile defined by EE_i is assumed fixed over the time horizon of 10 days. This is clearly a significant approximation because parameters such as interest rates and FX rates are assumed to have no impact on CVA volatility. However, a systematic increase in CDS spreads causes an approximately similar percentage increase in CVA. Hence, CVA VAR is clearly capturing the main volatility component of CVA. Evidence from initial calculations suggests that CVA VAR represents a charge similar to the impact of an approximately 100–200 bps increase in credit spreads. This seems plausible, given the time horizon involved and the overall volatility and correlations of credit spreads.

To give a very simple example of the impact of CVA VAR under the advanced method, we return to the four-trade portfolio defined in Section 9.5.1 which has a CVA of £257,905 for a flat CDS spread of 500 bps and recovery rate of 40%. The credit delta of this portfolio is £427, which is the impact of a 1 bp move in the CDS spread on the CVA. Assuming a worst-case scenario of a CDS spread widening of 140 bps,[33] the CVA increase is £427 × 140 = £59,780. Then, under a standard multiplier of 3, this would give rise to a capital charge of £59,780 × 3 = £179,340.[34] Hence, the capital charge appears comparable to the CVA value itself. With the requirement to compute CVA VAR with stressed market data, this capital requirement will be increased as the example in Section 17.4.7 will illustrate.

An obvious question is the capital relief that can be achieved via CVA hedges. Since the volatility of exposure is not considered, it is clearly not possible to recognise any other hedges other than those in relation to the credit spread volatility. The eligible hedges are,

---

[32] But does not include the IRC (incremental risk charge), which measures the impact of effects such as default and credit migration risk over a 1-year time horizon and is therefore similar to the Basel II IMM approach.

[33] This is estimated from an annual volatility of 300 bps for the CDS spread of 500 bps, which needs to be multiplied by $\sqrt{10/250} = 0.2$ to convert to a 10-day volatility and then by $\Phi^{-1}(99\%) = 2.33$ to approximate the impact of the 99% confidence level.

[34] This is the capital number rather than the RWA equivalent, which would need to involve a multiplication by 12.5 (the reciprocal of the minimum capital ratio of 8%).

therefore, single-name CDSs[35] (or single-name contingent CDSs), other equivalent hedges referencing the counterparty directly and index CDSs only. Only hedges used for the purpose of mitigating CVA risk, and managed as such, are eligible. Such eligible hedges may be removed from the standard VAR calculation.

With index CDSs, where an imperfect hedge clearly exists, the basis between the counterparty CDS and the index spread must be simulated in the VAR calculation (as indicated in Figure 17.8). Hence, a bank must not only estimate CDS spreads for many counterparties via curve mapping procedures (Section 10.3), but must also be able to simulate such spreads for VAR purposes. The extent to which this mapped spread is correlated to the relevant index then defines the benefit through hedging. The index can be modelled as a linear combination of its components. However, "If the basis is not reflected to the satisfaction of the supervisor, then the bank must reflect only 50% of the notional amount of index hedges in the VaR" (BCBS, 2011). As noted previously (Section 16.6.2), a 50% reduction is quite aggressive as it represents a high correlation[36] between the single-name and index spreads.

In the case of the more recently developed index-referencing contingent CDS (CCDS), described in Section 15.4.5, defining capital relief will be potentially more problematic. Since these will reference standard transactions, their hedging will be imperfect. The credit protection component of an index CCDS should be recognised, as with a credit index. However, the market risk component (driven by the exposure of the referenced transaction) cannot be accounted for as such risks are not modelled in the CVA VAR.

17.4.6 CVA VAR – standardised approach

For banks without the relevant IMM approvals to use the advanced approach for CVA VAR, there is the standardised approach. This involves a simple variance-type approach and is defined below for a given portfolio:

$$
2.33\sqrt{h}\sqrt{\left(\sum_i 0.5.w_i.\left(M_i.\text{EAD}_i^{\text{total}} - M_i^{\text{hedge}}B_i\right) - \sum_{ind} w_{\text{ind}}.M_{\text{ind}}.B_{\text{ind}}\right)^2 + \sum_i 0.75.w_i^2.\left(M_i.\text{EAD}_i^{\text{total}} - M_i^{\text{hedge}}B_i\right)^2}. \tag{17.5}
$$

In the above formula, 2.33 corresponds to a 99% confidence level for a normal distribution and h is the relevant time interval of 1 year. In terms of exposure, w_i is the weight applicable depending on the rating of the counterparty,[37] M_i is the effective maturity (see Appendix 17E) and $\text{EAD}_i^{\text{total}}$ is the total exposure at default (including netting and collateral) for the counterparty defined according to whatever method is used (Section 17.3). Hedges are defined by the terms B_i (notional of single-name CDS), B_{ind} (notional of index CDS), M_i^{hedge} (maturity of single-name hedge) and M_{ind} (weighted maturity of index hedge). The factors 0.5 and 0.75 effectively assume that 50% of the credit spread component is systemic and,

---

[35] Short bond positions are allowed if the basis risk is captured.
[36] As shown in footnote 29 in the previous chapter for equal volatilities, a reduction of 50% would imply a correlation of something in the region of 87.5%.
[37] Weights are 0.7%, 0.7%, 0.8%, 1.0%, 2.0%, 3.0% and 10.0% for AAA, AA, A, BBB, BB, B and CCC ratings, respectively.

therefore, can be hedged with a 50% weight to index hedges (aside from adjustments for maturity effects).

It is important to note that banks with the relevant approval to use the advanced CVA VAR approach cannot choose, instead, to adopt the standardised approach. This is especially important since, whilst simpler approaches tend to be generally more conservative, the standardised formula has been found by some market practitioners to give a lower capital number than the advanced approach.

17.4.7   CVA VAR example

In this section, we show example CVA VAR calculations for the standardised and advanced approaches described above and also illustrate the impact of hedges. The portfolio[38] concerned has a total of 156 interest rate and FX trades with an average lifetime of 8-years with two different counterparties with credit spreads (and ratings) of 384 bps (double-B) and 56 bps (double A). Whilst different portfolios could give rise to quite different results, we believe that this example provided a reasonable benchmark for illustrating some important features of the CVA VAR methods.

Figure 17.9 shows the CVA VAR capital charge for the example portfolio compared to the CVA itself. We see that the capital charge under the standard calibration follows the intuition of the simple example in Section 17.4.5 being less than, but comparable to, the CVA. The capital charge using the stressed calibration is, not surprisingly, higher and the requirement to sum the standard and stressed components creates a capital charge which is significantly higher than the CVA itself. The standardised formula gives a requirement slightly higher than the advanced approach as would be expected (although as noted above there is anecdotal evidence of some banks finding situations where the standardised method actually gives lower numbers).

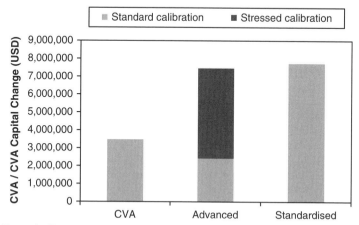

Figure 17.9 Example CVA VAR calculation showing the capital charge under the advanced and standardised approaches compared to the CVA itself. For the advanced calculation, the split arising from the standard and stressed calibrations is shown.

Source: Quantifi.

---

[38] This portfolio and the associated calculations have been provided by Quantifi and more detail can be found via www.quantifisolutions.com.

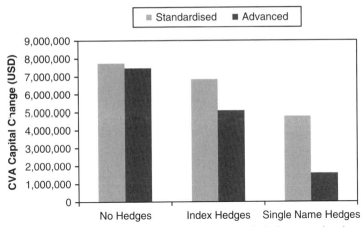

Figure 17.10 Example CVA VAR calculation showing the capital charge under the advanced and standardised approaches and the benefit achieved via index and single name hedges.
Source: Quantifi.

Next, in Figure 17.10, we show the reduction of the CVA VAR capital charge as a result of hedging.[39] The reduction arising from index hedges is moderate which is not surprising since, as described in Section 16.6.2, such benefit will be limited unless the correlation between the index and individual counterparty credit spread is very high. The capital relief achieved with a single name hedge is much better although not perfect since even a delta neutral hedge gives rise to some risk over a 10-day period, especially considering the capital charge is defined by the 99% worst case scenario.

This leaves a CVA desk in a difficult situation since they have to choose between hedging the CVA as defined by their own calculations and accounting rules and the CVA that implicitly appears within the CVA VAR formula. For example, as noted by Pykhtin (2012), the use of the alpha factor incentivises systematic overhedging of CVA. It could be argued that regulators should allow a closer alignment of CVA VAR with the typical CVA calculation of a bank and therefore better promote the hedging of CVA for capital reduction purposes.

17.4.8   Shortcomings and criticisms of CVA VAR

CVA VAR will create a significantly increased capital requirement for counterparty credit risk. CVA capital is likely to be multiples of current default risk capital and comparable with CVA itself. Some dealers claim that capital charges for some derivatives trades could be quadrupled. It is not surprising, given the significance and inherent complexity of the CVA VAR approach, that there remain significant criticisms over the methodology. Important context for these criticisms is that some believe the capital charge for CVA was driven by political pressure aimed to penalise the OTC derivative market and therefore push it towards central clearing.

---

[39] In these calculations, we have assumed a perfect alignment between the CVA as seen by the CVA desk of the bank (which would drive the magnitude of the hedges) and the CVA within the CVA VAR capital formula. As discussed in Section 17.4.8 there is unlikely to be a perfect alignment here and therefore in reality the capital relief from hedges may be weaker.

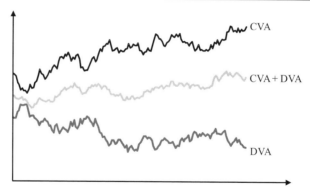

Figure 17.11 Illustration divergence in DVA treatment with respect to accounting and regulatory capital rules under Basel III. From an accounting point of view, a bank can offset the CVA with the DVA, thereby seeing a natural reduction in the volatility of the total. However, for the purposes of calculating CVA VAR, the DVA benefit must be ignored leading to a larger overall volatility.

A first and fundamental complaint made by some banks is the very nature of the formula in equation (17.4) and the reference to CDS spreads. Whilst large dealers have tended to calculate CVA in this way, trading book style, smaller banks have relied on historical default probabilities, essentially not recognising the mark-to-market of CVA, seeing it more as a banking book-style reserve or provision. Such a bank will be in a difficult position under Basel III as their definition of CVA for accounting and regulatory capital purposes will differ significantly. They may effectively be charged capital for PnL volatility that does not actually exist in their accounts.

Forcing banks to consider the current credit environment (via CDS spreads) and to quantify and hedge CVA dynamically would seem to be preferable to a backward-looking and static approach using historical data. However, the large non-default component in credit spreads (Section 10.1.6), the inability to define CDS spreads for most counterparties (Section 10.3), the illiquidity of CVA hedges and the experience of unintended consequences in CVA hedging (Section 16.5.4) may imply drawbacks to such an approach. The banking book versus trading book approach to CVA is at the heart of the CVA VAR debate as discussed by Gregory (2010). On the one hand, the trading book approach to CVA as advocated under Basel III is no different from the treatment of bonds held on a bank's trading books. However, ignoring CVA VAR would be equivalent to treating CVA as similar to a loan loss reserve for illiquid loans held on a banking book. We will discuss this again in the next chapter.

A second main criticism of CVA VAR is that the benefit of DVA (Chapter 13) is not included in either the standardised or the advanced approach. Clearly, a bank utilising DVA as a partial mitigant to CVA would desire DVA to be included in capital calculations. However, clear clarification that DVA should not be included has been given[40] and is explained as methodologies for including DVA being "either too complex, lacking conservatism, or relying too heavily on modelling assumptions". This is perhaps not surprising, given the controversial nature of DVA as explained in Chapter 13. Nevertheless, it should be emphasised that this creates another divergence between the definition of CVA from an accounting and a

---

[40] "Application of own credit risk adjustments to derivatives", Basel Committee on Banking Supervision, http://www.bis.org/press/p111221.htm. "Additionally, DVA gains must be derecognised from the calculation of equity – see http://www.bis.org/press/p120725b.htm" to ensure that an increase in the credit risk of a bank does not achieve an increase in its common equity due to a reduction in the value of its liabilities.

regulatory capital perspective, as shown in Figure 17.11. In the former case, a bank may[41] use DVA as an offset against CVA and the overall CVA and DVA mark-to-market volatility will be smaller than that of the CVA alone. However, from the point of view of calculating VAR, only the CVA volatility must be considered.

We note that the trading book-style treatment of CVA and the preclusion of DVA under Basel III are somewhat linked. The use of DVA from an accounting perspective, which reduces CVA and its volatility, in some sense partially moves from the trading book to a banking book-type approach. To understand this note that, as discussed in Section 13.3.4, only the systemic component of DVA can be realised via hedging. Removing this component from a credit spread (see Figure 10.4) should approximately remove the risk premium components, leaving only the real-world default probability. Not allowing CVA to be defined banking book style or allowing DVA benefit means that the definition of CVA under Basel III is incompatible with *both* ways in which banks tend to quantify and manage CVA.

Another strong complaint from the industry has arisen from the need to exclude exposure volatility and, therefore, any market risk hedges from the calculation, creating a "split hedge" issue. Not only will this fail to give capital relief for CVA market risk hedges (for example, those for interest rate risk), but these hedges will actually *increase* capital requirements by appearing in a bank's standard VAR calculation (as noted above, eligible hedges can be removed). Hence, a bank is given regulatory capital incentives **not** to hedge the market risk components of CVA.

Related to this point, we note that there is a misalignment between the expected exposure (EE) used in equation (17.4) and that used for a standard CVA calculation. This misalignment can arise from a number of components including (as noted previously, these were not included in the example in section 17.4.7):

• The use of risk-neutral vs real world parameters.
• The requirement to include the maximum of the standard and stressed EPE for capital purposes (section 17.4.1).
• The requirement to include an alpha multiplier in the EPE from the point of view of capital calculations (section 17.3.5).
• The requirement to use EEPE
• The requirement to calculate CVA VAR with stressed market data and add this to the standard CVA VAR (section 17.4.5).

This leaves a CVA desk in a difficult situation since they have to choose between hedging the CVA as defined by their own calculations and accounting rules and the CVA that implicitly appears within the CVA VAR formula. For example, as noted by Pykhtin (2012), the use of the alpha factor incentivises systematic overhedging of CVA. It could be argued that regulators should allow a closer alignment of CVA VAR with the typical CVA calculation of a bank and therefore better promote the hedging of CVA for capital reduction purposes.

We also note at this point that the capital charge for CVA is likely to be *procyclical* since CDS spread volatility tends to increase with increasing spreads. Hence, in good economic climates, CDS volatility and therefore CVA VAR will be low and it will tend to increase in more turbulent periods. The use of stressed CDS spread data will partially alleviate this problem. This behaviour is equivalent to market risk VAR behaviour and at first glance may not

---

[41] Indeed, under US GAAP and IFRS13 (introduced in January 2013), they must do this.

appear any more problematic. However, CVA is defined primarily by credit spreads which are strongly cyclical (in terms of overall level and volatility) and cannot be as well hedged as traditional market risks. Hence, a bank has limited control over their CVA capital charge increasing during turbulent periods.

Whilst the complaints against the CVA VAR methodology are strong, it is unlikely that any significant changes will occur in the short term. However, it seems local regulators may lift certain restrictions if lobbied to do so. For example, under CRD IV,[42] draft rules from the European Parliament in early 2012 proposed an exemption to the CVA charge for all non-financial counterparties and a draft version of CRD IV in March 2012 from the Council of the European Union proposed exempting trades with sovereign entities. The rationale behind such potential exemptions is a feedback loop similar to that illustrated in Section 16.5.4, as hedging of CVA increases CDS spreads which in turn increase CVA and create more hedging. Corporate and sovereign counterparties are argued to be particularly significant in this respect since they typically do not post collateral, leading to large exposures which will attract large hedges. Sovereign entities are especially problematic since they typically trade large notional interest rate swaps to hedge bond issuance. This can mean that a bank's entire sovereign exposure could increase simultaneously due to a significant interest rate move.

Local regulators allowing exemptions as described above seems to suggest that they agree that the entire premise of the CVA capital charge and associated capital relief through hedging is flawed, at least for certain counterparties. This raises again the banking book versus trading book approach to CVA discussed at the start of this section. To what extent unintended consequences of CVA hedging may further weaken the application of the CVA VAR capital charge in future will be interesting.[43]

17.4.9   Other relevant changes

In addition to the significant Basel III changes described above in the form of stressed EPE and CVA VAR, there are a number of other smaller changes that are relevant for the capitalisation of counterparty credit risk. These are outlined in more detail below.

Outstanding EAD

Outstanding EAD refers to the adjustment of EAD for CVA (and DVA). Incurred CVA is defined as the CVA value on the balance sheet of a firm. This should be recognised as being risk reducing, since it goes to zero in the event of a default. It can, therefore, be subtracted (with a floor at zero) from the EAD to reflect the fact that the CVA already defines an effective write-down of exposure. This reduction of EAD by incurred CVA losses does not apply to the determination of the CVA risk capital charge, but only to the determination of the default-related (Basel II) risk capital charge. Pykhtin (2011) argues that, in fact, the CVA should be subtracted from the product of EAD and LGD and include the *addition* of DVA benefit (DVA would therefore increase the capital requirements). Since the intention of this is to correct for counterparty risk already valued within a firm's accounting PnL, this would seem correct and not dependent on the BCBS's own view of the validity of DVA.

---

[42] The fourth Capital Requirements Directive, which is the vehicle implementing Basel III in Europe.

[43] With non-collateral posting counterparties (e.g., sovereigns and corporates) being subject to possible exemptions and collateralised trades (e.g., interbank) moving to central clearing, CVA VAR may even become largely irrelevant.

Specific wrong-way risk

Whilst general wrong-way risk is captured via the α multiplier (and additionally via the stressed EEPE calculation), specific wrong-way risk is treated separately. Specific wrong-way risk is defined as existing "if future exposure to a specific counterparty is highly correlated with the counterparty's probability of default", with the classic example of a company writing put options on its own stock (Section 15.4.3) being cited as an example.

Basel III required that there must be procedures in place to identify, monitor and control cases of specific wrong-way risk for each legal entity. Transactions with counterparties, where specific wrong-way risk has been identified, need to be treated differently when calculating the EAD for such exposures and must be considered as residing outside the netting set. Where specific wrong-way risk has been identified, a larger exposure must be assumed.

Furthermore, for single-name credit default swaps, where there exists a legal connection between the counterparty and the underlying issuer, and where specific wrong-way risk has been identified, the EAD should be 100%, less any current losses accounted for (e.g., via CVA). This is applied for other products also, such as equity derivatives, bond options and securities financing transactions that reference a single company which has a legal connection to the counterparty. In such a case the EAD must be defined assuming a default of the underlying security.[44]

Whilst this treatment of specific wrong-way risk appears quite straightforward, it does create requirements in having the ability to have the correct legal information. Furthermore, it must be possible to define netting sets based on wrong-way risk rather than legal data alone.

Increased margin period of risk

In certain situations, the margin period of risk (Section 8.5.2) must be increased from a minimum of 10 days for OTC derivatives to a minimum of 20 days. These situations are:

- For all netting sets[45] where the number of trades exceeds 5,000 at any point during a quarter (the longer 20-day period then applies for the following quarter).
- For netting sets containing one or more trades involving either illiquid collateral or an OTC derivative that cannot easily be replaced.
- If there have been more than two margin call disputes on a particular netting set, over the previous two quarters, that have lasted longer than the original margin period of risk (before consideration of this provision).

This will obviously require more data to determine whether each netting set should follow a 10- or 20-day assumption. Note that the margin period of risk must also include the contractual re-margin period of N days. If this is daily, then the period assumed is 10 or 20 days but otherwise it must be increased by a further $N - 1$ days.

It remains to be seen if the above rules actually improve collateral management practices, as there are potential problems and ambiguities with the above requirements. For

---

[44] If a LGD assumption is made elsewhere (e.g., IRC), the LGD must be set to 100%.
[45] Note that the margin period of risk applies to netting sets and not at the counterparty level (unless there is only one netting set).

example, if only a small fraction of the collateral is illiquid then the 20-day period assumed would be rather punitive. There could also be excess volatility from netting sets on the boundary (e.g., close to 5,000 trades) having unnecessary EAD volatility from switching between 10 and 20 days. Finally, market participants may behave sub-optimally, such as not disputing a collateral call to avoid triggering the move to a 20-day period, becoming less active in collateral management but reducing capital.

Asset correlation multiplier

Due to the realisation, during the crisis, that financial firms were significantly intercon-nected and their credit qualities therefore highly correlated, the correlation parameter in the Basel II IMM formula (Section 17.2.2) will be increased by a multiplier of 1.25 for the following cases:

- Regulated financial institutions whose total assets are greater than or equal to US $100 billion.
- Unregulated financial institutions.

This will create a corresponding increase in capital requirements via equation (17.1). Note that this applies to all assets, not just those for counterparty credit risk purposes.

Disallow rating triggers

Under the IMM methodology, any reduction in exposure at default, due to the ability to change collateral requirements based on deterioration in counterparty credit quality, is not allowable. The basis of this preclusion is clearly due to situations such as AIG and monoline insurers, where even an innocuous rating downgrade (e.g., Triple- to Double-A) caused a death spiral effect and, hence, was useless as a risk mitigant. An institution may still incorpo-rate mitigants, such as rating triggers, into their documentation but they cannot model their beneficial effects in their EEPE calculation.

Stress testing

There are more formalised requirements around stress tests, with the need to stress all princi-pal market risk factors (interest rates, FX, equities, credit spreads and commodity prices) and assess material non-directional risks, such as curve and basis risks, at least quarterly. Other requirements noted include:

- Proactively identify concentrations to specific directional sensitivities and concentrations of risk among industries and regions.
- Identify general wrong-way risk by considering exposure and counterparty credit quality jointly.
- Concurrent stress testing of exposure and non-cash collateral for assessing wrong-way risk.
- Stress testing of CVA to assess performance under adverse scenarios, incorporating any hedging mismatches. Severe historic or potential economic events may be considered.
- Integration of counterparty risk stress tests into firm-wide stress tests.
- Reverse stress testing (where scenarios are designed that create certain predefined losses) should also be used.

17.5   CENTRAL COUNTERPARTIES

The capital requirements for exposures to central counterparties (CCPs) have been outlined separately from the standard Basel III requirements.[46] Whilst CCPs are viewed as being of strong creditworthiness, it was viewed as important that exposures to them were not given zero capitalisation, as under Basel II. Clearly, a zero capital charge would create moral hazard problems and lead to the assumption that a CCP would never fail, even if this meant being bailed out as other financial institutions were in 2008.

17.5.1   Trade- and default fund-related exposures

The capitalisation of an exposure to a central counterparty is complex as there are a variety of different financial resources that are at risk when trading with a CCP, such as initial margins and default (or reserve) fund contributions (Section 7.2.5). In addition, the BCBS make distinctions between different CCPs, which will have different levels of riskiness.

There are two types of exposure to a CCP that need capitalising, so-called *trade-related* and *default fund-related*. Trade-related exposures arise from the current mark-to-market exposure and both initial and variation margin contributions. Such an exposure is only at risk in case of the CCP failure (not the failure of other CCP members) and it is this component that is given the relatively low risk weight of 2% for a qualifying CCP.[47]

It is the capitalisation of the default fund (described as the reserve fund previously in Chapter 7) that is more problematic. This is because it is possible for a CCP member to lose some or all of their default fund contribution, due to the default of one or more other CCP members, even if the CCP itself does not fail. Furthermore, it may be necessary to contribute additionally to the default fund (Section 7.2.5) in the event of relatively large losses from the default of other members. The fact that each CCP sets default fund contributions itself further complicates this approach as this implies that each CCP will represent a specific risk.

The default fund capital requirement is determined via three steps:

1. Calculation of the hypothetical capital for the CCP.
2. Calculation of the aggregate capital requirements of the CCP.
3. Allocation of aggregate capital to clearing members.

The quantity in step 2 above represents the extent to which the hypothetical capital exceeds the actual capital of the CCP. CCPs, where this is large, will essentially be more heavily penalised via larger default fund-related capital requirements imposed on their members.

17.5.2   Calculation of the hypothetical capital

The hypothetical capital is the amount of capital a CCP would have to hold if its trades, with all clearing members, were done in bilateral markets. It is required that the CEM method (Section 17.3.1) is used by a CCP to determine this amount. The CEM

---

[46] http://www.bis.org/publ/bcbs206.htm
[47] Committee on Payment and Settlement Systems (CPSS) and the Technical Committee of the International Organization of Securities Commissions (IOSCO). This is a CCP that complies with CPSS–IOSCO principles. The CPSS–IOSCO is responsible for the supervision and oversight of CCPs.

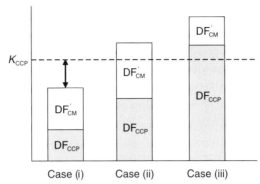

Figure 17.12 Illustration of the three possible cases relating to the aggregate capital requirements of a CCP ($DF_{CCP} + DF'_{CM}$) compared with the hypothetical capital requirements (K_{CCP}).

approach is simple enough to be adopted uniformly by all CCPs, although it will likely be conservative in the overall number produced.[48] Indeed, this is one of the main criticisms of the approach. Collateral held by the CCP, and default fund contributions, can be treated as being exposure reducing. Finally, the factor of 60% that defines the amount of current netting benefit that can be derived (Section 17.3.1) is increased to 70%. The hypothetical capital is defined as K_{CCP}.

17.5.3   Calculation of aggregate capital requirements

The aggregate capital requirements involve subtracting the CCP's own loss-bearing capital from K_{CCP}. The loss-bearing capital is related to the total default fund contributions of all clearing members. However, two times the average default fund contribution is subtracted from this. This is intended to avoid double counting the default fund contributions in the hypothetical capital, and actual capital, as the default fund contributions of any defaulted members (assumed two members in default) will not be available. The default fund contributions from the CCP itself and the clearing members (the later adjusted for two being in default) are denoted DF_{CCP} and DF'_{CM}.

Depending on the overall size of the aggregate capital, $DF_{CCP} + DF'_{CM}$, compared with the hypothetical capital, K_{CCP}, three situations are considered, as illustrated in Figure 17.12. Starting with case (iii), this is the ideal case since the CCP itself has contributed aggregate capital that exceeds the hypothetical capital and, hence, the default fund contributions of the clearing members are subject to the least risk in the event of default of another member. The capital requirement should therefore be the lowest. In case (ii), whilst the total default fund contribution exceeds the total hypothetical capital, the clearing members default fund contribution is at risk but only after DF_{CCP} has been used.[49] This case should, therefore, result in a higher capital charge. Finally, in case (i) the aggregate capital requirements of the CCP are smaller than the hypothetical capital

---

[48] Indeed, it is possible that this will change to allow a more advanced approach.
[49] This assumes that the CCP's own default fund contribution will be used before that of the members. The BCBS note that, in the case of a CCP where this priority is not followed, the capital formula must be adapted.

requirements. This is clearly a problem and should result in the highest capital charge, since a portion of the hypothetical capital requirements have not been met by the CCP.

Based on the above three possible states, a formula is created to give the aggregate capital requirements for all CCP members. The formula can be rewritten as the sum of the following terms:

- The amount of the default fund contribution that exceeds the hypothetical capital as exists in cases (ii) and (iii) above. This is given by $\alpha \times \min\left(DF'_{CM}, \max(DF_{CCP} + DF'_{CM} - K_{CCP})\right)$.[50] This is a low weight of between 0.16% and 1.6% because this component of the default fund exceeds the hypothetical capital.
- The amount by which the CCP hypothetical capital exceeds the CCP's default fund contribution. This is given by $100\% \times \max(K_{CPP} - DF_{CCP}, 0)$, which clearly has a weight of 100%, since this component of the default fund is a required component of the hypothetical capital and therefore is at significant risk in the event of default of CCP member(s).
- The amount by which the CCP hypothetical capital exceeds the CCP's aggregate capital (CCP's and members' contribution to default fund). This is given by $20\% \times \max(K_{CPP} - DF_{CCP} - DF'_{CM}, 0)$, which can be seen as an additional risk due to a hole in the aggregate capital as in case (i).[51]

17.5.4   Allocation of aggregate capital to clearing members

Finally, the aggregate capital requirements of the CCP defined above are allocated to each clearing member. This allocation is done based on the proportion of each clearing member's relative contribution to the default fund (assuming that this is in line with the way in which the CCP would allocate losses). A concentration factor is applied to account for the granularity of default fund contributions within the CCP.

17.6   SUMMARY

In this chapter we have described regulatory approaches to counterparty risk, in particular focusing on the regulatory capital requirements according to the Basel II and III guidelines. We have considered the different approaches available to compute counterparty risk capital charges, from the simple add-on rules to the more sophisticated internal model approach, to estimating capital based on EPE multiplied by a factor known as alpha. We have discussed repo-style transactions and the treatment of collateral within the various approaches of the Basel II framework. The treatment of double default effects of hedged (or partially hedged) exposures has also been examined. The more recent requirements of Basel III have also been addressed. This includes large additions to the capital framework, such as capitalisation of CVA volatility and exposures to central counterparties. Basel III also contains many smaller changes to the

---

[50] Here, $\alpha = \max\left(1.6\% / \left((DF_{CCP} + DF'_{CM})/K_{CCP}\right)^{0.3}, 0.16\%\right)$ is a decreasing function of between 0.16% and 1.6%.
[51] This could be seen as capitalising the need for clearing members to contribute more default funds in the case of a shortfall. However, the BCBS also make it clear that even if this is not the case then the additional capital charge still stands since trade exposures to a CCP are more risky in this case compared with a situation where a CCP had adequate coverage of hypothetical capital requirements.

regulatory regime, such as stressed EEPE and backtesting requirements, which have been covered in detail.

We have now discussed all the important aspects of counterparty credit risk, CVA and related subjects. The next chapter deals with the role of the CVA desk within an institution. This is the group with the responsibility to combine the many aspects to achieve the optimal management of counterparty risk and CVA under the many constraints such as an institution's risk appetite, risk mitigants, funding, accounting rules and regulatory capital requirements.

18

Managing CVA – The "CVA Desk"

> *A banker is a fellow who lends you his umbrella when the sun is shining, but wants it back the minute it begins to rain.*
>
> Mark Twain (1835–1910)

18.1 INTRODUCTION

In this chapter, we deal with the management of counterparty risk within a financial institution. Whilst some large dealers have utilised "CVA desks"[1] for many years to manage counterparty risk, this practice has spread to other banks only more recently because of the global financial crisis. The move to fair value accounting requires financial contracts such as OTC derivatives to have an adjustment applied to reflect the possibility of counterparty default. Whilst many institutions view CVA as purely an accounting need, it has become increasingly common for banks to charge for the expected loss of their credit risk (CVA). Furthermore, the Basel III regulatory changes are likely to catalyse all banks to have a CVA desk responsible for the pricing and management of CVA and the optimisation of regulatory capital. However, other peripheral components exist that may be centralised alongside CVA aspects. These include collateral management (Chapter 5) and funding aspects (Chapter 14).

It is not only banks that need CVA functions of some sort. Other large financial institutions, and/or significant OTC derivatives users, may deem it necessary to have centralised functions to manage their counterparty risk. Depending on the risk management sophistication of a particular institution and the overall amount of counterparty risk, the management approach will differ.

A CVA desk can add significant value to an institution's risk management. They can allow the firm to be competitive in certain transactions, but, just as importantly, realise when to walk away from business or transact with another counterparty. They may be able to facilitate increasing the level of business with a certain counterparty, whilst also reducing concentration risk by diversifying credit exposure. A CVA desk can focus attention in terms of risk mitigation on certain counterparties. In order to achieve all this, a close relationship with other groups such as collateral management, market risk, credit risk and credit trading is important.

---

[1] The term "CVA desk" has originated because of many banks pricing and managing counterparty risk through a front-office trading desk. Whilst we note that this is not always the case (for example, CVA may be handled within the risk management function), this term will be used throughout this chapter.

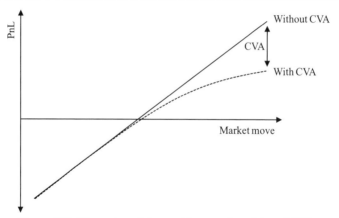

Figure 18.1 Illustration of the need for transfer pricing of CVA.

This chapter will aim to discuss the high-level issues around an overall strategy towards managing CVA, the main aim being protection of revenues, balance sheets and general financial integrity in case of default of counterparties. Mostly this will be biased towards banks, but the elements should apply to any institution setting up a dedicated CVA function of some sort.

18.2   THE ROLE OF A CVA DESK

18.2.1   Motivation

Not all traders and businesses can become experts in counterparty risk and CVA.[2] CVA can be a significant and exotic component of a valuation, as illustrated in Figure 18.1. Here, without CVA the PnL is a simple linear function of the market move, whereas CVA introduces a more complex non-linear behaviour. Due to the potentially complex nature of CVA, there is a need to centralise its management and decentralise the associated PnL from individual trading desks.

To achieve this, there are two primary needs (Figure 18.2):

- *Transfer pricing.* Counterparty risk arises very heterogeneously. Short-dated trades, high-quality and collateralised counterparties all lead to relatively small CVAs. On the other hand, long-dated trades, weaker credit quality, uncollateralised counterparties and wrong-way risk give rise to significant CVAs. It is important to charge the correct CVA to each trade, preferably at inception, accounting for important aspects such as up-front payments,

Figure 18.2 Illustration of the CVA charging process.

---

yield curve shapes and risk mitigants such as netting and collateral. This correctly accounts for the expected cost of the counterparty risk and incentivises the correct trading decisions. Indeed, CVA is a key determinant in the price of most OTC derivatives and may be the difference between being able to undertake a given trade or not.

- *PnL management.* It is reasonable to require the originator of counterparty risk to pay the CVA at inception, but the nature of transfer pricing is that future changes in CVA cannot impact the originator's PnL (similar to pricing in the insurance industry). Changes in CVA have caused huge swings in banks' profits, sometimes to the order of billions of dollars. It is therefore very important for a CVA desk to manage the CVA volatility arising from market moves. The primary way to achieve this is via hedging.

18.2.2 Mechanics of pricing

CVA pricing is best thought of as being similar to buying insurance. Suppose a trader in a firm is executing a trade with counterparty risk. Their CVA desk charges the trader a fixed amount, at inception, on the transaction that comes from the trading book's PnL. The trading book will then be indemnified against any future counterparty default. The trading book is likely then to incorporate this CVA in the price of the trade and require that their profit is *greater* than the CVA charge. The trader need not know anything about CVA but has effectively factored in the cost of counterparty risk in their pricing.

A CVA charge could be structured as an upfront or a running premium. From a trader's perspective, a running credit charge would be cleaner, since it can be matched with payments on a client trade (for example, receiving a spread on a swap leg). Traders can convert upfront to running CVA, as discussed in Section 12.4.3, although this does leave them with some annuity risk (since the running CVA they may charge a client is risky, as it is not received in default). However, since credit charges are normally relatively small and counterparty defaults are relatively unlikely events, the practical differences between running and upfront are not huge.[3]

The contract between the CVA desk and the originating trade essentially corresponds to a CCDS (Section 10.2.5) referencing the incremental exposure of the trade in question. This would be complex to document, but this is not needed since it is an internal trade.

If the counterparty defaults at any time during the life of the transaction, then the CVA desk immediately compensates the original trading desk for their loss with no adjustment for recovery (to avoid the desk having concern over the forthcoming bankruptcy process). This may be done in terms of the risk-free valuation of the transaction or the replacement cost. In the former case, the trader pays any additional replacement cost[4] whilst in the latter case the CVA desk bears this basis risk. The CVA desk will need to be involved in the workout process and deal with the payout of any relevant hedges (such as single-name CDSs). In the event of the relevant trading book having more than one trade with the defaulted counterparty, then they need only be compensated for the *net* replacement cost.[5] This is consistent with the charging of CVA being done on an incremental (or marginal) basis.

If the counterparty does not default then no part of the CVA charge is returned, since it will be required either for hedging costs or as part of a reserve to cover future losses on a

---

[3] Assuming a running premium would be correctly marked-to-market and not treated on an accrual basis by the trading desk.

[4] We note that, as discussed in Section 13.3.3, DVA may provide a benefit at this point.

[5] For example, if one trade has a positive value of 100 and another a negative value of 60 then both can be terminated and replaced at an overall cost of 40. The CVA desk will therefore compensate for this net loss. This, of course, assumes that netting is possible and has been accounted for in valuation.

portfolio basis. However, any other economic decision in relation to the trade (for example, unwind, option exercise, cancellation, termination) may trigger a CVA refund or an additional charge (see Section 12.4.5).

It is possible that the CVA desk will not insure the entire notional of a trade but, instead, leave some percentage or first loss with the originating trader to ensure they have some "skin in the game". This is similar to the use of excesses in the insurance industry to prevent moral hazard where the insured would have no incentive to monitor the underlying risk. In some client relationships, the originating trader or business may be the best placed to understand the nature of the counterparty risk, especially in relation to complex aspects such as wrong-way risk. By exposing the originating trader to some default losses, they may not knowingly enter into a bad trade (e.g., one with significant wrong-way risk) since the CVA desk does not insure them completely. However, this may unnecessarily penalise the originating trader in the case of a default over which they had no superior knowledge, expertise or mandate to hedge.

18.2.3   Mandate and organisational aspects

CVA desks typically are situated within the front office and report into the head of trading. In some circumstances, they may report to risk management or even other functions such as finance. The type of structure depends on the extent to which CVA is actively managed. For active hedging of CVA, a front-office structure is clearly important, whilst a more passive approach to counterparty risk management may suit a risk management-type reporting structure. Historically this split has been driven by the importance of counterparty risk (and therefore OTC derivatives) within the institution in question. Large dealers have typically followed the front office-style approach, whilst smaller banks (or those with large retail banking compared with their capital market activities) have employed the more passive risk management approach. These aspects will be discussed again below but we note that Basel III regulation effectively mandates the more active approach for all banks (Section 17.4).

Sometimes CVA trading is combined with loan trading. This is a reasonable idea from the point of view of centralising illiquid credit pricing and management. However, there are reasons why loan trading and CVA may be treated differently. Firstly, CVA tends to involve public counterparties rather than loans, which tend to be private. Secondly, loans carry only credit risk whilst CVA involves market risk also. Thirdly, CVA tends to be treated relatively dynamically and hedged accordingly whilst loans are typically dealt with more passively. The more active management of CVA, potentially required under Basel III, will increase this divide.

The above has represented the main historic mandate for a CVA desk. However, as counterparty risk has become an increasingly important and complex topic, there is a need for a CVA desk to be more intimately involved in other areas, as illustrated in Figure 18.3, including:

- *Regulatory capital.* CVA is not the only consideration in assessing the economic value of a trade with respect to counterparty risk. It is also important to understand the regulatory (and in theory economic) capital implications. Any profit, after CVA has been accounted for, should be compared with the required additional capital to support the trade and may be required to exceed a predefined "hurdle". Under Basel III (Chapter 17), capital requirements for counterparty risk will be large and not completely aligned to the actual volatility of CVA (indeed, hedging CVA can actually increase capital requirements for non-credit

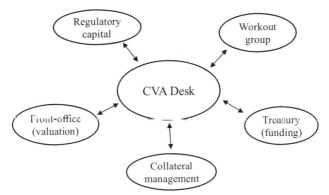

Figure 18.3 Illustration of the relationship of a CVA desk with other functions in a bank.

CVA hedges). It is therefore important for a CVA desk to balance the need to reduce CVA volatility with the need to reduce regulatory capital.

- *Collateral.* The calculation of CVA is very sensitive to assumptions around any existing collateral agreements (Section 12.5) and, therefore, the negotiation, management and legal enforceability of collateral is inextricably tied to the resulting CVA. In addition, the need to optimise collateral (Chapter 14), because of significant funding costs, has moved collateral management from a back-office to a front-office function.
- *Funding.* As discussed in Section 14.3, funding value adjustment (FVA) is a component similar to CVA and requires similar inputs for quantification. Furthermore, there is an important linkage between FVA and DVA, which must be treated consistently. The CVA desk may have expertise in valuing FVA into trades in a similar way to CVA. The same is true of CollVA discussed also in Chapter 14.
- *Valuation.* The calculation of CVA arises from an adjustment to the risk-free valuation of the underlying trade. As explained in Section 14.2, risk-free valuation is not the rather trivial problem it was once thought to be and is linked, in turn, to collateral agreements. CVA and risk-free valuation must be done consistently.
- *Workout.* The CVA desk is exposed to two recovery rates. It has exposure to the settled recovery (see Section 10.1.7) via hedging with CDS and bonds. However, it is also exposed to the settled or final recovery via the workout process. This refers to the process of negotiation that eventually leads to a recovery being received on claims with a defaulted counterparty. The CVA desk runs a basis risk on recovery and would be a key stakeholder in the workout process. In some cases, a CVA desk may even reduce their charges in anticipation of a favourable workout in the event of an actual default (see below).

18.2.4   Centralised or decentralised?

In an ideal world, an institution would have only a single CVA desk, since this maximises operational costs, expertise and the associated netting benefits. An alternative is the "decentralised" approach, where an institution may have several CVA desks (e.g., interest rates/FX,[6] commodity, credit) existing in silos. One rationale for this may be the limited

---

[6] Interest rates and FX tend to be combined in such an approach.

benefits from netting between these asset classes (although, whilst CVA may be largely unaffected by splitting up a netting set, such action can cause large increases in measures such as PFE). In addition, most counterparties with trades from more than one "silo" will be collateralised anyway (although then the underlying collateral modelling does become more problematic). One view is that the centralised approach is preferable and deviations occur only due to political reasons. Arguments against the centralised approach are that it may sometimes lead to less focus given to specific areas such as commodities, where the combined knowledge of asset class and client information is very important for CVA management. This is particularly relevant for the identification of wrong-way risk. In addition, many clients do not trade across asset classes and so the loss of netting benefits, arising via decentralised CVA management (i.e., splitting netting sets), is often not substantial. It is also easier to set up a decentralised CVA process as the data and analytical requirements can be rather more easily built on top of the existing data sources, risk management systems and trading systems.

A danger of a decentralised approach is that the individual CVA desks may report into the business area in question. This may cause problems if they benefit from the profits from that business line (e.g., in terms of bonuses) and therefore have a reduced incentive to manage CVA well on a long-term basis. Losses involving monoline insurers (for which the counterparty risk generally resides with the originating credit derivative business) are an example of this.

18.2.5 Coverage

Ideally, a CVA desk(s) would provide complete product coverage but in practice there needs to be some rollout process, due to the complexity around quantification. The main OTC derivatives products to consider are vanilla interest rates and FX products (including cross-currency swaps) and credit default swaps. Commodities, equity and exotics will be tackled when possible. Product coverage approximately follows an 80/20 rule (to cover the final 20% of the CVA may require 80% of the overall effort).

Another aspect of CVA coverage is collateralised (CSA) counterparties. These are often ignored, at least in the early stages of a CVA rollout, which, since CSAs reduce CVA, may seem reasonable. A first hurdle here is that CSA counterparties (such as banks) represent a large volume of trades and so the actual computation time will be significant. Furthermore, to compute collateralised CVA involves more in-depth calculations that require further, and quite subjective, assumptions over aspects such as gap risk (Section 9.7.4), the margin period of risk (Section 8.5.2) and wrong-way risk (Section 15.4.6). It is perhaps not surprising that many institutions look at CVA for uncollateralised counterparties only, although the results of Section 9.7.2 show that collateralised CVA is still material. Indeed, as seen in Section 13.1.4, even two banks trading with each other with the same CSA terms, and both using DVA, may still create a substantial CVA/DVA charge.

Trades with monolines and AIG (already mentioned in Section 13.3.2) tended, prior to 2007, to be excused CVA treatment due to the high credit quality of the counterparties concerned and the collateral terms.[7] In this example of banks utilising monolines and AIG to offload super senior risk to support their profitable structured credit businesses, an impartial centralised CVA desk may have been best equipped to identify the extreme wrong-way risk associated with such trades[8] (Section 15.5.2). This, in turn, would have curtailed growth in

---

[7] Although the collateral terms were linked to rating triggers, they were believed to have value.
[8] "An AIG failure would have cost Goldman Sachs, documents show", *New York Times*, 23 July 2010.

structured credit products and may even have reduced the impact, or possibly even averted the global financial crisis.[9] There is, therefore, a strong argument that CVA coverage should include all trades and counterparties, irrespective of the level of exposure, level of collateralisation and credit quality of the counterparties, since the exceptions often turn out to cause the biggest problems. This would imply that CVA for central counterparties (CCPs) should even be quantified, which tends not to be the case (and is not required under Basel III). Ignoring CVA with CCPs should be compared with ignoring CVA to monolines and AIG prior to 2007.

18.2.6 Profit centre or utility?

A CVA desk should price the new counterparty risk out to the maturity of a trade (potentially many years), considering correctly the implications of exposure, default probability and accounting for all risk mitigation (netting, collateral, hedging). In many institutions a CVA desk may not be judged on PnL generation, since any profit may ultimately come only at the expense of the trading desks and/or businesses within a firm. This normally means that CVA desks are typically referred to as utility functions, although the meaning of this is not always clear. For our purposes, we will use this term to indicate that the mandate of the CVA desk is to have a flat PnL. When not hedging, a neutral PnL can only be hoped for over a very long time horizon.

Whilst a zero PnL objective may seem to lead to incentive problems, it actually motivates traders more reasonably than traditional objectives.[10] A typical trader has a compensation profile that resembles being long a zero strike call option.[11] This is problematic, as increasing the value of an option can be achieved by increasing volatility. Hence, a trader is typically incentivised to take more risk to maximise profits knowing that they will not be penalised for losses. However, a typical CVA desk judged on zero PnL would have a profile somewhat similar to a zero-strike, short-straddle position.[12] This is because a PnL of zero should result in the maximum compensation for a CVA desk, as this implies the best performance in terms of neutralising counterparty risk. Large losses should obviously be penalised, as should large gains, as these might only be possible via excessive risk taking, which is not part of the CVA desk's mandate. A zero PnL mandate on an annual basis is still not ideal, however. For example, a desk making a profit at the end of a year is incentivised to create artificial losses to provide a cushion for the following year. A CVA desk must have a clear mandate and good explanation from where PnL is arising rather than a naïve annual goal of zero PnL.

There are several reasons why the above comments on a zero PnL target may not be realistic. Firstly, there are several ways in which a CVA desk might be able to make profit that it not directly linked to increased risk taking. Examples of this are:

---

[9] Whilst this may seem a significant claim, we note that monolines and AIG contributed to losses into hundreds of billions of dollars. Preventing such losses and significantly curtailing the growth of structured credit may have prevented the financial markets reaching the "tipping point", which ultimately led to events such as the failure of Bear Stearns, Lehman Brothers and AIG and created the fear that crystallised many other problems.

[10] Which can generally be summarised as make as much money as possible.

[11] This is because their compensation will be approximately proportional to any profit (at least up to a level) whilst any loss may result in a zero or small compensation. However, in the absence of any clawbacks, the compensation cannot be negative.

[12] A straddle is a combination of short call and put options at the same strike.

- *Unwinds and terminations.* A CVA desk may gain from the unwinding or termination of a transaction and may play some role in this.
- *Improved netting and collateral terms.* CVA gains may arise from improving netting and collateral terms (although we note as explained in Section 13.1.5, the use of DVA means that improved terms are not necessarily aligned to PnL gains).
- *Restructuring transactions.* CVA can be reduced via restructuring transactions with break clauses (ATEs), resets or re-couponing.
- *Improved workout recovery.* Achieving a higher recovery (than that assumed for valuation and hedging) during or at the end of the workout process will lead to a positive PnL for the CVA desk.

The above may constitute reasonable ways in which a CVA desk should generate PnL. However, there could be false incentives here. For example, a CVA desk may be incentivised to underestimate the benefit of risk mitigants to be able to generate future profit. PnL explain (Section 18.5.5) is important here to avoid the potential problem of real losses from the management of CVA being disguised. It could also be argued that any PnL generated from any of the above should be reallocated to the originating trading desks. An example of this is the impact of a negative incremental CVA that can arise from an unwind or favourable interaction of new trades with the existing netting set (Section 12.4.1). The CVA desk could charge a zero CVA and therefore make a profit[13] due to the reduction of their overall CVA. However, this profit potential may obscure losses and will not give the correct economic incentive for the unwinding of the transaction. Hence, it is probably most reasonable that it is paid to the originating trading book.

Other more obvious ways in which a CVA desk may generate PnL are:

- *Not hedging.* By choosing correctly not to hedge certain risks (most obviously credit spreads), a CVA desk may generate PnL.
- *Taking proprietary positions.* Obviously, PnL can potentially be generated by taking proprietary positions. A CVA desk may, arguably, have particular expertise and market knowledge on certain aspects and seek to benefit from this.

Whilst outright proprietary trading should not be the goal of a CVA desk, choosing not to hedge certain risks may certainly be within the mandate. For example, there is a subtle difference between a CVA desk being long credit and choosing (or not being able to) hedge and trading desk actively taking a proprietary long position in credit. The situation of not hedging credit risk in particular requires more thought later.

18.3   CVA CHARGING

A key aspect of the transfer pricing of CVA is that there must be a robust and industrialised process in place for calculation of CVA charges in real time. For example, OTC derivatives contracts with clients, such as corporates, can potentially constitute good business for banks, but only if the correct CVA can be priced into the trade at inception. Whilst for large, and/or complex, transactions it may be reasonable to have some delay in assessing the relevant CVA

---

[13] In practice, this can occur without the originating trader or business being aware of the negative contribution. Some CVA desks have also had formal agreements not to return negative incremental CVAs.

charge, in most cases the calculation will need to be capable of being achieved quickly and without the intervention of the CVA desk. To do this properly is complex from a systems point of view and simple methods are often used by necessity. Banks tend to provide pricing tools for trading, sales and marketing but these have varying levels of sophistication.

18.3.1 Lookup tables

A lookup table will provide a rapid estimation of a credit charge or CVA based on grids, which may be produced separately for each product type. For example, an interest rate desk may have a grid giving CVA charges as a function of maturity and credit quality (assessed by either counterparty rating or credit spread). Such calculations cannot, of course, account for trade specifics such as payment frequencies and currencies and, for this reason, the charges may be conservative in many cases (for example, an interest rate swap receiving quarterly fixed and paying 6-month LIBOR is unlikely to obtain the relatively small CVA charge it merits[14]). Lookup tables do not account for risk mitigants such as netting or collateral either but they do make for a very simple, rapid and transparent approach to charging for CVA.

18.3.2 Product-specific pricing

The next stage from pricing grids is stand-alone CVA pricing for different product classes. Such calculations may exist in spreadsheets and can be developed by the relevant quantitative research teams. For example, Appendix 12D (and Spreadsheet 12.2) gives an analytical formula for an interest rate swap CVA calculation. Such calculations will capture the specifics of a transaction (e.g., currency, payment frequency). Their main weakness will be the need to ignore any benefits from netting and collateral which is only relevant if all trades with a given counterparty are in the same direction.

18.3.3 Full simulation-based pricing

The calculation of CVA charges accounting for all aspects (especially including netting and collateral) can only be done accurately with the Monte Carlo-based approach for exposure described in Chapter 9. The key aspect is that, in order to calculate incremental CVA accounting for netting and collateral, it is necessary to have information on all other deals under the relevant netting and collateral agreements together with the contractual netting and collateral terms. Practically, this requires a simulation engine that generates all the relevant market variables and computes the values of the current transactions and the new transaction in many scenarios through time. From this data, the incremental CVA can be computed as described in Section 12.4.1.

As described in Section 9.6.4, rather than doing all calculations "on-the-fly", the simulation data for existing trades will probably be run in an overnight batch and then stored for aggregation with new trades during the next business day.[15] This prevents the ability to

---

[14] In this example, receiving the fixed rate in an upwards-sloping interest rate environment (Figure 8.14) and receiving quarterly against semi-annual payments (Figure 8.11) both reduce the CVA.

[15] Note that standard trades may also be run overnight to prevent the need to run these on an intraday basis.

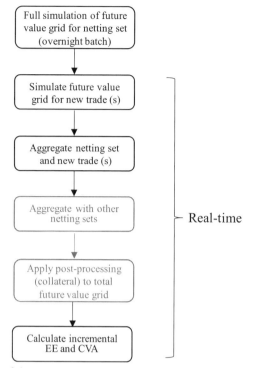

Figure 18.4 Illustration of the steps required in order to calculate incremental CVA. The future value grid has the dimensions of the simulation number and time step. Note that the aggregation with other netting sets and collateral post-processing are relevant only when there is a collateral agreement in place (which may cover more than one netting set).

capture intradaily trades and market moves which will be discussed in the next section on technology. It can also lead to PnL explain discrepancies (Section 18.5.5) as the CVA charge (s) and the actual PnL will not match.

Figure 18.4 illustrates the calculation flow required to calculate incremental CVA.

18.3.4 Unwinds, exercises, terminations and other special cases

Incremental CVA provides a credit charge covering the increase in total CVA for a counterparty. It is an instantaneous measure, giving the current CVA charge accounting for previous transactions and not, of course, accounting for any transactions in the future. As shown in Table 12.6, it depends critically on the ordering of the trades, which can appear unfair at some later time. However, new transactions can only be priced with information available at the time and it is (usually) not possible to predict what other offsetting transactions may be done in the future. Incremental CVA charges represent the only way in which a fixed charge[16] can be quoted and are therefore ideally the basis for all CVA charging.

---

[16] For example, marginal CVA charges would be "fairer" but change with subsequent trades and therefore would require later adjustments of a trading book PnL due to CVA.

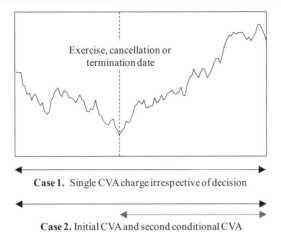

Case 1. Single CVA charge irrespective of decision

Case 2. Initial CVA and second conditional CVA

Figure 18.5 Illustration of the different ways in which to incorporate CVA charges in the case of optional exercises, cancellations and terminations. In the first case, a single charge is made which will incorporate the relative likelihood of the optionality. In case 2, two CVAs are paid, one at inception and a conditional one linked to the decision to exercise, cancel or terminate.

Institutions do sometimes deviate from charging incremental CVA, for example, a reduction is sometimes given on the first trade with a client in anticipation of later netting benefits. Another obvious deviation from incremental CVA is when more than one trade is executed in a short space of time. In such cases, a marginal analysis and CVA charges for the trades in question are relevant (see Section 12.4.2).

Unwinds or restructurings make another interesting case. However, an unwind is nothing more than the execution of the reverse trade and hence the incremental CVA will apply as usual. A trader unwinding may be expecting to receive a proportion of the original CVA charge back. However, market moves and subsequent trading with the same counterparty may significantly influence the appropriate "refund" that will be given via the incremental CVA. On the contrary, the refund may exceed the original CVA charge (for example, if the credit spread of the counterparty has widened) whilst there is no guarantee that the incremental charge will indeed be negative. In the latter case, this means that the trade may be charged twice. In practice, this is unlikely, as it requires a significant shift in the risk sensitivities of a netting set. DVA can also create counterintuitive behaviour, such as unwinds incurring addtional charges.

Option exercises and terminations (where the institution has the right to exercise), in theory, should also give rise to CVA charges as, like trade initiation and unwinding, they represent economic decisions that result in a change in CVA that should be transfer priced. However, a single upfront charge, which embeds the likelihood of exercise, is often used. Alternatively, charging CVA on an option exercise means that the exercise boundary is the correct one as it is based on the risky PnL (including CVA). There are, therefore, two alternatives here as illustrated in Figure 18.5. The simplest method is to have a single upfront CVA charge but this has the disadvantage that the initiating trader has no incentive to incorporate CVA in the optionality, since the CVA charge has already been paid. A more theoretically appealing way is to have initial and conditional (on exercise) CVA charges.

Examples of how the conditional charging of CVA could work in practice are:

- *Physically settled swaption.* The initiating trading book could be charged an initial CVA for the swaption and then a further CVA charge if the swaption is exercised. This means that the correct exercise decision is made (Section 12.4.5).
- *Cancellable swap.* There is an initial CVA charge for the entire life of the swap and then a refund[17] of CVA if the swap is cancelled. Note that a cancellable swap, where the option is very in-the-money, then converges to unwind situation.
- *Additional termination event (ATE).* The initial CVA charge could cover the exposure up to the (first) ATE time, whereupon there would be another charge if the termination does **not** happen. Alternatively, the full CVA could be charged initially and then, probably, a refund made if the trade is indeed terminated. The former option is probably preferable when the ATE is likely to be used and the latter otherwise.

The conditional charging mechanism is preferable as it creates the correct incentives with respect to optionality and allows subjective aspects like ATEs to be handled without creating moral hazard.[18] It also simplifies the CVA desk's hedging as, for example, it may reduce negative PnL jumps caused by sub-optimal behaviour.[19] However, conditional CVA charges influence the PnL of the originating desk who do not have the ability to charge this to clients. Operational simplicity and the ease of charging CVA to clients upfront means the single charge is mainly used in practice.

18.3.5   Reducing CVA charges

CVA charges, being a key pricing component of vanilla OTC derivatives, often define the competitiveness of a given institution. As such, it is not surprising to find a number of mitigants that tend to be used to reduce CVA. These include:

- *DVA.* The most obvious mitigant for CVA is DVA. The use of DVA is at least partially controversial, as discussed in Chapter 13. Sometimes CVA charges incorporate only a proportion of the DVA benefit or do not give the benefit when DVA exceeds CVA. These appear to be recognitions of the fact that the monetisation of DVA is imperfect (Section 13.3). We consider DVA in more detail below.
- *FVA.* It is becoming increasingly common to combine charges for funding value adjustment (FVA) together with CVA. In cases where the funding benefit is greater than the funding costs (e.g., see Section 14.3.5) then the overall FVA can be beneficial and reduce the charge.
- *Ignoring CVA for certain counterparties.* CVA for certain counterparties tends to be ignored completely. Examples tend to be very high credit quality sovereigns, supranationals and well-collateralised counterparties with whom a CVA charge would be impossible. Whilst there have been clear problems with such a strategy (e.g., monoline insurance companies – which had Triple-A ratings, Lehman Brothers – who posted collateral), it is likely to persist in the future with CVAs with central counterparties (for example) being ignored.

---

[17] This would be the incremental CVA at the cancellation time, which, whilst a refund is likely, we note could possibly represent an additional charge.

[18] In the single charging approach, a trader given the benefit of an ATE has no incentive to use it to minimise CVA.

[19] For example, a trader exercising an option on a risk-free basis even though the overall risky value is negative. In such a case, the CVA desk would experience a negative PnL jump which will be difficult (although not impossible) to hedge.

- *Higher ultimate recovery.* The assumption of a higher final recovery from a beneficial workout process may be incorporated, leading to a lower CVA charge (Section 12.3.2).
- *Blending of historical and risk-neutral default probabilities.* In some cases, banks blend historical and risk-neutral default probabilities on the basis that the latter are too large due to the embedded risk premiums (Section 10.1.6). We note that this practice may not appear completely in line with US accounting rules and the Basel III capital requirements.

Whilst applying no mitigants at all tends to produce CVA charges that are not competitive, the degree to which the above are rationale mitigants or artificial ways to reduce CVA is highly subjective.

18.3.6 Treatment of DVA

The question of whether or not to apply DVA in charging is a difficult one. On the one hand, especially in the interbank market, it will be impossible for trading terms to be agreed unless bilateral CVA charges are made. On the other hand, this leaves the CVA desk with the problem of monetising the negative component of the BCVA (i.e., the part that they essentially pay out to trading desks). Consider that an institution executes a swap with a counterparty, which has a similar credit quality such that the overall BCVA is zero (for both parties). The CVA desk does not receive a fee from the desk executing the trade but still has to manage the risk that the counterparty defaults. Furthermore, an institution with a relatively wide credit spread will have negative BCVAs for new deals, implying that the CVA desk should be paying trading desks and businesses when they execute new trades. In such a situation, a CVA desk would need to attempt to monetise the value of their institution's own default, for example via selling protection on highly correlated institutions. Yet this surely gives rise to new risks (such as when banks attempted to monetise DVA by selling protection on Lehman Brothers – Section 13.4.4). Even when banks do use DVA, they generally have rules whereby only a portion of the DVA benefit is included in prices.[20]

18.4 TECHNOLOGY

Given the ideal requirements to calculate incremental CVA in real time, regulatory requirements and hedging activities of a CVA desk, the technology requirements for counterparty risk are clearly significant. Below we outline the considerations and requirements for CVA technology.

18.4.1 PFE vs CVA

For around two decades, large derivatives dealers have invested significant resources in order to build sophisticated systems for quantifying potential future exposure (PFE). More recently, but for over a decade, some of these dealers have supplemented such systems with the ability to price (and hedge) counterparty risk via CVA. Regulatory rules in relation to backtesting and stress testing of EEPE and α and CVA VAR (Chapter 17) create further requirements. Despite this, many financial institutions do not have well-developed technology solutions for handling CVA and counterparty risk in general.

---

[20] For example, 50% of DVA is included subject to the overall value being positive (i.e., the DVA is not twice as big as the CVA).

For historic reasons, PFE and CVA systems have often been developed in isolation. In some sense, this is not unreasonable since PFE systems drive credit limit and regulatory capital decisions, whilst CVA systems are concerned with valuation and hedging. Another important aspect to consider here is the need to simulate real-world exposures for PFE purposes and risk-neutral exposures for CVA quantification (Section 12.2.2). Added to this is the fact that CVA VAR under Basel III (Section 17.4.4) is potentially most readily calculated via an institution's existing VAR engine. For the above reasons, having different systems for PFE and CVA (and CVA VAR) purposes is not unreasonable. However, the split in most institutions occurs more because the PFE system was developed first and could not reasonably be extended to cover CVA, which may require greater accuracy, speed and enhanced product coverage.

However, there are a number of reasons that a combined PFE and CVA system is preferable:

- *Data*. Legal data (legal entities, netting/collateral agreements) and trade data requirements are identical.
- *Market and historical data*. Whilst there is not a complete overlap of market data, as PFE tends to be driven from historic whilst CVA more from market data, there are certainly common market data components (e.g., interest rate curves and historical correlations).
- *Simulation engines*. The general simulation engines, whilst requiring potentially different data, will share common components. Aspects such as the simulation of collateral terms will be identical.

Figure 18.6 illustrates a potential typical data flow and reporting structure around a PFE and CVA system.

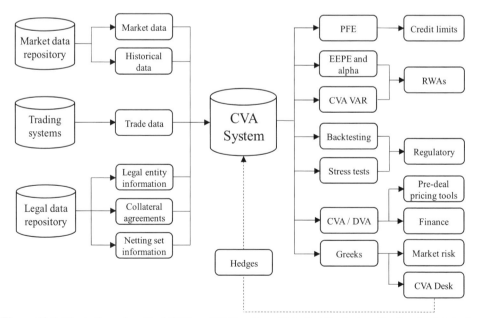

Figure 18.6 Illustration of an ideal CVA and PFE system. Note that the hedges feeding back into the CVA system represents their role in defining credit limits and RWAs.

18.4.2　Building blocks

The building blocks of the CVA system will be:

- *Databases.* Most institutions have multiple systems for legal, trade, market and historical data. Data collection and storage will be substantial and must be obtained from various front-office trading and back-office systems and external sources. The cooperation between various departments in order to retrieve such data is also crucial and has often proved a significant bottleneck for firms implementing a complex counterparty risk management system. Data requirements cover the following aspects:
  - trade population,
  - hedges,
  - legal entities,
  - netting agreements,
  - collateral agreements,
  - market data,
  - historical data (including stressed market data),
  - credit ratings,
  - credit limits,
  - credit spreads, default probabilities and recovery rates,
  - simulation data storage (for intraday pricing).

  Rapid data retrieval is also extremely important. For example, the retrieval of exposure simulations, probably at the netting set level (as discussed in Section 9.6.4) is required for exposure calculations and the pricing of new trades.
- *Monte Carlo simulation engines.* PFE generation is normally supported by a generic Monte Carlo simulation. This must be able to run a large number of scenarios for each variable of interest and revaluate all underlying positions up to the netting set level normally in a few hours (via an overnight batch).
- *Pricing functionality.* After generating a large number of scenarios, it is necessary to revalue every single product in each scenario. Whilst most common products, such as interest rate swaps, FX forwards and credit default swaps, are almost trivial and extremely fast to value, the scale is huge. Consider simulating one million trades at 100 time steps with a total of 10,000 scenarios. This requires one trillion valuation calls via the relevant pricing functions that can easily take many hours of CPU time. Valuations can be speeded up significantly via applying both financial and computational optimisations with parallel processing being common. The key point is not to refine valuations far beyond the error margins of the underlying variables being simulated, especially in the case of long time horizons where there is significant uncertainty. In such a context, multidimensional interpolation of prices, and the use of approximate pricing functions, should not necessarily be a major concern.
- *Collateral functionality.* It must be possible to track existing collateral, whether this be in cash or other securities, calculate the projected future collateral (post-processing described in Section 9.7) in each simulation and calculate the impact of this, and current collateral, on exposure.
- *Reporting.* Exposure metrics such as EE, PFE and EPE must be readily calculated from the simulation data, typically stored from daily (overnight) computations. It must also be possible to reaggregate on a real-time basis, including the impact of newly simulated trade(s) to look at the incremental impact on credit limits and CVA. It is highly desirable to

be able to calculate incremental CVAs for new trades in near real time, especially where the CVA may materially influence the profitability of the transaction in question. Traders and salespeople need to have access to such CVA calculations via simple tools. Reporting tools, showing credit limits breached, and allowing drill-down of exposure profiles (via marginal exposures discussed in Section 9.6.3) as well as risk sensitivities for hedging are required.

- *Greeks.* CVA hedging requires Greeks for all relevant risk factors covering both market and credit risk. The total number of Greeks is so large that many cannot even be calculated. Furthermore, most can only be practically calculated numerically by brute force (also called "bump and run") methods.[21] It is important to identify the key Greeks for hedging and risk limit purposes and to prioritise their calculation in the CVA batch.
- *Backtesting and stress testing tools.* As described in Section 17.4.3, Basel III is introducing significant requirements over the backtesting of EPE, which will involve the storage and tracking of hypothetical portfolios and the checking of PFE at multiple confidence levels and time horizons. This is a significant technology challenge, far more so than backtesting of traditional market risk VAR models. The ability to design and calculate stress tests will put additional pressure on systems, similar to requirements for Greeks. Stress testing functionality should support shifts to all current market data and the ability for non-standard changes, such as curve steepening or flattening, basis spread and correlation movements.

18.4.3   Wrong-way risk

We should note that systems for counterparty risk are typically built around the independence benefits of assuming no wrong-way risk. Indeed, historically, many systems were put in place long before extreme wrong-way risks embedded in products such as credit derivatives were appreciated. The inclusion of wrong-way risk products, such as credit default swaps in counterparty risk systems, is therefore challenging and requires either crude simplifications or major systems engineering. As shown in Section 15.3, it is possible to design portfolio wrong-way risk approaches that leverage on existing CVA approaches via the use of conditional exposure simulation (or conditional default probability assumptions). However, trade-level wrong-way risk approaches (Section 15.4), which require particular modelling of the precise relationship between risk factors and default probability, are more challenging to implement.

18.4.4   Intraday calculations

Rerunning simulations on an entire netting set of trades, every time a new trade needs to be priced, is generally not practical. The typical solution to this involves saving overnight simulations at the netting set level for each simulation and time step (Section 9.6.4). Incremental CVA pricing then involves simulating the new trade with the same scenarios[22] and aggregating with existing data.

---

[21] This is true for all market risk Greeks as they relate to partial derivatives on the exposure profile (Section 16.2.3), which is generated via Monte Carlo. Credit risk Greeks can be calculated without the need to re-simulate exposure, although only in the case of no wrong-way risk.

[22] We note that this is achievable even if it requires simulation of additional risk factors.

The above approach to achieving near real-time incremental CVA is generally used but it is only an approximation to the true PnL impact and the CVA desk is faced with some uncertainty if (as is likely) they commit to this as the CVA charge. Significant market moves, or other trades with the counterparty on the same day, are obvious cases where true intraday CVA calculations will be required. The calculation requirements of this are not particularly problematic. It must simply be possible to rerun simulations with current market and trade data to incorporate market moves and additional trade population. This may not need to be done for the entire counterparty population, but rather for selected counterparties with significant trading activity and/or sensitivity to particular market factors.[23] What is more of a challenge is to provide intraday feeds from front-office systems to CVA systems in terms of trade population and changes in collateral balances. Having the ability to, for example, transact twice within minutes with a given counterparty across different trading desks and capture all the relevant changes in CVA and PFE is the ultimate systems challenge.

18.5   PRACTICAL HEDGING OF CVA

We finally discuss the issues in designing a practical CVA hedging strategy. This is important for a number of reasons. Firstly, historically, institutions have dealt with CVA in very different ways from the actuarial approach (where there is no hedging) to the active approach (maximum hedging). Secondly, as discussed in Chapter 16, CVA hedging is far from straightforward, especially due to effects like cross-gamma (Section 16.5.2) and unintended consequences (Section 16.5.4) that potentially lead to spiralling hedging costs. Finally, it is important to note that a CVA desk faces a three-dimensional approach in terms of their role, which is to optimise the following components:

- *Actual economic risk*. The actual economic risk that an institution faces.
- *Accounting PnL*. The changes in CVA that drive accounting PnL under the relevant accounting rules.
- *Regulatory capital*. The regulatory capital for counterparty risk.

In an ideal world, the above would be perfectly aligned but, in reality, the misalignment can be significant. For example, a US or Canadian bank under US GAAP is required to account for DVA in their PnL but may not necessarily believe that this reflects the real economic risk they face, nor will they receive any capital relief for DVA. A CVA desk hedging interest rate risk will be reducing their economic risk and accounting PnL volatility but actually increasing their regulatory capital requirements under Basel III (Section 17.4.5).

It is therefore important that a CVA desk consider carefully the correct strategy for managing CVA accounting for the above points. Different institutions may favour different approaches depending on their own particular risk profile, regulatory environment, balance sheet and general trading and risk culture. Let us first look at the extremes for managing CVA, then consider the treatment of DVA and finally look to some conclusions for best practice.

---

[23] For example, a system may rerun all counterparties with significant FX exposure in the case of a large move in this market.

18.5.1   To hedge or not

Financial risk is – very broadly speaking – either prudently controlled and managed as in traditional risk management (for example, VAR) or dynamically hedged (for example, structured products). As discussed in Section 9.4.1, risk management is applied under the real-world probability measure, whereas dynamic hedging combines an appropriate trading strategy with risk-neutral-based valuation.

One particularly interesting feature of the quantification of counterparty risk is that it represents an intersection between the two distinct financial worlds of risk management and dynamic hedging. Potentially significant default losses, together with aspects such as wrong-way risk, provide convincing evidence for the need to hedge counterparty risk. Yet, as discussed in Chapter 16, the hedging of counterparty risk is challenging and is unlikely to be achieved without significant residual risks including those arising from the unintended consequences of CVA hedging (Section 16.5.4).

Let us consider two extremes of managing CVA, the "actuarial approach" based on real-world probabilities and risk management basics and the "market approach" based on risk-neutral pricing. These have also been associated previously with passive and active management of CVA, respectively.

18.5.2   Actuarial approach

In the actuarial approach, incremental (or marginal) CVA charges would act as insurance premiums, creating a collective buffer or reserve against counterparty defaults. This "actuarial CVA" should cover all **expected** future losses due to counterparty risk. However, additionally, there should be some charge relating to the unexpected loss, as illustrated in Figure 18.7, which would result from a greater than average number of defaults. The unexpected loss component is much harder to quantify, since it depends on the risk to all counterparties, as discussed in Chapter 11. This would be a complex calculation to make, unless some simple approximation, such as the alpha multiplier described in Section 11.3.4, were used.

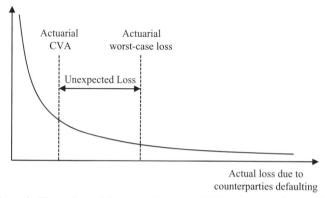

Figure 18.7 Schematic illustration of the quantification of CVA using the "actuarial approach". The figure shows the distribution of losses due to counterparty defaults (not including CVA charges received) over a time horizon covering the maturity of all trades. The "actuarial CVA" covers the expected loss, whilst the unexpected loss denotes the difference between this and a worst-case loss at some confidence level.

In the actuarial approach, the assessment of whether the counterparty risk is being well managed can only be accurately made over a long time horizon of many years. The CVA charges represent a buffer against future default losses. If this buffer is too small then significant additional losses may arise during periods when default rates are high. In contrast, a large buffer may mean overall losses are very unlikely, but may also suggest that business lines are being overcharged for counterparty risk. Ultimately, the uncertainty of the unexpected loss creates this difficulty.

18.5.3 Market approach

An alternative way in which to manage counterparty risk is the "market approach". The booking of a CVA leads to linear and non-linear risk sensitivities to all underlying variables and credit (all discussed in detail in Chapter 16). The market approach involves full hedging with respect to these sensitivities and hence quantifies the cost of *hedging* CVA as illustrated in Figure 18.8. Note that, in contrast to the actuarial approach, there is no unexpected loss component to consider. The risk-neutral CVA should define the hedging cost but a quantification of the residual hedging error is also required. The hedging error may reflect both uncertainty in hedging (symmetric effect) and a bias caused by aspects such as additional transaction costs (asymmetric effect). For a large investment bank, this "hedging error" can be potentially in the region of hundreds of millions of dollars.

It would be expected that the risk-neutral CVA would be significantly larger than the actuarial CVA, since it is calculated from market-implied parameters, which include substantial risk premiums as discussed in Section 10.1.6. Whilst performance is hard to assess in the actuarial approach (except over very long time horizons), this is not the case for the market approach as the PnL should ideally be relatively flat, with some expected volatility, due to imperfect hedging.

The actuarial and market approaches represent the extremes, with the most effective counterparty risk management representing a compromise in which only key sensitivities are dynamically hedged. In the last decade, institutions active in managing CVA have been moved, gradually, to more of a trading desk approach, aided by the development of the credit derivatives market. This will be catalysed further by Basel III regulation. However, it is important to note that the market approach for CVA (which is implied by the term "CVA

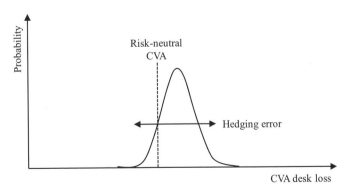

Figure 18.8 Schematic illustration of the quantification of CVA using the "market approach". The figure represents the "risk-neutral CVA", which should represent the cost of hedging in frictionless markets. There will be some additional hedging error as shown. This is likely to be positively biased due to transaction costs and other problems in hedging CVA.

desk") should not be compared too strongly with typical derivatives trading desks. Derivative trading generally involves hedging the majority of the underlying market risk, whilst accepting some residual risk ("hedging error" in Figure 18.8). Even exotic derivative trading desks are able to hedge the majority of their risk. By contrast, CVA is an exotic credit-contingent hybrid derivative and the proportion of the risk that can be truly hedged, whilst highly subjective, is limited.[24] The ideal management of CVA will therefore represent a balance between the actuarial and market approaches above, with other relevant aspects such as accounting PnL and regulatory capital also considered.

18.5.4 DVA treatment

The treatment of DVA differs from institution to institution, partly driven by different accounting rules and partly due to risk appetite. Essentially, we could consider three general approaches to DVA:

- *Ignore DVA*. Ignoring DVA may be preferred due to some of its controversial features. We note that this is only an option for banks not under US or Canadian GAAP, and will not be an option under IFRS13 accounting standards introduced in 2013.
- *Separate DVA into management PnL*. The separation of DVA into management PnL reflects a wish or requirement to account for DVA but not to incentivise the CVA desk to hedge the institution's own credit quality. This would mean that it would be difficult for a CVA desk to incorporate DVA in their charges, since the benefit will not be monetised. The CVA desk is essentially running a *long credit book*.
- *Incorporate DVA fully*. A full incorporation of DVA in the PnL of the CVA desk gives the potential to reduce charges and realise such reduction via hedging (albeit with various hedging problems as described in Section 13.3.4). The CVA desk is essentially running a *basis book* and attempting to manage the basis between their counterparties and their own credit spread. This basis book could reflect a net short credit position if the institution's own credit spread is significant enough.

18.5.5 PnL Explain

A key component for a CVA desk to have in place is the ability to explain PnL changes. This is a common requirement for trading desks to understand the performance of their hedging and the source of any material unhedged moves. PnL explain aims to decompose the PnL change into consistent components by looking at the impact of them independently. These components, broadly speaking, come from two sets of factors:

- *Managed risks*. This refers to risks that the CVA desk has the mandate to hedge, such as interest rate, FX and credit spread changes. The CVA desk performance should definitely depend on these aspects.
- *Unmanaged risks*. This may include aspects not under the control of the CVA desk, such as changes to netting and collateral terms. The CVA desk performance may not depend on these aspects, which may be accounted for in management PnL.

---

[24] Indeed, even in the period up to 2007 when banks were aggressively taking risk in exotic derivatives such as CDOs, credit hybrid businesses (similar in nature to CVAs) were limited partly due to the perceived complexities around pricing and risk management.

There are certain components of PnL that may be considered managed or unmanaged. One example is DVA; a CVA desk responsible for hedging DVA as part of a "basis book" (Section 18.5.4) should have DVA as a managed risk above. Alternatively, DVA handled in management PnL should consider DVA differently. Default risk is another difficult component: in an ideal world, it would be a managed component but it is not often possible to buy single-name CDS protection to protect against jump-to-default risk. Option exercises, as discussed in Section 18.3.4, may also create unhedgeable jumps in PnL. Finally, PnL explain should also include changes arising from new trades. The CVA charged by the CVA desk should match the change in PnL due to trade population. However, the operational inability to price the exact incremental and marginal CVA at trade time will create unexplained PnL.

18.5.6 Securitisation

The significant increase in regulatory capital required under Basel III, not surprisingly, has led banks to find other mechanisms for transferring CVA. Securitisation of CVA is one such alternative. Not only does this provide a new risk transfer method, but it potentially also allows hedging of the idiosyncratic risk from the many exposures to the counterparties for which there is no liquid single-name CDS market. A CVA securitisation can also give investors access to exposure to new credits. The idea of securitising counterparty credit risk is not new, with the first issue (Alpine Partners by UBS) issued in 2000 referencing a $750 million portfolio of interest rate exposures.

Unfortunately, CVA securitisation is difficult. From the modelling point of view, for both pricing and rating purposes, it requires quantification of CDO-type structures now considered so complex. In particular, the correlation modelling involves exposure correlation, default correlation and the correlation between exposure and default (wrong-way risk). The underlying complexity may put off investors who, in light of some of the problems in the financial crisis such as the pricing of MBS securities, require much more understanding of the specifics of a given portfolio, including correlation and industry concentration, and will not rely on ratings.

Another problem involves the confidentiality over the underlying reference counterparty names (only limited information such as rating, industry sector and geography may be available). Furthermore, the incorporation of collateral and treatment of the constantly changing counterparty exposures, and treatment of new trades, is challenging.

Not surprisingly, regulators have been cold on this form of risk transfer due to the complexities arising from both CVA and the process of securitisation, together with the role of the latter in the global financial crisis. On the other hand, if quantifying CVA VAR is possible, then pricing a CVA securitisation should also be achievable. Furthermore, one could argue that, if 50% capital relief (or more) can be achieved by hedging with a credit index that shares none of the individual names that make up an institution's CVA, at least as much relief should be obtained from a closer hedge in terms of portfolio composition arising from a CVA securitisation.

If done correctly then securitisation can be a powerful tool for beneficial risk transfer in capital markets. Done incorrectly, it can be highly counterproductive. It remains to be seen whether the strong need of banks to find ways to transfer their CVA can outweigh the underlying complexity of doing this, the caution of investors and the opposition of regulators.

18.5.7   Pragmatic approach to hedging

Whilst there is not much rationale for a CVA desk not to hedge certain liquid risks (such as interest rate and FX), the hedging of illiquid risks is more of a challenge. Illiquid, in this context, predominantly refers to credit risk since most counterparties will not be tradable in the single-name CDS market. However, it can also relate to other aspects, such as long-dated volatility, that may be difficult to hedge.

It is important to note that a CVA desk may not hedge a particular component for a variety of reasons, for example:

- *No hedge available.* There is no reasonable direct or indirect hedge available in the market.
- *Crowded trade effects.* Hedging is possible but due to crowded trade effects, hedging is relatively costly.
- *Choice.* The CVA desk believes it is better not to hedge (assuming this is a choice within their mandate and risk limits).

A very important consideration is that, by not hedging credit risk, as shown in Section 10.1.6, a CVA will expect to realise a significant positive gain (theta) over time[25] as transactions age. Whilst default losses will be experienced, the empirical results in Table 10.4, and well-known presence of risk premiums, suggest that these will only partially cancel out this positive theta. This creates the tantalising prospect that a CVA desk not hedging their illiquid credit risk will expect to generate PnL over the long-term, compared with one attempting maximum hedging, which will have an overall negative PnL due to hedging costs. This is illustrated schematically in Figure 18.9. Whilst the maximum hedging

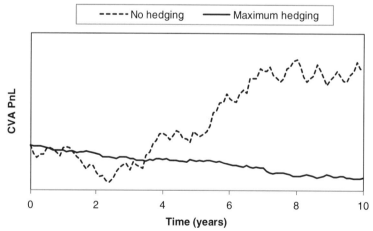

Figure 18.9 Schematic illustration of the PnL implication of no CVA hedging (positive drift, large volatility) and maximum hedging (negative drift, small volatility).

---

[25] We assume that the charging for CVA is market-based since, irrespective of the hedging needs of an institution, they would not want to be subject to the winner's curse by systemically under-pricing counterparty risk with respect to their competitors. We should also note that using DVA will introduce a negative theta as the benefit from an institution's own default is not hedged.

approach clearly benefits from a minimisation of PnL volatility (and regulatory capital requirements), the zero hedging approach is always preferable in the long-term.

Ultimately, holding rather than hedging CVA is the more profitable strategy. Regulatory requirements seem to direct banks to hedge CVA as much as possible. However, this leaves some obvious questions:

- Who will take the CVA risk away from banks?
- If CVA is transformed into other risks (e.g., via central counterparties) what really becomes of it?
- What are the potential unintended consequences of CVA hedging on a large scale?

18.6 SUMMARY

This chapter has considered the management of counterparty risk within a financial institution. We have outlined the important components to consider and the likely role and responsibilities of a CVA desk. CVA pricing and related technology considerations have been discussed. The operation of a CVA desk between the extremes of an insurance company (actuarial approach) and a trading desk (market approach) have been given careful consideration. We have explained that, whilst not hedging CVA at all may be naïve, the attempt to hedge actively may be dangerous also. The greatest challenge of a CVA desk is to know when to hedge and when not to.

19

The Future of Counterparty Risk

The only thing we know about the future is that it will be different.

Peter Drucker (1909–2005)

At the time of writing, counterparty risk represents one of the hottest topics within the financial markets, and the quantification and management of CVA is receiving much attention. It is also accepted that much work needs to be done in understanding complex components such as wrong-way risks and debt value adjustment (DVA). Areas related to counterparty risk, such as risk-free valuation and funding, are also receiving huge attention. Finally, the impact of mitigating counterparty risk through mechanisms such as hedging and central clearing is being debated. In this final chapter, we consider the key components that will define the subject of counterparty risk and related areas in the future.

19.1 KEY COMPONENTS

19.1.1 Regulatory capital and regulation

It was always inevitable, given the scale of the global financial crisis, that regulators would restrict leverage and impose much higher capital charges on banks. Nor was it surprising that, as one of the defining components of the crisis, counterparty risk would emerge as very severely hit in this respect (on a relative basis). Counterparty risk capital is defined as the sum of a number of components, such as the default risk charge, CVA VAR and charges with respect to centrally cleared transactions. In addition, different institutions may use simpler approaches (such as the current exposure method or the standardised approach for CVA VAR) or more complex ones (e.g., the internal model method or CVA VAR advanced approach). A number of changes required by Basel III, such as an increased margin period of risk and use of stressed data, are also required. A large part of the future landscape will be driven by capital requirements and the ways in which capital relief can be achieved. To some extent, only time will tell how well the capital rules are aligned with the actual risk-taking (and mitigating) practices of banks.

Additionally, regulators have imposed greater constraints around aspects such as backtesting, stress testing and wrong-way risk. This will create a significantly increased operational burden and require significant investments from a quantitative and technological perspective. However, it should also allow banks to avoid significant and unexpected losses and will provide regulators with greater confidence in banks' abilities to quantify counterparty risk correctly and avoid problems arising from significant co-dependencies.

19.1.2   Collateral

Collateral agreements are one of the strongest ways to reduce counterparty risk for one or both parties in a transaction. However, they can cause further problems that must be appreciated. The modelling of collateralised exposure requires more study, in particular with respect to the impact of the margin period of risk. The residual risk and CVA that exists with a CSA must also be better appreciated. The usefulness of collateral in mitigating wrong-way risk is also vital, although difficult to understand.

Standard collateral agreements are now accepted to contain a large amount of optionality due to the choices over the type of collateral that is posted. Collateral management is no longer seen as a back-office cost centre but more as a front-office important asset optimisation process where collateral should be utilised in the most economically beneficial way. It is likely that collateral agreements will be greatly simplified (e.g., the development of the standard CSA) to remove optionality and make the underlying valuation less complex. Collateral management also needs to embrace the highly automated OTC derivatives market, and rely less on manual processes. This can minimise operational risks and maximise the potential benefits of collateral.

19.1.3   CVA hedging

Whilst accurate hedging of highly complex structured products (exotics) is a challenging task, CVA takes hedging problems to a new level. The challenge of risk managing what is effectively an exotic multi-asset credit hybrid book is not to be underestimated. Furthermore, the assessment of how aspects such as DVA, wrong-way risk and collateral influence sensitivities (hedges) must be fully appreciated. A good CVA risk management strategy must involve a realisation and quantification of unhedgeable risks and a strategy to absorb idiosyncratic events and other unexpected losses. The unintended consequences of CVA hedging (for example, crowded trade effects) are also significant considerations, both for market practitioners and regulators. Whilst it is impossible to second-guess the impact of unintended effects, they will inevitably contribute to defining the way in which an institution chooses to manage their CVA.

Central counterparties (CCPs) have a key role to play in minimising counterparty risks for CDS protection buyers, which should help the CDS market develop. However, this must be balanced against the risk posed by a CCP itself.

19.1.4   The credit derivative market

The credit derivative market is almost a prerequisite for CVA as the single-name credit default swap is the most obvious instrument to use to define market-implied default probabilities. However, even if the single-name CDS market develops rapidly in liquidity then it is inconceivable that an institution will be able to define default probabilities in this fashion for any more than a small fraction of counterparties. Index CDSs therefore have a key role to play here, and the development of a more complex market with index CDSs being better developed across underlying credits, regions and sectors is important. Even then, the issue that an index CDS can (at most) provide only a good proxy for the counterparty credit spread in question remains a problem.

The CDS instrument is duplicitous within counterparty risk. On the one hand, it provides market-implied default probabilities for quantifying CVA and is a key hedging instrument. On the other hand, the potential presence of unpleasant wrong-way risks within CDS contracts creates additional complexity for those buying CDS protection. CVA hedging should ideally not create more counterparty risk within the hedging instruments. This would imply that all CDS hedges need to be centrally cleared.

19.1.5   Central clearing

A CCP apparently makes CVA disappear. On the surface, CCPs offer a quick single solution to many counterparty risk problems, such as the wrong-way risks embedded in credit derivative products. However, CVA is predominantly generated by institutions unable to post collateral against credit exposure, whereas CCPs operate only based on their members posting significant collateral. Therefore, CCPs do not directly solve the problems with non-collateral posting counterparties creating illiquid credit risks. Requiring such counterparties to borrow the necessary collateral simply creates significant funding liquidity risk. CCPs will not directly reduce CVA with counterparties such as corporates and sovereigns.

The major role of CCPs will rather be to mitigate counterparty risk between collateral posting counterparties such as banks and other significant financial institutions, whether they are clearing members or not. Here, a CCP could be argued to represent a key way to control counterparty risk via loss mutualisation and overall homogenisation of counterparty risk. However, significant moral hazard problems and systemic risk may exist. The benefits of central clearing may also depend on product type. For example, centrally clearing interest rate products may prove straightforward but credit derivatives are likely to be much more of a challenge, and the wrong-way risk that the CCP absorbs has the potential to cause severe problems as it did in the recent financial crisis. It is likely that market participants may also have strongly diverging views on the benefits of a CCP, some seeing it as the only realistic hub of the OTC derivatives market and others as introducing needless costs and complexity and even providing the basis of the next financial crisis.

It may be possible that a careful introduction of CCPs, in terms of their overall number, operating structures, capital bases and so on, will benefit greatly the OTC derivatives market. However, regulators need to carefully consider both the benefits and drawbacks of CCPs and heed the lessons to be learned by experiences such as the failure of supposedly high-quality counterparties such as monolines. CCPs must not be assumed too big to fail, as this will simply lead market participants to increase their exposure naïvely.

19.1.6   Too big to fail

Lehman Brothers was an unfortunate victim of the global financial crisis in the sense that they were not quite considered too big to fail at the time they became financially insolvent. However, rather than Lehman being *unlucky*, the situation was more that many failing institutions (and those heavily exposed to such counterparties) were *lucky* to be bailed out. Lehman is likely to prove to be a hugely important lesson in years to come, providing a constant reminder that large high credit quality institutions are not always too big to fail.

The "too big to fail" concept was at the heart of obscuring counterparty risks to the financial markets for many years. This is problematic since any institution that is deemed too big to fail will create moral hazards. Firstly, the institution itself may take unnecessary risks under the assumption that the taxpayer will effectively always be there to provide a last line of liquidity during turbulent times. Secondly, trading partners may naturally take larger exposures than they would otherwise do. A solid bilateral derivatives market is not based around too big to fail institutions but rather around institutions of varying creditworthiness, where credit quality has an impact on trading terms (CVA, collateral requirements, etc.), with institutions incentivised to have a strong creditworthiness by the more favourable terms available to them. Furthermore, in such a market the failure of any institution (even if unlikely) is always a possibility.

The mandate of CCPs does not sit well in the too big to fail debate. On the one hand, regulators are requiring too big to fail "systemically important financial institutions" (SIFIs) to hold greater capital and are even considering breaking them up into smaller bite-sized (non-SIFI) chunks. On the other hand, CCPs will inevitably attain SIFI status quite easily due to their positioning at the hubs of the financial network and the volumes of trades they clear. A key component for the future of counterparty risk will be whether CCPs are developing and expanding an effective form of counterparty risk mitigation and improving transparency or if they are just increasing the scale of the too big to fail problem.

19.2   KEY AXES OF DEVELOPMENT

19.2.1   Quantification

Counterparty risk is present in numerous transactions for banks, other financial institutions and many corporates. It covers many different instruments across all asset classes and contains both market risk (credit exposure) and credit risk (default probability and credit migration) components. It must be measured over a long time horizon (often many years), accounting for the many possible risk mitigants. Pricing counterparty risk must be done at the counterparty (netting set) level and not for individual transactions in isolation, and wrong-way risks and other subtle aspects must be given careful consideration. Counterparty risk at the portfolio level is complicated by the uncertainty of exposure as well as the problem of measuring default correlations. Good management of counterparty risk is certainly achievable but comes via careful control and quantification of many aspects simultaneously.

19.2.2   Infrastructure

There is huge interest around CVA as firms seek to build their systems' capability to actively price counterparty risk on a real-time basis and build CVA into all new transactions. Banks and other institutions are tending to form front-office-based CVA groups (often known as CVA desks in banks) that take overall responsibility for charging and management of counterparty risk. This is likely to continue to be a big effort, with any major user of derivatives needing to have state-of-the-art assessment of their counterparty risk on a dynamic basis. This is a key challenge due to the large number of asset classes that need to be included in such a system, the presence of exotics derivatives and wrong-way risk transactions such as credit default swaps. Furthermore, such systems must have all relevant netting, collateral and other contractual details for every counterparty. Finally, the computational requirements are extremely large.

19.2.3   Risk mitigation

Risk mitigation can be a double-edged sword: additional risk types are created and yet some of the original risk remains. The global financial crisis highlighted the fact that the complex documentation and legal terms relating to netting, collateral and entities such as SPVs are typically defined during normal times but mainly tested in crises, where they have sometimes been observed to fail. Clearly, any legal agreement used as a risk mitigant must be watertight under all market conditions, especially during crises or times of political and geopolitical troubles. Risk mitigation methods, seemingly favoured by regulators, such as collateral management and central clearing, convert counterparty risk into funding liquidity risk, legal risk and systemic risk. The extent of this conversion must not be ignored, especially since these forms of risk may be less well understood and more likely to be brushed under the carpet. CVA is complicated and difficult to manage, but perhaps preferable to some of the alternative risks that may be created when CVA is mitigated.

19.2.4   DVA

Bilateral CVA (BCVA) or DVA (debt value adjustment) in valuation is becoming rather standard especially for institutions with large amounts of OTC derivatives and counterparty risk. This is driven by the possibility of recognising one's "own credit" under fair value accountancy rules (SFAS 157, IAS 39 and IFRS 13) via pricing liabilities at market value on one's balance sheet. A key driver for institutions using DVA is simply that they cannot agree on transacted counterparty risk charges otherwise. Many users of DVA are uncomfortable with it as a general concept and agree that many features are counterintuitive; for example, the MtM benefits relating to an institution's deteriorating credit quality. Whilst some unpleasant features of DVA can be brushed under the carpet, the monetisation of the liability benefits of counterparty risk is a question that institutions will likely struggle with for some time to come. The apparent disagreement between the validity of DVA between accounting rules and capital requirements (Basel III) will also be an important consideration. Whilst accounting and capital rules differ in their intentions, they may need to converge to some degree on this issue.

19.2.5   Wrong-way risk

Wrong-way risk was brought to the fore by the failure of monoline insurers, bailout of AIG and the financial problems associated with various sovereign entities. Not surprisingly, there is a need to control wrong-way risk better. This will require improving methods to quantify so-called general wrong-way risk that occurs due to macroeconomic relationships, such as a correlation between credit spreads and interest rates. It will also involve identifying the potentially more toxic "specific wrong-way risk" that occurs more due to linkages between counterparty credit quality and exposure that may be a result of poorly chosen transactions (such as providing trades for heavy speculators). From a quantitative perspective, characterising the co-dependency that drives wrong-way risk is extremely challenging and historical data may be sparse and of limited use. Hedging instruments for wrong-way risk are also limited, although they may become more well developed (e.g., index CCDS) as banks attempt to find ways to hedge wrong-way risk and prevent the problematic cross-gamma that they otherwise are exposed to.

19.2.6   Links to valuation and funding costs

Counterparty risk has become associated with the issue of standard valuation and also the quantification of funding costs. CVA is defined with respect to the value of a financial instrument and therefore the two are inextricably linked. The most obvious representation would be to value "risk-free" and apply the CVA (and DVA) as an adjustment. However, defining "risk-free" value is no longer as straightforward as it requires issues such as "dual-curve" pricing to be resolved. In addition, the quantification of funding costs via FVA (funding value adjustment) is linked to DVA valuation and shares much of the technology and infrastructure required for counterparty risk. The valuation of collateral components via CollVA will also be important. It is likely that terms such as dual-curve pricing, FVA and CollVA will become common as derivatives valuation undertakes a complete regime shift.

19.2.7   Risk transfer

Ultimately, the problem of counterparty risk is that CVA is generated by the many participants in financial markets who cannot collateralise their transactions. Denying access to markets like OTC derivatives for such counterparties is not a viable solution as (for example) they have very significant and reasonable hedging needs. The question then is where the CVA should go. Banks are the natural holders of this uncollateralised and illiquid credit risk and they should, of course, be well capitalised against it. However, there is also a need for a market for counterparty risk transfer to exist.

The credit derivatives market is in a state of flux, with opinion divided somewhat between whether the underlying instruments represent important risk transfer and hedging tools or are simply dangerous weapons that will serve only to cause future disturbances within the financial markets. Central counterparties have a key role to play in making the credit derivative market more transparent, liquid and counterparty risk-free. This should improve hedging of CVA, at least with respect to the largest and most important counterparties. It will also allow hedging of the systemic component of illiquid credits (those that do not trade in the credit derivative market), although it is not obvious that transferring this systemic risk away from banks is definitely the most favourable solution.

Aside from hedging, banks will naturally look to other methods such as securitisation to hedge some of their illiquid counterparty risks. On the one hand, a regulator may view the securitising of CVA as far from innocuous since securitisation of far simpler underlyings was a major cause of the recent financial crisis. On the other hand, regulators are allowing capital relief of 50% or more when banks hedge with completely different portfolios (index relief for hedges under Basel III), and might reasonably be asked to look favourably at the more accurate hedges that securitisations would provide.

19.3   THE CONTINUING CHALLENGE FOR GLOBAL FINANCIAL MARKETS

Counterparty credit risk and CVA is a subject that will dominate practitioners, policymakers and academics for years. Banks and other institutions need to find the right way to manage their counterparty risk whether they have just a few or thousands of counterparties. CVA desks or groups will become the norm across banks and some other large financial institutions or significant derivatives users. Modellers need to work on the best and most pragmatic approaches to quantifying CVA. Technologists need to find the most efficient and cost-effective ways to implement systems that can cover all aspects of counterparty risk across products and counterparty type, providing real-time pricing and hedging together with accounting, reporting and regulatory functionality. Approaches to aspects such as DVA and wrong-way risk will be debated and improved upon recursively. Peripheral areas such as risk-free valuation and funding (FVA) will be studied alongside counterparty risk aspects. Regulators will attempt to provide the correct requirements such that institutions are capitalised against counterparty risk without choking economic growth and causing unpleasant unintended consequences.

The counterparty risk cocktail – including CVA, collateral, wrong-way risk, central counterparties, credit derivatives, DVA, FVA and regulatory rules – is likely to produce many headaches over the coming years. However, it is also likely to stimulate much active discussion and produce much new research, innovation and problem solving.

References

Acharya, V., Engle, R.F., Figlewski, S., Lynch, A.W. and Subrahmanyam, M.G. (2009) Centralized Clearing for Credit Derivatives, in *Restoring Financial Stability: How to Repair a Failed System*, Acharya, V. and Richardson, M. (eds), John Wiley & Sons Inc.

Albanese, C., D'Ippoliti, F. and Pietroniero, G. (2011) Margin Lending and Securitization: Regulators, Modelling and Technology, working paper.

Altman, E. (1968) Financial Ratios, Discriminant Analysis and the Prediction of Corporate Bankruptcy. *Journal of Finance*, 23, 589–609.

Altman, E. (1989) Measuring Corporate Bond Mortality and Performance, *Journal of Finance*, 44 (4, September), 909–922.

Altman, E. and Kishore, V. (1996) Almost Everything You Wanted to Know About Recoveries on Defaulted Bonds, *Financial Analysts Journal*, Nov/Dec.

Amdahl, G. (1967) Validity of the Single Processor Approach to Achieving Large-Scale Computing Capabilities, AFIPS Conference Proceedings, 30, 483–485.

Andersen, L. and Piterbarg, V. (2010a) *Interest Rate Modelling Volume 1: Foundations and Vanilla Models*, Atlantic Financial Press.

Andersen, L. and Piterbarg, V. (2010b) *Interest Rate Modelling Volume 2: Term Structure Models*, Atlantic Financial Press.

Andersen, L. and Piterbarg, V. (2010c) *Interest Rate Modelling Volume 3: Products and Risk Management*, Atlantic Financial Press.

Andersen, L., Sidenius, J. and Basu, S. (2003) All your hedges in one basket, *Risk Magazine*, November.

Arvanitis, A. and Gregory, J. (2001) *Credit: The Complete Guide to Pricing, Hedging and Risk Management*, Risk Books.

Arvanitis, A., Gregory, J. and Laurent, J.-P. (1999) Building Models for Credit Spreads, *Journal of Derivatives*, 6 (3, Spring), 27–43.

Baird, D.G. (2001) *Elements of Bankruptcy*, 3rd edition, Foundation Press, New York, NY.

Basel Committee on Banking Supervision (BCBS) (2004) An Explanatory Note on the Basel II IRB Risk Weight Functions, October, www.bis.org.

Basel Committee on Banking Supervision (BCBS) (2005) The Application of Basel II to Trading Activities and the Treatment of Double Default, www.bis.org.

Basel Committee on Banking Supervision (BCBS) (2006) International Convergence of Capital Measurement and Capital Standards, A Revised Framework – Comprehensive Version, June, www.bis.org.

Basel Committee on Banking Supervision (BCBS) (2009) Strengthening the resilience of the banking sector, Consultative document, December, www.bis.org.

Basel Committee on Banking Supervision (BCBS) (2010a) Basel III: A global regulatory framework for more resilient banks and banking systems, December (Revised June (2011), www.bis.org.

Basel Committee on Banking Supervision (BCBS) (2010b) Basel III counterparty credit risk – Frequently asked questions, November, www.bis.org.

Basel Committee on Banking Supervision (BCBS) (2011) Capitalisation of bank exposures to central counterparties, December, www.bis.org.

Basurto, M.S. and Singh, M. (2008) Counterparty Risk in the Over-the-Counter Derivatives Market, November. IMF Working Papers, 1–19, Available at SSRN: http://ssrn.com/abstract=1316726.

Bates, D. and Craine, R. (1999) Valuing the Futures Market Clearinghouse's Default Exposure during the 1987 Crash, *Journal of Money, Credit & Banking*, 31 (2, May), 248–272.

Bliss, R.R. and Kaufman, G.G. (2005) Derivatives and Systemic Risk: Netting, Collateral, and Closeout (May 10th), FRB of Chicago Working Paper No. (2005)-03. Available at SSRN: http://ssrn.com/abstract=730648.

Black, F. and Cox, J. (1976) Valuing Corporate Securities: Some Effects of Bond Indenture Provisions, *Journal of Finance*, 31, 351–67.

Black, F. and Scholes, M. (1973) The Pricing of Options and Corporate Liabilities, *Journal of Political Economy*, 81(3), 637–654.

Bluhm, C., Overbeck, L. and Wagner, C. (2003) *An Introduction to Credit Risk Modeling*, Chapman and Hall.

Brace, A., Gatarek, D. and Musiela, M. (1997) The Market Model of Interest Rate Dynamics, *Mathematical Finance*, 7(2), 127–154.

Brady, N. (1988) Report of the Presidential Task Force on Market Mechanisms, US Government Printing Office, Washington DC.

Brigo, D. and Masetti, M. (2005a) Risk Neutral Pricing of Counterparty Risk, in *Counterparty Credit Risk Modelling*, Pykhtin, M. (ed.), Risk Books.

Brigo, D. and Masetti, M. (2005b) A Formula for Interest Rate Swaps Valuation under Counterparty Risk in presence of Netting Agreements, www.damianobrigo.it.

Brigo, D. and Morini, M. (2010) Dangers of Bilateral Counterparty Risk: the fundamental impact of closeout conventions, working paper.

Brigo, D. and Morini, M. (2011) Closeout convention tensions, *Risk*, December, 86–90.

Brigo, D., Chourdakis K. and Bakkar, I. (2008) Counterparty Risk Valuation for Energy Commodities Swaps: Impact of Volatilities and Correlation. Available at SSRN: http://ssrn.com/abstract=1150818.

Burgard, C. and Kjaer, M. (2011a) Partial differential equation representations of derivatives with counterparty risk and funding costs, *The Journal of Credit Risk*, 7(3), 1–19.

Burgard, C. and Kjaer, M. (2011b) In the balance, *Risk*, November, 72–75.

Burgard, C. and Kjaer, M. (2012) A Generalised CVA with Funding and Collateral, working paper. http://ssrn.com/abstract=2027195.

Canabarro, E. and Duffie, D. (2003) Measuring and Marking Counterparty Risk, in *Asset/Liability Management for Financial Institutions*, Tilman, L. (ed.), Institutional Investor Books.

Canabarro, E., Picoult, E. and Wilde, T. (2003) Analyzing counterparty risk, *Risk*, 16(9), 117–122.

Cesari, G., Aquilina, J., Charpillon, N., Filipovic, Z., Lee, G. and Manda, I. (2009) *Modelling, Pricing, and Hedging Counterparty Credit Exposure*, Springer Finance.

Collin-Dufresne, P., Goldstein, R.S. and Martin, J.S. (2001) The Determinants of Credit Spread Changes, *Journal of Finance*, 56, 2177–2207.

Cooper, I.A. and Mello, A.S. (1991) The default risk of swaps, *Journal of Finance*, 46, 597–620.

Das, S. (2008) The Credit Default Swap (CDS) Market – Will It Unravel?, February 2nd, http://www.eurointelligence.com/Article3.1018+M583ca062a10.0.html.

Das, S. and Sundaram, R. (1999) Of smiles and smirks, a term structure perspective, *Journal of Financial and Quantitative Analysis*, 34, 211–239.

De Prisco, B. and Rosen, D. (2005) Modelling Stochastic Counterparty Credit Exposures for Derivatives Portfolios, in *Counterparty Credit Risk Modelling*, Pykhtin, M. (ed.), Risk Books.

Downing, C., Underwood, S. and Xing, Y. (2005) Is liquidity risk priced in the corporate bond market?, Working paper, Rice University.

Duffee, G. (1998) The Relation Between Treasury Yields and Corporate Bond Yield Spreads, *The Journal of Finance*, LIII (6, December).

Duffee, G.R. (1996a) Idiosyncratic Variation of Treasury Bill Yields, *Journal of Finance*, 51, 527–551.

Duffee, G.R. (1996b) On measuring credit risks of derivative instruments, *Journal of Banking and Finance*, 20(5), 805–833.

Duffie, D. (1999) Credit Swap Valuation, *Financial Analysts Journal*, January-February, 73–87.

Duffie, D. (2011) On the clearing of foreign exchange derivatives, working paper.

Duffie, D. and Huang, M. (1996) Swap rates and credit quality, *Journal of Finance*, 51, 921–950.

Duffie, D. and Singleton, K.J. (2003) *Credit Risk: Pricing, Measurement, and Management*, Princeton University Press.

Duffie, D. and Zhu, H. (2009) Does a Central Clearing Counterparty Reduce Counterparty Risk?, working paper.

Edwards F.R. and Morrison, E.R. (2005) Derivatives and the Bankruptcy Code: Why the Special Treatment?, *Yale Journal on Regulation*, 22, 91–122.

Ehlers, P. and Schönbucher, P. (2006) The Influence of FX Risk on Credit Spreads, working paper.

Engelmann, B. and Rauhmeier, R. (eds) (2006) *The Basel II Risk Parameters: Estimation, Validation, and Stress Testing*, Springer.

Figlewski, S. (1984) Margins and Market Integrity: Margin Setting for Stock Index Futures and Options, *Journal of Futures Markets*, 13(4), 389–408.

Financial Times (2008) Banks face $10bn monolines charges, June 10th.

Finger, C. (1999) Conditional Approaches for CreditMetrics Portfolio Distributions, *CreditMetrics Monitor*, April.

Finger, C. (2000) Towards a better understanding of wrong-way credit exposure, RiskMetrics working paper number 99-05, February.

Finger, C., Finkelstein, V., Pan, G., Lardy, J.-P. and Tiemey, J. (2002) CreditGrades technical document. RiskMetrics Group.

Fitzpatrick, K. (2002) Spotlight on counterparty risk, *International Financial Review*, 99, November 30th.

Fleck, M. and Schmidt, A. (2005) Analysis of Basel II Treatment of Counterparty Risk, in *Counterparty Credit Risk Modelling*, Pykhtin, M. (ed.), Risk Books.

Fons, J.S. (1987) The Default Premium and Corporate Bond Experience, *Journal of Finance*, 42 (1 March), 81–97.

Garcia-Cespedes, J.C., de Juan Herrero, J.A., Rosen, D. and Saunders, D. (2010) Effective Modelling of Wrong-Way Risk, CCR Capital and Alpha in Basel II, *Journal of Risk Model Validation*, 4(1), 71–98.

Garcia-Cespedes, J.C., Keinin, A., de Juan Herrero, J.A. and Rosen, D. (2006) A Simple Multi-Factor 'Factor Adjustment' for Credit Capital Diversification, Special issue on Risk Concentrations in Credit Portfolios (Gordy, M. ed.) *Journal of Credit Risk*, Fall.

Gemen, H. (2005) Commodities and commodity derivatives, John Wiley & Sons Ltd.

Geman, H. and Nguyen, V.N. (2005) Soy bean inventory and forward curve dynamics, *Management science*, 51 (7, July), 1076–1091.

Gemmill, G. (1994) Margins and the Safety of Clearing Houses, *Journal of Banking and Finance*, 18 (5), 979–996.

Ghosh, A., Rennison, G., Soulier, A., Sharma, P. and Malinowska, M. (2008) Counterparty risk in credit markets, Barclays Capital Research Report.

Gibson, M.S. (2005) Measuring counterparty credit risk exposure to a margined counterparty, in *Counterparty Credit Risk Modelling*, Pykhtin, M. (ed), Risk Books.

Giesecke, K., Longstaff, F.A., Schaefer, S. and Strebulaev, I. (2010) Corporate Bond Default Risk: A 150−Year Perspective, NBER Working Paper No. 15848, March.

Glasserman, P. and Li, J. (2005) Importance Sampling for Portfolio Credit Risk, *Management Science*, 51 (11, November), 1643–1656.

Glasserman, P. and Yu, B. (2002) Pricing American options by simulation: regression now or regression later?, in *Monte Carlo and Quasi-Monte Carlo Methods*, Niederreiter, H. (ed), Springer.

Gordy, M. (2002) Saddlepoint approximation of credit risk+, *Journal of Banking and Finance*, 26, 1335–1353.

Gordy, M. (2004) Granularity Adjustment in Portfolio Credit Risk Management, in *Risk Measures for the 21st Century*, Szegö, G.P. (ed.), John Wiley & Sons.

Gordy, M. and Howells, B. (2006) Procyclicality in Basel II: can we treat the disease without killing the patient?, *Journal of Financial Intermediation*, 15, 395–417.

Gordy, M. and Juneja, S. (2008) Nested Simulation in Portfolio Risk Measurement, working paper.

Gregory, J. (2008a) A trick of the credit tail, *Risk*, March, 88–92.

Gregory, J. (2008b) A free lunch and the credit crunch, *Risk*, August, 74–77.

Gregory, J. (2009a) Being two faced over counterparty credit risk, *Risk*, 22(2), 86–90.

Gregory, J. (2009b) *Counterparty credit risk: the new challenge for global financial markets*, John Wiley and Sons.

Gregory, J. (2010) Counterparty casino: The need to address a systemic risk, European Policy Forum working paper. www.epfltf.org.

Gregory J. (2011) Counterparty risk in credit derivative contracts, in, *The Oxford Handbook of Credit Derivatives*, Lipton, A. and Rennie, A. (eds), Oxford University Press.

Gregory, J. and German, I. (2012) Closing out DVA, working paper.

Gregory, J. and Laurent, J.-P. (2003) I will survive, *Risk*, June, 103–107.

Gregory, J. and Laurent, J.-P. (2004) In the core of correlation, *Risk*, October 87–91.

Gupton, G.M., Finger C.C. and Bhatia, M. (1997) CreditMetrics Technical Document, Morgan Guaranty Trust Company, New York.

Hamilton, D.T., Gupton, G.M. and Berthault, A. (2001) Default and Recovery Rates of Corporate Bond Issuers: (2000), *Moody's Investors Service*, February.

Hardouvelis, G. and Kim, D. (1995) Margin Requirements: Price Fluctuations, and Market Participation in Metal Futures, *Journal of Money, Credit and Banking*, 27(3), 659–671.

Hartzmark, M. (1986) The Effects of Changing Margin Levels on Futures Market Activity, the Composition of Traders in the Market, and Price Performance, *Journal of Business*, 59(2), S147–S180.

Hille, C.T., Ring J. and Shimanmoto, H. (2005) Modelling Counterparty Credit Exposure for Credit Default Swaps, in *Counterparty Credit Risk Modelling*, Pykhtin, M. (ed.), Risk Books.

Hills, B., Rule, D., Parkinson, S. and Young, C. (1999) Central Counterparty Clearing Houses and Financial Stability, *Bank of England Financial Stability Review*, June, 22–133.

Hughston, L.P. and Turnbull, S.M. (2001) Credit risk: constructing the basic building block, *Economic Notes*, 30(2), 257–279.

Hull, J. (2010) OTC Derivatives and Central Clearing: Can All Transactions Be Cleared?, working paper, April.

Hull, J. and White, A. (1990) Pricing interest-rate derivative securities, *The Review of Financial Studies*, 3(4), 573–592.

Hull, J. and White, A. (1999) Pricing interest rate derivative securities, *Review of Financial Studies*, 3(4), 573–92.

Hull, J. and White, A. (2004) Valuation of a CDO and an nth to Default CDS without Monte Carlo Simulation, Working paper, September.

Hull, J. and White, A. (2011) CVA and Wrong Way Risk, Working Paper, University of Toronto.

Hull, J., Predescu, M. and White, A. (2004) The Relationship Between Credit Default Swap Spreads, Bond Yields, and Credit Rating Announcements, *Journal of Banking & Finance*, 28 (11 November), 2789–2811.

Hull, J., Predescu, M. and White, A. (2005a) Bond Prices, Default Probabilities and Risk Premiums, *Journal of Credit Risk*, 1 (2 Spring), 53–60.

Hull, J., Predescu, M. and White, A. (2005b) The valuation of correlation-dependent credit derivatives using a structural model, *Journal of Credit Risk*, 6(3), 99–132.

Hull, J., Predescu, M. and White, A, (2005c) The Valuation of Correlation-Dependent Credit Derivatives Using a Structural Model. Available at SSRN: http://ssrn.com/abstract=686481.

International Swaps and Derivatives Association (ISDA) (2009) ISDA close-out protocol, available at www.isda.org.

Jamshidian, F. and Zhu, Y. (1997) Scenario Simulation: Theory and methodology, *Finance and Stochastics*, 1, 43–67.

Jarrow, R.A. and Turnbull, S.M. (1992) Drawing the analogy, *Risk*, 5(10), 63–70.

Jarrow, R.A. and Turnbull, S.M. (1995) Pricing options on financial securities subject to default risk, *Journal of Finance*, 50, 53–86.

Jarrow, R. and Turnbull, S.M. (1997) When swaps are dropped, *Risk*, 10(5), 70–75.

Jarrow, R.A. and Yu, F. (2001) Counterparty risk and the pricing of defaultable securities, *Journal of Finance*, 56, 1765–1799.

Johnson, H. and Stulz, R. (1987) The pricing of options with default risk, *Journal of Finance*, 42, 267–280.

Jorion, P. (2007) *Value-at-Risk: The new benchmark for managing financial risk*, 3rd edition, McGraw-Hill.

Kealhofer, S. (1995) Managing Default Risk in Derivative Portfolios, in *Derivative Credit Risk: Advances in Measurement and Management*, Jameson, R. (ed.), Renaissance Risk Publications.

Kealhofer, S. (2003) Quantifying credit risk I: Default prediction, *Financial Analysts Journal*, January/February, 30–44.

Kealhofer, S. and Kurbat, M. (2002) The Default Prediction Power of the Merton Approach, Relative to Debt Ratings and Accounting Variables, KMV LLC, Mimeo.

KMV Corporation (1993) Portfolio management of default risk, San Francisco: KMV Corporation.

Kenyon, C. (2010) Completing CVA and Liquidity: Firm-level positions and collateralized trades, working paper, www.defaultrisk.com.

Kolb, R.W. and Overdahl, J.A. (2006) *Understanding Futures Markets*, Wiley-Blackwell.

Kroszner, R. (1999) Can the Financial Markets Privately Regulate Risk? The Development of Derivatives Clearing Houses and Recent Over-the-Counter Innovations, *Journal of Money, Credit, and Banking, August*, 569–618.

Laurent, J.-P. and Gregory, J. (2005) Basket Default Swaps, CDOs and Factor Copulas, *Journal of Risk*, 7(4), 103–122.

Leland, H. (1994) Corporate Debt Value, Bond Covenants, and Optimal Capital Structure, *Journal of Finance*, 49, 1213–1252.

Levy, A. and Levin, R. (1999) Wrong-way exposure, *Risk*, July.

Li, D.X. (1998) Constructing a credit curve, Credit Risk: A RISK special report, November, 40–44.

Li, D.X. (2000) On Default Correlation: A Copula Function Approach, *Journal of Fixed Income*, 9 (4 March), 43–54.

Lomibao, D. and Zhu, S. (2005) A Conditional Valuation Approach for Path-Dependent Instruments, in *Counterparty Credit Risk Modelling*, Pykhtin, M. (ed), Risk Books.

Longstaff, F.A. and Schwartz, S.E. (1995) A Simple Approach to Valuing Risky Fixed and Floating Rate Debt, *The Journal of Finance*, L (3 July).

Longstaff, F.A. and Schwarz, S.E. (2001) Valuing American options by simulation: A simple least squares approach, *The review of financial studies*, 14(1), 113–147.

Martin, R., Thompson, K. and Browne, C. (2001) Taking to the saddle, *Risk*, June, 91–94.

Mashal, R. and Naldi, M. (2005) Pricing multiname default swaps with counterparty risk, *Journal of Fixed Income*, 14(4), 3–16.

Matthews, R.A.J. (1995) Tumbling Toast, Murphy's Law and the Fundamental Constants, *European Journal of Physics*, 16, 172–176.

McKenzie, D. (2006) *An Engine, Not a Camera: How Financial Models Shape Markets*, MIT Press.

Meese, R. and Rogoff, K. (1983) Empirical Exchange Rate Models of the Seventies, *Journal of International Economics*, 14, 3–24.

Mercurio, F. (2010) A LIBOR Market Model with Stochastic Basis, available at SSRN: http://ssrn.com/abstract=1583081.

Merton, R.C. (1974) On the Pricing of Corporate Debt: The Risk Structure of Interest Rates, *Journal of Finance*, 29, 449–70.

Milne, A. (2012) Central Counterparty Clearing and the management of Systemic Default Risk, working paper, Loughborough University School of Business and Economics.

Moody's Investors Service (2007) Corporate Default and Recovery Rates: 1920-(2006), *Moody's Special Report*, New York, February.

Morini, M. and Prampolini, A. (2010) Risky Funding: A unified framework for counterparty and liquidity charges, working paper. http://ssrn.com/abstract=1669930.

O'Kane, D. (2007) Approximating Independent Loss Distributions with an Adjusted Binomial Distribution, EDHEC working paper.

O'Kane, D. (2008) *Modelling Single-name and Multi-name Credit Derivatives*, John Wiley & Sons Ltd.

Ong, M.K. (ed.) (2006) *The Basel Handbook: A Guide for Financial Practitioners*, 2nd edition, Risk Books.

Picoult, E. (2002) Quantifying the Risks of Trading, in *Risk Management: Value at Risk and Beyond*, Dempster, M.A.H. (ed.), Cambridge University Press.

Picoult, E. (2005) Calculating and Hedging Exposure, Credit Value Adjustment and Economic Capital for Counterparty Credit Risk, in *Counterparty Credit Risk Modelling*, Pykhtin, M. (ed.), Risk Books.

Pindyck, R. (2001) The dynamics of commodity spot and futures markets: A primer, *Energy Journal*, 22(3), 1–29.

Pirrong, C. (2000) A Theory of Financial Exchange Organization, *Journal of Law and Economics*, 437.

Pirrong, C. (2009) The Economics of Clearing in Derivatives Markets: Netting, Asymmetric Information, and the Sharing of Default Risks Through a Central Counterparty. Available at SSRN: http://ssrn.com/abstract=1340660.

Pirrong, C. (2011) The Economics of Central Clearing: Theory and Practice, ISDA Discussion Papers Series Number One (May).

Piterbarg, V. (2010) Funding beyond discounting: Collateral agreements and derivatives pricing, *Risk*, 2, 97–102.

Polizu, C., Neilson F.L. and Khakee, N. (2006) Criteria for Rating Global Credit Derivative Product Companies, Standard & Poor's working paper.

Press, W.H., Teukolsky, S.A., Vetterling W.T. and Flannery, B.P. (2007) *Numerical Recipes: The Art of Scientific Computing*, 3rd Edition, Cambridge University Press.

Pugachevsky, D. (2005) Pricing counterparty risk in unfunded synthetic CDO tranches, in *Counterparty Credit Risk Modelling*, Pykhtin, M. (ed.), Risk Books.

Pykhtin, M. (2003) Unexpected recovery risk, *Risk*, 16(8), 74–78.

Pykhtin, M. (2012) Model foundations of the Basel III standardised CVA charge, *Risk*, July, 60–66.

Pykhtin, M. and Sokol, A. (2012) If a Dealer Defaulted, Would Anybody Notice?, working paper.

Pykhtin, M. and Zhu, S. (2007) A Guide to Modelling Counterparty Credit Risk, GARP Risk Review, July/August, 16–22.

Rebonato, R. (1998) *Interest Rate Options Models*, 2nd edition, John Wiley and Sons, Ltd.

Reimers, M. and Zerbs, M. (1999) A multi-factor statistical model for interest rates, *Algo Research Quarterly*, 2(3), 53–64.

Remeza, A. (2007) Credit Derivative Product Companies Poised to Open for Business, Moody's Investor Services special report.

Rosen, D. and Pykhtin, M. (2010) Pricing Counterparty Risk at the Trade Level and CVA Allocations, *Journal of Credit Risk*, 6 (Winter), 3–38.

Rosen, D. and Saunders, D. (2010) Measuring Capital Contributions of Systemic Factors in Credit Portfolios, *Journal of Banking and Finance*, 34, 336–349.

Rowe, D. (1995) Aggregating Credit Exposures: The Primary Risk Source Approach, in *Derivative Credit Risk*, Jameson, R. (ed.), Risk Publications, 13–21.

Rowe, D. and Mulholland, M. (1999) Aggregating Market-driven Credit Exposures: A Multiple Risk Source Approach, in *Derivative Credit Risk*, 2nd edition, Incisive Media, 141–147.

Sarno, L. (2005) Viewpoint: Towards a Solution to the Puzzles in Exchange Rate Economics: Where do we Stand?, *Canadian Journal of Economics*, 38, 673–708.

Sarno, L. and Taylor, M.P. (2002) *The Economics of Exchange Rates*, Cambridge University Press.

Segoviano, M.A. and Singh, M. (2008) Counterparty Risk in the Over-the-Counter Derivative market, IMF working paper, November.

Shadab, H.B. (2009) Guilty by Association? Regulating Credit Default Swaps, *Entrepreneurial Business Law Journal*, August 19, forthcoming. Available at SSRN: http://ssrn.com/abstract=1368026.

Shelton, D. (2004) Back to Normal, Proxy Integration: A fast accurate method for CDO and CDO-squared pricing, *Citigroup Structured Credit Research*, August.

Singh, M. (2010) Collateral, Netting and Systemic Risk in the OTC Derivatives Market, IMF working paper, November.

Singh, M. and Aitken, J. (2009) Deleveraging after Lehman – Evidence from Reduced Rehypothecation, March, *IMF Working Papers*, 1–11, available at SSRN: http://ssrn.com/abstract=1366171.

Sokol, A. (2010) A Practical Guide to Monte Carlo CVA, in *Lessons From the Crisis*, Berd,A. (ed.), Risk Books.

Sorensen, E.H. and Bollier, T.F. (1994) Pricing Swap Default Risk, *Financial Analysts Journal*, 50 (3 May/June), 23–33.

Soros, G. (2009) My three steps to financial reform, *Financial Times*, June 17th.

Standard & Poor's (2007) Ratings Performance: 2006Stability and Transition, New York, S&P, 16th February.

Standard & Poor's (2008) Default, Transition, and Recovery: 2008 Annual Global Corporate Default Study and Rating Transitions, April 2nd.

Tang, Y. and Williams, A. (2010) Funding benefit and funding cost, in *Counterparty Credit Risk*, Canabarro, E. (ed.), Risk Books.

Tavakoli, J.M. (2008) *Structured Finance and Collateralized Debt Obligations: New Developments in Cash and Synthetic Securitization*, John Wiley & Sons, Inc.

Tennant, J., Emery, K. and Cantor, R. (2008) Corporate one-to-five-year rating transition rates, *Moody's Investor Services Special Comment*.

Thompson, J.R. (2009) Counterparty Risk in Financial Contracts: Should the Insured Worry About the Insurer?, available at SSRN: http://ssrn.com/abstract=1278084.

Turnbull, S. (2005) The Pricing Implications of Counterparty Risk for Non-Linear Credit Products, in *Counterparty Credit Risk Modelling*, Pykhtin, M. (ed.), Risk Books.

Tzani, R. and Chen, J.J. (2006) Credit Derivative Product Companies, *Moody's Investor Services*, March.

Vasicek, O. (1997) The Loan Loss Distribution, KMV Corporation.

Vrins, F. and Gregory, J. (2011) Getting CVA up and running, *Risk*, October.

Wilde, T. (2001) The regulatory capital treatment of credit risk arising from OTC derivatives exposures in the trading and the banking book, in *ISDA's response to the Basel Committee On Banking Supervision's Consultation on The New Capital Accord*, May (2001), Annex 1.

Wilde, T. (2005) Analytic Methods for Portfolio Counterparty Risk, in *Counterparty Credit Risk Modelling*, Pykhtin,M. (ed.), Risk Books.

Index

Compiled by Indexing Specialists (UK) Ltd